WHO BUILT AMERICA?

WHO BUILT

WORKING PEOPLE AND THE NATION'S ECONOMY,

VOLUME TWO:

FROM

THE GILDED AGE

TO

THE PRESENT

AMERICAN SOCIAL HISTORY PROJECT

THE CITY UNIVERSITY OF NEW YORK

HERBERT G. GUTMAN, Founding Director

STEPHEN BRIER, Project Director and Supervising Editor

AMERICA?

POLITICS, CULTURE, AND SOCIETY

JOSHUA FREEMAN

NELSON LICHTENSTEIN

STEPHEN BRIER

DAVID BENSMAN

SUSAN PORTER BENSON

DAVID BRUNDAGE

BRET EYNON

BRUCE LEVINE

BRYAN PALMER

JOSHUA BROWN,
Visual Editor

ROY ROSENZWEIG,
Consulting Editor

94-1345

PANTHEON BOOKS
NEW YORK

Other permissions and credits are given on pages 695–700.

Library of Congress Cataloging-in-Publication Data

(Revised for vol. 2)
Who built America?
At head of title: American Social History Project,
The City University of New York.
Includes bibliographical references and index.
Contents: v. 1. From conquest and colonization through Reconstruction
and the great uprising of 1877—v. 2. From the Gilded Age to the present.
1. Working class—United States—History. 2. United States—
Social conditions. 3. United States—History.
I. American Social History Project.
HD8066.W47 1992

305.5′62′0973   89–43240

ISBN 0-394-54663-6 (v. 1)
ISBN 0-679-72699-3 (pbk.: v. 1)
ISBN 0-394-58650-6 (v. 2)
ISBN 0-679-73022-2 (pbk.: v. 2)
Interior design by Robert Bull Design

Manufactured in the United States of America

4689753

Title-page illustration: Children register their support for striking New York streetcar drivers in
September 1916. Prints and Photographs Division, Library of Congress.

CONTENTS

PREFACE

Who built the seven towers of Thebes?
The books are filled with the names of kings.
Was it kings who hauled the craggy blocks of stone?. . .
In the evening when the Chinese wall was finished,
Where did the masons go?

—Bertolt Brecht,
"Questions from a Worker Who Reads" (1935)

WHO BUILT AMERICA? surveys the nation's past from an important but often neglected perspective—the experiences of ordinary men and women and the roles they played in the making of modern America. As recently as thirty years ago, such a focus would have been virtually impossible. The research and writing (as well as teaching) of most U.S. historians remained focused on presidents, politics, wars, and the lives and values of the nation's elite—the familiar framework the historical profession consistently had favored. Most historians accepted the notion that there had been little fundamental social and economic conflict in America's past, that a broad consensus about the nation's basic values and its extraordinary prosperity had united the vast majority of its citizens.

In the past three decades much has changed. The social and political upheavals of the 1960s and early 1970s prompted a number of historians—including the authors of this book—to expand their inquiries into America's past. They made dramatic discoveries about the behavior and beliefs of groups traditionally slighted by the older historical synthesis: women; African-Americans, enslaved and free; Native Americans; farmers; factory and white-collar workers; and myriad immigrant groups. They also helped unearth a long and sustained history of conflict among Americans of different classes, races, national origins, and genders over the meaning of American ideals of liberty and equality and the distribution of the nation's enormous material wealth. Their discoveries allowed these historians to think and write differently about familiar topics, including the rise of industrial capitalism, U.S. overseas expansion, successive waves of internal migration and foreign immigration to the nation's cities, depression and war, the rise of industrial unionism, and the widening struggle for civil rights. Entire new fields of historical inquiry emerged, especially working-class and social history, while older areas of scholarly interest widened dramatically, including women's, African-American, and immigrant history.

Despite the enormous ferment in the profession, however, mainstream American history writing remained essentially unaffected by the new scholarship and the insights it offered. Moreover, debates about the significance of the new scholarship during the 1970s and 1980s were bottled up in the narrow confines of the historical profession, where academics talked only to one another about these issues.

The late Herbert G. Gutman—who inspired, cofounded, and collaborated in the American Social History Project until his death in 1985—was one of the first American historians to identify these problems and call for their correction. In 1982 Gutman called for "a new national synthesis" that would use the social and labor history he played so large a role in launching to recast the older economic and political analysis that continued to dominate writing and teaching about American history. This new synthesis would have much to tell ordinary citizens about their country and about the values and traditions that shaped and sustained it. Gutman forcefully argued for making the new synthesis accessible to a broad audience that encompassed general readers as well as students and teachers.

The American Social History Project was created by Herbert Gutman and Stephen Brier in 1981 to realize these ambitious ends. Supported by major grants from the National Endowment for the Humanities (NEH), the Ford Foundation, the City University of New York (CUNY), and others, the Project staff—numbering at times as many as a dozen researchers, writers, teachers, artists, and filmmakers—set out to produce a wide range of accessible educational materials, including books, videos, and viewer guides, and to train college, high-school, junior-high-school, and adult- and labor-education teachers to use them effectively. The two-volume *Who Built America?* text serves as the intellectual keystone of the Project's work.

Who Built America? offers a uniquely cast history of the United States. Its central focus and organizing theme are the changing nature of the work that built, sustained, and transformed American society over the course of almost four centuries and the changing conditions, experiences, outlooks, and conduct of the people who performed that essential labor. Special attention is given to the ways these working people affected and were affected by the more familiar economic, social, cultural, and political processes that together make up the national experience. This focus permits the integration of the history of community, family, gender roles, race, and ethnicity into the more familiar history of politics and economic development. Exploring the history of the nation's laboring majority, moreover, also renders more intelligible the beliefs and actions of the nation's economic, political, and intellectual elites.

For purposes of this book we have defined the category of "working people" broadly. Throughout much of its history, the nation's actual workforce embraced a wide spectrum of people laboring in very different conditions and settings—free and unfree; small proprietor and propertyless; agricultural and domestic as well as industrial, commercial, clerical, and service. Answering the question "Who built America?" therefore requires attention not only to wage-earning industrial laborers but also to indentured servants, slaves, tenants, sharecroppers, independent farm families, artisans, day laborers, clerks, domestic workers, outworkers, and women and children performing unpaid family labor—in short, the great majority of the American population at every phase of the country's development. Ignoring such people would thus not only fail to answer the question posed by our title, it would also miss the protracted, recurring, and complex processes out of which a modern working class emerged.

We have divided this study into two volumes. The principal theme of the first volume is the rise and subsequent decline of various precapitalist labor systems, especially racial slavery, and the parallel development and ultimate dominance of capitalism and its system of wage labor. The second volume carries the narrative and analysis to the present day. It considers the increasing significance of industrial capitalism and wage labor for the country's economy, social relations, domestic politics, foreign policy, popular culture, and intellectual life during the nation's second century and focuses on the corresponding growth and continual recomposition of the American working class. The volume's twelve chapters are divided into three parts:

- Part One considers the years between the great railroad strike of 1877 and the outbreak of war in Europe in 1914, exploring industrial capitalism's Gilded Age growth and the resulting rise of mass movements of protest, including the labor movement, Populism, and socialism. It also considers U.S. overseas expansion and the increasing racism and segregationist legislation that rolled back the gains won by African-Americans in the Reconstruction era, the massive wave of immigration from eastern and southern Europe that transformed the nation's cities after 1900, and the Progressive movement that emerged in response to the nation's growing political and economic crises.
- Part Two surveys the turbulent decades between the two world wars, examining the unparalleled growth and power

of U.S. political and economic institutions, and the continued recomposition of the American working class through a vast internal migration of Americans, black and white, from the rural South. Tracing the dramatic impact of the Great Depression, it details working people's unprecedented mobilization that gave birth to the industrial union movement and helped sustain the partial welfare state created by Franklin Roosevelt's New Deal, and America's entry and ultimate victory in World War II.

- Part Three examines life in post–World War II America, as U.S. military and economic ascendancy and tensions with the Soviet Union defined the Cold War era. It explores the triumph and decline of the industrial labor movement and the changing working-class experience. Highlighting the birth of the civil rights movement that transformed America's political culture and moral values, it also explores U.S. involvement in Vietnam and the rise of new social movements, such as the women's movement, in the 1960s and 1970s. Examining events of the 1980s, it considers America's fading industrial economy, the influx of new immigrants from Asia and Latin America, the rise of the New Right, and the collapse of the Cold War.

We have supplemented the text of each chapter with excerpts from numerous historical documents (letters, diaries, autobiographies, poems, songs, journalism, fiction, official testimony, and oral histories). These "first person" sidebars convey the experience and often the voice of working people during the various historical periods covered in the book. In the interest of clarity, we have sometimes modernized spelling and punctuation.

Each chapter also has drawings, paintings, prints, and photographs that derive from the historical periods covered. These images and their captions present some of the ways the topics considered in each chapter were portrayed and interpreted at the time, as well as how people received information and ideas. The visual record of the past— particularly regarding the lives of working men and women, immigrants, and people of color—requires careful consideration: our captions often alert the reader to distortions and gaps that pock the visual roadway. Pictures that were produced and viewed in specific historical eras can teach us a lot about working people's lives, but it is equally important to understand that there is much these pictures obscure or fail to show.

A book of this size and scope is, of necessity, the result of a team effort. The conception, structure, thematic and analytical emphases, outlining, drafting, and illustration of *Who Built America?* all involved extensive interaction and collaboration among the staff and contributing authors, the supervising and consulting editors, and members of the ASHP research, art, and education teams. ASHP staff members discussed the initial conceptualization of individual chapters at length, after which staff and contributing authors drafted individual chapters. These and subsequent drafts were critiqued several times by the authors of each of the volume's three parts and the supervising and consulting editors, a process of collaboration and revision that determined the final shape of this volume. However collaborative this process, though, in the end the chapters were the product of the work of individuals.

Part One: ASHP staff writer David Brundage wrote initial drafts of chapters 1, 3, and 4. Contributing writer Susan Porter Benson rewrote chapter 1 and drafted additional material for the other chapters in Part One. Contributing writer Bryan Palmer produced the original draft of chapter 2 and rewrote chapter 3, while ASHP staff writer Joshua Freeman rewrote chapter 4. Contributing writer David Bensman then edited the interim drafts of chapters 1, 2, 3, and 4. In the final stage, supervising editor Stephen Brier rewrote chapters 1, 2, and 3, edited the accompanying documents, and prepared the completed chapters for publication; staff member Bret Eynon rewrote chapter 4, edited the documents, and prepared the chapter for publication. Brier wrote the Part One introduction.

Part Two: Joshua Freeman drafted chapters 5, 6, and 7. The chapters were edited by David Bensman. Freeman then edited the chapters and the accompanying documents, and prepared them for publication. ASHP research and writing director Bruce Levine developed preliminary drafts of chapters 8 and 9. David Bensman completed and rewrote these chapters. Stephen Brier then edited chapters 8 and 9, as well as the accompanying documents, and prepared the chapters for publication. Freeman wrote the Part Two introduction.

Part Three: Contributing writer Nelson Lichtenstein drafted chapters 10 and 11. Bret Eynon edited these drafts and the documents for chapter 11, and prepared the chapter for publication. Lichtenstein edited the documents for chapter 10 and prepared it for publication. David Bensman wrote the initial draft of chapter 12. Lichtenstein rewrote chapter 12, which Brier edited and prepared for publication, along with the accompanying documents. Lichtenstein wrote the Part Three introduction.

Visual editor Joshua Brown wrote the volume introduction and the illustration captions.

A number of colleagues read and criticized parts or all of individual chapters or offered documents and sources. We would like to thank Jon Amsden, Betsy Blackmar, Eileen Boris, Susan Brand, Jennifer

Brier, Paul Buhle, Sally Deutsch, Barbara Melosh, Ruth Milkman, Martha Norman, Eric Perkins, Ricardo Romo, Ron Schatz, David Thelen, and Wendy Wolf for their thoughtful responses.

The writers were assisted over the years by a corps of research assistants, including Michael Hyman, Paul Mischler, and especially Michael Musuraca, who was responsible for the initial collection of the volume's first-person documents and participated with the authors and editors in rethinking the volume at a crucial stage of its development. Project administrators Elizabeth Sheehan, Aisha Khan, and Nately Donnell endured endless requests to print and mail drafts of the chapters.

A succession of researchers also contributed to the illustration of this volume. Kate Pfordresher's aesthetic and critical judgment was crucial to conceptualizing and collecting images in the early stages of the book's production. David Osborn and Marci Reaven also researched and located many images. Andrea Ades Vásquez played an important role in the latter stage of collection, combining insight about visual information with determination in tracking down elusive pictures. We also would like to thank a number of friends and colleagues for their help. Eric Breitbart, Jennifer Brier, Gideon Joslyn Brown, George Chauncey, Judith Evans, Mary Janzen, Charles Musser, Eric Perkins, Dorothy Rony, Marnie Schroer, Sally Stein, and Alan Sekula generously provided us with images, directed us to picture sources, or suggested approaches to captioning. Finally, we want to thank the staffs of research libraries (in particular, the New York Public Library), collections, archives, and photo agencies as well as private collectors who assisted us in securing the illustrations. The contributions of other individuals and institutions to the illustration of *Who Built America?*, too numerous to list here, are acknowledged in the picture credits.

We especially want to acknowledge and thank Roy Rosenzweig, the volume's consulting editor. That modest title does not do justice to Roy's contributions to this volume. He read innumerable drafts of the entire manuscript over the years, offering important conceptual insights, catching innumerable errors, and correcting sloppy writing. At a crucial stage in the volume's development Roy's criticisms led us to broaden the focus of the first-person documents. He offered myriad suggestions and ideas to realize that end and supervised the work of Kevin Smead and James Joy, who, along with Cynthia Meyers and Andrea Ades Vásquez, completed the gathering and preparation of the documents.

We are indebted to the Project's board of directors—Peter Almond, Ira Berlin, Eric Foner, Carol Groneman, Leon Litwack, and Roy Rosenzweig—for their continuing support and encouragement, particularly in the difficult period immediately following Herb Gutman's death.

We are grateful to the institutions that provided financial support to the Project and thus made possible the writing of *Who Built America?* Substantial grant awards from the National Endowment for the Humanities and the Ford Foundation allowed us to bring the Project staff together and sustained our labors through 1986. We want to thank Len Oliver and Jim Dougherty of the NEH and Susan Berresford, Sheila Biddle, Alison Bernstein, and Gladys Hardy of the Ford Foundation for their good advice and their patience. Without the support of former chancellor Joseph Murphy of the City University of New York, the Project would never have survived after 1986. We also want to acknowledge the support of the late Harold Proshansky, president of the CUNY Graduate Center, where we were based until 1989, and Deputy Chancellor Laurence Mucciolo, who helped assure CUNY's continuing support. The Project's transfer to Hunter College two years ago reinvigorated our work and provided a stimulating educational environment that enabled us to finish this volume. We want to thank President Paul LeClerc, Provost Laura Strumingher, Dean Carlos Hortas, Stuart Ewen, and many other Hunter faculty and administrators for their continuing encouragement and support.

Finally, we want to acknowledge and thank staff members at Pantheon Books and Random House for their energy and hard work. Bob Bull, Fearn Cutler, Peter Dimock, Kathy Grasso, Altie Karper, Jeanne Morton, Alan Turkus, and many others performed the tireless creative and administrative labor that turned this manuscript into a beautiful book. We also want to thank our line editors, Carol DeSanti and David Frederickson, who helped us express more clearly the arguments we wanted and needed to make in *Who Built America?* Thanks also to Cynthia Meyers and Dave Sutter for their careful proofreading of the galleys and to Margo Matwychuk, who typed the bibliographies.

In acknowledging the contributions to this volume, it would be difficult to exaggerate the role of Herbert Gutman. The impact of Herb's wide-ranging knowledge of American history—conveyed to us in four years of meetings, memos, chapter critiques, and individual consultations—was central to the conception of our task and the evolution of both volumes. Our collective and individual debts to Herb are, quite simply, immeasurable. In completing and publishing *Who Built America?*, it is our hope that we have succeeded in meeting the high standards he set for himself throughout his rich but too-brief career.

Stephen Brier,
Supervising Editor

"The Stride of a Century." Uncle Sam triumphantly, if uncomfortably, bestrides a united and prospering nation on its hundredth birthday in this 1876 Currier and Ives lithograph commemorating the Philadelphia Centennial Exposition.

INTRODUCTION

ONE HUNDRED YEARS!

It is 1876 and the United States has reached a venerable anniversary. The republic has survived for a century since declaring its independence. During that span its citizens have claimed new territories and the bounteous resources they hold; spread railroad and telegraph lines across the continent; built factories, invented new technologies, and joined Europe as a major industrial power; endured three major economic depressions; and fought two wars with England and one with Mexico. Perhaps most miraculously, the United States has just survived a bloody civil war.

United once more, Americans feel the nation deserves a spectacular birthday party. A centennial celebration will provide the occasion to display America's achievements in industry, science, agriculture, and the arts. This national fete should announce, with the kind of razzle-dazzle that will attract the attention of the rest of the world, that the United States is now the model by which all nations must measure "progress." The Centennial Exposition, which opens in Philadelphia on May 10, 1876, is designed to meet these heady expectations.

For six months, six days a week, twelve hours a day, ten million people, from every state and over thirty countries, flock to the Centennial (as it is popularly called). Visitors endure long lines at the entrance turnstiles, but the wait and the fifty-cent admission charge are immediately compensated for by the dramatic vista that lies before them.

Covering 450 acres of Philadelphia's Fairmount Park, the exposition grounds are situated on a lush plateau above the city. Five major exhibition buildings dominate the landscape, looming over a confusion of one hundred smaller pavilions; grand statues and cascading fountains are everywhere. Thousands promenade along the asphalt pathways, every turn presenting an attraction to please the eye, quell an appetite, or quench a thirst. There appears to be an endless choice

"1876—On Guard." Even as Americans celebrated the Centennial, they remained uneasy about the nation's future. In 1876 few could ignore the effects of three years of economic depression. But as this Currier and Ives lithograph indicates, many Americans blamed the nation's problems on agitators and ideas from abroad.

of restaurants, cafés, beer gardens (serving an extremely weak brew), popcorn stands, and ice cream soda fountains. For the more virtuous, ice water is provided at temperance society fountains. The grounds are immense, and those visitors willing to pay five cents choose to board one of the open cars drawn by locomotives along narrow-gauge tracks, or, for a far dearer sixty cents an hour, one of a fleet of rolling chairs driven by gray-liveried attendants.

Sooner or later the visitor must leave the open air and join the crowds entering the pavilions. The choice is vast. Large and small, their architectural styles competing for the visitor's attention, there are twenty-four state buildings, nine foreign government buildings, and an array of pavilions built by American businesses and organizations. The Singer Sewing Machine Building beckons, but so does the Shoe and Leather Building. Depending on where the visitor is from, his or her neighbors back home will want to hear about the exotic New England Log House or the Nevada Quartz Mill. The Bible Pavilion seems welcoming, the Centennial National Bank a wise choice, but you might decide to give the Burial Casket Building a wide berth.

The five major exhibition buildings are gigantic, unlike anything visitors have seen before. In this still largely rural nation, Agricultural Hall covers more than ten acres. Inside, the visitor can marvel at the latest mowing and reaping machines or grow nostalgic before a full-size windmill. The neighboring Horticultural Hall seems to be one great greenhouse thick with exotic plants (and electrically operated organ music), while Memorial Hall, devoted to the fine arts, displays painting and sculpture from around the world.

But as much as visitors have come to the Centennial to compare the work of America's farmers and artists with the rest of the world, the real attraction lies in the fair's Main Hall and Machinery Hall. Devoted to industry and manufacturing, these two buildings embody the latest technology in their very construction. Their glass walls glimmering in the sunlight, the mammoth structures are supported by a latticework of iron trusses and columns.

The Main Hall is the largest building in the world, two and a half acres of natural resources and manufactured products from America, Europe, Asia, and Africa. The centerpiece of the Exposition, however, lies in Machinery Hall. Weighing seven hundred tons, the majestic, forty-foot-high Corliss Double Walking-Beam Engine generates 1,400 horsepower, enough to drive all the other machines in the enormous

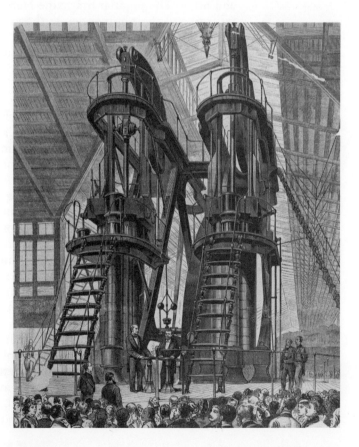

The Centennial begins. President Ulysses S. Grant and Dom Pedro, emperor of Brazil, start up the Corliss Engine in Machinery Hall on the opening day of the Philadelphia Centennial Exposition.

hall. Powered by a steam boiler in an adjacent building, the engine seems to run almost silently. It is an awesome creation, towering above the visitor, representing—in the beauty of its motion, design, and power—the new industrial age.

These massive, cavernous halls of iron and glass, flags and bunting draped overhead, herald the future. Everywhere, in almost choking profusion, are row after row of cases and display cabinets, stacks of products alternating with some piece of revolving machinery. One visitor complains there are too many sewing machines, while another lauds the largest loom in the world. Beneath the high ceiling and amid the clutter are to be found new, almost unbelievable inventions. Visitors view Thomas Alva Edison's telegraph, which can carry multiple messages on one wire. For fifty cents they can send a letter back home composed on the new Remington Arms typewriter. And they are provided with a demonstration of Alexander Graham Bell's curious new telephone (although many are prompted to ask, along with the New York *Tribune*, "Of what use is such an invention?").

For many a visitor a trip to the Centennial is a journey of discovery and pride. The popular magazine *Harper's Weekly* predicts that after returning to their homes across the vast nation, Americans'

> thoughts have been turned from old, worn channels, their feelings quickened and freshened. . . . For months to come there will be something for the farmer to talk about besides his crops; the views of the machinist and mechanic have been widened; . . . the merchant has had a thought of something different from banks and creditors tucked into his brain; and thousands of young people have had their minds enriched as by a visit to foreign countries. . . .

But the Centennial's sights, its grandeur, pomp, and play, are viewed differently by many other Americans. To these people, the Exposition is not so much a celebration of the nation's achievements as it is a diversion from a hard and bitter daily reality. Over the Centennial's seven months, this other America, neglected and stifled by the lavish festivities, occasionally peeks through.

Division characterizes the Centennial's Women's Pavilion. Paid for with contributions from across the country, the Pavilion presents visitors with crafts, inventions, and institutions established and conducted by women. From a power loom operated by a "lady engineer" to a cooking school, from a display of charitable organizations to a model kindergarten, the work of American women is laid before the public. But to many observers, it seems no more than a curiosity, a glimpse of a quaint and separate world. As if announcing the division between Pavilion planners who espouse the private, "domestic" sphere and advocates demanding a wider role for women in U.S. society, the National Woman's Suffrage Association holds its founding meeting in New York City on the same day as the Women's Pavilion opens at the Philadelphia fair. At the Centennial's July Fourth ceremonies, the feminists Elizabeth Cady Stanton and Susan B. Anthony disrupt the proceedings to read a Woman's Declaration of Independence.

Although African-American women helped raise funds for the Centennial, they find no place in the Women's Pavilion. It is a discriminatory condition that runs throughout the Exposition, reflecting the mixed experience of the ex-slaves freed by the victory of the North in the Civil War and made citizens almost eight years earlier by the ratification of the Fourteenth Amendment to the Constitution. No black workers were hired on the construction crews that built the Centennial, and visitors see African-Americans performing only menial tasks, or in the Southern Restaurant, where (as a guidebook describes it) "a band of old-time plantation 'darkies' . . . sing their quaint melodies and strum the banjo."

Only one exhibit addresses recent momentous events in African-American history: a statue located in Memorial Hall titled "The Freed Slave." A focal point for African-Americans visiting the Centennial, the statue comes in for particularly derisive criticism by commentators such as *Atlantic Monthly* editor William Dean Howells. It is, he writes, "a most offensively Frenchy negro, who has broken his chain, and spreading both his arms and legs abroad is rioting in a declamation of something from Victor Hugo; one longs to clap him back into hopeless bondage." Such expressions are replicated in deeds during the Centennial's opening ceremonies. Frederick Douglass—escaped slave, militant abolitionist, and acknowledged leader of the nation's four million African-Americans—is asked to sit on the opening-day speakers' platform, although he is not invited to speak. A policeman, convinced that no black man belongs among the invited dignitaries, bars his way until finally a U.S. senator intervenes on Douglass's behalf.

America's Native American population plays a more pronounced role than African-Americans in the Centennial proceedings, in a manner of speaking. The Smithsonian Institution constructs a massive exhibit of Indian artifacts in the U.S. Government Building, replete with pottery, weapons, tepees, totem poles (never before seen in the East), and life-size costumed mannequins. Native Americans, themselves, are superfluous, since visitors view the exhibit as an exotic counterpoint to the spirit of industrial progress that characterizes the rest of the fair. Indians represent a bygone age; the federal government finally permits them to leave reservations to visit the Centennial in the hope that they will more easily accept their fate after

"The Freed Slave." African-American visitors to the Centennial view the statue celebrating Emancipation in Memorial Hall.

seeing the resources of white civilization arrayed against them. But when news reaches the Centennial in July of the victory of Sioux and Cheyenne warriors at the Battle of Little Big Horn in Dakota Territory, where General George Custer and over two hundred of his men perish, many visitors see the exhibit as evidence of the Indians' unregenerate savagery. "The red man, as he appears in effigy and in photograph in this collection," writes William Dean Howells, "is a hideous demon, whose malign traits can hardly inspire any emotion softer than abhorrence."

Centennial visitors' responses to the many foreign exhibits also alternate between wonder and animosity. Fascinated by costumes, crafts, and buildings constructed by Japanese and Chinese exhibitors, many visitors prefer to rely on racial stereotypes rather than the evidence before their eyes. "The quaint little people with their shambling gait, their eyes set awry in their head, and their grave and gentle ways," comments one visitor, "how can it be in them ... to make such wonderful things?" Spurred by agitation that has turned violent against Chinese residents in California, some American visitors take to harassing people at the Centennial dressed in "foreign" costumes. The opening-day proceedings are marred by attacks on Chinese and Japanese dignitaries.

But perhaps the greatest problem confronting the Centennial lies literally at its doorstep. The celebration occurs not only on the hundredth birthday of independence but also in the third year of the worst economic depression in the nation's history. Instead of visiting Fairmount Park, thousands of unemployed haunt soup kitchens or scavenge through garbage, while homeless and destitute tramps roam the land.

The splendor of the Centennial, in fact, stands in sharp contrast to the shantytown just outside its gates. "Centennial City," as the shantytown is facetiously dubbed by its inhabitants and the police, stretches along Elm Avenue, a mile of tented concessions and cobbled-together sideshows, cheap hotels, and lowly saloons. For many visitors to the Exposition, "Centennial City" offers what the respectable and edifying attractions of the fair can't, especially a wide variety of alcoholic beverages. To many of Philadelphia's homeless, "Centennial City" is a convenient place to bed down. By September, Philadelphia officials have succeeded in evicting all the residents from Elm Street, and "Centennial City" is demolished.

Many employers see the Centennial as a way to ease workers' growing discontent with industrial capitalism. They urge their employees to view the wondrous sights of industrial progress as a way to help them forget the misery of the depression. For working people who possess the requisite admission fee, Sunday—the one full day they don't work—is the only day they can attend the fair. But on Sunday, thanks to pressure from local clergymen, the fairgrounds are closed.

Some companies arrange excursions to the Centennial for their workers during the week. Railroad and coalmining firms are particularly enthusiastic about such trips. They hope that a visit to the Exposition will soothe the bitterness felt by Irish mining families over the suppression of the recent "Long Strike" in eastern Pennsylvania and the destruction of their union. Even as the Philadelphia and Reading Coal and Iron Company sends eleven hundred men, women, and children from the Pennsylvania mines on an all-expense-paid trip to the Centennial, twenty miners are tried in a Schuylkill County courtroom as alleged members of a secret society called the Molly Maguires. They will be convicted of murder, largely based on evidence obtained by a detective hired by the railroad company, and hanged in June of the following year.

Philadelphia and Reading officers, along with corporate executives and officials in dozens of American states and cities, would soon perceive the Centennial as but a temporary respite in an atmosphere of mounting economic and political crisis. Even as the Exposition draws to a close on November 10, 1876, the festive aura of the fair is fading. The outcome of the presidential election that occurred three days earlier is in dispute; it will not be until February of the following year, after negotiations and secret agreements, that Rutherford B. Hayes finally is designated the nineteenth president of the United States. During the intervening months, many fear the republic will be sundered once again by civil war. Then, in the first year of the nation's second century, the vision of industrial progress hallowed by the Centennial meets its greatest challenge yet: the railroad strike of July 1877.

The Great Uprising, as it will be called in years to come, is brought on by the depression's hard times and the desire of the nation's railroads to continue to reap profits in a time of economic crisis. In March 1877, the presidents of the four largest railroads—the Pennsylvania, the New York Central, the Erie, and the Baltimore and Ohio (B&O)—decide to end their ruinous competition and to adopt a plan to cut their employees' wages. A wage cut is hardly necessary; the railroads have already cut costs substantially, and several continue to pay stock dividends to investors despite the economic downturn. John Garrett, president of the Baltimore and Ohio, explains the simple logic behind the railroads' actions: "The great principle upon which we joined to act was to earn more and to spend less."

Railroad workers have suffered one wage reduction after another since the onset of the depression. Their early resistance ended in defeat during the strikes of 1873–74. Beleaguered by hard times and the subsequent blacklisting of members, railroad unions have been virtually destroyed. But the new wage reduction pushes the workers beyond the limits of endurance.

The spark is lit when the B&O implements its 10 percent wage cut on July 16. Workers in Martinsburg, West Virginia, stage a spontaneous strike, vowing to shut down the railroad yards until wages are restored. Three days later, as the strike intensifies, President Hayes orders federal troops into West Virginia to protect the B&O and the nation from "insurrection."

Instead of suppressing resistance, the use of federal troops in a domestic labor dispute incites a wave of popular anger across the country. In Baltimore, the Maryland state militia fires on huge crowds of workers, leaving eleven dead and forty wounded. Work stoppages rapidly spread north and west along the railroad lines to Pennsylvania. There, the strike reaches its most dramatic climax.

The spark. A contemporary illustrated news weekly, *Frank Leslie's Illustrated Newspaper*, depicts striking railroad workers stopping trains in Martinsburg, West Virginia, on Tuesday, July 17, 1877.

Pittsburgh is dominated by the Pennsylvania Railroad, the largest corporation in America. Residents of the city have been particularly hard hit by the depression and blame the railroad for much of their misery. When Pittsburgh railroad workers go on strike on July 19 under the banner of the recently revived Trainmen's Union, they are also supported by the city's ironworkers. "We're in the same boat," says one iron-roller at a strike meeting held that evening. "I won't call employers despots, I won't call them tyrants, but the term 'capitalists' is sort of synonymous and will do as well." Much of Pittsburgh's population sympathizes with the railroad workers, including the city's militia companies, which are largely composed of workers. If Pennsylvania Railroad officials are to find help in suppressing the strike, it will have to come from outside Pittsburgh. On July 20, the adjutant general of Pennsylvania orders the Philadelphia militia to Pittsburgh. "My troops will see that the trains pass," asserts Pennsylvania Railroad president Tom Scott from his Philadelphia headquarters.

When Philadelphia troops reach Pittsburgh the next day, they are met by a large and angry crowd of strikers and sympathizers. Unnerved by their reception, soldiers suddenly thrust their bayonets at members of the crowd. Rocks are thrown at the troops, and they answer with a volley of rifle fire. A newspaper reporter at the scene describes the panic that follows: "Women and children rushed frantically about, some seeking safety, others calling for friends and relatives. Strong men halted with fear, and trembling with excitement, rushed madly to and fro, trampling upon the killed and wounded." When the gunfire finally ends, twenty Pittsburgh citizens, including a woman and three small children, lie dead.

News of the killing quickly spreads. Pittsburgh residents, including thousands of workers from nearby mills, mines, and factories, converge on the Pennsylvania Railroad yards. By dawn they have set fire to railroad property. New shooting erupts as the Philadelphia militiamen, who have retreated into the railroad roundhouse, now flee for their lives. Twenty more Pittsburgh residents and five soldiers are killed. Striking Pittsburgh workers and other residents quickly form citizens' patrols to restore calm to the city's streets and prevent looting by the unemployed. When federal troops finally arrive a week later, the citizens' patrols are disarmed and the local strike ended.

In the next few days the strike spreads across the Midwest. Workers take over entire towns, shutting down work until employers meet their demands. The same railroad and telegraph lines that have unified the nation and laid the groundwork for the full emergence of industrial capitalism also link and unify workers' protests. The strike spreads as far as Galveston, Texas, and San Francisco. Without any central organization (most national unions are defunct because of the depression), the conflict spawns local committees, many led by anarchists and socialists, that provide unity and direction to the strike.

In Chicago, the strike quickly becomes a citywide general strike that touches off open class warfare. Roving groups of strikers sweep through the city's industrial areas, calling workers out of shops and factories. City officials respond with extraordinary force. Chicago's bankers, lawyers, and merchants organize squads of special police to combat what they call "stray strikers and tramps." Police are ordered by the mayor to fire directly into crowds of strikers; two strikers are shot dead in the first confrontation at the giant McCormick reaper works. As police break up meetings and charge through working-class neighborhoods, men and women fight back with grim determination. "The women are a great deal worse than the men," says one journalist unsympathetic to the strikers, claiming that nearly one-fifth of the crowds are composed of women. The Chicago strike is also notable for the unity maintained between German, Bohemian (Czech), and Irish workers, thanks in large part to the strike's anarchist and social-

July 22, 1877. The interior of the Pennsylvania Railroad upper roundhouse the day after the battle between Philadelphia militia and Pittsburgh strikers.

ist leaders. Nevertheless, with the overwhelming appearance of federal troops and artillery on the streets of the city, the strike comes to an end.

Socialists are also active in the St. Louis strike, where thousands of workers participate in a largely peaceful general strike. They shut down virtually all of the city's industries while government officials flee the city. Black workers in St. Louis take an active role in the strike, closing down canneries and docks. When an African-American steamboat worker, addressing a crowd of white workers, asks, "Will you stand to us regardless of color?" the crowd responds, "We will! We will! We will!"

But racism prevails in other strikes, particularly in the Far West. In San Francisco a crowd gathers to discuss strike action but ends up rampaging through the city's Chinese neighborhoods, killing several residents and burning buildings.

The Great Uprising of 1877 lasts two weeks, leaving its mark on cities and towns across fourteen states and from coast to coast. In its wake, over a hundred people have died and millions of dollars' worth of property has been destroyed. It is the first truly national strike in American history and the first in which the federal government has placed its full power (in the form of the army) on the side of business. No matter which side they supported in the strike, as Americans recover from the shock of July 1877, few can any longer find solace— let alone pride—in the spirit of unmitigated industrial progress they had celebrated at the Centennial a short year before. The Great Uprising has demonstrated that the United States is condemned to suffer the class-based conflict that has plagued Europe since the birth of industrial capitalism.

That conflict would intensify at critical moments over the next hundred years, but it would never recur in quite the way it had in the summer of 1877. The chapters that follow detail the changing form and substance of the divisions that dominated American life in the century after the great railroad strike: first and foremost, the conflict between capital and labor; but also the struggles of women, African-Americans, and European, Latino, Asian, and Caribbean immigrants for inclusion in American society. As we will see, these struggles were played out in an international arena increasingly dominated by the United States but also fundamentally shaped by the American people's experience of war, economic dislocation, and ideological conflict.

WHO BUILT AMERICA?

PART ONE

MONOPOLY AND UPHEAVAL

1877–1914

THE GREAT railroad strikes of 1877, as the young labor leader Samuel Gompers noted, rang like an alarm bell heralding a new era of conflict and division in the nation. This conflict unfolded over the next four decades against a backdrop of extraordinary economic, political, and social changes wrought by industrial capitalism. The United States became the world's most powerful industrial nation in these years, giving rise to manufacturing enterprises of breathtaking and unprecedented size and output. In this same period, America launched a war with Spain that resulted in U.S. domination of Puerto Rico, the Philippines, Cuba, and Hawaii. Millions of immigrants from Europe, Asia, and Latin

America poured into the United States after 1900, feeding industrial capitalism's seemingly insatiable appetite for new workers. Urban America also took modern form and shape in this era, as the populations of New York and Chicago swelled beyond a million residents each and contemporary transportation, sanitation, and safety systems came into being.

Few Americans—old or new, factory worker or small farmer—could avoid being drawn into new forms of dependency, on wages or market relations, that U.S. capitalism imposed on their lives, as it did on those of millions of others who lived and worked under U.S. control in the Caribbean, Latin America, and the islands in the Pacific Ocean. As we will see in Part One, over the forty years from the 1877 strikes to America's entry into World War I, working men and women—African-Americans, native-born whites, and European, Latin American, and Asian immigrants—struggled repeatedly to find a place for themselves in industrial America as their communities were transformed by the growth of economic monopoly, unimaginable individual wealth, and unbridled political power.

Americans were sharply divided on the meaning of these changes. On one side stood industrial capitalists and their political and intellectual supporters: they justified capitalists' newly won wealth and power with an ideology that celebrated acquisitive individualism, laissez-faire economics, and the "survival of the fittest." On the other side, working men and women embraced the ideal of collectivity and the power of mutual, rather than individual, action to blunt the devastating impact of industrial capitalism on their work and family life and their communities.

The people and communities transformed by the dizzying growth of industrial capitalism, and the cultures of collectivity they created in response to that transformation, became the base from which working people launched a series of violent class wars unprecedented in the nation's history. The names and dates of individual battles—Haymarket, Homestead, Pullman, Coeur D'Alene, Lawrence, Paterson, Ludlow; 1886, 1892, 1894, 1912, 1913, 1914—became signposts along the tortuous road of industrial and political conflict that defined the era. Radical ideas—including Populism, feminism, anarchism, and socialism—animated many of these conflicts.

Out of this heady brew of labor struggle, political unrest, and a spate of tragic factory fires and coalmine explosions emerged a belief, shared by workers, middle-class professionals, and many business leaders, that the Gilded Age excesses of industrial capitalism required reform. This movement, known as Progressivism, articulated a modern notion that government should play a central role in regulating the nation's social, economic, and political ills.

Some of the issues facing the nation—child labor, factory safety, tainted food and drugs, political corruption, unchecked economic monopoly—proved amenable to the efforts of this diverse reform coalition to improve conditions of work and life in post-1900 America. But as war loomed over Europe, the particular conflicts that gave rise to Progressivism increasingly took a back seat to concern over the spreading international crisis. Nonetheless, Progressivism inaugurated a new era in U.S. politics, one in which the federal government took some small steps toward its now familiar role as guarantor of economic stability and the minimal safety and health of its citizenry.

"The Ironworkers' Noontime." Few painters chose industrial work as a subject in the late nineteenth century, its conditions seeming inappropriate for a medium that tended to highlight noble themes. Thomas Anshutz's painting, completed in about 1881, is therefore an unusual work, realistically portraying the weariness of skilled ironworkers at a Wheeling, West Virginia, nail factory, while also celebrating the workers' strength and craft pride.

PROGRESS AND POVERTY

THE GROWTH OF INDUSTRIAL CAPITALISM

INDUSTRIAL CAPITALISM'S EXPLOSIVE AND UNSTABLE GROWTH

THE NORTH'S victory in the Civil War inaugurated a period of extraordinary growth and consolidation of American industrial capitalism. Within fifteen years of war's end, Andrew Carnegie built his first steel plant, John D. Rockefeller organized the Standard Oil monopoly, and Alexander Graham Bell began manufacturing telephones. By 1894 the United States would become the world's leading industrial power, producing more than England, France, and Germany, its three largest competitors, combined. As a result, leading capitalists such as Carnegie and Rockefeller became unimaginably wealthy.

7

"The World Is My Market." Uncle Sam looks across the Atlantic for customers in this 1877 cartoon lauding the superiority of American over European products.

The northern victory in 1865 had in fact ensured industrial capitalism's successful development. By keeping the nation's political boundaries intact, the victory gave northern manufacturers access again to southern markets. In addition, during and immediately after the war the Republican Party, led by powerful iron manufacturers and coalmine owners, passed laws to stimulate industrial growth. Banking acts established a stable currency, high import tariffs protected American industry from foreign competition, and federal loans and huge land grants encouraged railroad expansion. An ideology that stressed the dignity of those who produced and the key role of labor in the expanding economy provided the philosophical justification for the Republican economic program and helped assure the party's political dominance in the postwar decades.

The nation's economic growth in the postwar era owed much to its abundance of natural resources: rich farmland provided food for a growing urban workforce, while extensive coal, iron, and mineral resources supplied the raw materials to feed the nation's mills and factories. But it was the dramatic expansion of the nation's railroad network after the war that made possible a veritable explosion of industrial growth. In the quarter-century following the completion of the transcontinental link in 1869, 100,000 miles of track were laid, giving the United States the most extensive transportation system in the world.

This surge in railroad-building required huge quantities of iron, steel, stone, and lumber, spurring the expansion of those industries as well. In 1882, for example, nine-tenths of the nation's entire production of steel went into rails. And by linking the United States into one vast national market, the railroads enabled manufacturers to reach consumers across the continent with their products. This, in turn, encouraged manufacturers to produce goods in larger quantities and to experiment with new, large-scale processes of industrial production. For example, the most important invention of the period, the Bessemer converter, which transformed pig iron into steel at relatively low cost, helped increase steel output by ten times between 1877 and 1892. Other industries grew, too: the output of copper rose seven times and that of crude oil four times. Pioneering electrical manufacturers already produced $23 million worth of goods in 1892.

The development of the transcontinental rail network and the national market that followed it did not come without difficulty. Until railroads agreed on a standard gauge for track (the actual distance between the rails), engines and cars filled with manufactured products could not move freely from one line to another. When a standard gauge was finally agreed on in the 1870s and 1880s, goods could move unhindered across the country. Small producers who had once dominated local markets—for example, a maker of iron stoves in Cincinnati—now faced competition from products made in distant factories and hauled, by the railroads, to markets all across the United States.

Despite these signs of prosperity and an expanding national market for manufactured goods, America's late-nineteenth-century economic growth was profoundly unstable. The eight years following the war's end were generally prosperous, but in late 1873 the nation paid the price for the excesses of its capitalists. Businessmen had engaged in a frenzy of investment in railroads and industries during the postwar prosperity, taking advantage of an unregulated financial and credit structure. In September, the collapse of Jay Cooke and Company, one of the country's largest investment houses, led to runs on a number of banks across the country and the closing for a week of the New York Stock Exchange. Five years of the most severe depression America had yet seen followed. One million workers lost their jobs; many faced outright starvation, and others tramped the land seeking relief and employment.

An upswing in the late 1870s brought a short-lived return of prosperity, which lasted barely four years. Industrial expansion was undercut once again by another depression, lasting from 1882 to 1885. This downturn was moderate compared to the longer and deeper depression that preceded it; but still, many industrial towns and working-class communities were hit hard. The worst was yet to come, however: a five-year-long economic collapse beginning in 1893 devastated rural and urban communities across the country. All in all, depression gripped the United States in almost half the years between 1873 and the turn of the century.

The "business cycle," this pattern of alternating rapid growth and sharp depression, boom and bust, haunted American workers and capitalists alike. Security became a fleeting memory. Few wageworkers, even those who were highly skilled, could count on full-time work all year round, even in the midst of a period of economic boom. Businessmen faced similar uncertainty. Those who avoided outright failure had to contend with the long-term decline in the prices of manufactured goods: from 1866 to 1890, average product prices shrank by over half. This decline affected nearly every sector of the economy, slashing profits and the wages businessmen were willing or able to pay their workers.

"A PATH IS OPEN'D FOR ALL TIME . . ."

This song, titled "The Pacific Railroad," was written by George F. Root, one of the best-known composers of his day, to celebrate the completion of the transcontinental railway system. The driving of the golden spike that connected the Union Pacific and Central Pacific railroad lines at Promontory Point, Utah, on May 10, 1869, seemed to Root and many other Americans to open up the endless bounty of the continent to all.

Ring out, O Bells! let cannons roar,
  In loudest tones of thunder,
The iron bars, from shore to shore,
  Are laid, and nations wonder.
Thro' deserts vast, and forests deep,
  Thro' mountains grand and hoary.
A path is open'd for all time,
  And we behold the glory.
Ring out, O Bells! *etc.*

We who but yesterday appear'd
  As settlers of the border,
Where only savages were rear'd
  Mid chaos and disorder—
We wake to find ourselves midway
  In continental station,
And send our greetings either way,
  Across the mighty nation.

We reach out to'ard the Golden Gate
  And eastward to the oceans;
The tea will come at light'ning rate,
  And likewise Yankee notions.
From spicy islands of the West
  The breezes now are blowing,
And all the world will do its best
  To keep the cars a-going.
Ring out, O Bells! *etc.*

The railroads illustrated how rapid growth, competition, and plummeting prices went hand in hand. Railroad companies had to pay high fixed costs for maintenance of equipment and track as well as substantial interest payments on bonds used to finance their construction, so they had strong incentives to continue operations even if they had to drop their rates to rock-bottom levels to do so. Low revenues were preferable to no revenues. Hauling empty cars was nearly as expensive as hauling the same cars loaded with freight, so railroad managers were willing to offer extremely low rates. As a result, freight costs fell by 70 percent over the last thirty years of the century, severely squeezing railroad profits. But because transportation costs made up such a large share of the final cost of manufactured goods, lower railroad rates also meant lower wholesale prices overall.

Industrial overproduction and intense competition among manufacturers also caused prices to fall. The Bessemer converter produced more steel than the market could absorb. Once expensive machinery was installed in a factory, manufacturers faced the same problem of high fixed costs as the railroads: they had to pay for the equipment even if it lay idle, so it was better to keep producing. Production outstripped demand, corporations aggressively cut prices, and profit margins disappeared.

America's extraordinary post–Civil War economic expansion contained within it the seeds of its own demise. The industrial system, which held out the hope of material plenty for all, was proving to be anything but predictable in the way it actually worked.

THE EMERGENCE OF URBAN-INDUSTRIAL LIFE

"We are fast drifting to that condition of society which preceded the downfall of [ancient] Sparta, Macedonia, Athens, and Rome," wrote a railroad carpenter in the late 1870s, "where a few were very rich, and the many very poor." Across the continent, many Americans shared the carpenter's dismay. Citizens in all walks of life found their accustomed ways of living and working disrupted. Although the new capitalist order created vast wealth and abundant individual opportunity, the very basis of the American republic—the ideal of economic independence for individual citizens—was in danger of being undermined.

For the first time, preindustrial groups—farmers, merchants, small-town artisans, indeed, most Americans—found themselves increasingly dependent on market forces and huge concentrations of power unprecedented in American history. A modern working class had emerged in just over thirty years of industrial growth, in a nation once dominated and even defined by preindustrial groups and ideals.

The human misery that had horrified American observers of English industrialization now scarred U.S. life as well. But those who saw a society divided neatly between the few rich and the many poor oversimplified the situation. Many Americans, especially skilled native-born workers and a new middle class, lived between these two dramatic extremes. The nation's class structure was fluid in the late nineteenth century, but it would be shaped by four key processes: the move from farm to factory; the rapid expansion of wage labor; the explosive growth of cities; and immigration. Each began before the Civil War, but sharply accelerated in the postwar years.

The first social transformation was the shift away from the land. Before the Civil War, the United States was still overwhelmingly an agricultural nation. About six of every ten Americans cultivated the soil, while fewer than three in ten were employed in industrial pursuits. By the end of the century, nonagricultural occupations employed nearly two-thirds of the labor force. The manufacturing workforce grew most dramatically of all, increasing four times, from 1.5 million workers in 1860 to nearly 6 million in 1900, while U.S. population in the same period increased two and a half times, from about 31 million to 76 million. For a society that had long regarded the independent farmer as the foundation of national virtue, agriculture's decline was alarming.

Beneath the shift from agriculture to industry lay a second, even greater social change: the eclipse of self-employment and the emergence of wagework as the way most Americans earned their livelihood. In 1860, as many people were self-employed as earned wages. By 1900, two of every three Americans relied on wages. The decline of the independent artisans or craftsmen who had produced and sold goods out of their own workshops had begun in the early nineteenth century and accelerated as factory production spread. Many working Americans still believed that hard work and individual sacrifice would pave the way from wage labor to economic independence, but industrial growth after the Civil War seemed to dash these hopes. Joseph Buchanan, a Colorado printer and labor leader in the 1880s, recalled:

> Twenty years ago, the [worker] could, by being industrious and economical, raise himself from the days-pay condition to a little business of his own. . . . Today the opportunity to start in his business for himself has been thrust from him by the greedy hand of the great manufacturers. . . . The man who can rise from the wage condition in these days must catch a windfall from his uncle or [find] a bank unlocked.

Third, industrial growth centered in cities during these years. Once manufacturers could use steam power instead of water power, they no longer had to locate their factories alongside rivers. Instead, they were able to build factories in urban areas where there was better access to railroads, raw materials, consumer markets, and not least of all, a ready supply of workers. By 1900, nine-tenths of all manufacturing took place in cities.

People followed factories into the cities, which grew twice as fast as the nation's population as a whole. The modern American city as we now know it was born in these decades, as were the essential urban services, including professional fire and police forces, sewers, extensive and safe water supplies, large hospitals, streetcars, and electric railways. By 1890, one of every three Americans already lived in urban areas. "We cannot all live in cities," the newspaper editor Horace Greeley mused, "yet nearly all seem determined to do so." In 1860, only three cities—New York, Philadelphia, and Brooklyn—had more than 250,000 inhabitants. By 1890, eleven cities had surpassed that size, while the population of Philadelphia topped 1 million, and New York exceeded 1.5 million.

Chicago grew most spectacularly of all. A city of 100,000 on the eve of the Civil War, its population had passed 1 million in 1890. A city expanding that fast could neither build housing nor deliver services as rapidly as its population expanded; overcrowding and squalor became commonplace. City lots that had housed single families were now subdivided and rebuilt until they held as many as thirty-two households crammed together in tiny apartments.

The cities were home to great wealth at the same time as they harbored the foulest and most degrading slums. Businessman Potter Palmer's mansion on Chicago's Lake Shore Drive boasted tapestried walls, marble floors, an eighty-foot tower, and mother-of-pearl washbasins. But in the tenements of the near North Side, outdoor privies overflowed in the courtyards where children played, and windows that faced the sun were prized.

Between these extremes were skilled workers and members of a new middle stratum, whose emergence was one of the distinctive features of late-nineteenth-century American society. Some skilled-worker families—hat finishers, for example—continued to live in industrial neighborhoods in houses they owned or rented; their low daily wages limited their mobility. Other highly paid skilled workers managed to save enough to move away from the noise and dirt of downtown urban life. In growing suburban and semisuburban neighborhoods, these craftsmen and their families lived next to members of a middle class, a group composed primarily of people of old American stock or of immigrants from the British Isles who worked either

"The Slaves of the Sweaters." An immigrant tailor's family returns from a contractor, carrying material to be sewn into garments back home. Scenes such as this of urban poverty were portrayed in the Gilded Age illustrated newspapers. Photography and individual "art" prints, however, tended to celebrate the city; the images were depopulated, focusing on the "grand style" architecture of new buildings or constructing distant bird's-eye views of ideal urban landscapes.

as self-employed businessmen or at white-collar or professional jobs. Merchant tailors, for example, who had once labored alongside their employees in nondescript workrooms, now dressed elegantly, received their customers in luxurious shops, and hid the actual manufacture of clothing in back rooms.

The new urban middle class not only labored and lived differently than their poorer working-class counterparts; they consumed differently as well. Industrial capitalism produced more than capital goods such as iron and steel; it also created a wealth of consumer-oriented "products." By the mid-1890s, 300,000 of the telephones Alexander Graham Bell had invented just two decades earlier were already used

Gibson girls. In the 1890s, Charles Dana Gibson's magazine illustrations of fashionable young women gained wide popularity. The physical type he portrayed became the standard of beauty, a romantic ideal that suggested a new independence while celebrating the privileges and glamour of elite society.

in homes and businesses around the country. Thomas A. Edison produced his first electric lamp in 1879 and was manufacturing more than a million light bulbs a year by 1890.

Building on these initial successes, entrepreneurs also began manufacturing consumer items once produced entirely in the home. These items were targeted initially at women who could afford to buy them, those in middle-class and high-income, skilled-working-class households. By the 1890s, for example, Royal baking powder, which was easier to use and faster than yeast, was being mass-produced. Firms such as Royal spent lavishly to promote their products, using catchy advertising slogans to capture the attention of this expanding market of "consumers." In 1882, the Procter Soap Company accidentally produced a bath soap that floated, named the mistake Ivory, and pitched it to the nation with the slogan "It floats!" Tired of the drudgery of daily baking and periodic soapmaking, many women responded enthusiastically to these and other newly packaged products.

The most important new consumer item in the late nineteenth century was ready-made clothing, produced in thousands of small factories and tenement sweatshops. Children's clothing and heavy outerwear were soon available for all members of the family. By the 1890s, businesses also began mass-marketing women's clothing. As the "Gibson girl" look became popular, women's skirts and shirtwaists (elaborate blouses) were available in every price range. Whereas Ivory soap and Royal baking powder offered women the opportunity to ease their household labors, store-bought clothes had an additional appeal: a chance for the "woman of the house" and her family to be "in style."

Merchants organized giant firms and chain stores to meet the growing demand for new consumer products. By 1900, department stores such as R. H. Macy in New York and Marshall Field in Chicago offered downtown shoppers vast arrays of merchandise along with free services and excitement. City neighborhoods far removed from downtown as well as smaller cities had their more modest retail counterparts. Small merchants in distant cities and towns felt the competition of chain stores such as Woolworth's and the A&P, while the lavish mail-order catalogs of Sears, Roebuck and Company and Montgomery Ward reached deep into the American heartland by the end of the nineteenth century.

While Americans—rural and urban, middle class and working class—increasingly came to share a thirst for new consumer products, sharp differences remained. In their new urban neighborhoods, the growing income of the middle class gave them access to innovations far beyond those available to the less affluent working class: the homes of the more affluent featured such comforts as central heating, electricity, and indoor bathrooms. But being middle class was often a state of mind as much as a matter of one's bank account; members of the middle class saw themselves as "respectable," observing their own rules about good taste and conduct. Much about the growth of urban-industrial life offended their sensibilities and seemed to menace their world: the sheer size of factories; the unbridled greed of capitalists; and most powerfully, the extreme poverty and "alien" culture of the urban-immigrant masses.

The great wave of immigration that swept into the United States was the fourth process shaping American society in the late nineteenth century. The largest worldwide population movement in human history brought 10 million immigrants, mostly from Europe, but from Asia as well, to the United States between 1860 and 1890. In the 1880s alone, as many immigrants came to this nation—5.25 million—as arrived in the first six decades of the nineteenth century.

Immigrants continued to arrive primarily from Ireland, Germany, and Britain, as they had before the war, but there were also smaller streams from all points of the compass: Scandinavia, Italy, and China sent hundreds of thousands of men to work on American farms, in the factories, and on the railroads. Lesser numbers came from among the various nationalities of the Austro-Hungarian Empire, particularly Bohemians from an area now in western Czechoslovakia. With the exception of the Irish, males predominated among these diverse immigrant groups.

Many came because they were forced off the land in their native countries. One and a half million Irish men and women left for America between the Civil War and 1890, for example, because of the consolidation of Irish agriculture, rapid population growth, and a major agricultural depression. Emigration from more developed economies such as Great Britain and Germany had a different cause: a long European industrial depression, triggered partly by competition from the United States, impoverished many European

" . . . THIS QUEER CONGLOMERATE MASS"

Jacob Riis—a journalist and photographer of industrial America, and himself a Danish immigrant—exposed the deplorable conditions of late-nineteenth-century urban life in his widely read book How the Other Half Lives, *published in 1890. Despite his immigrant background, Riis's attitudes mirrored the prejudices of the dominant culture toward "foreigners," as revealed in his description of an immigrant neighborhood on New York's Lower East Side.*

WHEN ONCE I asked the agent of a notorious Fourth Ward alley how many people might be living in it I was told: One hundred and forty families . . . one hundred Irish, thirty-eight Italian, and two that spoke the German tongue. Barring the agent herself, there was not a native-born individual in the court. The answer was characteristic of the cosmopolitan character of lower New York, very nearly so of the whole of it, wherever it runs to alleys and courts. One may find for the asking an Italian, a German, a French, African, Spanish, Bohemian, Russian, Scandinavian, Jewish, colony. Even the Arab, who peddles "holy earth" . . . as a direct importation from Jerusalem, has his exclusive preserves at the end of Washington Street. The one thing you shall vainly ask for in the chief city of America is a distinctively American community. There is none. . . . They [the native-born] are not here. In their place has come this queer conglomerate mass of heterogeneous elements, ever striving and working like whiskey and water in one glass, and with the like result: final union and a prevailing taint of whiskey.

"Bandit's Roost." Jacob Riis's photographs starkly exposed the plight of "how the other half lives" to the audiences who attended his lantern-slide shows or saw engraved versions in newspapers. But, as indicated in this photograph of a Mulberry Street alley, Riis often posed and framed his subjects in ways that were meant to arouse fear and distaste as much as sympathy among viewers.

artisans and factory hands during the same time period that America's demand for industrial labor took off.

To attract this much-needed labor force, railroad and steamship companies advertised throughout Europe and China the glories of American life. But potential immigrants were probably more convinced by encouraging words from those who had already come to America. Pioneering immigrants kept in touch with their Old World families and communities. The success of Francesco Barone, who prospered as a Buffalo saloonkeeper, spurred eight thousand people to move from his home village in Sicily to his adopted city, many with his direct assistance. Potential immigrants adjusted their plans according to the ups and downs of the business cycle: immigration fell sharply during the American depressions of 1873–78 and 1882–85.

On the other hand, in boom periods such as the late 1880s, immigrants accounted for as much as one-fifth of the country's total population growth.

Immigrants and their sons and daughters—the "second generation"—constituted a major proportion of the population, especially in the large cities. Nearly nine of ten Chicagoans were first- or second-generation immigrants by 1880. In New York, Milwaukee, Detroit, and St. Louis, the figure was about eight of ten. Approximately one of every three industrial workers in late-nineteenth-century America was an immigrant; but immigrants and their children especially dominated the industrial workforce of large cities. As a clergyman observed of Chicago, "Not every foreigner is a workingman, but in the cities, at least, it may almost be said that every workingman is a foreigner."

These movements—from agriculture to industry, from country to city, from economic independence to wage dependency, from the homeland of one's ancestors to a strange new land—fundamentally transformed all aspects of American life: the combined effect of these new forces left few untouched. The tentacles of urban-industrial life reached far into the countryside, drawing all into a market economy that was no longer local and face-to-face. The landowning farm family living in a rude sod hut on the Nebraska plains could order its dishpan from the Sears, Roebuck catalog; and the market price of the grain it grew now depended on decisions made in corporate headquarters in eastern cities as well as on the weather in grain-growing areas on the other side of the globe.

THE REMAKING OF THE AMERICAN WORKING CLASS

A diverse and stratified working class emerged in the wake of industrial capitalism's post–Civil War growth. Race and ethnicity, levels of skill, gender, and age separated working people. Men and women, adults and children, even members of the same family, often found very different opportunities open to them, and they lived and labored in ways informed by their various identities.

Skilled workers—who made up one-sixth of the workforce—were usually white men, and either native-born, or the native-born children of northern and western European immigrants. Such workers usually secured jobs through the intervention of family and friends, and so many trades took on a decidedly ethnic character. The sons of Irish immigrants often worked as plumbers, carpenters, and bricklayers. Germans came to dominate such urban crafts as furnituremaking, brewing, and baking, while the English, Welsh, and Scots—who had emigrated from the center of the world's first industrial revo-

Cigars and the news. While his fellow workers make cigars, one craftsman reads aloud from a newspaper. This arrangement, where cigarmakers pooled their wages to cover the pay of a designated reader, indicates how some skilled trades maintained preindustrial customs even as their work became subdivided and mechanized.

lution—filled the ranks of skilled machinists, metalworkers, and miners.

Skilled workers enjoyed high wages because employers relied on their craft knowledge and were prepared to pay a premium for it. Possession of a skill also meant independence and considerable control over daily conditions on the job, though such control varied from craft to craft. Skilled workers often refused to work in unsatisfactory circumstances and produced only what they agreed was "a good day's work." They demanded respect from the boss and unity among the workers in their trade.

The ideal of craft unity became almost a moral code for late-nineteenth-century skilled workers; collective action was as central to their world as belief in individualism and profitability was to capitalists such as Rockefeller and Carnegie. Skilled workers realized this collective ideal by forming unions to protect themselves, although no more than one-third of the workers in any nineteenth-century trade were union members. Their power rested as much on their personal ties and craft knowledge as it did on the strength of their formal organizations.

The unskilled—usually new European and Chinese immigrants, African-Americans, women, and children—were less able to control conditions on the job. Difficult financial circumstances usually forced them to take whatever work was available. Although women from England and Germany, like women born in the United States, could avoid work as domestic servants, far fewer first-generation Irish women escaped such a fate. One maid described the drudgery, isolation, and lack of independence of domestic work by suggesting how hard it was "to give up your whole life to somebody else's orders. . . . [You] always feel as if you was looked at over a wall, like." Similarly, employment opportunities for African-Americans, Mexican-Americans, and Asian immigrants were limited. African-American men could farm and do menial labor for wages; they served as gardeners, coach drivers, and doormen. African-American women also farmed, took in laundry, and, like young Irish women, worked as domestic servants. Mexican-American families worked southwestern farmlands they and their ancestors had occupied for generations prior to annexation by the United States in the late 1840s and early 1850s; Mexican men also labored on the railroads and in the expanding metal and coalmining industries of Colorado, New Mexico, and Arizona. Chinese men (few Chinese women emigrated) found work in laundries and restaurants in the Far West. Daughters of native-born and immigrant parents could take advantage of two rapidly growing white-collar occupations: retail selling and office work.

As a rule, wages varied directly with an occupational group's social power and status. Skilled craftsmen did considerably better than the unskilled: the best-paid craftsman (a locomotive engineer or a glassblower, for example) could bring home more than $800 a year; a textile worker's family had to survive on $350 a year. But the number of skilled jobs in the labor market was declining rapidly. In the late 1880s, workers without a skill were about evenly divided between those who eked out a living barely above the poverty line of $500 yearly and those who fell below even that meager standard. Unskilled laborers earned on average only about $1.50 per day—when they could find work. Male workers typically earned at least 50 percent more than women. And white workers commanded significantly higher wages than African-Americans, Mexican-Americans, or Chinese.

All working people, skilled and unskilled, also faced the prospect of unemployment or the threat that it was just around the corner. In 1878, as the five-year-long depression ended, between 500,000 and 1 million working people remained unemployed. Though employment soon picked up, by the mid-1880s as many as 2 million were out of work. Workers were long accustomed to lost time because of injury or illness, but the unemployment produced by the business cycle was a tremendous burden.

Despite chronic low wages and fear of unemployment, working-class families did benefit from the falling prices of goods. From 1870 until the end of the century, workers' wages at least remained fairly

The ironworkers sell soap. After Thomas Anshutz's painting was reproduced as a *Harper's Weekly* engraving in 1884, the popularity of the print prompted Procter and Gamble to exploit its theme to sell the company's Ivory Soap. Publishing a series of lithographs "suitable for framing" based on "The Ironworkers' Noontime," Procter and Gamble transformed the nobility of skilled labor articulated by Anshutz into a picture of grimy industrial work relieved by its "99 44/100% pure" product.

steady over the long run (despite wage cuts imposed by managers); in the same period virtually everything was becoming less expensive. The food that cost $1.00 in 1870 sold for just 78 cents a decade later, a notable savings at a time when more than half the income of a typical working-class family went for food. Thus the "real" wages of workers, adjusted for changes in the cost of living, actually rose slowly.

Despite the lower prices, many families had to send more than one family member out to work in order to survive. As the chief of the Massachusetts Bureau of Labor Statistics put it in 1882, "a family of workers can always live well, but the man with a family of small children to support, unless his wife works also, has a small chance of living properly." Consequently, the number of women and children in the labor force more than doubled between 1870 and 1890. In that year, there were 4 million women workers, and 1.5 million child workers between ages ten and fifteen.

From 1870 to 1900, one in every six or seven paid workers was a woman. In general, those women with the worst economic prospects most often worked outside the home: In 1900, African-American women were more likely to be in the labor force than white women, immigrant women more than native-born women, immigrant daughters more than the daughters of those born in the United States. With the exception of African-American women, these female workers were almost all young and unmarried. Still, a small but growing minority—one in every seven by 1900—of female wage-earners was married.

Everyone assumed that men would be in the labor force, but women's employment aroused controversy. Some insisted that women worked just for "pin money," "to decorate themselves beyond their needs and station"; others wondered if any woman who worked could ever be truly respectable. These persistent questions about the legitimacy of women's paid work dragged down both female workers' self-esteem and their earnings.

The vast majority of women took jobs because they had to support themselves or contribute to the family budget; the grim conditions of women's employment drove off those who could afford to stay at home. Wage-earning women experienced the same hardships as men—low pay, periodic unemployment, long hours, and dangerous conditions—but with a special twist. Employers often used the "pin money" argument to justify paying women less than men and laying them off first during hard times. But they were simply taking advantage of a needy group with very limited choices in the labor market. As an Iowa shoe saleswoman complained in 1886, "I don't get the salary the men clerks do, although this day I am six hundred sales ahead! Call this justice? But I have to grin and bear it, because I am so unfortunate as to be a woman." Many predominantly female occupations, such as domestic service and tenement house work, demanded extraordinarily long hours. And employment was hazardous to

"... LEAVES ME IN POOR CIRCUMSTANCES"

In his testimony before a U.S. Senate committee investigating conditions of labor and capital in October 1883, Thomas O'Donnell (who had immigrated to the United States from England eleven years earlier) describes the introduction of new production methods at the Fall River, Massachusetts, textile factory where he worked as a mule spinner. These changes allowed the mill's owners to employ children. O'Donnell describes the sharp decline in his family's living standards that followed.

[O'DONNELL:] THEY ARE doing away with a great deal of mule-spinning there and putting in ring-spinning, and for that reason it takes a good deal of small help [of children] to run this ring work, and it throws the men out of work.... There are so many men in the city to work, and whoever has a boy can have work, and whoever has no boy stands no chance. Probably he may have a few months of work in the summer time, but will be discharged in the fall. That is what leaves me in poor circumstances. Our children, of course, are very often sickly from one cause or another, on account of not having sufficient clothes, or shoes, or food, or something....

Q. How much [work] have you had within a year?—A. That would be about fifteen weeks' work.... I got just $1.50 a day....

Q. That would be somewhere about $133 [in annual wages], if you had not lost any time.—A. Yes, sir.

Q. That is all you have had?—A. Yes, sir....

Q. Do you mean that yourself and wife and two children have had nothing but that for all this time?—A. That is all. I got a couple dollars' worth of coal last winter, and the wood I picked up myself. I goes around with a shovel and picks up clams and wood.

Q. What do you do with the clams?—A. We eat them. I don't get them to sell, but just to eat, for the family. That is the way my brother lives, too, mostly. He lives close by us.

Q. How many live in that way down there?—A. I could not count them, they are so numerous. I suppose there are one thousand down there.

Q. A thousand that live on $150 a year?—A. They live on less....

Q. How long has that been so?—A. Mostly so since I have been married.

Q. How long is that?—A. Six years this month.

Q. Why do you not go West on a farm?—A. How could I go, walk it?

women's health: women wage-earners had a death rate twice that of other women.

Women bore additional burdens: they moved from a day of toil in the factory to an evening of work in the home; wage-earning did not buy women—married or single—exemption from household work. And in addition to wage discrimination, female workers sometimes faced sexual exploitation and abuse by male bosses and coworkers.

Children's labor also sustained millions of working-class families. About one of six children between ten and fifteen years old held jobs during the last thirty years of the nineteenth century. They toiled in textile mills, tobacco processing plants, and print shops; they roamed the streets as newsboys, bootblacks, and scrap collectors; they served as cash- and bundle-carriers in department stores.

Employers conceded little to youth. In a Chicago candy factory children worked eighty-two hours per week during the Christmas season, and southern children endured twelve-hour days, sometimes on night shifts, year round in cotton mills. A few states passed laws requiring school attendance and prohibiting child labor during these years, but the laws were loosely enforced and easily foiled by desperate parents and eager employers. Children's wages ranged from a few pennies to about 75 cents a day, half what an unskilled adult laborer could earn.

At the very bottom of the wage-earning class in terms of wages, hours, and working conditions were the families who labored in deplorable conditions in cramped tenement apartments. In 1892, nearly 11,000 people toiled in six hundred tenement workshops in Chicago. In a typical case, a family of eight lived and labored in a single three-

---

"... PAY IS TOO SMALL"

A number of states established bureaus of labor during the Gilded Age to investigate working and living conditions among industrial workers. Many of these reports, based on hundreds of individual interviews in workers' homes, emphasized the "moral, sanitary, physical, and economical conditions" of women workers. The following selection from the 1884 report of the Massachusetts Bureau of Statistics of Labor describes the circumstances under which "the working girls of Boston" toiled in the clothing industry. A typical young seamstress earned approximately $5 per week in wages.

A GOOD DEAL of complaint is made in regard to the low wages quite generally paid to working girls in all the various occupations in which they were found employed. The cause of complaint . . . is ascribed to the fact that girls living "at home," with little or no board to pay, work for very low wages. This is considered a great hardship to the lone working girl who is entirely dependent upon her own resources. The mothers in some cases have said that it takes more than the girls earn to feed and clothe them. . . .

In the manufacture of men's clothing, considerable complaint is made by the girls as to the very small wages . . . the cry was "pay is too small." . . . It is said that many of the girls get discouraged, as they hardly earn enough to pay running expenses, and are obliged to practise the most rigid economy. One girl says she "turns her clothes upside down, inside out, and outside in, not being able to make enough over living expenses to buy new clothes."

. . . Some of them have spoken very frankly about ill treatment by their employers. . . . One girl says she has been subjected to rough words and harsh treatment from the foreman in charge of the department. . . . Another girl says her employer is good natured according to his mood; if he does not like the way the work is done, he is apt to take it rudely from her hands and tell her to leave. . . .

The testimony of capable and honest women, of the heads of departments. . . of forewomen in shops, matrons of homes . . . is that the working girls are as respectable, as moral, and as virtuous as any class of women in our community; that they are making as heroic a struggle for existence as any class is a fact which all the statistics prove.

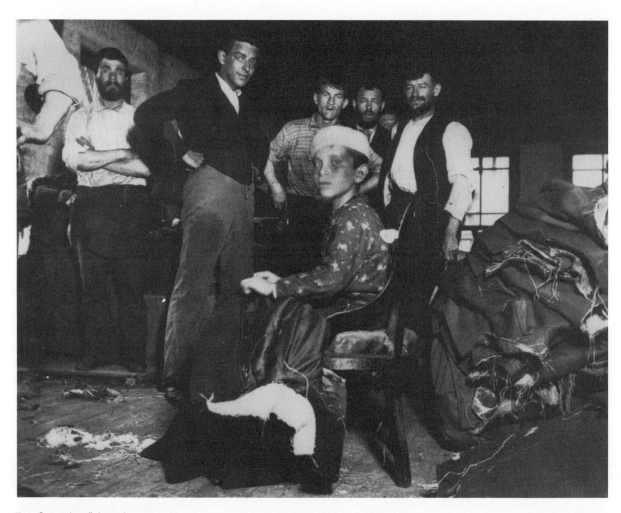

"In a Sweatshop." A twelve-year-old boy pulls threads in a New York City garment shop, photographed by reporter Jacob Riis in about 1889.

room flat. "The father, mother, two daughters and a cousin work together making trousers at 65 cents a dozen pairs," reported one investigator. "They work 7 days a week. . . . Their destitution is very great."

Divided as they were by skill, ethnicity, race, gender, and age, working people in the late nineteenth century nonetheless shared many common experiences. Hours remained long—six ten-hour days in a typical workweek. Only a few, such as skilled building tradesmen, achieved the ideal of an eight-hour day. Textile workers in Fall River, Massachusetts, complained bitterly of long hours in 1881: "I get so exhausted that I can scarcely drag myself home when night comes," said one.

Millworkers and other factory hands also toiled long hours in ever larger workplaces. Between 1870 and 1900, the average workforce in cotton mills and tobacco factories doubled. Steel mills replaced textile mills as the giants of the manufacturing world: by 1900, three steel mills had over 8,000 workers apiece. More and more workers faced the impersonality of the large factory, the sense of being an anonymous cog in a wheel.

Individual employers sought ways to reduce their workers' already meager wages through wage cuts or more indirect methods. Most notorious was the payment of wages in "scrip," or company-issued paper money, a common practice in mining areas. Mine owners also insisted that their employees shop exclusively at company-owned stores, which charged highly inflated prices. One mining company made $1,000 a month by selling powder to its men at $3.25 a keg, more than $1.25 over the going rate. As one miner explained, "A hint is conveyed to [the mineworker] in a roundabout way, that his prospects at the mine would be improved by trading at the store of his employer. If this has not the desired effect, he is laid off for a few days." Miners, according to one observer, became "virtually the slaves" of the scrip and company-store system.

In many industries, employers also expected workers to bear part of the cost of working. Clothing manufacturers often required workers to buy their own sewing machines, needles, and thread. One Kentucky factory owner required workers "to furnish their own stoves, fires, lights, and tools"; he calculated that they spent 8 percent of their wages in this way. The manufacture of clothing, artificial flowers, and other small items in workers' tenement apartments was a way of shifting the costs of rent, heat, and light onto the workers.

Some managers offered incentives in an effort to secure greater productivity and profits, and not coincidentally, their workers' continued loyalty. A few large capitalists, such as the Pittsburgh food processor H. J. Heinz, provided employees with

"BELL-TIME . . ."

Philip Hubert's 1897 description of a New England textile factory at quitting time captures the sense of sheer size of new industrial enterprises and their dehumanizing impact on factory workers who toiled within their walls.

ONE HOT EVENING in July last I stood on the brink of a little canal that skirts a row of noble buildings constituting the largest textile mill in New England . . . and watched hundreds and thousands of mill-hands pour over the bridge that connects the mills with the town of which they are the chief support and pride. As the great bell clanged forth its six peals, one could hear the cessation of toil for the day. The mighty turbines . . . ceased to revolve, the great Corliss engines that in recent years have come to the aid of water-power in all big mills, came to a stop; the three hundred thousand spindles, the eight thousand looms, and the thousand of other ponderous machines, ingenious and effective almost past belief, for picking, cleaning, roving, bleaching, printing, drying, and finishing the one hundred million yards of cotton and woolen goods turned out from these mills every year—all this vast mass of machinery, scattered over sixty acres of flooring came to a stop. Bell-time, as six o'clock in the afternoon is called in all New England mill towns, had come. In place of the hum and clatter of machinery, the patter of innumerable feet made itself heard. Then the first of the army of five thousand operatives began to come, first by driblets, comprising those who did not need to wash, or did not care to, then the larger streams as the doors of some great room were thrown open . . . and finally the dense stream of humanity, male and female, big and little, until the broad iron bridge was packed and shook under the strain. Browning's description of the rats as they came in answer to the three shrill notes of the Pied Piper came to my mind. . . .

"Caught in the Shafting." The *National Police Gazette* portrays, in characteristically lurid fashion, an industrial accident in a North Grosvenor, Connecticut, cotton mill. The *National Police Gazette* enthusiastically violated the mores of genteel culture, focusing on legal and illegal sports, violent crimes and accidents, and sex. Women were often depicted as perpetrators or victims of violence, providing titillation to the weekly magazine's male readership.

lunch and shower rooms and company-owned housing in an effort to "humanize the business system" and "end the spirit of enmity between capital and labor."

Most late-nineteenth-century businessmen continued to pursue arbitrary and careless policies with respect to their employees. They virtually ignored worker safety, largely because they had little financial incentive to make the workplace safer. Railroads, again, provide a classic example. Railroad work was very dangerous, essentially because most railroad companies simply refused to purchase the Westinghouse air brake and automatic coupler systems. Workers risked being maimed every time they ran along the tops of trains to set each car's brakes, or every time they stood on the tracks to drop a coupling pin as the railcars crashed together. In 1881 alone, long after safety devices were widely available, 30,000 U.S. railroad workers were killed or injured on the job. The courts repeatedly denied damages to injured workers, maintaining that they had accepted the risks of the job by going to work or that the workers shared the blame for the accident with the company. The Reverend Lyman Abbot acidly explained railroads' reluctance to use air brakes and automatic couplers: "So long as brakes cost more than trainmen we may expect the present sacrificial method of car coupling to continue."

Conditions of life and labor in the emerging industrial capitalist economy were exceedingly harsh. Sweatshops, long hours, payment in scrip, child labor, and lack of workplace safety all helped assure corporate profits. But they also resulted in a drastic deterioration of working conditions and engendered a bitterness among working people at their growing dependency and powerlessness. While workers sought ways to improve their condition under the new industrial order, their employers hoped to make the system even more productive and profitable.

BUSINESSMEN SEARCH FOR CONTROL

Like their working-class employees, businessmen confronted a chaotic economic world in late-nineteenth-century America. Economic and political forces appeared to block businessmen's best individual efforts to dominate their firms and their workplaces. Something more than worker-directed policies was needed. "Control" became the business watchword throughout this period: control of the markets in which they sold their products; of production within their firms and of the workers who toiled for them; and of the political environment in which they operated. To achieve this control, businessmen, especially in large-scale, "bulk" production industries such as iron and steel, expanded their firms ever larger, hoping to wipe out their competitors (or at least the worst forms of competition), guarantee supplies of necessary raw materials, and establish more effective ways to market their products. They also tried to replace "inefficient" practices inside their companies with more systematic methods of production and management. And finally, they sought "representation"

Railroad accident. The collapse of an old bridge at Calvary, Kentucky, in 1900 sends the engine, tender, and two cars of a Louisville & Nashville train into a creek. Reports of accidents filled newspapers and magazines during the late nineteenth century, feeding readers' interest in the sensational while also graphically illustrating railroad companies' disregard for safety.

of business interests in politics by buying control of public officials and politicians at every level of government.

Railroad executives pioneered the effort to secure control over markets. In the 1870s they organized themselves into "pools" to divide up traffic and set freight rates, an approach that seemed far preferable to an earlier era of cutthroat competition. But the pools collapsed. Some were undermined by a new breed of financial speculators, men who had little interest in running railroads but great interest in profiting from them. Financiers Jay Gould and Jim Fisk gained control of a number of railroads and then launched rate wars to drive down the price of railroad stocks and bonds temporarily so they could then buy up distressed roads at bargain prices.

Most of the time, railroad men broke their own pooling arrangements. In hard times, railroad executives slashed freight rates in an effort to win customers away from their competitors. Rival roads had no recourse but to follow suit when a pool member broke ranks; the agreements were unenforceable in the courts because they were not legal contracts.

When the pools collapsed in the 1880s, railroad managers turned to a new method of controlling competition: they built huge, self-sustaining systems to drive smaller lines out of business. Between 1880 and 1893, railroad companies leased more land, bought more equipment, and laid more track, enormously increasing the scale of their operations. Unfortunately, much of this new track was constructed from inferior materials along badly prepared routes and had to be rebuilt, at significant expense, within fifteen years. In the long run, individual railroads' efforts to improve their positions only produced an overbuilt national rail system with ruinous financial consequences. During the depression of 1893–98, scores of railroad lines went bankrupt.

Similar patterns of expansion, competition, and bankruptcy, of boom and bust, were also seen in large-scale manufacturing enterprises. As industrialists rushed into new markets, they quickly overbuilt capacity until initially high prices and high profits gave way to sharp competition, falling prices, and declining profits. In response, manufacturers organized "cartels," organizations dedicated to eliminating competition by limiting production and maintaining high prices. In the various branches of the hardware industry alone, more than sixty cartels appeared in the 1870s and 1880s. But industrial cartels worked no better than railroad pools: individual firms cut prices to steal customers when it suited them.

Again like the railroads, manufacturers turned to various forms of "horizontal" integration. Major producers in an industry merged to form a single firm with plenty of power to control prices and hopefully assure profit margins. John D. Rockefeller, who controlled the Cleveland petroleum business by 1871, saw his competitors as the main problem. Dismissing the cartels his rivals tried to organize as "ropes of sand," Rockefeller secretly merged his Standard Oil Company with competing firms, pledging the willing ones to secrecy and ruthlessly, even violently, coercing the unwilling. By 1880, Standard Oil controlled about nine-tenths of the nation's oil-refining capacity. Rockefeller now could set the price and control the output of oil virtually as he wished.

Rockefeller eliminated competition by gaining control of the *market*. Other manufacturers insulated themselves from competition by gaining control over their internal *costs*. The introduction of new technology often promised to lower the cost of manufacturing. If a manufacturer could cut expenses by installing a new production process, he could also imagine driving his overpriced competitors out of business once and for all, freeing himself to raise prices back to profitable levels. But technology did not solve manufacturers' financial problems; indeed, it often worsened them, for as soon as one manufacturer achieved a slight cost advantage over the competition, his rivals would match his improvement—and add new ones of their own. Moreover, big industrialists had to borrow massive amounts of capital to stay in the technology game. With prices falling, they couldn't easily repay their loans (and interest charges) and still show the profits needed to attract new investors.

Big manufacturers had one other option: "vertical" integration of their businesses (coordinating all aspects of production and distribution) rather than "horizontal" (linking different companies producing the same product). The steel industry was the best example of growth by vertical integration, especially as practiced by Andrew Carnegie, the Gilded Age's most powerful industrial capitalist. Annoyed by fluctuations in the price and supply of the pig iron with which steelmaking began, Carnegie began to expand his ironmaking operations in the 1870s to guarantee adequate pig iron supplies for his steel mills. Allying with Henry Clay Frick, Carnegie acquired sources of iron ore, coke, and coal and developed a fleet of steamships and a railroad for transporting them directly to his steel mills. "From the moment these crude stuffs were dug out of the earth until they flowed in a stream of liquid steel in the ladles," trumpeted one admiring observer, "there was never a price, profit, or royalty paid to an outsider."

Carnegie carried the techniques of vertical integration further than any of his contemporaries. Carnegie used his control over key oil fields, for example, to browbeat railroads into cutting the rates they charged for hauling his oil, and he coerced the railroads into giving him kickbacks on the inflated rates they charged his competitors.

"A VERY SAD, BITTER, AND RUINOUS EXPERIENCE . . ."

In his testimony before the U.S. Industrial Commission in 1899, George Rice, a small petroleum producer, offers a critical assessment of John D. Rockefeller's business practices. Rockefeller had succeeded in driving Rice into bankruptcy. Note the importance Rice attributes to the railroads in Rockefeller's plans to dominate the oil industry.

I AM A citizen of the United States, born in the state of Vermont. Producer of petroleum for more than thirty years, and a refiner of same for twenty years. But my refinery has been shut down during the past three years, owing to the powerful and all-prevailing machinations of the Standard Oil Trust, in criminal collusion and conspiracy with the railroads to destroy my business of twenty years ... wholly by and through unlawful freight discriminations.

I have been driven from pillar to post, from one railway line to another, for twenty years, in the absolutely vain endeavor to get equal and just freight rates with the Standard Oil Trust, so as to be able to run my refinery at anything approaching a profit, but which I have been utterly unable to do. I have had to consequently shut down, with my business absolutely ruined and my refinery idle.

This has been a very sad, bitter, and ruinous experience for me to endure, but I have endeavored to the best of my circumstances and ability to combat it the utmost I could for many a long waiting year, expecting relief through the honest and proper execution of our laws, which have as yet, however, never come. But I am still living in hopes, though I may die in despair. . . .

"SUBORDINATION IS A CARDINAL PRINCIPLE . . ."

Marshall Kirkman offered this admiring, if overly inflated, picture in 1896 of the ways he imagined systematic management principles creating almost military discipline inside a railroad company.

THE FORCE THAT runs a railway is like an army. It is methodically organized and drilled. It has its commanders, its rank and file; its officers, sub-officers and privates. . . .

Subordination is a cardinal principle of organized labor—subordination to the employer, subordination to each other according to rank and natural precedence. It is based upon a conception of the rights of men in their relation to property. . . .

The discipline of corporate forces is as absolute as that of a man of war [a battleship]. Obedience to superior authority is unqualified. . . . An order once given, must be obeyed. . . .

The work of those in the employ of railroads must be continuous, systematic and orderly. It is said that cleanliness is next to godliness. I think, however, that orderliness comes next, because it is the foundation of every beneficent thing whether of nature or man. . . .

Not every businessman tried to dominate his industry like Carnegie or Rockefeller, but virtually all were driven in these years to trim costs by carefully reshaping their firms' internal organization and the work that went on inside them. This more cautious strategy toward innovation was particularly evident in smaller manufacturing enterprises, such as woodworking and metal-turning firms where customized "batch" rather than larger-scale bulk production held sway.

In these smaller firms (most had fewer than a hundred employees), managers still responded to the demands of local rather than national markets. They therefore opted for more limited measures to increase their workers' productivity, to enhance management control, and to increase their firms' profits. For example, they might purchase a single new machine, identify a new local or regional market for their products, or modestly (rather than completely) reorganize the work process. Managers of small firms, like their counterparts in larger enterprises, faced internal and external imperatives to minimize waste and inefficiency. But they responded more cautiously to the new management innovations and production methods that swept corporate America in these decades.

The leaders of gigantic industrial firms, unlike their smaller counterparts, opted for a wholly new form of corporate direction and leadership. Big businessmen turned after 1880 to systematic management, a loose label for varied efforts to speed and coordinate industrial operations. Their intent was to create an orderly industrial world in which machines, workers, and the final product were subject to management initiative and prerogatives.

Initially these efforts were handicapped by the unsystematic and decentralized labor control systems that characterized most nineteenth-century factories. In most shops, each department was under the control of a foreman responsible for achieving customary production standards. Foremen attempted to "drive" their hands, but often they ended up having to cajole workers to get their jobs done; it was even common for foremen to negotiate with the work crew over output and pay.

Industrial workers resisted working continuously or at peak efficiency. Throughout the late nineteenth century, industrialists complained bitterly that much of their employees' labor time was "wasted" as even unskilled workers took breaks to rest or discuss the way the work was going or waited for machines to be repaired or for materials to be delivered. Factory workers also tried to set their own speed to give the boss what they considered "a fair day of work." Frederick Winslow Taylor, a manager who led the attack on such practices as an early exponent of systematic or "scientific" management, described this aspect of unskilled workers' control:

> This loafing or soldiering proceeds from two causes. First, from the natural instinct and tendency of men to take it easy, which may be called natural soldiering. Second, from more intricate second thought and reasoning caused by their relations with other men, which may be called systematic soldiering.

Employer efforts to overcome "soldiering" and increase workers' output took a variety of forms. First, managers attempted to create a more intense discipline about formal work rules and work time. Fines for minor infractions of work rules were common. "Minute thieves," foremen who shaved time off lunch periods and kept factories running after the official closing time, also squeezed a bit of unpaid work out of hourly employees. A New Hampshire factory headed its work rules: "NOTICE! TIME IS MONEY!" and went on to warn that washing up "must be done outside of working hours, and not at our expense."

Sensitivity to time was a recent development; it emerged with the completion of the national railroad network in the 1870s. The railroad's unprecedented speed made the local custom of telling time by the sun obsolete. Such traditional time-telling literally stood in the way of coordinated, predictable rail service. Finally, in 1883, all railroads agreed to convert to the four standardized time zones we still use today. An Indianapolis newspaper editor complained, "The sun is no longer boss of the job. People . . . must eat, sleep, and work as well as travel by railroad time." Industrialists and their factories soon fell into step. Two years after the railroads imposed their time zones on the nation, the time clock made its first appearance in American factories. It carried an unambiguous message: workers must now submit to the boss's idea of time.

When changes in work rules proved insufficient, manufacturers introduced machinery as a means of exerting control over their employees. Fuming at his workers' victory in an 1885 strike, Cyrus McCormick of Chicago's McCormick Harvesting Machine Company vowed, "I do not think we will be troubled by the same thing again if we take proper steps to weed out the bad element among the men." The "proper step" in this case meant installing $500,000 worth of molding machinery to "weed out" the skilled workers who had led the strike, crush their union, and replace them with low-paid, unskilled workers. Similarly, John D. Rockefeller used new barrelmaking technology in his Cleveland plant to break the power—and lower the wages—of the company's highly skilled and once-proud coopers (barrelmakers).

But it was Andrew Carnegie who developed the most coherent plan to gain total control over the work process, combining bold technological innovation and ruthless management of employees. Carnegie was well aware that the use of up-to-date machinery was only a first step toward systematic and therefore more profitable production. To control costs, Carnegie hired the renowned engineer Alexander Lyman Holley in the 1880s to design his new J. Edgar Thompson steelworks. Holley's design eliminated unnecessary manual handling, moving materials smoothly through the various stages of the steelmaking process. Elevated trains, for example, carried coal overhead throughout the huge mill, eliminating the need for hundreds of shovel-wielding laborers.

With such technological innovations in place by the late 1880s, Carnegie's steel plants were far and away the most technologically advanced in the world. The steel magnate, as we will see, then turned his attention to taming his workforce through a brutal lockout. After a long and ultimately successful struggle, Carnegie was able to increase the length of the working day in all of his plants while keeping the same daily rate of pay. In the mid-1890s, many of Carnegie's employees were working twelve-hour shifts, seven days a week. "We stop only the time it takes to oil the engines," said a worker at the giant Homestead plant. By 1900, Carnegie virtually dictated the price steel sold for across the country.

Despite such triumphs, profits for most big manufacturers continued to lag behind corporate needs and expectations in these years. Big businessmen saw politics as a means of further consolidating their control and increasing profits. Their influence pervaded all levels of government in the late nineteenth century, but they increasingly focused on the federal government in efforts to shape nationwide policies to match their far-flung national enterprises. The efficiency-conscious manager much preferred to deal with a uniform set of

Bessemer converters, 1886. An engraving conveys some sense of the dimensions, noise, and heat in one of Andrew Carnegie's Pittsburgh steel mills.

federal rules or laws than with a confusing and contradictory assortment of local and state enactments. Businessmen also found it easier to sway the federal government than state or local governments, which were usually more responsive to local interests.

Corruption and favor-buying in government, which had increased notably during the Civil War, persisted when peace came, in both the North and the South and in both political parties. "To the victors belong the spoils" became the motto of the American political system. So rife was vote-selling that one Ohio politician referred to the House of Representatives in 1873 as "an auction room." And the corruption became systematic. Political parties relied increasingly after the war on kickbacks from officeholders, who received their positions through the party system.

Republican dominance in Washington was increasingly challenged by the Democrats beginning in 1875, as they rebuilt their party from the shambles of the war. The revived Democratic Party, uniting most of the South with growing support among workingmen in northern industrial areas, seemed on the verge of victory in the 1876 presidential election. The party's candidate, Samuel J. Tilden, captured a majority of the popular vote and appeared to have won in the electoral college as well. Republicans disputed the returns in three key southern states that had seemingly gone for the Democrats, throwing the election into question. Nearly three months of wrangling and intrigue followed, with growing panic in the business community and fear in all quarters of renewed war between North and South.

Finally, pressure from businessmen and politicians forced a resolution (the Compromise of 1877) in late February, only a few weeks before the new president was to be inaugurated. The Democrats finally agreed to yield the presidency to the Republican candidate, Rutherford B. Hayes, in exchange for a fair share of federal appointments (including the appointment of at least one southerner to Hayes's cabinet), federal assistance to southern railroads, and the final removal of federal troops from the southern states.

A key figure in securing the compromise was Democratic iron magnate Abram Hewitt. A journalist described Hewitt as a man "with one hand upon his heart and the other hand in his pocket," announcing "I would prefer four years of Hayes's administration to four years of civil war." There was a powerful truth in this characterization: businessmen were coming to believe that they could best achieve their goals by supporting *both* parties. The 1877 compromise cleared the way for the subsequent complete removal of African-Americans from national and local politics, the withering of the Republican Party in the southern states, and the reassertion of Democratic control of a solid South.

The results of the 1876 election fed growing disillusionment with political corruption, particularly among businessmen annoyed with the uncertainty of the success of their bribe offers, but also among those with principles too strong or wallets too slim to join in the bribing. A campaign to clean up politics emerged in the late 1870s and gained momentum early in the next decade.

"The Bosses of the Senate." An 1889 cartoon from the satirical weekly *Puck* decries corporate control of the U.S. Senate. "This is a Senate of the Monopolists by the Monopolists and for the Monopolists!" reads the sign over the corpulent corporate spectators as they watch over the obedient legislators (many of whom were themselves millionaires). Meanwhile, the "Peoples' Entrance" to the Senate is barred shut.

Some businessmen and reformers had long argued for a civil-service system, which would select bureaucrats by merit and protect them against shifts in party power. In 1881, the assassination of Republican president James A. Garfield by a crazed job-seeker, who was a member of an opposing faction of Republicans, gave new urgency to the idea. Ironically, the Pendleton Civil Service Act, passed in 1883, freed political parties from financial dependence on their appointees, only to place them at the mercy of businessmen. Industrialists' and financiers' substantial contributions to the evenly matched Democratic and Republican parties assured them of the sympathy of whichever was in power. As a result, the writer William Allen White argued, senators represented not political but economic entities: "Coal and iron owned a coterie from the Middle and Eastern seaport states. Cotton had half a dozen senators. And so it went."

When popular sentiment demanded that the government rein in railroads or curb monopolies, business-oriented members of Congress could make sure that the resulting laws lacked muscle. Thus, businessmen used their influence to shape the two great measures of federal regulation of business during the late nineteenth century, the Interstate Commerce Act (1881) and the Sherman Antitrust Act (1890). For example, Senator Nelson Aldrich of Rhode Island described the Interstate Commerce Act, which established a federal system of railroad regulation, as "a delusion and a sham." Railroads soon made the Interstate Commerce Commission (the regulatory agency set up under the act) their servant instead of their master.

The most important and reliable bulwark of business power in federal circles, however, was the judiciary. Most federal judges had begun their careers in corporation law. Once they gained seats on the bench, they served their former business associates well. However weak the federal laws regulating business were, court decisions made them even more feeble. For example, the Sherman Antitrust Act was designed to curb the excesses of business monopolies. The courts rarely found corporations guilty of violating the act, however. But they did find the antitrust act useful in curbing labor unions, particularly by granting injunctions—cease-and-desist orders—against strikers and their unions.

As the nineteenth century ended, U.S. businessmen had taken major steps to reshape the world within which they operated. The sheer scale and influence of capitalist enterprise were absolutely without precedent. Yet businessmen had failed to tame the wild tiger of the American economy, whose instability was as bad at the end of the nineteenth century as it had been at the beginning of the post–Civil War era. Nor could businessmen count on their control of government. In spite of bribes and influence-peddling, their political influence was far from certain.

"THE SOUTH SHALL RISE AGAIN"

The growth of industrial capitalism profoundly transformed the South. The Compromise of 1877 cemented the rule of southern conservatives and made the region "safe" for northern business as it had not been during the social and political upheavals of the Reconstruction era. When the depression of the 1870s lifted, northern businessmen began to invest large amounts of money in the South.

They were welcomed by a new group of leaders who hoped to link their fortunes to those of northern industrial capitalists. Henry Grady, the editor of the Atlanta *Constitution*, envisioned a future for the "New South" filled with cities, immigrants, business, and industry. James Bryce, chronicler of Gilded Age America, called the South "a new country . . . whose advance is likely to be the swiftest."

But the story of the New South would not be a story of swift, steady progress, for the growth of industrial capitalism in the region prior to 1900 was shaped by southern dependence on cotton, the domination of northern business, and the legacy of slavery. The region's domination by northern capital made the lives of small farmers, black and white, who constituted the vast majority of the South's population, even more insecure, their suffering even more acute, than the lives of northern workers.

Northern business gained control of southern industry and banking after the Civil War. Southern capital had largely been invested in slaves and had thus been wiped out by emancipation. The collapse of the Confederacy and wartime destruction caused further losses. Federal action during Reconstruction reinforced southern dependency and the region's colonial status. Republican banking and currency legislation hampered the operations of those southern banks that had not failed outright. Furthermore, the nation's new financial system was oriented toward the promotion of industry, and the South was predominantly agricultural; it favored creditors, and the South was predominantly a debtor region. Northern, and to a lesser extent European, capital therefore bankrolled the growth of southern industry in the postwar period.

These outside investors placed their own profits before the region's welfare. They set up low-profit and low-wage operations that extracted raw materials or crudely processed products—lumber, coal, cotton, turpentine, seafood—from the South. Southern capital contributed to the establishment of cotton mills before the depression of the 1890s, but only in combination with northern capital. The only major southern-controlled industry was the tobacco industry, mechanized and increasingly dominated by North Carolinians. James B. Duke, noting that "tobacco is the poor man's luxury," played the role here that Carnegie and Rockefeller played in the North. Except in tobacco, outside investors called the shots in large southern enterprises, squeezing profits from the region as one might juice from an orange and leaving behind depleted resources, destitute people, and a dependent economy.

Railroads led the way in southern economic development, as they had in the North. Between 1880 and 1890, railroad laborers laid over 22,000 miles of track in the South, nearly doubling the region's rail network. In the process, large railroad companies swallowed up smaller ones. By the early 1890s, twelve large corporations, most of them directed from New York City, controlled half of all southern track. The Richmond and West Point Terminal Company, for example, bought up competing systems all across Tennessee, Virginia, and Georgia and emerged as the largest of the southern railroads. Of the twenty men on its board of directors in 1890, seventeen—including Jay Gould and Abram Hewitt—were New Yorkers.

The railroads, aided by probusiness state legislators who eagerly

Segregation in the workplace. White workers pause for a photograph in a Richmond, Virginia, cigarette factory.

opened up natural resources to speculators through generous land grants and lenient tax policies, helped create whole new industries in the South: coal, iron, and lumber. The growth of the iron industry in Tennessee, Virginia, and Alabama was particularly impressive. Birmingham, Alabama, which had not even existed in 1870, became one of the country's largest iron-, steel-, and coal-producing centers by century's end. Atlanta became the Southeast's transportation hub and developed a diversified industrial base.

The key to southern industrialization, however, was cotton manufacturing. Between 1880 and 1890, the number of spindles in the four leading textile states (Georgia, Alabama, and the Carolinas) increased ninefold, to just under four million. These new mills had two unbeatable advantages over their older northern counterparts: the newest, most efficient technology and a low-paid, impoverished workforce.

The South's colonial relationship to the North sharply limited southern industrialization. For all its growth, the South was further behind the North in 1900 than it had been in 1860, in large part because powerful northern interests crushed the South's few chances of catching up. For example, Andrew Carnegie and other Pittsburgh steelmakers, who believed that the South was "Pennsylvania's most formidable industrial enemy," demanded that railroads charge higher freight rates to Birmingham steel producers. Such discriminatory practices helped blunt the threat southern industry posed to its northern counterpart.

The burden of the region's economic dependency weighed heavily on its industrial wage-earners. Southern mills relied more on child labor than did those in the North. In 1896, one in four North Carolina cotton-mill workers was a child (as compared to only one in twenty in Massachusetts), and a North Carolina child earned less than four

African-American workers prepare tobacco in Richmond, Virginia, stripping stems from the leaves. As in most southern industries, black tobacco workers labored separately from whites and were relegated to the lowest-paying and least-skilled jobs.

cents for every dime a Massachusetts child earned. The difference for adults was a bit narrower, with North Carolinians earning from one-half to two-thirds what their Massachusetts counterparts did. Only the most skilled held their own against the regional differential: North Carolina cotton-mill machinists commanded wages only 8 percent less than those in Massachusetts.

The company town dominated southern textiles. Describing isolated Georgia mill towns in 1891, the social investigator Clare de Graffenreid painted a grim picture. "Rows of loosely built, weather-stained frame houses, all of the same ugly pattern and buttressed by clumsy chimneys," dominated the monotonous villages. The interiors, furnished by "a shackling bed, tricked out in gaudy patchwork, a few defunct 'split-bottom' chairs, a rickety table, and a jumble of battered crockery," testified to the inhabitants' poverty. Mill owners, like slaveholders before the Civil War, thought of themselves as kindly paternalists, but in fact they ruled their totally owned, unincorporated company towns with iron fists. Starvation wages, payment in scrip, and price-gouging company stores far outweighed low rent and subsidies for schools and churches.

Virtually all of the southern textile-mill labor force was white and born in the United States, in dramatic contrast to the immigrant-dominated workforce of the North. Race provided southern employers with a powerful weapon for dividing the workforce; whites tolerated exploitation the more willingly if assured that blacks were still worse off. Women in an Atlanta mill showed their determination to protect textile work as a white "privilege" when, in 1897, they struck fourteen-hundred strong against the employment of two African-American spinners.

A complex pattern of race and gender segregation marked work in southern cities. Few immigrants chose to come to the South, but those who did clustered in cities and, like their northern counterparts, made up a disproportionate part of the urban working class. One in twenty Richmond, Virginia, residents was an immigrant in 1880, but one in three of the city's unskilled white laborers was foreign-born. Cigar factories relied on African-American labor: women sorted and stemmed the leaves in filthy, hot, unventilated rooms while men made cigars or chewing plugs. Cigarette factories hired both blacks and whites, but segregated them. The vast majority of young African-American women in cities toiled by day as maids in whites' homes; they rejected live-in domestic work because its round-the-clock demands and close surveillance smacked of slavery. Older black women most often worked as laundresses in their own homes, where they could have more independence and keep an eye on their children.

Most southerners continued to farm the land, however, and even those employed in factories retained their ties to the soil. Many of the South's major employers—cigar and cigarette factories, seafood processors, and sugar refineries—offered only seasonal employment. In the off-season, their employees went back to farming. In Chatham County, Georgia, for example, African-American men often stayed on the farms all winter while African-American women worked in a nearby oyster-processing plant. In Tennessee and Virginia, men of both races went off to work in sawmills or coalmines while women tended the farms. Even though textile manufacturing had fewer seasonal ups and downs, cotton-mill workers periodically turned to farming as a respite from the discipline of the mills and as a means of supplementing low wages.

With the end of Reconstruction in 1877, former slaves had lost out in their efforts to own land and become economically independent; former slaveowners had also been effectively blocked from reestablishing slavery in a new form. The system that emerged shortly after the war was "share wages," which paid black workers not in cash but in a share of the harvested crop. Share wages were usually accompanied by overseers, the gang system, and violence; the "new" system looked a lot like the old one. With the Black Codes of 1865 and 1866 to back them up, white landowners had found a good substitute for slavery.

Former slaves insisted that share wages represented a *partnership* between themselves and the planters: one party provided the labor and the other provided the land. Freedpeople asserted their right to control their own work, struggling for shorter hours and a slower pace. African-American families wanted to get women out of the fields entirely so they could focus their energies on taking care of their own households.

The resulting conflict produced a totally new system, which began to emerge in large plantation areas across the South at the end of the 1860s. Gang labor and supervision virtually ended. African-American families now rented small plots of land, paying landowners a share of the crop at the end of each season. Blacks thus gained more control over their work than they had ever had before in the South. White planters still maintained a system of armed "riders" who monitored and disciplined them, and most important of all, whites retained the ultimate economic power of land ownership.

African-Americans had eked minimal gains out of an extremely oppressive situation: they had prevented the return of slavery, but had been robbed of their dreams of land ownership and self-sufficiency. The new arrangements, in fact, bore some similarity to the wage-labor system developing in the North: workers in both regions were legally free but economically dependent, all drawn into a large and uncontrollable market system.

But the southern economic system had a perverse twist. Even as they raised crops for the market, African-American farmers for the most part remained outside the money economy. Each family began the agricultural cycle by securing seed, supplies, and food from the landowner; these items were charged to the family and deducted from its share of the crop at harvest time. Even in the best of times, the family's share might prove inadequate, and as the price of cotton fell, this became more and more the case. The result was a deepening spiral of debt and dependency for sharecroppers in the 1880s and 1890s. The poverty of these families was remarkable even in this generally poor region: the typical African-American sharecropping woman kept house with only a straw broom, a laundry tub, a cooking kettle, and a water pail.

In this context, black families scrambled to make a bit of money, for every penny earned meant that much less dependency on the landowner. In addition to sporadic wage labor, men did day labor on nearby farms and women sold chickens, eggs, milk, cheese, and vegetables. The saying "chickens for shoes" summed up African-American women's diligent efforts to buy shoes for their children so they might go to school in the winter.

Sharecropping or one of its variants occupied the overwhelming majority of African-American farming families in the late-nineteenth-century South. Since 90 percent of African-Americans still lived in the South, and since 80 percent of those lived in rural areas, this system touched the lives of a substantial majority.

The transformation of southern agriculture also affected many white farm families. Although the wealthier slaveowning planters had wielded tremendous power in the antebellum South, most whites in the region had never owned slaves. Especially in the hill regions, they had remained relatively self-sufficient, producing foodstuffs for their own consumption or for trade with local artisans. But after the Civil War, southern white farmers shifted from subsistence agriculture to production for the market, as their northern counterparts had done a generation earlier. The southern white farmers naturally turned to cotton, the traditional route to power and wealth in the region.

Unfortunately, however, this shift coincided with the beginning of a long-term decline in the price of cotton on the world market. The dramatic increase in cotton production in Brazil, Egypt, and India, and—more significantly—a leveling off of international demand for cotton, led to a ruinous fall in prices. The record-breaking cotton crop of 1894 was two and a half times bigger than that of 1873, but it brought southern farmers less: prices had fallen to one-third of what they had been twenty-one years earlier.

"ALL MUST WORK UNDER MY DIRECTION"

This 1882 contract spells out the terms and conditions under which African-American tenant farmers could work small plots of land on the Grimes plantation in Pitt County, North Carolina. Although not a return to conditions of slavery, the contract gives the plantation owner extraordinary control over the conditions of field work and the division of the harvested crop. Sharecroppers were forbidden to keep any cotton seed from the harvest, which would have allowed them to plant their own crop without having to be furnished by the plantation owner.

TO EVERY ONE applying to rent land upon shares, the following conditions must be read and *agreed* to.

To every 30 or 35 acres, I agree to furnish the team, plow, and farming implements, except cotton planters, and I *do not* agree to furnish a cart to every cropper. The croppers are to have half of the cotton, corn and fodder (and peas and pumpkins and potatoes if any are planted) if the following conditions are complied with, but—if not—they are to have only two-fifths. Croppers are to have no part or interest in the cotton seed raised from the crop planted and worked by them. No vine crops of any description, that is no watermelons . . . squashes or anything of that kind . . . are to planted in the cotton or corn. All must work under my direction. All plantation work to be done by the croppers. . . .

All croppers must clean out stables and fill them with straw, and haul straw in front of stables whenever I direct. All the cotton must be manured, and enough fertilizer must be brought to manure each crop highly, the croppers to pay for one half of all manure bought, the quantity to be purchased for each crop must be left to me.

No cropper to work off the plantation when there is any work to be done on the land he has rented, or when his work is needed by me or other croppers. . . .

Every cropper must be responsible for all gear and farming implements placed in his hands, and if not returned must be paid for unless it is worn out by use.

Croppers must sow and plow in oats and haul them to the crib, but *must have no part of them.* Nothing to be sold from their crops, nor fodder, nor corn to be carried out of the fields until my rent is all paid, and all amounts they owe me and for which I am responsible are paid in full. . . .

The sale of every cropper's part of the cotton to be made by me when and where I choose to sell, and after deducting all they may owe me and all sums that I may be responsible for on their accounts, to pay them their half of the net proceeds. Work of every description, particularly the work on fences and ditches, to be done to my satisfaction, and must be done over until I am satisfied that it is done as it should be. . . .

Meanwhile, white farmers' costs rose. The railroad lines that spread through the southern back country linked farmers with a world market but simultaneously put them at the mercy of those controlling the railroads. Southern hill-country railroads established monopolies and raised rates, so that southern farmers did not benefit from the national decline in freight rates. Although the railroad was, for Henry Grady, the ultimate symbol of the "New South," for many poor farmers it symbolized exploitation and greed.

Even so, the railroads' worst offenses were minor compared to those of the "crop lien" system, which fed on southern hill farmers' consistent shortage of cash. In the immediate postwar shortage of banking facilities and credit, they had to borrow from "furnishing merchants" to buy their seed, tools, and other supplies. Using funds borrowed from northern banks, the merchant bought supplies and "furnished" them to the cash-poor white farmer on credit. To secure his loan, the merchant took a "lien" or a claim on the next harvest. Merchants usually insisted that borrowers grow cotton because it was readily marketable and, all things considered, the best bet. Credit customers paid significantly higher prices for goods than cash customers. And on top of these inflated prices the merchant added interest of 25 to 50 percent. In the fall, after the crop had been marketed, he collected his debt.

The small farmer found himself in a vicious circle: he could get credit only if he grew cotton; cotton prices kept falling, so he planted more to keep up his proceeds; the more cotton he planted, the less food he grew; the less food he grew, the more he had to borrow to buy food. Like the black sharecropper, the white farmer found more and more often that his debt surpassed the value of his crop. The farmer had no choice but to commit the *following* year's crop to the merchant as well. "The furnishing man was the boss, pure and simple," wrote a woman who watched the system work in Alabama. "His word was law."

In the end, many farmers lost their land to these merchants and became tenant farmers or sharecroppers, joining African-Americans on this lowest rung of the southern economic ladder. By 1900, one-third of the southern whites engaged in agriculture had been reduced to tenancy.

As the nineteenth century ended, black and white farmers in the South had much in common. They tilled the cotton fields laboriously by hand, using the simple plow and a heavy iron hoe. African-Americans were usually in debt to their landlords rather than to merchants, but the yoke of debt bore heavily on both races. Both peoples had had the goal of land ownership and economic independence; both now found themselves trapped in a system which made that goal ever more remote.

At the same time, racism and the rollback of the political gains of the Reconstruction era posed special problems for African-Americans. The whites-only hiring policy of the cotton mills prevented blacks from abandoning the land. Increasing violence—whether in the form of race riots started by whites, lynchings, beatings, or attacks on property—made resistance costly. More subtly, African-Americans suffered endless insults and humiliations simply because of their color. White southerners suffered as a class; black southerners suffered as a class *and* as a race. Most ominous of all, racism was being enforced by laws that restricted African-Americans to separate (and virtually always inferior) public facilities and that used transparent ruses to deny black men the vote they had so eagerly used in the aftermath of the Civil War. Southern African-Americans were not the only ones in the nation, or in the world, to be battered by a rising tide of American racism in this period, but the wave engulfed them with a terrible thoroughness.

HOW THE WEST WAS LOST

The American West experienced the same contradictory patterns of development as the Northeast and the South. Groups of white Americans—cattle drivers, sheep herders, farmers, miners, and others, all with conflicting visions of what the West should become—struggled with one another, often violently, for domination of the United States' last frontier.

The West entered by whites (and a few African-Americans) after 1870 was sparsely settled, but settled nonetheless. And therein lay a major source of conflict. Until about 1880, Indian resistance blocked white settlement in the level, treeless, semi-arid Great Plains (Kansas, Nebraska, the Dakotas, and surrounding areas). The destruction of the buffalo, the suppression of the massive Sioux rebellion of 1876, and the murder of its leader, Crazy Horse, by U.S. soldiers the following year breached what whites had for 250 years referred to as the "Indian barrier." The great pitched battles were over, but U.S. Army patrols, starvation, disease, and alcohol continued to take their inexorable toll on the Indians, while the federal government and the "Wild West" imagery of the cheap, mass-market "dime novels" attacked and distorted their culture.

The world of the Plains Indians was regulated by elaborate rituals and strong tribal ties. Unlike Native Americans of the Northeast or

Battle of Little Big Horn. One of a series of pictures drawn by the Sioux warrior Red Horse recording his memories of the 1876 battle, drawn five years later at the Cheyenne River Agency.

the Southwest, Plains Indians ranged widely in their hunts. Tribes, not individuals, owned land and shared the fruits of the land among all tribe members. The individualistic ways of the whites mystified the Indians; as Sitting Bull of the Sioux noted, "The white man knows how to make everything, but he does not know how to distribute it." The communal aspects of Plains Indian society deeply offended both the whites who wanted to carve the West up into private preserves and the humanitarians who equated civilization with individualism and private property.

The Dawes, or Indian Allotment, Act of 1887, by breaking up the reservation system, sought to transform Indians into American citizens and tribally held Indian lands into individually owned plots. The act allowed the president to grant U.S. citizenship to individual Indians willing to abandon their tribes and communal ways and adopt what the act called the "habits of civilized life," which the act made possible by granting ownership of 160 acres of land to individual Indian families. The law further allowed the government, with tribal consent, to sell the remaining reservation land to white settlers, holding the proceeds for the "education and civilization" of Indians. Finally, it reaffirmed the right of Congress to grant railroad and telegraph companies the right to build on Indian land. By promising the final destruction of tribal life, the opening of new lands for white settlement, and the "assimilation" of Indians into American culture, the act pleased Indian-hating settlers, railroad interests, and white humanitarians alike.

Even more important, the Indian Allotment Act permitted a massive transfer of land from Indians to whites. In 1880, Secretary of the Interior Carl Schurz had happily and correctly predicted that an allotment bill would "eventually open to settlement by white men the large tracts of land now belonging to the reservations, but not used by the Indians." When the Dawes Act was passed, Native Americans still held 138 million acres of land. Within thirteen years, their domain had shrunk to less than 78 million acres, virtually all of it unsuited to the agricultural life the federal government tried to foist on them. In the process, the Bureau of Indian Affairs destroyed many of the Plains Indians' traditional villages. One white observer described the remains of the Hidatsa village at Like-a-Fishhook in Minnesota a few years after allotment as "rings of dirt where the lodges used to stand, half-filled cache holes all covered with weeds."

The misery that resulted from the loss of reservation land and the destruction of villages was compounded by whites' relentless attempts over the next two decades to stamp out tribal customs. Moving Indians off of reservations was not enough, according to one Bureau of Indian Affairs agent:

Unless the Indians are removed some distance from their village, the tribal organization broken up, and they are deprived of the means, and the opportunities for dances and ceremonies, by scattering them out on farms it will in my judgment, be impossible to civilize and render them self-supporting.

Communal ceremonies—including the exchange of gifts and food, big feasts, and the performance of what Indian Bureau agents called "Indian dances"—were banned. Native American boys and girls were encouraged to attend boarding schools to learn the language and values of the newcomers.

Although they no longer possessed the means to openly resist this systematic destruction of their way of life, Plains Indians did not meekly accept their fate. Wovoka, a young man of the Nevada Paiutes, offered his demoralized people a ray of hope for the future. In 1888, Wovoka had a vision in which God urged peace on Indian and white alike and foretold the coming of a paradise when the earth would be restored to its primeval glory and returned to the Indians. The dead would spring back to life, and all would live peacefully and blissfully in eternal youth. Wovoka preached that this happy day could be brought nearer by the performance of a five-night dance. The Plains Indians deeply respected visions as a source of guidance, and the dance—dubbed the "Ghost Dance" by whites—spread rapidly throughout the West.

Although the dance and its accompanying rituals proceeded peacefully in most areas, the Bureau of Indian Affairs earnestly tried to wipe it out. But in the Dakotas the dance fed on the extreme misery of the Sioux and became linked to resistance to white rule. Already weakened in

---

"... A VERY SAD SIGHT"

American Horse, a Sioux leader, describes the massacre at Wounded Knee Creek on December 29, 1890.

THE MEN WERE separated ... from the women, and they were surrounded by the soldiers. Then came next the village of the Indians and that was entirely surrounded by the soldiers also. When the firing began, of course the people who were standing immediately around the young man who fired the first shot were killed right together, and then they turned their guns, Hotchkiss guns, etc. upon the women who were in the lodges standing there under a flag of truce, and of course as soon as they were fired upon they fled....

[T]he women and children of course were strewn all along the circular village until they were dispatched [killed]. Right near the flag of truce a mother was shot down with her infant; the child not knowing that its mother was dead was still nursing, and that especially was a very sad sight. The women as they were fleeing with their babies were killed together, shot right through, and the women who were very heavy with child were also killed. All the Indians fled ... and after most all of them had been killed a cry was made that all those who were not killed or wounded should come forth and they would be safe. Little boys who were not wounded came out of their places of refuge, and as soon as they came in sight a number of soldiers surrounded them and butchered them there....

Of course it would have been all right if only the men were killed; we would feel almost grateful for it. But the fact of the killing of the women, and more especially the killing of the young boys and girls who are to go to make up the future strength of the Indian people, is the saddest part of the whole affair and we feel it very sorely.

Mass burial. The day after the "Battle" of Wounded Knee, the dead—estimated by the U.S. Army at eighty-four men, forty-four women, and eighteen children—are buried in a mass grave at the scene of the slaughter on the Pine Ridge Reservation Agency, South Dakota.

1889–90 by malnutrition caused by a drought and reduced government food rations, many Sioux succumbed to epidemics of measles, whooping cough, and influenza. Taking advantage of a particularly inept Indian Bureau agent, they became restive and frantically danced the Ghost Dance. The War Department responded by dispatching army troops. Thousands of Sioux fled to the Dakota Badlands, although their unchallenged leader, Sitting Bull, remained on the reservation. Finally, in mid-December 1890, the army sent United States–trained Indian police to arrest him; the encounter ended with the deaths of Sitting Bull, seven of his supporters, and six policemen.

Deprived of their leader and under continuing pressure from the army, the Sioux prepared to surrender. The Seventh Cavalry—Custer's old regiment—entered the Sioux village at Wounded Knee Creek to search for arms. In the ensuing confrontation, a single shot rang out from the Sioux ranks. Army troops then massacred, by their own estimate, 150, many of them women and children (the Sioux claimed the actual number of dead was closer to 400). The resulting rage among the Sioux soon burned itself out, and their surrender marked the final, heartbreaking capitulation of once-proud Native American cultures to whites' notions of civilization.

To most westerners, the collapse of Indian resistance meant freedom to reshape the West as they wished. But this was a mirage; in fact they were as much tied into the expanding system of industrial capitalism as were northeastern wage workers or southern tenants and sharecroppers. Farm families migrating to the Great Plains and southwestern regions suffered less than their rural counterparts in the South, in large part because the former could own the land they farmed. But momentous changes throughout the West set the stage for massive social conflicts.

The westward expansion of agriculture led the way in the final white settlement of the American West. Between 1870 and 1900, American agriculture underwent a period of rapid expansion unprecedented in the nation's history. Within thirty years, the number of farms doubled and more land was brought under cultivation than in

"The Opening of the Fight at Wounded Knee." Dispatched to South Dakota to cover the Ghost Dance crisis, artist Frederic Remington never witnessed the violence at Wounded Knee or subsequently visited the scene. Nevertheless, he depicted the battle for the readers of *Harper's Weekly* in wash drawings that heralded the heroism of the Seventh Cavalry.

the previous two and a half centuries. The most rapid development occurred on the Great Plains, once dubbed "the Great American Desert" and written off as unsuitable for agriculture. In little more than a generation, however, the Great Plains became the heartland of American farming. White agricultural settlement also extended, although at a much slower pace, into the Southwest—the huge expanse of land annexed after the war with Mexico that stretched from Texas to the West Coast and would eventually comprise the states of Arizona, California, Colorado, Nevada, New Mexico, and Utah.

In the twenty years after the completion of the first transcontinental railroad in 1869, the national railroad network gave a tremendous boost to this western settlement and tied the region's farmers into distant markets. Anglo (European-American) settlers entered New Mexico and Colorado in the 1870s, for example, as the railroad was being completed. Within two decades the railroad and the market system it carried with it had transformed the region's economy and culture. Subsistence and communal farming and herding, as well as community-regulated common lands, had defined the region's economy for generations of Mexican farm families. This system now gave way to private homesteads based on commercial farming and cattle and sheep ranching linked by rail to distant markets. By 1889, nearly 72,000 miles of track sprawled west of the Mississippi River, connecting Plains and southwestern farms to the national and international economies.

Because farmers were intensely oriented to this market, they eagerly adopted mechanized techniques to increase their output. Thanks to harvesting and threshing machinery, agricultural productivity, especially on the Great Plains, grew enormously. Working by hand, a single farmer could cultivate about seven acres of wheat—as much as he could reap in the ten days when the grain was in its prime. Using automatic binders to cut and tie bundles of wheat, the same farmer could plant and harvest 135 acres in 1890, nearly twenty times more than in 1860. The resulting vast supply enabled the United States to export one-third of its wheat crop by 1900.

Despite rapid productivity gains, Plains agriculture was extremely unstable. In the early 1880s, boom conditions prevailed because of unusually heavy rainfall and rising wheat prices. But later in the decade, rainfall dropped to its normal level (well under the twenty inches a year usually required for agriculture), threatening drought. Equally important, the price of wheat on the world market resumed the downward course that had begun after the Civil War. A bushel of wheat that sold for $1.45 in 1866 went for 80 cents in the mid-1880s and under 50 cents in the mid-1890s. Yet transportation and storage costs continued to rise.

Like back-country southern farmers, Plains farmers were caught between falling prices and rising costs of production. They had to produce more and more just to stay even, but the more they produced, the lower prices fell. Developments outside the farmer's control further dragged down the price of his crops. Mechanization in conjunction with the opening of new grain-producing land in Argentina, Canada, and Russia flooded the world market with wheat and corn, resulting in depressed agricultural prices.

The railroads, America's largest business, were partially responsible. In many areas of the West, as in the South, farmers had access to only one railroad line and thus did not benefit from rate-cutting by competing lines. Roads charged as much as the traffic would bear in areas where they enjoyed monopolies, raising their rates to make up for losses on competitive routes elsewhere. Western freight rates could easily run from two to three times those farther east; many a farmer learned ruefully that the freight charges for a bushel of wheat cost more than the price it could fetch in the marketplace.

Plains farmers also had to pay high prices to the operators of elevators, the giant grain storage bins that loomed on western horizons. Like the railroads, the elevators were usually owned by large eastern corporations. The growing power of the railroads and elevators did much to weaken the market position of the western farmers.

The financial squeeze on western farmers also made daily life very difficult. Plains families perennially ran short of cash and had to resort to short-term, high-interest loans. Payments on machines, also at high interest rates, added to the farmer's fixed expenses. Anxiety over falling crop prices, unpredictable weather conditions, and crop diseases was constant.

The machinery in the fields of a Plains farm often contrasted starkly with the furnishings in the home. While a male farmer used expensive up-to-date machinery for planting, harvesting, and threshing, a farm woman operated a hand churn, carried water in a pail, and cooked at an open fireplace. Many a family set up housekeeping in a sod hut, a dark, dirty, leaky—if warm—structure made from large bricks of prairie sod. The less fortunate huddled in rude tarpaper shacks or dugouts. The difference between the equipment of house and field reflected the values assigned to men's and women's work on the Plains.

Almost invariably, men made the decision to move west, drawn by the prospect of available fertile land and the potential for economic success. Although a few women eagerly sought the journey west and thrived as independent homesteaders, most went reluctantly. Lavinia Porter confessed her misery at leaving a beloved sister behind:

I stood alone on that wild prairie. Looking westward I saw my husband driving slowly over the plain; turning my face once more to the east, my dear sister's footsteps were fast widening the distance between us. For the time I knew not which way to go, nor whom to follow . . . in spite of my brave resolve to be the courageous and valiant frontierswoman.

In the end, Porter chose her husband.

Once on their new farms, the struggle over very scarce resources marked the lives of many families; husbands and wives might argue over whether limited family funds should be invested in a new piece of farm machinery or on a new cookstove. For most men, farming on the Plains was a continuation of the agricultural work they had done before moving west; but for many women, resettlement brought far greater changes. The amenities of homemaking fell by the wayside, leaving grim drudgery and often requiring women to learn a whole new range of housekeeping skills. It was a full-time job just to keep the floors clean in a sod hut or tarpaper shack, and the constant labor ground down the most spirited of women. One seasoned western woman warned a friend in Missouri that frontier women had become mere "hewers of wood and drawers of water."

Women were also cut off from the connections to church, kin, and friends that had sustained them in the more densely populated regions from which they had come. "As soon as the storms let up, the men could get away from the isolation," wrote Mari Sandoz, the daughter of a Nebraska homesteader. "But not their women. They had only the wind and the cold and the problems of clothing, shelter, food, and fuel." Some farm women had more social contacts than Sandoz, but visitors could be a mixed blessing: in 1880 one Nebraska farm woman received over a thousand visitors, for whom she had to provide nearly eight hundred meals.

Over one million family farms sprang up in the West during the last forty years of the nineteenth century. Many bore little resemblance to the small farm of the yeoman ideal; by 1900, the average farm in the Dakotas measured 7,000 acres, and one single wheatfield extended for an astonishing 13,000 acres. Absentee investors owned some of these giant farms, working them with hired farmhands.

As western agriculture grew, cities sprang up quickly to serve the needs of western farmers and ranchers. Kansas towns such as Abilene and Dodge City originated as centers of the cattle trade. Farmers disliked cattle-shipping because the herds trampled their crops and the "cowboys'" freewheeling behavior flaunted traditional notions of law

The Sommers family pose in front of their sod-house home in West Custer County, Nebraska, in 1888.

and order. Thus, despite the economic interdependence of those who worked the land and those who herded cattle and lived in the cities, there were fierce social clashes between fundamentally different ways of life.

Farmers saw themselves as the guardians of settled and sober living in a region filled with lawlessness. In Kansas, for example, farmers joined with moral reformers in crusades against saloons, dance halls, and prostitution. They usually worked through conventional political channels but sometimes engaged in vigilante warfare with their foes. In Caldwell, Kansas, in 1884, reformers retaliated for the burning of an antiliquor editor's house by dragging a notorious gambler and whiskey dealer from his mistress's bed and lynching him in the stockyards.

Although grain farming dominated the western economy, each

region developed its own specialties: metal and coal mining in the Rockies and parts of the Southwest, cattle ranching on the Plains, lumber in the Pacific Northwest, and large-scale fruit and vegetable agriculture and metal mining in California. Until the late 1880s, for example, California's New Almaden Quicksilver Mine produced virtually half of the world's supply of mercury, a metal essential in the smelting of ore into silver. Fifteen hundred Mexican miners worked at New Almaden, ascending ladders and carrying two-hundred-pound sacks of ore strapped to their foreheads. Despite such primitive techniques, the mining industry yielded high profits and, along with ranching and commercial farming, attracted outside investors.

During the 1880s, in particular, European and eastern businessmen poured vast amounts of capital into such growth areas of the western economy. Scottish investors were especially important, pumping in funds to develop railroads, introduce new mining technology, and improve livestock breeding and marketing. Many investors ended up with little more than shattered hopes, but some reaped huge profits, particularly in metal mining and smelting. After 1879, when Colorado emerged as the nation's leading mining region, eastern capital and mining techniques along with western workers unlocked vast stores of mineral wealth, turning families like the Guggenheims into the American version of an aristocracy.

Hard-rock mining towns of the West seemed to be built overnight. With the discovery of silver in the Rocky Mountains, for example, Leadville, Colorado, went from a small cluster of log cabins in 1876 to a sprawling city of 15,000 people in 1880. Leadville's experience was repeated in towns across Colorado and Idaho in the 1880s. Creede, Cripple Creek, and Coeur d'Alene became urban outposts in the mountains almost overnight.

Although the mining towns soon developed a reputation for crudity and lawlessness, most also established stable community institutions. Even Deadwood, South Dakota, known as a sinkhole of gambling, prostitution, and violence, boasted schools, churches, and a theater within months of its founding. As two early residents reminisced, "On one hand could be heard the impassioned call of the itinerant minister of the Gospel. . . . In close proximity would be a loud-voiced gambler calling his game."

These towns owed their existence to the mines, but only a minority of their citizens worked in the mines. In Cripple Creek, for example, only one in four residents was a miner; the other three provided services ranging from prostitution to retailing. Adult men usually outnumbered adult women in these western towns, and saloons competed with the family as the center of social life.

In the mining towns, the western working class was extraordinarily diverse. Construction and service labor were the largest occupations for men. Women wage-earners—from the primly dressed "Harvey girls" at Fred Harvey's chain of cafeteria-style restaurants along the Santa Fe Railroad to the spangled prostitutes in Deadwood to the four female physicians in Cripple Creek—concentrated on service work. Mexican-American miners, Chinese laborers and launderers, Basque sheepherders, and African-American cowboys mixed with European immigrants and Anglo migrants from the East and South.

For many, the promise of the West soured, turning into the brutal reality of "unfree" labor. Just as indentured servitude and slavery had developed to ease the labor shortage in seventeenth- and eighteenth-century "frontier" Virginia, so various forms of bonded labor emerged on the late-nineteenth-century western frontier. These old labor systems became intertwined with modern capitalist enterprise, particularly in railroad construction. Railroad laborers had been recruited in China in the 1870s through a contract labor system much like indentured servitude. A similar system brought Italian workers to California agriculture and Greek laborers to Utah mining camps in the final two decades of the nineteenth century.

Conditions of life and work were in general harsher in the West than in the East, but for some the rewards were commensurately greater. Skilled workers in western cities such as San Francisco commanded higher wages than their counterparts in the East, and farmhands who earned from $16 to $25 per month in addition to room, board, and laundry probably ended up with more cash in their pockets than unskilled industrial workers did. But the tendency for regions within the West to rely on a single industry meant that even a slight downturn could bring harsh misery to an entire area. The boom-and-

---

". . . INDEBTED TO HER MASTER/MISTRESS"

Almost all of the Chinese who immigrated to the United States before 1900 were men. The Chinese Exclusion Act of 1882 not only banned additional immigration of Chinese laborers, it also prevented Chinese men who remained in the United States from bringing over wives from China to join them. Of the approximately 100,000 Chinese immigrants resident in the United States between 1880 and 1900, only 5,000 were women. Some found work as laundresses and servants; others arrived as indentured prostitutes. This 1886 contract describes the stringent conditions under which Xin Jin worked as a prostitute in San Francisco in exchange for payment of her fare from China.

THE CONTRACTEE Xin Jin became indebted to her master/mistress for food and passage from China to San Francisco. Since she is without funds, she will voluntarily work as a prostitute at Tan Fu's place for four and one-half years for an advance of 1,205 yuan (U.S. $524) to pay this debt. There shall be no interest on the money and Xin Jin shall receive no wages. At the expiration of the contract, Xin Jin shall be free to do as she pleases. Until then, she shall first secure the master/mistress's permission if a customer asks to take her out. If she has the four loathsome diseases she shall be returned within 100 days; beyond that time the procurer has no responsibility. Menstruation disorder is limited to one month's rest only. If Xin Jin becomes sick at any time for more than 15 days, she shall work one month extra; if she becomes pregnant, she shall work one year extra. Should Xin Jin run away before her term is out, she shall pay whatever expense is incurred in finding and returning her to the brothel. This is a contract to be retained by the master/mistress as evidence of the agreement. Receipt of 1205 yuan ($524) by Ah Yo. Thumb print of Xin Jin the contractee. Eighth month 11th day of the 12th year of Guang-zu (1886).

bust pattern of industrial capitalism that afflicted the rest of the nation hit western workers hard as well.

The frontier had, from early on in the nation's history, been seen as a land of opportunity. This attitude died hard. A western labor activist remembered with some bitterness that "the Golden West has been the Mecca in the dream of the misguided worker in all parts of the country. If I can only get West, has been his only thought." By the 1890s, however, the West, like the South, had been thoroughly caught up in the whirlwind of industrial capitalism.

INDUSTRIAL CAPITALISM AND THE MEANING OF DEMOCRACY

As the nineteenth century ended, industrial capitalism's rapid growth had transformed America. Life in the United States—now the world's richest nation—proceeded on a scale unthinkable to previous generations, thanks to the corporate successes of men such as Carnegie and Edison. The mechanization of both factory production and agriculture had changed forever the way most Americans worked and lived. By 1900, the railroad, the telegraph, and the telephone linked together in a vast national and even international market the miner in the Far West, the tenant farmer in the South, the steelworker in the Midwest, and the garment worker in New York City sweatshops.

Traditional institutions were also transformed by a vast internal and international migration of individuals and families seeking new opportunities in industrializing America: rural counties witnessed their young men's departure for the city; cities saw young working-class families try their luck in the West or set up businesses for themselves; poor families in agricultural areas in northern Mexico were drawn to the expanding economic opportunities of the Southwest; rural areas in China and Japan gave up their young men to the lure of the "Golden Mountain" in America; and the commercial revolution in European agriculture combined with industrial depression to push millions of young men and women away from farms, villages, and cities to a strange new "land of opportunity."

Yet beneath the technological progress and individual opportunity lay a pervasive discontent. As large industrial and financial institutions secured ever greater economic and political power, ordinary Americans—both those who could claim U.S. ancestry for many generations and those newly arrived—found themselves increasingly subject to forces beyond their control. The wages they earned for their labor and the prices they paid for goods were subject to arbitrary decisions made in remote corporate boardrooms or impersonal mechanisms of world trade. Factory managers used stopwatches to reshape the work process in the name of greater efficiency and increased profitability. In sweatshops and tenements, the cruel pinch of want served where the time clock could not go. Paupers and multimillionaires increased in number, even as a new middle class emerged that seemed to loathe the excesses of both.

Perhaps more disturbing than the glaring extremes, the autonomous farmer and the self-employed artisan—the traditional bulwarks of nineteenth-century American society—were being squeezed out. Lifelong wage-earning meant dependence, a betrayal of the longstanding American dream of being economically beholden to no one.

Throughout the final three decades of the nineteenth century, American workers and farmers—men and women, African-Americans, Mexican-Americans, native-born whites, and European and Chinese immigrants—searched for collective as well as individual solutions to the dramatic changes capitalism wrought. As the nation divided on the wisdom of such changes, its citizens struggled to find a place for themselves in a society transformed by economic concentration and previously unimaginable wealth.

The Bible against competition. An 1894 cartoon depicts the murder of Abel as a critical lesson about capitalism. Quoting George D. Herron, a critic of Social Darwinism, the caption reads: "Cain's hands were the first to grasp and wield COMPETITION as the weapon of progress: a weapon from which no economic theorists have ever been able to wash the blood of human suffering."

2

THE EMERGENCE OF WORKING-CLASS COLLECTIVITY

AS INDUSTRIAL capitalism reached into every corner of the nation's life, Americans disagreed on the merits of the newly emerging world. In *Democratic Vistas*, published in 1871, the poet Walt Whitman railed against the "hollowness of heart" and "depravity of the business classes" evident in the social relations of the new era. The humorist Mark Twain, in his 1874 novel *The Gilded Age*, described the whole country as living by a crass code of "money lust": "Get rich; dishonestly if we can, honestly if we must." Such critics thought that the new industrial order callously disregarded the human beings caught in its grasp. Others worshiped at the altar of capitalism's success. The writer W. R. Thayer concluded that material success came to those for whom it was intended: "That you have property is proof of industry and foresight on your part or your father's: that you have nothing is a judgment on your laziness and vices, or on your improvidence." The poor and the unemployed, Thayer believed, brought their misery upon themselves.

Many businessmen, politicians, and scholars went even further, distorting the British scientist Charles Darwin's theory of evolution to explain capitalism's new social relations. These "Social Darwinists" put forth a "scientific" explanation for the increasing impoverishment of the "unfit" masses, warning that interference in favor of the "weak" would doom American society. Columbia University president Nicholas Murray Butler argued against charity for the poor because "nature's cure for most social and political diseases is better than man's." The often ruthless actions of capitalists in building successful businesses were justified as "a survival of the fittest, the working out," according to John D. Rockefeller, "of a law of nature and a law of God."

The members of the new middle class—caught between the rich few and the growing numbers of poor—vacillated between supporting the new industrial order and criticizing it. Many small businessmen and professionals relied on working-class patrons for their liveli-

---

"... THE DUTY OF THE MAN OF WEALTH"

In The Gospel of Wealth and Other Timely Essays, *published in 1889, the industrialist Andrew Carnegie argued that individual capitalists were duty-bound to play a broader cultural and social role and thus improve the world.*

THIS THEN, IS held to be the duty of the man of wealth: To set an example of modest, unostentatious living, shunning display or extravagance: to provide moderately for the legitimate wants of those dependent upon him; and, after doing so, to consider all surplus revenues which came to him simply as trust funds, which he is called upon to administer, and strictly bound as a matter of duty to administer in the manner which, in his judgment, is best calculated to produce the most beneficial results for the community—the man of wealth thus becoming the mere trustee and agent for his poorer brethren, bringing to their service his superior wisdom, experience, and ability to administer, doing for them better than they would or could do for themselves. . . .

"A WORKINGMAN'S PRAYER"

Carnegie's point of view contrasts sharply with those of "A Workman," who published a satirical response to Carnegie's book in an 1894 issue of a Pittsburgh labor newspaper.

OH, ALMIGHTY ANDREW Philanthropist Library Carnegie, who art in America when not in Europe spending the money of your slaves and serfs, thou art a good father to the people of Pittsburgh, Homestead and Beaver Falls. We bow before thee in humble obedience of slavery. . . . We have no desire but to serve thee. If you sayest black was white we believe you, and are willing, with the assistance of . . . the Pinkerton's agency, to knock the stuffin[g] out of anyone who thinks different, or to shoot down and imprison serfs who dare say you have been unjust in reducing the wages of your slaves, who call themselves citizens of the land of the free and the home of the brave. . . .

Oh, lord and master, we love thee because you and other great masters of slaves favor combines and trusts to enslave and make paupers of us all. We love thee though our children are clothed in rags. We love thee though our wives . . . are so scantily dressed and look so shabby. But, oh master, thou hast given us one great enjoyment which man has never dreamed of before—a free church organ, so that we can take our shabby families to church to hear your great organ pour forth its melodious strains. . . .

Oh, master, we thank thee for all the free gifts you have given the public at the expense of your slaves. . . . Oh, master, we need no protection, we need no liberty so long as we are under thy care. So we commend ourselves to thy mercy and forevermore sing thy praise.

Amen!

hoods. This inclined them toward supporting working people's collective demands and struggles. But middle-class Americans owed much of their success to industrial capitalism's dramatic expansion. They shared with the industrial elite an enthusiastic belief in "acquisitive individualism," the idea that the individual pursuit of wealth was the highest realization of the American ideal of freedom.

Many workers, to be sure, embraced this philosophy as well, though more rejected it outright or at least understood its limitations. Whatever their individual hopes for prosperity and security, working people throughout the Gilded Age viewed with skepticism the idea of "making it" solely on their own. Their daily lives—on the job, at home, in their communities—rather than leading to greater independence and self-sufficiency, served instead to remind working people of their growing dependency on wage labor and the market.

Working people's actions in the final quarter of the nineteenth century thus reflected a profound tension. They sought individual advancement, but they remained connected to cooperative traditions. Working people survived the rigors of urban-industrial life by relying on group identity as much as on individual effort and initiative. These more collective values were drawn from an abiding belief in independence and liberty spawned by the American Revolution; they evolved from religious ideals of equality and justice inherent in evangelical Protestantism; and they emerged from the community institutions that linked individuals and families in urban neighborhoods and workshops and on farms and plantations.

Newly arrived immigrants carried similar cooperative values and traditions. Many were veterans of Europe's fierce social conflicts: Fenians who fought English rule in Ireland; Chartists who struggled for greater democracy in England; "48ers" who fought for social reform in Germany; socialists and anarchists from Europe's industrial regions. They remained fervent advocates of egalitarian principles after their arrival in the United States. Even nonrevolutionary immigrants relied on collective traditions and identities to help ease their entry into the new world of urban-industrial America. Most immigrants began by re-creating conditions in their homelands. City neighborhoods with names like "German Town," "Chinatown," and "Little Sweden" sprang up across Gilded Age America, each with its own churches, schools, saloons, and newspapers. German immigrants dominated Chicago's working-class neighborhoods, for example, after the Civil War. By the 1880s, German mutual benefit clubs, athletic and cultural associations, schools, military and drilling orders, and family-oriented saloons not only lent a particular cultural ambience to the city but also provided German immigrants with institutions that helped soften the worst effects of individual isolation.

Throughout the era, working people—immigrant and native-born, rural and urban alike—redefined and deepened these collective values and institutions, creating new, more militant organizations, forms of struggle, and ideologies: unions based on class rather than skill; strikes, not only for higher wages, but also to express solidarity with fellow workers; alternative and independent rural and urban political parties; and radical political ideologies such as socialism and anarchism.

To those who profited most from industrial capitalism, the growth of such militant working-class institutions and collective ideals seemed to threaten the new order's very survival. Its proponents increasingly came to see all working people, in the words of *Century* magazine, as "the vicious and disorderly classes." Workers countered such claims, arguing that if industrializing America had "dangerous classes," they lived, as a New York tailor put it, "in the mansions and villas."

By the mid-1880s, this debate would become a clash of diametrically opposed philosophies that pitted a newly revived labor movement and the values of mutuality and collectivity against the combined forces of capital and a supporting ideology that mixed Social Darwinism with acquisitive individualism. Labor reformer George McNeill, in his widely read 1887 book *The Labor Movement: The Problem of Today*, articulated working people's perspective on the growing struggle:

> [E]xtremes of wealth and poverty are threatening the existence of the government. In the light of these facts, we declare that there is an inevitable and irresistible conflict between the wage-system of labor and the republican system of government—the wage laborer attempting to save the government, and the capitalist class ignorantly attempting to subvert it.

Sharp conflict over industrial capitalism and its meaning for traditional American values and ideals dominated the national experience in the two decades that followed the great railroad strikes of 1877. In large cities and commercial ports and in rural communities, the older world of the self-sufficient, independent producer was relentlessly remade. That process posed both possibilities and problems for the individuals caught in its wake.

WORKING-CLASS ACCOMMODATION AND RESISTANCE

A tangle of paths cut across the landscape of industrial America—tracks left by individuals, families, and groups as they wrestled with the choices that lay before them. Two basic types of working-class responses to Gilded Age capitalism can be identified: complete accommodation to the new industrial order, and outright and even violent resistance. Few individuals remained fixed at one extreme or the other over the course of a lifetime; many changed their attitudes and behavior as their personal circumstances changed. Nonetheless, accommodation and resistance defined the boundaries of individual working-class behavior in industrializing America.

Accommodation was the route taken by those who grasped the promise of the expanding industrial economy; they searched for a comfortable fit between their own resources and circumstances and the opportunities presented. These individuals fell into three loose and often overlapping groups. First, many craft workers—most of old American stock, some immigrants and children of immigrants from England, Ireland, and Germany—secured privileged positions for themselves and their families. Dominating such trades as carpentry and iron- and steelmaking, these male skilled workers were proud of their respectability, of their male camaraderie, and of their capacity to support their wives and children comfortably; they were often referred to as an "aristocracy of labor." Some preferred to speak of themselves as "mechanics," or even as middle class, rather than workingmen. As long as they could protect their power and privilege from employers' attempts to undermine them, most craft workers wanted no social upheaval.

The second accommodationist strategy drew people into mainstream politics. The years before the Civil War witnessed the emergence of a new and expanded political process, laying the foundation for the well-oiled urban "machines" that controlled politics and jobs in Gilded Age cities. Both the Democratic and Republican parties traded municipal jobs for working-class votes, and many urban workers, native-born and immigrant alike, were only too willing to take advantage of the economic opportunities offered by politics.

Third, some working people chose the path of entrepreneurship. An extraordinary few rose from humble origins to fabulous wealth and power. But most working people who ventured along this path only managed to establish small and struggling businesses. Although such enterprises were always risky ventures, the lure of "being one's own boss" and escaping the dependency of wage-earning attracted the hopeful. Working-class neighborhoods in cities and small towns provided ready customers for the proprietors of groceries, saloons, barber shops, and variety stores. As in politics, those born in the United States shared the field with immigrants, who turned their native languages and knowledge of Old World preferences into business assets.

With notable exceptions, those who followed such accommodationist strategies did not necessarily wholly accept the individualist values of industrial capitalism. Most working-class accommodationists found that to succeed they still needed to join together with their families, ethnic kin, workmates, and coreligionists. In large cities, small industrial towns, and rural counties, local communities overflowed with benefit societies, church parishes and congregations, ethnic associations, and fraternal orders. These institutions enabled more fortunate working-class families to provide help to fellow community residents who were sick, injured, or unemployed and to share a sense of sociability and camaraderie. Of course, while accommodationists might not entirely embrace the values of acquisitive individualism, neither did they choose to challenge directly the power of the emerging industrial elite.

Resisters saw things differently. Drawing on the many antebellum critiques of political and social injustice, Gilded Age dissidents across the country, as we will see, espoused a wide range of causes: from staunch craft-union militancy to the strategy of organizing all workers, regardless of occupation or race, into the Knights of Labor; from Henry George's proposal for a single tax on land to populism (agrarian radicalism), anarchism, and the many varieties of socialism, some home-grown and some imported. Resisters, both moderate and militant, flourished inside a vibrant labor-reform environment. Every state with any industrial base nurtured dozens of working-class newspapers, debating societies, and radical enclaves. And in rural areas, crusading newspapers and outdoor protest meetings provided forums for radical critiques of capitalism's growing impact on farm families.

Accommodation and resistance often intersected. Deteriorating working conditions might transform an "accommodating" craft unionist into a militant socialist; being blacklisted by employers might push a radical union leader to abandon active struggle temporarily and open a small business in a new locale; ambition might lead a lifelong factory worker to open a neighborhood grocery or saloon. Individual strategies changed over time with the accumulation of experience; each was conditioned by a particular mix of ethnic, racial, gender, and regional identities, as well as by the nature of work and politics itself.

WORKING-CLASS EXPERIENCES

A close look at the lives of some of the people who lived through this phase of the making and remaking of the American working class conveys the human impact of the vast changes wrought by industrial capitalism. Several of these individuals were well known, even famous, in their time; most remained anonymous.

Andrew Carnegie—the wealthiest and most successful late-nineteenth-century U.S. capitalist—epitomized the outright embrace of

A sense of history. On the eve of the May Day 1886 eight-hour strike, workers at Chicago's Horn Brothers Furniture Company mark the occasion for posterity.

individual advancement in industrializing America. Carnegie was born in Dunfermline, Scotland, in 1835, the son of a linen weaver. Losing his job when the power loom was introduced, Carnegie's father, like so many displaced European skilled workers, moved his family to the United States. The Carnegies settled in 1848 in a Scottish neighborhood in Pittsburgh, then a small industrial outpost in western Pennsylvania. But America was not then the land of plenty for the Carnegie family; they barely eked out a living. His father wove and peddled linens, and his mother took in washing. To help out, young Carnegie found a series of low-paying factory jobs.

Within a few years, he landed a job as a telegraph operator, which put him in contact with members of Pittsburgh's growing business community. In 1853, Carnegie met Thomas Scott, the superintendent of the Pennsylvania Railroad's Western Division, who soon hired him as his secretary and personal telegrapher. As Scott's right-hand man, Carnegie familiarized himself with all aspects of the railroad business. When Scott was promoted in 1859 to Pennsylvania Railroad vice president, Carnegie, at age twenty-four, was given Scott's job. At the end of the Civil War, Carnegie quit to pursue a number of business opportunities, each of which substantially expanded his fortune.

Beginning in 1872, Carnegie decided to focus his energies on steel production; he spent the next quarter-century assuring his absolute domination over the steel industry. Carnegie built modern mills and acquired a number of steel companies from his competitors, adapting the management and marketing techniques he had learned at the Pennsylvania Railroad. Most importantly, Carnegie realized that to succeed on a truly massive scale his mills would need not only the most modern technology but also absolute control over his workers: he would have to break the power of the craft unions that traditionally protected skilled steelworkers' domination over production. In 1892, Carnegie ordered his managers to lock out all workers at his Homestead mill. The bitter, violent, and protracted struggle that followed, in which fourteen were killed and thousands lost their jobs, finally ended in victory for Carnegie and his new system of steel production and industrial management. By the end of the century, Carnegie-owned companies produced 25 percent of the nation's steel; he personally pocketed an annual profit of $25 million.

In 1901, tired from his business and labor battles, Carnegie decided to retire and devote himself to philanthropy. When he accepted J. P. Morgan's unheard-of offer of nearly $500 million for the Carnegie Steel Company, Carnegie became the richest man in the world. Andrew Carnegie had traveled an extraordinary distance in a half century from his humble origins. By distancing himself from the working class and by ruthlessly embracing the ideal of acquisitive individualism, he became the ultimate Gilded Age success story. He was also a phenomenal exception: very few wealthy capitalists rose from the kind of background that Carnegie did.

Booker T. Washington, the noted African-American educator, provides another example of working-class accommodation to industrialism. Born a slave in 1858, Washington lived in West Virginia after the Civil War, laboring with his stepfather in the salt furnaces of the Kanawha Valley. Washington soon moved to coalmining, where his dissatisfaction resulted in a fierce determination to escape mine labor. "One day, while at work in the coal mine," he remembered, "I happened to hear two miners talking about a great school for colored people somewhere in Virginia." That school, Hampton Normal and Agricultural Institute, launched Washington on the road to national prominence.

Washington quit the mines, found a job for five dollars a month as a servant for the mineowner's wife—a mistress whose compulsion for order, cleanliness, and honesty had a major effect on Washington—and prepared for the day when he would enter Hampton. He succeeded finally in the early 1870s, leaving behind, in his words, "the degrading influences of the slave plantation and the coal mines." Working his way through Hampton, Washington graduated, taught black students for a time in his old hometown, and then, in 1881, founded a Hampton-like school, Tuskegee Institute, in the "Black Belt" of Alabama.

Washington built his new school into a training ground for African-Americans to work with their hands. Acutely conscious of the narrow limitations whites placed on African-Americans' economic aspirations, Washington stressed that blacks must accommodate white people's, and especially southern whites', refusal to tolerate blacks as anything more than sophisticated menials. He urged blacks to "'cast down your bucket where you are'—cast it down in making friends in every manly way of the people of all races by whom we are surrounded." He told whites that "in all things that are purely social we can be as separate as the fingers, yet one as the hand in all things essential to mutual progress."

Washington's accommodationist language appealed to white politicians and businessmen eager to roll back African-American voting rights and secure blacks' continued status as a docile labor force. As a result, Washington possessed significant power to dispense patronage jobs and money to African-Americans and became the most powerful black man in late-nineteenth-century America. But he was unable to moderate his people's steady political and economic decline at the close of the nineteenth century.

If Carnegie and Washington accommodated the new order, Lucy Parsons offers a dramatic model of resistance. A militant anarchist and revolutionary of African-American descent, Parsons helped lead the organized working-class opposition to industrial capitalism. Parsons was probably born a slave in Texas in 1853. Carrying the scars of the African-American experience with her into the white, immigrant radical milieu she would inhabit, Lucy persistently denied her black ancestry, claiming instead to be the orphaned child of Mexican and Indian parents. However far she distanced herself from her real heritage, Lucy passionately denounced Ku Klux Klan rapes and lynchings that were commonplace in the Waco, Texas, region where she lived in the late 1860s. It was there in 1869 that she met Albert Parsons, her comrade and husband, when she was sixteen.

Albert and Lucy Parsons could not have come from more different backgrounds. The son of a prominent New England family, Albert Parsons numbered among his ancestors passengers on the *Mayflower*, graduates of Harvard and Yale, a pastor of an early Congregational church, and important military figures in the Revolutionary War. He eventually settled in Waco before the Civil War, where he apprenticed as a printer.

After his service in the Confederate Army ended, Parsons became a Radical Republican during Reconstruction, championing African-American rights, addressing meetings, and mobilizing black voters. His courageous stand earned him the respect of Texas blacks, including Lucy. When they set up house—state laws banned interracial marriage—in the early 1870s, they crossed over the line that forbade miscegenation, or "race-mixing." With Reconstruction's demise in Texas in 1873, Lucy and Albert Parsons thought it wise to move north.

They went to Chicago, where Albert found steady employment as a typesetter and joined the International Typographical Union. Lucy and Albert quickly made contacts among Chicago radicals. Socialist study groups began meeting in their home. Soon the two were at the center of factional struggles within an emerging American left caught between socialism and anarchism—both positions that challenged the notion of private property, with the former advocating government ownership of the means of production and the latter arguing that organized government was by its very nature oppressive. Albert lost his job because of his stirring speeches during the 1877 railroad strike; Lucy set up a dressmaking shop to support them both. For Lucy, the violence perpetrated by the police and the militia against working people in 1877 shaped her unyielding conviction that labor and capital could never be reconciled.

By 1885, Lucy and Albert Parsons were the most famous radical couple in Chicago. The "respectable" press regularly and viciously attacked them. The next year would witness Albert's legal frame-up, along with seven of his radical and anarchist comrades, for the Haymarket Square bombing that killed a Chicago policeman. Following her husband's execution in 1887, Lucy carried on their struggle for socialist and anarchist principles.

Most women and members of racial or ethnic minorities in Gilded Age America were less certain than Lucy Parsons about their attitudes toward industrial capitalism. But even those who wanted to accommodate to the new order still faced sexual and racial discrimination. They could never be sure that they would maintain whatever modest gains the new age afforded. Yet, despite enormous impediments to their individual advancement, few women and people of color embraced outright resistance to the new order.

Lee Chew, a Chinese immigrant, made a successful accommodation to American society, but one that was not without sacrifices. Chew left his Chinese village as a young man, hoping to find wealth "in the country of American wizards." He arrived in California just before the U.S. Congress passed legislation in 1882 prohibiting further Chinese immigration.

Learning American ways from the housewife who hired him, he worked as a domestic servant for two years. He sent money back to his family and saved to open a business. But he also dressed well and enjoyed theater and dinner parties in San Francisco's Chinatown. Lee and a partner opened a laundry (as did many Chinese), because it required little capital and demanded grueling labor that white Americans were only too happy to leave to others. Moving east to escape the anti-Chinese sentiment so prevalent in the Far West, Lee set up laundries in Chicago, Detroit, and Buffalo, but finally gave up laundry work altogether when factory-style steam laundries began to eat into his business. Finally, he settled in New York and established a successful business importing Chinese products.

"The Street of the Gamblers (by day)." Arnold Genthe's photographs of San Francisco's Chinatown provide information about the Chinese community at the turn of the century. His characterization of his subjects, however, often conveys a distorted and ominous message. Despite its title, the significance of this photograph of Ross Alley, taken sometime around New Year's, lies in its depiction of unusual daytime congestion resulting from the seasonal unemployment of many Chinatown workers after the holiday.

In America, Lee Chew found financial success but not peace of mind. He resented Americans' distorted images of his countrymen, the unpunished vandalism and outright violence that plagued Chinese communities from coast to coast, and laws that prevented Chinese men from bringing their brides into the country. Railing about America's outrageous treatment of the Chinese, Lee Chew asked, "How can I call this my home, and how can anyone blame me if I take my money and go back to my village in China?"

Margaret Getchell's successful business career at R. H. Macy & Company similarly reveals the limits of the opportunities open to women in the late nineteenth century. She began her career as a teacher, moving from school to school in her late teens. By the time she was twenty, she had used her hometown and family connections with R. H. Macy to secure a position in his department store as a cashier. Her mathematical ability quickly won her a bookkeeper's position. Then her administrative talents and personality propelled her into the superintendent's office in 1866, making her second in command to Macy himself.

Getchell married Abiel LaForge, a business associate of Macy's, in 1869. They rented rooms above the store, and LaForge joined the store staff so he could work alongside Getchell. They developed a smooth working relationship, with Getchell running the store and her husband focusing on merchandising. When their first child was born, Getchell gave up her position as superintendent; meanwhile, LaForge became a partner in the firm. Getchell continued to "help out" in the store at busy times, but her role as wife and mother now defined her status. Pregnant with her third child, she managed the store single-handed for three months while Macy and LaForge were on a European buying trip, but Macy gave her only a few small gifts in payment. Getchell refrained from protesting this treatment, and her connection with the store ended five years later, when LaForge died and she sold his share of the firm. Margaret Getchell stands out as perhaps the first American woman business executive. But her remarkable talents could not protect her from an interrupted career and demeaning treatment by Macy, who owed so much of his business success to her efforts.

Mexican-American farmers willing to adapt to the new industrial order also found opportunities for individual advancement in the southwestern territory in the last quarter of the nineteenth century. In 1871, the father of Elfido López (first name unknown), along with eleven of his fellow Mexican farmers from Trinidad in southern Colorado, filed separate claims for 160-acre private homesteads under the federal homesteading law.

The completion of the railroad had brought an economic boom to the area and encouraged López and other longtime Mexican residents of Colorado to give up traditional communal forms of farming and risk private homesteading. Only six of the twelve Mexican farmers, including López, had sufficient cash to buy shovels for digging irrigation ditches; they shared tools and other resources. Within the year López and his compatriots had planted three or four acres of wheat on each of their individual homesteads; they harvested crops communally, as was the long-standing Mexican custom in the Southwest.

But the financial difficulties inherent in this new system left López unable to support himself and his family, even though he did manage to acquire a small cattle herd. In 1876, López left his homestead to enter the region's growing wage economy. He traveled to the rail town of Las Animas, Colorado, with several hundred other men to work on the railroad line for cash to supplement his meager income. His family moved to Las Animas, too. His son Elfido herded cows for $1 per head per month and also sold the milk from the family's herd to gain additional cash. Finally, two years later, the López family returned to their homestead with a much larger herd. They also managed to open a small store.

It had been railroad work, not farming, that had allowed the López family to achieve a measure of success in the new industrial economy. The railroad brought opportunities and a market economy to the Southwest, but also cultural and social change. López and his fellow Mexican farmers were able to stay in the region and even prosper because they accepted and even embraced aspects of the new order. But their relative success also required changes: the abandonment of traditional communal work and land use for more individualized economic strategies.

Chew, Getchell, and López faced racial or sexual discrimination in their daily lives. But they also gained enough materially to make accommodation a reasonable choice. Other working people followed a very different path. Outraged at the injustices of American life, they steadfastly resisted industrial capitalism's growth.

Oscar Ameringer was one of these radicals. Ameringer arrived in Cincinnati as a teenager in 1886, a period of violent class conflict across the country. He had learned the skills of cabinetmaking and playing musical instruments from his father in Germany. But his abilities meant little in the furniture factories of the United States, where Ameringer initially sought employment. He found the labor there mundane and mind-numbing: "The work was monotonous, the hours of drudgery ten a day, my wages a dollar."

Ameringer eagerly responded to the labor movement's call. When the May Day strikes for the eight-hour day rocked Cincinnati in 1886, Ameringer left his job to march behind the Lehr und Wehr-Verein, a German workers' educational and protective society that had a labor battalion, four hundred strong, armed with Springfield rifles. Amer-

"YOU SHOULD TAKE ALLOTMENTS . . ."

Native Americans were not immune from pressures to accommodate to the new industrial order. This selection from the biography of Edward Goodbird, a member of the Hidatsa tribe in Minnesota, describes the period immediately following the passage of the Dawes Act in 1887, when Plains Indians were made to give up communal ways of life for individual family farms. Goodbird's experience was exceptional: he prospered under the new system, ultimately becoming an employee of the Bureau of Indian Affairs.

THE TIME CAME when we had to forsake our village at Like-a-fish-hook Bend, for the government wanted the Indians to become farmers. "You should take allotments," our [Bureau of Indian Affairs] agent would say. "The big game is being killed off, and you must plant bigger fields or starve. The government will give you plows and cattle."

All knew that the agent's words were true, and little by little our village was broken up. In the summer of my sixteenth year nearly a third of my tribe left to take up allotments. . . .

My father left the village, with my mother and me, in June. He had a wagon, given him by the agent. . . . We camped at Independence in a tepee, while we busied ourselves building a cabin. My father cut the logs; they were notched at the ends, to lock into one another at the corners. . . . The floor was of earth, but we had a stove. We were a month putting up our cabin. . . .

Our agent issued to every Indian family having an allotment a plow, and wheat, flax, and oats for seeding. My father and I broke land near our cabin, and in the Spring seeded it down. We had a fair harvest in the Fall. Threshing was done on the agency machine, and, having sacked our grain, my father and I hauled it, in four trips to Hebron, eighty miles away. Our flax sold for seventy-five cents, our wheat for sixty cents, and our oats for twenty-five cents a bushel. Our four loads brought us about eighty dollars.

I became greatly interested in farming . . . one day the agent sent for me. I went to his office.

"I hear you have become a good farmer," he said, as I came in. "I want to appoint you assistant to our agency farmer. . . . You are to measure off for every able-bodied Indian, ten acres of ground to be plowed and seeded. If an Indian is lazy and will not attend to his plowing, report him to me and I will send a policeman. . . ."

I began my new duties at once. . . .

inger and his countrymen signaled their revolutionary fervor by carrying red flags and *Arbeiter Zeitung,* a workers' journal printed on red paper; and they joined their voices in singing the "Arbeiter's Marseillaise."

Thirty-two thousand Cincinnati workers would eventually be involved in the May strikes. In their aftermath, most would find their way back to their jobs, their dreams of revolution dashed for the moment. Ameringer, however, had nothing to return to. He was blacklisted for assaulting a strikebreaker in front of the furniture factory where he worked. To make a living, he turned to the coronet, playing in the saloons that catered to the German working class. Ameringer's disillusioning experiences as a skilled worker in industrial America had propelled him into Cincinnati's German-American socialist community, where he remained a writer and agitator for several decades.

For Ameringer, socialism provided a vision of a world to come in which ownership of mines and factories would not entitle some to oppress and starve others, in which workers' dignity and right to a livelihood would be assured. As he saw it, the primary problem to be addressed was that of class conflict: the struggle between those who owned the mines and factories, and those who lived by the sweat of their brow.

Not all Gilded Age craft workers were as radical in their opposition to industrial capitalism. Patrick Henry McCarthy charted a different course, one that mixed trade-union militancy with a commitment to political accommodation rather than socialism.

Born in Ireland on Saint Patrick's Day in 1863, McCarthy arrived in the United States in 1880 as a carpenter's apprentice. After stops in Chicago and St. Louis, he settled in San Francisco in 1886. McCarthy helped found the Brotherhood of Carpenters and Joiners in the late 1880s, then organized the city's powerful Building Trades Council (BTC) in 1898, ruling it with an iron hand for twenty-four years. An imposing man who enjoyed great popularity at union dances, McCarthy relished luxuries such as fine furniture and diamond rings and developed a "lordly" public manner, his speech punctuated by frequent quotations from the classics.

But McCarthy's life was more than one man's success story. His prosperity was the result of his connection to the rich culture of San Francisco unionism. When McCarthy arrived in San Francisco in 1886, the city was already a center of trade union power. Ever since the heady days of the Gold Rush, when wages reached an astounding $14 an hour, building tradesmen were always in great demand in San Francisco because the city was so far removed from other industrial centers.

By organizing tightly, building tradesmen exercised strict control of the labor market. No one could work without a union card; everyone worked under strict union rules at good wages; employment was shared among union brothers; and all good union men informally restricted their output so there would be enough work for all. They were not afraid to strike, and in prosperous times they won more battles than they lost. These privileged workers jealously guarded the gates to their trade: some building unions barred all but their members' sons. A person of color—African-American or Asian—had virtually no chance of being admitted.

McCarthy was the czar of this labor fiefdom, little interested in unions outside of the building trades and even less concerned with the plight of San Francisco's unorganized workers. Despite such indifference, McCarthy and the organizations he led took a strong stand against the growing economic and political power of industrial capitalists. The Building Trades Council, for example, championed plans to free workers, albeit only those who were white, from the thrall of wage labor through cooperative enterprises and land reform. Their goal was to trim the overbearing influence of large capitalists such as Carnegie and Rockefeller, returning control of the new urban-industrial order to the broad mass of American citizens.

McCarthy's political agenda and social outlook nonetheless reflected his lofty status. He adopted the persona of "responsible pillar of the community," honest, upright, and pragmatic in his dealings with employers. He supported joint political action by employer groups and organized labor. He explained that "the Building Trades Council represents many thousands of property owners and tax-

Emancipation Day 1888. Crepe-paper bunting, American flags, and Lincoln's portrait grace the exterior of a general store as the African-American citizens of Richmond, Virginia, commemorate the twenty-fifth anniversary of the signing of the Emancipation Proclamation.

payers, who are as jealous of their interests as any . . . affiliated body, commercial, mercantile, financial or any other. . . . [The BTC] has always worked side by side with such bodies . . . for the selection of safe and competent officials." McCarthy's success testifies both to the extraordinary economic and political power exercised by skilled workers and their willingness, despite substantial personal prosperity, to continue to define their interests in class rather than individual terms.

For African-American workers the issue of race loomed at least as large as, often larger than, that of class. They were the most visible minority within America's growing working class; although every black person bore the special oppression of slavery and racism, their attitudes toward industrial capitalism varied. The lives of two African-Americans reveal very different responses: in one case, a commitment to work collectively through the emerging labor movement of the 1880s and 1890s to build interracial unionism; and in another, an individual struggle against the increasingly repressive world of the rural South.

Richard L. Davis, like the far more famous Booker T. Washington, was born in Virginia, a few months before the Civil War ended. At age eight, Davis already labored in a Roanoke tobacco factory. In 1881, "disgusted with the very low wage rate and other unfavorable conditions," he left for the newly opened West Virginia coalfields, as had Washington. A year later, Davis moved on to Ohio's Hocking Valley, a coalmining center torn apart by bitter strikes in the 1870s—strikes in which blacks had been brought in as strikebreakers.

Davis worked as a miner in the Hocking Valley, supported his family, and helped organize an interracial union local, no small feat in an area where memories of racial conflict were still fresh. But Davis did more than organize his home local. Throughout the 1890s he traveled to Ohio, West Virginia, and Alabama coal towns, educating miners of both races about the importance of interracial unionism and spreading the message of the newly formed United Mine Workers of America (UMWA). Twice, in 1896 and 1897, Davis won election to the National Executive Board of the UMWA; at the time he was the only African-American to hold national union office. He repeatedly battled segregation and the distorting influence of "the race question," arguing, "I think were we, as workingmen, to turn our attention to fighting monopoly in land and money, we would accomplish a great deal more than we will by fighting among ourselves on account of race, creed, color, or nationality."

Tragically, at the time of his death in 1900, at age thirty-six, Davis was penniless and out of work, blacklisted by the mine bosses for his efforts on behalf of the UMWA, shunned by many of his fellow black miners, who blamed him for leading them into a failed strike, and all but ignored by the national leaders of his union. Despite such defeats and disappointments, Davis never wavered in his commitment to labor unity and interracial unionism. He, and

"... LET US PROVE OURSELVES MEN"

In a July 1891 letter written to the National Labor Tribune, *a labor newspaper published in Pittsburgh, Richard L. Davis appealed to his fellow black miners to embrace the banner of unionism and not allow themselves to be used by white coal operators as strikebreakers.*

NONE OF US who toil for our daily bread are free. At one time ... we were chattel slaves; today we are, one and all, white and black, wage slaves, and it is just such [strikebreaking] actions as we have seen taken in the state of Washington that has for years been forging the chains of bondage around us more firmly.... I think the time has come that the Negro should know better than to run from place to place to break down wages, etc. He can plainly see that the money kings of this country are only using him as a tool to fill [their] own coffers with gold. Does any Negro think that an operator thinks any more of him than he does of a white man? If you do, you are sadly mistaken, for I remember several instances right here in this valley: whenever the colored men asked for that which was something like right and just, the answer was, whenever you colored men want the same as the whites do then we have no further need for you. This was the answer. Now then I would say to the Negro, of which race I am proud to be connected, let us be men; let us demand as much for our labor as any other nationality; let us not suffer ourselves to be trampled upon any more than any other people. We are a people; we are men; we constitute one-sixth of this great country so far as numbers are concerned, consequently it is not a white man's country; it is partly ours as well, so let us prove ourselves men and the equal of any others. We can do it. I want to say that the labor organizations will do more for the Negro than any political party can or ever will do. So let us get into them and try to make this country what it should be.

other trade unionists like him, had helped make the UMWA the largest interracial union (and indeed the largest interracial organization of any kind) in Gilded Age America.

Browne Cobb, like Richard L. Davis, struggled to secure a measure of independence and prosperity in a post-Reconstruction world bounded by racial and class discrimination. Born a slave in 1850 on an Alabama cotton plantation, Cobb, like many other freedmen after Emancipation, ended up laboring on white-owned land for a share of the crop; he occasionally supplemented his meager income with wages earned from sawing lumber and cutting railroad ties. Cobb married three times; his second wife, Liza, bore him a son, Ned, in 1885. Liza died in 1894, and Ned went to work with his father, plowing and chopping cotton on land owned by a white man, Clem Todd. Cobb was "furnished" with cotton seed and farming equipment, not by Todd, which was the typical arrangement, but by another white man, Lloyd Albee. In exchange for providing furnishings, Albee held a mortgage on half a dozen cattle Browne Cobb had managed to acquire over the years. Like most white landowners and furnishing agents, Albee wanted to exert greater control over the labor of his African-American "clients." He continually pressured Cobb to move to his land to live and work as a sharecropper.

In a dispute over the sale of one of Cobb's cattle, Albee tried again to force Cobb to move; when Cobb refused, Albee promptly had him thrown in jail for selling property that did not belong to him. Cobb was released from jail through the influence of yet another white man, Jasper Clay, in a deal that Cobb's son Ned later described as "a friendship business amongst the white race." In exchange for securing his release, Clay forced Cobb in 1899 to work Clay's land for shares. Clay's sharecroppers, who included both blacks and whites, plowed and chopped cotton in large gangs. They were supposed to receive "halves," 50 percent of the harvested crop. But Clay was widely known for taking the entire crop for himself while providing his sharecroppers with food that Ned Cobb remembered as consisting of "nothing but sorghum syrup and cornmeal."

Working for Clay for almost a year without receiving anything more than these meager rations, Browne Cobb was desperate to find a way to live and work independently. He proposed a deal: Cobb would use his considerable skill as a basket weaver to supply Clay with baskets to store his picked cotton. In exchange, Clay agreed to let Cobb and his family return to Clem Todd's land. Though Cobb was finally able to leave the Clay farm, the cycle of dependence and exploitation started over again. Cobb was tricked again by a white man, this time Ruel Akers, who made him sign a note, taking his whole cotton crop and everything he owned except some household furniture in exchange for furnishing cotton seed and equipment.

Once again Cobb was forced to flee to another white-owned plantation, where, as his son Ned later lamented, "he never did prosper none after that."

Although Browne Cobb struggled valiantly to gain a measure of independence from white control, the end of Reconstruction and the subsequent disfranchisement of African-Americans prevented him from a more collective form of resistance. Cobb's son Ned later explained that "white folks in this country didn't allow niggers to have no organization, no secret meetings. . . . The nigger wasn't allowed to have nothing but church services. . . ."

Like Browne Cobb, William Lamb was a southern man of the soil. But as a white man, Lamb was able to link his personal struggle with that of his fellow farmers and to stand and fight the changes imposed by the new industrial order. Coming of age without formal education in the post–Civil War South, Lamb's experiences paralleled those of many poor farmers and tenants: he moved from his native Tennessee to Texas, hired on as a farmhand, married at age twenty-three, and rented land to farm with his family.

By the mid-1880s, Lamb had become one among many rebellious southwestern farmers who quickly became angry champions of reform in response to falling farm prices and rising production costs. Lamb's conspicuous red hair and careful style of argument became well known to Texas farmers, whom he urged to cooperate and organize. When, in 1885–86, a strike pitted longshoremen and railway workers in pitched battles against corporate-hired marshals, Lamb urged his fellow farmers to support the working-class uprising and boycott the manufacturing interests of the region. Bluntly he declared that "those who are working against us are no good for us." To Lamb, the "labor question" was *the* central issue on which all were expected to show their true colors.

The "labor question" also encompassed women workers, who poured into the industrial labor force in huge numbers after 1860. An anonymous account, "Some Experiences of a Working Girl," published in *Lippincott's Monthly Magazine* in 1886, outlined the life history of one of the more fortunate of the "working girls" of this period. Turned out of her home at an early age, a mere eighty pounds in weight, she boarded in a room so tiny that she had to dress standing on her bed. To support herself, this working girl secured a job in the New York garment trades, first as an outworker making children's dresses at 25 cents apiece, then as a factory laborer and forewoman. Condemning the depressing monotony of women's factory work, the stern penalties and prohibitions imposed on female labor, and the grimy, dirty conditions of the workplace, she provided a powerful indictment of a system that devoured young girls, spitting out "hapless, voiceless workers . . . dead in spirit if not in body." Yet she organized no unions and led no strikes; she accepted her status in silence until her promotion as forewoman allowed her some freedom to speak out, albeit anonymously.

Not all women workers, to be sure, remained silent in the face of harsh conditions of work and life. One who would openly challenge the conditions of wagework was Leonora Marie Barry. Born Leonora Kearney, she arrived in upstate New York in the 1850s and for a time taught in a rural school. At age twenty-two she married an itinerant painter and musician, William E. Barry. For the next decade they were constantly on the move, having three children along the way. In 1881, Barry's husband and only daughter died, victims of one of the debilitating "fevers" of the time.

Faced with the necessity of providing for herself and her two sons, Barry took in sewing until the strain of this work damaged her eyes. She then took an unskilled job in an Amsterdam, New York, knitting mill, where she learned firsthand about grim working conditions and low wages—in her first week, she earned only 65 cents.

From then on she staunchly defended the interests of working women. In 1884, Barry joined the Knights of Labor, quickly rising to prominence as the nation's leading organizer of female workers. Mounting platforms from one end of North America to the other to praise "the dignity of labor," Barry was a popular speaker who lent her support to the causes of cooperation, temperance, safety legislation, abolition of child labor, and woman suffrage. With a "tall, commanding figure" and "warm voice," Barry was much respected in labor and reform circles.

"Union Against Union." A wry comment on the general refusal of working-class men and the trade union movement to consider women's maintenance of the household as work.

Although Barry believed that woman's proper sphere was still the home, she saw that women were being forced to join the paid labor force, and much of her reform activity was aimed at increasing women's opportunities to secure decent jobs. "If it were possible, I wish that it was not necessary for women to learn any trade but that of domestic duties," she said in 1889, "as I believe it was intended that man should be the breadwinner. But as that is impossible under present conditions, I believe women should have every opportunity to become proficient in whatever vocation they choose or find themselves best fitted for." But Barry warned women "who foolishly imagine that with marriage their connection with and interest in labor matters end," that they must be as politicized at home as in the workplace; the fight for working-class rights was a battle for family, not individual, needs.

Barry left the paid labor force upon her remarriage in 1890. In this she followed the path of the majority of white women workers. The most common pattern was that these women would labor for wages intermittently, usually in the years between late adolescence and marriage. Once married, they might well have to return to work to stave off a family crisis. Later, a husband's death, desertion, or disease might force them back into wage labor. Of course, when a male breadwinner was at hand and regularly employed, women worked unpaid at the never-ending routine of cooking, cleaning, and childrearing. We know little about the response of these women to their domestic toil. For some, the level of daily

"... WOMEN SHOULD DO ANYTHING THEY LIKED THAT WAS GOOD"

The commitment of the Knights of Labor to equality for women was more than rhetorical, as evidenced by the career of Mrs. Elizabeth Rodgers, the organization's Master Workman, or head, of the giant Chicago District No. 24. This 1889 portrait of Rodgers, offered by leading national antiliquor activist Frances Willard, underscores the desire on the part of many Knights, both men and women, to connect the struggle for labor reform with a broader vision that included vehement opposition to liquor.

SO I WENT; in an unfamiliar, but reputable, part of the city where the streetcar patrons are evidently wage-workers. I was welcomed to a small, but comfortable, modern house by a woman who came to the door with sleeves rolled up and babe in arms. She was the presiding officer over all the Knights of Labor in Chicago and the suburbs, except the Stock Yards division . . . including fifty thousand or more working men and women. . . . Probably no parallel instance of leadership in a woman's hands, conferred by such peers, can be cited in this country, if indeed in any other.

Mrs. Rodgers is about forty years of age. . . . She has been the mother of twelve children, ten of whom are now living. The youngest was but twelve days old when her mother started for the [1886] Richmond Convention, where the baby was made "Delegate No. 800," and presented by the Knights with a silver cup and spoon, and the mother with a handsome Knights of Labor gold watch.

"My husband always believed that women should do anything they liked that was good and which they could do well," said Mrs. Rodgers, proudly; "but for him, I never could have got on so well as a Master Workman. I was the first woman in Chicago to join the Knights. They offered us the chance, and I said to myself, 'There must be a first one, and so I'll go forward.'"

. . . Mrs. Rodgers got her training as the chief officer of a local board of the Knights of Labor, which office she held four years, and by the death of the District Master Workman became the chief for our great city.

"We take no saloon-keepers," she said, "not even a saloon-keeper's wife. We will have nothing to do with men who have capital invested in a business which is the greatest curse the poor have ever known; but wage-workers connected with the liquor business are not forbidden to join us." I told her I hoped the pledge of total abstinence might be made a test of membership, and she heartily acquiesced in the plan. . . . She seemed to me a sincere Christian, and warmly seconded my statement that "Mr. Powderly [the Knights' national leader] must have the help of God, or he could not speak and act so wisely."

drudgery seemed part and parcel of the deprivations of working-class life; others put the blame on a deserting or drunken husband. In any event, most resigned themselves to the tribulations of constant work in the house, just as their husbands adapted to the daily grind of workplace life.

For those who consciously chose neither to accommodate nor resist, acceptance of working-class life as it was brought daily grievances and uncertainty. Nonetheless, years of wage labor might eventually build a foundation of economic well-being. Those fortunate enough to hold on to jobs and remain in one locale might put savings aside in a bank or purchase a home.

William Turner, a skilled ironmolder who lived in Troy, New York, in 1880 with his wife and eight children, is a representative figure. Turner had emigrated in childhood from Ireland in 1850, along with his parents and three brothers. His father, James, had worked as a laborer in the Albany Iron Works, and by 1860 the three oldest Turner children, William included, worked in the same factory, where William soon became a skilled roller. The Turners' life revolved around work in the mill—six twelve-hour days per week—and time with the family. When Turner married, he moved to the same row of brick houses where his parents lived.

But the Turners also lived within Troy's Irish-American community. That community had organized nationalist groups such as Clan Na Gael and the Fenian Society, which supported the cause of Irish independence; it provided the backbone of the city's nine Roman Catholic congregations, especially St. Joseph's, the ironmolders' church; it participated in Troy's labor movement, led by the ironmolders' union; and it sustained a variety of clubs and fraternal organizations, fire brigades, baseball clubs, and ward-based political

Two homes. The Boston *Labor Leader* compares the homes of a union workman and a scab workman. In this view, strikebreaking is the logical outgrowth of the general moral and physical degradation of the one-room scab household; the "superiority" of the trade unionist is indicated in the modest but solidly domestic atmosphere of the family's parlor.

organizations. By the late 1880s, Troy's Irish-American working class had built quite an impressive world, considering how poor the immigrants had been when they fled Ireland and the difficulty of their early years as unskilled industrial workers.

Within the extended family networks and ethnic and religious organizations of Troy, William Turner had been able to adapt to the rigors of industrial capitalism. With the help of his family, his fellow unionists, and the Irish-American community, William supported his family and rose from the ranks of the unskilled to the more secure and comfortable position of a skilled worker. This was not the great American success story, but millions of Americans like William Turner never really dreamed of great success. It seemed sufficient to be able to make a decent life for his family, to perform the rituals and observe the commandments of his church, and to fulfill his obligations to the members of his workplace and ethnic community.

These, then, were some of the working people of Gilded Age America. The rapid, explosive, uneven growth of industrial capitalism before 1900 had shaped and reshaped workers' worlds, creating stable factory towns such as Amsterdam, New York, and mining boom towns such as Silver City, Idaho. People from every sort of background had entered these diverse worlds—former slaves; European, Asian, and Mexican peasants and craftsmen; and displaced farmers.

"... A PICTURE OF INFERNO SUCH AS DANTE NEVER PAINTED"

In her autobiography How I Became a Socialist Agitator, *noted Socialist Party leader Kate Richards O'Hare remembers as a young girl how her family's prosperous Kansas ranch was destroyed in the 1880s by one of the era's periodic depressions. Her father and the other members of her family, including Kate, were driven into the ranks of wage laborers in Kansas City, where she confronted urban poverty for the first time.*

MY EARLIEST MEMORY is of a Kansas ranch, of the wide stretches of prairie, free herds roaming over hills and coulees, of cowpunchers with rattling spurs and wide hats, free and easy of speech and manner.... Those were wonderful days and I shall never cease to be thankful that I knew them. Days that laid the foundation of my whole life, gave me health and strength and love of freedom, taught me to depend on myself, and to love nature, to honor rugged strength of mind and body and to know no shame in life....

Then came the memory of a Kansas drought, followed by one of the periodical panics which sweep over our country. Days and weeks of hazy nightmare when father's face was gray and set, when mother smiled bravely when he or we chil-

As they lived and worked, people blurred the differences between accommodation and resistance. Personal choice and inclination set individuals on their own paths, but few followed a single strategy for a lifetime. Nor did they act solely as individuals. The cultural heritage of working people, their religious beliefs, craft cultures, and political and ethnic traditions helped workers create new communities in which they could pursue their chosen strategies. As we will now see, the cultural vitality of these working-class places and cultures were a thorn in the side of those elites who sought cultural and political dominance over industrializing America.

CULTURES OF COLLECTIVITY: URBAN WORKERS AND REFORM

The spread of urban-industrial life was accompanied by the growth of new cultural and social forms, especially in working-class neighborhoods in cities and towns. These institutions—revolving around work, neighborhood, religion, and leisure—emerged in communities across Gilded Age America. And just as control over the workplace and politics would engender conflict between working people and their social and economic "betters," so too did the new social and cultural institutions of working-class life become contested terrain.

Of all the working-class institutions, the saloon was the most pervasive and drew the heaviest fire from middle-class critics. Temperance-minded employees and employers had, by the 1880s, come close to abolishing the early-nineteenth-century practice of drinking on the job. A gradual shortening of the workday to ten hours, especially for skilled workers, accompanied this tightening up of work discipline. Alcohol and beer consumption continued to play an important role in workers' lives, but now they drank in saloons during their leisure hours rather than at the workplace.

The drink industry became big business. The informal, unlicensed drinking establishments of the 1840s and 1850s, where liquor was sold (often by women) in the kitchens and bedrooms of working-class tenements, gave way to the larger

dren were near, but when we sometimes found tears upon her cheeks if we came upon her unexpectedly. Of course, it was all beyond our comprehension. A horrible something that we could not fathom had settled down over our lives, but the day when the realness of it was forced home came all too soon. The stock was sold, the home dismantled, and one day father kissed us good-bye and started away to the city to find work. He who had always been master of his own domain, who had hewn his destiny bare-handed from the virgin soil, was forced to go out and beg some other man for a chance to labor, an opportunity to use his hands. Though I could not comprehend it then the bitterness of it all was seared upon my memory and I never see a strong man vainly seeking and begging for work that my whole soul does not revolt.

Then came the day when we left the ranch and went to the city to take up the life of a wage-worker's family in the poverty-cursed section of the town. For, of course, no other was possible for us for father's wages were only nine dollars a week and nine dollars is not much to support a family of five. Of that long, wretched winter following the panic of 1887 the memory can never be erased, never grow less bitter. The poverty, the misery, the want, the wan-faced women and hunger pinched children, men trampling the streets by day and begging for a place in the police stations ... the sordid, grinding, pinching poverty of the workless workers and the frightful, stinging, piercing cold of that winter in Kansas City will always stay with me as a picture of inferno such as Dante never painted.

brewery-backed saloons of the 1880s, especially in immigrant-dominated northern cities. Chicago had 3,500 saloons in 1884, more than existed in all fifteen southern states combined.

Technological change made the shift possible. Before pasteurization and refrigeration techniques were perfected in the 1870s and 1880s, beer, the drink of the urban masses, had been limited to local markets. But once beer could be shipped in refrigerated railcars and safely stored upon its arrival, aggressive midwestern beer barons—Anheuser Busch, Schlitz, and Pabst—invaded the national market. They also pushed the small proprietor aside, backing the saloon-keeper who would rent their fixtures, promote their brand, and abide by their regulations.

Most saloongoers were working people; the elite and those with aspirations and pretensions drank at home, in private clubs, or at expensive hotels. "Watch the 'dinner pail' brigade as it files down, at nightfall, from the shops north of Lincoln Square and see how many men and boys drop into the saloons along the north end of Main Street," one Worcester, Massachusetts, observer noted in 1891. Popular taverns, usually located across the street from factories or down the road from the mine, attracted working-class customers who lined up three deep at the bar.

There were many negative aspects to saloons. Most important, they promoted alcoholism, with all its harmful effects on workers' health. Furthermore, because most saloons attracted male patrons exclusively, with the notable exception of establishments that catered to both German men *and* women, they widened and reinforced the gulf between men's and women's leisure time. And because they diverted wages from family support to the consumption of beer or liquor, saloons played their part in many individual tales of destitution and degradation.

Despite its faults, the saloon served tangible needs, material and social. Amid the urban squalor of working-class neighborhoods, a glass of clear, drinkable water was often hard to come by: winter cold froze pipes, and in summer small fish might drop out of faucets; backyard wells, next to overused privies, were usually contaminated. Milk was often adulterated or a few hours from souring. Beer was cheaper, commonly perceived to be of great nutritional value, easily available in glass or pail, and dispensed in a saloon that might well be the cleanest room in the neighborhood. Moreover, a nickel often bought a meal along with a beer. At Chicago's Workingmen's Exchange, a thin dime purchased "the special"—two huge porkchops, four slices of toast, a heap of fried potatoes, and a twenty-five-ounce schooner of beer. Tramps depended on such fare; an unemployed, homeless Boston workingman reported in 1889, "It is cheaper to live at the barroom than at the poor beaneries."

"Custer's Last Fight." Published in 1896 as a promotional print for Anheuser Busch of St. Louis, this lithograph was the best-known visual interpretation of the 1876 battle. At least 200,000 copies were distributed, the print's gruesome and imaginary depiction gracing the walls of saloons across the country. Its popularity continued into the twentieth century, when thousands of copies were sent out to American servicemen during the Second World War.

Furthermore, the saloon provided a place where male workers could read a newspaper, pick up a lead on a job, and enjoy good fellowship. Popular entertainments—boxing matches, cockfights, or gambling, sometimes illegal—enlivened the atmosphere. Trade unions and ethnic organizations connected with this culture, meeting in saloons when they lacked their own facilities.

Saloongoing confirmed working-class patrons in an experience of mutuality and collectivity that began with "treating"—standing the fellows to a round—and ended with the belief that "all men were equal before the bottle." Male workers who constantly faced the competition of the wage system readily pursued what the market had to offer beyond the job: a self-selected egalitarian refuge. For all its limitations it was, according to the Reverend George L. McNutt, "the one democratic club in American life." Trade unionists spent many an hour in this club, and one newspaper writer thought the third most popular kind of song heard in saloons—after those about "dear old Mother" and "the poor girl who was tempted"—was about "the organized workingmen and their nobility of character as compared with millionaire employers."

But drinking in saloons generally embodied just one part of

"THE WORKINGMAN'S CLUB"

This description, taken from a scholarly article titled "The Saloon in Chicago," conveys a sense of how the late-nineteenth-century saloon met a range of urban workers' social, economic, and cultural needs. The writer, a sociologist, calls the saloon "the workingman's club," comparing it to such institutions as the eating and political clubs that catered to the urban middle and upper classes.

THE TERM "CLUB" applies; for, though unorganized, each saloon has about the same constituency night after night. Its character is determined by the character of the men who, having something in common, make the saloon their rendezvous.... The "club-room" is furnished with tables, usually polished and cleaned, with from two to six chairs at each table. As you step in, you find a few men standing at the bar, a few drinking, and farther back men are seated about the tables, reading, playing cards, eating, and discussing, over a glass of beer, subjects varying from the political and sociological problems of the day to the sporting news and the lighter chat of the immediate neighborhood.... That general atmosphere of freedom, that spirit of democracy, which men crave, is here realized; that men seek it and that the saloon tries to cultivate it is blazoned forth in such titles as "The Freedom," "The Social," "The Club," etc. Here men "shake out their hearts together."...

In many of these discussions, to which I have listened and in which I have joined, there has been revealed a deeper insight into the real causes of present evils than is often manifested from lecture platforms.... This is the workingman's school.... Here the masses receive their lessons in civil government, learning less of our ideals, but more of the practical workings than the public schools teach. It is the most cosmopolitan institution in the most cosmopolitan of cities.... Men of all nationalities meet and mingle.... It does much to assimilate the heterogeneous crowds that are constantly pouring into our city from foreign shores. But here, too, they learn their lessons in corruption and vice. It is their school for good and evil.

working-class culture. Because so many male workers flocked to saloons in their leisure time, many politicians made saloons their unofficial headquarters, dispensing favors in the back rooms and buying "the boys" drinks at the bar. Saloon owners, who cashed workers' checks and often lent them money when they were short, were in a perfect position to become politicians in their own right; it was not uncommon for saloon owners to become important cogs in the political machine.

As a result, saloons were a target of labor reformers, who decried the debilitating consequences of drink and argued further that critics of wage dependency should shun dependency on alcohol. Terence V. Powderly, who headed the Knights of Labor, implored workers to "throw strong drink aside as you would an ounce of liquid hell." Some craft unions also militantly opposed drunkenness; the Amalgamated Association of Iron and Steel Workers and the Window Glass Workers' Association promoted temperance in their ranks, although it often seemed a losing cause. Such calls for temperance sought moderation in workers' alcohol consumption, not total prohibition.

Although saloons were the home of the least threatening aspects of workers' culture, those who feared "the dangerous classes" viewed saloons as dens of iniquity and crusaded to close them down. Factory owners led no-licensing campaigns after 1870, intending to close the doors of saloons catering to their workmen. Zealous, puritanical members of the religious community championed the cause as the righteous preservation of "peaceful, happy, prosperous homes." Most dramatically, bands of women occasionally marched on saloons to pray, sing hymns, push the "pledge," and shame proprietors into abandoning illegal or "immoral" activity.

"Father Come Home!" Temperance tracts emphasized the destructive effects of liquor consumption on familial relationships, framing messages in sentimental accounts of little children appealing to drunken parents to forsake the saloon and come home. Thomas Nast's cartoon "The Bar of Destruction" repeated a motif that dated back to Timothy Shay Arthur's antebellum bestseller *Ten Nights in a Bar-room.*

The Protestant elite crusaded most actively against saloons, fearing that the culture of the saloon undercut their capacity to command loyalty and respect from their social subordinates, especially the growing numbers of Catholic workers. Economic and social ends met in the creation of Citizens' Law and Order Leagues in the 1880s, their members drawn from the "who's who" of the manufacturing towns and industrial centers of the United States. Opponents of the saloon argued extravagantly that their reform efforts "greatly increas[ed] the efficiency of the city laborers . . . the men earn better wages, lose less time, do better work . . . while the relations between employers and workmen are most harmonious."

The saloon sustained its male working-class patrons materially and socially and provided space in which collective support could flourish, but it also drew them further into the commercialized world that was eroding working-class culture. Those eager to force respectability, sobriety, and efficiency on working people attacked the saloon, but so too did labor reformers who deplored the squandered wages and the dependency it fostered. The saloon in late-nineteenth-century America was undeniably a working-class institution, but one embedded in and in some ways serving the emerging capitalist order.

Women's leisure also became a battleground for class-specific cultural styles. During the late nineteenth century, working-class married women's leisure consisted of family-centered entertainment and neighborhood socializing. Unlike men, who retreated from the cares of daily life to the saloon, women mixed leisure with housework, child care, and cooking. When a woman had to pack a lunch, outfit the children in carefully laundered and ironed Sunday best, and supervise their conduct, an outing to the park was as much work as play. Still, married women developed ties of mutuality much like those of their husbands. Their grapevine paralleled saloon gossip, passing along vital information; they gave of themselves and of their meager resources to help one another. Networks of mutuality sometimes crossed ethnic lines: after an exhausting day scrubbing office floors, one Jewish woman walked far out of her way to fetch a Catholic priest to administer the last rites to a neighbor's dying child.

Whereas the leisure of married women was embedded in their daily routine, and precious moments of rest were often sacrificed for kin and neighbors, the leisure of young unmarried women increasingly merged with that of their male peers. By the 1890s, commercial dance halls, vaudeville theaters, amusement parks, and excursions were supplanting older, community-organized leisure forms. Unlike the saloon, these recreations mixed the sexes and provided new arenas for courting. The excitement and exoticism of the new diversions held out the promise of romance and adventure, but even these "cheap amusements" were often beyond the means of young working women who earned little and who were expected to contribute most of that to their families. The custom of "treating" evolved, but with a very different meaning than in men's saloon culture: women allowed men to treat them to food, clothing, and recreation in exchange for companionship and sexual favors. For most, the exchange stopped far short of intercourse or prostitution; the goal, after all, was to find a "steady" who would eventually become a husband.

Nevertheless, even these social activities at times merged with more political concerns. For example, "union girls" might insist that union men pick them, rather than unorganized women, as partners for promenades, balls, or picnics. Mary Kenney, an Irish bookbinder and labor organizer, recalled that in the 1890s she and her allies made sure that their male escorts' hatbands and cigar wrappers bore the appropriate label indicating that they were manufactured by union labor.

Middle-class and elite observers tended to look down on working-class women's styles of living as much as they did on working-class men's. Those with little direct contact with these women branded them un-American, slovenly, and lewd.

Antifemale attitudes grew out of a generalized rejection by the middle class of any and all forms of overt sexual expression and practice. In 1872, Anthony Comstock, a Connecticut dry-goods salesman and Young Men's Christian Association (YMCA) member, founded the New York Society for the Suppression of Vice with the backing of wealthy businessmen on the YMCA board of directors. Comstock immediately under-

"I HAD NO IDEA OF THE INWARD APPEARANCE OF A SALOON . . ."

The struggle against saloons reached its high point with the founding of the Woman's Christian Temperance Union (WCTU) in 1873. One of the union's most important leaders, Frances Willard, head of the Chicago chapter, was also prominent later in the woman suffrage movement. Willard linked her fight against liquor with her desire to protect the home and family against the ravages of the new industrial order. In this selection from her autobiography, Willard describes the WCTU's most widely known tactic: the praying-in-saloons crusade, in this instance in Pittsburgh in 1873.

WE PAUSED IN front of the saloon that I have mentioned. The ladies ranged themselves along the curbstone, for they had been forbidden in any wise to incommode the passers-by, being dealt with much more strictly than a drunken man or a heap of dry-goods boxes would be.

. . . The leader had already asked the saloonkeeper if we might enter, and he had declined, else the prayer meeting would have occurred inside his door. . . . At a signal we moved on and the next saloonkeeper permitted us to enter. I had no more idea of the inward appearance of a saloon than if there had been no such place on earth. I knew nothing of its high, heavily corniced bar, its barrels with the ends all pointed towards the looker-on, each barrel being furnished with a faucet, its shelves glittering with decanters and cut glass, its floors thickly strewn with sawdust, and here and there a round table with chairs—nor of its abundant fumes, sickening to healthful nostrils.

The tall, stately lady who led us placed her Bible on the bar and read a psalm. . . . Then we sang "Rock of Ages" as I thought I had never heard it sung before, with a tender confidence to the height of which one does not rise in the easy-going, regulation prayer meeting, and then one of the older women whispered to me softly that the leader wished to know if I would pray. It was strange, perhaps, but I felt not the least reluctance, and kneeling on that sawdust floor, with a group of earnest hearts around me, and behind them, filling every corner and extending out into the street, a crowd of unwashed, unkempt, hard-looking drinking men, I was conscious that perhaps never in my life, save beside my sister Mary's dying bed, had I prayed as truly as I did then. This was my Crusade baptism. The next day I went on to the West and within a week had been made president of the Chicago W.C.T.U.

"The Modern News Stand and Its Results." The frontispiece of *Traps for the Young*, an influential 1883 tract by Anthony Comstock, illustrates the threat purportedly posed by the "debased" commercial press. "They open the way for grossest evils," Comstock wrote. "Foul thoughts are the precursors of foul actions."

took a crusade for an anti-obscenity law, which culminated a year later in congressional passage, without debate, of "An Act for the Suppression of Trade in and Circulation of Obscene Literature and Articles of Immoral Use." Essentially a revision of the federal postal law, the Comstock Act, as it was popularly known, forbade the mailing of obscene, lewd, lascivious, and indecent writing or advertisements, including articles that aided contraception or abortion. Prior to the act's passage, both contraceptive aids (including douches, sponges, suppositories, and condoms) and abortion were widely available to and used by both middle-class and working-class women.

As an unpaid postal inspector, Comstock saw to it that his law was vigorously enforced. In 1875 alone, Comstock personally supervised forty-seven arrests (which yielded twenty-eight convictions) and the destruction of over 29,000 photos, leaflets, and rubber items. Comstock continued his crusade throughout the 1880s and 1890s, sustained by Congress, the courts, and the mainstream press. Although not aimed specifically at working-class women, Comstock's efforts nonetheless served to criminalize forms of social, cultural, and sexual behavior that deviated from an idealized middle-class norm that stressed sobriety, monogamy, and piety. Immigrant working women, as well as the nontraditional individuals—such as the sexual and political radicals Ezra Heywood and Victoria Woodhull—for whom the law was originally intended, bore the brunt of a growing middle-class wrath.

Not all middle-class reformers took such a dim view of the new, largely immigrant, urban working class. Settlement house workers—social workers who lived and worked in urban working-class districts—viewed their clients more sympathetically than Comstock and his followers, understanding the intense emotional bonds and self-sacrifice that sustained them. But even the best of social workers harbored mixed feelings about working-class women's culture. Lillian Wald, founder of New York City's Henry Street Settlement House, fiercely defended her neighbors from charges that they were "degraded human beings," encouraged them in forming trade unions, and mediated disputes between immigrant women and their Americanized daughters. But she also staged "coming-out" parties, modeled on the debutante balls of the elite, for members of the Henry Street Women's Club who reached age eighteen.

Other social workers attacked commercialized leisure more directly and aggressively, founding a network of working girls' clubs that tried to impose middle-class notions of domesticity and respectable leisure. "Working girls" responded to these clubs in many different ways, dividing by occupation, ethnic group, educational level, and politics, but the patronizing attitude of the middle-class organizers offended them all. By the turn of the century, most had voted with their feet, abandoning the clubs for other forms of recreation and self-improvement. The middle-class assault on working-class women's leisure was less shrill and more limited than the attack on the saloon, but working-class men and women alike confronted the pressures of patronizing middle-class disapproval.

Conflicts over public life and space often erupted into more intense struggles between working-class people and those who wanted to control them. Throughout the 1870s and 1880s, for example, boisterous Fourth of July celebrations featured brawls, beer, and boxing matches, and sometimes a hectic scramble after a squealing greased pig. In Pittsburgh, a parade featuring the city's ethnic, neighborhood, and occupational groups was followed by spectacles, contests, boat regattas, countless picnics, and drunken scuffling. These rowdy celebrations traced their origins to the annual urban parades of artisans and mechanics that commemorated the role of working people in winning American independence.

People of substance and standing saw the festivities as a breach of decorum and, worse, a threat to their property. For most of the 1880s, the respectable were sufficiently cowed by the patriotic façade of Independence Day celebrations that they dared not challenge the riotous behavior of holiday revelers. Noisy and unrestrained, the Fourth of July was a day when immigrant workers cut loose. "Among

"Work and Play in Gotham's Slave Pens." The *National Police Gazette* enjoyed thumbing its nose at Victorian morality. Often publishing sympathetic portrayals of the life and labor of working people, the *Gazette* also celebrated pastimes that violated the strict codes of public behavior prescribed for women. Such images, however, were designed to titillate male readers rather than advocate social reform.

people of refined tastes and sensitive nerves," social reformer Julia Ward Howe noted in 1893, " 'going out of town to avoid the Fourth' has been a phrase so common in my time that it ceases to awaken attention." But as the century closed, committees formed to impose "safe and sane" behavior on working-class patrons of the glorious Fourth.

The Fourth was only one day of the year, but workers' cultural activities managed to offend the rich and respectable all year round. In Pittsburgh, a patchwork of immigrant working-class neighborhoods supported theaters, sporting activities, and clubs as well as networks of tobacco shops, groceries, and small shops that served as centers of information and communication. Theater productions idealized the common man and conventional working-class values, spicing up the shows with references to local events and personalities. This culture conveyed a mixed message: it constantly pointed out the class nature of American society, but it failed to challenge inequality and indeed often nurtured the illusion that simple virtue could bring about justice.

Ruling elites could not tolerate even this equivocal message and waged a relentless war on popular working-class pastimes. In Pittsburgh, an Andrew Carnegie–funded museum, library, and music hall opened in 1895, promoting high culture for the masses. Free Sunday

"Our Metropolitan Picture Galleries." Two engravings present the cultural divide between classes in the late nineteenth century: genteel art admirers attend a private gallery opening, while a less-refined group ogles garish "cheap amusement" posters. Middle- and upper-class Americans increasingly defined their social status by how they pursued leisure activity. They saw "high" culture as edifying and uplifting compared to the "low" sensational and commercial pastimes of the working class.

"How the workingman enjoys the Museum on his only day of liberty." Some advocates of gentility endeavored to create cultural preserves sequestered from the taint of "cheap amusements." Prominent among such patrons of high art were the trustees of New York's Metropolitan Museum of Art, who resisted working-class demands for opening on Sundays until 1891.

organ recitals at the music hall, for example, tried to "develop the musical instincts of the people" by excluding "all music of low or vulgar character."

Those eager to redefine public space also tried to lure "the lower orders" to parks, away from the debaucheries of back alleys, houses of prostitution, gaming dens, and the saloon. Frederick Law Olmsted, the most influential landscape architect of the nineteenth century, summed up: "No one who has closely observed the conduct of the people who visit [Manhattan's] Central Park can doubt that it exercises a distinctly harmonizing and refining influence upon the most unfortunate and lawless classes of the city." Such hopes that parks would have a refining influence did not always succeed, however: middle-class citizens in Worcester, Massachusetts, constantly complained about the "unsavory and idle appearance" of the working people who relaxed on the city common.

Even the written word became the subject of struggle between workers and elites. Literacy increased notably in the United States during the late nineteenth century; by 1900, nineteen of twenty white native-born people and seven of eight white immigrants could read and write; for the first time, over half of the nation's African-Americans had achieved literacy. New technology and distribution networks made more reading material more widely available than ever before. Particular genres, especially a flourishing labor and ethnic press and "dime novels"—inexpensive stories of romance and adventure—appealed to the working class. Middle-class observers looked down on these favorite forms of working-class reading, the former for its subversive quality and the latter for their immorality.

In part as an attempt to reform working-class reading habits, members of the middle and upper classes urged the establishment of a new urban institution, the free public library. But most library buildings were forbidding edifices located outside working-class neighborhoods and were places where a respectable demeanor was required and considerable red tape stood between the applicant and a library card. Workers preferred to frequent their own institutions: the reading rooms established by the Knights of Labor in the 1870s and 1880s; Atlanta's Union Hall and Library Association, which during the mid-1880s drew some eight hundred people a week to read its collection of over 350 newspapers; and the Muncie, Indiana, Workingmen's Library, founded in 1900. Others, particularly white women and African-Americans who were largely excluded from the union culture dominated by white men, spent their pennies on books and newspapers and passed them from hand to hand.

Working-class leisure in the cities was thus a battleground in late-nineteenth-century America, but ethnicity and politics as well as class divided the combatants. Political opposition to the culture of

"THE MOST IMPORTANT AND FRUITFUL DISCOVERY . . ."

Literacy was not just for English-speaking workers. For Oscar Ameringer, who spoke and read only German when he first immigrated to the United States, the opportunity to read books in his native language opened up a whole new world. In this selection from his autobiography, Ameringer describes his discovery of American history books, translated into German, at the local public library.

THE MOST IMPORTANT and fruitful discovery I made in the winter of 1887–88 was the public library of Cincinnati, Ohio. I stumbled on the place by sheer accident. . . . The place looked good. It was warm and comfortable. In one of the large rooms of the ground floor people were reading newspapers and other periodicals, some of them in German, and all this was free. So I made myself at home. . . .

I discovered that the Cincinnati Public Library harbored the very place I hankered for. It was the history room up on the third floor, and there I settled down. The few others who patronized it occasionally were bespectacled young men who tended strictly to their own business, never spoke, and usually walked on tiptoe. There was the regular librarian, an elderly maiden lady who was always too busy crocheting to disturb the tranquility of the room. My particular method of reading history was to extract a large volume from the bookshelves, lay it on the table, spread my elbow-cradled face beween hands and if there were illustra-

rowdy indulgence appeared on both sides of the line dividing middle class from working class. Labor reformers, as well as middle-class reformers, sought to turn workers away from frivolous entertainments, although the former hoped by so doing to mobilize working people to fight for their class interests. Just as Knights of Labor leader Terence Powderly endorsed temperance, so too did he call for the workers' Fourth of July to link the labor movement with the republican heritage. An 1877 editorial in the *National Labor Tribune* spoke of the need for a "great change to be wrought" in the entire fabric of social life, blending "a sounder, deeper, and higher education of the people" with "a far higher degree of temperance in drink than now prevails" and "a higher type of practical Christianity than prevails in our gilded and painted churches." God and the republic, no less than the saloon and the park, became arenas of arm-twisting in an America divided by class.

WORKING-CLASS RELIGION AND POLITICS

For Americans of the antebellum era—worker and employer, slave and planter alike—religion, particularly evangelical Protestantism, had been a central way of making sense of the world. Evangelical churches had helped nourish a wave of social reform ideals that swept the country prior to 1860: antislavery, prison reform, and women's rights. After the Civil War, however, Protestant churches lost their hold on the reform impulse, particularly among working people. Nevertheless, the rhetoric, imagery, and spirit of the earlier evangelical Protestant movement continued to be a central cultural influence in American working-class life.

The character of urban development contributed to the decline of Protestant churches. As middle-class and elite Protestants left for the suburbs and founded new churches there, many of the downtown churches they had attended closed their doors. In the process, the churches lost touch with the needs of urban working people

tions, look at the illustrations. If there were no illustrations, I would snooze over the English text. . . .

One day when I passed too close to the elderly maiden lady, she looked up from her crocheting and asked me . . . "If you are so fond of history, would you mind if I selected a course of reading for you? I have noticed your reading is rather indiscriminate. You rarely selected the same book a second time."

I was caught. From now on, it was either read history or keep out.

The first book she handed me was a life of Tom Jefferson. It was written by a [18]48 revolutionist. . . . I should add that this life of Tom Jefferson was printed in German, thereby closing my last avenue of escape from reading it. I didn't snooze over that book. On the contrary, it kept me so wide awake that when "lights out" sounded that night I was still reading, and next morning was first on deck in the history room. This Tom Jefferson was a man after my own heart! His whole crowd belonged to my league. These fellows had no more respect for high priests, princes, kings, and hand-me-down authority than I had. They were rebels from the word go. They . . . had dissolved the unholy partnership between church and state. Declared that one man was as good as the next one and maybe a darned sight better. Had reveled in force and violence, going as far as I had in throwing bricks at scabs, or loyalists as they called them, when not riding the Tory strikebreakers tarred and feathered out of town on a fencerail.

The life of Jefferson swallowed in two bolts, the good teacher handed me the *Life of George Washington* by Washington Irving—still in German.

and became more exclusively oriented toward the upper class. The wealthy Protestant congregations produced nationally renowned ministers. Henry Ward Beecher, one of the best-known and most influential of these "princes of the pulpit," ministered to the privileged from his Brooklyn, New York, base. His social philosophy was profoundly conservative, sympathetic to the rich, and hostile to the poor. "No man in this land suffers from poverty unless it be more than his fault—unless it be his sin," Beecher proclaimed. "If men have not enough, it is owing to the want of provident care, and foresight, and industry." Even his extramarital affairs and his testimonial for Pear's soap—"If cleanliness is next to Godliness, soap must be considered as a means of Grace"—did not seem to affect his tremendous popularity with those who had a market-oriented morality. But for working people, the prominence of ministers such as Beecher made organized Protestantism less than relevant to their needs or their experiences.

Some nondenominational organizations, especially the Young Men's Christian Association, made efforts to bring the gospel word to city working people. But overall, urban Protestantism as an organized

"The Samson of Labor." Following the Great Uprising of 1877, a cartoon in the *Irish World* suggests there are biblical parallels to the struggle between labor and capital. Just as Samson destroyed the Philistine temple, so labor may bring down the Republic upon the railroads, "if his Righteous Claims are Mocked and his Wrongs are left Unrighted."

force was on the wane after 1877. In the words of one manufacturer, "the Protestant Church is too aristocratic for the clothes they [the working people] are able to wear." At the same time, rural Protestant churches continued to flourish: the vast majority of the nation's farmers, black and white, sustained and were sustained by countless small and often poor churches. In 1890, Protestant denominations still claimed more than six of every ten of the nation's church members.

By contrast, the Catholic Church—an institution brought mainly by poor Irish and German immigrants in the 1850s and 1860s—grew increasingly urban and working-class. The church's hierarchy remained extremely conservative on social issues throughout the late nineteenth century, readily excommunicating workers and priests who openly advocated resistance to capitalism. But at the local or parish level, poor priests—who were less closely tied to the elite than their counterparts were in much of Europe—braved their superiors' displeasure to defend the needs and aspirations of their working-class parishioners. Urban workers were tied further to the church through a parochial-school system that extended to the college level.

It would be a mistake to see the church's hold on the Catholic population as anything approaching monolithic. Many Irish immigrants had never seen a priest in Ireland, where English rule had constrained the church for centuries prior to the 1840s potato famine. Moreover, older Irish workers born to the Catholic faith before the famine rejected its conservatism in favor of a more activist and worldly orientation. One authority estimated that less than two-thirds of all New York City Catholics attended Sunday Mass; working-class participation probably was even lower.

Nevertheless, religion retained meaning for most American workers. Those who rejected the conservatism of the established Protestant and Catholic churches built a new form of labor evangelism on the rock of the old ideals of God-fearing America—the brotherhood of man, divine retribution against injustice, indignation at human suffering. The American Railway Union's newspaper pointed out the connection between religious doctrine and labor's perspective: "The arraignment of the rich by God Himself and His Son, the Redeemer, set the pace for all coming generations of men who would be free from the crushing domination of wealth." A midwestern worker stated in 1894: "God has given the earth to the children of men; that a few have stolen it all and disinherited the masses is no fault of God's, but the wickedness of man."

Religion in working-class America had not so much withered as shifted ground. Labor unions, argued the *United Mine Workers' Journal*, stepped into the space left when the churches abdicated their true mission: "Blessed are the union men. They are the salt of the

"Discord Amongst the Angels." The adultery scandal involving the Reverend Henry Ward Beecher, the nation's most famous clergyman, raised issues about the nature of religious faith in an age espousing individual advancement and the loosening of obligations to family and community. Beecher, despite the scandal, remained an influential and popular public figure—in part because his controversial position reflected the ambivalent attitudes of a new middle class toward older moral precepts.

earth which keeps uncontaminated the pure principles of brother-hood in the breast of their fellow toilers, and which, if allowed to die, would make us doubt the fatherhood of God." American workers had adapted religious ideals to reflect and interpret the growing class division. Many workers would have agreed with an unidentified worker's statement in 1898: "Jesus Christ is with us outside the church, and we shall prevail with God."

A similar shift occurred in popular politics. Nineteenth-century working-class political thought was permeated by an abiding belief in equality and independence that characterized the revolutionary era's republican heritage. The traditional ideology of republicanism placed all citizens who participated in American political and social life on an equal and fair footing, assuring all "producers" access to farmland or to a skill that would allow them to provide adequately for themselves and their families. To be sure, this ideology did not encompass women, who remained outside the bounds of formal political participation. Still, most Americans, male and female alike, accepted the notion that a sense of fairness and equal access to basic opportunity marked the difference between their country and the privilege-bound Old World.

By the 1870s, this older republican vision of a society of independent citizens was badly tarnished. The insurrectionary strikes of 1877, which revealed the ugly chasm that divided the broad mass of working people from the new economic wealth and political power of industrial capitalists, indicated how far the republic had traveled from the

"LABOR'S CATECHISM"

This catechism illustrates the ways the Gilded Age labor movement constructed an ideology in opposition to the values of acquisitive individualism. Like a religious catechism, this one was designed to instruct new recruits on the political and moral principles that guided the organization. The catechism—which was written especially for the power-loom weavers of Rhode Island by labor activists Bobba Chuttle and Betty Reedhook—appeared during the 1887 Christmas season in The People, *a Providence, Rhode Island, newspaper with close ties to the Knights of Labor and Christian Socialism.*

Q. What did thy masters promise for thee?

A. They did promise and vow many things in my name: First:—That I should renounce the comforts of life through working for less wages than the weavers in other towns, and starve my wife and hunger my children for the same cause. Second:—That I must not in any way try to better my condition, but be content to work at any price which they think proper to give; neither must I join the Knights of Labor as that is contrary to their by-laws. Third:—That I must bear patiently the insults of all that are put in authority over me, and a host of other things too numerous to mention.

Q. Dost thou not believe that thou art bound to do as they have promised for thee?

A. No, verily; for I have come to the determination to free myself, and to strive to get as much for my work as the weavers in other places for the same kind and quality, and that is the Knights of Labor's duty.

Q. Rehearse the articles of thy belief.

A. I believe in the Golden Rule—do unto others as you would have them do unto you—and in Honesty, his only son, who was conceived by our Common Right, born of the Virgin Truth, suffered under Cotton Treason, was crucified, dead, and buried in Rhode Island, for many years, but is now risen again, and sitteth on the right hand of Justice and Liberty.

Q. What dost thou chiefly learn from these articles of thy belief?

A. I learn to believe that the time has now arrived when I must make a firm stand for a fair share of the profits of my industry, which is nothing less than the Union List, have nine hours' work, seven hours' play, eight hours' sleep, and fair wages every day.

egalitarian promise of its eighteenth-century beginnings. The growing concentration of corporate economic might, compounded by what the German-American radical Friedrich Sorge dubbed "a true witches' sabbath of corruption . . . in official, business, and financial circles," mocked the traditional notion of equality. Labor editor John Swinton's *A Momentous Question: The Respective Attitudes of Labor and Capital*, published in 1895, summarized capitalism's effect on the era: "Great changes in the industrial world and in productive methods have taken place within the second half of our century," producing "a new state of things." Swinton spoke of dramatic technological advances, the concentration of wealth in the hands of a few, impoverished immigrants, and the depletion of available western land as the essential causes of these great changes. But for Swinton and other labor activists like him, it was the terrible human price working people paid for capitalist progress that made the question truly "momentous."

To the labor reformers of the Gilded Age, the debasement of politics and society rested in part on the capacity of the rich few to corrupt government power and use it for their self-interested ends. Thus labor reform undertook the social and moral regeneration not only of the "commonwealth of toil" but also of the nation's political soul. "We stand as the conservators of society," a Vermont labor leader declared in 1887, but he did not mean that the labor movement wanted to turn back the clock on industrial development. Rather, working people sought to cleanse and revive republican government in the new context of economic growth. Observing this effort, John Swinton reported with glee: "There will soon be but two parties in the field, one composed of honest workingmen, lovers of justice and equality; the other . . . composed of kid-gloved, silk-stockinged, aristocratic capitalists and their contemptible toadies."

In politics as in religion, then, workers protested the corruption of traditional American values. Neither the Democratic nor the Republican party offered workers alternatives to this process of republican decline. Both parties, however, made a point of throwing workers some crumbs from the sagging table of opportunity controlled by urban political machines. Tammany Hall, New York City's powerful Democratic organization, was the most notorious of these.

In a single day, a large number of New York's working-class families from many different parishes and social networks might come into Tammany's debt by way of its generous provision of vital social and personal services, including bail, relief (for example, support for a family burned out of its apartment), and financial support of various neighborhood social and cultural activities. But jobs were the glue that bound urban workers and political machines together: some 12,000 patronage jobs were dispensed by Tammany after its victory in

"THE MEAT QUESTION"

A satirical article published in 1890 in the Locomotive Firemen's Magazine *refuted the "scientific" claims of J. R. Dodge, a Department of the Census statistician, who concluded that Americans enjoyed the world's highest standard of living because they consumed the most meat.*

THE STUDENT OF history will not find it recorded that the men who laid the foundations of civilization and government in the United States were animated by considerations of "meat," that they might have more "meat." The Declaration of Independence does not refer to the meat question. The battles of the Revolution, from Concord to Yorktown, were not fought on the meat question. . . .

Mr. Dodge, the "scientist" ignores the declaration that "man shall not live by bread alone." There is something in the standard of living better than meat. Patrick Henry's immortal words were not "Give me meat or give me death. . . ."

Such "scientists" have greatly mistaken the purpose of American working-men. . . . They will continue to eat meat. . . . They will use knives and forks, have tables and dishes, sit in chairs, live in houses, dress decently, and do such other things as are becoming. They will be masters of themselves. They will read and think, meet and talk, agitate and organize, and in the near future, they will dictate policies, enact laws and teach scientists that "the standard of living" means much more than a large supply of meat. . . .

the 1888 elections. Tammany bosses helped young Irish women get jobs in the city's public schools, helped their brothers get jobs on the police force, and helped immigrants fresh off the boat get jobs as laborers constructing city streets, bridges, and buildings.

George Washington Plunkitt, a Tammany ward "heeler" or boss, liked to call this "honest graft," a fair exchange of cash, influence, liquor, and above all jobs for working-class votes. Plunkitt and his fellow Tammany bosses lined their own pockets, stealing millions of dollars from the public treasury while allowing important decisions on issues such as public transportation to be made by those private entrepreneurs willing to pay large bribes.

Labor reformers completely rejected political machines such as Tammany Hall and their accommodation of the capitalist system. Instead, they championed working-class self-organization and political activism, linking the economic struggle to truly oppositional contests in the electoral arena. The platform of the Workingmen's Convention, held in Chicago in 1886, vividly argued for the unification of the political and economic struggles:

> As the economic encroachments of aggregated wealth have caused the defensive organization of the producers into trade unions, Knights of Labor, Grangers [a farmers' support group], so must the political encroachments of the same aggregated wealth . . . inevitably force the people into defensive political organization as distinct and antagonistic to capitalist political parties as the trade union is to the club, cabal, or clique of the monopolist.

As we will see, this belief would find ample expression in 1886 with the founding of a number of local labor reform parties and in the candidacy of Henry George, a critic of the growing concentration of wealth, for mayor of New York City.

TWO GREAT QUESTIONS.   *Th. Nast.*

WHO STOLE THE PEOPLE'S MONEY?" — DO TELL. N.Y. TIMES.   'TWAS HIM.

"Who Stole the People's Money?" Critics of the urban political machine found a foe that was both charitable and corrupt. Thomas Nast's *Harper's Weekly* cartoons attacking the Tweed Ring supplied antimachine forces with a powerful weapon. His caricatures, accessible to everyone, succinctly conveyed a negative portrait of the machine and would influence popular perception of the political "boss" into the late twentieth century.

COLLECTIVITY IN THE COUNTRYSIDE

Community solidarity and mutual aid played important roles on the western frontier, where individual farm families struggled to overcome geographic isolation and economic fragmentation, so life on the Plains quickly developed a cooperative dimension. Farm men shared work to get the harvest in and houses or barns built, incorporating male rituals of hard drinking and demonstrations of physical prowess. Groups of women cooked for the men's "work bees" but also took part in such separate collective efforts as quilting and sewing bees and attending at births. On these occasions, women learned lore—some of it superstition (the first one to fall asleep on the wedding night would be the first to die) and some of it useful, practical advice—to sustain them in their solitary daily life. Even in their solitude, they partook of collective wisdom.

Leisure on the Plains echoed many of the patterns of urban leisure, but in a homegrown, less commercialized way. Church services and picnics offered easy sociability. Fourth of July festivities, the high point of the summer, mixed patriotism, fun, and the strengthening of social ties. As a Kansas woman noted, these celebrations "were the meeting place of the whole county, where once a year old friends met and new friends were made and new settlers were welcomed to the

A barn-raising. Jacob Roher and his neighbors take a break from their construction efforts on his farm near Massillon, Ohio, in 1888 to pose for a photographer.

county." Band music and singing on the Fourth of July delighted the music-starved settlers; at other times of year, a man who could fiddle or a woman who played the melodeon, a small organ, was popular indeed. Dances brought together young and old, good food and rollicking music. In contrast to city dance halls, the dancing was more traditional and less sexually suggestive. The only hint of commercialism was the passing of the hat to pay the local fiddler. Surprise parties, horseback rides, hunts, sleigh rides, and a variety of other social occasions further relieved the isolation. A Kansas woman, "well contented" with her new life, scoffed at "those who have never lived in a new country [and are] inclined to think such a life is full of privations, with no pleasures mixed in."

Women and men mobilized collectively to solve the problems of the frontier. In Kansas during the 1870s, desperate agricultural poverty caused by locusts and drought prompted the women of Wichita to mount a relief campaign for "families in the country whose only safety from starvation lies in the charity of the people." The men, meanwhile, tried to hush up the campaign for fear it would tarnish the image of the Golden West, and they were no more pleased when the women went on to crusade against drinking, gambling, and prostitution.

In the South, farmers as a whole were less isolated than their western counterparts; the color line, rather than gender, defined the most important fracture among the southern "plain folk."

The two extremes of southern society—the large cities and the rural areas—offered African-Americans the best opportunities to live independently. In the smaller southern towns, white control over blacks was exercised with ruthless barbarity. African-Americans fled these enclaves of racial supremacy to resettle the countryside in the late 1870s and 1880s or to migrate farther west, to places such as Kansas. Rural life meant economic subordination as African-Americans were increasingly drawn into the crop lien and sharecropping systems, but ironically the countryside also offered them a modest refuge from the violence, disfranchisement, and fraud of the post-Reconstruction South.

This rural African-American culture centered on the church. In Edgefield County, South Carolina, when blacks were driven out of higher-status occupations in the county seat at the end of Reconstruction, they migrated to the rural parts of the county and became tenant farmers and sharecroppers. Accommodationist leader Alexander Bettis founded some forty churches in this "open country." Around such churches grew African-American Masonic lodges, benevolent societies, burial organizations, schools, and a network of individuals who sponsored fairs and other social gatherings. This cultural foundation sustained blacks in "Bloody Edgefield," renowned for its lynchings. The connection between churches, a sense of community, and resistance worried a white writer for the North Georgia *Citizen* in 1879: "The meanest negroes in the country are those who are members of the churches; and, as a general thing, the more devout and officious they are, the more closely they need watching. . . . They have their schools and their houses of worship, but it does seem that instead of being benefited by these civilizing influences, they are daily made worse."

African-Americans could also fare better—within the severe limitations placed on every aspect of their lives—in the large cities, where black men and black women could secure menial jobs and some small measure of personal freedom. Some of the gains of the Reconstruction years persisted in cities. In Washington, D.C., for example, African-American illiteracy fell from 70 percent to less than 50 percent between 1870 and 1880. In Washington and other urban areas, a racially segregated culture of mutual aid and self-help eased the burdens of daily life for African-Americans.

White yeomen farmers in the South relied on similar cultural resources. Struggling for economic self-sufficiency, the southern yeomanry cherished the republican ideal of independence. Yet as small-scale producers they necessarily relied on one another for loans of much-needed cash or assistance when a large job needed doing quickly. Kinship connections reinforced this interdependence, and neighboring farm families "swapped work" and exchanged labor in ubiquitous "bees," much like their western counterparts. Independence and mutuality were thus intimately linked in this community of producers, especially as expanding rail lines and the tightening noose of credit drew the countryside more and more into the world market. These activities built on earlier efforts of the Grange, or Patrons of Husbandry, who were enthusiastic proponents of cooperative buying and selling across rural America as early as the 1860s.

Georgia hill farmers drew on such communal traditions to protect common grazing rights on unfenced land. Large merchants and landlords, stressing the "free market" and "private property," called for laws requiring farmers to enclose their livestock and designate land boundaries as legal fences for crop lands. Railroad companies, liable for damages if locomotives struck wandering animals, welcomed this attack on the open range. But poor white smallholders, landless whites, and the recently emancipated black freedpeople of the South saw the crusade as a threat to what little leeway the old common rights allowed them. "We as poor men and Negroes do not need the law," cried one Georgia farmer in 1885, "but we need a democratic government and independence that will do the common people good." As one yeoman argued, the stock law forcing fencing was "ultimately going to be the ruin of people and especially the poor people that have nowhere to keep their stock [and] . . . are entirely dependent on the landowners for pasture." Battles raged over elections called to determine if the land should be fenced. Even when the advocates of fencing won, they had trouble securing their victory. Outlaws lurked in the Georgia night, tearing down fences, smashing gates, and threatening advocates of enclosure.

"The Greatest Monopoly of the Age." An 1873 cartoon shows a Granger warning the complacent American public of the impending danger to their economic and political rights posed by the expanding power of the railroads.

The values and mutuality expressed in the stock-law struggle in Georgia were mirrored in other conflicts over enclosure across the country. In New Mexico, for example, Juan José Herrerra led a group of squatters of Mexican descent in a struggle against powerful cattle ranchers and landowners who began fencing the best pasturing and watering lands that had previously been held in common. Calling themselves White Caps, or Las Gorras Blancas, Mexican farmers in 1889 began burning fences, cutting barbed wire, and generally terrorizing cattlemen. At their peak, the White Caps claimed over 1,500 members. Their program was simply stated: "Our purpose is to protect the rights and interest of the people in general and especially those of the helpless classes." Their platform included statements opposing "land grabbers," political bosses, monopolizers of water, and race agitators.

The White Caps also fought against the railroads' encroachment on their land. During the building of the Santa Fe Railroad, the White Caps stopped sectionmen hauling ties, burned out part of the track, proclaimed the wage rates unacceptable, and penned threatening let-

"... WE ARE STARVING TO DEATH"

In this 1894 letter to the governor of Kansas, Susan Orcutt describes the devastation experienced by western Kansas farming communities caught in the iron grip of the depression (spelling and punctuation corrected).

▌TAKE MY Pen In hand to let you know that we are Starving to death. It is Pretty hard to do without anything to Eat here in this God forsaken country. We would of had Plenty to Eat if the hail hadn't cut our rye down and ruined our corn and Potatoes. I had the Prettiest Garden that you Ever seen and the hail ruined It and I have nothing to look at. My Husband went away to find work and came home last night and told me that we would have to Starve. He had been in ten countys and did not Get no work. It is Pretty hard for a woman to do without anything to Eat when She doesn't know what minute She will be confined to bed. If I was in Iowa I would be all right. I was born there and raised there. I haven't had nothing to Eat today and It is three o'clock.

"... WE ARE ROBBED OF OUR MEANS"

This 1891 letter from a Minnesota farmer to Ignatius Donnelly, the popular author and champion of the agrarian cause, suggests the increasing desperation that drove Plains farmers into taking collective action (punctuation and spelling corrected).

▌IN THE MINDS of the forlorn and the unprotected poor people of this and other states, I might say I am one of those poor and unprotected.... I settled on this land in good faith; built house and barn, broken up part of the land. Spent years of hard labor grubbing, fencing, and improving. Are they going to drive us out like trespassers . . . and give us away to the Corporations? How can they support them when we are robbed of our means? . . . We must decay and die from woe and sorrow. We are loyal citizens and do not intend to intrude on any Railroad Corporation. We believed and still do believe that the R.R. Co. has got no legal title to this land in question. We love our wives and children just as dearly as any of you. But how can we protect them, give them education as they should [get], when we are driven from sea to sea? . . .

ters to foremen. Their efforts garnered the support of the entire Mexican-American community and even of some Anglo farmers. When a group of White Caps were released from jail in 1889 after being held for fence-cutting, they paraded down the main street of Las Vegas, New Mexico, led by women waving the American flag and singing "John Brown's Body."

The New Mexico White Caps saw themselves not as an isolated regional group but as part of a larger collective movement of resistance against industrial capitalism. For that reason, they applied for membership as an assembly of the Knights of Labor, and in the early 1890s they affiliated with the radical agrarian People's (Populist) Party. The White Caps' efforts achieved a measure of success: the People's Party won several elections in New Mexico in the 1890s, railroad-building slowed, and so did the Anglo influx into those areas where the organization had support.

At about the same time, farther east, in the Cross Timbers region of Texas, neighborhood bands enforced their belief that ownership of the land did not convey the right to restrict free access to grass and water. Many of the settlers were of Scots-Irish and Irish descent, and their deep-seated, traditional dislike of landlords found its outlet in the cry "Land to the cultivator!" Brash fence-cutters left taunting notes behind: "We understand you have plenty of money to spend to build fences. Please put them up again for us to cut them down again. We want the fence guarded with good men so that their mettle can be tested."

"Settlers taking the law in their own hands." Custer County, Nebraska, homesteaders reenact how they cut down fifteen miles of wire fence erected by cattlemen in 1885.

In Texas, the defense of common rights was linked to growing opposition to those who monopolized land as well as credit. A former Indiana farmhand, Sam Bass, gained local popularity by stealing from the railroads. Celebrated in song and story as "the Robin Hood of Cross Timbers," Bass may not have considered himself a symbol of community resistance to capitalist speculation. But others saw him in that light: taking on the railroads, symbol of corporate capital in the Gilded Age, often won bandits such as Bass and the more famous Jesse James the applause of farmers and urban workers across the country.

COLLECTIVITY AND CONFLICT

As varied as was the working-class experience after 1877, the relentless forces of the wage system and market relations nonetheless led immigrant and native, black and white, man and woman, rural laborer and urban worker, to share a common fate: a growing sense of dependency and powerlessness. As this occurred, working people reached for diverse strategies to cope with the impact of industrial capitalism on their daily lives.

Working people drew on shared cultural values for sustenance—on the religious, political, ethnic, and craft traditions they carried with them—creating in the process new cultures of collectivity. These cultures, as we have seen, often resulted in and were colored by overt struggle, for Gilded Age America was a society increasingly divided along class lines and spoiling for a fight. Too much had happened too quickly to too many Americans. The fury of the great railroad strike of 1877 indicated how deep the gulf between working people and the leaders and supporters of the new capitalist order had become. As one contemporary noted, "The spontaneity of the movement shows the existence of widespread discontent, a disposition to subvert the existing social order, to modify or overturn the political institutions."

The 1877 insurrection was but a prelude to twenty years of intense and open class conflict. The people and communities transformed by industrial capitalism, and the cultures of collectivity that arose in response to that transformation, would be the foundation upon which workers' and farmers' organizations consolidated—a launching pad, as we will now see, for some of the most hard-fought and bitter class wars in the history of the United States.

March 1886: New York City Police
drive back striking streetcar workers
and their sympathizers as a lone
horsecar, operated by company
personnel, attempts to make its
usual journey along Grand Street.

3

GREAT UPHEAVALS

THE 1880s AND 1890s

WRITING IN the midst of the devastation of the 1877 railroad strikes, a St. Louis newspaper noted: "The country was in a feverish state of excitement from Boston to San Francisco, from the Lakes to the Gulf." That feverish state would recur repeatedly over the next two decades. Between 1877 and 1898 working people undertook a series of fierce battles with their economic and political antagonists. Craft unionists, Knights of Labor, Farmers' Alliance members, Populists, socialists, and anarchists struggled for a more egalitarian society and a more just economic system. As masses of working people shook their collective fist at the growing visibility of unbridled privilege, industrial capitalists dug in their heels in an organized defense of their wealth and power.

These struggles peaked twice: first in 1886, in an eruption of activism, organizing, and confrontation that came to be known as the Great Upheaval; and second in the 1890s, when Populism and the Homestead and Pullman strikes linked farmers and workers together in a loose coalition of resistance. At root, these epic confrontations of the 1880s and 1890s were working people's forthright responses to the unprecedented economic and political changes wrought by the new industrial order.

KNIGHTS, CRAFTSMEN, AND UNION FOR ALL

In 1876, the year that marked the centennial of the nation, only a handful of American workers belonged to labor organizations. The trade unions built by working people in the years immediately following the Civil War lay in ruins, victims of hard times and hardening employer opposition. Nevertheless, over the next ten years, as the economic gloom of the 1870s depression lifted, a labor movement of astonishing breadth emerged in the United States.

The first to organize were skilled craftsmen in the building trades, foundries, and small consumer-goods industries. An important manufacturing center such as Cincinnati, for example, already boasted thirty-five separate unions by the early 1880s. And because employers increasingly operated nationally, these local unionists understood the importance of affiliating with existing national organizations. By 1880, there were already eighteen national unions operating in North America; the following year they formed the Federation of Organized Trades and Labor Unions of the United States. At its peak in 1886, national union membership totaled only about 350,000, 3 percent of the nation's nonagricultural workforce.

Despite these limited numbers, craft unionists also came together to create strong central labor bodies in cities as scattered as Cincinnati, Boston, Chicago, Denver, New Orleans, and San Francisco. New York City boasted the largest of these. Its Central Labor Union (CLU) began in 1882 with just a dozen small unions, but within a few years, it was a virtual "parliament of labor," composed of over two hundred labor organizations. The CLU, moreover, sought to bring skilled and unskilled workers together under its banner; it also became a vibrant meeting ground for labor radicals of all stripes, from Knights of Labor to socialists and anarchists. As one printer put it, the CLU marked "an effort to organize the day laborer with the skilled mechanic," to replace the "little-minded, narrow-minded view of the interests of a single occupation" with that of "the general interests of all bodies of wage workers."

Skilled workers willing to make common cause with the unskilled not only joined citywide central labor organizations such as the CLU; they also poured into the Knights of Labor, the most important labor organization in the Gilded Age. When nine Philadelphia tailors organized the Noble and Holy Order of the Knights of Labor in 1869, they differed from other trade unionists mainly in their belief in secrecy and in the elaborate ritual of their meetings. Secrecy was a response by workers to employers' past use of firings and blacklistings to suppress unions. But the Knights were also influenced by the broad moral vision of their leader, Uriah Stephens. Born in New Jersey in 1821, Stephens had studied for the ministry before apprenticing as a tailor. His Protestant background shaped his thinking on the labor question, leading him, for example, to denounce long working hours as "an artificial and man-made condition, not God's arrangement and order." His religious beliefs also led him to call for the creation of an organization that would bring all workers together, regardless of race, nationality, or occupation.

Despite their broad and inclusive outlook, the Knights' rigid secrecy put sharp limits on their ability to grow. The railroad strikes of 1877, however, led the Knights' leaders to reassess the organization's commitment to secrecy. By demonstrating the tremendous reach and power of national corporations, the railroad strikes convinced many working people that only an open and public labor organization, built nationally rather than locally, could effectively do battle with the forces of capital.

In 1879, the Knights chose Terence V. Powderly as their "Grand Master Workman." An Irish Catholic machinist recently elected mayor of Scranton, Pennsylvania, Powderly would lead the Knights of Labor for the next fifteen years. The Order's programs reflected Powderly's deep beliefs in temperance, education, and land reform, as well as his conviction that the "wages system" should be abolished. Under his guidance, the Knights gradually put aside their secrecy.

After the Order shook off secrecy, native-born skilled workers flocked to the Knights, making common cause with the unskilled and the occasional "brainworker" (journalist, teacher, or white-collar worker) who gravitated to labor's cause. " 'Each for himself' is the bosses' plea; Union for all will make you free," read a banner carried by skilled barrelmakers in a Detroit labor parade.

But the Knights stood for more than just mutual support. In their view, they represented the last best hope for the American republic itself, a republic increasingly undermined by the combined forces of monopoly, political corruption, cutthroat competition, and—most important—wage labor. "We declare an inevitable and irresistible conflict between the wage system of labor and republican system of government," declared the Knights, who sought to preserve what was

"The Great Labor Parade of September 1st." A placard in an 1884 Labor Day march presents the struggle over inequality in the nineteenth century. "Wage slavery" has emerged as a new oppressive institution to take the place of racial slavery, defeated in the Civil War.

positive in the republican tradition and eliminate the political corruption and industrial degradation undermining the independence of the American citizenry.

With this commitment to republicanism went a deep faith in the broad social group that the Knights called the "producing classes." If properly mobilized, those who produced society's wealth—the worker, the farmer, even the honest manufacturer—could rescue America's endangered republican institutions from the hands of monopolists and other social parasites. "Nonproducers" such as bankers, speculators, lawyers, and liquor dealers were excluded from the ranks of the Knights of Labor. This division of American society into "producers" and "parasites" meant that the Knights did not necessarily keep employers out of their organization. As long as they respected the "dignity of labor" by employing union workers and selling union-made goods, "fair" employers could sit in the local assembly halls of the Order.

Few, however, were very comfortable there. The Knights remained an overwhelmingly working-class body, notable for the inclusion of immigrant factory hands, southern blacks, and working-class women in their ranks. Until the 1880s, women workers remained unorganized, the unskilled and immigrant masses were still locked out of the labor movement, and African-American participation was negligible. In joining the Knights, these groups transformed the organization.

Women factory operatives and millworkers fought their way into the Knights of Labor at an early date. Although in 1878 leaders of the Order spoke vaguely about "equal rights" and embraced the idea of equal pay for women, those leaders were less certain about admitting women as full members. Powderly, for example, refused to implement a resolution calling for women to be admitted to the Knights until rules "for the governing of assemblies of women" were prepared.

Meanwhile, working women took the initiative. In 1881, a group of "lady shoemakers" in Philadelphia won a bitter strike against their bosses and, in its wake, formed a labor organization called the Pioneer Garfield Assembly. At the convention of the Knights that year, the shoemakers' leader, Mary Stirling, presented herself as a delegate, forcing Powderly to take a stand. Finally he declared that "women should be admitted on equality with men." From that point on, women joined the Order in large numbers, constituting one in ten Knights by the mid-1880s.

Irish-American miners and laborers streamed into the Knights. Irish immigrants constituted a large proportion of the nation's working class, but it was not until the emergence of the Knights of Labor that Irish workers moved to the center of the American labor movement. Irish activism began as support for an organization of tenant farmers in Ireland known as the Land League. The league built an enormous following in the late 1870s by calling for an end to the oppressive Irish land system and raising the slogan "The land for the people." "The cause of the poor in Donegal [Ireland] is the cause of the factory slave in Fall River [Massachusetts]," proclaimed Patrick Ford, a New York City editor and advocate of the Irish cause. As Ford saw it,

"LABOR IS NOBLE AND HOLY"

The Knights of Labor employed elaborate rituals and symbols in their local assembly meetings. The initiation ceremony for new members, for example, relied heavily on religious imagery and language. The ceremony emphasized that all that was valuable and worthy in society derived from human labor. New Knights agreed to commit themselves to improve the conditions of all working people.

IN THE BEGINNING, God ordained that man should labor, not as a curse, but as a blessing; not as a punishment, but as means of development, physically, mentally, morally, and has set thereunto his seal of approval in the rich increase and reward. By labor is brought forward the kindly fruits of the earth in rich abundance for our sustenance and comfort; by labor (not exhaustive) is promoted health of the body and strength of mind, labor garners the priceless stores of wisdom and knowledge. It is the "Philosopher's Stone," everything it touches turns to wealth. "Labor is noble and holy." To glorify God in its exercise, to defend it from degradation, to divest it of the evils to body, mind, and estate, which ignorance and greed have imposed; to rescue the toiler from the grasp of the selfish is a work worthy of the noblest and best of our race.

You have been selected from among your associates for that exalted purpose. Are you willing to accept the responsibility, and, trusting in the support of pledged true Knights, labor, with what ability you possess, for the triumph of these principles among men?

the basic problem was monopoly, which took the form of rent-gouging in Ireland and labor exploitation in America. The result was the same, however, on both sides of the Atlantic: poverty and corruption on a massive scale.

From Pennsylvania mining villages and Rhode Island factory towns to Colorado railroad construction camps, thousands of Irish-American workers rallied to the Land League. Branches of the league emerged that were strikingly similar to the Knights of Labor in outlook. Powderly later recalled that in his own Scranton, Pennsylvania, "when the public, or Land League, meeting would be over, a secret meeting of the Knights of Labor would follow." In fact, Powderly maintained, "the American labor movement and . . . the Irish land movement" were "almost identical."

Not all immigrants were so easily integrated into the labor movement. The Chinese were the one group the Knights of Labor and most nineteenth-century white workingmen blatantly and even violently discriminated against. Chinese workers served as convenient scapegoats that American workers could turn against when times were tough. In the early 1880s, the major focus of the Knights' political activity in fact was to lobby for passage of a congressional bill to prohibit the Chinese from immigrating to the United States. When the Chinese Exclusion Act was passed in 1882, Knights hailed it as a step forward for "American" (meaning non-Asian) workers. Nonetheless, "American" workers felt the sting of the depression that began that year, even though they had succeeded in ending Chinese immigration.

As the depression deepened, anti-Chinese activity intensified. By 1886, conventions of workingmen hostile to the Chinese had been called up and down the West Coast, where Asian workers were concentrated in the greatest numbers. An 1885 attempt to boycott Chinese-made cigars in San Francisco crystallized the widespread and growing racism of white workingmen into an ugly anti-Asian campaign. Said one Knights of Labor–endorsed speaker: "This is the old irrepressible conflict between slave and white labor. God grant there may be survival of the fittest." As the Knights pushed the "white" label of the cigarmakers and other crafts, the union tag on the West Coast became less a symbol of union-made products than an open expression of antagonism to the Chinese. The most barbaric instance of anti-Asian violence surfaced in the mining communities of the West. At the Union Pacific Railroad coalmine in Rock Springs, Wyoming, for instance, the Chinatown was torched and its victims gunned down. As the ashes cooled the next day, twenty-eight Chinese bodies were found amid the dozens of buildings destroyed by rampaging whites.

WE PRACTICE WHAT WE PREACH

A KNIGHT OF LABOR

"An injury to one is an injury to all."
During the 1886 Knights of Labor
convention in Richmond, Virginia, the
Order's dedication to racial equality
and the prominent role played by
African-American delegates in the
proceedings impressed reporters
and artists covering the event.

If the Knights adopted a fundamentally racist stance in their approach to the Chinese, their relationship to black Americans was quite different. From the organization's very beginnings, it opened its doors to African-Americans. By the early 1880s, both all-black and integrated local assemblies flourished in the South. "The colored people of the South are flocking to us," trumpeted a Knights of Labor organizer. African-American coalminers in Alabama, West Virginia, and Tennessee, dockworkers in New Orleans, turpentine workers in Mississippi, and tobacco factory workers in Virginia all entered the Knights in the first half of the 1880s. In many instances, black workers became the mainstay of these fledgling local organizations of the Knights.

While heroic efforts were made to bring blacks and whites together in Knights of Labor halls, the Order's practice of organizing separate black assemblies conformed to the segregationist norms of the time. Some African-Americans also complained of continuing racism within the movement. A Durham, North Carolina, mason reported, "The white Knights of Labor prevent me from getting em-

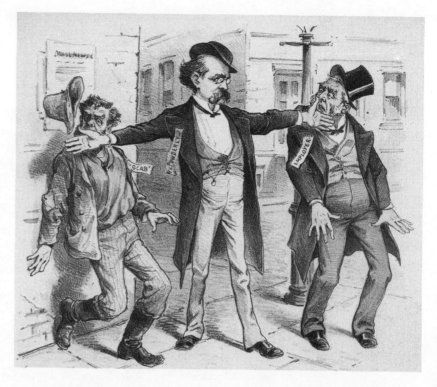

"The Gospel of the Knights of Labor." "We work not selfishly for ourselves alone," said Terence Powderly at the Richmond convention, "but extend the hand of fellowship to all mankind." In this 1886 cartoon, *Puck* editor/artist Joseph Keppler depicts Powderly's gesture as a hypocritical and aggressive act, a sentiment shared by other conservative editors unsettled by the increasing militancy and effectiveness of the Great Upheaval.

ployment because I am a colored man, although I belong to the same organization." Still, the Knights represented a significant advance for black workers previously excluded from labor organizations. Knights' local assemblies (which were the Order's version of a local union) provided the organizational context in which black and white workers could begin to make common cause.

When workers in Richmond, Virginia, hosted the Order's 1886 General Assembly, the racist southern press did not miss the opportunity to castigate the Knights' interracial delegations, pointing, with particular horror, to the mixing in public of white and black men and women. One editorial noted that the unprecedented meeting made "the two words 'nigger' and 'Knight' almost synonymous terms." Such hostility led some whites in the Order to urge caution and to back away from an attempt "to build a new social fabric" during their two-week visit to Richmond. But the organization stood its ground on the race question. The city's African-American workers responded by treating visiting Knights to a huge labor parade. One correspondent claimed "the entire colored population of Richmond was in attendance."

Fort Worth, Texas, Knights represented a united front of whites, African-Americans, and Mexican-Americans, the first coalition of its kind in state history. The Central Trades and Labor Assembly in New Orleans, where the Knights exercised significant influence, represented some 10,000 black and white workers who regularly combined forces in demonstrations and parades. Small wonder that a Brooklyn Knight wrote: "In view of the prejudice that existed a few years ago against the negro race, who would have thought that negroes could ever be admitted into a labor organization on an equal footing with white men?"

Membership in a Knights of Labor local assembly offered workers—black and white, male and female—a collective alternative to the promises of individual advancement held out by industrial capitalism. That alternative grew out of a set of institutions that reflected the Knights' ideals of mutuality and solidarity. The organization's assembly halls, for example, served as an alternative to the family-centered home and the commercial saloon. Such halls often provided workers with a cooperative store on the ground floor and an assembly room above. On one level their daily material needs would be met, while on another they could hear labor sermons, read a reform paper, listen to an agitator's speech, or debate politics and economics from a working-class viewpoint. Within the local assembly, workers found themselves surrounded with a symbolism and an imagery that emphasized labor solidarity and reminded all of the nobility and virtue of the labor-reform crusade and the dignity of honest work. In their hundreds of balls, picnics, and parades, the Knights

"LABOR HEADQUARTERS"

In this description of a Washington, D.C., Knights of Labor assembly hall in the late 1880s, the novelist T. Fulton Gantt conveys a sense of the diverse social, political, and intellectual functions that the meeting hall served for its members. Gantt recounts a discussion between the hero, Harry Wallace, a young and idealistic new member of the Order, and Jack Dolan, the Irish-born leader of the painters' union, concerning workers' use of the boycott and arbitration.

▼WO FLIGHTS OF narrow and well-worn stairs in the rear end of a business house, but a few steps from Pennsylvania Avenue and several blocks from the Capitol, leads to what is now known among the initiated as Knights of Labor Hall. A few of the [building] contractors suspect it to be a rendezvous of discontented workingmen. But the great public surging along Pennsylvania Avenue, even the colossal statesmen of this metallic age included, little dream that the murmur of voices occasionally floating from the third story windows to the street below emanate from the faithful pioneers of labor's greatest movement. . . .

Yet here they are, this bright Sunday afternoon, and in the chests in anteroom and hall might be found the charters of seven or eight assemblies since the first struggle of L[ocal] A[ssembly] 1644. Plasterers, carpenters, painters, tinners, plumbers, tailors, brickmakers, stone-cutters, etc., have been mingling together, making common cause of each other's wrongs. The meeting is informal, the hall being thrown open Sundays as a sort of club room for the Knights. . . .

The chief topic of conversation today was of a formal boycott declared by the painters, and endorsed by all the other assemblies. [Harry] Wallace asked Jack Nolan to explain fully the origin of this boycott.

"The fact is," said Nolan, "that this steamboat company we are boycotting first boycotted us. They blacklisted our entire assembly of painters; wouldn't give us work, and went to some trouble to get non-union men to paint the very boats they want us to ride on, and now we have concluded that we won't ride on their boats and shall tell everybody else why we don't patronize them. . . . This boycotting will do more for arbitration within the next year or two than strikes have done in a century. Why, we can boycott and live. We used to strike and starve.

". . . Here in Washington we learned very soon that, no matter how square we acted, they [the contractors] wouldn't arbitrate. We had learned a lesson from the Irish and introduced the boycott as an 'arbitration persuader,' and so far it has worked like a charm. . . . Establishing arbitration will dispose of these continued irritating fights now the result of the competitive wage system, and give us more leisure to work out a solution of the labor problem—that great problem that includes all the other problems on earth."

created distinctive forms of recreation and group expression. These recreational forms challenged both the limitations of the tavern and the offensive paternalism of company- or YMCA-sponsored leisure activities.

The Knights thus helped create an alternative cultural world, a world that unmistakably belonged to the producing classes. In Detroit in the mid-1880s the labor movement included not only trade unions and Knights of Labor assemblies, it also extended into the daily lives of the city's workers through prolabor weekly newspapers (published in English and German), a political room, theater groups, singing societies, a workers' militia called the Detroit Rifles (known to drill and practice target-shooting on the outskirts of town under cover of darkness), and nightly dances, balls, and educational events. The Knights' mixture of the seemingly mundane and the startlingly militant made America's capitalists more than a little uneasy. In 1886, their anxiety heightened.

1886: THE GREAT UPHEAVAL

"Killing" an engine on the Missouri Pacific. An incident during the Southwestern Railroad strike, depicted on the front page of *Frank Leslie's Illustrated Newspaper.*

With the Knights of Labor providing an unprecedented base, the workers' movement grew dramatically. The economic depression of the early 1880s and the drastic wage cuts accompanying it gave the labor movement its greatest impetus for growth. In 1884, unorganized shop workers throughout the West struck the giant Union Pacific Railroad when their wages were cut. When management rescinded the wage cuts four days later, the railroad strikers, buoyed by their success, entered the Knights of Labor in a body. A year later the Knights won an even greater victory against the Southwestern Railroad system controlled by Wall Street speculator Jay Gould.

In the wake of these victories, fought against two of the most powerful corporations in America, workers across the nation began to pour into the Knights. By 1886, the Order boasted 15,000 local assemblies representing between 700,000 and 1 million members. Nearly 10 percent of the country's nonagricultural workforce claimed membership in the Knights, a higher percentage by far than had ever before been enrolled in unions. In New York alone there were nearly 60,000 Knights, while Boston, Cincinnati, and Detroit each counted 17,000.

The American labor movement was riding a tidal wave as recent immigrants, the unskilled, and factory workers rushed to join. In Milwaukee, for example, where German-American craftsmen had played a dominant role in the Knights in the early 1880s, recently arrived and less-skilled Polish workers flooded into the organization in 1886; on a single day nearly a thousand Milwaukee Poles joined the Order. "The year 1886 will be known as the year of the great uprising of labor," proclaimed Massachusetts Knight George McNeill. "The skilled and the unskilled, the high-paid and the low-paid all joined hands."

"EIGHT HOURS FOR WHAT WE WILL!"

This poem, titled "Eight Hours," was written by I. G. Blanchard in 1866. Half a dozen years later Blanchard's poem was set to music by the Reverend Jesse H. Jones, who was closely associated with Boston's Eight-Hour League. The song became a rallying cry during the 1886 strike wave that demanded an eight-hour working day.

We mean to make things over,
　We're tired of toil for naught,
With bare enough to live upon,
　And never an hour for thought;
We want to feel the sunshine,
　And we want to smell the flowers,
We're sure that God has willed it,
　And we mean to have Eight Hours.
We're summoning our forces
　From shipyard, shop and mill;
Eight hours for work, eight hours for rest,
　Eight hours for what we will!

From the factories and workshops,
　In long and weary lines,
From all the sweltering forges,
　From all the sunless mines;
Wherever Toil is wasting
　The force of life to live;
Its bent and battered armies
　Come to claim what God doth give.
And the blazon on its banner
　Doth with hope the nations fill.
Eight hours for work, eight hours for rest,
　Eight hours for what we will!

The voice of God within us
　Is calling us to stand
Erect, as is becoming
　To the work of His right hand.
Should he, to whom the Maker
　His glorious image gave,
The meanest of His creatures crouch,
　A bread-and-butter slave?
Let the shout ring down the valleys
　And echo from ev'ry hill,
Eight hours for work, eight hours for rest,
　Eight hours for what we will!

There was never total harmony between these groups, of course, but the alliance was sufficiently stable to spark widespread fear among industrialists and their friends. During a Cleveland steel strike, employers called on police to intervene, a move that led to a number of violent confrontations at the mill gates. The city's daily newspapers launched a torrent of invective against the "un-American" Polish workers, labeling them "foreign devils," "ignorant and degraded whelps," and "Communistic scoundrels [who] have hoisted the red flag of Agrarianism, Nihilism and Socialism [and who] revel in robberies, bloodshed and arson." The fact that the striking workers were carrying not red but American flags was ignored. To those who were swept along in the Great Upheaval, what was important was not the color of labor's banners but the fact that people of such diverse backgrounds were marching together at all. "All I knew then of the principles of the Knights of Labor," the Jewish immigrant Abraham Bisno remembered, "was that the motto . . . was One for All, and All for One."

This call for unity was increasingly raised in efforts to win the eight-hour day, the "standard" length of the working day we now take for granted. American workers had been agitating for shorter working hours for decades. The struggle for an eight-hour day had played a particularly crucial role in the labor movement of the 1860s, and it surfaced again in 1884, when the Federation of Organized Trades and Labor Unions (FOTLU) resolved that "eight hours shall constitute a legal day's work from and after May 1, 1886." To back up this demand, the FOTLU proclaimed a general strike to begin on that day. "This is the workingman's hour," proclaimed the workers at Boston's Faneuil Hall on the eve of the May 1 strike.

Across the nation, nearly 340,000 workers went out on strike demanding the eight-hour day. By the end of the year there had been 1,500 strikes involving 400,000 workers, more than in any previous year of American history and a dramatic rise from the fewer than 500 work stoppages waged as recently as 1881. Centered in Milwaukee, Chicago, and New York, the movement spread to towns and cities across the nation. Despite the concerns of the Knights' national leadership regarding strike action, local Knights frequently found themselves at the head of the eight-hour movement. Though most of the strikes were only partially successful, they marked an important new phase in the mobilization of the unskilled and pushed many into the ranks of the labor movement.

Nearly as important as the eight-hour movement was the wave of boycotts mounted in the mid-1880s. An effort to win concessions from an employer by persuading other workers to stop patronizing his business, the boycott was especially effective in trades serving urban

Boycott fever. A cartoon in the satirical weekly *Life* comments on the ubiquity of the boycott. "Whereas," reads one boy, representing a committee of disgruntled candy-cart customers, "we find we don't git red color enough in our strawberry cream, nor enough yaller in our wanilla . . . to say nothin' o' the small measure of peanuts we gits for a cent; therefore, be it resolved . . . that all the stands in the city is boycotted until these things is righted."

working-class consumers. One business journal reported over two hundred boycotts in 1884 and 1885 against newspapers, street railways, and manufacturers of cigars, hats, carpets, clothing, shoes, and brooms. The movement hit its peak in 1886: countless campaigns touched the South, Far West, Midwest, and Eastern Seaboard; New York State alone was the site of some 150 boycotts. Eventually workers paid a price as customers. One disgruntled correspondent to *John Swinton's Paper* complained, "To be a sincere and systematic boycotter now, requires the carrying about of a catalog of the different boycotted firms or articles; and, if you have a family, another catalog is required for their use."

The spread of boycotts greatly alarmed employers, who denounced the tactic as "an un-American and anti-American offense" and turned to the courts for assistance. In the spring of 1886, New York courts ruled boycotting a form of criminal conspiracy and prohibited it, handing down indictments against over a hundred New Yorkers. In the most widely publicized of the subsequent trials, five workers who had organized a boycott against a local music hall were sentenced to long prison terms.

In response to these convictions, New York trade unionists turned to politics. Declaring that it was now time to "boycott" the Democratic and Republican parties, the Central Labor Union launched an independent labor party to run in the city election in the fall of 1886. Their candidate for mayor was a reformer and writer, Henry George. In 1879, George had published *Progress and Poverty*, a book that eventually be-

---

"LABOR NOWHERE HAS ITS FULL AND FAIR REWARD"

Henry George's 1886 mayoral campaign generated tremendous enthusiasm among New York working people, particularly trade union members. Although George campaigned for less than a month, he spoke more than one hundred times, sometimes addressing five or more labor unions and church groups in a single evening. This speech, presented to the members of Waiters' Union No. 3 in Manhattan, conveys George's identification with organized labor and his desire to channel the groundswell of working-class activism toward electoral politics.

WHEN THIS MOVEMENT commenced the politicians thought there was nothing in it. . . . The fact of the matter is, that the politicians and newspaper editors—not the newspaper reporters, but the newspaper editors—do not begin to appreciate the strength of this movement; they do not begin to understand the determination with which the workingmen of New York of all classes and of all occupations have taken hold of this movement. They do not realize that it is not a candidate who is looking for votes; it is the voters who are running the candidate on our side. I am your representative, put in the field by the accredited delegates of organized labor, and as their candidate I propose to run, and as their candidate I feel confident of election. . . .

All men who work for a living, whether by hand or head, are underpaid. Labor nowhere has its full and fair reward. Everywhere the struggle for existence, the difficulty of making a living, is far greater than it ought to be. This cannot be remedied by my election for Mayor; but a start will have been made; we shall at least have begun. From that time forth the questions of work and wages, the questions that concern the earning and the livings of us all, will get such an attention as they never had before. And the men who work for a living will have become conscious of the power of those questions. And the men who in Legislatures make the laws, and the men who on judicial benches interpret the laws, and the men who in administrative offices execute the laws—they, too, will become conscious of their power. . . .

If elected Mayor of New York it will be my duty to enforce the law. It will be at all times my duty to preserve order, at all times my duty to protect property; and that I will execute the law. . . . As a class workingmen have nothing to gain from disorder. . . . If the laws do not suit them, let them change the laws. Let there be no appeal to force so long as the ballot remains. That is the safer remedy for American citizens; to that remedy we propose at this election to appeal, and to appeal in tones that will ring through this land. . . .

came the most widely read tract in American history. George singled out private ownership of land as the main cause of inequality and corruption and proposed a complicated plan called the "single tax" to tax the parasitical landlord out of existence.

George's popularity, however, did not lie in this program. He focused attention on the central problems of the day—poverty, inequality, and the degradation of labor—and put forward what seemed like plausible solutions. Like the Knights, George embraced the republican tradition and tried to apply it, and his appeal was greatly enhanced by his regular denunciation of Ireland's landlords. This made him a great hero among the city's large Irish-American working class.

With the help of Father Edward McGlynn (a Catholic priest who embraced the gospel of labor reform), the Knights of Labor, and the New York Central Labor Union, Henry George generated tremendous working-class support for his campaign. But he drew equally intense opposition from employers and the Tammany (Democratic Party) machine, who joined forces to fight off the intrusion of class issues into politics. This united opposition fielded iron magnate Abram Hewitt as the Democratic Party nominee. George lost the election but captured 70,000 votes, one-third of the total and far more than the third-place Republican candidate, future president Theodore Roosevelt.

The George campaign was just the most prominent labor-reform effort; in almost every town or city where Knights of Labor assem-

"The Workingman between Two Fires." During the 1886 New York City mayoral campaign, many workingmen faced a dilemma when the Catholic Church hierarchy attacked the United Labor Party candidate, Henry George. As this cartoon from the humor weekly *Judge* indicates, although the ULP lost the election, the sizable turnout for George showed that many Catholic voters had ignored Archbishop Michael A. Corrigan's denunciations.

blies had been organized, workers discovered their political voice. In almost two hundred locales, "Union Labor" or "Workingmen's" parties elected aldermen, mayors, and school board officials. The United Labor ticket won more than one-quarter of the 92,000 votes cast in Chicago's 1886 elections, securing seats for five judges and several prolabor assemblymen. In Rutland, Vermont, the United Labor forces scored a stunning victory in 1886. Not only was their Knights of Labor candidate elected to the state legislature, but all fifteen labor-supported justices of the peace also took office. In other places labor managed to take control over one of the two established political parties.

In many towns the positive results of this political activity were quickly registered. Workers passed laws protecting trade unions and established the eight-hour day for public employees. Frequently just the threat of third-party action produced important concessions from the ruling authorities, who were stampeded into passing prolabor legislation or putting "friends of the workingman" on their slates. In Rochester, New Hampshire, the entry of the Knights of Labor into politics forced the Democratic Party to endorse the new labor ticket. The Knights claimed in November 1886 that they had also elected a dozen congressmen; almost all of them, however, came from the established parties and fused with the labor-reform forces.

Labor legislation first proposed by the Knights of Labor in the 1870s and early 1880s became law only later, when political mobilizations by trade unionists, working through labor parties as well as the major parties, gradually won approval in many states. These laws dealt with such issues as restricting child labor; inspecting factories, sweatshops, and mines; regulating women's labor; defining employer responsibility for employee accidents; establishing state machinery for arbitrating industrial disputes and state agencies for investigating the conditions and status of labor; and setting maximum hours for the labor of men. Although many of these laws were not strictly enforced, they helped to educate the public and provided the basis for more effective legislation in the years to come.

Democratic and Republican urban machines, badly shaken by the success of labor's political upsurge, attempted to co-opt many of these issues. In New York, the Tammany machine endorsed the establishment of a Bureau of Labor Statistics, called for a legal "Labor Day" holiday, and made a variety of other gestures to regain the following it had lost during the Henry George campaign. The machine also set up effective local organizations rooted in immigrant neighborhoods. But it was the patronage plum—the provision of municipal jobs to key supporters—that most effectively brought trade unionists into the political system. By the late 1880s, for example, there were more than four hundred Knights of Labor on Chicago's city payroll.

The Knights of Labor as a whole as well as many of its female members championed the cause of votes for women. But although the United States had long granted universal male suffrage, most women in the late nineteenth century still did not have the right to vote. Wyoming women were a notable exception, having successfully campaigned for suffrage in 1869 and helped elect a woman governor in the 1870s; some local governments also allowed women to vote. Thus while women Knights campaigned for labor tickets and called for political reform, they could not themselves cast ballots. In this narrow sense, the political activism of the Great Upheaval was a struggle for "working*men*'s democracy."

Looked at more broadly, however, neither woman suffrage nor labor issues were neatly divided between male and female; class divisions prevailed. The campaign for woman suffrage during the late nineteenth century was conducted primarily by middle-class women, and their attitudes toward their working-class sisters differed. Some middle-class suffragists refused to challenge the ideal of a separate domestic sphere for women's activities and ignored the social conditions of women's lives. Others, led by the dynamic and gifted organizers Elizabeth Cady Stanton and Susan B. Anthony, linked suffrage to the problems faced by wage-earning women and such working-class demands as the eight-hour day. In 1890, when the two camps finally united, the broad-based program put forward by Stanton and Anthony was pushed to the background.

Working-class women were far from indifferent to the vote, but saw it as only one element in the larger working-class struggle. As one woman wrote to a labor newspaper, "If women have the right of suffrage it will double the number of voices in the hands of the working people." The more progressive suffragists cultivated ties to the Knights of Labor because of the Order's crusade for "equal rights." Frances Willard of the Women's Christian Temperance Union, a broad-based organization with the slogan "Do Everything," belonged to the Knights of Labor, often addressed its meetings, and championed the labor movement of the 1880s. Praising the Knights' commitment to woman suffrage, equal pay, and temperance, Willard used a conventional metaphor: "I see that the Knights of Labor are also the Knights of the new chivalry. Who knows but these men shall bring in the new republic?"

And indeed, the Knights of Labor did provide an unprecedented opportunity for working-class women to struggle alongside men for equality. The eclectic reform vision of the Order linked women's industrial and domestic lives to broad social and political concerns, giving rise to what one historian has called the "labor feminism" of the 1880s. Far more effectively than feminist radicals such as Victoria Woodhull (who advocated abortion and "free love," which empha-

"Get Thee Behind Me, (Mrs.) Satan!" Illustrators and cartoonists often reserved their roughest treatment for women's rights advocates. Victoria Woodhull, outspoken proponent of the principle of free love, was a favored target. In this Thomas Nast cartoon, Woodhull is the devil, shunned by an oppressed housewife who intones, in the best tradition of the self-sacrificing guardian of family morality, "I'd rather travel the hardest path of matrimony than follow your footsteps."

sized freedom for men *and* women to choose sexual partners on the basis of mutual love) or disciplined immigrant socialist-feminists such as Augusta Lilienthal, the Knights mobilized support for equal pay for women, equal rights for women within all organizations, and equal respect for women's work, whether unpaid in the home or for wages in the factory or mill. The Knights succeeded in merging the struggle to overcome the special oppression of women and the exploitation of labor.

For American workers, then, the Great Upheaval was an exhilarating expression of solidarity. It was an explosion of militancy premised on the need for all workers to act in concert to change the very meaning of life in Gilded Age America. The vision of 1886 would last well into the 1890s and would, in fact, linger at the core of radical thought and action into the twentieth century. But the Great Upheaval was not to succeed in its purpose of transforming America.

THE EMPLOYER COUNTEROFFENSIVE AND THE RISE OF BUSINESS UNIONISM

Many of America's leading industrial enterprises were barely a decade old when Knights of Labor and craft unionists mobilized to challenge their power in the Great Upheaval. To counter and ultimately destroy labor's insurgency, capitalists mounted a sustained counteroffensive. Through their trade associations, they took concerted steps against workers, locking out those who joined unions and discharging strikers.

Employers also relied more and more on the coercive power of the government in these years. During the 1880s, legal charges such as "inciting to riot," "obstructing the streets," "intimidation," and "trespass" were first used extensively against strikers, and court injunctions restricting workers' rights to picket became commonplace; one judge, handing down the first injunction in a major labor dispute, proudly called it a "Gatling gun on paper." Blacklists of union activists were introduced and widely circulated. Labor spies, many of them employees of the rapidly growing Pinkerton Detective Agency, infiltrated labor organizations.

The Knights of Labor, whose weaknesses had been obscured by the spontaneous and heady expansion of the 1884–86 years, proved particularly vulnerable to this counteroffensive. Their most dramatic setback occurred on the same rail lines that had thrust the Order into public prominence. Overestimating their strength following the success of the 1885 strike, workers on the Southwestern Railroad lines struck again in March 1886, demanding wage increases and the reinstatement of a discharged Knight.

The Knights of Labor discovered that they could wring no concessions this time. Capitalists had concluded that placating workers' organizations fostered militancy and unionization and had consequently decided to yield nothing. On May 4, 1886, in the face of the railroad executives' intransigence, the Knights capitulated and called off their strike. In the course of the next several months the courts were jammed with workers as the railroads, aided by Pinkerton agents, charged scores with sabotage, assault, conspiracy, and even murder. Across the country, employers who had negotiated with labor in 1884–85 refused to follow suit in 1886–87. The Illinois Bureau of Labor reported that of seventy-six attempts to negotiate differences between labor and capital in 1886, capital rejected any discussion in thirty-two cases.

The employer counteroffensive coincided with labor's mobilization to win the eight-hour day. While the trade unions had initiated the campaign, political radicals played a prominent role in the agitation, especially in Chicago, where German socialists and anarchists—most notably Albert Parsons, August Spies, Michael Schwab, and Samuel Fielden—were leaders. On Saturday, May 1, 1886, with the anarchists in the forefront, some 40,000 Chicago workers struck for the eight-hour day. Parsons himself led the parade, 80,000 strong. The day passed without incident, but two days later, on Monday, May 3, a clash between pickets and scabs at the McCormick Reaper Works ended in police beatings and the fatal shooting of two unarmed workmen. August Spies, who witnessed the bloodshed, issued a fiery leaflet, calling Chicago's workers to a protest rally at Haymarket Square the following evening.

Given poor weather and the haste with which the Haymarket rally was called, attendance on Tuesday, May 4, was small. As rain threatened, the small crowd began to melt away, leaving no more than three hundred workers in the square. Before Samuel Fielden could finish speaking, the police moved in to break up the meeting. At that instant, and without warning, a bomb was thrown, killing one policeman. The police opened fire immediately, in the words of the Chicago *Tribune*, "blinded by passion" and "as dangerous as any mob." The police killed one person in the crowd and wounded many more, including some in their own ranks. It was, a Chicago *Herald* reporter wrote, a scene of "wild carnage."

Chicago's civic leaders, whipped into an antiradical, antiimmigrant frenzy by the Chicago press, needed little prodding to seek revenge for the policeman's death. Eight anarchist leaders were quickly arrested, charged with conspiracy to commit murder, tried, convicted, and sentenced to be executed. No evidence was ever offered connecting any of the accused with the bomb-thrower, who was, in fact, never identified. But in the wave of hysteria produced by the Great Upheaval, none was needed. Spies, Parsons, and two of their

Wanted. The police dispatch for Rudolph Schnaubelt, the immigrant machinist who was the only indicted Haymarket anarchist to escape arrest. Finally settling in Argentina after fleeing the United States and traveling about Europe, Schnaubelt became the favored choice for the bomb-thrower for both the police and some anarchists. The blame, however, seemed largely predicated on his physique (for the police) and his successful escape (for the anarchists).

comrades went to the gallows in November 1887. One condemned prisoner, Louis Lingg, committed suicide; the three remaining anarchists were pardoned years later.

The legal lynching of the Chicago anarchists divided and demoralized the labor movement. Militant action in the industrial and political arenas faded fast. Powderly refused to support Parsons, a fellow member of the Knights of Labor, or to criticize the courts. "Better," Powderly said, "that seven times seven men hang than to hang the millstone of odium around the standard of this Order in affiliating in any way with this element of destruction."

The hanging of the Haymarket anarchists emboldened capitalists as much as it undercut labor unity. In the second half of 1886, some 100,000 workers were locked out of work by their employers. Laundry workers in Troy, New York; packing-house workers in Chicago; and knitters in Cohoes and Amsterdam, New York, suffered harsh defeats. All the strikes involved the Knights of Labor; these defeats signaled the Order's increasing inability to protect its members' workplace rights.

Prior to the confrontation in Chicago's meat-packing plants, the Knights of Labor claimed 40,000 members in the city. Less than a year later that number had shrunk to 17,000. And after a bitter and unsuccessful strike by coal handlers and longshoremen in New York, the Order's District Assembly membership fell from 61,000 to 33,000. In ten pivotal districts in the Northwest, the Knights of Labor lost almost 180,000 members between July 1886 and July 1887. Across the nation the Order, which had boasted perhaps 1 million supporters at its peak in 1886, slipped to 500,000 dues-

---

"... I DIE HAPPY ON THE GALLOWS"

The Chicago radicals convicted of the Haymarket Square bombing remained openly defiant to the end. In his final address to the court, twenty-one-year-old carpenter Louis Lingg enthusiastically embraced the principles of anarchism and the violence he thought was necessary to emancipate the working class. Lingg refused to ask for mercy or to allow the state to execute him. He chose to hang himself in his cell several months after his conviction and sentencing.

ANARCHY MEANS NO domination or authority of one man over another, yet you call that "disorder." A system which advocates no such "order" as shall require the services of rogues and thieves to defend it you call "disorder."

The Judge himself was forced to admit that the state's attorney had not been able to connect me with the bombthrowing. The latter ... charges me with being a "conspirator." How does he prove it? Simply by declaring the International Working People's Association to be a "conspiracy." I was a member of that body, so he has the charge securely fastened to me. Excellent! Nothing is too difficult for the genius of the state's attorney!

It is hardly incumbent upon me to review the relations which I occupy to my companions in misfortune.... The universal misery, the ravages of the capitalistic hyena have brought us together in our agitation, not as persons, but as workers in the same cause. Such is the "conspiracy" of which you have convicted me.

I protest against the conviction, against the decision of the court. I do not recognize your law, jumbled together as it is by the nobodies of bygone centuries, and I do not recognize the decision of the court....

I repeat that I am the enemy of the "order" of today, and I repeat that, with all my powers, so long as breath remains in me, I shall combat it. I declare again, frankly and openly, that I am in favor of using force. I have told [Chicago Police] Captain Schaack, and I stand by it, "if you cannonade us, we shall dynamite you." You laugh! Perhaps you think, "you'll throw no more bombs"; but let me assure you I die happy on the gallows, so confident am I that the hundreds and thousands to whom I have spoken will remember my words; and when you shall have hanged us, then—mark my words—they will do the bombthrowing! In this hope do I say to you: I despise you. I despise your order, your laws, your force-propped authority. Hang me for it!

"Photographing criminals." As part of its coverage of the Haymarket incident, one newspaper displayed this scene in Chicago's police headquarters, showing the construction of a criminal identification system based on photographs. The "Rogues' Gallery" would serve as an archive to identify individual criminals (including political dissenters and labor activists) and to discern, according to contemporary scientific beliefs, what "physiognomic" traits (such as skull shape and facial characteristics) indicated innate criminal tendencies.

paying members a year later. By 1890, the Knights claimed only 100,000 members. The Great Upheaval was over.

The legal repression visited on the labor movement after the Haymarket bombing, and the rapid decline in the membership of the Knights of Labor, sharpened the conflict between the Order's more inclusive social and organizational vision and the narrower, craft orientation of the surviving national unions of skilled workers. Before the crisis of 1886, many skilled workers, ranging from railway employees to urban craftsmen, happily joined both the Knights and a trade union. Moreover, both the Knights and the unions had agitated for the eight-hour day, mounted mass strikes, used boycotts, and supported efforts to pass reform legislation. But in the aftermath of the Great Upheaval, the national trade unions chose increasingly to take

The "typical" anarchist—hairy, disheveled, and perched above the deadly tools of his "trade"—stares out from the cover of an 1886 edition of *The New York Detective Library*, one of the many weekly "dime novels" eagerly read by working people in the late nineteenth century.

a narrower view of their purpose as labor organizations. This strategic decision allowed the national unions to gain greater organizational stability and coherence than ever before, but the broad inclusiveness that had characterized the labor movement during the Great Upheaval would never again be realized.

The philosophical breach between the Knights and the craft unions widened significantly during 1886. Samuel Gompers, an immigrant cigarmaker and former socialist who was one of the leaders of the Cigar Makers' International Union (CMIU), was furious with the Knights of Labor national organization for supporting a socialist-dominated cigarmakers' local that had challenged the CMIU leadership. In May 1886, Gompers invited leaders of all the national unions to meet to formulate a common position with respect to the Knights. There followed halfhearted negotiations between the two organizations during which the craft unions insisted on exclusive jurisdiction over their members. The Knights' leaders would not accept this. When negotiations broke down, trade unionists organized the American Federation of Labor (AFL), a loose alliance of independent national unions, in December 1886. Gompers was elected AFL president, a position he was to hold for most of the next four decades.

Most of the trade unionists drawn to the AFL still possessed skills that gave them the ability to bargain effectively with their employers. Molders, machinists, brewers, building tradesmen, and others whose skills had been only partially eroded by technological change could still secure concessions from employers as long as they limited their demands to improved wages and working conditions. Disillusioned with the defeats of mass strikes and broad reform programs that could no longer win immediate material gains, these craft unionists sought to define an organizational strategy that could maximize their power and minimize their vulnerability.

With Samuel Gompers as their spokesman, the trade unionists developed the practice of "business unionism." Central to their approach was the national union of skilled workers, a strong organization possessing both exclusive jurisdiction within a specific craft and control of ample strike funds paid for out of relatively high dues assessments. National union leaders wanted to be able to make sure that their locals did not call unwinnable strikes. A second feature of business unionism was its focus on collective bargaining with the employer as the means of winning concrete material gains. Political action might be necessary—to fight for protective tariffs or against competition from prison labor—but business unionists avoided involvement in broad-based political movements. Implicit in business unionism was an overall acceptance of the prevailing social and political order and the capitalist economic relations upon which that order rested.

TWO ROADS FOR THE WORKINGMAN—ONE LEADS TO PROSPERITY, AND THE OTHER TO VIOLENCE AND RUIN.

"Two Roads for the Working Man." No admirer of the labor movement, *Puck* depicts the warring trade unions and Knights of Labor as essentially the same, taking workers down the "road of Lawlessness and Disorder." Meanwhile, in the background, P. M. Arthur of the conservative Brotherhood of Locomotive Engineers chugs forward toward prosperity, progress, and, most important, order.

The Knights of Labor did not simply disappear. While the Knights' leadership remained in the hands of skilled English-speaking labor reformers, the Order's sustaining forces in the late 1880s and early 1890s shifted to rural blacks, western and southern miners, and unskilled immigrants. In the South, for instance, a whole new chapter in the Order's history was being written. At the same time as the organization lost strength among industrial workers in the late 1880s, it continued to *grow* in the southern countryside. The new members were not independent yeoman farmers, who occasionally joined the Knights in other areas of the country. Rather, they were overwhelmingly tenants, miners, rural day laborers, and domestic workers—the bulk of them African-Americans. Long known for their advocacy of African-American rights, the Knights of Labor in the South became increasingly a black organization as the 1880s gave way to the 1890s.

The early growth of the United Mine Workers of America (UMWA) offers a good illustration of the continuing impact of the Knights of Labor philosophy. Founded in 1890 with the support of dozens of Knights of Labor local assemblies in coalmining areas, the UMWA embraced the Order's broader, more inclusive vision of labor organization. Unlike many other unions, the UMWA struggled from the outset to build interracial, industrial unions in the mining regions of Alabama and West Virginia as well as in older coal states, such as Ohio. During this period Richard L. Davis, the African-American miner from Ohio profiled earlier, won election to the union's executive board in and traveled all over the South, successfully organizing his fellow black miners into the UMWA.

In the southern West Virginia coalfields, for example, the UMWA, encouraged by the efforts of Davis and other organizers and building on earlier organizing successes of the Knights in establishing local assemblies, achieved remarkable success in bringing black and white mineworkers together to form dozens of local unions. One explanation for the UMWA's progress in West Virginia in the 1890s was the realization by black and white miners alike of the importance of electing union officials of both races. A succession of African-American miners were in fact elected to the West Virginia district vice presidency between 1891 and 1898. Black miners rewarded this commitment to interracial leadership by being the most stalwart supporters of the UMWA in West Virginia in these years. A similar commitment by black miners to the UMWA cause was evident in the Alabama coal mines in the same period.

The UMWA was unfortunately unique in the American labor movement in these years. Between 1890 and 1894, the UMWA remained affiliated with both the Knights and the AFL, a position atypical of other national unions in the years following the Great Upheaval. While the UMWA attempted to preserve the Knights' commitment to interracialism and broad industrial organization, most

Have guns, will travel. Prepared to suppress labor trouble anywhere in the Philadelphia and Reading Railroad's domain, whether on the rails or underground, the company's Railroad and Coal and Iron Police pose in front of their traveling headquarters in 1888.

"The Perils of Street-car Traveling in New York During a Strike." An 1889 cartoon shows a passenger in a streetcar that has barely survived a blockade by striking transit workers. "Let me out at Vesey Street, please," he peeps. City transit workers represented one of the trades that continued to affiliate with the Knights of Labor through the late 1880s.

national unions increasingly became narrow organizations of skilled, white, male workers. Rejecting the miners' inclusive approach to organizing, craft unions—notably the building trades unions and the railroad brotherhoods—systematically excluded black workers and the unskilled from membership. The increasingly businesslike and racist policies of craft unionism had overwhelmed the Knights' broader vision of working-class organization.

Despite this retreat into narrow exclusivity and racism, the national federation and its constituent unions did not lack for militancy. The national unions often stood as champions of the efforts of craftsmen to obtain the eight-hour day, to defend their organizations, and to fight off employer encroachments on their traditional control over the job. The number of strikes actually increased in the late 1880s, and strikes became more organized, disciplined, and successful. In a period when the majority of strikes ended in defeat for workers, more than 60 percent of the strikes waged in 1889 and 1890 were victories. Nor was this wave of strikes narrowly based on the desire of particular occupational groups or crafts to win wage increases. The AFL championed the early use of sympathy strikes, the refusal to work by one group of workers in support of striking workers in another place or group. Such sympathetic job actions increased nearly fourfold in the early 1890s. When New York's cabinetmakers struck to preserve their union in 1892, for example, they were joined by more than eleven other craft groups employed in over a hundred firms.

Between 1888 and 1891, the craft unions affiliated with the AFL consolidated their influence, paced by the building trades' largely successful struggle for the eight-hour day and the molders' successful implementation of a national trade agreement. In reaction to these victories, capitalists decided to confront the power of the craft unions head-on. The steel industry would be the center of this renewed employer offensive in 1892.

HOMESTEAD

During the 1870s and 1880s, skilled iron and steel workers won high wages based on their knowledge and command of the production process as well as their unity in dealing with employers. Although rapid technological change in the steel industry did much to undermine steelworkers' power by the early 1890s, they remained strong. At Andrew Carnegie's Homestead works, one of the most advanced mills in the world, skilled workers had won an important strike in 1889. The victory gave them wages one-third higher than those at neighboring mills. The 1889 wage settlement also pegged the wages of the unorganized Homestead laborers, some of whom were recent eastern

European immigrants, to those of the skilled English-speaking craftsmen in the Amalgamated Association of Iron and Steel Workers.
When skilled unionized workers won a major wage increase, it benefited the unskilled, nonunion helpers as well. Craftsman or laborer,
organized or unorganized—by 1890 workers in Homestead shared
common interests.

Community ties strengthened those formed at the mills. The
twelve mills at Homestead employed 3,800 men, making it one of the
nation's largest industrial complexes. The town itself had only 11,000
residents; virtually every household sent at least one person to toil in
the mills. Most of the townspeople spoke English; less than a fifth of
the workforce was from southern and eastern Europe. Steelworkers
dominated the town, heading its city government and police department and owning most of its modest homes. A late-nineteenth-
century version of republican ideology shaped their outlook;
unionism was a right of citizenship, a bulwark against dependency,
and a protector of the workers' positions as homeowners in a community they had made their own. As a state militia officer wonder-
ingly remarked, "They believe the works are theirs quite as much as
Carnegie's."

Carnegie wanted a cheap and docile labor force; to get it, he had
to break the Amalgamated Association, which stood in his way. Sail-
ing for a vacation in Scotland, Carnegie left the dirty work of union-
busting to his associate Henry Clay Frick. In June 1892, Frick
announced that the company would only deal with men on an individual basis and would not renew its contract with the Amalgamated
Association. Frick knew that the union could not accept this new
policy. He therefore prepared for battle, surrounding the mills with
three miles of twelve-foot-high steel fence topped with barbed wire;
workers dubbed it "Fort Frick." Frick also hired three hundred armed
Pinkerton agents to protect the scab workers he planned to bring in;
they were to land directly from the river onto company property. On
July 2, Frick shut down the Homestead works and announced that he
would reopen them with nonunion labor.

The Homestead workers had made their own preparations. The
Amalgamated Association formed a forty-man advisory committee,
which successfully recruited the unskilled workers, and indeed virtually the entire town, for the coming struggle. The committee organized the town on a military basis: it took control of the local
utilities; patrolled all access to the town by land, water, and rail; and
closed the saloons. Public support for the committee ran so deep that
the county sheriff was unable to raise a posse to protect the mills from
the workers.

On July 5, the heavily armed Pinkertons approached the plant
from a barge on the Monongahela River. But the locked-out workers

had been tipped off; armed with guns, rocks, and a small cannon, an intimidating crowd, including workers and their enraged wives, met the detectives at the river's edge. In the twelve-hour battle that ensued, nine strikers and seven detectives were killed, and many more were wounded. The Pinkertons finally surrendered to the strikers.

This spectacular victory prompted the Carnegie company to turn to the state government for assistance. The governor of Pennsylvania, after some hesitation, responded to Frick's request and sent in the state militia. A spokesman for the union welcomed them with the statement: "On the part of the Amalgamated Association I wish to say that after suffering an attack of illegal authority, we are glad to have the legal authority of the state here." But the general in command of the troops was less gracious: "I do not recognize your association, sir. . . . We have come here to restore law and order."

In the days that followed, the confrontation spread beyond Homestead as other Carnegie mills were shut down by sympathetic strikes or lockouts. By August the militia was escorting repairmen, mechanics, and strikebreakers into Carnegie's plants, the courts were clogged with cases of union men accused of violent crimes, and scabs were being hired from as far away as Ohio. Pittsburgh juries refused to convict union men, and the Amalgamated Association hung on for four months.

Although the workers believed they had right on their side, might was against them. By September nearly all of the mills and departments were running, albeit poorly, with scab labor. On November 18, the striking unskilled workers petitioned the Amalgamated Association to release them from their strike pledge. Two days later the union called off the strike; the Amalgamated leaders were fired and blacklisted. Frick cabled Carnegie: "Our victory is now complete and most gratifying. Do not think we will ever have any serious labor trouble again."

"TO PROTECT THEIR HOMES AND FAMILIES . . ."

Written by George Swetnam in 1892, "Song of a Strike" commemorates the Homestead strikers' courage in defending their homes and their jobs against the overwhelming might of the Carnegie Steel Company and their hired "bum detectives" (Pinkertons).

We are asking one another as we pass the time of day,
Why workingmen resort to arms to get their proper pay.
And why our labor unions they must not be recognized,
Whilst the actions of a syndicate must not be criticized.
Now the troubles down at Homestead were brought about this way,
When a grasping corporation had the audacity to say:
"You must all renounce your union and forswear your liberty
And we will give you a chance to live and die in slavery."
Now this sturdy band of workingmen started out at the break of day,
Determination in their faces which plainly meant to say:
"No one can come and take our homes for which we have toiled so long,
No one can come and take our places—no, here's where we belong!"
When a lot of bum detectives come without authority,
Like thieves at night when decent men were sleeping peacefully—
Can you wonder why all honest hearts with indignation burn,
And why the slimy worm that treads the earth when trod upon will turn?

When they locked out men at Homestead so they were face to face
With a lot of bum detectives and they knew it was their place
To protect their homes and families, and this was neatly done,
And the public will reward them for the victories they won.

"An Awful Battle at Homestead, Pa." The *National Police Gazette* portrays the July 6, 1892, fight between striking steelworkers and Pinkerton strikebreakers on the Monongahela River. Directed to male readers, many of whom were workers, the *National Police Gazette* occasionally covered labor conflict, expressing sympathy toward strikers while also exploiting the more sensational aspects of the events.

The defeat of the Homestead strike dealt the skilled men of the Amalgamated Association a severe blow. Their union was shattered, their faith in their powerful craft organization and their republican ideals severely compromised. They had learned what capital's new power was all about, and they had experienced firsthand the role of government in labor-capital conflict. Long gone were the days when the craftsmen had only to "withhold our skills . . . until such time as [the bosses] agree." Regardless of the important connections forged during the strike between skilled Anglo-American workers and their unskilled immigrant helpers, this had not been sufficient to carry the day against Carnegie. "The Amalgamated Association made a big mistake in the beginning by attempting to form an 'aristocracy of labor,'" argued one Homestead worker following the defeat. "They left out the salaried men and laborers. . . . The union should have included every man connected in every way with the steel mill."

Perhaps more important, technological change had eroded skilled workers' centrality in the production process and made them increasingly vulnerable. In the two decades after 1890, productivity at Homestead tripled; far fewer steelworkers produced much more steel. And they earned 20 percent less for a twelve-hour day and a seven-day week.

The crushing of the Homestead strike was the opening shot in the second phase of capital's war to tame workers' militancy. Days after the Homestead strikers returned to work, another incident of armed warfare broke out between strikers on the one side and strikebreakers and company guards on the other in the silver-mining region of Coeur d'Alene, Idaho. Here also the state militia was called in, the governor declared martial law, and again the striking workers met with defeat.

Like the Homestead strike, Coeur d'Alene indicated that the center of political power was shifting from the local to the state level, while economic power was becoming increasingly national. Large corporations could exert far greater influence over governors than they could over mayors and aldermen—especially in communities where the political power of working people remained significant. And within this new political context, employers made it clear that

Martial law in Coeur d'Alene. The interior of a "bull pen," one of the makeshift prison sheds erected by federal and state troops in 1892 to hold arrested union miners and sympathizers, and resurrected seven years later by federal forces during the 1899 mining war.

they would do everything possible to crush the labor movement. Under these circumstances even the most strenuous efforts of workers in 1892 could not produce strike victories: switchmen in the Buffalo railway yards, Knights of Labor in the Tracy City, Tennessee, coalmines, and black and white workers in New Orleans united in a general strike experienced defeats similar to those of the Homestead and Coeur d'Alene workers.

Faced with this record of crushing defeats, AFL president Samuel Gompers asked, "Shall we change our methods?" He answered in the negative, preferring to see the very survival of trade unions in the face of the employer offensive as proof of the correctness of his policies. Gompers had a point. The AFL combined membership held steady despite the setbacks in 1892. But he missed the larger meaning for the labor movement of that year's crushing losses. In the face of overwhelming defeat, the mutuality and culture of solidarity that many skilled craft workers had expressed and lived by for thirty years was in decline. Narrow self-interest and a businesslike approach now increasingly defined craft unionism. If 1886 represented the defeat of the Knights' broad vision of labor unity, in 1892 craft unionism met a similar defeat.

1894: DEPRESSION, THE PULLMAN STRIKE, AND GOVERNMENTAL POWER

"The Americans are a people of magnificent achievements and of equally magnificent fiascoes," commented a British journalist in September 1893. "At present they are in the throes of a fiasco unprecedented even in their broad experience." The writer was referring to the major financial panic that struck the New York Stock Exchange four months earlier. By year's end, some 500 banks and 16,000 businesses had shut their doors in bankruptcy. "Never before has there been such a sudden and striking cessation of industrial activity," observed the *Commercial and Financial Chronicle* in August 1893. "Mills, factories, furnaces, mines nearly everywhere shut down in large numbers, and commerce and enterprise were arrested in an extraordinary degree."

By the middle of 1894, over 150 railroad companies, with 30,000 miles of track and a combined capital worth $2.5 billion, had gone bankrupt. Just as the railroads led the economy into growth, so their collapse now pushed it into depression. The failure of major railroads triggered a collapse of a number of other industries with which they were intertwined. The steel industry that had produced the rails was hardest hit: more than thirty steel companies went bankrupt in the first six months of 1893. The agricultural economy exhibited similar weaknesses. Farmers' earnings declined steadily after 1888. And when farming fell on bad times, it dragged down farm machine manufacturers, grain elevators, and a wide variety of rural and small-town businesses.

The severe economic depression, which lasted five years, brought misery on a scale not previously experienced in industrial America. The effects of the depression were brutal. Plant closings threw Americans out of work in staggering numbers. The AFL estimated the unemployed at over 3 million in 1893. In New York, police reported that 20,000 homeless people sought shelter in the city jails. Chicago, with 1 million residents, counted more than 100,000 unemployed. Many traveled the country in search of work or relief. In the winter of 1893–94, Chicago police stood guard at the railroad stations to prevent more tramps from entering the city.

As millions of families stared starvation in the face, labor demanded public aid for the needy. In December 1893, the annual convention of the American Federation of Labor declared that "the right to work is the right to live" and called for the establishment of the eight-hour day to spread available work among a larger number of workers and the federal issue of $500 million in paper money to fund public works.

Detroit mayor Hazen Pingree put the unemployed to work growing vegetables on vacant lots. Described as "municipal farming for the poor," the "Pingree Potato Scheme" was copied in Buffalo, Brooklyn, New York, Cincinnati, and many other cities. Yet such relief efforts, public and private, did not come close to meeting the needs of workers and their families. Small wonder: in a society where the wealthy and powerful believed that "getting something for nothing" was a sin against God and nature, relief was viewed with heartfelt distaste. Even Josephine Shaw Lowell, who had devoted much of her life to improving the situation of the unfortunate, echoed prevailing opinion when she lashed out against "the socialistic teaching" that the poor should be given charity; instead she advocated that unemployed men be given work only that was "continuous, hard, and underpaid."

Faced with miserable conditions and the contempt of their social "betters," workers soon erupted in protest. The year 1894 was one of the most conflict-ridden in American history. A mass movement of the unemployed marched from one end of the country to the other, while an awesome strike wave involving hundreds of thousands of workers paralyzed the nation.

Some of the unemployed rallied behind Ohio businessman Jacob S. Coxey, who had a simple plan: the Good Roads Bill, introduced by Coxey's sympathizers in Congress, promised simultaneously to improve American roads and put thousands of people back to work. Congress's hostility to the plan provoked Coxey to take more dramatic steps: "We will send a petition to Washington with boots on." With these words, he announced the formation of an "industrial army" of the unemployed, to leave Massillon, Ohio, on Easter Sunday 1894 in a grand march on Washington. He predicted that a hundred thousand would march, but only a hundred left Ohio. The press denounced Coxey's movement as one of wild visionaries and dangerous anarchists.

As the army moved east, other despairing men joined its ranks. By the time they reached Homestead, Pennsylvania, they numbered six hundred, with thousands more cheering them on in every industrial town they passed through. A young sociologist named Thorstein Veblen captured the most important dimension of the event: what distinguished Coxey's Army from earlier movements was that it appealed to the federal government for relief and, in so doing, asserted that the federal government had a basic responsibility for the people's welfare. For the men who joined Coxey's Army, Veblen argued, "the classic phrase is no longer to read 'life, liberty, and the pursuit of happiness'; what is to be ensured to every free-born American

On the road to Washington, D.C. Members of Coxey's Army march into Alleghany, Virginia, their progress marked by a Chicago reporter on horseback.

citizen under the new dispensation is 'life, liberty, and the means of happiness.' "

The federal government, however, was far from ready to endorse this interpretation of its role. As the Coxeyites neared Washington, President Grover Cleveland, a Democrat, made clear his determination to enforce a law prohibiting parades on the Capitol grounds. When Coxey's Army finally arrived in Washington, D.C., on the morning of May 1, 1894, they were greeted by enough police, according to one observer, "to take every single Coxeyite into custody." A riot resulted.

Coxey's movement was only the most famous of fully seventeen industrial armies that set out for Washington in 1894. In the Far West, the armies were much larger, numbering in the thousands. Although they traveled mainly on foot, they sometimes seized trains. The federal government moved as forcefully against them as it had against Coxey. President Cleveland's attorney general, former railroad lawyer Richard C. Olney, played a particularly important role in shaping administration policy. Olney obtained federal court injunctions, deployed large numbers of U.S. marshals, and finally brought in U.S. troops to end the train seizures. These measures led to considerable conflict, including at least one gun battle between lawmen and workers (who were aided by sympathetic townspeople) in Billings, Montana. But they ended train hijackings and, more important, halted the eastward march of the industrial armies.

The Cleveland administration used harsh tactics again when it intervened in the American Railroad Union (ARU) strike and nationwide boycott of the Pullman Palace Car Company. Located just south of Chicago in Pullman, Illinois, George Pullman's company town was a throwback to the paternalistic mill villages of the 1830s and

---

" . . . AN ULCER ON THE BODY POLITIC"

The men and women who labored in George Pullman's "model" town during the 1893 depression endured starvation wages and deplorable living and working conditions. They especially loathed Pullman's paternalistic control over all aspects of their lives. This statement from a Pullman striker, delivered at the June 1894 Chicago convention of the American Railway Union, suggests the depth of the strikers' hatred of their employer and their commitment to the ARU.

WE STRUCK AT Pullman because we were without hope. We joined the American Railway Union because it gave us a glimmer of hope. Twenty thousand souls, men, women, and little ones, have their eyes turned toward this convention today, straining eagerly through dark despondency for a glimmer of the heaven-sent message you alone can give us on this earth.

In stating to this body our grievances it is hard to tell where to begin. . . . Five reductions in wages, work, and in conditions of employment swept through the shops at Pullman between May and December 1893. The last was the most severe, amounting to nearly 30 percent and our rents had not fallen. . . . No man or woman of us all can ever hope to own one inch of George Pullman's land. Why even the very streets are his. . . .

Pullman, both the man and the town, is an ulcer on the body politic. He owns the houses, the schoolhouses, the churches of God. . . . The revenue he derives from these, the wages he pays out with one hand—the Pullman Palace Car Company, he takes back with the other—the Pullman Land Association. He is able by this to bid under any contract car shop in the country. His competitors in business, to meet this, must reduce the wages of their men. . . . And thus the merry war— the dance of skeletons bathed in human tears—goes on, and it will go on, brothers, forever, unless you, the American Railway Union, stop it; end it; crush it out.

1840s. Pullman was not the model town that its founder asserted it to be; rather, it was an overcrowded, tightly controlled environment, and conditions only worsened with the depression of 1893. George Pullman forced a 25 to 40 percent wage cut on his employees; he did not reduce their rents, however. Some workers literally took home pennies after rent was deducted from their wages. When a committee of workers formed in May 1894 to discuss the matter with Pullman, he responded by firing three of its members on the spot. The Pullman workers appealed to the ARU for support; the union responded by calling for a nationwide boycott and strike.

Formed in 1893 by Eugene V. Debs and a group of western railroad workers who had remained in the Knights of Labor, the American Railway Union, along with the United Mine Workers, stood at the forefront of the industrial union movement of the 1890s. Disgusted with the narrow craft exclusiveness of the traditional railroad brotherhoods, the ARU threw open its doors to workers of all skill levels and to anyone who worked for a railway company. The union's quick victory over the Great Northern Railroad earlier in 1894 won the ARU enormous prestige and influence among rank-and-file railroad workers. By 1894 the ARU's membership stood at over 150,000, more than all the other railroad unions combined.

With the important exception of black workers, who were not allowed to join the organization, the ARU embraced the idea of working-class mutuality. In the early 1890s, this commitment took the form of the sympathy strike, the refusal to work in support of striking workers in another place or industry. The potential power of the sympathy strike was so great that Debs would hail "the Christlike virtue of sympathy" as "the hope of civilization and the supreme glory of mankind."

Unlike the largely spontaneous revolt of 1877, the "Debs Revolution," as the Pullman strike was called, was preceded by widespread organizing activity by the ARU. The strike was directed by a centralized labor organization with representatives from each participating local union. Committees across the Southwest and Midwest and in California coordinated activities with Debs and the strike's Chicago headquarters. On June 26, the ARU inaugurated its planned boycott of all trains hauling Pullman cars.

But employers had also perfected their weapons of industrial warfare since 1877. The General Managers' Association, an organization of the twenty-six Chicago railroads, rallied to George Pullman's aid, ordering the discharge of any workers who refused to handle Pullman cars. Railroad workers responded by shutting down entire lines and bringing most of the nation's rail traffic to a halt by the end of June. From an isolated labor dispute the boycott became, in Debs's words, "a contest between the producing classes and the money power of the country." An estimated 260,000 railroad workers joined the battle, nearly half of them unaffiliated with the ARU; as many as 500,000 may have been idled because of the boycott. The Chicago *Tribune* boldly proclaimed the strike and boycott "an insurrection" and called for firm and immediate action to crush it.

Railroad managers then played their trump card: they sought the intervention of the federal government. Attaching mail cars to trains containing Pullman cars enabled the government to charge strikers with interfering with the mails. Attorney General Olney, building on the tactics he used earlier against Coxey's Army, obtained a sweeping injunction in early July from the federal courts, effectively outlawing the boycott. The Chicago *Times* astutely noted that the injunction's purpose was "to lay a foundation for calling out the United States troops."

Federal troops and state militia were quickly dispatched in six states. The arrival of the U.S. Army in Chicago on the Fourth of July precipitated a violent confrontation that left thirteen dead, more than fifty wounded, and hundreds of thousands of dollars of railroad property destroyed. Working-class resistance to the troops spread rapidly across the country over the course of the next week, encompassing twenty-six states in all from Maine to California. "The strike is now war" screamed a headline in the Chicago *Tribune*. By July 11, an estimated thirty-four people were killed; Debs and other ARU leaders were arrested.

The final blow to the Pullman strike was delivered by Samuel

"Chicago under the mob." An ardent admirer of the military, artist-reporter Frederic Remington displayed no sympathy for the Pullman strikers in his reports for *Harper's Weekly*. Endorsing suppression, Remington described the strikers as a "malodorous crowd of foreign trash" talking "Hungarian or Polack, or whatever the stuff is."

"King Debs." Eugene Debs was lambasted by much of the press during the Pullman strike. But while this *Harper's Weekly* cartoon, among many other published pictures, portrayed Debs as a tyrant paralyzing the country's commerce, it also made the face of the American Railway Union president familiar to readers across the nation.

Gompers and the AFL. Rather than back the revolt, as many within its ranks urged, the AFL leaders quashed appeals for the general strike called for by Debs, voted a paltry $1,000 in support of Debs's legal defense, and called on strikers belonging to AFL affiliates to return to work. By mid-July, the strike was over and the ARU routed. In the bitter aftermath, Debs and other union leaders were convicted of civil contempt and sentenced to prison; many strikers were blacklisted.

Clearly paralleling the Pullman events was the national bituminous coal strike that began earlier in the year. Though the UMWA's official membership stood at only 20,000, over 125,000 miners immediately rallied to the union cause when the strike began in April 1894. Direct action, including use of roving bands of pickets, quickly spread the strike across the country. Miners from Spring Valley, Illinois, marched to neighboring La Salle, where they appealed to their fellow miners to join them, addressing a mass meeting in a dozen different languages. Striking miners also engaged in violent confrontations with strikebreakers, local police, and state militia in Illinois, Ohio, and Pennsylvania. But the severe impact of the depression undercut the miners' impressive solidarity; within two months, West Virginia and Virginia mines were operating with nonunion labor. Although finally overwhelmed by the armed might of the state and starved into submission, coalminers had achieved something new: the 1894 strike was the first truly nationwide miners' uprising. That year also marked the first time in American history that coalminers and railroad workers, workers in the two largest industrial occupations in the Gilded Age, went on strike at the same time; not surprisingly, miners and railroad workers accounted for the bulk of the year's unprecedented half a million strikers.

The Pullman strike and boycott and the UMWA strike were the most visible expressions of a general political crisis shaking America in the early 1890s; 1894, like 1886, was a year in which class relations sharply polarized. For the first time since 1877, more than half a million workers were out on strike; and more than six in ten of these job actions were sympathy stoppages called in support of other striking workers. The battles of 1894 revealed the organized and coordinated character of strike activity, the increasingly national orientation of strikers, and the extent to which "the habit of solidarity" was expressed in class conflict.

One railroad worker summed up the lessons of 1894, claiming that it demonstrated "to the laboring men that they must get together; that no single organization can win." The workers, he concluded, "have seen the united press against them; they have seen the united clergy against them; they have seen the entire officeholders of the country against them, and all the old-time [labor] organizations." Faced with this concerted opposition, the leaders of both the ARU and the United Mine Workers urged labor to change the government at the ballot box, not on the picket line. In so doing they pointed toward the rapidly rising Populist movement, one of the largest and most powerful third parties in American history. For a brief moment the "producing classes" flirted with the idea of linking working people together as a political force in the cities and the countryside.

ALLIANCEMEN, POPULISTS, AND THE POLITICS OF PROTEST

In 1893, a leading journalist posed a prophetic question: "Are we perhaps," he asked, "on the eve of another political uprising similar to that of 1886, though on a grander, a more national scale?" The answer was yes. The People's Party, commonly known as the Populists, mounted one of the most potent challenges to the two-party system that America has ever seen.

Populism's roots were planted in the cooperative crusade of the Farmers' Alliance, which began in Texas in the late 1870s. Headed by Charles Macune, the Alliance published a widely read journal, the *National Economist*, which promoted the organization's simple message: "The Alliance is the people and the people are together." This

"We feed the world." Grangers, predecessors of the Farmers' Alliance and Populists, gather in the woods near Winchester, Scott County, Illinois, in August 1873.

message was communicated by an army of lecturers at small local meetings, larger county gatherings, and massive Fourth of July encampments.

The Alliance took action first in Texas, where farmers challenged the market system through cooperative buying and selling. They began by "bulking," selling their crops as a group instead of individually: one bulk sale in Fort Worth brought participating farmers a crucial 5 percent more than those who sold their crops as individuals. The tactic proved successful despite deep opposition from local merchants and manufacturers.

Alliance organizers also formed hundreds of suballiance chapters committed to other cooperative functions: recovery of stray animals; the use of vigilante methods to protect farmers from thieves and ranchers hungry for grazing land; and support for poor agriculturalists victimized by land company agents who used fraudulent methods to steal settlers' land.

As the Alliance gained momentum in the early 1880s, it spread throughout the South and across the Great Plains. In Minnesota, for example, the Alliance grew to 15,000 members by 1889, spurred by the stump oratory of the lecturer, utopian novelist, and aspiring politician Ignatius Donnelly. Donnelly's widely read novel *Caesar's Column*, published in 1889, communicated the mixed ideological signals of the farmers' crusade. Anticlerical and strongly opposed to eastern commercial interests, the novel also lapsed into scapegoating and crude anti-Semitism. At its peak the Alliance claimed hundreds of thousands of members and supporters nationwide. Approximately one-quarter were the wives or daughters of farmers.

The Farmers' Alliance nonetheless exhibited crucial weaknesses that would continue to haunt farmer protest into the 1890s, flaws that held the democratic impulses of rural agitation in check. First, the Alliance drew on diverse groups of farmers, merging the interests of dirt farmers and large planters. Second, the cooperative program of the Alliance spoke primarily to those who still owned their land and marketed their crops. It did not address the problems of wage-earners or landless rural people, however much the rhetoric of Alliance lecturers might appeal to such dispossessed people. Third, the Alliance excluded African-Americans from membership. The deep racism of most southern Alliancemen, whose fathers had often been in direct competition with slaveholding planters, led them to oppose any efforts to organize black sharecroppers or rural laborers.

By keeping blacks out, the Alliance excluded nearly half of the agriculturalists of the South, failed to challenge the deepening white supremacy of the new South, and undermined its own goal of building solidarity among all producers. A separate Colored Farmers' Alliance did emerge in the 1880s and by 1890 probably encompassed 250,000 members. It made considerable headway with its white counterpart and was accepted as an ally by some white farmers. But large numbers of African-Americans in the southern countryside continued to place their trust in the Republican Party as the vehicle of their liberation, fearing that the growth of the Alliance would actually intensify their oppression by strengthening the small white producers who habitually subjected them to racist jibes and direct assault.

None of these weaknesses was fully apparent during the 1880s. When members of the Southern Alliance met in 1889 with a parallel organization from the Great Plains in St. Louis to discuss a merger, the future looked bright. Though the meeting did not lead to a united body, there was a general consensus on the need to nationalize the railroads, prohibit large landholding companies, abolish national banks, and institute a graduated income tax.

But the St. Louis gathering did produce a new idea: Charles Macune's innovative plan for a federal subtreasury that would provide farmers with storage space for their crops in government-owned warehouses until prices climbed to acceptable levels. While the crops piled up, farmers were to receive state loans of up to 80 percent of the current market price for their crop, the loan to be repaid when the price rose to the point that a sale might be undertaken. Over the next few years the subtreasury plan captured the imagination of farmers across the nation.

In 1890, farmers plunged directly into the political fray, capturing local Democratic parties in the Southwest and forming independent parties of their own in the Plains states. The level of involvement by the rural poor astonished America. Sixteen hundred wagons pulled up for one meeting at Hastings, Nebraska. Rural Kansas typically had open-air rallies of 25,000 people. The summer of 1890 would long be remembered in the Midwest as "that wonderful picnicking, speech-making Alliance summer."

The farmers' movement spawned a group of extremely effective orators. "Sockless" Jerry Simpson, a Kansas farmer whose poverty earned him his nickname, spoke a language in perfect pitch with that of his followers. Mary Elizabeth Lease, who urged the movement to place woman suffrage at the heart of its agenda, was the most effective of all. An Irish-born lawyer, Lease delivered hundreds of speeches across Kansas in 1890, arguing that women "should be heart and hand in this Farmers' Alliance movement."

This political upsurge produced dramatic results. In the South, the Alliance elected four governors and more than forty congressmen and took control of eight legislatures. Great Plains farmers made gains as well, electing state legislators and congressmen in Kansas, Nebraska, and South Dakota. Many farm activists reasoned that if such results could be secured in the absence of effective party machinery, the possibilities for a well-organized third party seemed limitless.

The People's Party, founded in February 1892, held its first

"... MONOPOLY IS THE MASTER"

The Populist leader Mary K. Lease held crowds of midwestern and southern farmers spellbound with her fiery oratory. In this selection from one of her many 1890 speeches to large audiences of Kansas farmers, Lease attacked the eastern moneyed interests, whom she accuses of dominating the lives of southern and western farmers.

THIS IS A nation of inconsistencies. The Puritans fleeing from oppression became oppressors. We fought England for our liberty and put chains on four million of blacks. We wiped out slavery and our tariff laws and national banks began a system of white wage slavery worse than the first.

Wall Street owns the country. It is no longer a government of the people, by the people, and for the people, but a government of Wall Street, by Wall Street, and for Wall Street.

The great common people of this country are slaves, and monopoly is the master. The West and South are bound and prostrate before the manufacturing East.

Money rules, and our Vice-President is a London banker. Our laws are the output of a system which clothes rascals in robes and honesty in rags.

The [political] parties lie to us and the political speakers mislead us.... The politicians said we suffered from overproduction. Overproduction, when 10,000 little children, so statistics tell us, starve to death every year in the United States, and over 100,000 shopgirls in New York are forced to sell their virtue for the bread their niggardly wages deny them....

We will stand by our homes and stay by our fireside by force if necessary, and we will not pay our debts to the loan-shark companies until the government pays its debts to us. The people are at bay; let the bloodhounds of money who dogged us thus far beware.

convention in July in Omaha, Nebraska. Here 1,300 delegates adopted a platform that combined a biting attack on economic and social conditions with a hopeful call to action. "We meet in the midst of a nation brought to the verge of moral, political, and material ruin," declared the preamble to the Omaha platform. "The fruits of toil of millions are boldly stolen to build up colossal fortunes for a few, unprecedented in the history of mankind; and the possessors of these, in turn, despise the Republic and endanger liberty."

The Populist Party's demands—for free coinage of silver, which would increase the amount of circulating currency (thereby aiding cash-poor farmers); a graduated income tax; government ownership of railroads and telegraph lines; and establishment of the cooperative-inspired subtreasury system—spoke most immediately to the needs of farmers. Other planks in the Populist program—direct election of U.S. senators (who were at this time still elected by state legislatures), restriction of presidents to a single term, and use of the initiative and referendum to ensure democratic participation in decision-making on major issues—had broader appeal. Finally, the call for a shorter working day and for immigration restriction represented attempts to speak to the concerns of organized labor.

Coin's Financial School. William Harvey's slim volume seemed to be everywhere in 1895. "[It] is being sold on every railroad train by the newsboys and at every cigar store," reported one congressman. Published by prosilver advocates, the book's direct prose and numerous illustrations blamed the farmer's plight on the manipulation of gold by international bankers. "Coin" Harvey's arcane conspiracy theories struck a responsive chord in many readers looking for explanations for the devastating economic depression.

WHAT IT COSTS A FARMER TO DINE AT A FIRST-CLASS CHICAGO RESTAURANT.

In the 1892 elections, the Populists garnered over one million votes and elected governors in Kansas and Colorado. Nevertheless, the electoral results failed to live up to the high hopes of the party's supporters. Urban workers did not vote for the People's Party, despite massive efforts to bring them into a farmer-labor alliance. Furthermore, the party remained virtually unknown in much of the nation in 1892.

Helped by the 1893 depression, the Populist vote in the 1894 election increased by one-half over 1892, passing the 1.5 million mark. As a result, the party had to be taken seriously: the Democrats, in order to win back their supporters, began selectively to endorse parts of the Populist program.

By 1894, it had become clear to Populist leaders that their movement had reached its maximum strength in the countryside; if the party was to push forward, it would have to find ways of attracting urban working people. The potential power of a farmer-labor alliance was central to the producer ideology of the Gilded Age's reform milieu, but AFL leaders did not give it much support. Samuel Gompers dismissed working-class efforts to ally with the People's Party as "unnatural," explaining that "composed, as the People's Party is, mainly of *employing* farmers without any regard to the interests of the *employed* farmers of the country districts or the mechanics and laborers of the industrial centers, there must of necessity be a divergence of purposes, methods, and interests."

But however logical Gompers's position might have been, it was contradicted by political experience. Workers in the mountain West who supported Populist candidates in large numbers in 1892 had little cause for regret. Colorado, where miners helped put Populist Davis Waite in the governor's mansion, rapidly became one of the most prolabor states in the nation. Waite sent in the state militia to protect miners from their employers' private army in an 1894 strike, publicly supported the Pullman strike, and defended the rights of Coxey's followers to make their way across the state.

In the November 1894 elections, proponents of the farmer-labor alliance focused their attention on Illinois. Here leaders of the Chicago labor movement and the state's agrarian activists sought to overcome their ideological differences and launch a united movement. With the intellectual reformer Henry Demarest Lloyd pointing the way and trade unionists embracing the cause, the Illinois movement hoped for a substantial victory.

On election day many Illinois coalminers and railroad workers did indeed follow their union leaders in voting Populist. But many other urban workers cast their lot with a party that appealed directly to their narrow economic interest and their ethnic loyalties. Republicans, not Populists, fared best in the "distinctively workingmen's districts." Proclaiming "a full dinner pail" for all, the party won over many workingmen to the notion of a protective tariff on foreign goods as the key to renewed prosperity. This was an acute reminder that a farmer-labor coalition was always a fragile entity and that political reform could easily take a backseat to the lure of a quick economic fix.

The story was much the same in other parts of the nation. In some areas—Milwaukee, the Ohio Valley coal communities, and in the Irish Catholic mining regions of the West—Populists succeeded in turning working-class disgust with the Democrats into votes for the People's Party. But the Republicans were the decisive winners among workers. In the biggest victory in the history of Congress, the Republicans gained 117 seats. In New England and the Midwest the Democrats were overwhelmed; they even lost ground in the South. The 1894 elections broke through the deadlock of two-party competition and stalemate that had dominated American politics since the close of the Civil War. The Republicans became the clear-cut majority party.

At the AFL's convention in Denver one month later, these Republican victories set the stage for a crucial debate over the political course of the AFL. For a year prior to the convention, socialist trade unionists led by Socialist Labor Party member and Chicago Populist Thomas J. Morgan had canvassed the national unions affiliated with the AFL on behalf of a broad program of independent farmer-labor action and social and political reform. The socialists' program, which was based on the platform of the British Independent Labour Party, called for compulsory education; inspection of mines and factories; abolition of sweatshops; municipal ownership of streetcar systems and gas and electric utilities; nationalization of telegraphs, telephones, railroads, and mines; and collective ownership by all the people of all means of production.

Many trade unionists—the mineworkers, cigarmakers, tailors, brewery workers, painters, electrical workers, and machinists—responded favorably to the socialists' program. But at the AFL convention in Denver in December 1894, Morgan and his allies were outmaneuvered. While the delegates did embrace most of the socialist platform, Gompers and his allies were able to prevent ratification of two crucial planks: the call for social ownership of the means of production (socialism), and outright endorsement of independent political action.

To defeat these two planks, Gompers forged an alliance with "racketeers" such as William Columbus Pomeroy (well known for extracting "subsidies" from the Republicans and the Democrats) and conservative business unionists. The socialists retaliated against

"The Supreme Court—as It May Hereafter Be Constituted." *Puck* presents an unabashedly cosmopolitan view of how the Supreme Court might appear if the Populists won the 1896 election. "Gold Bugs and Millionaires" huddle in a "waiting pen," their fate in the hands of nine justices who collectively embody the rustic "old geezer" stereotype: sporting unkempt goatees, their dress severe but informal, their behavior unsophisticated in its lack of ceremony.

Gompers by denying him reelection to the AFL presidency, the only break in his nearly forty-year tenure as the leader of the AFL.

Thus, while the Denver AFL convention demonstrated the depth of worker disenchantment with the industrial order, it did not further the cause of the most potent challenger to that order: independent political action in the form of Populism. But the biggest blow to the People's Party was yet to come. With the 1896 elections approaching and the Democratic Party facing almost certain defeat, its rank and file moved to adopt as their own one of the most appealing planks in the Populist platform: free silver.

Free silver was only one aspect of the Populists' program. At the 1892 Omaha convention, delegates had given the demand for government ownership of the railroads much heartier approval than that for free silver. Still, prosilver sentiment ran deep in the country at large. Especially after the Panic of 1893 and the sharp deflation that followed, Populists emphasized this issue as a way of attracting support among western silver miners and credit-starved farmers unattracted by other aspects of their program.

This emphasis on silver, however, proved to be the Populists' undoing. In their party convention of 1896, Republicans nominated

Ohio governor William McKinley and held fast to their hard-money theories, which linked the dollar's worth to a rigid gold standard. Democrats, however, confounded all predictions by endorsing the unlimited coinage of silver and nominating a young Nebraska journalist, William Jennings Bryan, as their presidential candidate. Bryan lashed out at the Republican advocates of hard money, declaring, "You shall not crucify mankind upon a cross of gold."

The Populist movement now literally tore itself apart on the issue of whether to endorse "fusion" with Bryan and the Democrats or maintain political independence. In the end the former road was chosen, and Bryan received the official nomination of the People's Party. Although some Populist leaders, such as Henry Demarest Lloyd, vigorously dissented from this wholesale desertion of the broad reform program enshrined in the Omaha platform, there was little they could do in the face of fusion sentiment.

Despite the fervor of the campaign, which one commentator said "took the form of religious frenzy," McKinley overwhelmed Bryan. The Republican's margin of victory was the most lopsided in twenty-five years.

Though the People's Party lived on for twelve years after 1896, it put its worst face forward to the public, lapsing into vile racism and supporting the movement to take the vote away from African-Americans. Populism as a force in American life, and as an attractive possibility for workers, was dead. With its demise, an alliance of the producing classes of town and country was tarnished for a generation and more.

NATIVISM, RACISM, AND THE DECLINE OF PRODUCER IDEOLOGY

The election of 1896 marked not only the end of Populism but also the emergence of Republican domination of American politics. Much of the support for the Republicans came from urban working people attracted to the party's promise to protect American goods and jobs from foreign competition by imposing high duties or tariffs on imports. By promising to ease unemployment, the Republican tariff policies gained popularity during the crisis of the 1890s. But there was a second factor solidifying working-class support for this established party of American capital: Republicans exploited nativist sentiments that reappeared in the aftermath of the labor upheavals of the 1880s, and fed on the fear of foreign-born radicals. Shortly after the Haymarket affair, the American Party was organized in California. The state's businessmen were disturbed by the important role that Irish-Americans, like San Francisco's building trades president Patrick McCarthy, played in its labor movement, and their American Party sought sweeping immigration restriction, a tightening of requirements for citizenship, and a ban on the "alien" ownership of property. Outside California, however, the party was not effective in converting Republicans to its cause.

Labor organizations had also been advocates of restriction, especially in California and on the Pacific Coast, where the anti-Chinese movement had grown quite strong in the mid-1880s, building on white workers' fears of competition from Chinese immigrants for jobs. Labor organizations, including the AFL, actively lobbied for extending the Chinese Exclusion Act, originally passed in 1882, when it came up for congressional renewal in 1892. In general, however, sentiment for immigration restriction was at least as widespread among employers as in labor unions in these years. Though industrialists sought a cheap and steady labor supply, their desires were more than counterbalanced by their belief that immigrants were a source of labor strife, violence, and radicalism. The New York *Tribune* called "Huns" (Hungarians) the most dangerous of labor unionists and strikers: "They fill up with liquor and cannot be reasoned with." When immigrant strikers killed Henry Clay Frick's chief engineer in 1894, the Pittsburgh *Times* reported the region "trembling on the brink of an insurrection. Never before were the dangerous foreigners so thoroughly aroused."

As the 1893 depression deepened, however, some workers, searching for an explanation for the sudden sharp drop in their economic fortunes, embraced nativist ideas. This was particularly true of workers of U.S. birth or older immigrant origins. As conditions worsened, incidents multiplied. Italians, who were just beginning to appear in large numbers in the workforce, were often scapegoats for workers' anger: striking miners in Colorado massacred six Italian workers implicated in the death of a saloonkeeper in 1895; in Wheeling, West Virginia, miners struck when their employer refused to fire two Italians; and Detroit workers threatened to "chase the Dagos back to Italy."

Such attacks were based on more than economic insecurity and ethnic prejudice; they also stemmed from a revived fear of the growing power of the Catholic Church in America. Anti-Catholicism became an organized force with the formation of the American Protective Association (APA). With the Panic of 1893 and the general social crisis that the depression ushered in, the APA grew substantially. It attracted many supporters among skilled workers and small businessmen in the Mississippi River valley and in the Rocky Mountain region.

Reaching a peak of about half a million members in 1894, the APA declined steadily thereafter. But the nativist cause now found a new and more respectable home in an organization known as the Immigration Restriction League. The upper-class Boston intellectuals who formed the league left a lasting imprint on the immigration debate by drawing a line between "old" and "new" foreigners. To do this they advanced the notion of a racial gulf between the old-stock Anglo-Saxons (political reality forced them to include the Irish in this group) and the newest immigrants from southern and eastern Europe. Although the distinction was entirely without substance, it became the linchpin of the anti-immigration crusade.

The Immigration Restriction League hit upon the idea of a literacy test to curb immigration. All immigrants would have to demonstrate an ability to read and write their native language to be allowed admission into the country. Although this approach was not perfect (e.g., Polish and Russian Jews—a leading new immigrant group—had high rates of literacy), the test would generally work against unlettered peasants from eastern and southern Europe. The strategy paid political dividends. Republicans demanded laws that excluded those who could not pass a literacy test, and the party's 1896 platform justified such restrictive practices on the grounds that they would protect American "citizenship" and "the wages of our workingmen against the fatal competition of low-price labor."

Urban working people—particularly Protestants in small and medium-size midwestern cities—gave the Republican Party unprecedented support. This support was due in part to the fact that workers tended to blame the depression on President Cleveland and the Democrats; it also had to do with the Republican claim that a high protective tariff would ease the unemployment situation. But when Republicans added immigration restriction to their program, the final tumbler fell into place: they won over a great portion of the white working class, those Protestant skilled workers who were increasingly alienated from a northern Democratic Party dominated by immigrant, Catholic, and unskilled workers.

Nativism thus played an important role in shaping the victory of the Republican Party. Ironically, racism played a similar role in enhancing the Democrats' strength in the South. Though reduced to the status of a minority party at the national level, by the end of the 1890s southern Democrats had effectively defused the Republican and the even more ominous Populist threats in their region. By 1900, the South was, as people said, "solid"—meaning solidly Democratic. The ideology of racism and a policy of racial disfranchisement and segregation played important roles in assuring this outcome.

The belief in the racial inferiority of African-Americans had a long history in the South. But segregation of blacks and whites in social life had never been a prominent feature of southern life under slavery, although it was informally practiced with rigor in many northern communities such as New York City. When industialization introduced new social, political, and economic relations in the South after the demise of Reconstruction, formal segregation of public facilities began in southern cities. Segregation helped employers cement control over a restless and incompletely formed industrial workforce, offering white workers privileges denied African-Americans.

There was also a political purpose to segregation. "Jim Crow," as the system was called, was intended to disfranchise African-Americans. For all the social and economic setbacks that had accompanied the end of Reconstruction in the 1870s, blacks had still been able to participate in politics in many areas of the South and to win some elective offices at local, state, and even federal levels; some upper-class southern leaders continued to count on black votes to prevent potentially dangerous poor whites from exercising political power. But when small Populist farmers began to make unprecedented appeals across racial lines for the political support of black farmers, the situation changed dramatically. Now it was the southern elite of planters, industrializers, and merchants—in slightly different combinations in different states—who moved decisively to eliminate African-Americans from the political process. Nor did they stop there; they disfranchised many of the "poorer sort" of whites at the same time, the better to consolidate their power.

Beginning in Mississippi in 1890, southern governments began systematically to impose residency requirements, poll taxes, and the literacy test so highly vaunted by northern nativists. South Carolina adopted the Mississippi formula in 1895, and over the next twelve years the remaining southern states followed suit.

The destruction of voting rights was accompanied by a renewed wave of horrifying violence against black people. Between 1890 and 1900, an average

"... OUR CONDITION IS PRECARIOUS IN THE EXTREME"

The intensity of racist violence against African-Americans during the 1890s was truly astonishing. In this report printed in Philadelphia's Christian Recorder on March 24, 1892, the Reverend E. Malcolm Argyle describes the situation in Arkansas and cries out for help.

THERE IS MUCH uneasiness and unrest all over this State among our people, owing to the fact that [black] people all over the State are being lynched upon the slightest provocation.... In the last 30 days there have been not less than eight colored persons lynched in this State. At Texarkana a few days ago, a man was burnt at the stake. In Pine Bluff a few days later two men were strung up and shot.... At Varner, George Harris was taken from jail and shot for killing a white man, for poisoning his domestic happiness. At Wilmar, a boy was induced to confess to the commission of an outrage, upon promise of his liberty, and when he had confessed, he was strung up and shot. Over in Toneoke County, a whole family consisting of husband, wife and child were shot down like dogs. Verily the situation is alarming in the extreme.

At this writing 500 people are hovering upon wharves in Pine Bluff, awaiting the steamers to take them up the Arkansas River to Oklahoma.... What is the outcome of all this? It is evident that the white people of the South have no further use for the Negro. He is being worse treated now, than at any other time, since the [Confederate] surrender. The white press of the South seems to be subsidized by this lawless element, the white pulpits seem to condone lynching.... The Northern press seems to care little about the condition of the Negroes [in the] South. The pulpits of the North are passive. Will not some who are not in danger of their lives, speak out against the tyrannical South ... speak out against these lynchings and mob violence? For God's sake, say or do something, for our condition is precarious in the extreme.

"THE COLORED CITIZENS DESIRE . . . THAT SOME ACTION BE TAKEN"

Memphis, Tennessee, newspaper editor Ida Wells-Barnett was the leader in the national effort to get the federal government to stop lynchings of African-Americans. Born into slavery in Mississippi in 1862, Wells-Barnett became part owner and editor of the Memphis Free Speech, *an outspoken advocate for the area's African-American citizens, in the late 1880s. A brutal lynching of three young African-American businessmen in 1892 launched Wells-Barnett's national antilynching crusade. Despite her unstinting efforts, she never succeeded in securing a federal antilynching law before her death in 1931.*

In the following 1898 petition to President William McKinley, Wells-Barnett, accompanied by the Chicago delegation of Illinois congressmen, protested the lynching of a South Carolina African-American postmaster. The federal government took no action.

MR. PRESIDENT, THE colored citizens of this country in general, and Chicago in particular, desire to respectfully urge that some action be taken by you as chief magistrate of this great nation, first for the apprehension and punishment of the lynchers of Postmaster Baker, of Lake City, S.C.; second, we ask indemnity for the widow and children, both for the murder of the husband and father, and for injuries sustained by themselves; third, we most earnestly desire that national legislation be enacted for the suppression of the national crime of lynching.

For nearly twenty years lynching crimes, which stand side by side with Armenian and Cuban outrages, have been committed and permitted by this Christian nation. Nowhere in the civilized world save the United States of America do men, possessing all civil and political power, go out in bands of 50 and 5,000 to hunt down, shoot, hang or burn to death a single individual, unarmed and absolutely powerless. Statistics show that nearly 10,000 American citizens have been lynched in the past 20 years. To our appeals for justice the stereotyped reply has been that the government could not interfere in a state matter. Postmaster Baker's case was a federal matter, pure and simple. He died at his post of duty in defense of his country's honor, as truly as did ever a soldier on the field of battle. We refuse to believe this country, so powerful to defend its citizens abroad, is unable to protect its citizens at home. Italy and China have been indemnified by this government for the lynching of their citizens. We ask that the government do as much for its own.

of over 175 African-Americans were lynched every year in the South for violating the "rules" of the new order. African-Americans fought courageously against this wave of violence, organizing a national antilynching movement through letters, petitions, and the creation of the Antilynching Bureau under the leadership of Ida B. Wells-Barnett. But these valiant efforts were to no avail. A decade of racist violence was capped by a brutal riot in 1898 in Wilmington, North Carolina, where rampaging whites killed eleven blacks and injured many others.

By the end of the decade northern political and business leaders were more prepared than ever to acquiesce in these developments. As late as 1889, Republican leaders such as Henry Cabot Lodge had still sought to use federal power to guarantee African-American voting rights —black votes were still deemed necessary to the survival of the GOP in the South. With the sweeping Republican victory of 1896, however, that pressure was removed. Few protests against the "color line" would be raised in the later 1890s. The die was cast when the U.S. Supreme Court upheld the South's introduction of formal segregation in its famous 1896 decision in *Plessy* v. *Ferguson*. The Court enshrined as law the position that "separate but equal" public facilities were constitutional. The ruling would remain law until 1954.

Under these circumstances, little room remained for blacks to exercise the political rights won nearly three decades earlier with the passage of the Fourteenth and Fifteenth amendments to the Constitution, guaranteeing citizenship and the right to vote. The Republican Party, a channel of political activity for African-Americans for three decades, was now effectively closed to them, and the limited openings that the People's Party had provided were shut tightly after the Populists' 1896 electoral defeat and retreat into racism.

END OF A CENTURY; END OF AN ERA

"The North Carolina Race War," By the Mayor of Wilmington

COLLIER'S WEEKLY

A SCENE IN THE RACE DISTURBANCE AT WILMINGTON, N. C.

"The North Carolina Race War." Many national periodicals expressed little sympathy toward African-American victims of the 1898 Wilmington riot. In a fashion reminiscent of "Redemptionist" arguments at the close of Reconstruction, commentators claimed that the "misrule" of corrupt black Wilmington officials had brought the violence upon themselves. The illustration of gun-toting terrorists appearing on the cover of Collier's Weekly only bolstered popular misconceptions about black aggression.

Class conflict defined the final two decades of the nineteenth century as working people confronted, with extraordinary creativity, the profound changes wrought by industrial capitalism. The first truly national working-class movement emerged in these years out of the militant protests and oppositional ideas of workers and farmers across the country. In creating a culture of resistance, the late-nineteenth-century labor movement rejected not only capitalists' growing control over the nation's economic and political life but also the twin ideologies of acquisitive individualism and Social Darwinism that served to justify that control. While the movement's programs were eclectic, its philosophies diverse, and its outright victories few, it nonetheless succeeded in galvanizing millions with an alternative vision of industrial America.

But the bitter defeats suffered by the Knights of Labor in 1886, by the Homestead workers in 1892, by the Pullman workers and coalminers in 1894, and by the Populists in 1896 eroded the power of this alternative vision and marked the end of an era. As a result, many working people in cities and the countryside retreated into insular cultures that included strong elements of racism and nativism. The nineteenth century closed with the labor and agrarian movements fragmented and their broad, organizing efforts defeated.

There was some hope for the labor movement as the century ended. The post-1896 growth of socialism beyond isolated communities of immigrants and native-born radicals indicated that oppositional ideas retained some resiliency. And the craft unions that made up the American Federation of Labor came out of the depression of the 1890s largely intact, a significant improvement over the record of earlier labor organizations. As the U.S. economy stood poised to rebound after 1898, so too did the craft unions and the socialists.

But the bitter defeats of the 1880s and 1890s left permanent scars. The United States would never again witness such a broad or fundamental challenge by working people to the claims of capital. Racial, nationality, gender, skill, and ideological divisions came to define the labor movement after 1900, displacing the working-class unity that had characterized the earlier movement. Though the labor wars continued and the nation's leaders began to express concern over the growing conflict, capitalists stood primed as the new century dawned to take full advantage of the widening divisions in labor's ranks.

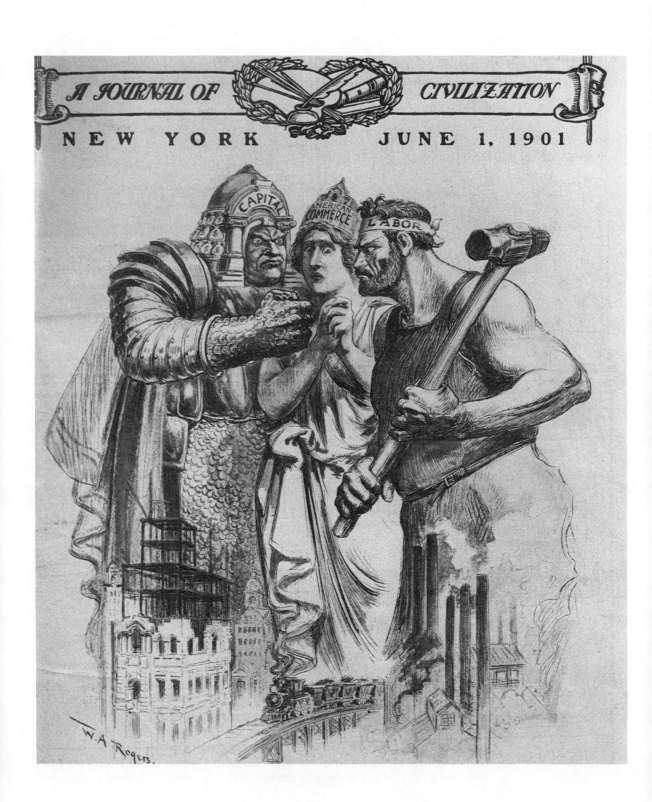

4

WORKING PEOPLE AND REFORM

"Come, brothers, you have grown so big you cannot afford to quarrel." William A. Rogers depicts Capital and Labor as evenly matched—with American Commerce a beleaguered referee—on a 1901 cover of *Harper's Weekly*. Variations on this theme frequently appeared in the Progressive Era's mainstream press. Commerce alternated with other allegorical figures such as the "nation" or the "public," suggesting that organized labor now represented a powerful "interest," equal to capital and equally oblivious to how its actions affected the well-being of ordinary Americans.

AS THE twentieth century began, many Americans believed a new age was dawning. To an extent, they were right. The very look, feel, and pace of American life were undergoing dramatic transformations as telegraphs, telephones, electricity, and automobiles became more common. In the cities, ever-taller office buildings, steam heating, subways, and motion pictures were part of a seemingly endless stream of new technical marvels. Overhead flew the first, crude airplanes.

The most basic change was not in the material fabric of everyday life, however, but in the nation's economic and social organization. Corporate enterprise had grown rapidly since the Civil War; by the turn of the century its dominance was no longer in question.

After the bitter defeats of the Homestead and Pullman strikes and the demise of the Populists' broad democratic vision, few realistically believed any longer in the nineteenth-century republican ideal of a nation of equal citizens, one made up of small, independent producers. Even the most ardent critics of industrial capitalism now recognized that the large-scale production and distribution of goods had rendered obsolete these older social ideals.

But industrial capitalism's triumph brought neither social harmony nor political consensus. The chasm that divided social classes grew ever larger. "We assemble thousands of operatives in the factory, and in the mine," lamented Andrew Carnegie in 1900, "of whom the employer can know little or nothing, and to whom he is little better than a myth. Rigid castes are formed, and, as usual, mutual ignorance breeds mutual distrust. . . . Often there is friction between the employer and the employed, between labor and capital, between rich and poor."

During the first decades of the new century, the friction between labor and capital at times approached the level of full-scale war. But industrial conflict was hardly a new problem, nor was it the only one that worried Americans. In the cities, huge numbers of new immigrants clustered in miserable ghettos. They were mostly poor, often unhealthy, and, in the eyes of some, a threat to the established order. At the same time, political and economic corruption was rife, continuing largely unchecked since the Gilded Age. Even corporate giants that loomed over society, such as Standard Oil and U.S. Steel, faced difficulties: continued competition cut into their profits, while their labor policies, often shoddy products, and immense power fed a growing chorus of public criticism. That criticism, along with continued fears of class conflict, would finally crystallize in a movement for political, economic, and social reform called Progressivism.

In an era of enormous and disquieting change, a single event sometimes focuses attention on the very real human costs of economic and political transformation and comes to symbolize the need for reform. One such event occurred on the warm spring afternoon of March 25, 1911. A small fire broke out in a bin of rags in one of the many crowded garment factories on New York City's Lower East Side. In less than an hour 146 people—most of them young Italian or Jewish women who had recently arrived in America—died from asphyxiation or, fleeing the flames, jumped ten stories to their deaths. The victims had been trapped by blocked exit doors and faulty fire escapes. The fire at the Triangle Shirtwaist Company—one of the worst industrial fires in the nation's history—horrified Americans of all classes and became a galvanizing symbol of industrial capitalism's excesses and the pressing need for reform.

The Triangle tragedy brought together New York's middle-class reformers and working people, including survivors of the fire. That coalition demanded and won the creation of a state commission to inquire into unsafe factory conditions; it also ultimately secured passage of landmark laws to protect the health and safety of New York workers. Such local events and personal tragedies as the Triangle fire helped convince Americans everywhere of the need for laws to regulate industrial capitalism.

The call for factory reform was part of a broader movement that had emerged around the turn of the century to address the social, economic, and cultural problems engendered by capitalism's dramatic growth. This movement gave birth to what historians have labeled the "Progressive Era," the period between 1900 and the outbreak of World War I. But scholars have been unable to agree on exactly what Progressivism was. In fact, Progressivism encompassed many distinct, overlapping, and sometimes contradictory movements: it was working people battling for better pay and control over their working lives; it was women campaigning for more equality and the right to vote at the same time as African-Americans were being disfranchised in the South; it was corporations and their allies pushing to make city governments more businesslike; it was middle-class reformers closing saloons by prohibiting the sale of alcohol; and it was politicians and presidents extending the power of the government to "bust trusts" and regulate corporate activity. Sometimes these various reform forces worked together, sometimes they fought each other. Each responded in some way to the profound economic and social changes of the Gilded Age, but they differed in their interpretation of problems and solutions. As coalitions shifted, these diverse campaigns laid the foundation of modern American politics.

THE SEARCH FOR NEW MARKETS

One of the hallmarks of the new era was American expansion overseas. For most of its history, U.S. political and military activities had focused primarily on North America. Although expansion involved military conflict, including the Indian wars and the 1840s war with Mexico, these conflicts took place within the limits of the North American continent. But as the nineteenth century ended and the western frontier was officially declared "closed," the United States began increasingly to involve itself in world affairs. Driven, in many ways, by economic needs, this overseas expansion would have broad social and political consequences in the twentieth century.

The U.S. interest in expanding its international influence was sparked in part by the example of the leading European nations. In the late nineteenth century, Britain, France, and Germany carved out large colonial empires in Asia and Africa. These overseas empires augmented the colonizing nations' political and military clout and gave their businesses special investment and marketing opportunities.

As the American economy struggled out of the depression of the early 1890s, American business leaders, inspired by Europe's example, hoped that overseas markets might absorb the nation's surplus production. U.S. farmers also argued for seeking foreign markets in which to sell the nation's substantial agricultural surplus. Economic considerations such as these encouraged political leaders to seek overseas expansion.

The class conflict of the 1890s had also spurred politicians and religious leaders to voice a strident nationalism, and this too prompted America's entry into overseas adventures. Patriotism, once linked to egalitarian notions of republican virtue, grew more aggressive and jingoistic. The 1890s saw the emergence of organizations such as the Daughters of the American Revolution as well as a new cult of the American flag. Schools began requiring students to salute the flag each morning. Furthermore, some conservatives saw war—which they believed to be the highest form of patriotism—as a way of calming the turmoil of the depression years. According to a Kansas newspaper, war "would clear the atmosphere and stamp out the growth of socialism and anarchy, discontent and sectional prejudices that are gaining a foothold in this nation."

In April 1898, the United States entered its first overseas

"TAKE UP THE WHITE MAN'S BURDEN . . ."

In 1899, the British novelist and poet Rudyard Kipling wrote a poem titled "The White Man's Burden: The United States and The Philippine Islands," which urged the United States to take up the "burden" of empire, as had Britain and other European nations. Theodore Roosevelt, soon to become vice president and then president, copied the poem and sent it to his friend Senator Henry Cabot Lodge, commenting that it was "rather poor poetry, but good sense from the expansion point of view."

Take up the White Man's burden—
  Send forth the best ye breed—
Go send your sons to exile
  To serve your captives' need
To wait in heavy harness
  On fluttered folk and wild—
Your new-caught, sullen peoples,
  Half devil and half child

Take up the White Man's burden
  In patience to abide
To veil the threat of terror
  And check the show of pride;
By open speech and simple
  An hundred times made plain
To seek another's profit
  And work another's gain

Take up the White Man's burden—
  And reap his old reward:
The blame of those ye better
  The hate of those ye guard—
The cry of hosts ye humour
  (Ah slowly) to the light:—
"Why brought ye us from bondage,
  Our loved Egyptian night?"

Take up the White Man's burden—
  Have done with childish days—
The lightly proffered laurel,
  The easy, ungrudged praise.
Comes now, to search your manhood
  Through all the thankless years,
Cold-edged with dear-bought wisdom,
  The judgment of your peers!

"The Spanish Brute Adds Mutilation to Murder." Grant Hamilton's bestial Spaniard, bespattered in American blood, typifies how the U.S. press sensationalized news coverage and exploited patriotic sentiments to support U.S. intervention in Cuba.

war. The immediate issue was Cuba, just ninety miles off the coast of Florida. As Cuban guerrillas fought to free their island from Spanish colonial rule, they aroused popular sympathy in the United States. Popular support for war was fed by sensationalized (and sometimes falsified) newspaper reports and an unexplained explosion aboard the U.S. Navy's battleship *Maine* as it lay anchored in Havana Harbor. When Congress declared war on Spain and vowed to guarantee Cuban independence, the public reaction was enthusiastic.

The war in Cuba was brief. Only ten weeks of fighting were needed before the Spanish power was broken. A young assistant secretary of the navy, Theodore Roosevelt, gained fame by quitting his job and leading a group of cavalry volunteers known as the Rough Riders. Lesser known but equally important were the many African-American soldiers, including the highly decorated Ninth and Tenth cavalries.

Much of the war was actually fought in the Philippine Islands, Spain's colony in the Pacific Ocean. The U.S. Navy sailed into Manila Bay before any action was taken in Cuba. At first, U.S. troops met a warm welcome from the Filipinos, who also were battling Spanish rule. Filipino guerrillas even captured Manila for their American "allies." But once Spain was beaten, the United States asserted its right to control the Philippines. President William McKinley declared that he considered it appropriate to use "every legitimate means for the enlargement of American trade."

As it became clear that the United States intended to rule the Philippines as a colony, guerrilla leader Emilio Aguinaldo took to the hills in an effort to drive the Americans out. It took 63,000 U.S. troops and three years of brutal fighting to suppress the independence movement. U.S. troops killed 14,000 Filipinos in the first year of the war alone. Racism heightened the war's brutality. Reports came back to the United States that "picking off niggers [Filipinos] in the water" was "more fun than a turkey shoot."

As war dragged on, Congress debated whether to annex the Philippines. Presidential adviser Mark Hanna explained that annexation would allow the United States to "take a large slice of the commerce of Asia. . . . We are bound to share in the commerce of the Far East and it is better to strike for it while the iron is hot." Congress approved annexation of the Philippines and, for good measure, grabbed another former Spanish possession, the Caribbean island of Puerto Rico. Like Filipinos, Puerto Ricans were given little voice in this decision that profoundly shaped their future.

Some Americans opposed efforts to establish United States dominance abroad. Labor leaders such as Eugene Debs and Samuel Gompers joined Democratic politician William Jennings Bryan in denouncing American annexation of the Philippines. Mark Twain turned his scathing wit on America's betrayal of its earlier support for independence struggles: "As for a flag for the Philippine Province, it is easily managed. We can have a special one . . . our usual flag, with the white stripes painted black and the stars and stripes replaced by a skull and crossbones."

Opponents of America's imperial aspirations were few compared to the businessmen, farmers, and urban working people who felt that

"THE AMERICAN INVASION RAISED GREAT HOPES IN OUR BREASTS . . ."

In 1898 the United States took control of the Caribbean island of Puerto Rico, intending to use it as a base for strategic naval operations. Most of the island's 900,000 inhabitants (descendants of the Arawak and Carib peoples, enslaved Africans, and Spanish colonists) welcomed the end of Spanish rule. But they were divided about the U.S. presence. Some hoped links with the United States would lead to increased trade and prosperity; others wanted total independence. Some who initially welcomed the United States became disillusioned. In 1899, a group of cigarmakers from the town of Cayey wrote: "The American invasion raised great hopes in our breasts. We thought that by belonging to a nation of such progressive instincts that the condition of the honest laborer would change, but up to the present this has not been the case."

Under Spain, Puerto Rico's economy had been almost entirely agricultural, divided between medium-sized sugar and coffee estates and small, independent farms. The invasion of U.S. capital after 1898 prompted the growth of huge estates, some of them owned by U.S. investors. Small farmers had difficulty competing with these large estates; many had to sell their land. Some joined the existing class of field laborers, or peons; others tried to learn manufacturing trades. This process eventually spurred a series of bitter revolts by field laborers. It also led many Puerto Ricans to migrate, first to the island's cities, such as San Juan, and eventually to the United States.

In 1899, Severo Tulier, a small farmer from Vega Baja, had to sell his farm; he worked first as a field laborer, and then moved to San Juan to learn a trade. He described the conditions of life among farmworkers to Henry K. Carroll, the special commissioner for the United States to Puerto Rico, who interviewed hundreds of Puerto Ricans as part of his effort to formulate U.S. policy for governing the island.

TULIER: The usual rate [of wages] is 25 centavos and breakfast, and 37 ½ centavos to the better class of workmen. A few laborers who have some special skill receive as high as 50 centavos a day, but it should be borne in mind that where 50 centavos is paid, payment is made in vales, which are mere tokens . . . redeemable at the company's store. . . .

The customary hours of work are from six to six; that is, for work in the field.

the United States had the right and duty to extend its influence. As he justified the drive for empire, Senator Albert Beveridge of Indiana blended the desire for economic gain with an appeal to the near-religious themes of "Manifest Destiny." "Shall the American people continue their march toward commercial supremacy of the world? Shall free institutions broaden their blessed reign as the children of liberty wax in strength, until the empire of our principles is estab-lished over the hearts of all mankind?" Ohio ironworker and trade unionist Michael Mc-Govern wrote a poem in 1899 that expressed the patriotism and masculine bravado that led many workingmen to support America's overseas expansion:

You wealthy ones, who fear to
  fight
Make room for those who dare,
Consign the flag—now
  threatened—to
The fighting workingmen's
  care.

With the support of many Americans, businessmen and government leaders soon settled on a policy of aggressively pursuing economic expansion while generally avoiding the explicit colonization that characterized European empires. In Latin America this policy was carried out with a heavy hand. Theodore Roosevelt, who became president in 1901 following Mc-Kinley's assassination, argued that the U.S. government should exercise what he called "international police power" in the Western Hemisphere. In 1898, the United States pledged to guarantee Cuban independence, but after the war ended the United States refused to with-

For work in the shops and on the sugar machinery, they have to go earlier, sometimes as early as 4 o'clock in the morning. . . .

CARROLL: What do they have to eat in the evenings?

TULIER: The basis of their evening meal is a big plantain, which they sometimes make into a mess with rice and beans. . . . They have meat only on Sundays. . . . Their food improves a little during the corn season, as that forms an addition to the daily diet. Their three chief articles of food, it may be said, are sweet potatoes, plantains, and corn. . . .

CARROLL: What about their houses?

TULIER: The house is made of poles, thatched about with palm, and about 4 or 5 varas square [a vara is about 33 inches] partitioned off into a parlor, a bed-room and a kitchen. . . . The kitchen has no flooring, and the parlor and bed-room flooring is badly laid. Frequently the house lets in the rain. . . . Their wardrobe consists of two changes—one that is being worn and the other that is being washed. . . . The children, as a rule, have only one shirt, and while the mother is washing that one they must run about without any cloth-ing. . . .

The number of [infant] deaths caused from want of medical assistance is not considerable, because the women lead a free, out-of-door life, but owing to want of proper nourishing food, a great many [infants] succumb from weak-ness. . . . The poor people are absolutely in want of medical assistance in the country places, and if they go to the village to obtain medical aid they can only do so through the charity of the doctors, as they are not able to pay for such services. . . .

Usually about five persons live in a house of the kind I have described. They all sleep together—father, mother, grown-up sons and daughters—and when they haven't sufficient beds, they sleep on piles of palm leaves. . . .

The peasant is naturally intelligent, and his mind is as fertile as the land which he works and is only waiting the implements of education. As a proof of this I will cite an instance. When it was known that autonomy was to be granted and that suffrage was limited to men of 25 years of age who knew how to read and write, I formed a class in my district and offered to teach free all men of that age and over, to fit them to vote. I had men in the class whose ages ranged from 25 to 60 years, and some of them after a few lessons knew the letters of the alphabet at sight and could write them. This was done without the aid of any modern appliances used in teaching, a piece of rough board and chalk being the only materials at hand. . . . The desire of everybody to learn was manifest.

"Benevolent assimilation." American troops guard nationalist prisoners, captured in Pasay and Paranque, during the Filipino-American War.

draw its troops, reserving the right to intervene in Cuba whenever it felt that order was not being maintained. U.S. troops were sent to Cuba in 1906, 1912, and 1917 to prop up governments sympathetic to American business interests.

The U.S. government similarly asserted its power in 1902, when the legislature of Colombia rejected a proposed treaty giving the United States the right to build a canal across the northern part of their country. The U.S. government conspired with a group of Colombian businessmen and politicians who suddenly declared northern Colombia to be an independent country, Panama. Immediately, Panamanian leaders gave the United States the canal rights it sought; construction soon began, and the Panama Canal was opened in 1914.

Backed by this government muscle, U.S. corporations increased their activity in South and Central America. Exports to Latin America more than doubled between 1900 and 1914, helping to answer American industrialists' call for new markets. U.S. corporations treated Latin America as their private preserve and sought to limit competition from European capitalists anxious to penetrate new international markets. Elsewhere, the United States could not pursue such a bold policy. In Asia, European powers already had extensive economic interests, having set up colonies or exercised strong influence over local governments. The United States thus advocated an "Open Door" policy in Asia, arguing that all industrialized nations should be given equal economic access, hoping in this way to gain new markets and raw materials in areas where other nations already dominated.

Access to foreign markets was only one goal of American international economic activity. In fact, American investment abroad increased much faster than exports. Direct U.S. investment in Latin

America was particularly significant. The United Fruit Company owned more than a million acres of land in Central America by 1913, where it grew bananas for the U.S. market. It also owned railroad lines throughout Central America, controlled the docks and communications network of Guatemala, and ran a fleet of merchant ships. American businessmen controlled more than 40 percent of Mexican property and more than half of its oil production before a revolution made such foreign control illegal. By 1914, American businessmen had more than $3.5 billion invested in other countries, making the United States one of the four largest investor nations in the world. U.S. capitalism had truly become international.

The global expansion of the United States increased the nation's wealth, and millions of Americans benefited. Cheaper raw materials, for example, meant cheaper finished goods, while some foods, such as bananas and coffee, once luxury items, became commonplace in the American diet. Meanwhile, U.S. influence reshaped the lives of millions of men and women in Puerto Rico, Cuba, and the Philippines. It also led the United States to become involved politically and militarily in the internal affairs of other Asian and Latin American countries—involvement that would profoundly shape the twentieth-century experience.

BIG BUSINESS AND THE REMAKING OF THE WORKING CLASS

Aided by new overseas markets and sources of supplies, America's industrial economy once again began to boom, achieving astonishing size and strength in the first decade of the new century. Employers' introduction of new technology continued to spur industrial growth. But the deepest changes were ones of scale and organization. In 1870 only a handful of factories, such as the McCormick plant in Chicago, had employed more than 500 workers. But by 1900 nearly 1,500 factories reached that size. Some had become truly gigantic. The Cambria Steel factory in Johnstown, Pennsylvania, employed nearly 20,000 people in 1909; General Electric employed 15,000 at its factory in Schenectady, New York, and 11,000 at another plant, in Lynn, Massachusetts.

As industrial production boomed, so too did the demand for industrial workers. After 1900, however, factory owners increasingly hired unskilled and semiskilled workers (including increasing numbers of women and new immigrants) instead of the skilled craftsmen who had long dominated the industrial workforce. Capitalists introdbced technologically advanced equipment to perform tasks that craftsmen used to do. Capitalists also continued to perfect the techniques, pioneered in the Gilded Age, of "scientific management," which divided up skilled tasks to maximize labor by the least-skilled

The science of repetition. With small lights attached to his arms and hands, a worker performs his job for efficiency experts. This "cyclegraph," a photograph taken by an open-shutter still camera, was invented by time-and-motion specialist Frank Gilbreth to chart workers' movements in mass-production jobs. In Gilbreth's scheme, cyclegraphs would help eliminate useless movement and turn work into a rigid arrangement of "efficient" motions.

and lowest-paid. Semiskilled workers would learn, for example, how to operate one machine, but not how to set it up, repair it, or operate similar equipment. Lacking generalized knowledge of production, semiskilled workers had less bargaining power than those they replaced.

From the owners' point of view, this strategy provided increased control over the labor force. Skilled workers, of course, saw threats to their jobs and to their fiercely defended sense of autonomy. Less-skilled workers, many of them new to industrial work, took the new jobs eagerly, though they often later rebelled against wage cuts, unsafe conditions, and dehumanizing work. As we shall see, recurring conflicts between these groups—owners, skilled workers, and less-skilled workers—would shape the industrial landscape of the Progressive Era.

Economic growth posed other challenges for businessmen. As the economy gained strength, they again confronted the Gilded Age problems of low profits and intense competition. Businessmen thus resumed efforts to merge companies and organize trade associations to reduce competition. Beginning in 1898, businessmen engaged in a frenzy of merger activity. By 1904, three hundred giant firms controlled nearly two-fifths of the manufacturing capital in the nation. As corporations grew ever larger, effective control was concentrated in fewer hands.

The biggest new combination, U.S. Steel, formed in 1901 from 150 smaller corporations, was capitalized at over $1 billion. U.S. Steel was so large, it could dictate prices; competition in the steel industry virtually disappeared. At the same time, following Carnegie's earlier example, U.S. Steel was "vertically integrated," making the giant corporation invulnerable to suppliers' price increases and labor problems.

Some attempts at combination failed. Although General Electric and Goodyear ultimately became household words, U.S. Leather and United Button did not survive. In industries that did not require large investments in expensive machinery, new competitors could more readily emerge and challenge the trusts. Other parts of the economy remained highly competitive, with thousands of firms battling for a slice of the market. The leather, printing, clothing, and construction industries conformed to this latter pattern.

By 1910, there were two distinct economic sectors. Small firms competed feverishly in industries that did not require heavy capital investment. But very large corporations dominated capital-intensive industries. The problem of how to deal with these huge concentra-

Eat, drink, and be merry. The managers of the nation's competing steel companies gather together in 1901 to celebrate their merger into the giant U.S. Steel Corporation.

tions of wealth and power became one of the driving issues of the era of reform.

The resurgence of America's industrial economy after 1898 and the strategies pursued by industrialists had a profound impact: American industry created millions of new jobs for both skilled and less-skilled workers; changes in the global economy and advances in transportation technology helped manufacturers draw this labor force from the world's vast pool of poverty-stricken peasants and agricultural workers. As new immigrants, migrants, and women moved into the factories, they took part in yet another major reshaping of the American working class.

This process varied according to region. In the industrializing areas of the South (Alabama, Tennessee, Virginia, and West Virginia), African-Americans continued to be pushed out of the building trades and other skilled crafts, but increasing numbers found jobs in coalmining and lumbering, on the railroads, and as unskilled urban laborers. By 1910, well over a million African-Americans were working in the industrial sector.

In the Far West and Southwest, an already ethnically diverse labor force, which included native-born white Americans, Mexican-Americans, African-Americans, and Chinese, absorbed an influx of tens of thousands of new Japanese and Mexican immigrants. Between 1898 and 1907, when an agreement between Japan and the United States ended the immigration of Japanese laborers, more than 80,000 Japanese, the vast majority young men, entered the United States; nearly half settled in California. Most had been unemployed or landless agricultural workers and farmers in Japan; they came to the United States with the intention of settling down and importing brides from their homeland. Most Japanese labored for wages on the railroads, in agriculture, and in service work in hotels and private homes. A significant number opened small businesses serving the Japanese community; some also set up truck farms that provided western cities with specialized fruits and vegetables.

Unlike the Japanese, immigrants from Mexico after 1900 entered long-standing Mexican-American communities in the Southwest and West that traced their origins back for generations. There were probably 100,000 people of Mexican descent living and working in the United States at the end of the nineteenth century. Economic and political crises that culminated in the Mexican Revolution pushed tens of thousands of Mexico's rural and urban poor to immigrate to the north between 1900 and 1914, tripling the total Mexican population in the United States. Like the Japanese, new Mexican immigrants worked in railroad construction and maintenance and

Steelworkers at a Russian boardinghouse. Lewis Hine photographed immigrant steelworkers in Homestead, Pennsylvania, during 1907 and 1908 for the Pittsburgh Survey, the first extensive study of a major industrial city. Hine's photographs represented a new form of documentary evidence for social scientists as they attempted to understand the impact of industrial capitalism on turn-of-the-century America. In addition, Hine's photos conveyed a new reform message about the immigrant to the American public; in contrast to the detachment and distaste of Jacob Riis's pictures, Hine constructed a view of worthy newcomers deserving a role in and the benefits of American society.

agriculture. They concentrated in the expanding sugar beet industry, which increasingly replaced sugarcane as the primary source of raw sugar. Mexican immigrants also found significant employment opportunities in the expanding coal and metal mines and smelters throughout the Southwest.

The most striking changes took place in the northeastern and midwestern states, the heartland of American industry; there, European immigrants met industry's needs for labor. After 1896, increasing numbers of immigrants arrived from southern and eastern Europe. The influx reached staggering proportions. During the 1890s, an average of less than half a million newcomers arrived each year. In contrast, more than a million immigrants arrived in each of six different years between 1905 and 1914. The mushrooming of immigration and the rise of various ethnic groups gave America a new look, particularly in the manufacturing cities of the East and Midwest.

As in the past, European immigrants left lands that were in economic and political turmoil. Rapid population growth in Europe put tremendous pressure on peasant economies. As peasant families passed land on to their sons in ever smaller plots, it grew harder to survive. Improved overseas transportation meant that European agriculture now faced competition from Canada, the United States, and Argentina. European farmers needed to adopt new production techniques, but this entailed money that most peasants did not have. As a result, in large areas of Hungary and Poland peasants lost their farms and fell into the ranks of agricultural and urban wage laborers.

Eastern European Jews faced different problems. Living in crowded towns on the western edge of the Russian Empire, they were legally prohibited from owning land. Most engaged in trade or artisan labor. The increasing industrialization of eastern Europe undermined their traditional ways of life. At the same time, anti-Semitism grew, spurred by government officials looking for scapegoats for the region's economic problems and political unrest. Life for Jews became less secure.

As change swept eastern and southern Europe, some displaced farmers and workers responded with protests. Rural labor unions, some espousing revolutionary programs, emerged in southern Italy in the 1880s and 1890s. In 1897, Hungarian workers undertook a strike to force the government to introduce welfare measures. Rumanian peasants revolted in 1907. In Russia, a growing revolutionary movement drew in peasants, urban workers, and oppressed minorities, especially Jews.

Emigration was another way for individuals to respond. Peasants, workers, and Jews left their homes and moved not only to the United States but also to Canada, Argentina, Australia, and more prosperous industrial regions in Europe as well. To millions of individuals, emigration seemed a more sensible alternative than enduring continued economic hardship or battling oppression. Janos Kovacs, a Hungarian peasant who could "earn only enough for bread and water," concluded that "there was but one hope, America."

Different emigration patterns emerged. Young Italian and Slavic men left Europe without their families, hoping to earn enough money to return to their homelands and buy land, marry, or set up small businesses. Between 1899 and 1924, fewer than half the Italians who came to the United States became permanent American residents. Most returned to Italy. Jews, by contrast, like Japanese, seldom returned to their homeland. Theirs was the migration of an entire people; Jews often came in family groups, and almost half were women. Despite these differences, there was one constant: the vast majority of emigrants were young.

If the new immigrants' reasons for coming to America resembled those of earlier immigrant streams, their experiences in the United States were different. Most previous immigrants had been either English-speaking or Protestant or both. The newcomers rarely spoke English, and most were Catholic or Jewish. As a result, they faced greater prejudice than most of their predecessors, with the important exceptions of the Irish and the Chinese. In addition, most newly arriving workers brought agricultural and craft skills that were not particularly valued in America's rapidly advancing industrial economy. They tended to enter the American economy largely as unskilled or semiskilled laborers.

The "old" northern European immigrants (such as Germans, Scandinavians, and the Irish) and their American-born children still represented a large percentage of the American working class. Some prospered as farmers or businessmen; others found a measure of security in the skilled trades. With the industrial economy expanding, there were plenty of opportunities for those already established to move up into the ranks of foremen and the skilled. In 1900, for example, Germans dominated the brewing industry and were well represented in metalworking and other crafts. The English and Welsh were found throughout the mining industry. The Irish moved into the building trades, though they continued to work at unskilled labor to a greater extent than other old immigrants. Women in all these groups moved into new clerical and sales jobs created by capitalism's expansion.

The remaking of America's working class thus meant growing divisions. In the Northeast and Midwest, the labor market was divided by nationality, with new immigrants tending to hold less-skilled positions. In the South and the West, race and nationality served as the most obvious dividing lines, with African-Americans, Mexicans, and Asians performing largely unskilled labor. Nationwide, this division had deep significance both on and off the job. Unskilled and semiskilled workers still typically earned less than half what skilled workers did, although the gap between the two groups narrowed between 1900 and 1914. More broadly, skilled and less-skilled workers tended to live differently, fought separately for their rights, and had distinctly different relationships with their employers.

This last distinction was readily apparent in the steel industry. In an attempt to defuse the skilled steelworkers' militancy further, corporate execu-

"... MOSTLY WE BROUGHT RAGS AND BONES"

Immigrant working people often had to take whatever jobs they could find. Rocco Corresca left the slums of Naples with the help of a labor agent named Bartolo, who placed him in a rooming house in Brooklyn, New York. In December 1902 he recalled his first day in America.

THE NEXT MORNING, early, Bartolo told us to go out and pick rags and get bottles. He gave us bags and hooks and showed us the ash barrels. On the streets where the fine houses are the people are very careless and put out good things, like mattresses and umbrellas, clothes, hats and boots. We brought all these to Bartolo and he made them new again and sold them on the sidewalk; but mostly we brought rags and bones. The rags we had to wash in the backyard and then we hung them to dry on lines under the ceiling in our room. The bones we kept under the beds till Bartolo could find a man to buy them. Most of the men in our room worked at digging the sewer.

"THE MACHINES GO LIKE MAD ALL DAY ..."

Some immigrants found semiskilled work. Sadie Frowne did domestic work and sewing as a child before she began working in a garment factory in Brooklyn, New York, at age fifteen. She described her work in an article in The Independent *magazine in 1902:*

AT SEVEN O'CLOCK we all sit down to our machines and the boss brings each one the pile of work that he or she is to finish during the day. ... This pile is put down beside the machine and as soon as a skirt is done it is laid on the other side of the machine. Sometimes the work is not all finished by six o'clock and then the one who is behind must work overtime. ... The machines go like mad all day, because the faster you work the more money you get. Sometimes in my haste I get my finger caught and the needle goes right through it. ... The machines are all run by foot power, and at the end of the day one feels so weak that there is a great temptation to lie right down and sleep. But you must go out and get air, and have some pleasure. ...

The Surrender of New York Town

"The Surrender of New York Town."
The wave of new immigration
spawned hostility among many
native-born Americans, particularly
those who saw their power
diminishing in the changing world of
urban politics and business. The
satiric New York weekly *Life*
repeatedly published anti-Semitic
cartoons that wallowed in racial and
ethnic stereotypes. It was not alone
among turn-of-the-century
publications.

tives did more than crush unions, as Carnegie had done at Homestead. Companies also provided skilled workers with decent housing,
streetlights, and electricity; built parks and libraries; and sponsored
baseball teams. In the mills, skilled workers had opportunities to join management. Outside the workplace, management
involved the skilled workers in churches, schools, and company-
dominated political parties. By the time World War I began, steel mill
owners had succeeded in making skilled steelworkers a more stable
and decidedly less rebellious segment of the labor force.

The steelmakers' strategy for dealing with less-skilled immigrant
laborers contrasted sharply. A survey conducted in 1910 concluded
that if a millhand worked the standard shift—twelve hours per day,
every day of the year—he still could not earn enough to support a
family of five. Foremen drove their men to work at a killing pace, and
layoffs were common. The steelmakers wanted their unskilled labor
force to turn over rapidly so that no solid body of **aggrieved workers**

would develop. As a result, steel-mill laborers, many of them young and single, moved from one bleak steel town to another in search of steady work. Immigrants who remained in America for several years often sent home to their villages in Europe for their wives, or for a bride. Immigrant families established distinctive ethnic neighborhoods surrounding factories, and here, family and work were deeply intertwined.

The home lives of steelworkers mirrored the differences between the work experiences of the skilled and the unskilled. Skilled workers' families lived in relative comfort on weekly wages of approximately $20. They could buy a small house away from the smoke and stench of the mill, thrive on a varied, healthy diet, and take pride in decent furniture and housing, insurance, and even some savings. Amenities such as pianos and hand-operated washing machines were within reach.

The unskilled earned an average of $10 a week, about half the wage of skilled workers. It was barely enough to rent a dilapidated two-room tenement without running water, subsist on a substandard diet, and purchase the most minimal private insurance—a necessity for workers daily exposed to workplace hazards and unprotected by any form of governmental insurance. Such a budget provided only the crudest furniture and clothing and made infant and child mortality a constant threat.

An unskilled worker's income was not enough to keep a family going. Other family members had to provide the margin of survival. Women generally had charge of the family budget, struggling constantly to stretch an inadequate income. One-third of immigrant families took in boarders, a practice that produced extra income at the cost of overcrowding for the whole family and extra work for women and girls, who cooked, laundered, sewed, and kept house for the boarders. Industrial homework—piecework manufacture of items such as clothing, artificial flowers, or costume jewelry—provided another way of earning money at home. Children, especially girls, often joined their mothers at this work. Boys (and a few girls) as young as ten sold newspapers, shined shoes, or scavenged in the streets. And more than a quarter of a million children under age fifteen worked in mines, mills, and factories in 1900.

The connections between work and family went beyond budgets. In New Hampshire's huge Amoskeag Mills, as well as in California or Colorado agriculture, people often got jobs through family ties; relatives substituted for one another on the job. That an immigrant laborer worked alongside his brother, in the same factory or field as his father and daughter, sometimes made the harsh work conditions easier to endure.

The nature of women's participation in the workforce varied by

Breaker boys in coal chute, South Pittston, Pennsylvania, January 1911. Lewis Hine took hundreds of pictures as staff photographer for the National Child Labor Committee from 1908 to 1918. Hine traveled across the country, photographing children in textile mills, canneries, glass and shoe factories, mines, and fields to reveal the extent of child labor and the need for enforcement of reform laws. "No anonymous or signed denials can contradict proof given with photographic fidelity," Hine wrote. "These pictures speak for themselves, and prove that the law is being violated. . . ."

ethnic and racial group. Whereas unmarried Polish women in Buffalo, New York, often took jobs in factories or as domestic servants, their counterparts from southern Italy preferred to do industrial work in the home (such as garment production) or even seasonal agricultural labor. The differences were even greater among married women: many African-American married women worked for wages, but few married immigrant women did so.

Overall, the number of married women in the labor force was growing. In 1890, just over 3 percent of married women worked for wages, but this figure climbed to nearly 10 percent by 1920, due to changing patterns of family organization. First, women had about half as many babies at the end of the nineteenth century as they did at its start. This meant that in 1900 women spent ten fewer years of their lives raising children than had their grandmothers. It also meant that households were smaller. Second, technological change and the growth of the consumer market meant that home production of domestic goods continued to decline. Particularly in cities, it became easier after 1900 to purchase prepared food and finished clothes than to make them.

Middle-class women benefited the most from the availability of new services and household technology such as washing machines, vacuum cleaners, and gas ovens. Poor women still struggled with dirt, noise, unpaved streets, and the lack of sewers, garbage collection, and running water. Most working-class households used wood and coal stoves into the 1920s. It took a lot of hard physical labor to run such a household. But to help pay the bills—to buy clothes, canned goods, and other household items—an increasing number of married women joined their young single daughters in the wage labor force.

Women had limited job options, as the labor market was strictly divided by gender. Women usually found work in garment and textile manufacturing, teaching, domestic service, nursing, retail sales, and clerical work. These jobs usually paid less and carried less prestige than equivalent male positions.

Teaching, clerical work, and other white-collar women's jobs attracted immigrants' daughters as well as women of native-born parentage. Immigrants' daughters, in fact, often entered the white-collar world before their brothers. In Chicago, Italian female teachers outnumbered Italian male teachers by six to one; in New York, by four to one. Nursing, in contrast, drew few new immigrants and remained a preserve of native-stock Americans.

Nursing was, along with teaching, at the top of the female job hierarchy. While nurses were enrolled in what was basically an apprenticeship program in hospital schools, they were used as cheap labor. But upon graduation, most went into private nursing, caring for patients in their own homes or in hospitals on a fee-for-service basis, paid directly by the patient. These nurses developed independent work styles similar in some ways to those of skilled male craftsmen. At the same time, their work placed them in an uneasy subordination to the patient and the patient's family. Some of their work was disconcertingly similar to that of domestic servants, and the isolation of private duty weighed heavily on them, especially in contrast to the shared experience of training school. Even the most desirable of women's jobs had serious drawbacks, reflecting women's second-class position in the labor market.

Domestic work was a more common experience for women. In 1910 more than 2.5 million women, more than a third of the entire female workforce, were engaged in domestic or personal service. In the South, most domestic workers were black women who lived in their own homes. In the North, domestic servants were more likely to be native-born whites or northern European immigrants, many of whom lived with their employers.

Although domestic service paid low wages, some women found they could still save money, because their jobs often provided room and board. However, many found domestic work to be psychologically as well as physically taxing, especially for live-in servants, since it involved intimate surveillance by an ever-present employer. Women with other choices abandoned domestic work in droves: one former servant reported how happy she was to leave behind the "de-

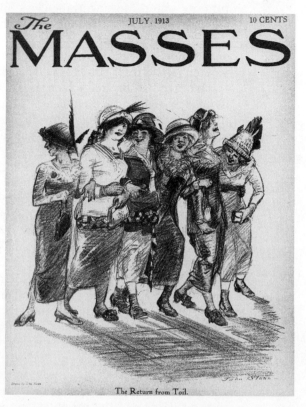

The Return from Toil.

"The Return from Toil." John Sloan's cover illustration for the radical magazine *The Masses* presented working women in a new way. As in earlier pictures, women were often portrayed in *The Masses* as the victims of oppressive working and labor conditions; but the magazine's artists also tried to break away from the standard sentimental or wretched stereotypes, instead showing working women as strong, independent, and exuberant.

grading sense of servility." Factory work may have been harder, but at least it offered the camaraderie of a group and greater control over leisure time.

America's industrial life had been transformed in myriad ways after 1900. A dramatic expansion in the size of the working class accompanied unprecedented growth of the economy. Workers were more divided than ever along gender, nationality, and racial lines. Working women and men did not remain passive in the face of such changes, however. Their responses to these profound changes would shape the very nature of Progressive Era politics and help bring into being a new urban-industrial culture.

A NEW URBAN WORLD

The changes sweeping America at the turn of the century were particularly visible in New York City, Chicago, Pittsburgh, and other northeastern and midwestern metropolitan centers. The public architecture of the day celebrated the dynamic power of urban America at the turn of the century. Travelers entered major cities through magnificent new railroad stations built of granite and steel, with vast train sheds and high-ceilinged waiting rooms. Nearby were tall office buildings, whose previously unreached heights were made possible by new construction techniques. Large corporations located their headquarters in these skyscrapers, to advertise their dominant position in American life. Downtown department stores competed for the most opulent displays and the greatest assortment of goods, while expensive restaurants, music halls, and nightclubs offered the middle and upper classes exciting and varied entertainment.

Urban skilled workers with sufficient incomes lived in residential areas, removed from the bright lights of the central city and the mill gates of the industrial neighborhoods. They rented or bought one- or two-family homes on blocks they shared with small businessmen and white-collar workers, an occupational group that grew as corporations expanded their management ranks.

Immigrant working-class districts, often located near the mills, were another world altogether. Cheap tenements and wood-frame houses pressed tightly together to save developers the cost of high-priced central real estate. In dark, cramped apartments, families and boarders squeezed together, sleeping in shared beds or on couches, chairs, and sometimes floors. Privacy was nowhere to be found, nor were indoor toilets. The streets provided the only escape. There peddlers sold food and clothing, holidays were celebrated, news and gossip exchanged, and politics debated. Mothers socialized on front steps and porches, and children played in streets and alleys.

Outsiders viewed the immigrant neighborhoods as chaotic assemblages of unconnected, disoriented people. But they missed the dense cultural and institutional life immigrants created. As immigrants entered the country, they sought out relatives or someone from their village in the "old country" for help in finding a job and a bed to sleep in. Enterprising immigrants, particularly those semiskilled and skilled workers who earned higher wages, set up boardinghouses, often serving newcomers from one village or region. In time, neighborhood grocery stores, butcher shops, and saloons sprang up to meet the special needs and tastes of particular ethnic groups.

Networks based on extended families and Old World village ties met many of the immediate needs of immigrant workers, but other problems demanded more collective solutions. For instance, if a community of immigrants from the Abruzzi region of Italy wanted a church with a priest who spoke Italian, they had to enlist the help of Neapolitans or Romans in making their request to Catholic officials. This experience might create a greater sense of common identity, especially because the English-speaking majority tended to ignore regional differences among Italians. Ethnic consciousness gradually evolved.

"BLAYBT ER LIGN TOYT IM HOL" (HE LIES DEAD IN THE HALL)

The "new" immigrants of the Progressive Era added to the diversity of American culture by bringing with them the cultural forms and practices of their homelands. Drawing on the Yiddish language and musical traditions of eastern Europe, Jewish immigrants created expressive musical shows in Lower East Side bars and theaters. This Yiddish song "Di Nyu Yorker Trern" (New York Tears), written earlier but first published in 1910, comments on the difficulties and tragedies of immigrant life in urban America.

New York bubbles like a pot
There's constant tumult and hubbub
You see a lot of people rushing around and
Often you see people's tears.
Misfortunes happen here at every step
And yet this hell is called Freeland
They put a family out on the street
Because they can't pay the rent on time
It rains, it pours, the tears flow
And the poor things sit depressed and forlorn

That's the New York tears
Which can never stop
A sob, a scream, a sigh and a woe
That's what you hear all the time
That's nothing new; wherever you go
You see the New York tears

Who hasn't heard of the murder
That took place not long ago on Montgomery Street
They found three people stabbed
A man, a wife, and a mother-in-law in a pool of blood
And there you hear a boy shot his friend
Two children were playing with a pistol
A boy of fourteen, what has he seen of life
The second boy, still younger, aimed at him
When he felt the shot
He screams "mama" loudly
And, running from the third floor
He lies dead in the hall

Immigrants also created secular ethnic and fraternal organizations, such as the Sons of Italy, the Polish Union, and the Jewish *Landsmanschaft* organizations, to provide mutual assistance and a familiar cultural milieu. They started newspapers and magazines in dozens of languages, filled with news from the old country and advice to newcomers. Neighborhood-based machine politicians, including many saloonkeepers, dispensed jobs and emergency financial aid to immigrants in return for votes.

Although class and ethnic divisions characterized the turn-of-the-century city, new forms of commercial culture were emerging that provided common experiences. At about this time, newspapers achieved mass circulation by appealing to diverse audiences. Adorned with bold headlines and illustrations, filled with advertising, and hawked by thousands of newsboys, newspapers like Joseph Pulitzer's New York *World* included sports and fashion news, household tips, color comics, and short stories. Although many immigrants stuck to the foreign-language press, the new dailies were popular with both working-class and middle-class readers.

Amusement parks (built at the end of trolley lines to stimulate traffic) also achieved broad appeal, especially to the legions of young immigrant men and women who flocked to the parks on their days off. New York's Coney Island was the most famous of these wonder worlds, but every major city had at least one. Pittsburgh's "Dream

Maxwell Street market. A scene in Chicago's immigrant Jewish neighborhood, photographed in about 1905.

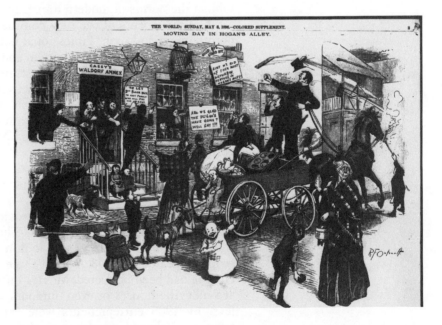

"Moving Day in Hogan's Alley." Richard F. Outcault's color comic, first appearing in the New York *World* in 1896, lovingly portrayed the immigrant, working-class urban neighborhood as energetic and comically chaotic. "Hogan's Alley" (also known as "The Yellow Kid," named after the strange, hairless child in a yellow dress who appeared in each installment) instituted the serialized color comic strip as one of the many features in the new mass-circulation newspapers. Like the movies, newspapers now gained a broad audience by offering a range of features designed to please every taste.

City," for instance, opened in 1906 with dance halls, skating rinks, theaters, pony rides, wooded grounds, picnic sites, and "shoot the chutes," the favorite ride of the day. These elaborately decorated, highly mechanized amusement parks seemed to some a vision of paradise, a release from the dullness of the workaday world. "It is just like what I see when I dream of heaven," one young woman exclaimed on her first visit to Coney Island. Yet amusement parks also had distinctly sexual overtones: the Tunnel of Love had an obvious purpose; more active rides lured young men and women by asking, "Will she throw her arms around your neck and yell?"

Young working-class immigrant women participated avidly in the new urban culture. Many unmarried immigrant women struggled to hide some part of their wages from their families, scrimping to purchase shirtwaists, stylish hats, and other "American clothes." They stretched their pennies even further by "dating" young men, who paid for an evening's food, drink, and entertainment in return for female companionship and the possibility of sexual experimentation. These young working women were the pioneers of a new mixed-sex world of leisure; previously, women's leisure had largely been restricted to family activities or female-only activities. Now, at dance halls and amusement parks, the young could meet and enjoy each other's unsupervised company. In seeking excitement and some measure of independence, young immigrant women and men helped establish the norms of modern romantic companionship.

Not all aspects of the new commercial culture were enjoyed by both women and men. Professional boxing and bicycle racing found more devotees among businessmen and workingmen. Baseball, on its way to becoming the "national pastime," drew an enthusiastic male following in these years, although women also cheered their home teams, both amateur and professional. In some immigrant neighborhoods, sandlot diamonds were the only open spaces in the smoky, dirty, thickly populated landscape. As hard-hitting, slick-fielding children of immigrants made their way up from neighborhood pickup games to local semipro teams and then to the major leagues, inner-city residents could begin to feel they were part of the larger American society.

Of all the new cultural forms, movies were perhaps the most popular, attracting massive audiences. The first moving pictures, peep shows seen by a single viewer looking into a hand-wound Kinetoscope, appeared in 1893. Within three years, large-screen projection cinema had been perfected. Movies initially were shown as novelties at vaudeville houses or even outdoors, on sheets stretched across alleys. By 1905 entrepreneurs were setting up theaters, sometimes simply a darkened storefront, to show continuous programs of short films. These "nickelodeons," so named because the price of admission was a nickel, were an instant success; by 1908 more than 300,000 people went to movies *every day* in New York City.

At first, as the comedian Milton Berle later remembered, "the movies were something for the lower classes and immigrants. Nice people didn't go to the 'flickers.'" But in workers' districts, movies were the rage, especially with children, who could afford the low admission price. Married immigrant women patronized movies extensively: admission was cheap, they could take the children along, and the early shows were brief enough to fit into a busy household routine. Immigrant life provided the topic for many early films, and immigrant producers competed for places in the early filmmaking industry. Silent movies crossed many barriers of language and culture: "It doesn't matter whether a man is from Kamchutka or Stamboul . . . ," wrote one movie theater manager, "he can understand pictures." For many of the foreign-born, movies were the first sustained contact with mainstream American society.

Middle- and upper-class disapproval of "the flickers" was not only an issue of class snobbery; it also reflected a broader cultural conflict. Spokesmen for genteel America—ministers, college presidents, and political leaders—had long advocated a public culture of Victorian virtue; sponsoring symphonies and museums, they sought to edify the masses and encourage industriousness, self-control, and moral uplift. Though they had never fully succeeded in controlling the diverse cultural lives of working Americans, the genteel had long held sway over the middle class and dominated the official vision of American culture.

The new commercial culture of movies, amusement parks, and spectator sports challenged the dominance of genteel ideals. While manipulative and designed to make a profit from leisure, it was also more exuberant, sensual, and irreverent. The genteel, including some Progressive reformers, saw this new culture as exploitative and dangerous. One essayist called Coney Island "a disgrace," a place where "humanity sheds its civilization and becomes half child, half savage." Another critic elaborated:

> Looping the loop amid shrieks of stimulated terror or dancing in disorderly saloon halls are perhaps natural reactions to a day spent in noisy factories and in trolley cars whirling through the distracting streets, but the city which permits them to be the acme of pleasure and recreation to its young people commits a grievous mistake.

Immigrants and other working men and working women paid little heed to such elite criticism. Commercial culture eventually triumphed in part because it provided opportunities for excitement and escape from the daily stresses of industrial life.

Genteel culture would soon lose its hold on middle-class Americans as well. In the 1910s, in places such as New York's Greenwich Village, artists, writers, and other middle- and upper-class rebels such as the journalist John Reed, the playwright Eugene O'Neill, and the political activist Emma Goldman gave voice to scathing criticism of middle-class values. In the next decade, as we will see, even main-

"Picturesque America." Illustrator Harry Grant Dart's vision of the increasingly aggressive and intrusive character of advertising in turn-of-the-century America appeared in a 1909 issue of *Life*.

stream middle-class Americans would experiment with a new morality and less genteel cultural styles. Eventually, from the cultural cauldron that was the turn-of-the-century industrial city, would emerge the popular mass culture of twentieth-century America.

THE RESURGENCE OF CRAFT UNIONISM

In the early years of the new century, working women and working men not only ran industrial machines and helped shape the emerging modern culture; they also fought bitter battles with employers to defend their rights and improve their lives. The turbulent conflict affected the actions of reformers and politicians and, ultimately, the shape of the whole Progressive Era.

Turn-of-the-century labor battles can be divided into two categories. Skilled craft workers fought, often with great militancy, to retain and extend previously won shop-floor rights; these battles were led by established craft unions, most of them members of the American Federation of Labor (AFL). Less-skilled workers, though excluded from AFL unions, engaged in militant labor struggles of their own. Skilled workers often looked down on these newcomers, and employers often helped erect walls of misunderstanding between the two groups. This division between skilled and less-skilled workers played an important role in shaping the labor battles of the Progressive Era.

As the economy expanded after 1897, AFL-affiliated craft unions enjoyed a resurgence, in part because industrial growth had created a labor shortage. Companies were sometimes hard-pressed to find the skilled workers they needed. Accordingly, skilled workers grew less fearful of the possible consequences of collective action, renewing their long-standing struggle to preserve control over the work process and extend union organization. Between 1897 and 1904, the number of working people organized in unions—especially on the railroads and in metalworking, construction, and coalmining—climbed from under 500,000 to more than 2 million.

The resurgence of craft unionism was concentrated in the Northeast and Midwest and primarily involved men of northern and western European stock. The upsurge, however, extended to the South and West as well. It even included a few organizations of unskilled workers, in "federal labor unions" chartered by the AFL. In Birmingham, Alabama, the industrial center of the New South, African-American workers moved rapidly into such unions and for a time were welcomed by white union officials. The Alabama State Federation of Labor, organized in 1900, included all-black as well as integrated unions and boasted a number of African-American leaders until 1905. Its white secretary exhorted white workers to "lay aside all malice and prejudice against color, creed, or nationality."

AFL leaders typically resisted the integration of nonwhite workers into the organization. In Oxnard, California, 1,200 Mexican and Japanese farm laborers organized the Japanese-Mexican Labor Association (JMLA) and won a hard-fought strike in 1903 against sugar beet growers. But the AFL notified the JMLA that it would grant its request for a charter only if it excluded the Japanese, whose very presence in the United States the AFL strenuously opposed. AFL president Samuel Gompers had attacked all Asian labor in a widely read pamphlet published by the federation and titled *Meat* vs. *Rice*. J. M. Lizarras, the Mexican secretary of the JMLA, refused to accept an AFL charter under these conditions. He wrote to Gompers:

> In the past we have counseled, fought and lived on very
> short rations with our Japanese brothers, and toiled with

them in the fields. . . . We would be false to them and to
ourselves and to the cause of unionism if we now accepted
privileges for ourselves which are not accorded to them.

Most AFL craft unions excluded women as well as immigrants
and the unskilled from their ranks. Women were cut off even from
potential membership because they were barred from skilled occupations by employers. Even when women worked alongside men, as
in the cigar industry, unions treated them with hostility. Defining
their goals in narrow, "bread and butter" terms, craft unions fought
for the "family wage," which would enable men to support their families "in a manner consistent with their responsibilities as husbands,
fathers, men, and citizens." Although the demand for a family wage
dignified male workers' struggles, it devalued women's paid work and
limited their participation in labor issues.

The AFL's Samuel Gompers increasingly thought of unions as
"business organizations of wage-earners." Like other business organizations that enjoyed stable and centralized organization, most
unions were now directed by professional leaders who held their posts
for long tenures and received handsome salaries. Changes in the
United Brotherhood of Carpenters illustrate the transformation of
craft unionism. In the 1880s the union's founder, the socialist P. J.
Maguire, ran it almost single-handed; the political education of the
working class was his urgent mission. Two decades later, the real
power in the brotherhood was held by full-time union officials known
as "business agents," whose duties included negotiating with contractors and assigning jobs to union members. While increasing numbers of business agents helped the United Brotherhood of Carpenters
and other craft unions grow more stable and effective, these officials
also tended to frame union goals solely in terms of wages and working
conditions.

But the growth of craft unions also depended on older traditions
and forms of struggle, including boycotts, sympathy strikes, and
other tools of class solidarity pioneered by the late-nineteenth-
century labor movement. Such traditions were passed on by older veterans of the labor movement to newer industrial workers. British and
American coalminers, for instance, taught new immigrants to avoid
subservience to bosses. One longtime miner told an investigator how
"he had given a lesson in the ways of the mines to a newly landed
'hunky' who was working as his laborer: 'Come here, Frank, says I.
Here's the boss. Don't work. Always sit down when the boss is
around.'"

Some immigrants needed no such prompting. When coalminers
undertook a long and brutal strike in 1903 against Colorado Fuel and
Iron, recent Italian immigrants, many with long careers in Italy's an-

archist and socialist movements, were the strike's most militant supporters. The International Hod Carriers, Building, and Common Laborers Union also had a large Italian membership whose bonds of solidarity had similarly been forged in Italy's nationalist and radical movements. Rhode Island's Providence *Journal* captured this ambience in its description of a 1910 parade of striking hod carriers, who responded to a song tribute to the Italian nationalist leader and guerrilla general Giuseppe Garibaldi:

> The Italian Royal March was succeeded by the Socialist Anthem, and the American National Anthem by the Garibaldi March. Whenever the band struck up the well-known strains of the Garibaldi March, all the marchers took their hats off and applauded enthusiastically.

The upsurge of craft unionism prompted some industrialists to seek a peaceful solution. Hoping to promote a cooperative approach to industrial relations, corporate leaders gathered in 1898 to found the National Civic Federation (NCF). Oil magnate John D. Rockefeller, former President Grover Cleveland, Catholic Bishop John Ireland, and such labor leaders as James O'Connell of the Machinists' Union and Samuel Gompers joined the federation. They sought to solve "the labor problem" by fostering employer acceptance of conservative forms of unionism. NCF leaders denounced all forms of radicalism, but they also condemned anti-union employers, arguing that "organized labor cannot be destroyed without debasement of the masses."

The NCF urged employers to seek harmony by negotiating industry wide labor agreements through newly formed trade associations. Employer organizations such as the National Metal Trades Association and the Newspaper Publishers' Association reached agreements with national unions. Agreements were also signed in the mining, ironmolding, and pottery industries. Briefly, it appeared that the war between owners and skilled workers might end.

But the moment soon passed. In one industry after another, rank-and-file skilled workers refused to accept the weakening of their workplace control. In 1900, the National Metal Trades Association and the Machinists' Union leaders signed an agreement that provided for a reduction in work hours from ten to nine and the elimination of sympathy strikes. But militant locals across the country insisted that employers raise hourly wages so they would not suffer any loss of income. Local protests forced leaders of the Machinists' Union to call a nationwide strike.

Such displays of worker militancy convinced most corporate leaders that labor peace was too costly. They rejected union demands and crushed the ensuing strikes. By 1903 many employers had broken with the NCF, reverting to earlier union-breaking tactics: labor spies, professional strikebreakers, and blacklists of union activists. Employer associations in the machinery and metal trades let national trade agreements collapse. In the structural iron industry, the breakdown of labor-management cooperation led to a long struggle, with workers resorting to dynamite when the strike weapon proved insufficient.

New organizations such as the National Association of Manufacturers (NAM) and the Citizens' Industrial Association called for "the open shop." Although the open shop seemed to mean that workers were free to decide whether to join a union, it really meant that employers were free to bar unions from factories. The National Association of Manufacturers sought to influence public opinion by circulating millions of antilabor pamphlets to schools and churches as part of their open-shop crusade. The initial Citizen's Industrial Association bulletin captured well the movement's anti-union spirit:

> Do you hear the murmur and the mutterings and see the lightning flashes of the storm of public indignation rolling up in mighty grandeur? . . . The 14,980,000 decent, upright, peaceful voters who love work and demand liberty are now arising in their might, and the text on the wall . . . proclaims that the slimy red fingers of anarchy shall be crushed by the mailed hand of the common people and their law.

The open-shop drive, together with fluctuations in the economy, slowed and then halted the spread of craft unionism. In the metal trades, no more than 11 percent of machinists were organized in the years prior to 1913. Membership in the AFL decreased by nearly 200,000 in 1905, after nearly seven years of growth. And for the next four years, unions did not recover these losses in membership.

Many factors influenced the employers' ability to turn the tables on AFL unions. Widespread structural changes in the economy had enhanced capitalists' control of the workplace, especially their ability to use machinery to replace skilled workers with the less skilled. And organizations such as the NAM had increased businessmen's ability to shape public opinion. In comparison, workers had more difficulty than employers in sustaining permanent organizations. The union movement was also undercut by social divisions between skilled and less-skilled, immigrant and native-born, black and white, women and men. Most important, it was undermined by the AFL's reluctance to bridge these gaps.

LABOR WARS

As the craft unions' upsurge slowed, the focus of labor conflict shifted. In the years between 1905 and 1917, less-skilled immigrant workers engaged in epic struggles, especially strikes in the Lawrence, Massachusetts, textile mills in 1912 and the Paterson, New Jersey, silk mills in 1913. The less-skilled played pivotal roles in other battles as well. The skilled steelworkers' effort to organize U.S. Steel in 1909, for example, failed because the company was successful in winning the loyalty of some craftsmen and because craft unionists were isolated from the mass of unskilled immigrants.

The most successful efforts to organize the semiskilled focused on clothing workers, nearly 400,000 of whom joined unions between 1909 and 1913. Concentrated in New York City, the industry had tens of thousands of small, marginal firms and just a few large manufacturers with modern plants. The workforce was almost exclusively immigrant, heavily female, and largely Jewish and Italian; many immigrants possessed skills learned in European workshops.

Garment unions made little headway in the early years of the century. Short, spontaneous strikes were common; lasting organizations were rare. Garment workers, though, had a radical tradition; the anarchist movement had considerable influence among recent Italian immigrants, and many Jewish workers had been involved in European socialist or trade-union activities.

In the fall of 1909 the garment industry exploded. The first breakthrough came with workers who produced the fashionable shirtwaists or long blouses worn by many urban working-class and middle-class women. These workers were mostly young Jewish and Italian women, who worked both to help support their families and to gain a measure of security and independence. A series of wage cuts and other grievances sparked a wave of small walkouts by these young women. Then, at a dramatic meeting at New York's Cooper Union, the shirtwaist workers called a general strike. Within two days, 20,000 workers walked out. A month later the strike spread to Philadelphia. The conflict dragged on until February 1910, when the International Ladies' Garment Workers' Union (ILGWU) and the manufacturers reached a settlement. Although employers refused to recognize the union, they reduced hours, improved conditions, and agreed to arbitrate future disputes through a board of community and religious leaders.

Within months, two other groups of garment workers walked out. In New York, 60,000 mostly male cloakmakers began a general strike. Then, at Chicago's Hart, Schaffner, and Marx, a huge manufacturer of men's clothing, fourteen young women walked out over a cut in their

"A PINT OF TROUBLE FOR THE BOSSES . . ."

The 1909 shirtwaist workers' strike saw young immigrant women step to the forefront of the labor struggle. Fifteen-year-old shirtwaist worker Clara Lemlich, a Jewish immigrant from Russia, emerged as a key organizer and speaker. A reporter from the New York Sun witnessed this attack by anti-union thugs on Lemlich and other strikers.

THE GIRLS, HEADED by teen-age Clara Lemlich, described by union organizers as "a pint of trouble for the bosses," began singing Italian and Russian working-class songs as they paced in twos before the factory door. Of a sudden, around the corner came a dozen tough-looking customers, for whom the union label gorilla seemed well-chosen.

"Stand fast, girls," called Clara, and then the thugs rushed the line, knocking Clara to her knees, striking at the pickets, opening the way for a group of frightened scabs to slip through the broken line. Fancy ladies from the Allen Street red-light district climbed out of cabs to cheer on the gorillas. There was a confused melee of scratching, screaming girls and fist-swinging men and then a patrol wagon arrived. The thugs ran off as the cops pushed Clara and two other badly beaten girls into the wagon.

I followed the rest of the retreating pickets to the union hall, a few blocks away. There a relief station had been set up where one bottle of milk and a loaf of bread were given to strikers with small children in their families. There for the first time in my comfortably sheltered, Upper West Side life, I saw real hunger on the faces of my fellow Americans in the richest city in the world.

piece rate. The women picketed alone for three weeks before co-workers began to take them seriously, but eventually 40,000 workers throughout the city's clothing industry joined them. Both strikes ended with compromise agreements that left many issues to arbitration. But they added greatly to the momentum of union organizing. By the eve of World War I, new unions had made deep inroads in the clothing, fur, and millinery industries.

The strikes by garment workers sparked action from a range of diverse groups. Middle-class female reformers, appalled by conditions in the garment industry and the spread of social conflict, were particularly active in aiding the strikers. Even some large garment manufacturers and buyers came to support unionization. They realized that unions, by stabilizing wages and conditions, might lessen the cutthroat competition and ensure more predictable prices and supplies. The agreement ending the 1910 cloakmakers' strike, for instance, was worked out by Louis Brandeis, a lawyer and reformer acting on behalf of Boston department store owner A. Lincoln Filene.

The garment workers' uprising also demonstrated the growing influence of the Socialist Party (SP) on the labor movement. Many garment union activists belonged to or sympathized with the party, which had been formed in 1901 by the merger of several socialist groups. The party's best-known spokesperson was Eugene V. Debs, leader of the Pullman strike seven years earlier. Jailed for his role in the Pullman strike, Debs had become convinced that only the collective ownership of industry would guarantee a democratic society and individual rights. "I am for Socialism," he wrote, "because I am for humanity. We have been cursed with the reign of gold long enough. Money constitutes no proper basis of civilization."

By 1908 the Socialist Party had 41,000 dues-paying members in over 3,000 local branches. That year, running for president on the Socialist ticket, Debs received over 400,000 votes. Four years later, party membership peaked at 118,000, and Debs received 900,000 votes in the presidential election. And it became increasingly common for Socialists to win municipal elections. In 1911, Socialist Party candidates won 73 mayoral seats and 1,200 lesser offices in 340 cities and towns nationwide.

Some middle-class women and Christian socialists backed the Socialist Party. The SP also enjoyed substantial rural backing, especially in the Southwest, where many farmers were being forced to sell their land and become tenants. But the core of the party's strength was among urban workers. At first the party was popular mostly with skilled workers, including many German immigrants. By 1909 it was winning more and more support from "new" immigrants. This mixture of diverse groups and traditions made the SP a volatile and exciting organization.

Socialist Party leaders were critical of the policies of the American Federation of Labor. They denounced AFL officials for cooperating

"The Red Special." Eugene Debs and Socialist Party staffers during his 1908 presidential whistle-stop campaign.

with businessmen through the National Civic Federation and attacked the AFL's lack of interest in unskilled workers. Many Socialists argued that the policy of organizing unions along narrow craft lines, instead of more broadly by industry, had turned the federation into the "American Separation of Labor."

Despite these criticisms, most party leaders supported the AFL, hoping to "bore from within" to change its policies. Socialists had considerable influence in many unions, including those of the machinists, the mineworkers, and the ILGWU. Their attacks on Gompers' participation in the National Civic Federation won widespread support from AFL workers. At the 1912 AFL convention, a Socialist running against Gompers for the AFL presidency received a third of the votes. But long before that, other Socialists had given up hope that the AFL would ever change.

In 1905, dissident Socialists, including Debs, came together with other radicals and industrial unionists to found a new labor organization, the Industrial Workers of the World (IWW). In contrast to the AFL, the IWW sought to abolish the wage system and create a society where workers would own and control their factories. Western hard-rock miner Big Bill Haywood opened the IWW's founding convention by announcing: "Fellow workers, this is the Continental Congress of the working class. We are here to confederate the workers of this country into a working-class movement that shall have for its purpose the emancipation of the working class from the slave bondage of capitalism."

The IWW shared some ideas and leaders with the Socialist Party, but its underlying strategy was different. IWW leaders, sometimes called "syndicalists," believed that a revolutionary union, not a working-class political party, should be the vehicle for radical economic and political change. Organizing all workers in one big militant union, IWW leaders believed, would lead to a massive general strike in which capitalism would be overthrown, leaving industry to be run in a decentralized, democratic fashion by the people as a whole.

The IWW's broad concern with the social order contrasted sharply with the "bread and butter" approach of most AFL unions. The IWW's other distinctive contribution was its commitment to organizing the most impoverished workers. The IWW was the most egalitarian labor organization in American history, organizing skilled and unskilled, men and women, blacks and Mexicans, and, in a break with tradition, Chinese and Japanese workers.

The IWW emerged, in part, from a decade of struggle by the Western Federation of Miners (WFM), representing 30,000 hard-rock miners in the Rocky Mountain region. Through a series of bitter strikes in Idaho, Montana, and Colorado between 1894 and 1904, against

Mr. Block. Ernest Riebe's comic strip about a willfully ignorant and gullible worker appeared in the IWW's *Industrial Worker*. The strip conveyed the organization's attitude toward workers who lacked class consciousness or subscribed to the AFL's conservative craft unionism, inspiring IWW songwriter Joe Hill's lyrics: "Oh, Mr. Block, you were born by mistake. / You take the cake. / You make me ache. / Tie a rock to your block and jump in the lake. / Kindly do that for Liberty's sake." The adventures of the beleaguered Mr. Block, as indicated here, also took swipes at the reform wing of the Socialist Party.

some of the largest corporations in America, the WFM's leaders had come to reject capitalism and embrace industrial unionism. After the state of Colorado threw its resources into crushing miners' strikes in 1903 and 1904, the WFM intensified its efforts to build alliances with workers in the East, an effort that culminated in the 1905 founding convention of the IWW in Chicago.

But the IWW also drew on the Knights of Labor's belief in organizing across ethnic and racial lines, the shop-floor democracy of skilled craftsmen when they exercised control over production processes, and the industrial unionism of coalminers and the American Railway Union. It was a heady combination, and the "Wobblies," as they were popularly known, frightened both industrialists and AFL leaders.

At first, factionalism, government harassment, and the economic downturn of 1907–8 stymied the Wobblies. In 1907 the WFM seceded from the IWW, leaving it with fewer than six thousand members. But things changed in 1909, when unskilled immigrant workers at the Pressed Steel Car Company in McKees Rocks, Pennsylvania, struck to protest an incentive pay system. Joined by skilled workers, the strikers shut down the plant. After a split developed between immigrant and native-born workers, and the latter returned to work, IWW leaders arrived to take charge of the walkout. Led by the Wobblies, unskilled workers displayed fierce solidarity. After eight weeks the company offered concessions, the strike ended, and the IWW won nationwide attention.

The IWW also led a series of "free speech" fights in the West. Unable to reach lumber and agricultural workers on the job, where they were dispersed over vast regions, the IWW began appealing to them in western cities, where they rested between jobs. Local authorities responded by banning IWW street speakers. The Wobblies defied these bans in Spokane, Washington; Fresno, California; Kansas City; and elsewhere. Deliberately seeking arrest, IWW members filled local jails, where they were often brutalized. But as arrests mounted—four hundred Wobblies were locked up in Spokane—city officials often had to retreat.

The IWW's reputation soared in 1912, when it led a massive textile strike in Lawrence, Massachusetts. The struggle began in January, when a hundred women, many of them Poles, quit work after discovering that millowners had lowered their weekly pay. Already upset by long hours and a recent speed-up, this was the last straw for Lawrence's 30,000 textile workers. Half of the mills' labor force were young women between fourteen and eighteen, many already suffering from malnutrition and overwork. Two days after the pay cut was announced, more than 20,000 workers of forty nationalities were on strike. Called in by the local chapter, national IWW leaders—includ-

Happy Hooligan. Beginning in 1900, Frederick Opper's comic strip featuring the hapless tramp was a major attraction of William Randolph Hearst's New York *Journal.* Unlike Riebe's Mr. Block, Happy Hooligan was the undeserving victim of the abuses and insanities of American society—including, in this strip, popular hysteria about anarchists and the police penchant for summary justice.

ing Joseph Ettor, Elizabeth Gurley Flynn, and Italian socialist Arturo Giovannitti—helped coordinate the battle that followed.

To prevent ethnic splits from developing, the IWW organized separate strike and relief committees for each nationality. They translated speeches and literature into every language. Strikers threw up massive picket lines around the mills and regularly paraded through the city's streets. Women were especially active. Some provided food for the strikers. Consiglia Teutonica later remembered, "My mother made sure no one goes hungry or cold, not on our block." Other women joined picket lines not because they were forced to but because, as one woman put it, "we feel it is but [our] duty." Women strikers harassed strikebreakers, policemen, and soldiers, using weapons ranging from words to red pepper to hefty lengths of pipe.

Millowners and government officials mobilized a massive show of force. After a woman picketer was shot and killed, Ettor and Giovannitti, who were three miles away at the time of the shooting, were arrested as "accessories to the murder" and held in jail without bail for eight months, awaiting trial. Martial law was declared and all public meetings banned. After the state militia was called in to help the police, a militiaman killed a fifteen-year-old Syrian boy with his bayonet.

Strikers began sending their children out of Lawrence, where they would be safe. Margaret Sanger, a nurse who later became famous for her work in promoting birth control, accompanied the children on a train to New York City. She testified that "out of the 119 children, only four had underwear on . . . their outerwear was almost in rags . . . their coats were simply torn to shreds . . . and it was the bitterest weather we have had this winter."

The departure of the children from Lawrence generated so much sympathy for the strikers that the authorities decreed that children of strikers would no longer be allowed to leave. When strikers tried to send more of their young ones to safety, the police attacked them. A witness testified:

> When the time came to depart, the children arranged in a long line, two by two in an orderly procession with the parents near at hand . . . the police closed in on us with their clubs, beating right and left with no thought of the children who then were in desperate danger of being trampled to death.

This was the turning point. Throughout the country, public outrage grew at the employers' tactics. In March, the Lawrence millowners agreed to a settlement providing pay raises, overtime pay, and other improvements.

Although Lawrence demonstrated that immigrant workers could unite in militancy and solidarity, the victory did not open the way for

"We want bread and roses, too." Textile strikers confront National Guardsmen, Lawrence, Massachusetts, 1912.

widespread industrial organization of immigrant workers. The next year, the IWW met a serious defeat in a silkworkers' strike in Paterson, New Jersey. The Paterson strike was remarkably similar to the uprising at Lawrence. Once again, thousands of immigrant women, men, and children walked out of the mills. IWW leaders again organized effective picket lines and enthusiastic rallies over the course of seven months. Once more, repression by the authorities passed all bounds; Socialist Frederick Sumner Boyd was arrested for reading the free-speech clause of the New Jersey state constitution at a strike meeting.

But in Paterson, employers exploited divisions within the silkworkers' ranks. The skilled, English-speaking workers and their craft unions scorned the unskilled and skilled immigrants. One craft unionist said of the Jewish and Italian workers: "If an organization is formed today, they want to strike tomorrow. They don't seem willing to stick to any organization any length of time unless they have a strike." English-speaking workers were also put off by the anarchism of many of the Italian and Jewish workers. When the immigrant workers walked out of the mills, it took three weeks for the English-speaking skilled workers to follow. During the strike, employers re-

"...IT WAS A MURDER AND NOTHING LESS"

The brutal massacre of strikers and their families at Ludlow, Colorado, stunned the nation and led to numerous investigations and reports. Below are two documents about the massacre. The first is an excerpt from a newspaper reporter's account that appeared in the New York World. The second is a portion of John D. Rockefeller's testimony before the Commission on Industrial Relations, set up by the U.S. government in 1914 to investigate labor conditions. Rockefeller is questioned by Commission chairman Frank Walsh, a noted reformer.

New York World

THEN CAME THE killing of Louis Tikas, the Greek leader of the strikers. We saw the militiamen parley outside the tent city, and a few minutes later, Tikas came out to meet them. We watched them talking. Suddenly an officer raised his rifle, gripping the barrel, and felled Tikas with the butt.

Tikas fell face downward. As he lay there we saw the militiamen fall back. Then they aimed their rifles and deliberately fired them into the unconscious man's body. It was the first murder I had ever seen, for it was a murder and nothing less. Then the miners ran about in the tent colony and women and children scuttled for safety in the [underground] pits which afterwards trapped them.

We watched from our rock shelter while the militia dragged up their machine guns and poured murderous fire into the arroyo from a height by Water Tank Hill above the Ludlow depot. Then came the firing of the tents. . . . The militiamen

peatedly invited craft union leaders to speak in Paterson against Wobbly-style unionism. Ultimately, despite a spectacular fund-raising pageant held in New York's Madison Square Garden, the movement collapsed; the English-speaking millworkers agreed to return to work on a shop-by-shop basis, leaving the striking unskilled immigrants high and dry.

Such divisions weakened Paterson workers in their battles against employers. Wage and skill differentials, cultural gaps, and organizational conflicts between the AFL- and IWW-affiliated unions made it difficult to work together. Employers encouraged these divisions and often tried to play one group off against the other.

The United Mine Workers of America (UMWA) showed that these difficulties could be overcome. Coalminers were unlike most other AFL members. Though highly skilled, the miners had no tradition of apprenticeship, which prevented them from controlling entry into the trade. Partly as a result, many miners were recent immigrants or African-Americans. The UMWA shaped its organization to take such factors into account.

Drawing on the Gilded Age legacy of interracial unionism left by the Knights of Labor and black UMWA activists such as Richard Davis, the UMWA extended its commitment to organize all who worked in and around the mines. This included a growing number of unskilled newcomers from eastern and southern Europe. By 1910, nearly one-third of all coalminers were unionized, compared with one-tenth of the broader American labor force. But the mine owners remained fiercely anti-union, and they fought back.

In 1913, John D. Rockefeller's Colorado Fuel and Iron Company led other companies in an open-shop drive, which prompted more than 10,000 miners to launch a major strike in September. The battle was long and bitter. Women joined the strike not as workers, as they had in Lawrence and Paterson, but as wives with their own grievances against the owners.

were thick about the northwest corner of the colony where the fire started and we could see distinctly from our lofty observation place what looked like a blazing torch waved in the midst of militia a few seconds before the general conflagration swept through the place.

Testimony of John D. Rockefeller

CHAIRMAN: And you are willing to go on and let these killings take place . . . rather than go out there and see if you might do something to settle those conditions?

ROCKEFELLER: There is just one thing . . . which can be done, as things are at present, to settle this strike, and that is to unionize the camps; and our interest in labor is so profound . . . that interest demands that the camps shall be open [nonunion] camps that we expect to stand by the [Colorado Fuel and Iron Co.] officers at any cost. . . .

CHAIRMAN: And you will do that if it costs all your property and kills all your employees?

ROCKEFELLER: It is a great principle.

CHAIRMAN: And you would do that rather than recognize the right of men to collective bargaining? Is that what I understand?

ROCKEFELLER: No, sir. Rather than allow outside people to come in and interfere with employees who are thoroughly satisfied with their labor conditions—it was upon a similar principle that the War of the Revolution was carried on. It is a great national issue of the most vital kind.

"Class War in Colorado." John Sloan's June 1914 cover for *The Masses* was unusual: portraying the devastation and death wrought by the National Guard and Rockefeller-hired private police on the miners' tent colony, Sloan nevertheless emphasized strikers fighting back.

The poverty of the mining towns made women's lives a nightmare of drudgery; they also faced demands for unpaid domestic service in the bosses' homes and occasional threats of sexual harassment while their men were in the mines. Despite the determination of the miners and their wives, the owners refused to recognize the union, evicted strikers from their homes, and brought in deputies and the state militia to break the strike. Finally, the militia attacked a strikers' tent camp in Ludlow on Easter night in 1914. Firing machine guns and setting fire to the tents, they killed fourteen, including eleven children.

In the wake of the Ludlow massacre, the UMWA issued a "call to arms." Miners armed themselves and headed into the foothills. For ten days a virtual war between miners and troops raged in southern Colorado, until the miners were finally disarmed by federal troops. Wobbly leader Bill Haywood concluded that the country was gripped by "an irreconcilable class struggle" between workers and capitalists. Other observers might not have used the same terms, but they would have agreed that at Ludlow, Lawrence, and across the country, the industrial system had generated a terrifying social conflict, one that seemed to threaten the very stability and promise of American life.

AN AGE OF REFORM

The labor struggles of the early twentieth century capped the series of turbulent battles between working people and their employers that had plagued the nation since the 1870s. These conflicts, and the sense that corporate power was out of control, engendered a growing belief among not only working people, but also middle-class Americans, that the industrial order needed fundamental reform. The Populist political upheaval in the 1890s, the massive influx of new immigrants, and the evident corruption of urban government all contributed to this national sentiment.

Millions of Americans responded to this challenge by taking part in progressive reform activities on a wide range of issues. Some were particularly concerned with the problem of business monopoly, others with municipal corruption, and still others with the needs of working people and the poor. Although in 1912 a Progressive Party was founded, reformers could be found among Democrats, Republicans, and independents as well. Most reformers worked outside the two-party system, yet they helped spur a fundamental reshaping of American government and politics.

The movements for reform involved Americans from many classes and groups, but the white, Protestant middle class was the group most often identified with Progressivism. Some descendants of long-established families felt that their status was now being usurped by new industrial entrepreneurs. Through reform politics, they sought to reassert their values and place in American society. The movement sprang from a spirit of optimistic evangelical Protestantism and included many "social gospel" ministers. But unlike Protestant reformers of the 1830s and 1840s, Progressives did not believe that moral persuasion alone would solve social ills. Rather, they believed in the power of science and of rational inquiry. By analyzing society's ills and applying knowledge to their solution, Progressives believed they could build a better society. In general, social-gospel Progressives thought that America's problems stemmed not so much from industrial capitalism as from the chaotic manner in which it developed. They believed that society had to be reformed if its democratic character was to be preserved.

This group of prominent reformers built alliances with a range of social groups. They found allies among members of a new professional class—physicians, businessmen, engineers, managers, and scientists—who experienced industrial society as chaotic, inefficient, and inhumane. Reform coalitions also involved more radical activists, including socialists and feminists who sought to advance women's rights as part of a larger vision of social transformation. And on many issues, reform movements also included American working women and men, who sought to meet their own needs and impose their own sense of order. Members of this diverse coalition found common ground as citizens concerned with preserving democratic government, and as disgruntled consumers resentful of high prices, shoddy products, and the monopolistic corporations that created them.

Crusading newspapers and "muckraking" magazines played a vital role in linking the elements of reform coalitions and informing the public about the problems of corruption and monopoly. In many cities, newspaper editors assigned reporters to expose political bosses' abuses of power, hoping to spur public outrage. New mass-circulation magazines such as *McClure's* and *The Independent* added to the clamor for reform. Investigative reporters such as Lincoln Steffens and Ida Tarbell exposed corporate wrongdoing, targeting, among others, Rockefeller's Standard Oil Company, the stock market, and the meat-packing industry. Crusading journalists helped create the sense that there was a broad public whose interests as citizens and consumers were ill served by the dominant political and economic institutions.

Despite broad agreement that reform was necessary, Progressives often disagreed on how to bring about necessary changes. The effort to reform city government and improve urban life, for example, varied according to region. In midwestern cities such as Milwaukee and St. Louis, and western cities such as San Francisco, reformers' attacks on corrupt state and local government drew support from working people and trade unions as well as middle-class citizens. These insurgencies often developed a strongly antibusiness character, yielding electoral reforms that opened up the political system to the influence of working people. In the South and on the East Coast, in contrast, reformers were more likely to view working people as part of the problem, not as part of the solution, and reforms often functioned to limit popular participation in the political system.

Hazen Pingree, a four-term mayor of Detroit, was a pioneer of the more democratic reform movement. First elected in 1889, Pingree increased taxes on corporations and provided public services such as electricity and sewers. Pingree's program and his support of striking railroad workers won him the support of local unions and the city's immigrants. When Pingree organized a municipal streetcar company in 1896, his democratic politics began to draw national attention. By the first decade of the twentieth century, campaigns for public ownership of municipal utilities were triumphing throughout the nation.

The movement for reform blossomed in St. Louis in 1900, during a strike by unionized workers against the local street railway, which had used its monopoly position to charge high prices for poor services. When the Central Trades and Labor Union and the Building

"The Boss." The standard reform perspective of the urban political machine, as illustrated in *Collier's* in 1906. Graphically, the conception of the Boss had changed very little since Thomas Nast's Tweed Ring caricatures of the 1870s.

Trades Council called on citizens to boycott the streetcar line, the entire community turned to "every conceivable vehicle . . . excepting balloons and baby buggies" to punish the hated monopoly.

This working-class action spurred middle-class reformers to undertake a series of legal and political battles with the railway and its allies—bankers, corporation heads, and the St. Louis political machine. One reformer, St. Louis district attorney Joseph Folk, took the crusade against corruption to a new level, running for governor in 1904. After working people helped him sweep to victory, Governor Folk successfully prosecuted Standard Oil and other monopoly corporations for overcharging Missouri consumers.

To strengthen the reform coalition, Folk, Pingree, Wisconsin's Robert LaFollette, and other midwestern Progressives moved to open up the political process to their working-class allies. With the support of unions and some middle-class groups, they pushed for direct primaries, which shifted the power to pick candidates from party bosses to the voters themselves. They also established the procedures known as the "initiative" and the "referendum," which enabled voters to put popular issues directly on the ballot. These Progressives also fought for passage of the 1913 constitutional amendment that replaced the election of senators by state legislatures with direct popular election.

On the East Coast and in the South, efforts to reform local government tended to go in a different direction. These movements were dominated by businessmen and other elites seeking to make local government more efficient and less costly. Aiming to seize control

---

"GIVE THE PROPERTY OWNER A FAIR SHOW . . ."

Some reformers sought to eliminate from urban government the power and influence of what they thought of as the ignorant working masses. The first document comes from the elite Voters' League of Pittsburgh, which campaigned in 1911 for removing workingmen from local school boards, suggesting that "a man's occupation ought to give a strong indication of his qualifications for membership. . . ." In the second document, Rear Admiral F. E. Chadwick, a leader in the municipal reform movement in Newport, Rhode Island, argued for changing local government to ensure a larger voice for "property owners."

Voters' League of Pittsburgh

EMPLOYMENT AS ORDINARY laborer and in the lowest class of mill work would naturally lead to the conclusion that such men did not have sufficient education or business training to act as school directors. . . . Objection might also be made to small shopkeepers, clerks, workmen at many trades, who by lack of educational advantages and business training, could not, no matter how honest, be expected to administer properly the affairs of an educational system . . . where millions of dollars are spent each year.

Rear Admiral F. E. Chadwick

OUR PRESENT SYSTEM has excluded in large degree the representation of those who have the city's well-being most at heart. It has brought in municipalities . . . a government established by the least educated, the least interested class of citizens.

It stands to reason that a man paying $5,000 in taxes in a town is more interested in the well-being and development of his town than the man who pays no taxes. . . . It equally stands to reason that the man of the $5,000 tax should be assured a representation in the committee which lays the tax and spends the money which he contributes. . . . Shall we be truly democratic and give the property owner a fair show or shall we develop a tyranny of ignorance which shall crush him?

of local government and destroy often corrupt political machines, they saw working-class voters—especially immigrants and African-Americans—not as allies but as part of the problem. Such reformers sought to strip African-Americans, immigrants, and the children of immigrants of the vote. And in the urban East they pushed social reforms to improve immigrant behavior, and immigration reform to reduce the influx of "undesirable" newcomers.

In hundreds of small and middle-size cities, especially in the South, business groups introduced "city commission" or "city manager" systems, shifting power from popularly elected councilmen to professional administrators. Designed, as John Patterson of the National Cash Register Company put it, to place municipal government "on a strict business basis," such systems ultimately took power away from working-class communities.

Other electoral reforms had similar effects. Political parties had long issued their own ballots, which voters carried with them to the polls. In the Progressive Era, reformers promoted the publicly printed "Australian ballot," which listed all the candidates. While it discouraged corruption, the new system also made voting more difficult for non-English-speaking immigrants, since they had to be able to read

"... HAMMERING AT THE TRUTH"

Although Progressive Era reforms in southern states limited the rights of African-Americans, the diverse Progressive movement also included individuals who fought for racial justice and equality. The Niagara Movement brought together a loose association of blacks and whites committed to this struggle. In 1910, members of the Niagara Movement helped organize the National Association for the Advancement of Colored People, which would play a leading role in the twentieth-century civil rights movement. W. E. B. DuBois, an eloquent and insightful African-American scholar and activist, gave this speech at a 1906 convention of the Niagara Movement.

THE MEN OF the Niagara Movement coming from the toil of the year's hard work and pausing a moment from the earning of their daily bread turn towards the nation and again ask in the name of ten million the privilege of a hearing. In the past year the work of the Negro hater has flourished in the land. Step by step the defenders of the rights of American citizens have retreated. The work of stealing the black man's ballot has progressed and the fifty and more representatives of stolen votes still sit in the nation's capital. Discrimination in travel and public accommodations has so spread that some of our weaker brethren are actually afraid to thunder against color discrimination as such and are simply whispering for ordinary decencies.

Against this the Niagara Movement eternally protests. We will not be satisfied to take one jot or tittle less than our full manhood rights....

to distinguish between candidates. The new system also gave public officials new power to eliminate third-party candidates from the ballot.

Southern reformers proposed and passed "antifusion" laws, which further diminished the effectiveness of workers' and farmers' protests. Throughout the late nineteenth century, disgruntled workers and farmers organized their own parties and then used them to support a major party candidate who backed their demands. This "fusion" of parties had been important to the development of Populism in the 1890s, but by the turn of the century numerous states passed laws that prohibited two parties from supporting the same candidates, making it more difficult for working people to wield power through third parties.

A more direct method to limit workers' political power was the adoption of literacy requirements for voting. All southern states and nine states outside the South had adopted such laws by 1920. In some instances, reformers changed electoral procedures specifically to check the growth of the Socialist Party, which was achieving considerable success on the local level. In the South, literacy was used as a tool to disfranchise African-Americans.

Literacy requirements were one factor in the dramatic decline in voter participation across the country. In an average 1870s election, 80 percent of those eligible voted; by 1920, only 60 percent voted in the northern states and under 30 percent voted in the South. The decline in voting also reflected a broader erosion of the popular politics of intense partisanship and spectacular election campaigns that had flourished in the nineteenth century. In the early twentieth century, once-vibrant party loyalties diminished, and a new, less participatory style of politics emerged.

This decline in formal voter participation was countered in part by the spread of nonelectoral forms of citizen participation. Americans employed other means to confront the problems

In detail our demands are clear and unequivocal. First, we would vote; with the right to vote goes everything: Freedom, manhood, the honor of your wives, the chastity of your daughters, the right to work, and the chance to rise. . . .

Second. We want discrimination in public accommodations to cease. Separation in railway and street cars, based simply on race and color, is un-American, undemocratic, and silly. . . .

Third. We claim the right of freemen to walk, talk, and be with them that wish to be with us. . . .

Fourth. We want the laws enforced against rich as well as poor; against Capitalist as well as Laborer; against white as well as black. . . .

Fifth. We want our children educated. . . . And when we call for education, we mean real education. . . . Education is the development of power and ideal. We want our children trained as intelligent human beings should be, and we will fight for all time against any proposal to educate black boys and girls simply as servants and underlings. . . .

These are some of the chief things which we want. How shall we get them? By voting where we may vote, by persistent, unceasing agitation, by hammering at the truth, by sacrifice and work. . . .

Courage, brothers! The battle for humanity is not lost or losing. All across the skies sit signs of promise. The Slav is rising in his might, the yellow millions are tasting liberty, the black Africans are writhing towards the light, and everywhere the laborer, with ballot in his hand, is voting open the gates of Opportunity and Peace. The morning breaks over the bloodstained hills. We must not falter, we may not shrink. Above are the everlasting stars.

of the industrial age. These means ranged from municipal and national commissions such as the Commission on Industrial Relations, established by President Wilson in the aftermath of the Ludlow massacre to investigate the era's industrial unrest, to voluntary associations such as the National Association for the Advancement of Colored People (NAACP), founded in 1910 by white and black reformers to fight the rise of segregation and lynching of African-Americans. This participatory style, pioneered by nineteenth-century women reformers, increasingly defined struggles for political and social change during the Progressive Era and beyond.

One of the most dynamic vehicles of Progressive reform was the "settlement house." Beginning in the late 1880s and continuing into the first decade of the twentieth century, hundreds of young men and women from middle- and upper-class homes moved into immigrant and working-class neighborhoods. There they organized settlement houses to address social problems related to the changing nature of urban-industrial life and labor. Reformer Jane Addams's Hull House in Chicago was the most famous of these. Addams and other settlement house workers focused their efforts particularly on poor and working-class immigrants. Although their work was initially humanitarian and "nonpolitical," settlement house workers and their allies helped transform American politics and government.

Through the settlement houses, reformers initially sought to provide social services otherwise unavailable to immigrants and the urban poor. Settlement house workers organized kindergartens, adult education classes, health programs,

---

"THEN WE'D HAVE SOME CAKE AND COFFEE . . ."

Immigrant men and women had a wide range of experiences with settlement house reformers. Some immigrants encountered the settlement houses as places of refuge and caring; at other times they found reformers to be arrogant and patronizing. This document, which describes a positive encounter, is drawn from the oral memoirs of Rosa, an Italian immigrant who lived and worked at a Chicago settlement house, Chicago Commons.

IN THE FIRST beginning we always came in to the club and made two circles in the room. One circle was for those ladies who could talk English and the other was for the ladies who talked German. Mrs. Reuter talked German to the German ladies and Miss Gray talked English to the other ladies. But I guess they both did the same preaching. They used to tell us that it's not nice the drink the beer, and we must not let the baby do this and this. Me, I was the only Italian woman—where were they going to put me? I couldn't talk German, I went in the English Circle. So after we had about an hour or an hour and a half of preaching, they would pull up the circle and we'd play the games together. All together we'd play the games—the Norwegian, the German, the English and me. Then we'd have some cake and coffee and the goodnight song. . . .

Pretty soon they started the classes to teach us poor people to talk and write in English. The talk of the people in the settlement house was different entirely than what I used to hear. I used to love the American people, and I was listening and listening how they talked. That's how I learned to talk such good English. Oh, I was glad when I learned enough English to go by the priest in the Irish church and confess myself and make the priest understand what was the sin! But I never learned to do the writing in English. I all the time used to come to that class so tired and so sleepy after scrubbing and washing the whole day—I went to sleep when they starting the writing. . . .

I have to tell about another good thing the settlement house did for me. That winter my [baby] Leo died we were still living in that little wooden house in the alley. All my walls were thick with frosting from the cold, and I got bronchitis on the lungs, with blood coming up. So one of those good ladies from the Commons, she arranged and sent me to a kind of home in the country where people go to get well. They had the nice nurses in that place and they cured me up good. I had a good time there, too. . . .

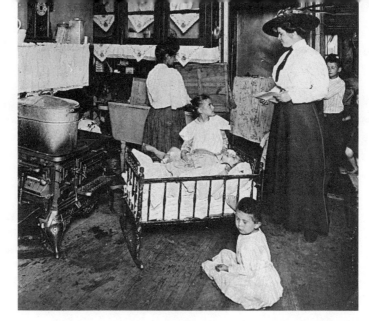

Settlement worker and immigrants. A photograph documenting the activities of a settlement house worker captures the complicated relationship between reformers and the people they "served." The reformers' altruism was offset by their belief in the superiority of middle-class mores, which they imposed on immigrants to get them to relinquish "un-American" customs.

and employment bureaus. The houses themselves served as meeting places where poor people could gather, learn, discuss, and organize. By 1910, hundreds of thousands of working people were using more than four hundred settlement houses nationwide.

The settlement houses also served as training grounds for a generation of reformers. Many of these reformers were unmarried, college-educated women reluctant to return to a life restricted to a middle-class Victorian home. In the settlement houses they found that they could engage more directly with the world. Influenced by their experience in the settlement houses and by the ideology of feminism, these women went on to become "spearheads of reform" in a variety of social and political movements.

Feminist reformers, including settlement house workers, played an important role in efforts to organize women workers. In 1903, New York reformers and their wealthy supporters established the national Women's Trade Union League (WTUL), seeking to combine trade unionism and feminism. League leaders believed that working women were more oppressed as workers than as women, but at the same time, that women of all classes shared important "bonds of womanhood." Supporting the unionization of working women, they enlisted the support of middle- and upper-class women who sympathized with their sisters. This strategy proved especially successful in the campaigns to organize garment workers in New York and Chicago. The WTUL also supported such female labor leaders as Rose Schneiderman, who became a key organizer in the garment district, and Agnes Nestor, who led glovemakers in Illinois.

"FOR WHY MUST I TELL YOU ALL MY BUSINESS?"

Some immigrants found reformers to be interfering and insensitive. This excerpt from "The Free Vacation House," a short story written by Jewish immigrant Anna Yezierska, illustrates this unpleasant aspect of the encounter between immigrants and reformers.

HOW CAME IT that I went to the free vacation house was like this:

One day the visiting teacher from the school nursery comes to find out why don't I get the children ready for school in time; for why are they so often late.

I let out on her my whole bitter heart. I told her my head was on wheels from worrying. . . .

"My dear woman," she says, "you are about to have a nervous breakdown. You need to get away to the country for a rest and vacation. . . ."

Later, in a few days, I just finished up with Masha and Mendel and Frieda and Sonya to send them to school, and I was getting Aby ready for kindergarten, when I hear a knock on the door, and a lady comes in. She had a white starched dress like a nurse and carried a black satchel in her hand.

"I am from the Social Betterment Society," she tells me. "You want to go to the country?"

Before I could say something, she goes over to the baby and pulls out the rubber nipple from her mouth, and to me she says, "You must not get the child used to sucking this; it is very unsanitary."

"Gott im Himmel!" I beg the lady. "Please don't begin with that child, or she'll holler my head off. She must have the nipple. I'm too nervous to hear her scream like that."

When I put the nipple back again in the baby's mouth, the lady takes herself a seat, and then takes out a big black book from her satchel. Then she begins to question me. What is my first name? How old I am? From where come I? How long I'm already in this country? Do I keep any boarders? What is my husband's first name? How old is he? How long he is in this country? By what trade he works? How much wages he gets for a week? How much money do I spend out for rent? How old are the children, and everything about them.

"My goodness!" I cry out. "For why is it necessary all this to know? For why must I tell you all my business? What difference does it make already if I keep boarders, or I don't keep boarders? If Masha had the whooping-cough or Sonya had the measles? Or whether I spend out for my rent ten dollars or twenty? Or whether I come from Schnipshnock or Kovner Gubernie?"

"We must make a record of all the applicants, and investigate each case," she tells me. "There are so many who apply to the charities, we can help only those who are most worthy."

"Charities!" I scream out. "Ain't the charities those who help the beggars out? I ain't no beggar. I'm not asking for no charity. My husband, he works. . . ."

"If your application is approved, you will be notified," she says to me, and out she goes.

Female settlement house workers and reformers often became ardent suffragists, infusing that movement with the energy of the new social feminism. They argued that if women could vote, they would bolster the broader cause of reform. Before social feminists entered the woman suffrage movement, the cause faltered as a result of class divisions. In the 1890s, upper-class women had taken over leadership of the National American Woman Suffrage Association, and the movement's base had narrowed. But the alliances that settlement house workers and WTUL reformers forged with working women reversed that trend. After women reformers rallied to support striking female shirtwaistmakers in 1909, young women from the sweatshops began marching in suffrage parades. By 1915, Jewish and Italian men in the garment shops were voting for women's right to vote in statewide referendums.

As the movement broadened its base, it shifted tactics as well. Local suffrage organizations with large working-class memberships began holding open-air meetings and massive parades. They built alliances with socialist activists, who were also concerned with suffrage and women's rights. The new approach brought results: in 1910, male voters in Washington State extended the franchise to women. By 1912, four more states had followed suit.

But as the drive for woman suffrage grew, so did the opposition. The Catholic Church disapproved of female voting, while liquor interests, machine politicians, and some business groups feared that women voters would support reform efforts. Referendums on woman suffrage were defeated in Pennsylvania, Massachusetts, and New York. The battle over a constitutional amendment franchising women grew increasingly heated in the years leading up to World War I.

While progress toward woman suffrage was slow, social feminists affected politics and government in other ways. Throughout the nineteenth century, women reformers had pushed to expand the definition of "women's sphere" to include education, health, public morals, and social welfare—any activities, in other words, that involved women and children. They sought to address problems in these areas through private agencies, such as churches and voluntary groups. By the early twentieth century, as a result of their experiences in settlement houses and labor and suffrage struggles, many women reformers had concluded that the problems were so deep-rooted that only the power of government was adequate to the task. As these social feminists and their allies undertook new strategies based on this understanding, they succeeded in helping to redefine the social responsibilities of American government.

Social feminists thus sought to improve the wages and working conditions of women and children through legislation. Onetime settlement house worker Florence Kelley led a coalition that won passage of a factory inspection act in Illinois; she then went to Oregon, where she helped force the state legislature to enact a law limiting the workday of women laundry workers to ten hours or less. Social feminists often worked closely with labor activists as they battled for protective legislation for women and child workers. Progressive politicians such as Robert LaFollette also realized that working people's support was necessary to prevail against political machines. They broadened their concerns to include women's and labor issues.

The struggle for protective legislation was aided by a 1908 U.S. Supreme Court decision that upheld the Oregon ten-hour law. Progressive lawyer Louis Brandeis argued, in a brief based on research by Josephine Goldmark of the National Consumers League, that limitations were needed because the "two sexes differ . . . in the amount of physical strength [and] in the capacity for long continued labor." In upholding the Oregon law, the Court justified its decision by noting that women would always depend on men for "protection." The decision was double-edged. Although it benefited working women, its underlying logic reinforced male domination. Nevertheless, the decision broke with previous legal doctrine that gave employers total control over the terms of their workers' employment.

The growing acceptance of protective legislation reflected a fundamental reorientation of the social and political beliefs of many middle-class citizens. Most Progressives rejected the rampant acquisitive individualism of the Gilded Age. Instead, they spoke increasingly of the importance of "society" or "social bonds." This new view marked a departure from nineteenth-century ideas and gave intellectual support for increased governmental intervention in the nation's economic and social life.

A MODERN FORM OF GOVERNMENT

As distrust of big business and its excesses grew, the struggles of middle-class reformers to enhance the role of government achieved a wider resonance. Socialist activists had long argued that only governmental authority could control the power of giant corporations. Now growing popular pressure for reform engulfed more mainstream political leaders at the local, state, and even national levels. Even machine politicians and Republicans, usually allied with business interests, wanted to be seen marching under the reform banner. Building coalitions with such politicians allowed reformers and their working allies to win concrete changes. In some cases, however, the involvement of mainstream forces allowed business interests to limit the real impact of reform.

Among the most important of political converts to reform was Theodore Roosevelt. Roosevelt assumed the presidency in 1901, the year before the United Mine Workers of America called a major strike in the Pennsylvania anthracite coalfields. At first the president was sympathetic to the operators, as had been earlier presidents confronted by nationwide labor disputes. But public opinion began to turn against the mine owners after one of their leaders, George Baer, refused to bargain with the UMWA, saying, "The rights and interests of the labor man will be protected and cared for—not by the labor agitators—but by the Christian men to whom God in his infinite wisdom has given control of the property interests of this country." Meanwhile, UMWA leaders followed a moderate course, which won them support. Worried that a strike would cripple the nation's economy and swayed by the weight of public opinion, Roosevelt pressed the operators to settle. After threatening to order U.S. troops to seize the mines, Roosevelt succeeded in getting the coal operators to negotiate. The ensuing settlement boosted the cause of the UMWA and unionization nationwide.

The coal strike taught Roosevelt that bashing big business could be good politics. Thereafter, he took pains to show the public that he was not afraid to use government power against large corporations. During his presidency, the Justice Department filed forty-five cases under the Sherman Antitrust Act, earning Roosevelt the nickname "trustbuster." Each suit fed public concern about business behavior. Roosevelt's most celebrated success was the breakup in 1907 of Standard Oil, which had achieved monopoly control of the nation's oil business.

Yet the Standard Oil case proved to be an exception. Many antitrust suits were dropped after corporate leaders visited the White House seeking presidential assistance. Roosevelt's decision not to break up more trusts was based on his belief that "bigness" had become inevitable. What was important, in his mind, was that the federal government possess the power to regulate corporate behavior, so that no corporation was so powerful as to be beyond the law's reach.

Between 1904 and World War I, government regulation of business grew rapidly. In 1906, Congress gave the previously weak Interstate Commerce Commission (ICC) the power to regulate railroad rates under the Hepburn Act. In the same year, after Upton Sinclair's sensational novel *The Jungle* exposed unhealthy practices in the meat-packing industry and *McClure's* exposed fraud in patent medi-

WILSON'S SUGGESTION FOR A CARTOON

"If I were a cartoonist I would draw a picture of the biggest monopolies of the United States, drawn up in line and in front Mr. Roosevelt trying to lead them in a hallelujah chorus."— *Woodrow Wilson.*

—*Ireland in Columbus Dispatch*

Teddy the trust-buster. A critical view of Theodore Roosevelt's reputation as a regulator of corporate abuses, appearing in the Columbus (Ohio) *Dispatch* during the 1912 presidential campaign.

cines, a popular uproar spurred passage of the Pure Food and Drug Act and the Meat Inspection Act.

Although corporate executives usually opposed regulation, they learned to live with the new regime. Some even turned it to their advantage by helping shape regulatory legislation, agencies, and boards. Following an economic panic in 1907 and the ensuing public pressure for monetary reform, bankers embraced calls for federal regulation of the banking system. When Congress approved the Federal Reserve Act in 1913, bankers had to accept a measure of public control over their industry. But they quickly learned how to make federal regulation work to their benefit. Bankers soon dominated the boards of the regional Federal Reserve banks and shaped the policies of the Federal Reserve Board, both of which regulated the nation's currency and credit systems. Lobbyists and leaders in other industries, including meat-packing and railroads, also managed to influence the boards and commissions set up to regulate their businesses. These businessmen used Progressive Era regulation as a means of achieving orderly markets and reducing competition.

Government regulation was supported by other unlikely groups. The 1911 Triangle Shirtwaist fire that killed 146 workers provided the impetus for New York City's machine politicians to embrace the reform banner. New York's state government had long resisted legislation to regulate working conditions, but the furor over the Triangle fire convinced urban Democrats, who controlled the legislature, that the time was right to join the reform crusade. Responding to socialist agitation and intense pressure from both working-class and middle-class reformers, the legislature voted to establish a factory commission to investigate the Triangle tragedy and recommend ways to prevent future incidents.

By naming AFL president Samuel Gompers and National Consumers League representative Frances Perkins to the Factory Commission, politicians acknowledged well-established national reform forces. But crucial to the commission's success were two Tammany Hall politicians, Robert Wagner and Alfred E. Smith. Over the course of the commission's four years of work, Wagner and Smith permitted hundreds of workers to testify about unsafe working conditions. The commission sponsored fifty-six laws to improve wages and working conditions and, because of the leadership of Wagner and Smith, many of these laws were passed. By wrapping itself in the banner of reform, New York's Democratic Party succeeded in undercutting the growing influence of socialists and others among its working-class constituents.

Southern Democrats felt no such pressure to enact reforms to maintain the allegiance of their working-class supporters. Two weeks after the Triangle fire, on April 8, 1911, a violent explosion ripped through the Banner coalmine outside Birmingham, Alabama; 128 convict miners, mostly African-Americans jailed for minor offenses, were killed. Unlike that of their immigrant counterparts at the Triangle Company, the fate of the African-American convict miners elicited little sympathy among white Alabamans and other Americans. Although clear evidence supplied by the federal Bureau of Mines indicated the presence of high levels of dangerous methane gas in the mine, a state investigating commission announced that the miners' own ineptitude caused the explosion.

Middle-class reformers and Alabama's trade union movement called immediately for abolition of the nearly century-old policy of leasing out convicts as laborers. But a coalition of Democratic state legislators and big businessmen intent on protecting the substantial profits each group garnered from the convict labor system quickly quashed the proposed legislation. Coal continued to be mined by convicts in Alabama for nearly two more decades before the infamous system was finally abolished in 1928. The failure of even such modest Progressive Era reforms in the South had much to do with the overall weakness of the region's trade union movement and the virulent racism that continued to divide reform forces and dominate southern political life during these years.

Although the strength of the movement was uneven, by the second decade of the twentieth century an unlikely alliance of reformers, radicals, feminists, unionists, and machine politicians had placed the social needs of working people squarely on the nation's political agenda. In 1912 alone, thirty-eight states passed child labor laws and twenty-eight states (mostly northern and western) set maximum hours for women workers; legislators in southern states resisted such reforms. Some reform legislation affected male workers as well; by 1915, workmen's compensation laws were on the books in thirty-five states. In twenty-five states, some categories of male workers were also protected by limitations on working hours.

Ironically, the AFL and its leader, Samuel Gompers, were among the last to accept the government's role in reform. During the early years of Progressivism, believing it was better for working people to make gains through collective bargaining, Gompers advocated a course known as "voluntarism." The AFL minimized its involvement in electoral politics and reform crusades. Though it supported protective legislation for women and children, the federation did not seek laws to improve conditions for men.

Later in the era, in response to a series of judicial actions that clearly aided employers, the AFL changed its attitude toward government involvement in labor issues. In 1904, the courts began reinforcing employer campaigns against unionization by liberally issuing injunctions that prohibited strikers' picket lines and the distribution of strike benefits. In 1908 the U.S. Supreme Court severely limited the use of boycotts, ruling that the Sherman Antitrust Act blocked unions as well as companies from restraining interstate commerce. These court actions overcame the AFL's aversion to politics. Gompers and his allies rejected a call by Socialists in the labor movement for independent political action, which could have strengthened the Socialist Party. Instead the AFL tried to push the two major parties to support labor issues. The Democrats responded more positively, and the AFL began moving into the Democratic camp.

In the election of 1912, three major candidates ran for the presidency and, in a tribute to the power of the reform tide, all claimed to be progressives. The incumbent president, Republican William H. Taft, had been Theodore Roosevelt's handpicked successor in 1908. Roosevelt grew disenchanted with Taft, however, and in 1912 decided to seek the GOP nomination himself. When the Republicans chose Taft, Roosevelt joined with other reformers to form the Progressive Party. The Democrats nominated Woodrow Wilson, a reform governor from New Jersey who saw trusts as economically inefficient and called for government efforts to restore competition. Meanwhile, the Socialist Party ran Eugene Debs, who won 6 percent of the vote and pushed the debate even further in the direction of fundamental change. With support from middle-class voters and AFL unions, Wilson won the presidency by a narrow margin.

As president, Wilson rewarded labor by backing the 1914 Clayton Act. Gompers called the legislation labor's "Magna Carta," believing the law would free labor from oppressive court interpretations of the Sherman Antitrust Act. Wilson also championed a model federal workmen's compensation statute, an eight-hour-workday law for railroad workers, and a federal child labor law. The result of years of pressure from working people and reformers, these bills established, for the first time, the federal government's interest in regulating the conditions of labor.

Wilson responded to some but not all of the items on the reform agenda. He dragged his feet on the call for woman suffrage and showed almost no sympathy for the problems of immigrants and African-Americans. On the other hand, Wilson set up the Federal Reserve system to oversee the national banking industry; and he agreed to the creation of the Federal Trade Commission, which was charged with preventing corporate practices that inhibited competition. These efforts continued a trend, begun a decade earlier under Roosevelt, of concentrating federal power in the executive branch, creating a large administrative bureaucracy to mediate conflicting social pressures.

Progressivism responded to the economic, social, and political dislocations that accompanied industrial capitalism's dramatic growth during the Gilded Age: rapid technological change; intense and episodic conflict between capital and labor; the influx of enormous numbers of new immigrants from southern and eastern Europe, Asia, and Latin America; and the growing national and international reach of American capitalism. Each of these problems posed a special challenge to older American ideals of individual independence and equality.

Progressivism looked to an active government to blunt the worst of capitalism's economic and social problems. Working people, in coalition with socialists, radicals, and feminists, were key participants in Progressive reform struggles, helping to win passage of prolabor legislation, especially the federal Clayton Act, which established a basic "bill of rights" for labor unions. These reforms helped lay the foundation for our modern notion of government and were among Progressivism's most lasting contributions to American political life.

But by the time war broke out in Europe in 1914, the central role many Progressives desired for government had been only partially realized: federal, state, and local laws minimally regulated the economy and industrial relations while extending limited protections to consumers and women and children. Assembling the cross-class coalition that made Progressive reforms possible had involved significant compromises. Only a relatively small number of working people—those organized into skilled-craft unions and those working in the industries covered by limited factory reforms—fully benefited from the passage of Progressive legislation. Many others—unskilled and manual laborers, domestic servants, agricultural wageworkers, and sharecroppers—remained outside Progressivism's protective sphere.

African-Americans experienced the Progressive Era quite literally as a tightening noose: the federal government repeatedly ignored the wanton lynching of hundreds of blacks by southern whites. At the same time, the modest political and economic gains African-Americans had made during Reconstruction were rolled back in a flood of Progressive Era disfranchisement laws and the purging of African-Americans from federal jobs by the Wilson administration.

Despite these very real limitations, Progressivism represented a watershed that marked the beginning of a new relationship between working people and the government. The era's limited reforms inaugurated a period of governmental involvement in economic and social affairs that would intensify in coming decades. As a result, working people would look increasingly to government to ameliorate the worst excesses of industrial capitalism. Progressivism set the terms of this new relationship, as working people's experiences in their struggle for a better life were now linked inextricably to national political, economic, and social developments.

PART TWO

WAR, DEPRESSION, AND INDUSTRIAL UNIONISM

1914–1945

BETWEEN 1914 and 1945 two world wars and a prolonged economic depression created unprecedented crises in the United States and the rest of the globe. Nearly 15 million died in the first international conflict while as many as 60 million perished during World War II. The Great Depression threw scores of millions out of work. The devastation and misery that characterized these decades ushered in dramatic changes in the economic, political, and social order.

The central role played by the United States in winning each of the wars transformed the international balance of power. The global struggles not only made the United States the world's most powerful military force; along with Depression-era reforms they also made the federal government the dominant force in American economic and social life.

America's military and economic ascendancy rested on foundations already in place. The United States acquired little new overseas territory and no new states entered the union between the start of World War I and the end of World War II. While the U.S. population continued to grow—from roughly 100 million to nearly 150 million—it increased much more slowly than in the past. By the outbreak of World War I, the basic industrial infrastructure—railroads, mines, ports, steel mills, and the like—was already well developed and would not be altered substantially until World War II. Many basic institutions that still characterize modern American life—national corporations, the financial system, and the main political parties—also were in place by World War I.

As we will see in Part Two, war transformed the nation's workforce. Tens of millions of women and men moved into industrial labor, some migrating thousands of miles to find work. During and after both wars, African-Americans and poor whites from the rural South as well as Mexican and French-Canadian immigrants filled many industrial jobs previously taken by southern and eastern European immigrants, whose entry into the United States was restricted by quotas in the interwar years.

War also provided a favorable environment for union growth. With the economy booming during World War I, unions signed up millions of new members and made significant political gains. After the war, unionists hoped to capitalize on their advances with a drive to organize basic industry and improve pay. But the offensive failed, as companies and the government unleashed a wave of repression, using techniques they had pioneered during the war against radicals and dissenters. By the early 1920s, the labor movement was in full-scale retreat.

In the interwar years the production of consumer goods became the most dynamic sector of the economy. Major innovations in manufacturing, distribution, and marketing and radical changes in popular culture and everyday life stimulated the new consumer economy. Most Americans thought the basic economic challenge facing the nation was no longer how to produce enough goods to meet its citizens' needs but how to find enough customers to buy everything its economy produced. In spite of impressive economic growth during the 1920s, this challenge was not met; while many prospered, many others remained impoverished. Extreme economic inequality helped trigger the Great Depression that followed.

By the 1930s, depressions had been a regular part of American life for over a century. But never before—or since—did an economic downturn have such great or lasting political impact. The Great Depression discredited business and political leaders while sparking a series of mass protest movements.

During the presidency of Franklin Roosevelt, American life was further transformed. In the face of widespread misery and popular discontent, the federal government launched an extensive economic recovery program and took on many new responsibilities. Most important was the creation of what we now call a welfare state that included a national pension system, unemployment insurance, jobs programs, public housing, and aid to dependent citizens. Such government intervention failed to end the Depression, although it helped tens of millions of Americans survive it.

Workers benefited from these initiatives, but their greatest gains came from the dramatic growth of industrial unions. The Depression changed the balance of power between labor and capital, temporarily giving the labor movement an advantage. Even before Roosevelt took office, a new working-class combativeness emerged. When the new administration endorsed the right to join unions, it set off a wave of successful organizing drives. Then, in 1934, came an extraordinary series of large, violent strikes. These struggles resulted the following year in the passage of strong, pro-union federal labor legislation and the rise of a new, dynamic force—the Congress of Industrial Organizations—that enrolled millions of factory workers once thought unfit for organization. Over the next six years, these workers undertook a series of dramatic struggles that unionized the nation's mass-production industries.

World War II ended the Great Depression and made the United States the most powerful nation in the world. With the fighting almost exclusively on foreign soil, wartime America boasted a sense of confidence and good fortune that contrasted sharply with the extreme suffering the war visited on the rest of the world. As the worldwide conflict entered its final year, America's economic and military might proved pivotal in defeating Germany and Japan.

The Allied victory brought joy to Americans. It also raised troubling questions. How should America's military might, especially its newly unleashed atomic bomb, be used in the coming era of peace? What role should the government play in the peacetime economy? And would the democratic rights and values for which the country claimed to have fought be extended to all its own citizens? These questions would be debated in the postwar era amid a prosperity and power that would have been almost impossible to imagine thirty years earlier.

No man's land. Caught on one of the barbed-wire barricades that webbed European battlefields during the First World War, a soldier's corpse hangs unburied between the trenches of the opposing armies.

5

WARS
FOR
DEMOCRACY

BIG WARS bring big changes in how people live. To fight on the scale of World War I required the warring nations of Europe and North America to take drastic steps to mobilize their economies and maintain political unity. Although the United States did not enter the war until 1917, as a major exporter of supplies to the battling nations it was affected well before then. And once it became a combatant, virtually every aspect of American life was touched.

To coordinate the war effort, the federal government immensely expanded its role in economic, social, and political life. The need to win working-class cooperation in war production forced the government to pay close attention to workers' concerns. The "labor question," already a major national issue, influenced virtually every aspect of government policy. In these circumstances, working people made unprecedented organizational and political gains.

Workers also benefited from a labor shortage that developed as war production grew. With jobs easy to get, workers pressed for better wages and conditions and for recognition of their unions. Often they won major concessions, though sometimes they were harshly repressed. The shortage of labor also sparked a major population redistribution, as rural southern blacks moved north to fill industrial jobs, and immigration from Mexico surged. Simultaneously, women were recruited for jobs from which they traditionally had been barred.

World War I started as a result of long-standing rivalries between the capitalist powers in Europe; it ended in a political and economic crisis that threatened the very existence of the world capitalist system. The war undercut the moral, political, and economic bases of the old regimes of Europe. In Russia the collapse was complete, with the czarist regime replaced by a revolutionary socialist government. In half a dozen other countries, revolutions were attempted or seemed just around the corner. Never before had the foundations of capitalism seemed so shaky.

The United States was the only country to emerge from the war economically stronger. Also, it had far fewer war dead than the other combatants. Accordingly, the postwar political crisis was less severe in the United States than elsewhere. Still, as the fighting ended, the country faced a fundamental question: Would it return to its prewar ways, or would a new type of postwar society be constructed?

NEUTRALITY OR WAR?

When World War I broke out in the summer of 1914, the leaders of all the nations involved expected a short struggle. The immediate cause of the war was a dispute between Serbia and Austria-Hungary following the assassination of the heir to the Austro-Hungarian throne by a Serbian nationalist. This local conflict quickly escalated to involve most of Europe. Over the previous decades the European powers, competing for markets, colonies, and raw materials, had built up their armed forces and signed a series of secret treaties that established two major blocs—the Allied Powers of Great Britain, France, Russia, and Italy; and the Central Powers of Germany, Austria-Hungary, and Turkey. Now the clash between these alliances was at hand.

Each side confidently predicted a quick victory. Instead, the war turned into a grinding, gruesome battle of attrition. Even more than the American Civil War, World War I was an industrial war. The combatants fielded huge armies and cranked out mountains of supplies and equipment. Defensive measures such as trenches, fortifications, and machine guns effectively blocked advances. The result was a stalemate. On the Western Front, running through eastern France, and the Eastern Front, running across Poland, millions of troops were pinned down in parallel lines of trenches. Forward thrusts led to death and maiming on an unprecedented scale. For example, 600,000 soldiers were killed during the 1916 German offensive at Verdun, which barely changed the position of the front.

As soon as the war in Europe began, groups of Americans began advocating radically different views on what the United States should do. At one extreme were the peace forces. Some were out-and-out pacifists, opposed to all wars. Others, including many socialists, strongly objected to this particular conflict, which they saw as the product of capitalist greed. At the other extreme were the so-called preparedness groups, which urged the United States to begin military mobilization. Many leaders of these groups had ties to East Coast banking and commercial interests and were strongly pro-British and pro-French.

At first the Wilson administration urged strict American neutrality. The very nature of the war, though, made this difficult. All the warring parties needed myriad supplies to sustain their massive armies and civilian populations; each side tried to stop the other from getting these from neutral countries. The British, possessing the most powerful navy in the world, were able to blockade the Central Powers, turning back ships carrying war-related goods, including food. The Germans eventually retaliated by using a new weapon, the submarine, to sink Allied supply ships.

The British blockade and long-standing patterns of international commerce meant that U.S. firms traded more extensively with the Allies than with the Central Powers. As the war went on, American businesses developed even stronger ties to England and France and an ever greater economic stake in their victory. Once Germany began submarine warfare in February 1915, incidents involving Americans were inevitable. Americans traveling on British boats were killed during submarine attacks, and a few American ships were sunk by mistake.

Some opponents of the war, including Secretary of State William Jennings Bryan, urged Wilson to take steps to prevent shipping and trade issues from sucking the United States into the conflict, even calling for barring American commercial ties with the combatants. Wilson refused, arguing that the United States had to maintain its freedom of trade and freedom of the seas. The real issue, though, was not the abstract principles of international law, but how the war would affect the United States's international economic position and its domestic politics.

Like most business and political leaders, Wilson believed that

America's continued prosperity and tranquillity depended on expanded investment abroad and growing international trade. The main obstacle, in his view, was European-style imperialism: colonies, exclusive spheres of influence, and high tariffs. The Underwood Act of 1913, which lowered U.S. import duties, was designed to be a first step toward an international free-trade system. Wilson meant his policies not simply to aid American industry and raise the standard of living; he also saw the spread of free-trade, democratic capitalism as a deeply moral project, a concrete expression of his Christian belief and the values he cherished in American life.

In spite of his professed belief in democratic self-rule, though, Wilson repeatedly defended U.S. colonialism in the Philippines, which he called a sacred trust. He also put or kept U.S. troops in Cuba, Haiti, Nicaragua, and the Dominican Republic to defend American property and make sure that debts were paid. In addition, the United States became deeply involved in Mexico's revolution, which had begun in 1911 with the overthrow of the longtime dictator Porfirio Díaz. Wilson, worried about threats against U.S.-owned prop-

Invading forces. A 1914 Mexican postcard shows a company of American soldiers marching along the Avenida Independencia in Vera Cruz.

Soldados Norte-Americanos llegando por la Avenida Independencia

erty, backed first one Mexican faction and then another, twice sending U.S. troops to occupy parts of Mexico.

World War I presented Wilson with a profound dilemma. Both sides were seeking to strengthen precisely the sort of imperialism he opposed. Since the United States faced no immediate military threat, it could stay aloof. However, Wilson, who was emotionally and ideologically sympathetic to Great Britain, feared that if the Allied Powers were defeated, Germany would emerge as a dangerous economic and military rival to the United States. Furthermore, Wilson worried that if America remained neutral it would be unable to help shape the postwar world.

Wilson faced strong, conflicting domestic political pressures. Americans of German heritage generally favored the Central Powers; those from British backgrounds backed the Allies for the most part. Most Irish-Americans, though no special friends of Germany, opposed aid to Britain, especially after the abortive 1916 Easter rebellion in Ireland led to a new, more intensive phase of the Irish independence struggle.

Beyond these ethnic considerations, many Americans saw the war controversy as an opportunity to promote their own particular social goals. Many conservative businessmen, for example, used preparedness as a cover for anti-union, antiradical, and nativist campaigns, associating their cause with patriotism. Joining them were representatives of the old elite, such as Theodore Roosevelt, who for years had been trying to use militarism to infuse the country with the values they held dear: order, self-discipline, and individual achievement.

One of the most dramatic examples of the deep social divisions behind the war debate took place in San Francisco. In July 1916 the local chamber of commerce, which had just launched an open-shop campaign, sponsored a Preparedness Day parade. The city trade-union movement, which was heavily Irish, denounced the march, with the powerful Building Trades Council forbidding its members to take part. Amid this tense atmosphere a bomb exploded along the parade route, killing ten and injuring forty. Within a week six radical labor activists were charged with the bombing. Although the evidence against them was flimsy, two men, Tom Mooney and Warren K. Billings, were convicted of murder. The following autumn, open-shop employers capitalized on the fear of labor violence that followed the bombing to win passage in a general election of an antipicketing ordinance.

Just as many conservatives embraced preparedness, many reformers advocated nonintervention. Most feminists and suffragists opposed the war, including Jane Addams and Carrie Chapman Catt, president of the National American Woman Suffrage Association, who together founded the Women's Peace Party. So did many Progressive journalists and settlement house workers, and the old Populist Tom Watson. In Congress a large bloc of southern and midwestern Democrats joined rural Progressives George Norris and Robert La Follette in criticizing preparedness. Even a few prominent industrialists joined the peace camp.

Radicals were nearly unanimous in their opposition to intervention. The IWW, the Socialist Party, and assorted anarchists all denounced the war as an imperialist conflict. Their position carried considerable weight; although relatively few Americans belonged to radical organizations, a growing number were sympathetic to their ideas. In 1914 a Socialist from New York City's Lower East Side was elected to Congress, and two years later another was elected mayor of Milwaukee. Two groups in particular were turning toward socialism: new immigrants and middle-class intellectuals. Tens of thousands of recent immigrants joined special Socialist Party ethnic federations, while many artists, writers, college students, and reformers were caught up in a wave of socialist enthusiasm.

As the war debate raged, President Wilson vacillated. After first supporting neutrality, in the fall of 1915 he came out for a program of military buildup. A few months later he switched positions again. The reason was politics. In 1912 Wilson had been elected with only a minority of the vote in a three-way contest; if he was to be reelected in 1916 he would have to win over a sizable bloc of new supporters. To do this he launched a liberal offensive aimed at Progressive, labor, and antiwar voters.

First came the appointment of leading Progressive Louis Brandeis to the U.S. Supreme Court. Next Wilson supported a rural credits bill he had previously blocked, bolstering his support among farmers (many of whom were antiwar). Then he backed a series of prolabor bills. Finally, once the campaign got under way in the summer of 1916, Wilson began championing the cause of peace. The main Democratic slogan was "He kept us out of war."

Wilson's twists and turns di-

"LET THE CAPITALISTS DO THEIR OWN FIGHTING . . ."

Radical and socialist opposition to the war was near-absolute, growing out of a sense that the war resulted from inevitable capitalist rivalry for international markets and raw materials. Eugene Debs, industrial union leader and Socialist Party presidential candidate, expressed this intense antiwar attitude in the following editorial, published in August 1914 in the working-class newspaper National Rip-Saw, *immediately after the outbreak of fighting in Europe.*

THE CAPITALISTS TELL us it is patriotic to fight for your country and shed your blood for the flag. Very well! Let them set the example.

It is their country; they own it and therefore according to their logic it is their patriotic duty to fight and die for it and be brought home riddled with bullets and covered with flowers as shining examples of patriotic duty to the youth of the nation. . . .

You never had a country to fight for and never will have as much as an inch of one as long as you are fool enough to make a target of your bodies for the profit and glory of your masters.

Let the capitalists do their own fighting and furnish their own corpses and there will never be another war on the face of the earth.

vided the AFL, which initially was united against the war. When Wilson came out for military expansion, many AFL unions and local labor councils opposed him, especially wherever the left was influential or where there were many Irish or German unionists. However, in a January 1916 speech to the National Civic Federation, Samuel Gompers abandoned his longtime pacifism and came out for preparedness. "Though we may realize the brutality of war," he said, "yet we know equally well what would be the effects upon the lives and minds of men who would lose their rights, who would accept denial of justice rather than hazard their physical safety."

Wilson's 1916 return to an antiwar position convinced many unionists that the AFL should endorse him, as it had in 1912, rather than resume its previous policy of neutrality in presidential elections. Even many left-leaning unions, such as the miners and machinists, came out for Wilson. Wilson's strong labor backing was attributable not only to his peace platform but also to the fact that his administration had amply repaid the AFL for its support.

One of Wilson's first acts in office in 1913 had been to choose members for the Commission on Industrial Relations, authorized by Congress in response to the growth of labor radicalism and labor violence. As chairman he selected Frank P. Walsh, a Kansas City lawyer, social worker, and reformer highly sympathetic to labor. Walsh used a series of public hearings to expose what he called "industrial feudalism." Walsh believed that poor conditions, autocratic management, and the concentration of wealth were the underlying causes of labor violence. The commission's final majority report, issued in 1915, was perhaps the most sympathetic document about labor released by the federal government to that time. It called for an inheritance tax to finance education, social services, and public works; a child-labor law; equal pay for women and men; and legislation protecting the rights of workers to join unions and bargain collectively.

Although the Wilson administration ignored most of these recommendations, organized labor's political mobilization finally paid off. In 1914 Congress passed the Clayton Act—the AFL's paramount legislative goal—which exempted the labor movement from antitrust action. The next year, Congress approved the Seamen's Act, which eliminated the system of debt peonage and semimilitary discipline that had made sailors among the most abused American workers. (The law also barred Asians from working on U.S. ships and restricted some maritime jobs to citizens.) And in 1916 came a federal child-labor law and the Adamson Act, which granted railroad workers the eight-hour day, the first time a group of private workers had their working hours regulated by the federal government.

Some of these legislative victories were later undercut by the courts: the labor provisions of the Clayton Act were severely weakened by court interpretations, and the child-labor law was soon declared unconstitutional. Nevertheless, most trade union leaders believed that the AFL's de facto alliance with Wilson had paid rich dividends, so they renewed it in 1916.

Wilson's election-year stance also won him strong Progressive support. With the exception of the followers of former President Roosevelt—who had abandoned third-party politics to return to the Republican fold—most Progressives backed Wilson with extraordinary enthusiasm. Wilson seemed to be supporting everything they believed in: an active federal role in upgrading work and living conditions; the settlement of domestic and international conflicts through conciliation; and more broadly, the notion of a new world built on principles of rationality and social harmony. Wilson's reform image was so powerful that many Socialists deserted their own party to support the president. Meanwhile, the Republican candidate, Charles Evans Hughes, hampered by Roosevelt's militaristic speeches and bitter divisions within his party, ran a confused campaign. For Wilson, it was lucky that he did, since the Republicans were still basically the dominant national party: When the votes were counted, Wilson won the popular ballot by less than 600,000 votes, and the electoral college by a majority of just 23.

Many Progressives believed that Wilson's reelection would usher in an era of peace, progress, and social cooperation. Within months they faced devastating disappointment. In late January 1917 Wilson called for a European "peace without victors," a "peace among equals." But only days later the German government announced that it was resuming unrestricted submarine warfare, which it had suspended in mid-1916, and would attack all ships headed for Britain. Relations between Germany and the United States quickly deteriorated, and on April 2—just twenty-nine days after he began his second term—Wilson asked Congress to declare war. It did so four days later by overwhelming majorities.

LABOR ON THE OFFENSIVE

Well before the United States declared war, the fighting abroad was profoundly affecting the American economy. To finance the war, Europeans were forced to sell to Americans some $3 billion worth of investments they had in the United States. In addition, they borrowed over $2 billion from American banks and the federal government. By the end of the war, the United States had reversed its historic position as a net debtor and become a net lender. New York was well on its way toward replacing London as the world's most important financial center.

Much of the money that the United States loaned came back immediately to pay for food, raw materials, and manufactured goods needed by the warring countries of Europe. The Allied Powers, for example, increased their U.S. wheat purchases sevenfold. J. P. Morgan & Co., acting as the exclusive purchasing agent for England and France, placed over $3 billion worth of wartime orders. By the end of 1915, American goods were flowing to Europe in massive quantities.

Trade with other regions also increased. With the warring countries concentrating on military production, American businesses were able to enlarge their share of export markets long dominated by European countries, particularly in Latin America. U.S. companies also developed new ties to raw-materials producers around the world.

Stimulated by exports, the American economy pulled out of the recession that had plagued it from 1913 to the middle of 1915. By 1917 the gross national product was 20 percent above what it had been three years earlier. Manufacturing output increased by nearly 40 percent, mining by over 30 percent.

Employers suddenly faced an unfamiliar problem: a shortage of labor. At the very moment when more workers than ever before were needed in mines, factories, and fields, the flow of immigrants across the Atlantic was sharply diminished by the European war. In 1914 over 1 million Europeans had come to America; in 1915 the number fell to under 200,000, and in 1918 to just 31,000. By 1918 the unemployment rate had fallen to 2.4 percent, down from over 15 percent just three years earlier.

Workers were quick to take advantage of their improved bargaining position. Individually, they began shopping for better wages and conditions, switching jobs frequently. Collectively, they joined established unions, formed new ones, bargained with employers, and went on strike. Hard-pressed to replace fired workers or find strikebreakers, many companies with steady, highly profitable orders to be filled accepted higher labor costs rather than face prolonged stoppages.

Inflation contributed to the labor unrest. In 1915 consumer prices, after a long period of relative stability, began to rise sharply as a result of the war. By 1920 they doubled. Even when wages went up, purchasing power often declined. Traditional relationships between wage levels were disrupted by the upward spiral of pay and prices. Frequently workers in one type of job, used to making more money than workers in another, found themselves falling behind and responded by striking.

In every year from 1916 through 1920 over a million workers went on strike—a higher proportion of the workforce than during any equivalent period before or since. Workers of all sorts struck: unionists and nonunionists, the skilled and the unskilled, women and

SCHWAB'S BONUS MEN By Edward Mott Woolley

"Schwab's Bonus Men." A May 1916 cover of *Collier's* presents a romantic portrait of the industrial worker, reflecting the steel companies' sudden turn to extolling the virtues of their workers in the face of a labor shortage.

men, immigrants and natives, day laborers and those with steady jobs. The many strands of worker militancy that had developed since the turn of the century converged in a massive outpouring of protest.

Many war-era walkouts occurred on a very large scale, with workers from different companies or even different industries striking in support of one another. In the summer of 1915, for instance, a wave of strikes hit the booming munitions industry in the Northeast. In Bridgeport, Connecticut, machinists from eighteen different shops, including a giant Remington Arms plant, struck demanding an eight-hour day and union recognition. Most employers quickly agreed to a shorter workweek. Inspired, thousands of unskilled Bridgeport workers—from corset and textile factories, garment shops, and laundries—left their jobs too, demanding shorter hours and other improvements. In spite of the fact that few of these workers belonged to unions, they won many concessions. "A ten-hour center like Bridgeport," the New York *World* observed, "was converted overnight into an eight-hour community, a result that ten years of agitation under normal conditions might not have accomplished."

Unionized craft workers took advantage of the favorable wartime bargaining climate to pursue long-sought goals. For example, metalworkers, who took part in more wartime strikes than any other group, repeatedly struck for shorter hours, higher pay, and union recognition. Their ongoing battle against scientific management was particularly intense during the war, as manufacturers tried to capitalize on steady production runs

". . . HAVE THE WOMEN ORGANIZED IN SEPARATE LOCALS"

As a militant spirit spread among American workers, women joined unions in growing numbers. But most did not become active members. In the article below, Alice Henry, editor of the Women's Trade Union League newspaper, analyzed some of the obstacles to women's participation and proposed a solution.

THE COMMONEST COMPLAINT of all is that women members of a trade union do not attend their meetings. It is indeed a very serious difficulty to cope with. . . .

At first glance it seems curious that the meetings of a mixed local composed of both men and girls, should have for the girls even less attraction than meetings of their own sex only. But so it is. A business meeting of a local affords none of the lively social intercourse of a gathering for pleasure or even of a class for instruction. The men, mostly the older men, run the meeting and often are the meeting. Their influence may be out of all proportion to their numbers. It is they who decide the place where the local shall meet and the hour at which members shall assemble. The place is therefore often over a saloon, to which many girls naturally and rightly object. Sometimes it is even in a disreputable district. The girls may prefer that the meeting should begin shortly after closing time so that they do not need to go home and return, or have to loiter about for two or three hours. They like meetings to be over early. The men mostly name eight o'clock as the time of beginning, but business often will not start much before nine. Then, too, the men feel that they have come together to talk, and talk they do while they allow the real business to drag. Of course, the girls are not interested in long discussions on matters that they do not understand and in which they have no part and naturally they stay away, and so make matters worse, for the men feel they are doing their best for the interests of the union, resent the women's indifference, and are more sure than ever that women do not make good unionists. . . .

Where the conditions of the trade permit it by far the best plan is to have the women organized in separate locals. The meetings of women and girls only draw better attendances, give far more opportunity for all the members to take part in the business, and beyond all question form the finest training ground for the women leaders who in considerable numbers are needed so badly in the woman's side of the trade union movement today.

"... THOSE WHO HARVEST THE HARVESTER"

In a 1915 article, E. F. Doree, a leader of the Agricultural Workers' Organization, described the conditions harvest workers faced and the preparations by farmers and unionists for the upcoming season.

THE EXCEEDINGLY LONG work day is the worst feature of the harvesting so far as the worker is concerned. The men are expected to be in the fields at half past five or six o'clock in the morning until seven or half past seven o'clock at night with from an hour to an hour and a half for dinner. It is a common slang expression of the worker that they have an "eight-hour work day"—eight in the morning and eight in the afternoon. . . .

. . . The workers are sometimes paid so much per hundred bushels, and the more they thresh the more they get. On this basis they generally make more than "goin' wages," but they work themselves almost to death doing it. . . . Twenty-five men died from the heat in one day last year in a single county in Kansas. . . .

In North and South Dakota no worker is sure of drawing his wages, even after earning them. Some farmers do not figure on paying their "help" at all and work the same game year after year. The new threshing machine outfits are the worst on this score, as the bosses very seldom own the machines themselves and, at the end of the season, often leave the country without paying either worker or machine owner. . . .

. . . The harvesters move almost entirely by "freight," and here is where the train crews get theirs. With them it is simply a matter of "shell up a dollar or hit the dirt." Quite often union cards are recognized and no dollar charged, and the worker is permitted to ride unmolested.

It is safe to say that nine workers out of every ten leave the harvest fields as poor as when they entered them. Few, indeed, are those who clear $50.00 or more in the entire season. . . .

The last six months has seen the birth of two new organizations that will operate during the coming summer. . . . The ostensible purpose of the National Farm Labor Exchange is to handle the men necessary for the harvest systematically, but its real purpose is to flood the country with unnecessary men, thus making it possible to reduce the wages, which the farmer really believes are too high. . . .

News has come in to the effect that the farmers are already organizing their "vigilance committees," which are composed of farmers, businessmen, small town bums, college students and Y.M.C.A. scabs. The duty of the vigilance committee is to stop free speech, eliminate union agitation, and to drive out of the country all workers who demand more than "goin' wages."

Arrayed against the organized farmers is the Agricultural Workers' Organization, which is made up of members of the I.W.W. who work in the harvest fields. It is the object of this organization to systematically organize the workers into One Big Union, making it possible to secure the much needed shorter workday and more wages, as well as to mutually protect the men from the wiles of those who harvest the harvester.

by introducing new manufacturing methods that diminished the role of skilled workers.

Other strikes involved workers who had previously seemed indifferent to collective action. A new militancy among unskilled immigrant workers, noticeable before the war, accelerated. Many immigrants from southern and eastern Europe, who had planned to return to their native lands with money saved in America, found themselves stranded by the wartime disruption of transatlantic travel. Once willing to tolerate miserable job conditions because they saw their situation as temporary, many immigrants now sought immediate improvements.

Many Europeans who had come to America in the decade prior to World War I had been exposed back at home to ideas unknown to earlier immigrants. Throughout Europe, socialism, anarchism, and unionism were on the rise, even in rural districts. The repression that followed the failed 1905 Russian Revolution sent thousands of eastern European political activists into exile in America. As their influence spread in immigrant communities, workers grew increasingly receptive to collective action and political radicalism.

In Bayonne, New Jersey, for example, Polish refinery workers who had long accepted low pay, long hours, and dangerous

"... THERE WERE DOZENS TO TELL HER THAT SHE MUST NOT BUY FOWL"

In February and March 1917, there were repeated protests in New York City against rising food prices. On the city's Lower East Side Jewish women organized successful boycotts of onions, potatoes, and other items. The following article from the New York Times describes the reaction of shoppers when they discovered that butcher shops had sharply raised the price of poultry.

■MMEDIATELY THEY SHOWED their resentment. So far as could be learned, there was no meeting, no formal resolution, but simply a widespread outburst decreeing that no poultry should be bought. The pickets who were out to enforce the onion and potato boycott turned their attention to poultry, and the hundreds of women who refused to purchase at the prevailing prices joined them. Whenever a woman, basket or bag on arm, approached a poultry market there were dozens to tell her that she must not buy fowl of any kind. If she ignored the warning and emerged with a chicken she was seized, as was the chicken, which was torn limb from limb.... Several hundred women in the chicken market at Stanton Street and the East River became frenzied by the sight of a crate of chickens, and set upon it. The crate was destroyed, the chickens were seized and dismembered, and the crowd poured through the street, waving the heads and wings and mutilated bodies of chickens.

working conditions walked off their jobs in 1915. Although virtually the entire local Polish community supported their struggle, violence by police and hired thugs broke the strike. The journalist Mary Heaton Vorse wrote that when visiting Bayonne "you realize that you are in a terrorized city, and that fear is in the very air that you breathe." Still, even though five strikers were killed by gunfire, the Bayonne refinery workers struck again the next year.

Migrant farm laborers, led by a new unit of the IWW, the Agricultural Workers' Organization (AWO), also joined the wave of collective action. Without abandoning the IWW's revolutionary ideology, the AWO stressed winning immediate demands. After signing up thousands of midwestern harvest workers, it succeeded in gaining better pay and conditions from wheat farmers more eager to take advantage of high grain prices than to battle labor.

The success of the AWO led to a general revival of the IWW, which had gone into decline just before the war. In 1916 the Wobblies began an intensive organizing campaign among northwestern lumber workers. IWW organizers were repeatedly arrested, and many strikers were beaten or shot by police and employer strong-arm men. Nonetheless, IWW influence spread. In the same year, the IWW took over the leadership of a strike of ten thousand miners in the Mesabi iron range of northern Minnesota. A virtual reign of terror unleashed by police and over five hundred company guards helped defeat the walkout, but once the miners returned to work, employers upgraded pay and conditions.

Between 1914 and 1917, labor militancy helped push up average annual employee earnings by 26 percent; however, inflation erased these gains. Frustration grew so great that violent protests broke out against higher prices. Women played the key role in these actions. In most working-class homes women did the shopping and were in charge of the family budget; they were the ones who each day saw the rising cost of bread, potatoes, vegetables, and meat. In early 1917

Food riot, 1917. Wartime inflation severely taxed the limited budgets of working-class families. On February 20, 1917, after confronting pushcart peddlers who were charging exorbitant rates for necessities, thousands of women marched to New York's City Hall to demand relief. The "food riot" precipitated a boycott campaign that eventually forced pushcart prices down.

women in New York, Philadelphia, and Boston took to the streets in fury when yet another round of price hikes began. They attacked pushcarts and stores, organized demonstrations, and, in a few instances, even battled the police.

The high level of working-class protest during World War I placed labor issues near the top of the national political agenda. Along with the political tactics of the AFL, it helped the union movement win an unprecedented series of political and legislative victories. Equally important, once the United States formally entered the war, government leaders were forced to take the reaction of labor into consideration in all of their plans.

MOBILIZING FOR WAR

To raise an army and mobilize the economy for war, the federal government worked closely with a variety of private groups as the inordinate demands of modern war led to a partial fulfillment of the Progressive vision of a society rationalized through public-private cooperation. The financier Bernard Baruch, who played a key role in coordinating the wartime economy, later recalled that "many businessmen . . . experienced, during the war, for the first time in their careers, the tremendous advantages, both to themselves and to the general public, of combination, of cooperation and common action."

Although the Allies wanted the United States to send troops to Europe quickly, to be integrated into existing French and British combat units, Wilson refused. Instead, he accepted his military staff's recommendation that wholly American units be organized under U.S. command. But the United States had only a small army and few experienced officers, so preparations took time.

The first step was the draft, authorized in May 1917. To insulate the federal government from criticism and create the illusion that conscription was a voluntary community act, local draft boards were set up, charged with registering, classifying, and calling up fighting-age men. (A quarter of the registrants were found to be illiterate, a third physically unfit.) Slowly an army was raised, equipped, and trained. When the war ended, over four million American men were in uniform, almost half of them in Europe.

Although proponents of conscription had argued that a draft would strengthen American democracy by bringing young men from different ethnic and class backgrounds into close, cooperative relationships, the reality was quite different. Immigrants who had not filed naturalization papers were exempted from call-up. Many of the foreign-born who were drafted were put into ethnically segregated units or "development battalions," where they were taught English and civics. The nearly 400,000 African-Americans who served in the military suffered severe discrimination. The marines remained exclusively white; the navy's African-Americans served only as messmen. The army, too, at first declined to take black draftees. Racial tension built. In August 1917 a group of black soldiers in Houston—men who had joined the army well before the war—became fed up with local Jim Crow laws and continual harassment. They armed themselves and attacked white residents, killing thirteen. With extreme haste an equal number of black soldiers were court-martialed and hanged; six more were later executed. That fall, when African-Americans began to be drafted in large numbers, they were assigned to all-black units.

Under pressure from African-American groups and the National Association for the Advancement of Colored People (NAACP), the

"At last," an army medical examiner exults, "a perfect soldier." Robert Minor's cartoon in the July 1916 *The Masses* was published before the United States entered the war. A year later, the magazine's antiwar position would lead to its suppression under the 1917 Espionage Act.

Largest Murder Trial in the History of the United States.
Scene during Court Martial of 64 members of 24th. Infantry U.S.Q
on trial for mutiny and murder of 17 people at Houston Tex. Aug 23, 1917
Trial Held in Gift Chapel. Ft Sam Houston
Trial Started --- Nov 1, 1917 - Brig. Genl. George K. Hunter, Presiding.
Col. J.A. Hull - Judge Advocate.   Counsel for Defense.
Maj. D.V. Sulphin, Asst. .   Maj. Harry S. Grier.
Prisoners guarded by 19th. Infantry Co "C" Capt. Carl J Adler

The largest murder trial in American history. African-Americans in uniform incensed white southern society. Members of the 24th Infantry Regiment trained in Houston, Texas, were subjected to harassment by whites and beatings by the city police. On August 23, 1917, a gunfight broke out between black troops and white citizens, leaving 17 dead. In the ensuing trial of 64 soldiers for murder and mutiny, 13 were sentenced to death and 40 to life imprisonment.

military made some concessions. A black officers' training school was set up, with its graduates assigned to black units under white supervision. More important, over half the blacks in the army were put into combat units rather than less prestigious support groups. But the army remained segregated, and the basic pattern of racism was unchanged.

As part of their induction procedure, nearly two million soldiers were given a newly developed "IQ" test, which purported to measure innate intelligence. According to the psychologists in charge, the results indicated that the average soldier had the mental age of a thirteen-year-old, and half could be classified as "morons." Furthermore, they claimed that the tests proved that northern and western Europeans were more intelligent than southern and eastern Europeans, who in turn were more intelligent than African-Americans.

In reality the IQ tests were so flawed in design and administration that the results were virtually meaningless, as even the army recognized at the time. For example, one question asked: "Christy Mathewson is famous as a: writer, artist, baseball player, comedian." If anything, the tests measured literacy in English and familiarity with mainstream American culture, not intelligence. Nonetheless, the army program legitimized IQ testing, which was widely used after the

> ## To the colored soldiers of the U. S. Army.
>
> Hallo boys, what are you doing over here? Fighting the Germans? Why? Have they ever done you any harm? Of course, some white folks and the lying English-American papers told you that the Germans ought to be wiped out for the sake of humanity and democracy. What is Democracy? Personal Freedom, all citizens enjoying the same rights socially and before the law! Do you enjoy the same rights as the white people do in America, the land of Freedom and Democracy? Or aren't you rather treated over there as second class citizens? Can you go into a rest urant where white people dine, can you get a seat in a theater where white people sit, can you get a Pullman seat or berth in a rail roadcar or can you even ride, in the South, in the same street car with white people? And how about the law? Is lynching and the most horrible cruelties connected therewith a lawful proceeding in a democratic country?
>
> Now, all this is entirely different in Germany, where they do like colored people, where they treat them as Gentlemen and not as second class citizens. They enjoy exactly the same social privileges as every white man, and quite a number of colored people have migthy fine positions in business in Berlin and other big German cities.
>
> Why then fight the Germans only for the benefit of the Wallstreet robbers to protect the millions they have lent to the English, French and Italians? You have been made the tool of the egotistic and rapacious rich in England and in America, and there is nothing in the whole game for you but broken bones, horrible wounds, spoiled health or — death. No satisfaction whatever will you get out of this unjust war. You have never seen Germany, so you are fools if you allow ____ to teach you to hate it. Come over to see for yourself. ____ to the fighting who make profit out of this war; do ____ em to use you as cannon food. To carry the gun in ____ ce is not an honor but a shame. Throw it away and come over to the German lines. You will find friends who help you along.

"To the colored soldiers of the U.S. Army." A propaganda leaflet dropped by German airplanes behind American lines.

war, and gave a pseudoscientific gloss to existing prejudices. The exam was used to justify immigration quotas and served as the model for the Scholastic Aptitude Test.

While the military slowly geared up for combat, a battle took place to mobilize the economy fully. Allied war orders already were threatening to overtax the economy; the added need to supply American fighting forces meant even more competition for raw materials, production facilities, transportation, and labor. Only centralized coordination could possibly prevent chaos. Accordingly, the federal government took charge of the economy to an extent previously approached only during the Civil War.

In the summer of 1916, Wilson established the Council of National Defense (CND) to plan economic measures that would be needed if America entered the war. Much of the council's work was carried out by its civilian advisory board, made up of leading businessmen and public representatives (including the AFL's Samuel Gompers). Once war was declared, a host of other agencies were established.

In a few cases the federal government took charge of strategic industries directly. The Railroad Administration, for example, ran the nation's entire railroad system as one unit. Similarly, the Shipping Board took control of existing merchant ships and launched a massive shipbuilding program.

More generally, however, the federal government worked to rationalize the economy through cooperative agreements rather than direct control. Working closely with business groups, federal agencies determined production priorities, fixed prices, and facilitated orderly operations. Since many government agencies were staffed by businessmen on paid leaves of absence, it was, in effect, a system of government-sponsored industrial self-regulation.

The Food Administration, a key wartime body, was typical of the new economic bureaucracy. Huge European food orders and small harvests in 1916 and 1917, the results of bad weather, had driven food prices sky-high, which in turn had led to the food riots. The head of the Food Administration, Herbert Hoover, a mining engineer who had led a London-based Belgian relief organization, resisted pressure for coercive measures such as food rationing or retail price-fixing. Instead he used persuasion, threats, patriotic appeals, and the profit motive to increase production, streamline distribution, and encourage conservation. Hoover guaranteed wheat farmers high prices, for example, so they would plant larger crops. To stabilize prices and further stimulate production, the government bought and sold vast amounts of farm commodities, including the entire Cuban sugar crop. Profit margins for food processors were fixed, and food storage and transportation facilities were coordinated. Hoover also recruited tens of thousands of volunteers to urge housewives to conserve food. Special "meatless" and "wheatless" days were promoted in the name of patriotic self-sacrifice.

To enable industrywide arrangements, Hoover encouraged farmers to organize. To this end he helped finance a network of county farm bureaus, usually led by local agricultural agents. These rather conservative, businesslike groups became the successors to the old-style, more radical farm protest organizations. With farm income rising, often to new highs, many farmers embraced the bureaus. Once the war ended, the bureaus banded together as the American Farm Bureau Federation to become a major lobbying group.

Many wartime agencies increased production by standardizing parts, products, and procedures. Before the war, to take one example, typewriter ribbons were produced in 150 different colors; by its end, in only 5. Simultaneously, businesses took advantage of steady wartime production and cost-plus contracts, which guaranteed manufacturers all their costs plus a fixed-percentage profit, to expand facilities and introduce new production methods. The Ford Motor Company used a navy boat contract to begin construction of its giant River Rouge complex, while continuing car production at existing plants. Arms manufacturers built new plants and introduced machinery that lessened their dependence on skilled workers. Many other contractors also experimented with new ways of organizing production, using the military budget to subsidize private innovation.

In the six months following the declaration of war, workers—led by unionists in the metal trades, shipbuilding, and coalmining—launched a massive strike wave that deprived the economy of more than six million workdays. Workers struck for many reasons, but most common was the effort to offset higher prices with increased wages. Also, there was an intensification of struggles over discipline, control of work processes, and payment plans. The government's relentless pressure on industrial firms to increase production meant renewed pressures on workers to accept scientific management. Incentive pay plans, which offered workers sizable pay increases if they would boost their normal output, were especially popular with employers, and just as feared and hated by unionists. Despite the best efforts of the federal government—and Gompers—to keep production lines rolling without disruption, there were repeated strikes against incentive pay plans at such crucial factories as Pittsburgh's Westinghouse Electric and Mesta Machine shops.

Labor's militancy forced the federal government to establish a series of labor relations agencies. Most were tripartite commissions composed of labor, business, and public representatives, a favorite Progressive device pioneered by the National Civic Federation. This in itself was a major victory for organized labor. Never before had unions been given so extensive a role in determining and administering federal labor policy. Also, Progressives sympathetic to unionism—such as Felix Frankfurter, W. Jett Lauck, and Frank Walsh—were appointed to key agency positions.

The wartime labor bureaucracy accepted in broad terms the analysis Walsh had put forth in his Commission on Industrial Relations report. Strikes, Frankfurter and others argued, were largely the results of real grievances and the lack of established channels for collective bargaining. Agency officials, hoping to forestall strikes and reduce labor turnover, pressured employers to raise pay, shorten working hours, and upgrade conditions.

Actual unionization, however, remained highly controversial. Many labor agency officials believed that a strong union movement would assure industrial peace by directing worker discontent into orderly procedures for negotiation and arbitration. Wilson himself said, "Our laws and the long-established policy of our government recognize the right of workingmen to organize unions if they so desire." Other officials, though—particularly in the Justice, Commerce, and Agriculture departments, the military, and the War Industries Board—opposed unionism.

In theory, wartime federal regulations forbade employers to interfere with the right of workers to join unions. Enforcement, however, was spotty. Some businesses were forced to rehire workers fired for organizing; others were not. Only rarely were businesses required to sign union contracts. As an alternative, federal agencies made some companies set up shop councils, employee-elected committees empowered to discuss working conditions and grievances. Although these were not unions, unionists were often elected to them. The government also occasionally imposed mediation or arbitration to settle labor disputes.

As contradictory as this policy was, it generally aided organized labor. The meatpacking industry provides a good example. In the summer of 1917, the Chicago AFL began organizing the city's huge packinghouses. Union organizers made a concerted effort to recruit both black workers, who made up about a quarter of the workforce, and whites (although they kept union locals segregated). Within a few months union membership tripled, to 28,000. The employers at first refused to bargain, but under pressure from Washington they yielded to some union demands and sent others to federal arbitration. In March 1918 an arbitrator set the basic working day in packing plants at eight hours, with overtime thereafter, and raised pay rates substantially. "It is a new day," proclaimed union leader William Z. Foster to a meatpackers' rally. "You men and women, black and white, have not only an eight-hour day but you are on an equality." Other federal directives that followed also favored labor. Claiming credit for these gains, the stockyard unions grew rapidly; by the time the war ended, the Amalgamated Meatcutters' Union put its national membership at over 62,000.

Such federal benevolence was a quid pro quo for the prowar position taken by the AFL—it was not extended to unions that refused to make at least token gestures of support for the war. Nevertheless, for most of the labor movement the war was a time of unparalleled organizational gain. By 1919 the International Association of Machinists had 331,540 members, six times its membership a decade earlier. The Amalgamated Clothing Workers' Union doubled in size during the war, in part because of the skillful way its president, Sidney Hillman, cultivated ties to federal officials in charge of labor policy and clothing purchases. The railroad brotherhoods mushroomed; while the government ran the railroads, virtually all white railroad workers became union members, making transportation the country's most heavily unionized industry. (Most railroad unions barred nonwhites.) All told, union membership increased by nearly 70 percent between 1914 and 1920, to over 5 million, with close to one of every five nonagricultural workers belonging to a union.

TO THE PROMISED LAND

Perhaps the most important long-range domestic effects of World War I were the occupational and demographic shifts it set off. With European immigration drastically reduced, employers accepted and in some cases actively sought workers they had previously spurned, easing discriminatory practices that had long reserved many types of jobs for white men. This stimulated massive population movements and helped change social attitudes.

The war accelerated the long-term shift of the American population from the countryside to cities. For instance, the rapidly expanding auto industry, in addition to attracting many workers from the rural Midwest and Canada, recruited workers from the rural South. Between 1910 and 1920, over half a million white southerners moved out of the region. The mountain areas of the upper South were particularly ripe for an exodus. Farming in the Appalachian Mountains had always been difficult, and by World War I much of the area's timber had been cut down and many local coalmines were worked out. High birth rates contributed to the region's poverty. When the war opened up high-paying jobs in nearby northern cities, a massive migration ensued. By one estimate over 50,000 West Virginians moved to Akron, Ohio, alone, the center of the booming rubber industry.

Similar forces contributed to a parallel migration of black southerners to the North, in what has been called the "Great Migration." Although some African-Americans had been moving out of the South since the end of Reconstruction, in 1910 the geographic distribution of the country's black population was still pretty much what it had been a half century earlier: four of every five African-Americans lived in one of twelve southern states, and within those states they lived overwhelmingly in rural areas.

There were plenty of reasons why blacks wanted to leave the rural South: disfranchisement, segregation, poverty, racial violence, lack of educational opportunities, and the drudgery of farm life. Until World War I, however, racial discrimination had severely limited job opportunities for African-Americans in the North. The wartime labor shortage changed this. Employers in desperate need of workers began hiring African-Americans for jobs they previously had been shut out of. Some companies even sent agents to the South to recruit black workers. Other recruiters worked on their own, providing labor for a fee.

Most black migrants did not have to be recruited. The year 1916 was a particularly bad one in the South: the boll weevil was attacking the cotton crop, and floods caused extensive damage. "The two calamities," wrote one black Georgian, "left the average farm laborer with nothing to start out with to make a crop for next year . . . he wants to migrate to where he can see a chance to get work." Northern black newspapers such as the Chicago *Defender* were widely circulated in the South, spreading the word about jobs and conditions up North; southern African-Americans responded.

White southerners did their best to stop the migration. African-Americans were crucial to the southern agricultural economy. Even if enough workers remained to plant and harvest the crop, a decrease in the labor supply would drive up wages. State and local governments revived or passed laws designed to put labor recruiters out of business. Plantation overseers used violence and threats of violence in an effort to keep workers from leaving. But while some who wanted to migrate were prevented from doing so, many more managed to leave.

Like transatlantic immigration, the Great Migration quickly developed self-sustaining momentum. Recent migrants wrote home urging others to join them, enclosing money when they could. Kinship and social networks soon linked particular areas of the two regions: migrants from Virginia, the Carolinas, and Georgia tended to move to the Northeast. African-Americans from Mississippi, Alabama, Louisiana, Arkansas, and Texas usually headed to the Midwest—above all to Chicago—or to the West, particularly to Oakland, California, the western terminus of the Southern Pacific Railroad.

"... PASS US AWAY FROM HERE TO A BETTER LAND"

The anonymous letter below was typical of the letters from southern African-Americans that flooded into the office of the Chicago Defender *asking for assistance in coming to the North. The passes referred to were for free railroad transportation; they were sometimes distributed by recruiters looking to hire black workers for jobs in the North.*

Daphne, Ala. 4/20/17

Sir:

I am writing you to let you know that there is 15 or 20 familys wants to come up there at once but can't come on account of money. . . . We can't phone you [because] they don't want us to leave here . . . [but] we want to get away if we can. If you send 20 passes there is no doubt that every one of us will come at once. We are not doing any thing here we can get a living out of. . . . Some of these people are farmers and some are cooks, barbers, and blacksmiths. . . . These are nice people and respectable. . . . We all want to leave here out of this hard luck place that does need this kind of people.

I am a reader of the *Defender* and am delighted to know how times are there & [would be] glad to know if we could get some one to pass us away from here to a better land. . . . Please find some one that need this kind of people and send at once for us. We don't want anything but our wareing and bed clothes and have got no money to get away from here with and begging to get away before we are killed and hope to hear from you at once.

Between 1910 and 1920 about 500,000 blacks left the South, most after 1916. During that decade the African-American population of Chicago nearly doubled, to over 100,000, while the number of blacks in New York topped 150,000, making it the largest African-American center in the country. There were major black communities in Philadelphia, Detroit, Cleveland, St. Louis, Baltimore, and Washington, D.C. After the war the migration continued, accelerating during the 1920s.

Although African-Americans had been attracted to the North by the promise of better jobs, better housing, and greater equality, they did not escape racism. Most men who made the trek northward found jobs in heavy industry. (By contrast, northern-born black men were more likely to work in hotels or restaurants or in other service positions.) The steel, meatpacking, auto, shipbuilding, and mining industries all were major employers of African-Americans. Even these industries, however, practiced discrimination. Some firms refused to hire any blacks, while others placed them only in particular plants. African-Americans usually were restricted to unskilled jobs, often the dirtiest and most physically taxing. Generally they were paid less than white workers, though still much more than they could earn in the South. Black women had a hard time getting factory work at all. In 1920 nearly half of all employed black women worked in personal or domestic service; less than 7 percent worked in industry. African-Americans also faced discrimination in housing. Legal or customary bars kept blacks out of most white neighborhoods, forcing them into increasingly overcrowded ghettos.

Many northern blacks resented the southern newcomers. Like the German-American Jews who had looked down on later Jewish immigrants from eastern Europe, established northern blacks were often embarrassed by the rural, unsophisticated ways of southerners and worried that a white reaction against the migrants would threaten their own tenuous position. Northern-born African-Americans, however, were well on their way to becoming a minority in their own communities; by 1920 half the black residents of the North had been born in the South.

The influx of southern African-Americans did lead to a dramatic increase in racial tension in northern urban areas, as whites and blacks competed for jobs, housing, and political power. (Unlike in the South, in the North blacks generally had the right to vote.) Many white workers feared that blacks would take their jobs or force down their wage rates. Some white unionists tried to sign up the newcomers, while others sought to keep them out of what were considered "white" positions.

Under pressure from African-American unionists and groups such as the NAACP and the Urban League, the AFL issued occasional statements on the need to organize black workers. In practice, however, it did little. Many AFL unions continued to bar black workers entirely or to segregate them in locals with restricted voting and job rights. While some African-American workers persisted in lobbying the AFL to drop its racial bars, others formed small, independent, all-black unions. In the port area of Newport News, Virginia, for example, R. T. Sims, a former IWW organizer, established the National Brotherhood Workers of America, which enrolled hundreds of black shipyard workers. But in the face of the AFL's indifference, many African-Americans rejected unionism altogether. Black ministers, politicians, and editors often encouraged this, arguing, as Booker T. Washington had, that blacks were more likely to find allies among white employers than among white workers.

These divisions within the African-American community hurt the wartime AFL campaign to organize the Chicago stockyards. Although the AFL brought in black organizers from the mineworkers' union to aid recruitment efforts, its campaign was opposed by the rival American Unity Labor Union, which urged blacks not to "join any white man's union." Only 15 percent of the African-American stockyard workers joined the AFL campaign, compared to nearly 90 percent of the Poles and Slovaks.

The vicious circle of job competition and racism that was developing throughout the North exploded in July 1917 in East St. Louis. Local manufacturers had recruited southern African-Americans in an effort to drive down wages. White

---

"... WE LOST EVERYTHING BUT WHAT WE HAD ON"

In the following letter to a friend, a victim of the 1917 East St. Louis riot recounts the terror of being caught in the midst of the violence.

3946 W. Belle
St. Louis, Mo.
Dearest Louise:

Was very glad to hear from you. Your letter was forwarded from what used to be my house.

Louise, it was awful. I hardly know where to begin telling you about it. First I will say we lost everything but what we had on and that was very little. . . .

It started early in the afternoon. We kept receiving calls over the phone to pack our trunks and leave, because it was going to be awful. We did not heed the calls, but sent grandma & the baby on to St. Louis & said we would "stick" no matter what happened. At first, when the fire started, we stood on Broadway & watched it. As they neared our house we went in & went to the basement. It was too late to run then. They shot & yelled some thing awful, finally they reached our house. At first, they did not bother us (we watched from the basement window), they remarked that "white people live in that house, this is not a nigger house." Later, someone must have tipped them that it was a "nigger" house, because, after leaving us for about 20 min[utes] they returned & yelling like mad "kill the 'niggers,' burn that house."

It seemed the whole house was falling in on us. Then some one said, they must not be there, if they are they are certainly dead. Then some one shouted "they are in the basement. Surround them and burn it down." Then they ran down our steps. Only prayer saved us, we were under tubs & any thing we could find praying & keeping as quiet as possible, because if they had seen one face, we would have been shot or burned to death. When they were about to surround the house & burn it, we heard an awful noise & thought they were dynamiting the house. (The Broadway Theater fell in, we learned later.) Sister tipped the door to see if the house was on fire. She saw the reflection of a soldier on the front door—pulled it open quickly & called for help. All of us ran out then & was taken to the city hall for the night—(just as we were). The next morning we . . . were sent on to St. Louis. Had to walk across the bridge with a line of soldiers on each side . . . in the hot sun, no hats, & and scarcely no clothing. . . .

On Tuesday evening . . . our house was burned with two soldiers on guard. . . . We were told that [the crowd] looted the house before burning it. . . .

workers responded by organizing a whites-only union. Racial friction also developed over access to housing and recreational facilities. When a strike at an aluminum factory was defeated through the use of black strikebreakers, the local union movement launched a campaign to drive recently arrived African-Americans out of town. A shooting incident touched off a full-scale riot. White mobs invaded black neighborhoods; bystanders were assaulted, shot, and lynched. At the end of two days, forty blacks and nine whites had been killed.

But in spite of all the problems African-Americans encountered, they kept coming North. One former southerner wrote back home: "I should have been here twenty years ago. I just begin to feel like a man. . . . My children are going to the same school with the whites and I don't have to humble to no one. . . . Will vote in the next election and there isn't any 'yes, sir, and no, sir.'" Such tastes of freedom spurred on a growing determination in northern black neighborhoods to fight for full and equal rights.

During the war era immigration from Mexico dramatically increased. In the years before World War I, new railroads had opened up northern Mexico; many Mexicans left crowded central provinces for the region near the U.S. border. At the same time, railroads and irrigation stimulated rapid growth in the southwestern United States, creating a labor shortage. The Mexican Revolution acted as a catalyst, setting off mass migration across the border. The inflation, violence, and social chaos that accompanied the Mexican Revolution—which had begun as a fight over presidential succession but turned into a broad social conflict that lasted through the war years—led many Mexicans to flee to the United States. Some came only temporarily, hoping to save money and return home quickly. Others came intending to stay, entering long-standing Mexican-American communities across the Southwest.

The U.S. entrance into World War I initially reversed the population flow. Many Mexicans working in the United States feared that they would be drafted. In addition, a 1917 immigration law banned contract labor and imposed a literacy test and a head tax on immigrants. Mexican labor had become so vital to the southwestern economy, however, that major employers pressured the federal government to assure Mexican workers that they were exempt from the draft. Also, the new immigration restrictions were suspended for Mexican agricultural workers, and then for mine and railroad workers. With these steps, immigration resumed.

According to official statistics, over 185,000 Mexicans entered the United States between 1910 and 1919. Many more crossed the border without going through legal procedures and remained uncounted. Some estimates indicate that the total number of people of Mexican heritage living in the United States doubled during this decade, to about 750,000.

Most Mexican immigrants settled in the Southwest, particularly in Texas, California, Arizona, and Colorado. Agriculture provided the most jobs. Although wages were very low by U.S. standards, they were seven to twenty times what was being paid in Mexico. Railroads and mines also hired large numbers of Mexican workers. As the southwestern labor supply swelled, some Mexican-Americans, many with roots in the region as far back as the 1840s, left for better-paying industrial jobs in the Midwest.

Mexican-Americans faced many of the same problems as African-Americans. Segregated schools, theaters, restaurants, and neighborhoods were common in the Southwest. Often Mexican workers were paid less than the Anglos who worked beside them. However, there were instances of cooperation between the two groups. A series of mine strikes in New Mexico and Arizona in 1917 brought together Anglo and Mexican miners in struggles aimed at eliminating unequal wages and winning recognition for the Western Federation of Miners and the United Mine Workers of America. These strikes ended when thousands of Mexican-born strikers were arrested and many deported. The two miners' unions were not typical; most unions ignored or excluded Mexican-Americans or placed them in separate locals.

There was a strong radical strain in the Mexican-American community. Before the revolution many critics of the Mexican government had gone into exile in the United States, where they organized political parties, put out newspapers, and developed ties with U.S. radicals. The revolution itself strengthened Mexican-American radicalism. Both the Socialist Party and the IWW had large Mexican-American memberships.

"IRON ROAD"

Many songs composed by Mexican immigrants expressed homesickness, disappointment, and concern over the adoption of "American" values. In the song below, the completion of a railroad line stretching over six hundred miles from Victoria, Texas, to central Mexico is portrayed as an occasion for alarm rather than celebration.

EL FERROCARRIL	IRON ROAD
La máquina pasajera No puede hacer cosa buena Porque "oscurece" en su casa Y amanece en tierra ajena.	She's like a bird of passage Who never can do the right thing. She leaves her home every evening Just to see what the morning might bring.
¡Ay! ¡qué dolor! Tendrían los mexicanos Al ver el ferrocarril Que traen los americanos.	Oh, what pain Will visit those Mexicans When they hear her steaming down the track, The train of the Americans.
La máquina chiquitita Es la que ha quedado aquí Y la quieren llegar Hasta San Luis Potosí.	Just a little bitty steam engine Is all they left for me And they really think it'll go from here To San Luis Potosí.
Oigan y oigan El ferrocarril bramar, Él que lleva a los hombres Y nunca los vuelve a traer.	Listen, listen, Hear her roar down the track, She's coming for a load of men That she won't be bringing back.

Many Mexican immigrants, however, avoided involvement in unions or protest, concentrating instead on amassing enough money to buy land or businesses back home. But like the Slavs and Italians who had come before them, many Mexican immigrants eventually settled down permanently and grew more receptive to collective action. Enhanced by this new immigration, the long-established Spanish-speaking communities of the West and Southwest became an increasingly important element in the fastest-growing region of the country.

The war profoundly altered the status of women. Unable to find enough male workers, many wartime employers hired women for traditionally male jobs. The number of female railroad workers, for instance, tripled, and in many cities women were hired as streetcar conductors. Women were also hired for metalworking and munitions

Arms and the woman. Recently hired women operate equipment in a Bloomfield, New Jersey, munitions plant, 1917.

jobs, often as part of management efforts to reduce skill levels. Some of the women who took these jobs were entering the paid workforce for the first time. More switched over from lower-paying jobs in female-dominated occupations.

Sometimes male unionists accepted women as coworkers, helped them to organize, and fought for equal pay for equal work. More often, though, they resisted the hiring of female workers, fearing that their own jobs would be threatened and their pay rates reduced. In part for this reason, the gains women made in blue-collar work proved temporary; once the war ended, most women left or were forced out of these positions. But the war did speed up a permanent expansion of white-collar jobs for women. Between 1910 and 1920 the number of female clerical workers more than doubled, while the number of female domestic servants declined.

Even the temporary opening of nontraditional jobs to women helped change social attitudes. Women war workers demanded greater social and political rights, advancing the growing movement for woman suffrage. Many working-class suffragists saw a close link between the vote and the conditions of everyday life. A leaflet put out by the Wage-Earners' Suffrage League in New York City asked: "Why are you paid less than a man? Why do you work in a firetrap? Why are your hours so long? . . . Why does the cost of living go up while wages go down?" Its answer: "Because you are a woman and have no vote. Votes make the law. Votes enforce the law. The law controls conditions." During 1917 women won at least partial voting rights in eight states, including New York, long a major battleground. The struggle to pass a federal constitutional amendment granting woman suffrage likewise heated up.

Like many other reform movements, the suffrage movement was split by the war. In 1916 a new militant suffrage group, the National Woman's Party, formed. Refusing to support the war, its members began picketing the White House the next year, demanding that "democracy should begin at home." When arrested, imprisoned pickets began hunger strikes; they were brutally force-fed. The largest suffrage group, the National American Woman Suffrage Association, took the opposite tack—supporting the war, encouraging its members to do war work, and cementing an alliance with Wilson.

In January 1918 the House of Representatives, under strong pressure from the suffrage movement, passed a constitutional amendment giving women the vote. In spite of Wilson's declaration that woman suffrage was "vital to winning the war," the Senate initially rejected the amendment, but in June 1919 it too approved the measure. The following August, after Tennessee became the thirty-sixth state to ratify the amendment, it went into effect. The long, long battle for woman suffrage was over.

> ## "... WE DON'T WANT OTHER WOMEN EVER TO HAVE TO DO THIS OVER AGAIN"
>
> *Polish-born suffragist Rose Winslow (her given name was Ruza Wenclawska) started working in a Pennsylvania textile mill at age eleven, quitting eight years later when she developed tuberculosis. In 1917 she was one of five protesters sentenced to seven months in prison for obstructing traffic in front of the White House. After she and National Woman's Party founder Alice Paul began a hunger strike, they were transferred to a prison hospital. Winslow smuggled out an account she kept of her stay.*
>
> ■F THIS THING is necessary we will naturally go through with it. Force is so stupid a weapon. I feel so happy doing my bit for decency—for our war, which is after all, real and fundamental.
>
> The women are all so magnificent, so beautiful. Alice Paul is as thin as ever, pale and large-eyed. We have been in solitary for five weeks. There is nothing to tell but that the days go by somehow. I have felt quite feeble the last few days—faint, so that I could hardly get my hair brushed, my arms ached so. But to-day I am well again. Alice Paul and I talk back and forth though we are at opposite ends of the building and a hall door also shuts us apart. But occasionally—thrills—we escape from behind our iron-barred doors and visit. Great laughter and rejoicing!
>
> My fainting probably means nothing except that I am not strong after these weeks. I know you won't be alarmed.

CONSENSUS, FORCED AND ENCOURAGED

While the war helped propel the woman suffrage amendment toward ratification, its overall impact on the Progressive movement was devastating. When America joined the war, reformers felt confident they had the power and knowledge to create a more rational, stable, and just society. But the war—and especially the effort to force a consensus for war—unleashed powerful conservative tides, even among the Progressives themselves. By war's end, the reform movement was shattered.

Woodrow Wilson had long made it clear that if the United States entered the war, dissent would not be tolerated. However, even as the country geared up to fight, it remained deeply divided. One of nine Americans had been born in one of the Central Powers or had a parent born there. Adding disaffected Irish, the number of people inclined to oppose the war on ethnic grounds alone was immense. Then there were ideological opponents: isolationists, pacifists, socialists, Wobblies, and agrarian radicals. Further, some Progressives who had supported Wilson joined the antiwar camp, bitterly disillusioned with their onetime leader.

I told about a syphilitic colored woman with one leg. The other one was cut off, having rotted so that it was alive with maggots when she came in. The remaining one is now getting as bad. They are so short of nurses that a little colored girl of twelve, who is here waiting to have her tonsils removed, waits on her. This child and two others share a ward with a syphilitic child of three or four years, whose mother refused to have it at home. It makes you absolutely ill to see it. . . .

Alice Paul is in the psychopathetic ward. She dreaded forcible feeding frightfully, and I hate to think how she must be feeling. I had a nervous time of it, gasping a long time afterward, and my stomach rejecting during the process. I spent a bad, restless night, but otherwise I am all right. The poor soul who fed me got liberally besprinkled during the process. I heard myself making the most hideous sounds. . . . One feels so forsaken when one lies prone and people shove a pipe down one's stomach.

This morning but for an astounding tiredness, I am all right. I am waiting to see what happens when the President realizes that brutal bullying isn't quite a statesmanlike method for settling a demand for justice at home. At least, if men are supine enough to endure, women—to their eternal glory—are not. . . .

. . . Don't let them tell you we take this well. Miss Paul vomits much. I do, too. . . . We think of the coming feeding all day. It is horrible. The doctor thinks I take it well. I hate the thought of Alice Paul and the others if I take it well. . . .

All the officers here know we are making this hunger strike that women fighting for liberty may be considered political prisoners; we have told them. God knows we don't want other women ever to have to do this over again.

In local elections in the summer and fall of 1917, the vote for the Socialist Party was unusually high, an expression, many observers felt, of antiwar sentiment. In Chicago the Socialists won a third of the votes in a municipal election in which the Democrats and Republicans backed a united ticket to prevent a Socialist victory. Opposition to the war was also strong in many rural areas. The most dramatic protests were in the Southwest, where clandestine tenant farmer groups urged armed resistance to military conscription. There was even a brief, abortive antiwar insurrection in eastern Oklahoma, the so-called Green Corn Rebellion. "Now is the time to rebel against this war with German boys," read one Oklahoma poster. "Get together, boys, and don't go. Rich man's war. Poor man's fight."

Believing that dissent hindered the nation's ability to win the war, the Wilson administration, with the aid of state and local authorities, launched an extraordinary campaign to create a consensus in favor of its policies. It used both persuasion and force. In the spring of 1917, the federal government set up the Committee on Public Information (CPI) to disseminate war news and progovernment propaganda. Heading the CPI was a prominent Progressive journalist, George Creel, who recruited well-known muckrakers and even a few Socialists to aid him. Creel and his colleagues made sophisticated use of mass propaganda techniques to sell the war. Some 75 million pamphlets explaining government policy, written in many languages, were distributed; slick ads were placed in magazines; prowar films were produced; and 75,000 speakers were signed up to give short talks before any audience they could find. As the war went on, the CPI abandoned the pretense that it was a neutral information source, and began to spread wildly exaggerated stories alleging German atrocities. More propaganda came out of the Treasury Department; "Liberty Bonds," used to finance the war, were sold through patriotic campaigns that employed Boy Scouts, movie stars, and local community leaders.

THAT LIBERTY SHALL NOT PERISH FROM THE EARTH
BUY LIBERTY BONDS
FOURTH   LIBERTY   LOAN

The power of pictures. In the mobilization for war, the U.S. government quickly recognized the power of effective, if often fantastic, imagery to shape public opinion. Most illustrators and especially editorial cartoonists eagerly produced prowar work; nevertheless, the government instituted a Bureau of Cartoons, which issued the weekly *Bulletin for Cartoonists* with suggestions about appropriately patriotic themes and, in some cases, instructions for specific pictures.

Wilson and his backers promoted the war as a selfless act by the American people, a war not for national conquest or economic gain but to "make the world safe for democracy." Because the March 1917 Russian Revolution had overthrown the czar, Wilson could argue that all the Allied Powers were democracies, while Germany, with its kaiser, and Austria-Hungary, with its emperor, were autocratic. Casting the conflict in this light helped win popular support.

In November 1917, however, another uprising in Russia, this time led by the communist Bolshevik Party, overthrew the new parliamentary regime. The revolutionary government, headed by V. I. Lenin, initiated peace talks with Germany and called on European workers and soldiers to stop the war. It also published previously secret treaties between the various Allied governments that revealed long-existing plans to take over territory and colonies from the Central Powers in the event of war.

The second phase of the Russian Revolution created a severe crisis for Wilson and the Allies. The publication of the secret treaties revealed that Wilson's characterization of the war was bogus. In Europe a yearning for peace grew rapidly. Furthermore, inspired by the Russian Revolution, radicals in other countries, including the United States, gained strength. For many, Lenin, not Wilson, now seemed the towering figure of the age.

To counter the Russian initiative, in January 1918 Wilson issued a new statement of war aims, his famous Fourteen Points. He called for free trade, freedom of the seas, a reduction in armaments, arbitration of international disputes, and the adjustment of European borders along ethnic lines—all to be arrived at through open negotiation of fully public treaties. Making the principle of national self-determination the centerpiece of his program, Wilson proposed that an international association of nations maintain peace by guaranteeing the political independence and territorial integrity of its members.

During the last year of the war, the Fourteen Points were the main platform on which the war was sold, both in the United States and Europe (even though the Allies never formally endorsed them). Russia, though, remained a problem. In March 1918 it signed a peace treaty with Germany and dropped out of the war. Within months the United States joined England and France in sending troops to Russia—soon reorganized as the Union of Soviet Socialist Republics—in an ill-fated effort to overthrow the Bolshevik regime and maintain military pressure on Germany from the east. Wilson seemed to be contradicting his own principles even before the war ended.

When the United States declared war, many employers, civic groups, and local governments eagerly joined the crusade. Steel companies

TO THE RUSSIAN ENVOYS
President Wilson and Envoy Root are deceiving Russia.
They say We are a democracy. Help us win a world war.
so that democracies may survive.
We, the women of America, tell you that America is not a democracy.
Twenty million American Women are denied the right to vote. President
Wilson is the chief opponent of their national enfranchisement.
Help us make this nation really free. Tell our government that it
must liberate its people before it can claim free Russia as an ally

Hands across the water. Demonstrators in front of the White House in July 1917 appeal to representatives of the new Russian government to support American woman suffrage as a condition for Russia's remaining in the Allied camp. The banner aroused the ire of patriotic passersby, and soon after this photograph was taken an angry crowd attacked the suffragists.

sponsored parades, flag-raising ceremonies, and bond-selling drives. School districts instituted loyalty oaths and offered federally prepared "war study courses." Colleges taught similar courses and enlisted students in the new Reserve Officers' Training Corps, which replaced earlier college military training programs.

Repression often went hand in hand with persuasion. Some professors who protested the use of educational institutions to promote the war were fired. Steel companies told their workers that it was "a bond or your job." The harshest measures came from the federal government. The Espionage Act, passed in June 1917, and the Sedition Act, passed a year later, gave federal authorities wide powers to suppress dissent. Using "disloyal, profane, scurrilous, or abusive language" about the American form of government, the Constitution, or the flag was made punishable by twenty years in prison.

Press censorship was extensive. In the summer of 1917, the Post Office Department began refusing to deliver newspapers and magazines critical of the war, the draft, or even of how the war was being conducted. Hardest hit was the Socialist Party; socialist periodicals

"This is for traitors." The pillory, a device used in colonial New England to punish through public opprobrium, is resurrected in Cincinnati in 1918. Placed in a public square, this pillory was "a warning to citizens of Cincinnati as to what they may expect in case of disloyalty." Unable to find a convenient dissenter immediately, the photographer of this picture had to make do with an acquiescent volunteer.

with a combined prewar circulation of over a half million were banned from the mails. The foreign-language press was also closely watched: a federal law required that articles discussing the war or the government be submitted in translation for prior approval, a process so costly that many papers either folded or began promoting progovernment views to win exemptions.

The battle against radicals and dissidents led to a significant expansion of the police bureaucracy. On the federal level the Department of Justice's small Bureau of Investigation, forerunner of the FBI, was enlarged. In addition, the army set up a special unit to spy on civilians. Many states also went into the spy business, and several set up or expanded state police forces.

Critical voices were silenced through arrest. Fifteen hundred people were put on trial for opposing the war or counseling draft resistance. In addition, over six thousand German and Austrian nationals were detained as potential threats to national security. In mid-1918 Eugene Debs, who opposed the war but had kept his views private, took to the stump to protest these violations of civil liberties and reaffirm his revolutionary beliefs. "They tell us that we live in a great free republic," he said in Canton, Ohio, "that our institutions are democratic, that we are a free and self-governing people. This is too much, even for a joke." Alluding to the current conflict, he continued: "The master class has always declared the wars; the subject class has always fought the battles. The master class has had all to gain and nothing to lose, while the subject class has had nothing to gain and all to lose—especially their lives." For this speech Debs was arrested and sentenced to ten years in prison.

As the prowar campaign intensified, a vigilante spirit grew. German-Americans were harassed, beaten, tarred and feathered, made to kiss the flag, and, in at least one instance, lynched, simply because of their nationality. Radicals, opponents of the war, even those who simply refused to buy war bonds, were subjected to similar treatment. A whole series of "loyalty" organizations were formed to spy on neighbors and coworkers. The largest, the American Protective League, had a quarter of a million members and was given funding and quasi-official status by the Department of Justice. Often local businessmen and reactionaries used loyalty groups to harass radicals and unionists in the name of patriotism.

The Wilson administration was especially concerned about antiwar sentiment among workers. Both the Department of Labor and the CPI deluged factories with posters, slogans, and speakers in an effort to counteract the widespread working-class belief that America was fighting a businessmen's war. To influence working-class opinion further, the government launched an unprecedented campaign to manipulate the political direction of the union movement, aiding those segments of organized labor that supported the war while harassing or destroying those that opposed it.

After Congress declared war, most labor leaders rallied behind the war effort. Many saw it as a positive opportunity; by supporting the administration they hoped to win greater say over federal labor policy and boost public support for organized labor. With secret funding from the CPI, Gompers set up the American Alliance for Labor and Democracy to counter antiwar agitation. Acting on behalf of the administration, he also tried to defuse growing antiwar sentiment among European unionists. This was the start of an ongoing alliance between some top union officials and the government to promote American policy abroad. Gompers's activities met with considerable resistance within the AFL, particularly from heavily Irish and German unions, but he survived all challenges.

While ties between the AFL and Washington were growing closer, the Wobblies came under fierce government attack. Although the IWW, which had been one of the most vocal critics of the European conflict, downplayed its antiwar propaganda once the United States joined the fighting, it refused to endorse the war and led militant struggles in a number of war-related industries. In September 1917 federal agents raided every IWW office in the country, arresting some three hundred union leaders. Within six months two thousand Wob-

"The I.W.W. and the Other Features That Go With It." The kaiser's features portray the Wobblies' traitorous intent, according to the New York *Globe* in 1917.

blies, including the entire IWW executive board, were in jail awaiting trial. Most were eventually convicted of violating wartime statutes and sentenced to long jail terms.

The federal government was particularly determined to break the IWW's hold on northwestern lumber workers. At first federal officials tried to end a series of Wobbly-led strikes and slowdowns by pressuring lumber companies to grant an eight-hour day and other improvements. At the urging of Gompers and other AFL officials, they also suggested that if the companies recognized a "responsible" union, by which they meant an AFL affiliate, the IWW would disappear. The employers, however, stood pat.

In October 1917 an army lieutenant, Bruce P. Disque, was sent to resolve the situation, accompanied by a division of military lumberjacks who could be used to break strikes and increase production. Disque briefly tried promoting the Progressive formula of improved conditions and AFL recognition, but soon turned to more drastic measures. While all but forcing the owners to grant the eight-hour day, he set about smashing the Wobblies, organizing as a replacement the Loyal Legion of Loggers and Lumbermen, essentially a company union. Wobbly organizers were driven out of the area, and the AFL was ignored. Disque's carrot-and-stick approach ended the IWW threat but left lumberworkers unprotected by any bona fide union.

All over the country Wobblies faced coordinated government-employer attacks. In Bisbee, Arizona, a local sheriff, with the aid of the Phelps Dodge mining company and executives from other corporations, deputized two thousand townspeople to round up twelve hundred alleged Wobblies, aliens, and subversives and place them in railroad cattle cars, which were towed to the middle of the desert and abandoned. Vigilante violence and government raids left the IWW fighting for its life.

Immigrants faced a particularly hard time during the loyalty crusade. Although nativism and racialism were firmly rooted American ideologies, the war provided fertile soil for their growth. Even before America joined the conflict, some people began speaking of the danger of "divided loyalty" among "hyphenated" Americans—German-Americans, Polish-Americans, and so forth. Immigrants were seen as potentially treasonous, possibly more loyal to their countries of birth than to their adopted land. Wilson spoke of the need for "100 percent Americanism," while Theodore Roosevelt called for "America for Americans." Such views drew on both long-standing fears among old-stock Americans that their position and values were being threatened by newcomers, and the common association of immigrants with radicalism. The fear of sabotage further inflamed anti-immigrant feelings.

The "Americanization" campaigns were one response to concerns

deportation of I.W.W's July 12, 1917

Loading men on train

The Bisbee deportation, July 12, 1917. Under the watchful eyes—and loaded weapons—of town vigilantes, strikers are loaded onto cattle cars headed for the New Mexico desert.

about immigrant loyalty. Supported by social workers, civic groups, and government agencies, these campaigns tried to bind immigrants more closely to the United States. Some emphasized teaching immigrants English and civics and encouraging them to apply for citizenship. Others had a harder edge, stressing obedience, antiradicalism, and the need to break Old World ties.

Employers took a special interest in Americanization because they believed it would help them retain their experienced workers at a time of severe labor shortages and instill in the workforce what were deemed positive attitudes and values. Henry Ford, for example, believed that immigrants had to "be taught American ways, the English language, and the right way to live." Foreign-born workers, who made up a majority of the Ford Motor Company workforce, were encouraged to move out of ethnic neighborhoods and told not to take in boarders. If they did not speak English they were required to attend the Ford English School. There they were not only taught the language but also lectured on work habits, personal hygiene, and table manners. They were even indoctrinated with American racism: a Ford text said that blacks "came from Africa where they lived like other animals in the jungle. White men brought them to America and made them civilized."

Although the impetus for Americanization came primarily from nonimmigrants, many immigrants welcomed the opportunity to learn English, become citizens, and more fully share the way of life of native-born Americans. Often immigrants were encouraged to do

"... THESE MASSES OF FOREIGNERS MUST BE EDUCATED"

Some employers used nurses not only to take care of sick and injured employees but also as agents of Americanization. The following 1916 report was made by Florence S. Wright, a nurse employed by the Clark Thread Company in Newark, New Jersey, to a meeting of the National Safety Council, an employer-controlled industrial safety group. Notice that one of her examples is an "American mother"; "foreigner" apparently was a synonym for "poor" as much as an indication of a person's place of birth.

WHEN MOST OF the workers were English-speaking and either American-born or from European countries whose standards of living are not so different from ours, many problems did not arise which now cause us the most anxiety. With laborers coming from the four corners of the globe, speaking strange languages, and bringing with them their own traditions, superstitions, diseases, religions, it becomes necessary for the employer who is awake to his own needs and to those of the company to do something toward educating these masses in habits of cleanliness, health, morality, and thrift, and especially in suitable standards of living and in adapting their lives to changed conditions.

We see an Italian family of six living in three rooms, taking boarders. They do this, not because the man does not earn enough, but to get money to buy a home, and because they were used to being crowded in Italy. They do not know that conditions which did not injure health in the warm, sunny, outdoor life of the homeland become a menace when every one works indoors and when doors,

so by leaders in their own communities. Many immigrant shopkeepers, lawyers, and small businessmen, once primarily concerned with the politics of their native lands, were becoming increasingly American-oriented, urging their conationalists to concentrate on self-help and immediate advancement.

Other aspects of the wartime experience besides Americanization led many immigrants to identify more closely with the United States. Tens of thousands of immigrants entered the armed forces and fought in the war. In the process, they and their families often developed intense feelings of patriotism and a new sense of belonging to their adopted homeland. Also, the wartime labor shortage opened many job opportunities to immigrants. Men who had known only unskilled or semiskilled employment were upgraded; more women joined the paid workforce. Along with steady work and overtime, this brought many immigrant families significant improvements in their living standards.

The shift was dramatically apparent in the steel industry,

windows, and cracks are stopped up to keep out the cold. . . .

A Russian father cannot control his boys because they speak a language he does not know and in their new surroundings have become ashamed of the homeland ways.

An American mother loses a baby each summer because she cannot nurse her children. She has no idea of cleanliness, using a long tube nursing bottle in which the milk is often clotted solid and which is never cleaned. . . .

These instances could be related for hours from memory of actual cases and results, accomplished and not accomplished, but is it not proven that these masses of foreigners must be educated in cleanliness, homemaking, and infant care; in fact, that they must be made into good Americans as fast as possible?

No one can do this who does not reach the homes, and who can reach the homes except the visiting nurse?

She goes out in the morning with a list of names and addresses. . . . She finds the Italian family taking boarders. She goes slowly and keeps the family on her list. In time each member will accept her advice without question. The father has his chest examined, is found to be an incipient tuberculosis case, and after a period of rest and education is given outdoor work suited to his strength. The mother is taught to buy and to cook. The children are sent to open-air school. It takes time but in the end the boarders are no longer there, the father is well and doing suitable work, the children are gaining, and the mother is making a home of which the family and the nurse are proud.

Incidentally, the nurse has increased her Italian vocabulary and has six firm friends. Needless to say the unseen employer who sent the nurse also has six loyal friends although he may never know of their existence. . . .

where before the war corporate management had counted on rapid turnover in the ranks of the unskilled and semiskilled as a safety valve for discontent. Now the steel companies built housing for immigrant workers, raised their wages, granted promotions, and conducted citizenship classes. C. S. Robinson, general manager of the Youngstown Sheet and Tube Company, urged his foremen in March 1917 to show a "spirit of helpfulness and consideration" toward foreign-born workers: "These men are needed by our company." Where once the battle for survival had priority, it was now possible to think of a decent life.

While immigrants often had positive reasons for embracing Americanization, they also feared the consequences of resisting it. They had reason to worry. As the war went on, nativism grew increasingly crude. Sometimes it was silly, like renaming sauerkraut "liberty cabbage." Often, though, it was deadly serious. Egged on by respectable leaders such as Roosevelt, mobs attacked German-American stores and drove German-American performers off the stage. Many Americans with German names changed them.

Amid this hysteria, Congress passed several measures with a nativist slant. In 1917 a law enacted over Wilson's veto imposed a literacy test and other restrictions on immigration, beginning a process of limiting entrance into the United States that continued after the war. The AFL was one of the staunchest supporters of this measure. In that same year Congress passed the Eighteenth Amendment to the Constitution, banning the manufacture or sale of alcoholic beverages; ratification was completed in 1919. Many temperance supporters had long advocated prohibition on moral grounds, while others thought it would increase productivity. But nativism was involved, too: alcohol was commonly associated with immigrant life, and more specifically with German-Americans, who dominated the brewing industry.

E PLURIBUS UNUM

Out of the melting pot and into the ... The 1916 graduates of the Ford English School at the finale of commencement exercises. The graduation included a ritual of citizenship where the graduates, dressed in traditional national costumes, disembarked from an immigrant ship and disappeared into a gigantic melting pot (center of photo). Their teachers then vociferously stirred the pot with ladles, and the graduates finally emerged dressed in "American" clothes and waving flags.

Prohibition, like many aspects of the wartime loyalty campaign, had little to do with the direct requirements of fighting a war. Rather, World War I provided an opportunity for the Protestant elite to make sweeping changes to counter political and cultural challenges. The international crisis legitimized the use of government power to enforce social, political, and cultural orthodoxy. Although many wartime measures were temporary, the campaign for enforced consensus had permanent effects: radical groups were severely weakened, European immigration was virtually cut off, and foreign-born Americans were put on the defensive. The atmosphere of fear and intolerance created during the war would prove very harmful to labor in the postwar era.

THE SHAPE OF THE PEACE

For all the debate and preparation, the United States ended up playing only a minor military role in World War I. Large numbers of American troops entered combat in mid-September 1918. Within two months the German army, exhausted by an offensive the previous spring, collapsed, and an armistice was signed ending the war. Although many American soldiers saw battle, few experienced the prolonged trench warfare that characterized the war. A total of 112,000 American soldiers and sailors died during the conflict, over half from disease (mostly influenza or pneumonia). By comparison, 1.8 million Germans, 1.7 million Russians, 1.4 million French, 1.2 million Austro-Hungarians, and over 900,000 British died. To put these figures in a different perspective, according to conservative estimates in 1917 and 1918 nearly 24,000 Americans were killed and nearly 3 million injured in industrial accidents.

The war's end brought social crisis to much of Europe. By comparison, the United States was much more stable. Nevertheless, in 1919 it too experienced intense conflict. For Americans, two questions dominated the political agenda: What new international arrangements would grow out of the war? What kind of postwar society would emerge in the United States itself?

When Woodrow Wilson arrived in Europe late in 1918 to begin peace negotiations, he was greeted by cheering crowds. At the peace conference in Versailles, however, he found little support for a treaty based on his Fourteen Points. The Italian, French, and English governments were all led by conservative statesmen determined to exact severe penalties from Germany and to promote their own economic and political interests.

A number of factors weakened Wilson's bargaining position. First, he had just suffered a political defeat at home; in the fall 1918 elections the Republicans recaptured control of

---

"YOU BOYS GIVE 'EM HELL FOR ME"

Even a brief experience with front-line combat could be harrowing. The following entries from the diary of Elmer Sherwood, a corporal from Linton, Indiana, describe fighting on the Western Front near the end of the war.

●CT. 8. . . . Two of our fellows had already been wounded by an explosion near our kitchen this morning, but I was determined to go back for some mess because I was so confounded hungry. . . . I had just got a panful of slum and started eating, when I saw part of the temporary trench I had left, screened by an exploding shell. I thought it had come over the trench, but no—just then Smithy and Netterfield jumped out calling for stretchers.

I dropped my mess and ran to the trench and looked in. Poor Art was dead, one arm completely severed from his body. Danny had a hole in his stomach and we placed him on a stretcher and sent him back to the first aid station. . . . Dan looked at me with a smile on his face as we loaded him into an ambulance. I gave him a word of cheer and he said, "I don't know, Doc, old boy. I've got a pretty bad wound in my stomach. You boys give 'em hell for me." [He died the same day.]

I have seen many die, but none have been so close to me as these fellows. I have worked with them and fought beside them every day since I joined the outfit, and they have been my best pals.

But we must carry on, whatever happens. I ran back to the trench and rescued the battered switch board. . . . We are experiencing a fierce cannonading as I jot down these lines.

Oct. 30. Last night Fritz [the Germans] put on a whale of a bombardment, and I don't see how any of us escaped to tell the story. In the thick of it our communications were knocked out and I was detailed to repair the telephone line. How kind they are to me! Well, I thought of all the mean things I had done in my life, breathed a little prayer, climbed out of my fox hole, and darted out into the inferno.

Flashes of exploding artillery at intervals lighted up the blackness of the night. Explosions of enemy shells on every hand and the scream of big ones going over head to back areas added to the thunderous roar so that I could not have heard my own voice had I dared to speak. Boy! I was glad when I came to that break in the line. I was splicing the wire when—Shriek! Bang! a ton of steel came over me. Just as I finished the job—hell's bells—another hit knocked the line out of place.

For once I lost my cocky self-assurance, for I wasn't so certain that I would ever see home and Mother again. But finally, after stumbling over the body of a dead German, I came upon the next break and spliced it in a hurry. Then I raced back to my hole after reporting communications in order.

both houses of Congress. Second, Wilson was unwilling to ally with the strongest forces opposing a punitive peace treaty, the European socialist parties, which were growing rapidly in the aftermath of the Russian Revolution. The new Soviet government, like the German government, was not even invited to the peace conference. Third, Wilson's advocacy of self-determination was undercut by his support for the continuation of colonialism. Irish-Americans, for example, were upset by Wilson's acquiescence to British refusal to discuss Irish independence. And when a young Vietnamese nationalist, later known by the name Ho Chi Minh, came to the conference to plead for greater autonomy for Vietnam, then a French colony, the American delegation ignored him.

The treaty that finally emerged from Versailles blamed the war on Germany. It forced Germany to cede considerable territory to France and called for huge German reparation payments to the Allies. To fulfill the national aspirations of various ethnic groups and surround the Soviet Union with a cordon of hostile states, a number of new countries—Austria, Hungary, Poland, Yugoslavia, Czechoslovakia, Estonia, Latvia, Finland, and Lithuania—were formed from the Austro-Hungarian Empire (which was broken up) and parts of Germany and the old Russian Empire.

Wilson's major achievement at the conference was the inclusion of a plan for a League of Nations in the peace treaty. The League— meant to resolve disputes between member nations and guarantee their territorial integrity—was empowered to consider collective action in response to aggression. But when the president returned to Washington after months of arduous bargaining, it became clear that his negotiating victory was in jeopardy. Even before Wilson presented the Versailles Treaty to the Senate for ratification, Republicans were voicing strong opposition. Frustrated by lengthy hearings being held by the Senate Foreign Relations Committee, in September 1919 Wilson began a speaking tour to drum up support for the pact. Late that month, exhausted by the effort, he collapsed. After being rushed back to Washington, he suffered a severe stroke. For the remaining seventeen months of his presidency, Wilson was an invalid, often unable to conduct business. Meanwhile, the Senate twice refused to ratify the Versailles Treaty. Ultimately, the League of Nations was established without U.S. membership.

As the Versailles Treaty was being written and debated, a fierce struggle was occurring between labor and capital over what postwar America would be like. In 1919 four million workers—fully one-fifth of the nation's workforce—went on strike. It was not just the extent of the 1919 strikes that was startling; in a variety of ways, organized labor put forth a more fundamental challenge to the established order than at any other time in the twentieth century. Repression by business and government forces was unmatched in its ferocity as well.

Many labor leaders had looked forward to the war's end, believing that the vast wartime increase in union membership, as well as labor's growing influence on federal policy, meant that it would be the beginning of a better day for American workers. Excitement over the Russian Revolution further heightened hopes. Sidney Hillman, himself a Russian immigrant, wrote to his daughter in 1918: "Messiah is arriving. He may be with us any minute. . . . Labor will rule and the world will be free."

In addition to solidifying and extending wartime organizational gains, unions urgently sought to recapture real income being lost to a sharp postwar inflation. Businessmen had a very different agenda. Generally, they wanted a rapid dismantling of the government's expanded economic apparatus. They also sought to roll back the wartime gains of labor. The result was a series of titanic clashes.

The Seattle General Strike early in 1919 set the tone for the year. Seattle was a strong union town. The city's 35,000 shipyard workers, through an alliance of craft unions, had succeeded in winning higher

The Seattle General Strike. The General Strike Committee issues groceries to union families.

wages than elsewhere in the country. But during the war a government panel had limited further increases in an effort to equalize wages nationally. In January 1919 the shipyard workers responded by going on strike. Two weeks later 25,000 other Seattle workers joined them in a general strike that paralyzed the city.

One hundred and ten local unions—mostly AFL craft groups—took part in the shutdown. For five days the city was largely run by a General Strike Committee, which set up twenty-one community kitchens to feed strikers and other residents, issued special permits to allow milk delivery for children and laundry service for hospitals, established collective butcher shops and laundries, and even organized some five hundred uniformed war veterans to patrol the streets. The General Strike Committee exuberantly declared that working people were "learning to manage" the local economy.

Although the strike was completely peaceful, the city's mayor and local businessmen charged the labor movement with attempting revolution. Fearful national labor leaders successfully pressured the Seattle labor movement to call off the strike before the shipyard workers had won their demands. Still, it had been a remarkable demonstration of unity and organization.

In industry after industry, workers displayed similar militancy and solidarity. In New York, 50,000 men's clothing workers struck for thirteen weeks, winning a forty-four-hour workweek. Theater actors struck too, under the banner of Actors' Equity. In New England and New Jersey, 120,000 textile workers stayed away from their jobs. Also in New England, a strike of female telephone operators forced the Post Office Department, which had taken over the nation's telephone system during the war, to grant higher wages. Late in the year 400,000 soft-coal miners walked away from the coalpits, defying a plea from Wilson and a federal court injunction that barred their union from organizing the strike. Despite determined federal efforts to put down the uprising, the miners stayed out until they were granted an immediate wage hike of 14 percent, and arbitration of their other grievances.

No one seemed immune from the spirit of labor militancy. In Boston a local police-

"OVER FAIR"

In 1919 striking actors in New York City satirized the popular prowar song "Over There," which had been written by George M. Cohan. Cohan, a Broadway producer as well as a songwriter, playwright, and performer, had spoken out against the actors' union and tried to break their strike.

Over fair, over fair,
We have been, we have been over fair.
 But now things are humming
 And the time is coming
 When with Labor we'll be chumming
Everywhere.
So beware, have a care,
Just be fair, on the square, everywhere.
 For we are striking, yes, we are striking,
And we won't come back till the managers are fair.

men's organization affiliated with the AFL, outraging the police commissioner, who responded by suspending nineteen policemen. The police then struck. Almost immediately the city was hit by a wave of rowdyism, theft, and violence. While local unionists debated calling a general strike in support of the police, Massachusetts governor Calvin Coolidge announced that none of the strikers would be rehired. State troops were mobilized, the general strike failed to materialize, and an entirely new police force was recruited from among unemployed veterans.

Although the 1919 strikes were notable more for their size and tactics than their demands, which centered on wages, hours, and other traditional issues, a spirit of radicalism was infusing the labor movement. The Bolshevik victory in Russia and the growing strength of the British Labour Party inspired many Americans. The United Mine Workers of America demanded the withdrawal of U.S. troops still in Russia. In Seattle and San Francisco, longshoremen refused to load guns being sent to groups trying to overthrow the Bolsheviks. Equally important, the wartime experiences of railroad workers and miners had taught vivid lessons about the virtues of coordinated bargaining and of government administration of industry. In 1919, the railroad unions endorsed a plan proposed by Glenn Plumb for government ownership of all railroad lines, with labor participation in the management of the enterprise. At the same time, the UMWA debated nationalization of the coal industry.

Even as socialist sentiments grew more common, though, the Socialist Party—already weakened by wartime repression—was being torn apart by disagreements over the Russian Revolution and other issues. In the summer of 1919, the party splintered into three factions. One, which kept the name Socialist Party, continued electoral activities in the belief that it would eventually become the majority party, enabling it to legislate democratic control of the economy. The two other factions held out the Bolsheviks as their model, and went underground to organize an American revolutionary movement. Eventually, these groups merged to establish the Communist Party. Wrapped up in disputes with one another, all three factions failed to play a major role in the postwar strike wave.

Adding to the sense of crisis that gripped the country in 1919 was a new wave of racial violence. In July a race riot in Washington, D.C., resulted in six deaths and a hundred injuries. Later that year four people were killed in a racial incident in Omaha and perhaps as many as twenty-five blacks and several whites died in rural Arkansas, where black sharecroppers had begun to organize and arm themselves.

The worst riot was in Chicago. Like many racial clashes, it began on a hot summer day at a public facility uneasily shared by whites

(*Left*) The scourge of Bolshevism. "Progress" and "Civilization" are annihilated by the bestial revolution in a 1919 *Leslie's Illustrated Weekly Newspaper* cover.

(*Right*) "Society Note from Moscow." One of a series of cartoons by Alfred Frueh in the radical weekly *Good Morning* celebrating the Bolshevik Revolution's impact on Russia's aristocracy: "Count Parasitsky will not occupy his palatial residence in the mountains this summer," reads the caption. "He expects to remain in the city and do uplift work."

and blacks, in this case a beach. When a young black swimmer, who had drifted to a white section of the beach, was killed by a thrown rock, fighting broke out. It quickly spread to the city proper, fed by pent-up resentment over housing, job competition, and segregation.

In the past, when white rioters had invaded black neighborhoods, the inhabitants had hidden or fled. But in 1919, Chicago blacks fought back, reflecting the commitment that had developed during the war among northern African-Americans to refuse to accept second-class citizenship. Recently returned veterans, some of them armed, took the lead in defending black areas. Along the borders between black and white neighborhoods, full-scale battles occurred. For five days the riot raged; by the time it ended, thirty-eight people had died and more than five hundred were injured.

In September, the most important strike of 1919 began. Since the turn of the century the steel industry had been overwhelmingly nonunion. Dominated by U.S. Steel, the largest corporation in the world, the industry had used its financial strength and political connections to crush organizing efforts, exploiting tensions among various groups of workers and between competing unions.

During the war, the labor shortage and the government's democratic rhetoric had revived interest in unionism among iron and steel workers. Aware of this, in mid-1918 John Fitzpatrick and William Z.

Foster, leaders of the union drive in the Chicago meatpacking industry, won AFL approval for a campaign to organize the steel industry. Fitzpatrick and Foster used the same techniques they had pioneered in the packinghouses. For one thing, they hired organizers fluent in all the languages spoken by steelworkers. For another, to prevent destructive wrangling among the many craft unions that claimed jurisdiction over skilled steelworkers, they created temporary "federal locals" to govern new recruits during the campaign. Only after organizing was completed would skilled workers be transferred from these units—which were directly affiliated with the AFL—to existing craft unions.

At first the organizing drive was most successful in the Chicago region and among immigrant workers. Gradually, though, other workers began signing up. By the summer of 1919, union leaders felt sufficiently confident to begin recruiting in the Pittsburgh region, the heartland of the industry. The only group they failed with was African-American workers. For years unions in the iron and steel industry had excluded blacks, and some continued to do so. Few African-Americans were willing to throw in their lot with a movement that had so frequently spurned them.

For months the steel companies refused to negotiate with the committee coordinating the union drive. Instead, in factory after factory they fired active unionists. Faced with this intransigence and an increasingly restless membership, on September 22, 1919, the unions struck, ignoring appeals from Wilson and Gompers for a postponement. Virtually the entire industry was shut down as over 300,000 workers left their jobs.

Although temporarily crippled, the struck companies fought back, unleashing, with the cooperation of local authorities, a reign of terror. In city after city, strikers and their supporters were beaten, arrested, shot, or driven out of town. In Pittsburgh the sheriff deputized five thousand U.S. Steel employees and prohibited outdoor meetings. Nearby, in Clairton and Glassport, state troopers clubbed strikers attending peaceful gatherings. In Gary, Indiana, federal troops took control. Such government action enabled the companies to keep many of their mills open throughout the strike.

To justify this repression, the steel companies had to win public support, no mean feat considering that their initial refusal to meet with the unions, even at the president's request, won them widespread scorn. To gain popular sympathy, the companies portrayed the conflict not as a labor dispute but as an attempted revolution. The press began printing stories about Foster's syndicalist past, claiming that he had forced the strike "for the purpose of revolutionizing industry." The fact that a large number of strikers were immigrants lent credence to the steel companies' charges, since native-born

How do you spell strike? The strike ballot distributed by the National Committee for Organizing Iron and Steel Workers—printed in English, Croatian, Hungarian, Italian, Slovak, and Polish—indicates the range of nationalities composing the industry's workforce in 1919.

"... WE OUGHT TO HAVE THE RIGHT TO BELONG TO THE UNION"

"... WE OUGHT TO HAVE THE RIGHT TO BELONG TO THE UNION"

Frank Smith, a Hungarian-born steelworker, testifies at a Senate committee investigation of the 1919 steel strike, and explains why he thought he had the right to join a union.

STATEMENT OF FRANK SMITH

THE CHAIRMAN: What is your nationality?

MR. SMITH: I am an Hungarian.

THE CHAIRMAN: You are not naturalized?

MR. SMITH: No, sir.

THE CHAIRMAN: How long have you been in this country?

MR. SMITH: Thirteen years. The reason that I am not naturalized is that I never stayed in one place; stayed long enough to get my papers.

THE CHAIRMAN: Do you expect to be naturalized?

MR. SMITH: Yes ... because I have got my family here, my woman and five children ... and I would like to know how a man is going to make a living for himself and his wife and five children on $4.73 a day.

THE CHAIRMAN: How many hours do you work?

MR. SMITH: I work 10 hours a day and I get paid for straight 10 hours time.

THE CHAIRMAN: And how many days in the week do you work?

MR. SMITH: Seven days—sometimes six days and sometimes seven days....

THE CHAIRMAN: Are you a union man?

MR. SMITH: Yes, I am a union man.

THE CHAIRMAN: Do they treat you in that way because you belonged to the union?

MR. SMITH: Oh, they won't allow us in there if they know that we are union men.

THE CHAIRMAN: Are you sure about that?

MR. SMITH: Yes, I am sure about that.

THE CHAIRMAN: And you want the right to belong to the union, too?

MR. SMITH: Yes, sir; we do. This is the United States and we ought to have the right to belong to the union.

SEN. MCKELLAR: Did all of you boys buy Liberty Bonds?

MR. SMITH: Yes, sir; every one of us.... We were all for the United States. We worked day and night for that....

Americans often associated immigrants with radicalism. According to the New York *Tribune*, the issue was "Americanism vs. Alienism."

The organizing unions squabbled with one another with more enthusiasm than they contributed funds to their joint effort. While money for strike relief ran out, the companies stood firm. Maintaining production wherever they could, they worked to split the strikers along ethnic and racial lines. In late October, they started bringing in African-American and Mexican strikebreakers. Back-to-work movements, aimed in particular at skilled and native-born workers, grew increasingly successful. Slowly the strike fell apart, and in January 1920 it was officially called off.

It had been a heroic display and a terrible defeat. The immigrant steelworkers had demonstrated a capacity for sustained militancy and discipline, the steel industry had shown itself capable of crushing even the most massive of walkouts, and the craft form of organization had proved utterly unsuitable for mass-production industry, even with the modifications Fitzpatrick and Foster had introduced. It would be fifteen years before another major effort would be launched to organize such basic industries as steel, auto, and electrical equipment manufacturing.

THE RED SCARE

The mobilization of municipal police forces, state militias, and federal courts against strikers was but part of a larger postwar business-government offensive against radicals and labor militants. This offensive, which focused on the foreign-born, took place despite the fact that by the fall of 1919 the worldwide advance of radicalism had been largely checked. An attempted revolution in Germany had been suppressed, and a Soviet government in Hungary had been quickly toppled. In the United States the socialist movement was splintered, while the IWW was devoting much of its energy to defending members facing trial on wartime charges. Nevertheless, official and unofficial "loyalty" organizations intensified their antiradical crusade.

Foremost among the red-hunters was Attorney General A. Mitchell Palmer. In November 1919, Palmer's agents arrested 250 members of the Union of Russian Workers, beating up many though recommending only 39 for deportation. The next month 249 aliens were shipped off to the Soviet Union. Most had never been charged with a crime. Some, like the well-known anarchist Emma Goldman, had been in the United States for decades.

The largest of the Palmer raids took place in January 1920, when federal agents arrested 6,000 alleged Communists in thirty-three cities across the country. Many were arrested without warrants and were not allowed to contact lawyers or their families. Confessions were sometimes coerced. Some of those arrested had no connections whatsoever to radical activities, but were detained for up to a week nonetheless.

The excesses of the January raids eroded support for the anti-red campaign. The Labor Department, which was in charge of deportations, ended its cooperation with the Justice Department. Only 600 of the January arrestees were eventually forced to leave the country. Developments in New York State also helped brake the red scare. In April 1920 the New York State Assembly expelled five duly-elected Socialist Party legislators. Protests against this action were widespread, and critics included such mainstream Republicans as Charles Evans Hughes and Ohio senator Warren G. Harding. The public was growing tired of the red issue. So were many businessmen; once the steel strike was defeated, they began worrying more about alienating their foreign-born employees and less about the danger of revolution.

Palmer hoped to use the red scare to further his presidential ambitions, but he overplayed his hand when he warned that revolutionaries were planning a wave of violence on May 1, 1920. Police were mobilized, buildings guarded, and political leaders protected, but the day passed quietly. Discredited, the anti-red drive began dying down. Nevertheless, until 1924 the Department of Justice continued its antilabor and antiradical activities, working closely with state governments, businesses, and private detective agencies. Private groups such as the American Legion also continued to harass left-wing activists.

One case in particular kept the issue of political repression alive.

"Under the Stars and Stripes." Daily representations of subversion and menace, like this Bolshevik serpent in the Philadelphia *Inquirer*, also carried a strong anti-immigrant message, fueling the 1919 red scare.

On May 5, 1920, two Italian-born anarchists, Nicola Sacco and Bartolomeo Vanzetti, were arrested in Brockton, Massachusetts, and charged with killing two men in the course of an armed robbery. Both men protested their innocence, insisting that they were being persecuted for their political beliefs. At the time of their arrests Sacco and Vanzetti had been organizing protests against the death two days earlier of another Italian radical who had fallen—or, some suspected, had been pushed—out of a fourteenth-story window while in federal custody. Following a trial marked by questionable evidence and procedures, the defendants were convicted of first-degree murder and sentenced to death.

For many people in the United States and abroad, the Sacco and Vanzetti case came to symbolize government injustice. As legal appeals were pursued, protests flared, first among Italian-Americans, then among non-Italian radicals, and finally among a broad spectrum of intellectuals and civil libertarians. Under pressure, the governor of Massachusetts appointed a committee of prominent citizens to review the case, but it found no reason to reverse the sentence. On August 22, 1927, as crowds gathered throughout the world to protest, Sacco and Vanzetti were executed.

After the executions—Boston, August 1928. Thousands of mourners follow behind the funeral carriages of Sacco and Vanzetti.

America's domestic battles in 1919 were part of a larger struggle over the shape of the post–World War I world. For a few moments during and just after the war it looked like a realization of Progressive hopes for controlled reform and a more peaceful, fairer international order based on liberal democratic capitalism might emerge from the bloodshed. A more radical alternative, the spread of socialism beyond the Soviet Union, also seemed possible. But neither came to pass.

Nonetheless, the United States was forever changed by the war. After the war the government continued to play an enlarged if less visible role in the economy, in labor relations, and in shaping public attitudes. Wartime suspicion of "foreigners" contributed to the end of open immigration, while population shifts that began during the war, from the South to the North and from Mexico to the Southwest, continued. Women retained a greater degree of political equality even as most of their wartime economic gains were reversed. Immigrants, in spite of increased prejudice, held on to a greater sense of themselves as full-fledged Americans.

During the war, the labor movement had loomed large in national political and economic life, and unions had grown stronger, more political, and more radical. But when the war ended, so did many of the conditions that favored labor. With production levels falling and four million men who had been in the armed services reentering the workforce, the labor shortage abated. At the same time, forces unleashed by the war—intolerance, fear of foreigners, fear of radicalism—played into the employers' hands. Corporations, swelled by wartime profits and aided by government repression, were able to withstand even long interruptions in production, while labor's radical allies were weakened by bickering. As a result, business was able to turn back labor's offensive in 1919 and in the years immediately thereafter. By the early 1920s, business no longer had to deal with a confident, politicized working-class movement. It would be well over a decade before the labor movement again exerted much weight on a national scale.

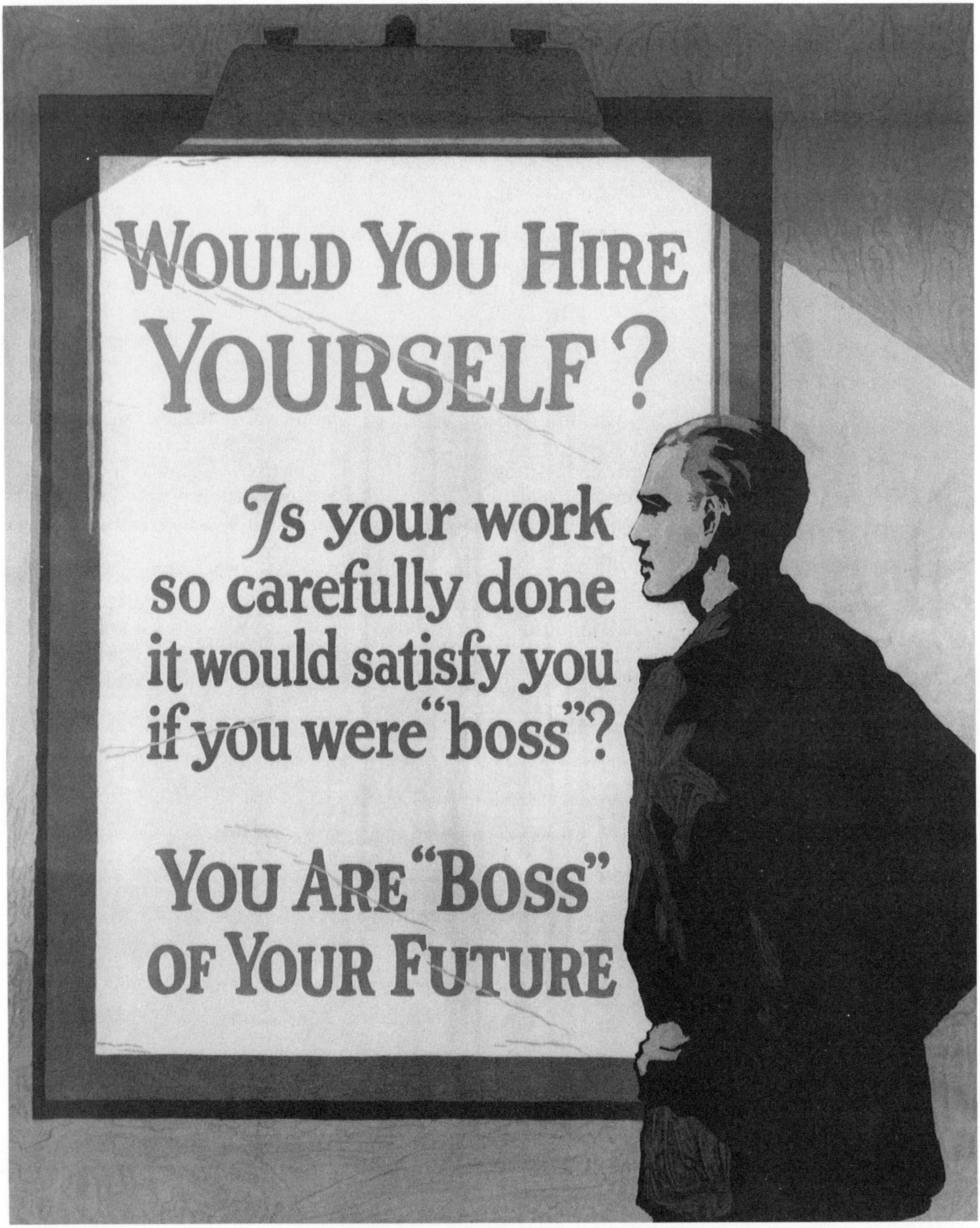
WOULD YOU HIRE
YOURSELF?
Is your work
so carefully done
it would satisfy you
if you were "boss"?
YOU ARE "BOSS"
OF YOUR FUTURE

6

"THE NEW ERA"

MASS SOCIETY AND BUSINESS TRIUMPH

"You Are 'Boss' of Your Future." One of a series of posters commissioned by the U.S. government in 1929, emphasizing how personal success could be achieved through hard work, discipline, and, implicitly, obedience to authority. The posters were never distributed; in the aftermath of the October 1929 stock-market crash, the posters' "self-made man" message may have seemed unconvincing.

AMERICANS usually think of the 1920s as an era of speakeasies, bootleggers, and high living, a carefree moment between World War I and the Great Depression. Indeed, for many people it was a time of good fortune. "The whole upper tenth of a nation," the novelist F. Scott Fitzgerald wrote, was "living with the insouciance of a grand duc and the casualness of chorus girls." But the glitter masked as much as it revealed about fundamental changes that were taking place in American society. Following a brief depression after World War I, industrial output and national wealth soared. The manufacture of consumer goods such as cars, radios, and refrigerators accounted for much of the growth.

269

Construction boomed. With economic expansion came major changes in social structure and the fabric of everday life. The 1920 census was the first to show more than half the population living in cities and towns; urbanization continued unabated during the decade. Far fewer immigrants came from Europe in the 1920s than earlier, but more came from Mexico.

As working hours decreased and income rose, the entertainment industry thrived. New mass media promoted consumerism and competed with family and community in transmitting ideas and values. Out of the ethnic and regional subcultures of the past, a new mass culture was created, dominated by an ethos of fast moneymaking and feverish acquisition.

For two decades the "labor question" had been a central concern of virtually every sector of society, but in the 1920s this was no longer the case, as big business rapidly established its dominance. By 1923 the postwar strike wave was over and the labor movement was in steep decline. Industrialists introduced far-reaching changes in the organization of production with relatively little interference. For many workers the trade-off for a loss of control on the job was a rising standard of living.

But the prosperity of the 1920s was very uneven. While the rich got much richer, the average worker's income rose slowly. In some industries workers experienced falling wages and massive unemployment. Many farmers, too, suffered through most of the decade. And as usual, blacks fared worse than whites.

Social conflict declined in the 1920s, but divisions remained. Race relations were tense (though there were fewer riots than during the war era). Violent strikes convulsed ailing industries such as textiles and mining. Disagreements over culture and religion deepened. To some extent these conflicts reflected growing disparities in living standards as some groups entered the new mass-production, mass-consumption economy while others remained outside.

Corporate growth transformed American society without eliminating large pockets of poverty and economic stagnation; it even created some new ones. The unequal distribution of wealth, though generally ignored by political and business leaders, was a central feature of the 1920s, ultimately leading to the economic collapse that ended the era.

"THE BUSINESS OF AMERICA IS BUSINESS"

The First World War strengthened business, increased its popularity, and forged close working relationships between corporate executives and government officials. The war also intensified workers' grievances and raised their expectations. Despite fierce worker militancy, business turned back the 1919 strike wage. But when the 1920s began, labor was far from impotent; the craft unions still had considerable clout, and hundreds of thousands of wartime recruits swelled labor's ranks. Questions about who would control the levers of power in the postwar economy remained open. Would government continue to regulate economic activities, as it had during the war? Would unions continue to have significant bargaining power despite being excluded from the rapidly expanding industrial sector?

In late 1920, boom gave way to depression. Prices fell sharply, unemployment rose, and a hundred thousand firms went bankrupt. In just two years the number of manufacturing employees fell by 25 percent. Many businesses tried to compensate for falling prices by slashing wages and increasing hours, often in violation of union contracts. Employers saw the economic downturn as an opportunity to reverse the wartime gains of labor. Building on wartime patriotism, they launched an "open-shop" campaign, portraying union shop contracts, which required all employees to be union members, as infringing on traditional American liberties. The open shop, in which union membership was not required and often forbidden, was called the "American Plan."

Unions fought back. Between 1920 and 1922, there were major strikes in the textile, clothing, printing, meatpacking, shipping, coal, construction, and railroad industries. Although some unions, such as the Typographers and the Amalgamated Clothing Workers, were able to preserve their bargaining status and prevent or minimize the deterioration of wages and working conditions, the anti-union drive took its toll. In San Francisco, when construction unions rejected a 1921 arbitration decision that would have lowered wages by 7.5 percent, employers organized a lockout that broke the power of the local AFL Building Trades Council and ended the union shop. Similarly, a 1923

"WHAT IS TH' OPEN SHOP?"

Chicago newspaperman Finley Peter Dunne (1867–1936) created an extraordinarily popular character in "Mr. Dooley," a fictional Irish saloonkeeper. Dunne had Mr. Dooley speak in dialect, but portrayed him as a shrewd social observer. Here he comments to Mr. Hennessey, his steady customer, on the justifications for the open shop.

"WHAT'S ALL THIS that's in the papers about the open shop?" asked Mr. Hennessey.

"Why, don't ye know?" said Mr. Dooley. "Really, I'm surprized at yer ignorance, Hinnissey. What is th' open shop? Sure, 'tis where they kape the doors open to accommodate th' constant stream av' min comin' in t' take jobs cheaper than th' min what has th' jobs. 'Tis like this, Hinnissey: Suppose wan [one] av [of] these freeborn citizens is workin' in an open shop f'r th' princely wage av wan large iron dollar a day av tin [ten] hours. Along comes anither son-av-gun and he sez t' th' boss, "Oi think Oi could handle th' job nicely f'r ninety cints." "Sure," sez th' boss, and th' wan dollar man gets out into th' crool woruld t' exercise hiz inalienable roights as a freeborn American citizen an' scab on some other poor devil. An' so it goes on, Hinnissey. An' who gits th' benefit? Thrue, it saves th' boss money, but he don't care no more f'r money thin he does f'r his right eye. It's all principle wid him. He hates t' see men robbed av their indipindence. They must have their indipindence, regardless av anything else."

"But," said Mr. Hennessey, "those open-shop min ye menshun say they are f'r unions if properly conducted."

"Shure," said Mr. Dooley, "if properly conducted. An' there we are: an' how would they have them conducted? No strikes, no rules, no contracts, no scales, hardly iny wages, an' dam' few mimbers."

strike of New England telephone operators, faced with management's refusal to bargain, ended without gains after a month and led to the demise of telephone unionism throughout the region.

Perhaps the worst loss was in the railroad industry, long a bastion of organized labor. In July 1922 some 400,000 railroad shop workers struck to prevent wage cuts. Although President Harding criticized the owners for spurning federal mediation, his administration eventually turned against the strikers. On September 1, Attorney General Harry Daugherty secured the most sweeping federal restraining order ever issued against a group of strikers. The walkout soon collapsed. The defeated unions managed to win agreements with some railroads that maintained their status as bargaining agents, but other railroads reverted to nonunion operation.

By 1923 union membership had fallen to 3.6 million, from a high of over 5 million in 1920. Most membership losses were in the very industries that had seen the greatest wartime gains: shipbuilding, meatpacking, transportation, and metalworking. By the time the open-shop drive wound down in late 1923, unions were excluded from heavy industry, weakened by heavy membership losses, and disheartened by strike defeats.

The 1920 presidential election set the political tone for the decade that followed. Both major parties resolved internal disputes by nominating bland, middle-of-the-road Ohio politicians: the Republicans, Senator Warren G. Harding; the Democrats, Governor James Cox. Since the candidates debated few major issues, the election became a test of what the voting public thought of the Wilson years.

On Election Day the Democrats were thoroughly repudiated. Harding carried thirty-seven of the forty-eight states, winning 61 percent of the popular vote, the highest percentage since before the Civil War. But less than half the eligible voters had gone to the polls, the lowest percentage in nearly a century. Harding's victory ended the eight-year Democratic interlude that had resulted from the 1912 split in the Republican Party. Once again the Republicans were the dominant national party. Only in the South could the Democrats depend on support, and even there Harding made inroads.

The Democratic defeat reflected, above all, the fact that millions of Americans had tired of the moral righteousness and unceasing urgency of the Wilson administration. Harding brilliantly capitalized on this mood when he declared that the country needed "not heroism but healing, not nostrums but normalcy, not revolution but restoration." "Normalcy" became the catchword of the day.

The Harding administration's "normalcy" meant extraordinary corporate influence on national policy; during the 1920s the political power of big business climbed to unprecedented heights. Harding's

The business of America is accommodation. Battle flags captured by northern troops during the Civil War are returned to aged Confederate veterans in a 1927 ceremony in front of the Capitol supervised by President Calvin Coolidge. Such rites of reconciliation between old enemies obscured the repressive state of race relations in the South during the 1920s.

cabinet was dominated by Secretary of the Treasury Andrew Mellon, one of the richest men in America, and Secretary of Commerce Herbert Hoover, an engineer and business executive. When Harding died suddenly in 1923, he was succeeded by Vice President Calvin Coolidge, who had risen to national prominence as Massachusetts governor by crushing the 1919 Boston police strike. Reelected in 1924, Coolidge in turn was succeeded four years later by Hoover.

More than any of their predecessors, these Republican presidents identified the fortune of America with the fortune of business. Business, Coolidge argued, "is one of the greatest contributing forces to the moral and spiritual advancement of the race." If business prospered, so would the country as a whole, for, as he put it, "The business of America is business."

When they spoke of business, Republicans and most Democrats meant privately operated business. At the end of World War I, both parties sought to return quickly to private hands businesses operated by the government during the war emergency. The key test was the railroad system. The railroad brotherhoods, which had prospered while the government ran the railroads, proposed that the government buy the railroad system and operate it through an agency composed of government, labor, and management representatives. Congress ignored the proposal (which was backed by the AFL), and restored the railroads to corporate control in 1920.

Some leading Republicans, including Mellon, felt that the government could best aid business by reducing spending, lowering taxes (particularly for the well-to-do), and minimizing federal intervention in the economy. In 1926 Mellon succeeded in halving the maximum income-tax rate. Estate taxes were drastically lowered as well.

Other Republican officials, however, including Hoover and Henry C. Wallace, Harding's secretary of agriculture, concluded from the country's wartime experience that the government should be actively involved in promoting and coordinating private economic efforts. Under Hoover, the Commerce Department sponsored studies of industrial waste, pushed for the further standardization of parts, helped set up trade associations, and worked with the State Department to increase exports. Antitrust action was kept at a minimum, which encouraged corporate cooperation. Similarly, the Department of Agriculture urged farmers to keep prices up through cooperative marketing arrangements and voluntary crop reduction.

As secretary of state in the early 1920s, Charles Evans Hughes actively used federal power to assist American business expansion overseas. The American leaders' willingness to "send in the marines" was a key factor in the growth of U.S. investment in Venezuelan oil, Chilean copper, Cuban sugar, Argentine beef, and Central American fruit. In 1926, for example, years of American intervention in Nicaragua culminated in the marines' suppression of the nationalist rebellion led by Augusto Sandino and the imposition of the Somoza dictatorship that would last for over half a century. Private U.S. investment abroad increased fivefold from 1914 to 1930, and by the latter year the United States led the world in exports.

Between 1919 and 1929, adjusting for inflation, the gross national product rose 39 percent, while corporate profits nearly doubled. The real earnings of employed wage-earners also rose, though more modestly; in 1929 they averaged about one-quarter higher than a decade earlier. People were living longer (life expectancy went from age forty-seven in 1900 to fifty-nine in 1930), eating better (e.g., fruits and vegetables became a more important component of the urban diet), and becoming better educated (27 percent of all seventeen-year-olds graduated from high school in 1929, up from 16 percent in 1920).

The booming economy transformed the physical landscape. Taller and taller skyscrapers were built, not only in the largest cities but also in smaller ones such as Memphis and Minneapolis. At the same time many factories and warehouses moved to the cities' edges, where land was cheap; trucks made downtown water and rail connections less vital. By 1925 over $1 billion was being spent on roads, parkways, bridges, and tunnels to handle the exploding volume of motor traffic. Public construction of schools, courthouses, and irrigation projects took place on an unprecedented scale.

All across the country, builders scrambled to ease a serious housing shortage. Between 1922 and 1929 six million new homes went up—twice as many as in any previous seven-year period. Well over half were single-unit dwellings. "To possess one's own home is the hope and ambition of almost every individual in our country," Presi-

Goodwill. The 1928 Havana Pan-American Conference found Calvin Coolidge defending U.S. intervention in Nicaragua from attacks by Latin American delegates. U.S. press coverage largely ignored the controversy, preferring to herald transatlantic aviator Charles Lindbergh's arrival in Havana with a message of "goodwill." "How sweet it sounds in the ears of the Pan-American delegates," commented the New Masses in the caption to this cartoon, "but how different it looks to Sandino and the Nicaraguan patriots."

dent Hoover said. "Those immortal ballads 'Home Sweet Home,' 'My Old Kentucky Home,' and 'The Gray Home in the West' were not written about tenements or apartments. . . . They never sing songs about a pile of rent receipts."

The new houses going up were beyond the means of most working-class families. A third of all families lived in houses categorized by one expert as below "any decent standard." But the growing availability of mortgage financing made it possible for more families than ever before, even from the working class, to own some sort of home. Banks were not the only lenders; some employers provided low-cost mortgages to their skilled workers, hoping to win their loyalty. A few unions also helped underwrite mortgages or, in the case of the Amalgamated Clothing Workers, sponsored cooperatively owned apartment buildings. Altogether, during the 1920s the dollar amount of mortgage borrowing tripled.

Still, residential patterns remained segregated along economic and racial lines. As cities grew, the middle class and better-off workers moved outward, while poorer families took over the neighborhoods they abandoned. Suburban areas grew twice as rapidly as the center cities; by 1930 nearly one of six Americans lived in the suburbs. To keep out African-Americans, Asians, Mexicans, and Jews—or simply the less affluent—many suburbs used zoning regulations or restrictive covenants (special clauses in deeds) to regulate the sale of land and houses.

Dramatic changes took place inside the average home. "The homely broom," wrote sociologist Robert Lynd, "unchanged since the time of the early Egyptians, is giving way to an expensive piece of electrical equipment," the vacuum cleaner. This was possible because most city and town dwellings now had electricity (though most farms did not). Also, by 1930 half of all homes had flush toilets, up from one of five a decade earlier. Even in working-class households oil furnaces, radios, toasters, irons, and washing machines commonly could be found.

Like homeownership, the widespread purchase of major household goods was stimulated by a rapid expansion of consumer credit. By one estimate, 75 percent of all radios and 60 percent of all cars and furniture were paid for in installments. Credit was even used to buy clothes. In Flint, Michigan, young single working women often went into debt to keep up with the latest styles. A Department of Labor study reported that their fashion-consciousness stemmed from their belief that the nation "naturally favored the better-dressed girls." An ethic of spending was replacing an ethic of saving.

The increased production of durable consumer goods was largely responsible for a near doubling of manufacturing output between 1921 and 1929. The manufacturing workforce, however, barely grew;

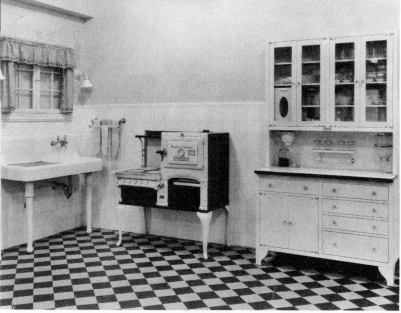

Model kitchens. A quarter of a century separates these two "model kitchens," indicating how technology and new consumer products—including gas stoves, washing machines, and vacuum cleaners—changed housework. The wood stove in an 1899 kitchen, for example, stands in sharp contrast to the 1924 showcase electric stove. Nevertheless, some innovations were far beyond the means of many American families; over one-third of all American households still had wood or coal stoves in 1940.

almost the same number of workers produced twice as many goods. Several factors accounted for this sharp rise in productivity. Some gains came from new technology. During and after the war, manufacturers invested heavily in more efficient machinery, often converting from steam to electric power. They also installed mechanical devices to replace unskilled labor, which became more expensive once immigration was limited in 1924.

Productivity gains also came from speed-up—simply having workers work harder and faster. This practice was particularly prevalent in the southern textile industry. One female mill hand recalled having nightmares about a speed-up: "I just sweated it out in my dream just like I did when I was there on the job; wanting to quit but [knowing] I couldn't afford to."

Soaring manufacturing productivity and modest productivity gains in mining, transportation, and agriculture changed the occupational structure. Most new jobs were in construction or white-collar work—clerical employment alone increased by nearly a million jobs during the 1920s—while the proportion of workers engaged in manufacturing, mining, agriculture, and railroading declined. By 1929 one-third of all jobs were in sales, service, or finance. Furthermore, most of the growing occupations—construction was the key exception—heavily employed women. In 1930, for example, more than half the country's clerical workers were female.

FORDISM

Taken together, a series of new methods in manufacturing, labor relations, and consumer sales perfected during and after World War I constituted a virtual second industrial revolution. The automobile industry was the seedbed for many key innovations. During the early 1920s, the term "Fordism" was widely used to describe the highly automated production of complex consumer goods on a vast scale. Although within a few years a new term, "mass production," came into vogue, the original phrase was apt, for Henry Ford and the Ford Motor Company pioneered many techniques later adopted throughout the economy.

Three major developments accounted for the inordinate influence of the Ford Motor Company on American life: the Model T, the assembly line, and the five-dollar day. Although automobiles had been built in America since the 1890s, the early models were luxury items. But in 1907 Henry Ford, a machinist and engineer born on a Michigan farm during the Civil War, developed a simple, low-cost car that could travel even over poor roads. The Model T was an instant success. By 1914 the Ford Motor Company was producing 250,000 Model T's a year. When production was finally halted in 1927, 15 million Model T's had been made.

The Model T paced a rapid expansion of the entire automobile industry. In 1921 a total of 1.5 million vehicles were produced and 10.5 million registered; in 1929 a total of 4.8 million were made and 26.5 million registered. By the latter year almost half the families in the United States owned a car. By comparison, an equivalent level was not reached in England and Italy until 1970.

In 1929 the automobile industry accounted for nearly 13 percent of the value of all manufactured goods, making it central to the

American economy. The industry employed 375,000 workers directly and millions more indirectly. Fifteen percent of all steel went into vehicles and 80 percent of all rubber into tires. A host of related businesses burgeoned, from gasoline stations to road construction to tourism. The vast rubber plantations of the East Indies were developed largely to meet the American demand for tire rubber. Whole cities grew up around automobile production. Detroit went from a population of 285,000 in 1900 to 1.5 million in 1930. Flint, Michigan, where General Motors had numerous plants, increased in population twelvefold.

To produce the Model T, Ford first built a plant for 14,000 workers in Highland Park, Michigan, on the edge of Detroit. Then, during World War I, he developed the even larger River Rouge complex in nearby Dearborn. This was a thoroughly integrated operation, with a port, steel plant, power plant, railroad, and the world's largest foundry. At its height the River Rouge complex employed over 75,000 workers, making it the largest factory in America.

Key to the Ford Motor Company's success was its ability to manufacture cars so cheaply that a mass market was created. This required standardization. "The way to make automobiles," Henry Ford said, "is to make one automobile just like another . . . to make them come through the factory alike—just like one pin is like another pin." For twelve years, the only cars Ford sold were black Model T's. Having just one model lowered costs and allowed Ford engineers to scrutinize every phase of the production process minutely.

Ford factories borrowed innovative techniques from the metalworking industries. The company spent freely for the best machine tools, and designed and built new ones when necessary. The steady production of standardized parts made it economical to introduce machines capable of doing only one operation, but doing it very efficiently. For example, to produce engine blocks, a Ford drill press simultaneously drilled forty-five holes from four angles, which normally would have required many separate operations. Single-purpose machines had the added advantage of requiring operators with only limited training.

The capstone of the Ford production method was the assembly line. Early on, Ford positioned machines according to their sequence in the production process—not by type, the usual practice—so that each part went directly from one machine to the next. Still, parts had to be hand-carried between work stations and then to a central area where they were assembled by skilled mechanics. In 1913, Ford engineers began experimenting with gravity slides, rollways, endless chains, and conveyor belts to move parts between stations. They also began assigning each worker only a few simple operations on parts that passed before him, instead of numerous tasks on stationary objects. These techniques proved so efficient that they were quickly introduced throughout the Ford operation. The crowning achievement was a continuous moving chain to which frames were attached. As the frames were pulled along, various subassemblies—motors, axles, gearboxes, and so forth—were delivered by feeder lines to workers who added them on, until all that was left to do was to lower a body onto the chassis and drive the completed vehicle to a parking lot. By this means, the final assembly time for a Model T was reduced from twelve and a half man-hours to less than two.

It is true that continuous materials-handling systems had been tried before, but it was Ford who perfected the assembly line. Soon company after company was adopting "Fordist" methods. The assembly line transformed the very nature of manufacturing by addressing in a new fashion the old problem of increasing the work pace; instead of quotas, piecework wages, or foremen setting the pace of production, the machinery itself determined how fast work was to be done. For companies, this meant enormous savings. For workers, it was an exhausting, nerve-racking, alienating experience.

Even without heavy labor, assembly-line work was draining. "The weight of a tack in the hands of an upholsterer is insignificant," one worker noted, "but if you have to drive eight tacks in every Ford cushion that goes by your station within a certain time, and know that if you fail to do it you are going to tie up the entire platform, and you continue to do this for four years, you are going to break

---

"... WE RODE THE PUBLIC A LITTLE OURSELVES ..."

To sell its Model T, the Ford Motor Company established a national network of sales agencies. These were independent businesses, but as one rural dealer recalled, they were forced by Ford to meet sales quotas. To do so, they sometimes used unethical practices.

WHEN I FIRST took the agency I was my own boss like any other business man, selling as many cars as I could and buying more when I needed them.... Then one day a representative of the [Ford] Company came to see me ... and said ten cars a month was not enough for a dealer like me to sell. It seems the Company had made a survey of my territory and decided that the sales possibilities were much greater. Benson [the Ford representative] said my quota had been fixed at twenty cars a month, and from then on that number would be shipped to me.

Naturally, I got a little hot under the collar at this kind of a proposition, and I told Benson where he could get off at.... Benson was pretty hard boiled.... Either I could buy twenty cars a month or the Company would find another agent....

Well, I finally decided to take a chance on twenty cars a month rather than lose the agency.... But I sure got it in the neck when the slump of 1920 came on. If anyone wants to know what hard times are he ought to try to do business in a Western farming community during a panic.... From September to January of that year I sold exactly four cars....

I am willing to confess that we rode the public a little ourselves while we were getting rid of our big surplus of cars. There are always people that you can sell anything to if you hammer them hard enough. We had a salesman named Nichols who was a humdinger at running down prospects, and one day he told me he had a fellow on the string with a couple of hundred dollars who would buy a car if we would give him a little extra time on the balance. This prospect was a young fellow that had come out West on account of his health and was trying to make a living for his family as an expert accountant. Just at that time the referee in the bankruptcy was doing most of the accounting business around town, and I knew the young fellow wasn't getting on at all. He had about as much use for a car as a jack rabbit....

Well we went ahead and made the sale, but we never got any more payments. The young fellow took to his bed just after that, and the church people had to look out for him and his family until he died. In the final showdown it turned out that the two-hundred dollar equity in the car was everything they had on earth, and by the time we replevined it and sold it as a trade-in there wasn't anything at all. I gave twenty dollars toward his funeral expenses.

Assembly line, 1928. Automobile workers at the end of an assembly line at the Ford River Rouge plant put the finishing touches on a Model A.

under the strain." A worker's wife wrote to Henry Ford, "the chain system you have is a *slave driver! My God!*, Mr. Ford. My husband has come home and thrown himself down and won't eat his supper— so done out!" Monotony and boredom were severe; as another employee put it, "a man checks his brain and his freedom at the door when he goes to work at Ford's." In 1936 Charlie Chaplin brilliantly captured the dehumanizing effect of the assembly line in the movie *Modern Times*, based in part on a tour he had taken of the Highland Park plant.

Worker discontent increased dramatically when Ford's new methods were introduced. A number of unions, including the IWW, began making headway in auto plants. But a more immediate threat to employers came from extraordinarily high worker turnover. In 1913, the year the assembly line was developed, Ford had to hire 52,000 workers to maintain a workforce of 13,600.

Although the Ford situation was extreme, high turnover plagued most of American industry. Semiskilled and unskilled workers were particularly prone to quit. With little chance for advancement and few ties to their employers, if they disliked a foreman, wanted a vacation, or saw a better opportunity elsewhere, they felt free to move on. Their mobility was costly to employers; new workers constantly had to be hired, trained, and tolerated until they mastered their jobs.

To keep out unions and reduce turnover, in 1914 Henry Ford dramatically announced a reduction in the workday in his plants from nine hours to eight, and a wage increase to five dollars a day. For laborers and semiskilled workers, this was double the prevailing wage in the Detroit area. Workers rioted at the doors to Ford's Highland Park plant, seeking jobs. The wage policy had some catches, however. All workers received a basic wage, but only some got an additional profit-sharing payment that could bring the total up to five dollars. To qualify for the latter, they had to meet certain standards both on the job and in their home life. A sociological department was set up to investigate workers' lives and administer the plan. During the war, the profit payments were also connected to Ford's Americanization program. The promise of higher pay thus was used as a lever to re-shape workers' lives, both on and off the job.

Supporters of Fordism argued that high wages were important not only to maintain labor peace but also to enlarge the pool of purchas-ers for consumer products. The Boston reformer and department-store owner Edward A. Filene saw mass production as "large-scale production based upon a clear understanding that increased produc-tion demands increased buying, and that the greatest total profits can be obtained only if the masses can and do enjoy a higher and ever higher standard of living. . . . Mass production is . . . *production for the masses.*"

By keeping costs and prices low and volume and wages high, Henry Ford achieved enormous success; in 1921 his company con-trolled 55 percent of the U.S. automobile market. Even then, however, Ford's main rival, General Motors, was developing an alternative ap-proach to automobile production that ultimately undercut Ford's suc-cess. GM president Alfred P. Sloan, Jr., realized that as incomes rose, cars could be sold on the basis of comfort and style as well as price. Accordingly, GM began introducing a wide range of differently priced car styles, which they changed every year. The ideas was "to keep the consumer dissatisfied" with what he or she had, and therefore eager to buy a newer and fancier model. Sloan called this "the 'laws' of Paris dressmakers . . . in the automobile industry."

To help customers buy more expensive cars than they could afford out-of-pocket, GM set up its own credit agency. To produce many different, rapidly changing models, the company maintained five separate car divisions, ranging from Cadillac, which made the fewest but most expensive cars, to Chevrolet, which mass-produced low-priced vehicles.

By the mid-1920s, GM was eating away at Ford's market share. As makers of consumer goods competed fiercely for a limited number of consumer dollars, GM's stress on marketing proved effective against Ford's stress on manufacturing. Ford was forced to abandon the Model T, introduce new models, imitate GM's practice of heavily advertising each style change, and move toward more flexible manufacturing methods. The original version of Fordism, based on extreme standard-

Automobiles and Milady's Mood. A 1927 advertisement originally printed in color, for Paige-Jewett cars suggests how manufacturers and advertising firms used colors and new styles to differentiate their products from those of competitors. Buying became confused with self-expression as consumers were urged to purchase products as a way to display individual taste and distinction.

ization and price reduction, was on its way out. Replacing it was a more sophisticated form of mass production, based on creating and then fulfilling ever-changing consumer demands. Like other consumer industries, the automobile industry began manufacturing not only products but also desires.

MASS CULTURE AND THE CHANGING FAMILY

Cars, advertising, movies, and radio all contributed to the emergence of a new, national popular culture. Each acted to pull previously isolated groups into the mainstream, penetrating the family to reach its members individually. Each also created new wants and new aspirations.

"Mass culture" had the most dramatic impact in the countryside. Farmers and people in small towns, for instance, were the first to purchase cars in massive numbers; cars filled a real and obvious need. Even many poor farmers, by saving and scrimping, were able to buy secondhand vehicles. In the Black Belt of Georgia, 50 percent of the white and 40 percent of the black sharecroppers owned a car by the

"... A SINGLE MAIDEN, NEVER WED"

Graham McNamee was the most popular radio announcer of the 1920s. The flood of mail he received from listeners included many letters, like this one, asking for help in finding a spouse.

DEAR Mr. McNamee:

Knowing that your great station and its very pleasing official voice reaches into many homes and distant places, it occurred to me that, in view of the fact that I have given the early years of my life to educational advancement by studying nights and working by day, I am now in the thirties, in the best of health, with several degrees and now completing a course in Radio Engineering.

I own a farm on the highway to ——, built my own home and garage, but am waiting for a suitable bird to put in the nest. I have partitioned off nothing so far, but want a Protestant girl of settled habits, strong moral fiber, of German, Scotch, or American parentage, of the old school, who can cook the old-fashioned way, loves children, nature, flowers, who will be a real mother and home-maker.

Probably among your many listeners there is a *single maiden, never wed,* who is looking for such an opportunity, for I am a bachelor self-made in every sense.

Yours,

P.S. You may read my letter to your listeners.

mid-1930s. Car ownership transformed social relations. This was particularly true in the South. Autos weakened the tyrannical grip of plantation owners and local merchants as farmers gained access to more distant stores, banks, and cotton gins. Many white southerners fumed when they saw a black family taking a Sunday drive.

The automobile affected life in the city, too. Cars enabled people to live farther from work and away from public transportation, contributing to the growth of suburbs and the eventual breakup of older working-class neighborhoods. Equally important, cars gave people a sense of freedom and control over their lives. As work became increasingly routinized, the automobile added to a growing feeling that recreation should be part of everyday life, not just an occasional event.

While the automobile lessened distance, radio obliterated it. Commercial broadcasting began in 1920; within two years, three million radios had been sold. By the mid-1930s, 70 percent of all homes had one. Even in the country, radios were common, powered by batteries or windmill generators. For the first time millions of Americans could hear the voice of their president, the sounds of the World Series, weather and agricultural reports, drama, comedy, and professional musicians. One Missouri farmer wrote to a radio station in 1923 that "we hill-billies out in the sticks look upon radio as a blessing direct from God. We farmers are going broke anyway, but we would like to have our radios to sorta ease the pain."

Movies, too, reduced isolation. Before World War I, moviegoers were mainly urban, working-class immigrants. During and after the war, however, movie theaters sprang up even in remote towns. Carrboro, North Carolina, for instance, was a small mill town without electricity; baseball, hunting and fishing, conversation, and music had provided the only entertainment. Now a gasoline generator powered a new movie theater, and mill families could see the latest newsreels and Hollywood productions. Meanwhile, in the cities, to attract

Music and milking time. Pausing to tune in to his favorite program, this farmer represents an extreme example of radio's broad popularity during the 1920s.

more middle-class audiences, film distributors began building large, ornate movie palaces that showed films running an hour or more. To fill these theaters, in the late 1920s they introduced "talking pictures." By 1930 a total of 100 million movie tickets were being sold every week.

For immigrants and their children, for farmers, miners, millworkers, and laborers, movies provided a window on the outside world, on ways of life with which they had no direct contact. Films taught about life in middle- and upper-class America. Kate Simon, a writer who grew up in a New York immigrant neighborhood, recalled that from movies "we learned how tennis was played and golf, what a swimming pool was and what to wear if you ever got to drive a car . . . and of course we learned about Love, a very foreign country like maybe China or Connecticut."

Movies and radio as well as glossy magazines and tabloid newspapers were shaping the values of the younger generation. No longer were parents or local communities the main channels for children's access to the outside world. Often this led to conflict, especially in immigrant homes. Grace Gello, who grew up in an Italian family on New York's Lower East Side, remembered that she and her fiancé "weren't allowed to go out alone, even with groups." But occasionally they would take the afternoon off from work to go to the movies. "We didn't do this too much because we were afraid of my father. He would say, 'If I catch you, I'll break your neck.' "

Young people, and many adults, too, began modeling their clothes, speech, and behavior after stars from the movies, vaudeville, radio, and professional sports. There had been popular idols in the nineteenth century, but the celebrities of the 1920s were different. Many came from working-class, immigrant backgrounds. Rudolph Valentino, Hollywood's top male romantic actor, was born in Castellaneta, Italy. The magician Harry Houdini was the son of a Jewish tailor. And the greatest celebrity of all, baseball slugger Babe Ruth, came from a poor Catholic immigrant family.

Mass culture was a vast Americanization program, but one that was redefining national values. Many of the celebrities of the 1920s were popular precisely because they spurned Protestant middle-class ways. Part of Valentino's attraction was that he was exotic and defied established sexual taboos. Ruth was celebrated not only for his extraordinary athletic accomplishments—his career home-run record lasted four decades—but also for his oversized appetites for food, clothes, alcohol, and sex.

The extraordinary impact of mass culture on the young worried both parents and the traditional arbiters of public values: ministers, political leaders, police officials, social workers, and academics. In the aftermath of the fixing by gamblers of several 1919 World Series games, major-league baseball owners appointed a commissioner of baseball, Kenesaw Mountain Landis, a federal judge known for his virulent antiradicalism. Similarly, to forestall widespread efforts to

First-nighters. Movie fans crowd under the marquee of New York's palatial Warners' Theatre before the premiere of the 1926 film *Don Juan*.

have local authorities censor movies (some states and cities already had censorship laws), the film industry hired Will Hays, Harding's postmaster general, to set up a system of industry self-policing. Landis and Hays instituted some cosmetic changes, but the old cultural elite no longer had enough credibility or support to reassert control.

Many businessmen embraced the new popular culture because they believed it would stimulate consumption. People wanted to own the cars and clothes and apparently everything else they saw in movies and magazines. After Hays's office decreed that films could not show even married couples together in bed, there was a boom in sales of twin beds.

Advertising, which directly encouraged consumer spending, more than doubled in dollar volume between 1918 and 1929. Although some ads simply promoted the virtues of a particular product, others tried to create new wants by associating certain commodities with a desirable life-style. "Men at the top are apt to be pipe-smokers," read an ad for Edgeworth Pipe Tobacco. Advertisements aimed at women often tried to undermine their confidence in traditional sources of advice and authority—mothers, friends, neighbors—so they would

"THE NATIONS MOST IMPORTANT ASSET . . ."

In 1912, the Children's Bureau was established within the Department of Labor. The Children's Bureau's responsibilities expanded during the 1920s from offering advice on maternal and child health to providing information on nutrition and hygiene, establishing well-baby clinics, and offering prenatal care in rural areas. (Many of these programs were ended by Congress in 1929.) Letters to the Children's Bureau, like those following, reflect the concerns of women about themselves and their children.

Mrs. M. A., Minnesota
(October 19, 1921)

Dear Miss Lathrop:—

Two or three years ago, I wrote you for some pamphlets on "Care of the Baby" etc. I . . . found them very useful. But after my last Babe was two years old I gave away . . . the pamphlets to a relative who has since gone away.

I'm to have another Babe in Jan. and I want very much a pamphlet of some kind containing instruction on the first things to do when the Baby arrives, the tying of the naval cord etc. We are 7 ½ miles from a Dr. and tho that isn't far in summer when cars are running, it's quite a distance in winter, when roads may be bad and one must depend on teams to get the Doctor when needed. I want to get some practical directions so that a woman could do all the necessary things if the Dr. was not in time. . . .

rely instead on the assertions of the ads themselves. Advertisers also pointed out the dire consequences of not purchasing their products: "A single contact with inferior toilet paper," warned a Scott Paper ad, "may start the way for serious infection—and a long, painful illness." Famous personalities—from entertainment, sports, and even politics—routinely endorsed products. The presidents of U.S. Steel, the B&O Railroad, and the AFL all praised Parker pens.

Many families, of course, could not afford the products they saw in movies and magazines. In spite of the country's overall prosperity, tens of millions of Americans were living frugally or in poverty. Even when they had steady work, many blue-collar workers could barely afford to shelter and feed their families. When unemployment, seasonal layoffs, or sickness struck, their families were plunged into desperate circumstances. "When my husband's working steady," the wife of a roofer said, "I can just manage, but when he's out [of work], things go back. First I stop on the damp wash, then on the food, and then the rent goes behind." With advertising and the mass media raising expectations, even families with rising incomes were often unable to achieve the life-style they desired.

To help their families survive or live more comfortably, during the 1920s more married women took jobs outside the home. The increase was modest; in 1930 less than 12 percent of all married women were wageworkers, while the percentage of all women who worked outside the home held steady over the prior decade at just below 25 percent. But the long-term trend of women replacing children as second family wage-earners continued.

A number of changes in family life made it easier for married women to take jobs. Household appliances and prepared foods somewhat eased the burden of housework. More important, the trend toward smaller families continued. The movement to make birth control readily avail-

I have been reading quite a bit about the work of the Children's Bureau. Naturally, I am much interested in the things being done for children. I consider them the Nations most important asset, tho I sadly fear that some of our politicians are blind to that fact. . . .

Sincerely Your Friend

Mrs. W. M. (February 10, 1925)

Dear Friend:—

I am enclosing a stamp for an answer & am taking the liberty to ask you for advice. You have helped me before & told me I could write & ask your advice anytime.

I am pregnant a little over 6 months. I had a longing for strawberries for breakfast one day; I thought about them before I got up, and while in the bathroom com[b]ing my hair, I wiped out the corners of my eyes with my fingers. I thought, well, it doesn't matter even if I haven't eaten any strawberries yet. I asked a neighbor about it, & she told me I sure must of marked the baby. . . . if you have an appetite for anything & don't eat it, & put your hand on your face, or scratch your face, that it will mark the baby sure. I'm just worried sick. Its on my mind all the time. . . . I worry every time I wash or put my hand to my face that I'm marking the baby because I couldn't get or didn't eat what I longed for last. Does this come from worry? . . . I couldn't tell this to anyone else but you, as I have no mother, & no one else cares. . . . I have your book on "Prenatal Care," but it doesn't say anything about longing for things to eat. . . . Please keep this confidentially.

able, which had been strongly associated with radicalism and feminism, became more respectable as it was taken over by middle-class doctors and eugenicists—advocates of "improving" the human gene pool through population control. At the same time, popular psychological literature stressed the need for parents to pay closer attention to childrearing, an easier task when families were small. And as child labor became less common, children were no longer an economic asset to poor families but a liability.

Employers had strong opinions about what was "women's work" and what was not. Stereotypes, often deriving from women's subordinate role in the family, pervaded the workplace. Women were considered suitable for jobs that involved serving others or doing precise but routine tasks. Jobs involving independent action or policy-making were reserved for men. But the classification of jobs by sex often varied with labor market conditions. Automakers, for instance, employed few women, and assigned those they did hire to a narrow range of jobs—nearly a third operated sewing machines. By contrast, electrical equipment manufacturers deemed women suitable for a great deal of assembly work; women held a third of all jobs in the industry. No matter how they categorized particular jobs, though, almost all employers viewed women mainly as cheap labor for the bottom rungs of the occupational ladder. During the 1920s the gap between male and female wage rates widened; by 1929 the average working woman earned only fifty-seven cents to a man's dollar.

Complex patterns of sex stereotyping went on in white-collar as well as blue-collar employment. New methods of cost accounting and recordkeeping, introduced during the first decades of the twentieth century, required an ever-growing number of clerks, bookkeepers, and accountants. But clerical work was changing. To lower costs, companies introduced calculating machines, tabulators, comptometers, and Dictaphones. Scientific management was used to divide the work process into narrow, highly routinized jobs and speed the pace of production. By the 1920s large typing pools and accounting departments were more like light manufacturing plants than the small company offices of an earlier era. Both men and women could be found in all types of clerical jobs, but employers preferred women for the most routine tasks. Men were more likely to be hired for sales and general clerical posts that both paid better and had greater promotional opportunities. Even women who held jobs with varied responsibilities were rarely promoted to managerial positions.

For a relatively few, mostly middle-class women, new career opportunities did open up. Certain professions were heavily female—nursing, librarianship, teaching, and social work—and a small but growing number of women found jobs as lawyers, bankers, religious

"Teaching old dogs new tricks." The slinky style of the "flapper" was celebrated in the popular press, most notably in the cartoons of John Held, Jr. The cartoons of high-stepping, bootlegging high society, however, quickly lost their appeal after the 1929 stock market crash.

leaders, and editors. All told, though, less than 15 percent of wage-earning women were in professional positions in 1930. By contrast, 20 percent of all female workers were domestic servants, and nearly as many held clerical positions. By 1930 more women were employed in offices than in manufacturing. Most were white. Although out of economic necessity a higher percentage of black than white women worked outside the home, the black women were highly concentrated in agricultural labor and service occupations.

The slowly expanding place of women in the workforce was part of a broad but limited change in female and family life during the 1920s. Ratification of the woman suffrage amendment to the federal Constitution led to the extension of some other legal rights to women—by the early 1920s, for example, women could serve on juries in twenty states. But property, marriage, and divorce laws remained unfavorable to women. An equal rights amendment to the Constitution, the focus of many middle- and upper-class women activists, repeatedly failed to pass Congress. And the long-standing hope of suffragists that women would use the vote to win greater social and economic equality was largely unfulfilled. Fewer women than men voted throughout the decade, as voter participation in general declined and the major parties displayed indifference toward women voters and women's issues. Many women would have agreed with Amanda Miles, a Chicago laundress, who felt "there was no need wasting time by voting" because it made no difference to her

"Mother," a young flapper says with a sigh, "when you were a girl, didn't you find it a bore to be a virgin?" Former *Masses* cartoonist Art Young comments on the gulf between the views of two generations of women about sexuality and propriety.

life. When women did vote, their choices were shaped not just by gender but also by class, region, age, race, religion, and a myriad of other factors.

Still, habits and customs were changing. One study indicated that women born after 1900 were twice as likely to have premarital sexual relations than women born earlier. Although few women lived like the provocative "flappers" who captured so much public attention, the social restrictions on female behavior loosened. For example, drinking and smoking in public, once taboo for women, became far more common.

Magazines, movies, and literature of the 1920s often celebrated the "new woman," stylish, adventurous, with a career of her own. But the "new woman" was a middle-class woman. For working-class and farm women, the 1920s brought less isolation and a wealth of new aspirations and role models, but only modest improvements in employment opportunities, economic well-being, political rights, and social freedom.

WORKERS' AND FARMERS' MOVEMENTS IN DECLINE

Throughout the 1920s, industrialists and bankers hailed what they called "the new capitalism" or, more broadly, "the new era." "The economic revolution of the 1920s will appear as vital as the industrial revolution in England," declared the president of Remington Rand. Charles E. Mitchell, of National City Bank, claimed that "a revolution in industry . . . is raising all classes of the population to a more equal participation in the fruits of industry," bringing nearer "the day when poverty would be banished." Even the boom-bust business cycle had been conquered, according to Nelson A. Taylor, head of the American Bankers' Association: "We need not fear a recurrence of conditions that will plunge the nation into the depths of the more violent financial panics such as have occurred in the past."

But the experience of millions of workers and farmers gave the lie to such rosy statements. The growth of mass production, mass consumption, and mass culture, as impressive as they were, excluded a very large segment of the population. Economic growth, rather than diminishing the gap between the rich and the poor, increased it. Also, despite Taylor's assertion, the economy remained highly cyclical.

The unbalanced nature of the American economy became clear during the short depression that began in late 1920. This was the first time that the giant, integrated firms, formed in the wake of the depression of the 1890s, had faced a major economic contraction. Most failed to adjust their production levels quickly to compensate for the decline in demand. As a result, huge inventories developed, throwing some firms into crisis. As the slump deepened, many large companies—especially manufacturers in industries dominated by a relatively few companies, such as auto and steel—laid off workers and cut production, thereby reducing inventories and keeping up prices. Such measures enabled these corporations, unlike many small businesses, to return to profitability rapidly, which in turn sparked an overall economic recovery that lasted through 1929.

In the oligopolistic industries employers also were able to pay their employees relatively high wages to promote stable labor relations. Ford's five-dollar day was only the most dramatic of a wide range of paternalistic plans adopted by large employers. Among the benefits offered were stock-purchase plans, pensions, subsidized housing or mortgages, insurance, and sports programs. In southern textile towns companies even built churches and paid ministers' sal-

Welfare capitalism and its conceits. A 1929 installment of J. R. Williams's popular comic strip *Out Our Way* pokes fun at the illusions held by some of the workers who bought stocks in their companies.

aries. Some of these programs, collectively dubbed "welfare capitalism," were specifically aimed at reducing labor turnover, particularly among skilled workers. Unskilled workers often did not qualify for welfare benefits.

Frequently, welfare programs were run through company unions—employer-sponsored groups that workers were pressured or required to join. Some company unions were mere paper organizations, but others were more elaborate affairs, with elected officers, signed contracts, and other features mimicking independent unionism. Although company unions predated the war, during the 1920s they were used more frequently as a tool to keep out bona fide worker-controlled unions, build employee loyalty, and settle grievances. In 1928 there were 869 company unions in 432 companies, covering 1.5 million workers. Along with welfare programs, these organizations had some success in limiting worker protest and reducing turnover. Increasingly, employees of major manufacturing firms came to view their jobs as long-term mutual commitments.

By contrast, in industries with many small, competing producers, the recovery from the 1920 depression failed to materialize. Workers in these industries were generally paid more poorly and treated more harshly than in industries controlled by a few large firms. Small manufacturers lacked the financial reserves needed to cut production. Instead, as prices dropped they often increased their output in an effort to maintain their cash flows. With thousands of producers reacting the same way, overproduction intensified. Prices continued to fall, as did profits and wages.

The problems of the soft-coal industry were typical. High bituminous-coal prices during World War I led to the opening of many new mines, particularly in Kentucky and West Virginia. But the postwar economic slowdown

---

"AMOSKEAG DID ALL THIS TO KEEP HARMONY . . ."

The Amoskeag Corporation in Manchester, New Hampshire, operated the world's largest textile mill, employing some 14,000 workers. The company ran a whole series of welfare programs for workers and their families. Joseph Debski, who began working at Amoskeag in 1910 when he was fourteen years old, described one company benefit.

THE AMOSKEAG HAD a textile club; anybody over eighteen who worked there could belong to it. It had a reading room, canteen, billiard and pool tables, and card tables; and they used to have dances, probably once a month in the wintertime. They had a golf course with a clubhouse; and in 1927 they took over the Intervale Country Club. . . . Then they had the Amoskeag Textile Field, which was a baseball field.

There was a general fund to operate things like a Christmas party for employees' children. They'd take all the equipment out of the garage—it was all bare floor—and prepare it for fifteen to twenty-five hundred children from five to fifteen, free of charge. They would try to take the hard cases, people who probably couldn't afford a good Christmas party of their own.

The textile club had an annual meeting at the Jolliet Hall . . . and there'd be fifteen hundred to two thousand people there. They'd have a big dinner and entertainment. We had committees on bowling, athletics, photography. . . . They had about twenty different committees. . . .

Amoskeag did all this to keep harmony amongst its employees. The board of directors established the textile club. . . . During the strike of 1922, the textile club functioned the most because people didn't have anywhere else to go. They would go play cards, play pool. They didn't draw any lines and say people couldn't come in because of the strike. . . . The club kept going . . . until the mid-thirties. . . . It was when the mill was shut down [in 1936] that everything was demolished.

lessened the demand for coal, which continued to fall as more efficient boilers were introduced and as oil, natural gas, and hydroelectric power became more widely used. By 1926 only half the coal that could be produced was being sold, resulting in a drastic drop in coal prices. There were simply too many mines and too many miners.

In the early 1920s the United Mine Workers of America, the country's largest and most powerful union, endorsed nationalization as the best solution to the coal industry's problems. But with radicalism in decline, such a proposal was futile. Miners were forced to rely on their own strength to maintain wages and conditions in the face of falling prices.

In 1922, 600,000 coalminers struck for over four months to resist proposed pay cuts. Most unionized northern coal operators eventually gave in, but the UMWA failed to win contracts covering nonunionized mines in western Pennsylvania, Tennessee, and West Virginia. Even though a 1923 pact with northern operators maintained wages and conditions for another three years, the UMWA faced mounting trouble. Nonunion mines with lower wage costs were capturing a growing share of the coal market. To compete, many unionized firms began closing mines, breaking contracts, or shifting operations to nonunion subsidiaries. By 1926 over 65 percent of the nation's soft coal came from nonunion pits. Moreover, massive overcapacity meant that most miners—union and nonunion—worked only part-time. Because of unsteady work, even miners earning union wage rates were living in poverty. Then a disastrous strike in 1927 further weakened the UMWA. The union's membership in soft-coal mining dropped from 500,000 in 1920 to just 80,000 in 1928. Safety standards deteriorated, the average workday grew longer, and wages fell. Meanwhile, the union was racked by factionalism and demoralized by the autocratic methods of its president, John L. Lewis.

Agriculture was plagued by many of the same problems as coal and other highly competitive industries: overcapacity, overproduction, falling prices, and declining income. The first two decades of the twentieth century had been a period of relative prosperity for farmers. Before World War I, agricultural prices had risen faster than industrial prices, increasing farmers' purchasing power. The extraordinarily high wartime demand for agricultural products further improved conditions in rural America. But the 1920 economic downturn hit agriculture particularly hard. By 1921, farm prices had fallen to prewar levels, and total farm income was back to where it had been in 1910. A bushel of Nebraska corn that sold for $1.22 in 1919 brought only $0.41 a year later. Although industrial prices were also falling, they did not drop to the same extent. The net result was a major decline in the real earnings of farm families.

Overproduction and falling demand led to the farm crisis; debt made it worse. Large wartime European orders for American farm products had prompted farmers to expand their acreage, often using borrowed money. When conditions in Europe returned to normal, demand dropped. As the value of both farm products and land declined, nearly half a million farmers, unable to meet their debt payments and other costs, lost their farms.

Several long-term trends exacerbated overproduction. Throughout the 1920s, agricultural productivity was increased through the growing use of fertilizer and the introduction of new crops and management techniques. A tenfold increase in tractor use also boosted productivity while freeing for cash crops millions of acres that had been used to grow horse feed. There simply was not a market for everything farmers could grow; domestic demand was near its limit, and the United States faced increasing foreign competition from Canada, Australia, Argentina, and Brazil.

But farmers couldn't check falling prices simply by cutting production. For one thing, they generally had heavy debt payments—for land, equipment, and supplies. For another, with so many farmers growing each crop, even when a sizable group agreed to reduce production it had only a limited impact on prices. So to survive, when prices fell many farmers planted larger crops instead of smaller, only worsening the problem of overproduction and falling prices.

Although by 1923 the overall economy was well on its way to recovery, agriculture remained severely depressed. Furthermore, the price relationship between the countryside and the city had been changed. In 1923, for instance, a suit of clothes cost the equivalent of 31 bushels of wheat, up from 21 bushels ten years earlier. The average annual per capita farm income in 1929 was only $273, compared to a nonfarm average of $750.

Many farmers simply gave up. Between 1920 and 1930, the total number of farms declined for the first time in the nation's history. Thirteen million acres of cultivated land were abandoned. Other farmers were forced into debt or tenancy. By 1930 a total of 42 percent of the country's farmers were tenants and an equal percentage of all farms were mortgaged.

Not surprisingly, the crisis in agriculture led to a revival of rural protest and political activism. Farmers, though, were not of one mind; they belonged to a variety of organizations that proposed different solutions to the farm problem.

At first the most successful protest group was the Non-Partisan League. Founded in North Dakota in 1915 and centered in the upper Midwest, the league adopted many of the old Granger and Populist programs. It called for state ownership of grain elevators, packinghouses, and flour mills; state hail insurance; a grain inspection system; easy rural credit; and tax exemptions for farm improvements. In 1916 league candidate Lynn Frazier was elected governor of North Dakota. Within four years the league had effectively taken over that state's government and had instituted much of its program. In Minnesota the league allied with organized labor, leading to the eventual formation of the Farmer-Labor Party. However, in 1921 opponents of the Non-Partisan League forced a recall election in North Dakota that resulted in the ouster of the governor and the attorney general. Thereafter, the league's influence waned.

The more conservative Farm Bureau flourished as the league declined. The Farm Bureau stressed cooperative marketing by farmers to increase their bargaining power. In the early 1920s the federal government exempted farm marketing cooperatives from antitrust action, raised import duties for certain agricultural products, and made more farm credit available. But these measures had relatively little impact.

A more thoroughgoing solution was proposed in the McNary-Haugen bill, introduced in Congress in 1924 with the support of the Department of Agriculture. This rather complex plan was designed to restore the prewar relationship between farm prices and industrial prices—what came to be known as parity. The bill would have set up a government corporation to purchase enough of the agricultural surplus to raise prices to the parity level. These crops would have been sold abroad, with any loss made up through a small tax on farmers. In effect a two-tier agricultural market would have been established, with domestic prices, protected by a tariff, above world prices.

Opposed by Coolidge and many southern Democrats, the McNary-Haugen bill was defeated in the House. Congress passed revised versions in 1927 and 1928, but Coolidge vetoed them. Still, the bill had a major, long-term effect on agricultural policy. The principle of government action to maintain parity prices was given a major boost; it was adopted during the 1930s and has been a cornerstone of American farm policy ever since.

Discontented farmers and unionists joined together in 1924 to back a third-party presidential bid by Wisconsin senator Robert La Follette. The railroad brotherhoods, disgusted with the federal role in defeating their 1922 strike, initiated the campaign; they were joined by the Non-Partisan League, the Socialist Party, and La Follette's own supporters. Even the AFL endorsed La Follette, the only time in its history that it backed a third-party effort.

La Follette's platform harked back to prewar Populism and Progressivism. "The great issue," it argued, was "the control of government and industry by private monopoly." To rectify this situation it called for government ownership of railroads and water power, a ban on antilabor injunctions, more aid for farmers, and a restructured tax system. To prevent the U.S. Supreme Court from blocking reform, it advocated a congressional veto over Court decisions.

With the Democrats deeply divided—it took their 1924 national convention 103 ballots to settle on a compromise candidate, corporate lawyer John W. Davis, for president—the Republicans concentrated their attack on La Follette, implying that he represented Soviet Bolshevism. But despite a lack of campaign funds, La Follette made a decent showing. Although he carried only his home state, he received close to 5 million votes, compared to 8 million for Davis and 15 million for Coolidge. Undoubtedly the industrial recovery helped the Republicans.

After 1924 farmers continued to press for government aid, but with little success. A gradual rise in agricultural prices diminished many farmers' political fervor. Also, their efforts were hampered by growing differences among farmers in income, life-style, and political perspective.

A new pattern was emerging in American agriculture. Large, well-financed farms were accounting for more and more of the country's agricultural output. By 1930 half the farms produced nearly 90 percent of the cash crop. These farms did relatively well. However, farmers without enough land or capital to operate at peak efficiency

"Here!! You can't run—you might win!" Many commentators thought that La Follette had a good chance of carrying California in the 1924 presidential election. But as this cartoon in the Cleveland Press indicates, La Follette's hopes for an electoral victory were hampered when the Progressive Party was prevented from getting on the state ballot. La Follette subsequently ran on California's Socialist Party ticket.

suffered. And suffering even more were the millions of sharecroppers, tenants, and agricultural laborers.

For example, those midwestern grain growers who could afford large farms and mechanized equipment prospered during the late 1920s. Identifying themselves as businessmen, they often shared business's hostility to unionism. Large truck farmers and fruit growers in California and Florida also thrived, shipping fresh produce to colder regions of the country in the winter. By contrast, southern cotton growers continued to face hard times, particularly in years when bumper crops drove prices down. Those renting land or working on shares were particularly hard-pressed. As Alabama farmer Ned Cobb put it, "Every time cotton dropped, it hurt the farmer. Had to pay as much rent, had to pay as much for guano [fertilizer], but didn't get as much for his crop."

At the bottom of the agricultural economy were farm laborers, particularly migrant workers. During the 1920s, estimates of the number of farm laborers in California alone ranged up to 200,000. The California fruit and vegetable industry, made possible by large-scale, government-financed irrigation, was utterly dependent on hired labor. Planting and harvesting an acre of lettuce, for instance, took ten times the labor needed for an acre of wheat. In 1929 daily wages for farm workers averaged only $2.30, the same as they had been, adjusting for inflation, in 1914.

Seventy-five percent of California's farm laborers were Mexican. Since the demand for agricultural labor peaked at harvest time, these workers moved from region to region as different crops ripened. Then, in the winter, they either returned to Mexico or moved into the Mexican districts that had grown up in virtually every southwestern city. Whole families, including children, worked side by side in the fields. There was little opportunity for social life or schooling on the road. And conditions in migrant camps were often atrocious, as evidenced in a minister's description of a settlement in California's Imperial Valley:

> Shelters were made of almost every conceivable thing—burlap, canvas, palm branches. . . . Calves and horses wandered at will about the shelters. There was a huge pile of manure close by the houses. . . . We found one woman carrying water in large milk pails from the irrigation ditch. . . . This is evidently all the water which they have in camp. There were no baths.

Two years later Mexican cantaloupe workers in the valley struck for higher wages and improved conditions, foreshadowing the agricultural strikes that rocked California in the early 1930s.

The growing disparity of income among farmers was just one aspect of a more general development: during the 1920s, the gap in wealth between the well-off and the not-so-well-off widened greatly. Between 1922 and 1929, wages rose an average of about 40 percent, but in the latter year the 36,000 wealthiest families received as much income as the 12 million poorest. Even within the working class there were growing disparities. Between 1923 and 1929, for example, annual earnings of construction workers barely rose—up an average of less than 4 percent—and coalminers and cotton spinners saw their hourly wages drop.

The weakness of the union movement left most workers with little bargaining power. After 1923 the sharp drop in union membership ended, but a modest decline continued. The union movement made virtually no progress in organizing such rapidly growing industries as autos, electrical equipment, and petrochemicals. Only unions like those in the building trades and the Teamsters—which dealt with small, local employers unaffected by technological change—continued to grow.

"LET'S STAND TOGETHER, WORKERS"

The 1929 Communist-led strike at the Loray Mill in Gastonia, North Carolina, captured national attention, in part because of the violence that accompanied it. Following are two very different appeals in support of the strikers. The first is a song, "Mill Mother's Lament," written by Ella May Wiggins, a twenty-nine-year-old millworker and mother of five who was killed by vigilantes during the strike. The second is contained in a reporter's description of a strikers' prayer meeting.

We leave our home in the morning,
We kiss our children goodbye,
While we slave for the bosses
Our children scream and cry.

And when we draw our money
Our grocery bills to pay,
Not a cent to spend for clothing,
Not a cent to lay away.

And on that very evening,
Our little son will say:
"I need some shoes, dear mother,
And so does sister May."

How it grieves the heart of a mother
You every one must know.
But we can't buy for our children,
Our wages are too low.

Faced with stiff business opposition, a conservative political climate, and declining membership, AFL leaders grew increasingly cautious after 1924. Few top unionists were interested in repeating such radical gestures as the La Follette campaign. The death of Gompers in 1924 and his replacement by UMWA secretary-treasurer William Green only strengthened the power of conservative craft unionists within the federation.

When unionists did try to organize new members, they found an unsympathetic legal system to be an almost insuperable barrier. A series of U.S. Supreme Court decisions prohibited labor organizers from attempting to sign up workers who had promised when they were hired that they would not join a union. These decisions enabled employers to force millions of workers to sign legally binding "yellow-dog" contracts.

Stymied by the courts, some unions tried to win employer acceptance by indicating a willingness to aid efforts to increase productivity. "Labor," William Green told a 1925 gathering of industrial engineers, "is understanding more and more that high wages and tolerable conditions of employment can be brought about through the excellency in service, the promotion of efficiency and elimination of waste." However, although there were several well-publicized experiments in union-management cooperation, few nonunion employers embraced unionism as a way to increase profits.

Unions also tried to attract or hold members by providing them with a greater range of services. Many unions set up their own banks and began offering insurance and other benefits. The Amalgamated Clothing Workers even established a women's department, but in the face of male opposition closed it after a year. However, with few serious efforts at organizing under way, such measures failed to stop organized labor's decline.

Unionists advocating militant policies became increas-

It is for our little children
That seems to us so dear,
But for us nor them, dear workers,
The bosses do not care.

But understand, all workers,
Our union they do fear,
Let's stand together, workers,
And have a union here.

THE STRIKERS TODAY went back to the fundamentals which they brought with them from the mountains. Kneeling on an old store counter salvaged out of the wreckage of the strikers' headquarters, H. J. Crabtree, minister of the Church of God, prayed for divine guidance of the strike. As the old man prayed, a group of strikers stood with bowed heads and as he came to a close fully a dozen joined in the "Amen." . . . Brother Crabtree then preached. His text was "Deliver me, oh Lord, from the evil man; preserve me from the violent man." "I call God to witness who has been the violent man in this strike," the preacher said. "But we must bear it. Paul and Silas had to go through with it, and today they sit a-singing around the great white throne. In a few days you'll be a-singing through the streets of Loray with good wages. God's a poor man's God. Jesus Christ himself was born in an old ox-barn in Bethlehem. He was kicked about, speared about, and finally nailed on a cross. And for what? For sin. It's a sin that's causing this trouble. Sin of the rich man, the man who thinks he's rich. . . .

"All the wealthy men in this here crowd hold up their hands. I'll hold mine up, for one. My father owns this whole world. He owns every hill in this world and every tater in them hills."

ingly isolated. The leading center of left-wing unionism was the Trade Union Education League (TUEL), set up by William Z. Foster in 1920 to promote the amalgamation of craft unions into industrial units and the formation of a labor party. Initially the TUEL attracted wide support. But its ties to the Communist Party (which Foster secretly joined in 1921), its failure to support La Follette, and growing opposition from top AFL leaders soon undermined its backing. In the mid-1920s TUEL supporters and opponents waged bitter battles in several unions. Only in the small furriers' union did the left wing come out on top. Then, in 1928, on orders from the Communist Party, the TUEL abandoned its efforts to "bore from within" the AFL. Instead, a new Communist-dominated group, the Trade Union Unity League (TUUL), tried to set up independent "revolutionary" unions.

Some nonunionized workers, all but forgotten by the AFL, attempted on their own to force their employers to improve conditions and wages. This occurred most dramatically in the southern textile industry, where a wave of strikes erupted in 1928. In most cases either the AFL's textile union or its Communist-led rival stepped in to take over these struggles. But regardless of the leadership involved, the power of the southern mill owners and the willingness of local authorities to use violence to crush strikes were simply too great for the workers to succeed.

The contrast between organized labor at the beginning and at the end of the 1920s was stark indeed. Right after World War I the labor movement was growing, militant, and willing to experiment with new forms of organization; in 1929 it was shrinking, increasingly conservative, and generally content to provide a small elite of craft workers with union representation while leaving most other workers to fend for themselves.

AFRICAN-AMERICAN LIFE IN THE 1920s

America's economic expansion in the 1920s brought great changes to the lives of African-Americans, as it did to the lives of whites. Blacks continued their movement to the growing cities, taking jobs in the expanding industrial sector. But most African-Americans did not share in the profits of the oligopolistic economy.

Between 1920 and 1930, a net total of 824,000 African-Americans moved from the South to the North. (Nearly as many whites also made the move.) The black population of New York, Chicago, and Cleveland more than doubled; in Detroit it tripled. Some growth came from West Indian immigration; by 1930 there were 50,000 foreign-born blacks in New York. In the South, the African-American urban population grew by a third between 1920 and 1930, to 2.6 million. Thus, while in 1930 over half the country's black population remained in the rural South, one of five African-Americans lived in a southern city, and an equal number lived outside the region.

A major occupational shift accompanied the continuing black migration. By 1930 more African-American men held blue-collar jobs than worked in agriculture. Black female employment in industry also increased, though most northern African-American women continued to work in white homes. In Milwaukee, for instance, roughly 75 percent of black working men were in manufacturing in 1930, while 60 percent of black working women were in domestic service.

Racial discrimination in industrial life was still widespread. Auto companies, for example, hired blacks only in small numbers and at selected factories; most auto plants were all-white. When African-Americans were hired, they were usually given the least attractive jobs.

Ford was an exception; 5 to 10 percent of its Detroit-area workers were black. About half the black Ford workers were assigned to the River Rouge foundry, but there were also African - American assembly-line workers, craftsmen, clerical workers (mostly men), and foremen. Henry Ford believed that whites, as a "superior" race, were obligated to help blacks establish decent lives. But his hiring practices were not strictly altruistic. As his company expanded it needed a steady supply of labor. And Ford found that the African-American workers his company recruited—generally through local ministers—were unusually loyal, an important consideration given his fear of unions. By 1926 the company had roughly ten thousand African-American employees.

As the northern black population expanded, opportunities opened up for African-American professionals and businesspeople. In most northern cities

---

"THEY RAISED THE PEOPLE'S CHILDREN . . ."

In the South as well as the North, domestic service was one of the few occupations in which African-American women could find work. In an interview with the author Susan Tucker, Cecelia Gaudet described what it was like. Gaudet, born in Mobile, Alabama, in 1897, had moved to Chicago in the early 1920s. But the man she married there—another Mobile native—preferred the South.

MY HUSBAND WAS a boner ... for Swift's [a Chicago meatpacker]. But he heard from his sister that they were losing some of their property [in Mobile]. So we came back in 1924. I got a job working at housekeeping for a gentleman. He had lost his wife, and he had a sister there. She was an old maid, but they were rich, and she never didn't know nothing about housekeeping.

She and his two children and him, they fell in love with me. He said I was a perfect housekeeper and cook. I was like their mother. I stayed there until I bought me a place in town. They lived too far out, and my husband said it was too hard on me to go out there.

Then, for a good while, I just did work here and there. This family I'd worked for some before, her son got typhoid pneumonia. I nursed him. Then, her daughter she got grown and married, and whenever she wanted something special done, then she'd come around me—for serving parties. And when these babies in white families were born premature, well, I nursed them.

I took a little girl—she wasn't but six years old—and I raised her because I didn't have no children of my own that lived. So I took care of her and sewed at home and sold vegetables, flowers, chickens, eggs. And sometimes I'd go out and serve parties or weddings. . . .

The majority of [black] people here in Mobile worked. And the majority of them made their living working for white people or washing and ironing for them. Everybody couldn't be teachers, and that was the only thing for them to do. They had to work for white people as cooks, housekeepers, maids.

And it's some people that just done it for a lifetime . . . from young people till they got old for the same family. They raised the people's children, and they raised the children's children.

there had long been a small black middle class that included lawyers, doctors, musicians, saloonkeepers, and dressmakers; its clientele was heavily white. However, as the African-American working class grew, there emerged a new middle class that provided services to blacks: ministers, newspapermen, hotel and drugstore owners, real-estate and insurance agents, funeral directors, and the like. In Harlem, the country's largest African-American community, blacks owned or managed 35 percent of the real estate. The African-American class structure was becoming more complex.

Throughout black America, a new political militancy emerged after World War I. Heightened racial pride characterized what was often called "the New Negro." As the Chicago riot had shown, blacks were determined to resist white attacks. African-American news-papers and leaders urged northern blacks to arm and defend them-selves and, if need be, retaliate against what the poet Claude McKay called "the murderous, cowardly pack."

Even before the war there had been signs of growing black impa-tience with white injustice. The war and migration catalyzed these feelings. After the armistice many African-Americans who had fought in or supported the war sought greater democracy at home. Black migrants to the North found themselves facing problems they thought they had left behind: inadequate housing, discrimination in employment, and racial violence. Many concluded that if blacks were to improve their lot they would have to fight on their own behalf.

Initially, the NAACP benefited most from this new spirit; by 1919 it had 91,000 members. However, its membership soon declined. Dominated by whites and well-off blacks—what W. E. B. Du Bois termed "the talented tenth"—it concentrated on opposing segrega-tion through lawsuits, public inquiries, and other moderate tactics. This failed to win the allegiance of poor African-Americans in either the North or the South.

Instead, it was Marcus Garvey's Universal Negro Improvement Association (UNIA) that won massive support. Garvey, a printer by trade, founded the UNIA in his native Jamaica in 1914. Two years later he came to the United States, in part to study Booker T. Wash-ington's black self-help projects. Impressed by the progress African-Americans were making during the war, Garvey settled in New York City.

Part of Garvey's appeal was his Pan-Africanism. Garvey argued that blacks throughout the world were one people; the struggle for black rights outside Africa was necessarily linked to the fight to free Africa from colonial rule. To help liberate Africa, he encouraged African-Americans with needed skills to return to their "African homeland." He urged other blacks to struggle for advancement where they were.

During November 1922, the NAACP ran this full-page advertisement in the New York *Times* and other newspapers, pressing for passage of the Dyer antilynching bill. Passing in the House of Representatives by a two-to-one majority, the antilynching bill was subsequently filibustered and defeated in the Senate.

Perhaps even more important to Garvey's appeal was his assertion of pride in being black. Garvey publicized black achievements, opposed interracial marriage, and, in a reversal of the norm, looked down on light-skinned African-Americans. Critical of the NAACP's push for racial integration, he argued that African-Americans would make most progress by developing their own, separate institutions. The UNIA urged blacks to begin commercial enterprises of all sorts and itself set up various businesses, including a shipping company, the Black Star Line. Financed by 35,000 small investors, the line was meant to link blacks together throughout the world through trade.

The Black Star Line. An advertisement in Marcus Garvey's newspaper, *The Negro World.*

After World War I, the UNIA grew with remarkable speed. Within a few years it had half a million members in the United States, as well as branches in the Caribbean and Africa. West Indians, recent migrants from the South, and members of the new black middle class were particularly strong Garvey supporters, but the UNIA attracted followers from virtually every segment of black America.

The UNIA's success made it a target. Many black leaders, including NAACP officials, Socialists, and followers of Booker T. Washington, were highly critical of Garvey. Both the American and British governments harassed the UNIA, and in 1922 Garvey was indicted by the federal government for mail fraud in connection with the Black Star Line. Convicted, he was sent to prison in 1925 and deported two years later. Garvey's removal broke the back of the UNIA, but his ideas remained influential.

Throughout the 1920s many political groups, including the major political parties, competed with the UNIA and the NAACP for black support. As the northern African-American population grew, black votes became increasingly important to the predominantly white urban machines, opening up opportunities for black politicians. Although most black voters were Republicans—one black New Jerseyite said that "being a black Democrat was like announcing one had typhoid"—both parties courted African-American support. By maneuvering among white factions, black political leaders were able to win influence, patronage, and some social gains. In New York City, for example, blacks began to be hired by previously all-white police, fire, and other municipal departments. In Chicago, Oscar De Priest, an Alabama-born son of ex-slaves, was elected the city's first African-American alderman in 1915. In 1928 he became the first black representative ever elected to Congress from the North.

Radical groups also attracted some African-American support. One small group of activists, impressed by the Irish and Russian revolutions, formed a secret radical organization, the African Blood Brotherhood, which eventually merged into the Communist Party. A somewhat larger, more influential group, including A. Philip Randolph and Chandler Owen, joined the Socialist Party. These black leftists stressed the need for African-Americans and organized labor to ally.

But black trade unionists faced enormous problems. Many black leaders, including Garvey and disciples of Booker T. Washington, discouraged African-Americans from joining white-led unions, urging them instead to seek good relationships with their employers. They justified this position by pointing to the many unions that refused to admit African-Americans or denied them full union rights.

In spite of these obstacles, as the number of black industrial workers grew, so did African-Americans' interest in unionism. In 1925 the Urban League set up a department of industrial relations, black Communists founded the American Negro Labor Congress, and Socialist Frank R. Crosswaith set up the Trade Union Committee for Organizing Negro Workers. And in that same year the most important black union in the country's history, the Brotherhood of Sleeping Car Porters (BSCP), was founded.

Sleeping car porters held a special place in black America. Most—about 15,000—worked for the Pullman Company, the country's largest employer of African-Americans. Although Pullman working conditions were awful—typically a porter worked 400 hours a month and traveled 11,000 miles—compared to other jobs open to blacks the pay was good. As a result, many of those who took porter jobs were highly able, politically sophisticated, well-educated men, often leaders in their communities.

In 1925 a small group of porters set out to organize a union. To head it they recruited A. Philip Randolph, who turned his newspaper, the *Messenger*, into the union's official organ. Thousands of porters soon joined the BSCP. But the Pullman Company refused to recognize the union, fired several of its leaders, and began hiring Filipino porters as a warning to African-Americans that they could be replaced. In 1928 the BSCP threatened to strike, hoping to force the federal government to become involved. But when the Coolidge administration failed to act, Randolph called off the walkout. Many porters quit the union in disgust. Desperate for help, Randolph applied for a national union charter from the AFL. Refused, he finally accepted a compromise under which individual BSCP locals affiliated directly with the AFL. By the end of the 1920s, the BSCP was down to a few hundred members, but these survivors kept alive the dream of a black national labor union.

The postwar surge in African-American political militancy was paralleled by a flowering of black culture. In New

---

"... I COULD NOT EAT THE POEMS I WROTE"

Langston Hughes, one of the country's leading twentieth-century poets, recalls the spirit of the Harlem Renaissance, and its underside.

WHEN I CAME back to New York in 1925 the Negro Renaissance was in full swing. Countee Cullen was publishing his early poems, Zora Neale Hurston, Rudolph Fisher, Jean Toomer, and Wallace Thurman were writing, Louis Armstrong was playing, Cora Le Redd was dancing, and the Savoy Ballroom was open with a specially built floor that rocked as the dancers swayed. Alain Locke was putting together *The New Negro* [an anthology of black literature]. Art took heart from Harlem creativity. Jazz filled the night air—but not everywhere—and people came from all around after dark to look upon our city within a city, Black Harlem. Had I not had to earn a living, I might have thought it even more wonderful. But I could not eat the poems I wrote. Unlike the whites who came to spend their money in Harlem, only a few Harlemites seemed to live in even a modest degree of luxury. Most rode the subway downtown every morning to work or look for work.

Downtown! I soon learned that it was seemingly impossible for black Harlem to live without white downtown.... It was not even an area that ran itself. The famous night clubs were owned by whites, as were the theaters. Almost all the stores were owned by whites, and many at that time did not even (in the very middle of Harlem) employ Negro clerks.... And almost all the policemen in Harlem were white. Negroes couldn't even get graft from themselves for themselves by themselves. Black Harlem really was in white face, economically speaking. So I wrote this poem:

Because my mouth
Is wide with laughter
And my throat
Is deep with song,
You do not think
I suffer after
I have held my pain
So long?

Because my mouth
Is wide with laughter,
You do not hear
My inner cry?
Because my feet
Are gay with dancing,
You do not know
I die?

The Crisis. Heralding the style and substance of the Harlem Renaissance, the NAACP's magazine, edited by W. E. B. Du Bois, reached from 60,000 to nearly 100,000 readers monthly.

York—the country's foremost center for black writers, artists, and intellectuals—an explosion of creativity, the Harlem Renaissance, burst forth. In poetry, novels, plays, dance, painting, sculpture, and photography, blacks celebrated African-American spiritual and cultural traditions, rejecting white values and stereotypes. The leading figures of the renaissance also rejected Victorian literary and artistic forms, self-consciously experimenting with new modes of expression.

Extraordinary for its intellectual and artistic accomplishments, the Harlem Renaissance was primarily a movement of the African-American elite. Relatively few working-class or rural blacks were exposed to it. But more popular African-American cultural forms also flourished. Singers such as Florence Mills and Ethel Waters and dancers such as Bill Robinson starred on a growing circuit of black nightclubs, theaters, and vaudeville houses. Noble Sissle and Eubie Blake broke new ground in the musical theater with such all-black Broadway plays as *Shuffle Along.* And then there was jazz, America's greatest contribution to world music. The culmination of centuries of African-American musical development, jazz emerged in the 1920s in cities such as New Orleans, Kansas City, Chicago, and New York as an immensely popular and highly sophisticated musical form. At the same time, in the South, string bands, blues singers, and jug bands reached new heights of accomplishment and popularity, entertaining at house parties, in "juke joints," and in traveling tent shows. Leading blues singer Bessie Smith's first recording, "Downhearted Blues," made in 1923, sold 750,000 copies in just six months.

Some middle-class whites were drawn to black culture, finding it an escape from the sterility and materialism of their own milieu. In a variant of older stereotypes, they saw African-Americans as symbols of freedom, passion, and sensuality. "Slumming" became fashionable, with whites venturing into black neighborhoods to go to cabarets, dance halls, and jazz clubs or to frequent literary salons. (Some of the largest Harlem clubs admitted only whites.) Most whites, though, had contact with African-American culture secondhand, through white entertainers who copied black styles. Band leaders such as Paul Whiteman, for instance, built large followings by imitating and incorporating black musical innovations. But in spite of such backhanded recognition of African-American artistry, when white mass culture portrayed blacks, most notably in the movies, racist depictions still prevailed.

CULTURAL POLITICS

The discrimination against blacks in white mass culture was one facet of a larger truth about the mass-consumption culture that emerged in the 1920s: it sharply divided the American people. The extraordinarily rapid spread of consumerism; changes in the arts, literature, and popular entertainment; and shifts in life-style were eagerly embraced by some but vehemently rejected by others.

The differing reactions to mass culture reflected, at least in part, the uneven economic development of the country. In places such as Flint, Michigan, where the booming auto industry was at the heart of the new mass-production, mass-consumption society, there were large numbers of young workers, many of whom had recently come to the city. Unfettered by community traditions or heavy family obligations, they eagerly adopted the ethic of consumption, buying cars and fashionable clothing on the installment plan. Workers from all over the city flocked to movie theaters, dance halls, and bowling alleys in Flint's downtown, the physical home of the new culture.

By contrast, in the declining mining towns of western Pennsylvania and West Virginia, where most families had to struggle to make ends meet, and where large numbers of young men were leaving for northern cities, mass culture made little headway. When hard-pressed working people in economically stagnant communities borrowed money, their creditor was more likely to be the butcher or the grocer than an auto dealer.

But cultural cleavages were more than a matter of economics. In many of the nation's large cities, and in many smaller industrial towns as well, ethnic enclaves continued to be the home of a "workers' world" where old traditions were preserved and family obligations were stressed. As late as 1940, New York had 237 foreign-language periodicals; Chicago, 96; and Los Angeles, 25. English was not spoken in the homes where 22 million Americans were raised. Immigrant parents often sent their children to religious schools that fostered Old World traditions while portraying the movies, popular dances such as the Charleston, and the new jazz music as instruments of Satan.

New ways and old were not always in contradiction. Adherents to older cultural forms found that they could use the new media toward their own

---

"RED BANDANAS I DETEST . . ."

Cultural conflict also divided the growing Mexican-American community in the Southwest. This Texas canción, or popular song, called "Las Pelonas" ("The Bobbed Heads" or "The Flappers") laments the free-and-easy conduct of young Mexican girls in San Antonio. These young Mexican-American working women copied the clothing and hairstyle of the era's flappers, much to the dismay of more traditional Mexican immigrants.

Los paños colorados	Red bandanas
Los tengo aborrecidos,	I detest,
Y ahora las pelonas	And now the flappers
Los usan de vestidos.	Use them for their dress.
Las muchachas de San Antonio	The girls of San Antonio
Son flojas pa'l metate.	Are lazy at the *metate.*
Quieren andar pelonas	They want to walk out bobbed-haired,
Con sombreros de petate.	With straw hats on.
Se acabaron las pizcas,	The harvesting is finished,
Se acabó el algodón.	So is the cotton.
Ya andan las pelonas	The flappers stroll out now
De puro vacilón.	For a good time.

ends. The radio, for example, could not be dismissed easily as an instrument of the devil if it brought news of the old country into the home. Scores of radio stations carried foreign-language programs; in neighborhoods such as Boston's Italian-American North End, many more people listened to such broadcasts than to English-language programming. Stars of foreign-language radio shows became important figures in the ethnic enclaves, making frequent personal appearances in neighborhood restaurants, dance halls, and cultural centers.

Even the movies, the great purveyors of the American dream, could be adapted to the needs of ethnic communities. Eastern European Jews created a Yiddish movie industry in the 1920s, with its own directors, movie stars, and theaters. The conflicting aspirations of European-born parents and their "American" children were a major theme of this emerging cinema. There was a small, independent black movie industry as well.

Many rural Americans resisted the new culture, too. In the early 1920s, a movement arose among fundamentalist Protestants to stop the teaching of biological evolution in schools. Although the immediate issue was hostility toward a theory that ran counter to a literal reading of the Bible, the fight against Darwinism was a rallying point for Protestants unhappy with the spread of secular thought, with liberal forms of Christianity (Bruce Barton's bestseller *The Man Nobody Knows* described Jesus as a

"WE DIDN'T JOIN AMERICAN ORGANIZATIONS . . ."

Joe Rudiak, a Polish-American steelworker, described growing up in the ethnic enclave of Lyndora, Pennsylvania, home to coalminers and steelworkers.

AND OF THE things my mother insisted on, education . . . was one of them. Mother insisted, with a few other families, at least to educate us [in] our own native tongue and [in] writing [at the] language schools. They formed language schools through the churches. And that was a must with most families. . . . I don't know why they did it. I guess it was on account of their background, [out of] loneliness and everything for their own countries. And my mother insisted that we all become musicians. . . . Seven of us became musicians. Every day—about two hours every day—there was catechism. And during . . . school vacation we had to attend the language schools. The Polish church was a good distance away. There was the problem of shoes, clothing, and weather conditions and all that. And sure we were down a good distance away also from the public school. Mother insisted that we go to the Greek [Orthodox] church; they had the language school. When they had a problem of not having any money, we joined the Ukrainian Orthodox. So I've learned how to speak Ukrainian, but it wasn't my mother's tongue. It meant another language, which came in very handy.

We celebrated various holidays together. We did it as musicians, you see, in our family. And different churches went out caroling, and they gathered money for support of the band and their cultural activities. And this was done during Christmas. We each had costumes of our own native lands. You know, the Slovaks had [boys dressed as] sheep herders going from house to house singing. The women would have embroideries of different colors. It was beautiful, beautiful, made out of linen. It was all hand made. . . .

Since we went to the Ukrainian school, [we kids spoke Ukrainian. And] my mother spoke very good Ukrainian and my father spoke good Ukrainian because he spoke it in Europe. So there was no problem as far as learning the language [was concerned], because you got to repeat [it] at home after you came from elementary school. But when the Polish friends would come in, then it was Polish language. It just happened that most of them lived around their own churches, tried to get as close as possible to their social activities. And the church was part of their social activity.

We didn't join American organizations though. There was no drive on among the nationality people, no drive on by the politicians. You've got to understand that they didn't want these people to vote in the first place. The companies controlled the towns. They controlled the courthouse. They controlled the police. They controlled the state police, the coal mine police. There was no encouragement for people to vote up until the Depression.

Billy Sunday. George Bellows's 1923 lithograph of William Ashley Sunday, the professional baseball player turned evangelical minister, captures the atmosphere of revival meetings during the 1920s. Preaching a return to "old-time religion," traveling evangelists such as Sunday relied on techniques inspired by forms of mass entertainment in the period.

successful salesman), and with the increasingly prominent role of non-Protestants in American life.

The battle came to a head in 1925 when a Tennessee schoolteacher, John T. Scopes, was arrested for violating a recently passed state law that outlawed teaching "that man has descended from a lower order of animals." Scopes's trial received enormous national attention. His defense team of prominent liberal lawyers was headed by Clarence Darrow, who had defended many political and criminal celebrities. Aiding the prosecution was former secretary of state and Democratic presidential candidate William Jennings Bryan. The high point of the trial came when the defense put Bryan on the stand as an expert on the Bible. Darrow exposed Bryan's deep ignorance, ridiculing him before the court and the nation. But Scopes was convicted (his sentence was later thrown out on a technicality), Tennessee's anti-evolution law remained on the books until the 1960s, and thousands of schools throughout the country stopped teaching Darwin's theory of evolution.

Many observers saw the Scopes trial as part of a broad clash between an emerging secular, multiethnic culture, centered in the large cities, and an older Protestant culture, based in small towns and rural areas. Many of the best-known writers of the 1920s, including Sinclair Lewis, Sherwood Anderson, and Ernest Hemingway, portrayed small-town life as narrow, hypocritical, and spiritually impoverished. When the *New Yorker* magazine was founded in 1925, its advertising slogan was "Not for the old lady in Dubuque."

This clash of beliefs, however, was not strictly geographical, as evidenced by the reemergence of the Ku Klux Klan. The new Klan, founded in 1915, was inspired by the Reconstruction-era organization of the same name. Like the earlier Klan, it was profoundly racist, surrounded itself with mystical trappings, and regularly used violence to silence its foes. However, unlike those of the first Klan, its antiblack activities were overshadowed by a powerful anti-Catholicism. Moreover, the new Klan was heavily urban; at its height, in the early 1920s, roughly half of its two million members lived in metropolitan areas. And although the Klan had considerable support in the South, it was strongest in the Midwest and the Southwest.

The intolerance and vigilantism fostered by the national government and leading public spokespersons during World War I paved the way for the Klan's rise. Farmers going through hard times, underpaid workers facing competition from immigrants and blacks, and small businessmen losing out to national manufacturers and chain stores all lashed out through the Klan against those they saw as threatening their economic well-being. But cultural as well as economic tensions fueled the Klan's growth. In the cities old-stock Protestants felt displaced by Catholics and Jews. Country dwellers resented the diminishing importance of rural virtues in the national culture, which seemed to denigrate their way of life.

In the early 1920s, Klan leaders gained strong influence over the

White sheets in Washington, D.C. Forty thousand members of the Ku Klux Klan march down Pennsylvania Avenue on August 8, 1925. Organized to counter reports of faltering enrollment, the "konklave" succeeded in attracting national attention but marked the peak of Klan power in the 1920s.

state governments in Texas, Oklahoma, Oregon, Louisiana, Kansas, and above all Indiana. An Oregon law, passed by initiative, virtually eliminated Catholic schools by requiring public-school attendance for those aged eight to sixteen. However, within a few years the Klan was in decline. A series of sexual, financial, and political scandals tainted the organization, and established political leaders in several states moved against it. But the cultural antagonisms that the Klan capitalized on continued through the end of the decade, symbolized by the issue of prohibition.

The 1919 ratification of the Eighteenth Amendment to the Constitution, which made it illegal to manufacture, sell, transport, import, or export drinking alcohol, did not lead to a national consensus in support of prohibition. Although alcohol consumption declined, perhaps by as much as half, tens of millions of normally law-abiding Americans broke the law or abetted those who did. Even President Harding had a favorite bootlegger.

The vast profits that could be made from illegal liquor fed organized crime. Criminal gangs grew in size, sophistication, and power. Prostitution, loansharking, and labor racketeering supplemented bootlegging. Utilizing the latest technology—from fast automobiles

Raids and refreshment. Wine pours into the streets of a Brooklyn neighborhood after federal agents raid an illegal distillery—and local children rush to catch as much of the illegal brew as they can.

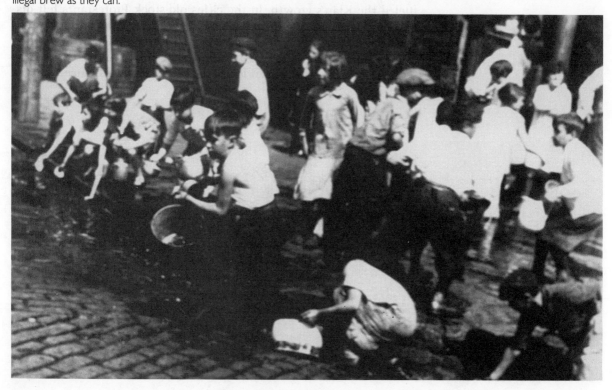

to Thompson submachine guns—gangs fought one another to establish regional fiefdoms. Politicians and police were bought off wholesale. In some cities, gangs became an integral element in the local political apparatus. With profits rolling in, organized crime provided poor Italians, Jews, Poles, and Irish with a path of upward mobility. Gangsters such as Al Capone became celebrities: their latest doings—and especially their elaborate funerals—received full newspaper coverage and became the talk of the town. The "grand experiment" of prohibition, begun as an effort to use the power of government to enforce morality, ended up undermining respect for the law itself.

Throughout the 1920s cultural clashes spilled over into national politics, with prohibition the foremost political issue of the decade. The Republicans were united in supporting prohibition laws, though not necessarily in obeying them. But the Democrats were deeply split over prohibition and other cultural issues. Ranged against one another were the southern and western wings of the Democratic Party: the old Bryan supporters, who supported prohibition; and the immigrant-led urban machines, which opposed it. The 1924 Democratic national convention was virtually paralyzed as the two evenly balanced groups bitterly debated prohibition and the Ku Klux Klan.

But by 1928, the balance of power within the Democratic Party had shifted decisively toward the cities. In that year New York's governor, Al Smith, easily

---

"THERE WAS ANOTHER UNUSUAL FEATURE OF THE FLOWER SHOP BASEMENT . . ."

The criminal lawyer George Bieber's first job was in a Chicago bootlegging establishment. The job paid well enough, according to Bieber, to enable him to pay his college tuition.

■ WAS FIFTEEN when the Volstead Act [enforcing prohibition] went into effect, working in the Division Flower Shop. . . . The owners weren't interested in selling flowers. They kept a dozen bunches in the windows, but if some stranger came in and placed a big order, they'd fill it through a genuine florist nearby and send it out under the Division label. That was my job, standing around in the front of the shop and handling people who actually wanted to buy flowers.

The boss was Vincent "Schemer" Drucci. They nicknamed him that because of the wild schemes he was always thinking up to defeat the law. The real business of the Division Flower Shop was converting denatured alcohol into drinkable liquor. Drucci and his partners had first set up a hair tonic plant. This entitled them to buy No. 39B alcohol. . . .

Up to a point, the Cosmo Hair Tonic Company was legitimate. They advertised widely. . . . And they sold quite a few bottles. Not nearly as many as their books showed. To deceive the government inspectors, they would sell a few hundred cases to a friendly wholesale distributor and throw in a few hundred more as a bribe. The books would then show sales of thousands, and on the basis of such a big volume the government would allot the company corresponding amounts of 39B alcohol.

The conversion to drinkable liquor took place in the basement of the flower shop under the direction of the chemist we all called Karl the Dutchman, who was formerly employed by a toothpaste manufacturer. . . . To fake scotch, bourbon, rye, or whatever, Karl would let the rectified alcohol stand for a few weeks in charred barrels in which authentic whiskey had been aged. I would pick up those barrels from a cooperage on Lake Street. They brought enormous prices—as high as $50 or $60 a barrel. The owner's son would help me load them onto a truck, and I remember he wore a diamond ring the shape of a barrel. . . .

Some of Drucci's customers came from out of town, and if he figured a man was a *shnook*, he would sell him the liquor in a trick 5-gallon can. This can had a tube soldered inside to the top and bottom. Only the tube contained whiskey. The rest of the can was filled with water to give it weight, as the *shnook* would discover when he got it home.

There was another unusual feature of the flower shop basement—a life-size picture of a cop. The boys used it for target practice. . . .

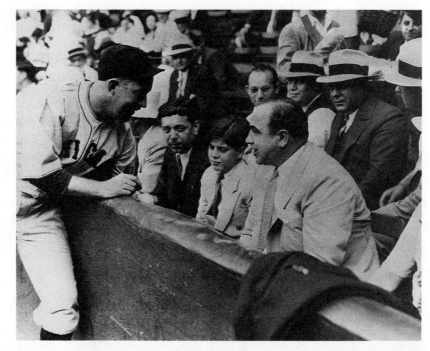

Two celebrities. Catcher Gabby Hartnett exchanges pleasantries with "Scarface" Al Capone (who was known to wield a bat himself on occasion) as the Chicago Cubs player autographs a baseball for the gangster's twelve-year-old son at a charity game in Comiskey Park.

won the party's presidential nomination. The contrast, at least in image, between Smith and his Republican opponent, Herbert Hoover, could not have been greater. Smith was a "wet" (an opponent of prohibition), a Catholic, and a product of urban, ethnic, working-class life. Radio coverage of the campaign made his heavy New York accent familiar throughout the nation. Hoover stressed his boyhood in rural Iowa, professing his love for fishing and the simple, small-town life, although in fact he was a sophisticated businessman, the first president to rise to power from the ranks of the managerial elite rather than through party politics.

During the campaign Smith was attacked as the candidate of foreigners and immoral drinkers. Many Protestant leaders proclaimed that like any Catholic he was unfit to serve as president, since he would place obedience to the pope above loyalty to his country. Hoover, by contrast, had a basic advantage: the Republicans were receiving credit for the country's prosperity. The result was a landslide victory for Hoover; he received 444 electoral votes to Smith's 87. Still, the Democrats made significant gains; helped by increased voter participation among immigrants, Smith outpolled Hoover in the country's twelve largest cities, marking the emergence of the Democrats as the party of urban America.

Hoover's victory capped his long, successful career in industry, relief work, and government. Fate, though, and the economy can be cruel. Within a year of Hoover's election, the country was plunged into a devastating depression. By the early 1930s, Hoover's mishandling of the crisis had destroyed his political reputation. The man who, along with Ford, perhaps best symbolized America in the 1920s ended up as one of the most hated men in the country.

After World War I, American businessmen reached many of the goals they had been seeking for fifty years. They crushed organized labor, perfected the machinery of industrial production, and made the federal government an ally in the pursuit of corporate profit and economic growth.

Oligopolistic arrangements helped corporations tame excess competition in many industries, and the growth of mass consumption created new and rapidly growing markets. The mass media played a role in the transformation of the society by helping to create not only new consumer demands but also a mass culture at odds with many American traditions.

Rising agricultural production worldwide forced many rural people to move to cities, where a new system of mortgage financing made it possible for many Americans to buy new homes for the first time. For those fortunate enough to be employed in dynamic economic sectors, living standards improved during the 1920s, particularly as consumer credit brought cars, refrigerators, washing machines, and vacuum cleaners within reach.

The rapid growth of mass production, mass consumption, and mass culture planted the seeds of a new social order that was to flower after the Second World War. But during the 1920s the economy had a fatal weakness: industry's productive capacity far outstripped the American people's ability to consume. The problem was easiest to see in agriculture and mining, where hundreds of thousands of farms and mines had to be abandoned for lack of markets. Even in the heart of the mass-production, mass-consumption economy, workers' wage increases trailed far behind corporate profits.

Until the stock market crashed in 1929, most Americans were oblivious to these structural faults. But in the bleak years that followed, many Americans questioned whether the promises of the new era would ever be realized as long as business so totally dominated the government and the economy.

7

THE GREAT DEPRESSION AND THE FIRST NEW DEAL

Detroit, July 1930.

"WE IN AMERICA today are nearer to the final triumph over poverty than ever before in the history of any land. We shall soon . . . be in sight of the day when poverty will be banished from this nation." So Herbert Hoover told the American people as he accepted the Republican nomination for president in 1928. And apparently the people agreed, for Hoover was elected by a wide margin the following November.

As the 1920s neared an end, big business seemingly had solved many of America's social problems. Corporate leaders had replaced the intense competition of the late nineteenth century with oligopolistic arrangements in many large industries. Living standards had risen at home, while America's diplomacy and military expansionism had secured plentiful opportunities to make profitable investments and obtain cheap raw materials overseas. Political opposition to industrial capitalism had lessened in response to regulatory reform, the patriotic fervor generated by the First World War, and the Red Scare.

The "labor problem" also seemed to have been resolved. The open-shop drive of the early 1920s had broken the back of the labor movement, the Red Scare had driven radicals into retreat or underground, and the welfare policies of many large businesses had apparently softened the animosity that characterized earlier labor-management relations.

But all was not as it seemed. Underneath the veneer of prosperity the social peace, American society was riven by economic and social conflict. When American capitalism was gripped by yet another of its periodic bouts with economic depression and mass unemployment, the corporate solutions of the 1920s were abandoned or discredited. Old questions reemerged concerning economic and industrial democracy, the proper role of government, and the subordinate place of women and minorities. Amid widespread suffering, America's working people, with renewed militancy, helped redefine the nature of U.S. society and their own place in it.

THE CRISIS OF THE NEW ORDER

When Herbert Hoover was sworn in as president in March 1929, he told the American people that the nation's prosperity was permanent. But as he delivered his inaugural address, the rapid industrial expansion that had fueled the optimism of the 1920s was already finished; it had lasted just five years, from 1922 to 1927. By the beginning of 1928, consumer spending was declining and construction slowed. As consumers reduced their purchases, manufacturers' inventories grew alarmingly; in 1929, industrial corporations began reducing production and laying off workers. By the summer, the nation was in the midst of an economic contraction.

Hoover knew that America's economy was in trouble, but he said nothing for fear of destroying the optimism necessary to sustain a speculative boom. Then, during a few dramatic weeks between early September and mid-November, the stock market collapsed. "Black Thursday," October 24, 1929, began with a rush of sell orders at the New York Stock Exchange, sending prices tumbling. As fear and panic threatened to get completely out of hand, the directors of the stock exchange and worried bankers tried to stabilize the situation. But by the following week it became clear that efforts to prop up stock prices had failed.

Relatively few people were directly affected by the stock market crash, since the vast majority of Americans did not own stock. Nonetheless, a severe economic slump followed the debacle on Wall Street. Between October and December the number of unemployed workers jumped from fewer than 500,000 to over 4 million. At first, many people thought that this was just a normal downturn and that business would soon pick up. But in mid-1931 the economic slide accelerated; a catastrophe was at hand. By the spring of 1933, 15 million people were out of work, nearly one of every three wage-earners. Millions more were working only part-time. Average real wages fell 16 percent in just two years.

Between 1929 and 1933 the gross national product, the sum of all the goods and services produced in the country, fell 29 percent. Construction was down 78 percent, manufacturing 54 percent, and investment a staggering 98 percent. In the summer of 1932, the steel industry operated at only 12 percent of its capacity. Fewer miles of railroad track were built in 1932 than in any year since the Civil War. Many cities went broke, unable to pay their bills or employees.

Breadlines and soup kitchens sprang up in the large cities in 1930. So many men sold apples on street corners that the Bureau of the Census classified apple-sellers as employed. President Hoover defended this action by arguing that "many persons left their jobs for the more profitable one of selling apples." More than a million desperate, unemployed people took to wandering around the country, hitching rides or hop-

---

"... THE HAWK HAD COME"

In 1929 Gordon Parks—later a world-famous photographer—was sixteen years old, living alone and attending high school in St. Paul, Minnesota. To support himself he worked part-time as a bellboy at an exclusive club. Here he describes the impact of the stock market crash on his life.

WORKING evenings and weekends at the club I overheard talk of Hoover, A.T.&T., General Motors, U.S. Steel, General Electric, the Federal Reserve Bank and other such names. And, although I didn't know what the conversations really meant, I sensed a certain optimism in them. . . .

The employees' locker room at the club was unusually quiet when I arrived at work on Wesnesday. Waiters who had known each other for years were sitting about as though they were strangers. The cause of the silence was tacked to the bulletin board. It read: "Because of unforeseen circumstances, some personnel will be laid off the first of next month. Those directly affected will be notified in due time. The management."

"That Hoover's ruining the country," an old waiter finally said. No one answered him. I changed into my suit of blue tails, wondering what had happened.

By Thursday the entire world knew. "MARKET CRASHES—PANIC HITS NATION!" one headline blared. The newspapers were full of it, and I read everything I could get my hands on, gathering in the full meaning of such terms as Black Thursday, deflation and depression. I couldn't imagine such financial disaster touching my small world; it surely concerned only the rich. But by the first week of November I too knew differently; along with millions of others across the nation, I was without a job. All that next week I searched for any kind of work that would prevent my leaving school. Again it was, "We're firing, not hiring." "Sorry, sonny, nothing doing here." Finally, on the seventh of November I went to school and cleaned out my locker, knowing it was impossible to stay on. A piercing chill was in the air as I walked back to the rooming house. The hawk had come. I could already feel his wings shadowing me.

ping freight trains in what the National Resources Committee called a "migration of despair." Woody Guthrie, the hoboes' balladeer, described the traveling life:

> I could see men of all colors bouncing along in the boxcar. We stood up. We laid down. We piled around on each other. We used each other for pillows. I could smell the sour and bitter sweat soaking through my own khaki shirt and britches, and the work clothes, overalls and soggy, dirty suits of the other guys.

Compared to previous periods of depression, however, the 1930s was a time of relative geographic stability: most Americans stayed put, struggling to deal with economic and personal insecurity in their own communities.

In the fall of 1930 one New Jerseyite wrote to President Hoover, "Can not you find a quicker way of Executing us than to Starve us to death?" Although outright starvation was unusual, it was not unknown; in 1931 ninety-five people were reported to have died of hunger in New York City alone. In Colorado, a survey found that half of all schoolchildren were insufficiently fed. With inadequate diets came disease; the incidence of dysentery, tuberculosis, pellagra, and typhoid all rose.

To understand why prosperity was so quickly transformed into mass hunger and joblessness, we must look at the boom psychology that distorted businessmen's economic decision-making in the 1920s, as it has so often before and since. In capitalist economies there is a tendency, when times are good, for businessmen to assume they will stay good. During and after World War I this led to heavy investment in expensive capital equipment, which, along with technological innovations and mass production methods, dramatically increased the country's industrial capacity. Tens of thousands of corporations and entrepreneurs, all sharing a belief that markets would expand forever, built more mines, machines, and factories than were needed. Real estate, too, suffered from overinvestment; in most major cities more office space was constructed than could be rented. To build the factories and office buildings, businessmen went heavily into debt, but they didn't worry; if demand kept rising and prices kept increasing, they'd have no problem repaying creditors.

This assumption proved unrealistic. By the late 1920s, the markets for many of the new products that stimulated the economy after World War I were saturated. For instance, most people who could afford a car or a radio already owned one. As excess capacity, competition, and rising wages lowered the rate of profit in goods production, investors grew reluctant to put more money into industries that would yield only diminishing returns. Many turned instead to short-term, highly speculative investments, hoping to reap quick windfall profits. The boom in Florida real estate was one example of this trend.

The stock market was the main focus of speculative mania. With the blessing of the Federal Reserve System, which traditionally pursued an easy credit policy, most Wall Street investors bought their stock on "margin": they gave their brokers only 10 percent of the cost of the stock they bought, promising to pay the other 90 percent when they sold it. This was fine as long as stock prices were generally rising. But once Wall Street's optimism was shattered, stock prices collapsed in waves of panic selling. By November 1929, the value of all stocks had fallen from a high point of $87 billion to $56 billion. At the stock market's bottom point, in 1933, the same stocks were worth just $18 billion.

The stock market crash shattered public confidence. Those with money to spend reduced their purchases, while corporations canceled plans for new investment. As the demand for both capital and consumer goods fell, companies began laying off workers. This further diminished consumer demand. A downward spiral of declining confidence, declining demand, and declining income thus began.

The major reason the economy failed to rebound was underconsumption. Although the country's productive capacity had soared in the 1920s, its ability to consume what its factories produced had lagged far behind. The primary culprit was the extremely uneven dis-

Have faith. Instead of its usual movie advertisement, a Boston theater sound truck tours the streets in December 1931 chiding citizens who, fearing impending financial failure, had withdrawn their deposits from local banks.

tribution of income and wealth, the result of business's insistence on paying low wages. Treasury Secretary Mellon's "soak the poor" tax policies reinforced this problem. The bottom 40 percent of the population got only one-eighth of all the personal income American families received in 1929, while the top 5 percent took in almost one-third. Many workers and farmers could not afford much more than basic necessities, and there was only so much that the rich could consume. Furthermore, immigration restriction and the incorporation of the last southwestern territories (Arizona and New Mexico became states in 1912) meant that the domestic market was no longer growing simply as a result of population and territorial expansion.

The failure of the economy to recover from the Great Crash also resulted from the sick state of U.S. agriculture and the resulting impact on the banking system. Farmers had been plagued by low prices since the early 1920s. By the time of the Wall Street plunge, the average farmer's income was just one-fourth of the national average. Many farmers went deeply into debt, hoping that future high prices would solve their problems.

The onset of the Depression devastated agriculture. As the Federal Reserve reduced the money supply, prices fell and farmers' incomes dropped. By November 1930, hundreds of thousands of farmers declared bankruptcy. When they stopped paying off their loans, hundreds of rural banks failed. Their failure spread to their urban counterparts. By 1931, five thousand banks had closed their doors, wiping out 9 million savings accounts. When people saw their local banks stumble into financial difficulty, they rushed to withdraw their savings, which exacerbated the problems not only of the banking system but ultimately of the entire economy.

Since the United States was the world's leading economic power, its troubles quickly spread abroad, hastened by the 1930 Smoot-Hawley Tariff Act, which sharply raised tariffs on imported goods. The resulting decline in imports into the United States was a serious blow to the already shaky economies of Europe, where rapid inflation and mass unemployment had already wreaked havoc throughout the 1920s. The situation in Europe reached crisis proportions in 1931, when several major banks collapsed and England abandoned the gold standard.

Now Europe's economic problems came back to haunt the United States. The spread of the Depression and the disruption of the international financial system led many countries to adopt stiff tariffs and other measures that further curtailed world trade. The erection of these trade barriers, combined with losses suffered by American businesses on their overseas investments and loans, intensified the slide in the U.S. economy.

"A Wise Economist Asks a Question." In a 1931 Chicago *Tribune* cartoon, John McCutcheon suggests how commonplace American beliefs about thrift were undermined by the onset of the Great Depression.

As the Depression deepened worldwide, rising unemployment led to massive discontent. The European political crisis that had grown out of World War I intensified. Instability developed in country after country, with ruling groups challenged from both the right and the left.

In the early 1930s, communist and socialist parties grew throughout the world. Although many socialists sought alliances with centrist parties against the growing power and influence of the far right, communist parties, believing revolution was imminent, spurned such coalitions and attacked socialist leaders as witting or unwitting allies of big business.

Fascism was also on the rise. In Italy, a fascist government led by Benito Mussolini had been in power since 1922. In Germany, in most of eastern Europe, and in France and Britain, fascist movements were gaining strength. Usually these movements drew their greatest support from the lower middle class by calling for strong, centralized governments that would do away with parliamentary democracy, destroy the left, and mobilize industry. Extremely nationalistic, they typically blamed the Depression on foreigners or ethnic minorities, particularly Jews. Although they used anticapitalist rhetoric to build support, most had ties to corporate leaders or large landowners.

The contest between left and right was most intense in Germany, where the weak postwar government was unable to overcome severe economic problems that grew out of the Versailles Treaty and the international Depression. In 1932, the fascist National Socialist (Nazi) Party won more seats in the German legislature than any other party. A year later the Nazi leader Adolf Hitler was appointed chancellor. Almost immediately his government began jailing opponents, outlawing all opposition parties, destroying trade unions, and launching a campaign of violence and legal restrictions against Germany's Jews.

In the United States, the Depression did not cause so severe a political crisis. Nevertheless, the prolonged economic slump undermined the legitimacy of American governmental and business institutions and paved the way for major transformations in the nation's political economy. The Depression reached a low point in 1932. For the rest of the decade, while there were ups and downs, the economy would remain largely stagnant until another world war broke out.

HARD TIMES

During the nineteenth century, when times were bad many workers survived by raising their own food in garden plots, returning to family farms, or even rejoining their families in Europe. In the 1930s, some unemployed people could still take these steps. For instance, Charles Denby, an African-American autoworker who left an Alabama cotton plantation for Detroit in 1924, returned home in 1930. Although he had once sworn not to go back South until "all the roads were paved and there was electricity and water in every house," he had little choice; he could find no work in Detroit.

In the early years of the Depression, more people moved from cities to farms than in the other direction. Between 1930 and 1935, more than a million acres of previously uncultivated land was farmed by people fleeing the cities. And many workers in rural areas—Appalachian coalminers, for instance—began growing more of their own food.

By the 1930s, however, most workers were long cut off from the land and completely dependent on wages for survival. Unemployment meant family disaster. Joblessness was the greatest problem the country faced. Workers in all parts of the country and in all occupations were affected.

The employment situation was generally worst in the large cities, among unskilled blue-collar workers, and among nonwhites. White-collar workers in retail and wholesale trade, communications, banking, and insurance fared somewhat better than blue-collar workers.

Hooverville, 1933. A squatter settlement built by homeless people in Seattle, Washington.

Government employees were less likely to lose their jobs than workers in the private sector. And unemployment in the South was not quite as bad as in the North, in part because many of the South's manufacturers were so marginal and in debt that they could not afford to reduce production and thus risk a further reduction in income.

The country's largest manufacturing firms generally tried to retain as many of their experienced workers as possible. Rather than fire valuable employees, they reduced the number of hours or days each worked so that more people could be kept on the payroll. "They'd just say, 'You come in Monday. Take the rest of the week off,'" one GE worker remembered. Some companies fired unskilled workers and gave skilled workers their jobs (at lower pay rates). By reducing hours and reassigning jobs, the Westinghouse Electric Corporation retained almost all employees with over ten years' seniority at its huge East Pittsburgh plant.

Most construction companies and smaller manufacturers could not afford to retain excess workers, even part-time. Between 1929 and 1933, building employment dropped by over 80 percent. And at one point in New York City, only 10 percent of the members of the Amalgamated Clothing Workers' Union were working.

Joblessness was the worst but not the only problem workers faced. Those with jobs earned greatly reduced incomes because of shorter hours and lower pay. One New York subway conductor, for example, saw his annual earnings fall from over $2,000 in 1930 to just over $1,200 two years later. Many people, employed and unemployed, could not keep up rent or mortgage payments, which meant losing their homes. In Philadelphia, 1,300 homes and apartment buildings were being sold each month at sheriffs' sales. Evictions became so common in the Quaker City that young children made a game of it. "We ain't got no money for the rent, so's we moved into a new house," a youngster told his teacher. "Then we got the constable on us, so we's moving again."

At any given time during the 1930s, roughly one of five wage-earning women was out of work. This was lower than the unemployment rate for men; the number of working women actually increased substantially during the Great Depression. One reason was hunger. So many millions of male breadwinners lost their jobs that millions of wives and daughters had no choice but to seek employment. Also, in a job market sharply segregated by gender, most women worked in occupations less hard hit by the Depression than those dominated by men. Less than 18 percent of working women were in manufacturing, while 75 percent were in domestic and personal service, clerical occupations, professional service (mostly as teachers and nurses), or trade. When men lost their jobs in factories, they did not often apply for jobs as maids, secretaries, or salesclerks.

Nonetheless, as unemployment rose, so did discrimination against working women. Many people felt that married women who worked were taking jobs away from unemployed men; women were assumed to be working only to make extra "pin money." This was usually not the case, but when layoffs occurred, married women were often the first to be let go. Both New England Telephone and Telegraph and the Northern Pacific Railroad, for instance, fired all married women in 1931. Most cities banned married women from teaching. The American Federation of Labor, which had hundreds of thousands of female members, was so distressed by widespread unemployment that in 1931 it adopted a program that sought to counter the "unfortunate trend in family life": the entry of women into the labor market. Federation leaders proposed that "preference of employment" be given for "those upon whom family or dependency rests," by which they meant men.

When they had jobs, women routinely were paid less than men, even for the same work. Along with irregular employment—for example, women worked an average of only twenty-six to thirty-five weeks a year in the garment, glove, and textile industries—this meant that the average annual income of women was roughly half that of men ($525 versus $1,027 in 1937). Millions of women—heads of households with children to support—lived on the edge of destitution.

Statistics on women's work and wages tell only part of the story of what women had to do to survive the Depression. As household income shrank, women's unpaid work at home greatly expanded. Women had to stretch food farther than in better times (though partly because of falling food prices there was less malnutrition during the 1930s than in earlier depressions), and when once they might have bought new clothes, now they darned socks, shortened pants, let out waistlines, and hemmed dresses.

Finally, the Depression imposed one more cost on working women: it limited their mobility into better jobs. White women had rapidly entered white-collar work between 1910 and 1930; in the 1930s that movement virtually came to a halt. Hundreds of thousands of women had to lower their expectations and face a working life of diminished pay and satisfaction.

The contraction of the economy also led to a rise in racial and ethnic discrimination. Some employers and white workers insisted that white citizens be given preference in employment. Mexican-Americans were perhaps the foremost victims of this revived racism. In California, joblessness and inmigration of whites from the Southwest mushroomed at the same time that agricultural production declined. As a result, the pool of available agricultural workers swelled; by 1933 over twice as many people were looking for work in California farms as there were jobs. It soon became the standard practice to hire Anglos rather than Mexicans, even though many of the latter had been recruited to come to the United States by the growers themselves. Similarly, many nonagricultural employers laid off Mexican workers first.

During the Depression, nearly 500,000 Mexican nationals and their United States—

"WHERE WOMEN GO . . ."

Meridel LeSueur, poet and journalist, described the plight of unemployed women, of which she was one, in the worst years of the Depression. "Jungle" was a common term for a homeless encampment.

IT'S one of the great mysteries of the city where women go when they are out of work and hungry. There are not many women in the bread line. There are no flop houses for women as there are for men, where a bed can be had for a quarter or less. You don't see women lying on the floor at the mission in the free flops. They obviously don't sleep in the jungle or under newspapers in the park. There is no law I suppose against their being in these places but the fact is they rarely are.

Yet there must be as many women out of jobs in cities and suffering extreme poverty as there are men. What happens to them? Where do they go? Try to get into the Y.W.[C.A.] without any money or looking down at the heel. Charities take care of very few and only those that are called "deserving." The lone girl is under suspicion by the virgin women who dispense charity.

I've lived in cities for many months broke, without help, too timid to get in bread lines. I've known many women to live like this until they simply faint on the street from privation, without saying a word to anyone. A woman will shut herself up in a room until it is taken away from her, and eat a cracker a day and be as quiet as a mouse so there are no social statistics concerning her.

born children returned to Mexico, most of them before 1933. Many left voluntarily; others were pressured or forced to depart. Because this outmigration was heavier from the countryside than from cities, its net effect was to redistribute the Mexican-American population; by 1940 most Chicanos were living in urban areas.

To encourage Mexicans to leave the country, several states barred noncitizens from employment on public works projects. Many local governments and private relief agencies paid rail fare as far as the border for Mexicans who were willing to leave, sometimes making emergency relief contingent on agreement to do so. And various groups, such as the Los Angeles Chamber of Commerce, began campaigns to scare Mexicans into leaving the country. The federal government cooperated in these efforts; although relatively few Mexicans were formally deported—a process that required lengthy, complex hearings—the deportations that did occur were heavily publicized. In Michigan, the Immigration Service transported "welfare cases" as well as deportees to the Mexican border. In 1932, three of four of Detroit's Mexican inhabitants returned to Mexico. Chicago relief authorities organized a massive repatriation campaign that resulted in the departure for Mexico of several thousand Chicano steelworkers.

Chinese immigrants also experienced a revival of racism in the Depression's early years. Chinese had long dominated the laundry business in New York and other large cities, laundry work being one of the few jobs open to them. With the introduction of mechanized washing machines and steam presses during the 1920s and the downturn in business caused by the Depression, competition dramatically increased between small Chinese-owned hand laundries (usually operated by a single individual or family) and the newer, large-scale steam laundries owned by non-Chinese. When Chinese launderers in New York refused to abide by a minimum price scheme set by a citywide laundry organization in 1932, the trade association retaliated by organizing a massive boycott of Chinese-owned establishments. A racist proboycott poster showing a bucktoothed Chinese laundryman spitting into a pile of wet clothing appeared in store windows throughout New York City. Early in 1933, the laundry trade association intensified its efforts to drive Chinese laundries out of business by convincing the Board of Aldermen to pass an ordinance calling for registration fees and a $1,000 bond for all one-person laundries.

The Chinese laundrymen fought back. With the help of the Chinese consul, they got the New York police to convince storeowners to take down the offensive posters. And ignoring the conservative Chinese Consolidated Benevolent Association, which had long dominated social and political life in Chinatown, in April they formed the more militant Chinese Hand Laundry Association (CHLA), which immediately challenged the bond ordinance in court. The Board of Aldermen finally relented, lowering the bond to $100. Within a month, the CHLA claimed 2,400 members. The formation of the CHLA altered the power structure in Chinatown and served as a base for more progressive political activities later in the Depression decade.

African-Americans, too, suffered from increased racism and discrimination, both on and off the job. All over the country, black factory workers found themselves being laid off before whites, reversing some of the progress blacks had made in moving into industrial jobs. At the same time, whites began seeking and securing low-status jobs—especially in heavy labor and service work—they once willingly left for African-Americans.

Sometimes drastic measures were used to oust black workers. In Atlanta, African-American bellhops were arrested on trumped-up charges so their jobs could be given to whites. In Louisiana, vigilantes launched a reign of terror against black railroad firemen, killing ten, to force them off the rails. In Milwaukee, white workers at the Wehr Steel Foundry struck, demanding that their African-American co-workers be fired.

African-American workers were concentrated in occupations that were particularly affected by the economic downturn: unskilled manufacturing, construction, mining, the lumber industry, and domestic labor. Along with racial discrimination, this led to a substantially higher unemployment rate for blacks than for whites. Meanwhile, Depression era wage cuts drove hundreds of thousands of working African-Americans to the brink of starvation—and beyond. After surveying conditions in Cleveland, where half the workers in the largest African-American ghetto were without work, one observer expressed the belief that "the race is standing on a precipice of economic disaster."

Racial oppression away from the workplace also intensified, particularly in the South, where three-quarters of the African-American population still lived. Lynchings, for example, grew in number, with twenty-four black Americans killed in 1932 alone. The terror that southern blacks faced received national attention with what became known as the Scottsboro case. In 1931, nine blacks, one only twelve years old, were falsely accused of raping two white women on a freight train near Scottsboro, Alabama. In a trial riddled with prejudice, procedural error, and questionable evidence, eight of the defendants were convicted and sentenced to death. Their case, taken up first by the Communist Party and then by the NAACP, became an international *cause célèbre*, much like the Sacco and Vanzetti case had been during the 1920s. Eventually the death sentences were thrown

Scottsboro defense. The *Daily Worker* announces one of the many demonstrations sponsored by the Communist Party in support of the Scottsboro defendants.

out, but five of the defendants served long prison terms for a crime that never occurred.

Suffering was also intense in rural America. The coal industry, already sick in the 1920s, was particularly hard hit. With the Depression the demand for coal fell to its 1904 level. Coalminers worked an average of only 27 hours a week and 146 days during 1932. Some eastern Kentucky coal towns were without a penny of income. People tried to live on a diet of dandelions and blackberries, without success. Readers were horrified by reports of starving babies with bloated stomachs, and children so hungry that they chewed up their own hands.

Between 1929 and 1932, net farm income fell by two-thirds. This was due to decreased production and to falling prices. The price of raw cotton, for instance, fell by over two-thirds during the first three years of the Depression. Many farmers found that it was not even worthwhile to harvest the crops they had planted. Plunging agricultural income in turn led to economic collapse in small towns and villages that served local farmers.

Farmers were less dependent on the market for survival than nonfarm workers, since farmers at least could grow some of their own food. But with their income dropping, many farm families found it impossible to meet mortgage payments, repay loans, or pay their taxes. As a result, tens of thousands lost their farms. During just two years in Iowa County, Iowa, a once-prosperous corn-growing area, one of every eight farms was sold at auction. An Indiana woman wrote the secretary of agriculture in 1930 that her family was about to lose its 250-acre farm. "[We] worked to death with no income, no leisure, no pleasure and no hope of anything better. . . . We are a sick and sorry people. . . . My nearest neighbor has turned bootlegger, I can smell the mash brewing in his still." In the South, many landowners could not afford to lay out provisions and advances to tenant farmers, who were left to fend for themselves.

If farmers faced only economic problems, their situation would have been bad enough, but during the very depth of the Depression another disaster arrived: drought. At first the lack of rain was most severe in the East, but then the center of the dry spell moved to the Great Plains, where temperatures reached 118 degrees in Nebraska in 1934. Normal rainfall did not return to the southern plains until 1941.

With the drought came a series of dust storms that hit the Plains states from 1932 through the end of the decade. These storms, which could last from an hour to several days, were terrifying. Clouds of dirt as high as eight thousand feet would roll in, sometimes accompanied by thunder, lightning, and powerful winds. One storm, in March 1935, carried off twice as much dirt as had been dug during the building of the Panama Canal. The storm destroyed half the wheat crop in Kansas and the entire wheat crop in Nebraska. Occasionally, children

Dust storm. A wall of dirt and sand descends on Spearman, Texas, on August 14, 1935.

On the road. Their worldly possessions piled on two rundown vehicles, a migrant family pauses en route to California in February 1936.

caught outside when dust storms came died of suffocation in drifts of dirt. Dust seeped everywhere, into homes, beds, food, and clothes. The worst-hit area was the so-called Dust Bowl, which encompassed parts of Kansas, Oklahoma, Colorado, New Mexico, and the Texas Panhandle. Some places were turned into virtual deserts. Crops, live-stock—and a whole way of life—were destroyed.

The immediate cause of the Dust Bowl was dry weather. But droughts were not new to the southern plains; what was new was the destructive way farmers had been cultivating the land. When farmers began settling in the region in the 1890s they plowed up the grasses that kept the topsoil in place. When the 1930s dry spell hit, the result was one of the worst man-made ecological catastrophes ever to have occurred.

The huge outmigration of residents of the southern plains caused by the Dust Bowl began on a massive scale in 1935. Not until four years later, though, when John Steinbeck published his novel *The Grapes of Wrath*, did most Americans become aware of this extraordinary exodus. Over three million people left Plains states farms during the decade. "I didn't sell out back there," complained one migrant, "I give out." Some migrants moved only short distances, but many headed west, particularly to California. Sometimes the dust had destroyed their farms, but just as frequently the introduction of mechanized agriculture had forced migrants to leave land their families had worked for generations. Joining onetime farmers in the stream of "Okies" and "Arkies" moving west were families fleeing the economically ruined towns and cities of the southern plains.

Material deprivation was only part of the human cost of the Depression. The psychological strains were also severe. Almost everyone felt insecure. Those with jobs feared losing them; those without work worried about what would become of them. In the early years of the Depression, people generally blamed themselves for their troubles. A ruined wheat farmer whom writer Sherwood Anderson met on the road was typical: "It's my own fault," he said. "I was not smart enough." Men who lost their jobs often felt that their status in their families and communities was diminished. Many women found it hard to keep on going with their deeply depressed husbands moping around at home. Larry Van Dusen, the son of a carpenter, remembered: "My father led a rough life: he drank. During the Depression, he drank more. There was more conflict in the home." Many young people, uncertain of their futures, held off starting families; marriage and birth rates both dropped in the early 1930s.

Although middle-income Americans were better prepared financially for the Depression than were most workers, they were often less prepared psychologically. Committed to an ethic of individual accomplishment, many of them felt deep shame about even modest economic setbacks. They stopped going to churches and clubs, shunned their former friends, and turned down social invitations. The problems of middle-class Amer-

"AND THEN WE WERE IN CALIFORNIA ..."

Even from areas outside the Dust Bowl, families streamed into California. Cesar Chavez's father owned a small plot of land in Arizona until a bank foreclosed on his loan. He and his family were forced to become migrant farmworkers in the mid-1930s at a time when labor was plentiful, wages extremely low, and discrimination against Mexican-Americans growing. Many years later Chavez help found the United Farm Workers' Union.

WE all of us climbed into an old Chevy that my dad had. And then we were in California, and migratory workers. There were five kids—a small family by those standards.... I was about eight. Well, it was a strange life. We had been poor, but we knew every night there was a bed *there*, and that *this* was our room. There was a kitchen. It was sort of a settled life, and we had chickens and hogs, eggs, and all those things. But that all of a sudden changed. When you're small you can't figure these things out....

"Following the crops," we missed much school. Trying to get enough money to stay alive the following winter, the whole family picking apricots, walnuts, prunes. We were pretty new, we had never been migratory workers. We were taken advantage of quite a bit by the labor contractor and the crew pusher....

Coming into San Jose, not finding—being lied to, that there was work. We had no money at all, and had to live on the outskirts of town under a bridge and dry creek....

We got hooked on a real scheme once. We were going by Fresno on our way to Delano. We stopped at some service station and this labor contractor saw the car. He offered a lot of money. We went. We worked the first week: the grapes were pretty bad and we couldn't make much. We all stayed off from school in order to make some money. Saturday we were to be paid and we didn't get paid. He came and said the winery hadn't paid him. We'd have money next week. He gave us $10. My dad took the $10 and went to the store and bought $10 worth of groceries. So we worked another week and in the middle of the second week, my father was asking him for his last week's pay, and he had the same excuse. This went on and we'd get $5 or $10 or $7 a week for about four weeks. For the whole family.

So one morning my father made the resolution no more work. If he doesn't pay us, we won't work. We got in a car and went over to see him. The house was empty. He had left. The winery said they had paid him and they showed us where they had paid him. This man had taken it.

Traveling to the Arkansas Delta to pick cotton, members of a South Texas family were photographed by the Farm Security Administration's Dorothea Lange in August 1936.

icans were intensified by the fact that they were also less likely than workers or farmers to live surrounded by extended families to whom they could turn for emotional and material support. Even when their immediate financial situation was not dire, many felt that their world was falling apart.

GOVERNMENT AND BUSINESS RESPONSE TO THE DEPRESSION

During the early days of the Depression, most business leaders downplayed the significance of the stock market crash and the subsequent economic slide. Optimistic about a rapid recovery, businessmen initially opposed any strong government response to the crisis; they felt it was unnecessary and might lead to greater government regulation of the economy. Willis H. Booth, head of the Merchants' Association of New York, believed that there was "no fundamental reason why business should not find itself again on the up-grade early in 1930." Thus, when the business leaders who made up the National Economic League were asked in January 1930 what the country's "paramount problems" were, they listed first, "administration of justice," second, "Prohibition," and third, "lawlessness." Unemployment was eighteenth on their list!

Some members of the Hoover administration agreed that there was no need for government action. Treasury Secretary Andrew Mellon, a member of one of the nation's richest families, thought that the crisis was "not altogether a bad thing." "People," he argued, "will work harder, live a more moral life. Values will be adjusted, and enterprising people will pick up the wrecks from less competent people." Hoover himself kept telling the American people that the economy was "on a sound and prosperous basis" and would soon recover. But privately he believed that the Depression would be severe.

In dealing with the Depression, Hoover thought that the primary role of the federal government should be to coordinate private, state, and local efforts rather than launch major initiatives of its own. The key to recovery, he believed, was restoring business confidence, which meant avoiding unsettling actions and balancing the federal budget.

Hoover had some initial success in winning cooperation from business. At his request, many major corporations agreed not to cut wages, in an effort to maintain spending power. A host of presidentially endorsed business committees were set up to promote relief and recovery through voluntary, private action. In the end, though, little was accomplished. Many companies that froze wages negated the economic impact of this action by cutting hours and laying off employees. Then, in 1931, U.S. Steel announced a 10 percent wage cut that was widely copied.

Hoover did initiate some direct federal action. He sharply increased spending on public works to $700 million, an unprecedented sum; he set up the Reconstruction Finance Corporation to extend up to $300 million in credit to failing banks and businesses; and he boosted aid to farmers. Compared to nineteenth-century presidents who had watched depressions afflict the nation, Hoover pursued an activist program. The relief situation, however, illustrates how woefully inadequate this federal action was.

At the time of the stock market crash, poor relief was provided largely by local governments and private charities. Only eight states had any form of unemployment compensation. Furthermore, even after unemployment became widespread, many relief agencies treated the poor as if their plight was their own fault. Before receiving aid, relief applicants were often required to submit to humiliating interviews. In many places the relief they received was largely in the form of "food orders," which could be used only to purchase groceries. This system was deeply resented; as one Pittsburgh relief recipient put it, "Does a man's status change when he becomes unemployed, so that, while he was perfectly able to handle money while he had a job, he can't be trusted with it when he is out of work?" Frequently, little or no money was provided for rent, clothes, or medical care.

"Fundamentally the ship was sound." *New Yorker* cartoonist Richard Decker comments on the obstinate outlook of conservative business leaders in the face of the nation's mounting economic and social crisis.

Of course WE CAN DO IT!

● We dug the Panama Canal, didn't we? And they said we couldn't do that.

● We put an army in France four months after we entered the World War, didn't we? And surprised the world.

● Now we've got a tough one to crack right here in our own back yard.

Men are out of work. Our men. Our neighbors. Our citizens. Honest, hard-working folk.

They want jobs. They're eager to work. But there aren't jobs enough to go 'round. Somebody's got to tide them over.

Who's going to do it? The people who dug that ditch. The people who went to France, or bought Liberty Bonds, or went without sugar—Mr. and Mrs. John K. American.

That means you—and *you*—and Y O U!—every one of us who is lucky enough to have a job.

We're going to share our luck with the folks out of work, aren't we? Remember—there's no National fund they can turn to for relief. It's up to us! And we've got to dig deeper than we did last winter.

But if we all dig deep enough we can keep a roof over every head, food in every pantry, fuel on every fire, and warm clothing on every needy man, woman and child in America.

That will beat Old Man Depression and lead the way to better days. Can we do it? Of course we can do it. Give . . . and give generously.

WHERE TO GIVE: There is no National Agency through which you may contribute. The way for you to give is through your *local* welfare and relief organizations, through your Community Chest or through your emergency unemployment committee if you have one.

THE PRESIDENT'S ORGANIZATION ON UNEMPLOYMENT RELIEF

Walter S. Gifford *Director*.
(WALTER S. GIFFORD)

COMMITTEE ON MOBILIZATION OF RELIEF RESOURCES

Chairman
(OWEN D. YOUNG)

● The President's Organization on Unemployment Relief is non-political, and non-sectarian. Its purpose is to aid local welfare and relief agencies everywhere to provide for local needs. All facilities for the nation-wide program, including this advertisement, have been furnished to the Committee without cost.

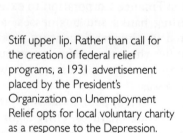

Stiff upper lip. Rather than call for the creation of federal relief programs, a 1931 advertisement placed by the President's Organization on Unemployment Relief opts for local voluntary charity as a response to the Depression.

Even so, by 1931 most local governments and many private agencies were running out of money for relief. Sometimes needy people were simply removed from the relief rolls. According to one survey, in 1932 only about one-quarter of the jobless were receiving aid. Many cities discriminated against nonwhites. In Dallas and Houston, African-Americans and Mexican-Americans were denied any assistance. Furthermore, the payments that were given were wholly inadequate. In New York, the average family grant in late 1932 was only

J. Egbert Haggle, prominent Chicago packer, is encouraging a movement for the rich to devote two minutes of silent meditation before beginning their Christmas dinners. "This should cheer up the unemployed by letting them know they are being thought about," Mr. Haggle said.

Salomon De Pischer, leading department store owner of New York thinks the trouble with the unemployed is that they are hoarding their money. When asked for his cure for unemployment, the great merchant, without a moment's hesitation, said: "Spend More."

Graves S. Close-Fist, eminent Brooklyn banker, thinks high-living has caused poverty and unemployment. Addressing the exclusive "Four Hours For Lunch Club," Mr. Close-Fist summed up his advice to the unemployed in two words: "Save More."

"Interviewed On Unemployment." The December 1930 edition of the League for Industrial Democracy's *The Unemployed* satirically presents three business perspectives on the unemployment "problem."

$2.39 a week, and only half of all qualified families received even this tiny sum.

Cities soon began taking desperate measures. In Youngstown, Ohio, an abandoned police station was turned into a flophouse. In Hamtramck, Michigan, welfare officials cut off relief to all families with fewer than three children. In Detroit, Frank Murphy, who was elected mayor in 1930 with strong labor backing, opened emergency lodges in empty factories, set up municipal feeding stations serving 14,000 daily, and promoted "thrift gardens" for the jobless on vacant city land. But within two years deteriorating city finances forced Murphy to give in to fierce pressure from the banks—from whom the city needed loans—to cut relief spending sharply.

Even as the crisis worsened, Hoover refused to commit federal funds for basic needs. Relief, he argued, was a local responsibility; federal involvement would strike at "the roots of self-government" and destroy "character." Only in July 1932, under ever-increasing popular pressure, did Hoover sign a bill that established federal relief spending.

During his reelection campaign in 1932, Hoover blamed international economic problems for the continuing Depression at home. He was convinced that the failure of the American economy to revive was the result of the economic crisis in Europe and the breakdown of international trade and monetary relations. Only a negotiated, international restoration of trade and finances, he contended, could restore the world economy. The president had succeeded in winning a one-year moratorium on intergovernmental debt and World War I reparation payments but had failed to get broader agreements. While there was some truth to Hoover's analysis, his three years of minimizing the seriousness of the Depression and the degree of suffering it caused embittered millions of people who knew from firsthand experience just how bad conditions had become.

POPULAR AND RADICAL RESPONSES
TO THE DEPRESSION

Stunned and disoriented by the sudden collapse of the economy, many workers—employed and unemployed—turned inward, retreating to sullen reflection and resignation. But not all working people responded passively to the Depression. Throughout the country, unions and community organizations established self-help programs to aid the unemployed.

In Detroit, members of the Typographical Union voted to tax themselves to provide $25 a week for families and $10 for single jobless men. In Flint, Michigan, the city's worker-managed Industrial Mutual Association provided jobless benefits for 1,200 workers and their families in 1930–31. In Seattle during the summer of 1931, job-less workers founded the Unemployed Citizens' League. This "repub-lic of the penniless" arranged for idle fishing boats to be made available to unemployed workers; arranged with farmers to allow the jobless to dig potatoes and pick apples and pears; and gained permis-sion from landowners for the cutting down of trees for firewood. League members mended clothing, rebuilt furniture, gave haircuts, and repaired shoes as the city's economy reverted to barter. The suc-cess of the league inspired imitation; by the end of 1932 there were 330 similar organizations in 37 states, with a membership exceeding 300,000.

Informal self-help was even more significant. In New York's Har-lem and on Chicago's South Side, African-Americans raised money to forestall eviction by organizing rent parties. Jazz musicians, many of whom, like Willie (The Lion) Smith and Fats Waller, later became world-famous, provided entertainment. "A hundred people would crowd into one seven-room flat until the walls bulged," Smith re-called. "Food! Hog maws and chitlins with vinegar—you never ate nothing until you ate 'em. Beer and gin. When we played the shouts, everyone danced." In the anthracite fields of western Pennsylvania, self-help took the form of a gigantic illicit industry: more than 6,500 miners made their living by illegally taking coal from abandoned mines.

Even early in the Depression there were signs of anger at the suf-fering working people were experiencing. In 1930 over 3,000 Flint workers, only a handful of whom were union members, struck a GM body plant to protest cuts in piecework rates. Generally, however, em-ployed workers avoided job actions, fearing that if they lost their jobs they would be unable to find others. It was among the unemployed and farmers that massive protests first began.

Within months of the stock market crash it became obvious that the institutions to which working-class families traditionally turned in times of trouble—churches, ethnic associations, local political machines, unions—were unable or unwilling to deal with mass un-employment and its effects. This created a vacuum into which vari-ous radical groups moved: the Socialist Party, independent socialist groups led by minister-turned-labor-leader A. J. Muste, and especially the Communist Party.

In late 1929, the Communist Party organized the first of what was soon a nationwide network of "Unemployed Councils." These Communist-led neighborhood groups worked to aid the unemployed with immediate problems of rent and food, to apply pressure for im-proved relief programs, and finally to recruit new members to join the party. On March 6, 1930, the Communists held a series of rallies on what it dubbed "International Unemployment Day," demanding government action. In city after city, the turnout far exceeded expectations. In both Boston and Chicago there were 50,000 protesters; in Milwaukee, 40,000; and in Detroit, perhaps as many as 100,000. In New York, when demonstrators tried to march on City Hall, police attacked the huge throng. The New York *Times* reported that "hundreds of policemen and detectives, swinging nightsticks, blackjacks, and bare fists, rushed into the crowd, hitting out at all with whom they came into contact." The leaders of the demonstration were arrested and sentenced to six months in jail.

The Unemployed Councils called for improvements in local relief and a national unemployment compensation system. To promote this program, the Communist Party organized demonstrations, petition drives, and two "hunger marches" on Washington. In some cases protests won upgraded relief benefits from local authorities and less humiliating procedures. The campaign failed in the short run to win federal legislation, but it was an important factor in the eventual creation of a national system of unemployment insurance.

Much of the day-to-day work of the Unemployed Councils centered around organizing rent strikes and anti-eviction battles. When landlords or banks evicted families, council members would round up as many people as possible and move the families back into their homes. Delegations also went to housing courts to pressure judges to refuse to order evictions. Sometimes attempts to move people back into their homes led to clashes with the police. Several times police killed demonstrators during such battles; occasionally police, sheriffs, or landlords gave in. Once, in Chicago, the head of a police detail facing a hostile crowd passed his hat to collect money for an evicted family's rent, rather than provoke a battle. Eventually, the Unemployed Councils became so well known in the African-American neighborhoods of Chicago that, according to one account, when eviction notices were received "it was not unusual for a mother to shout to the children, 'Run quick and find the Reds!'"

Anti-eviction fights were effective because they mobilized existing, informal community networks. Most of those who took part were not Communists but simply people outraged at conditions and eager to help their neighbors. The success of the Unemployed Councils led other radical groups to set up their own groups of the unemployed. In 1936, separate organizations of the unemployed led by the Socialist Party, A. J. Muste, and the Communist Party merged to form the Workers' Alliance of America. Nonradicals got into the act, too: in 1932 James Cox, a Catholic priest, led 12,000 unemployed Pittsburgh workers on a march in Washington.

Of all the unemployment activities led by the Communist Party, the most dramatic was the "Ford Hunger March." On March 7, 1932, over 3,000 protesters—organized by the small, Communist-led Auto

Workers' Union—marched on the main Ford plant in Dearborn, Michigan, demanding jobs for laid-off Ford workers, a slowdown of the company's assembly line, and a halt to evictions of ex-Ford workers. When the police tried to stop the march, a fight broke out and police and members of the Ford security force began firing their revolvers into the crowd. As the marchers retreated, the police opened up with machine guns. Four marchers were killed, and over sixty were injured. For Dave Moore, who began his political activity fighting evictions in Detroit, the Hunger March was "the turning point in my life. . . . When I saw the blood flowing there on Miller Road, that was the point I became a radical." The following Sunday, a crowd estimated at 20,000 to 40,000 followed the caskets of the slain men to a cemetery, where they were lowered into the ground to the strains of the "Internationale," the Communist anthem. Henry Ford, a hero of the 1920s, became a much-hated man in the city of Detroit.

For tens of thousands of people, unemployment protests were their first experience in organized political activity. Many went on to be active in union and other struggles. Furthermore, both in northern communities such as Harlem and in southern cities such as Chattanooga and Atlanta, whites and blacks worked together in Unemployed Council activities. This proved an important precedent for future interracial efforts.

In the South, the Communist Party tried to organize not only industrial workers and the unemployed but also what it called "the black peasantry." The southern party operated virtually as an underground organization because of severe local repression. In May 1932, for instance, when a young African-American Communist, Angelo Herndon, tried to organize a demonstration of the unemployed in Atlanta, he was charged with insurrection under an 1866 law and sentenced to twenty years in prison. (The U.S. Supreme Court eventually overturned his conviction.)

The Communist Party was particularly active in Alabama, where its membership was predominantly black. In Birmingham, the party attracted many steelworkers; in the countryside, black sharecroppers. As cotton prices plummeted, sharecroppers were pressed ever harder by landlords and merchants. Some landowners cut off food advances to their tenants, reduced wages for day labor, and forced sharecroppers to work off real-estate taxes—the responsibility of landowners—by doing roadwork. When the Communists organized the Sharecroppers' Union (SCU) in Tallapoosa County, Alabama, in 1931, many African-Americans joined in spite of the enormous risk.

Within months, local landowners and authorities struck back. In July 1931 a sheriff's party raided a Sharecroppers' Union meeting near the town of Camp Hill, touching off a series of gun battles that resulted in the wounding of two officials and the death of a sharecropper. As the Communist Party's role in organizing the SCU and in defending the "Scottsboro boys" became known, more Alabama blacks joined the party. In 1932, a second shoot-out between authorities and SCU members resulted in the death of at least two sharecroppers and the imprisonment of five others.

The collapse of cotton prices was a regional catastrophe, affecting not only sharecroppers but landowners, independent farmers, merchants, and banks as well. In an effort to force up cotton prices in 1931, Louisiana governor Huey Long had his state's legislature pass a bill prohibiting any planting of cotton the following year. Mississippi, South Carolina, and Texas followed with more modest plans contingent on the passage of similar laws in all the cotton-growing states. However, when the Texas Supreme Court overturned that state's law, the movement for a moratorium on cotton planting collapsed.

"WEREN'T NO USE UNDER GOD'S SUN TO TREAT COLORED FOLKS LIKE WE BEEN TREATED . . ."

Ned Cobb, a sharecropper and staunch supporter of the Alabama Sharecroppers' Union, describes how he resisted an attempt by his landlord, Mr. Taylor, to foreclose on another sharecropper, Clint Webster, in 1932. Cobb ended up spending twelve years in prison for defying the authorities in this incident.

I happened to be at Clint Webster's house one mornin' when Mr. Taylor sent the deputy sheriff [Mr. Woods] over to attach everything the man had and bring it away from there.... Well, I knowed I had to take a stand right there because ... I was going to be next.... I stretched out my arms and said, "Mr. Woods, please, sir, don't take what he's got. He's got a wife and children and if you take all his stock and everything else, you'll leave his folks hungry." He told me ... "I got orders to take it, and I'll be damned if I don't." ... So I just politely told him that he weren't goin' to do it....

Then the deputy raised sand with me about it. He jumped up and told me, "I'm going to Dadeville to get [Sheriff] Carl Platt and bring him down here. He'll come down here and kill the last damn one of you, shoot you in a bunch."

Now, a organization is a organization, and if I don't mean nothin' by what I say and do, I ought to keep my ass out of it; but if I'm sworn to stand up for myself and stand up for all the poor class of farmers, I have to do it. Weren't no use under God's sun to treat colored folks like we been treated here in the state of Alabama, weren't no sense in it. Work hard and look what's done to me....

Mr. Woods come back that same day ... with four sheriffs.... There were several men in Clint Webster's house when that bunch of sheriffs arrived, five or six of them. But when the sheriffs walked up in the yard, I was standin' outside....

Many midwestern farmers also believed that their plight would be eased only if farm prices were raised. Instead of taking a legislative approach, however, they turned to direct action. In 1932 the Iowa-based Farmers' Holiday Association organized a moratorium on agricultural sales. Wisconsin dairy farmers held a similar farm "strike." In some instances, they forcibly stopped trucks and trains carrying farm products to market. But like the cotton reduction movement, farm "holidays" failed to raise prices.

More effective were efforts to stop auctions of farms for overdue taxes or mortgage payments. Often a farmer's neighbors would intimidate potential bidders and then buy the farm themselves at a token price, returning it to its original owner. Emil Loriks, of Arlington, South Dakota, remembered that in his county "farmers would crowd into the courtroom, five or six hundred, and make it impossible for the officers to carry out the sales. Deputies would come along with whole fleets of trucks and guns. One lone farmer had planks across the road. They ordered him to remove them. They came out with guns. He said, 'Go ahead and shoot, but there isn't one of you S.O.B.'s getting out of here alive.' There were about fifteen hundred farmers there in the woods. The trucks didn't get through."

As threats of violence and actual clashes became more common, several states passed laws blocking sales of farms for taxes or debt.

The protest against Depression conditions that most captured national attention was the "Bonus March" in the summer of 1932. After World War I, Congress had passed a bill promising each veteran a cash "bonus" to be paid in 1945. As the Depression deepened, veterans began demanding that the bonuses be distributed immediately. In May 1932 a group of vets from Portland, Oregon, set out to Washington, D.C., to press their

I said, "Fellas, here they come, here come the officers." God Almighty, they jumped up and run out of that house goin' out the back way into the field and the forest, clean out of there.... Then [Deputy Sheriff] Grant, be standin' in front of me holdin' a shotgun straight on me; wouldn't budge, just standin' there lookin' at me, wouldn't say nothin' ... just lookin' at me and holdin' that gun, the muzzle part of it....

And bless your soul, I got tired standin' there.... So I walked off. I just decided I'd go on in the house. And when I started up the doorstep, [Deputy Sheriff] Meade ... grabbed me by my right arm and just pressured it, but I absolutely flung him off like you would fling off a leech.... I just commenced a steppin' right on in the house. And Mr. Grant shot me three times, in the back.... But I didn't stop walkin' when he shot me. Shot me twice more, right quick before I could get in the house. Boom! Boom! Same place, every time he shot me. I just still kept walkin', never did weaken.

Now the door to the north room of that house was open comin' off a hallway. I just walked in that door to the north room and looked back. Mr. Grant still had that gun on me, and I started workin' out with him. He jumped behind a big oak tree and I just kept working' out with my .32 Smith and Wesson. I had that gun on me when I come there that mornin', and they didn't know it. I didn't go there actin' a fool, less'n a person will call me a fool for what I said. My finger was on that trigger all the time and the gun was in my hand. I had on a pair of big overalls, brand new, and the pockets was deep and my hand in the pockets. And I had on a white cowboy hat—that's the way I was dressed and my jumper and a pair of Red Wing boots, about knee-high.... And when Mr. Grant shot me—shot me three times, in the same place—my blood came near to fillin' them boots.... I was just sloshin' in my blood every step I took.

Well, I shot six times, and when I got done shootin', all of them deputies done cleared out from that house, every one of 'em run away from there.

The Spirit of '32. Three striking farmers mimic Archibald Willard's "The Spirit of '76," the popular 1876 painting celebrating the American Revolution. When asked by a reporter how he justified Farm Holiday protest actions that broke the law, one elderly man replied, "Seems to me there was a Tea Party in Boston that was illegal, too."

case. Their movement—reminiscent of Coxey's Army forty years earlier—quickly caught on. Soon 20,000 ex-servicemen were camped out in the capital.

Although the House passed a bonus bill, it was defeated in the Senate. When Congress adjourned, many veterans left town; others stayed, some bringing their families to join them. In late July, the Hoover administration evicted protesters camping in unoccupied government buildings. Two veterans were killed in skirmishes that followed. Using this as an excuse, the administration called out the regular army to force demonstrators out of their main campground. Under the command of General Douglas MacArthur (assisted by Dwight Eisenhower, then a major), cavalry troops, tanks, and soldiers firing tear gas routed the veterans and their families and set fire to their tents.

MacArthur claimed that he had saved the nation from revolution. Hoover, too, defended the assault, asserting that many of the protesters were Communists or "persons with criminal records." Few Americans took seriously the idea that the veterans had threatened the stability of the government. Instead, millions were horrified by the image, reproduced in newspapers and newsreels, of a battle-equipped army pushing out of Washington a ragtag collection of men who had faithfully served their country and were now desperately seeking help. Hoover's already low public standing fell even further. Like

Anacostia flats and flames. The Bonus Marchers' shantytown burns down in sight of the Capitol on the afternoon of July 28, 1932, after federal troops disperse unemployed demonstrators.

Ford, Hoover went from being hailed in the 1920s as a representative of all that was best about America to being widely hated in the 1930s as a symbol of all that was worst.

THE FIRST NEW DEAL

Although most Americans did not join protest movements, the growing evidence of discontent caused many observers to worry that revolution was around the corner. Lorena Hickock, a newspaperwoman hired by the federal government to report on social conditions, wrote that "vast numbers of the unemployed in Pennsylvania are 'right on the edge' . . . it wouldn't take much to make Communists out of them." John Burke, head of the Pulp and Paperworkers' Union, reported in 1933 that he had "never known a time . . . when there has been so much discontent among the working people in our industry." By then it had become common to think that if economic conditions did not soon improve, capitalist democracy would be endangered. AFL president William Green warned in August 1932 that if the country did not "get at the fundamentals in an orderly, constructive way, we shall be swept aside by a tide of revolt."

Even several years into the Depression, some businessmen continued to downplay the crisis. But by 1931 concern was growing in corporate circles, and various business leaders were proposing sweeping recovery programs. Many looked back to the World War I experiment with government-business cooperation for a model. The most widely publicized plan, put forth by Gerald Swope, president of General Electric, called for a system of national planning in which each industry, through a trade association, would standardize products, set prices, and coordinate production. Employers and employees would jointly finance pension and social insurance systems, and a national economic council would provide overall direction.

The two main parties avoided such large-scale proposals during the 1932 presidential campaign. Hoover, running for reelection, concentrated on defending his administration. The Democratic nominee, New York governor Franklin D. Roosevelt, vaguely pledged "a new deal for the American people."

In a massive repudiation of Hoover, Roosevelt easily won, carrying all but six states. Although the Democrats made significant gains among immigrant and working-class voters, Roosevelt's campaign failed to generate much enthusiasm. Roosevelt did not receive a mandate for specific new policies, since he hadn't proposed any. In the South, where Roosevelt won especially strong backing, he was popular with Democratic leaders because they saw him as a party regular, unlikely to lead a popular revolt.

Between Roosevelt's election in November 1932 and his inauguration in March 1933, the economy slid to its lowest point of the entire Depression. Particularly worrisome was a wave of bank failures. In mid-February 1933, to prevent the collapse of banks in Detroit, Michigan's governor ordered all the banks in the state to close for eight days. Depositors elsewhere, fearful that their banks would also collapse or be closed, began withdrawing massive amounts of money. The banks did not have enough liquid assets to cover this sudden flood of withdrawals. In state after state—forty altogether—the authorities were forced to order bank closings. Even the New York Stock Exchange shut down.

Not since Lincoln had a president taken office in such dramatic and difficult circumstances. For Roosevelt, it was a golden opportunity. A master of the radio, he used his inaugural address to assure the nation that "the only thing we have to fear is fear itself." When Hoover made similar pronouncements, they rang hollow, but FDR's enormous self-confidence and his aristocratic, paternal manner calmed the country. Furthermore, Roosevelt launched a whirlwind of activity.

Few programs during the first phase of Roosevelt's presidency— the "first New Deal"—were terribly innovative. Most had been tried in one form or another either during World War I or under former Republican administrations. Together, though, they represented federal action on a scale unprecedented in peacetime. Secretary of the Interior Harold Ickes described the first hundred days of the Roosevelt administration as "a new world. . . . It's like quitting a morgue for the open woods."

Virtually overnight an "alphabet soup" of new agencies sprang up: the AAA, NRA, CCC, FERA, PWA, CWA, FDIC, and so on. Agency heads scrambled to find personnel and office space. Many key New Deal officials were young men and women, just out of law or graduate school, who were given extraordinary responsibility. Other New Dealers were veterans of the Progressive movement or the World War I bureaucracy. Many posts dealing with relief or labor relations were filled by women long active in social reform movements, including Secretary of Labor Frances Perkins, the first female cabinet officer. Bright, energetic, self-confident sometimes to the point of arrogance, the New Dealers improvised solutions to the nation's myriad problems; they also jockeyed for the attention of the president, who liked to play them off against one another.

Throughout his first years in office, Roosevelt could count on congressional cooperation. The same election that brought Roosevelt to power resulted in an unusually liberal Congress. During the "first hundred days" of the Roosevelt administration, Congress passed a flood of legislation to provide immediate relief, promote economic recovery, and strengthen government regulation of the economy. These laws did not reflect any one ideological outlook but rather resulted from pressure from business leaders, politicians, reformers, and the growing mobilization of popular discontent.

Roosevelt's first step was to declare a national "bank holiday," closing all banks; he then called Congress into special session. Although popular anger at the banking system was at such a pitch that Congress was ready to nationalize the banks, the Roosevelt administration proposed a bill that merely empowered the government to lend money to troubled banks, reorganize failed ones, and stop the hoarding of gold. Within a week the government began allowing those banks it found to be solvent to reopen. It quickly became clear that public confidence had been restored; more money was deposited in these banks than withdrawn.

Roosevelt and the Congress then fulfilled two Democratic campaign promises. First, a constitutional amendment ending Prohibition was passed. Second, over protests from veterans' groups, veterans' benefits were slashed and federal salaries lowered. Although later FDR would be thought of as a big spender, during the 1932 campaign he had criticized Hoover for failing to balance the federal budget, a goal to which Roosevelt always remained at least theoretically committed.

Roosevelt's style gave the impression that he had embarked on a bold new course, but his early legislation was actually the program of the most conservative wing of the Democratic Party. Cutting federal

THE BLUE EAGLE SOON APPEARED EVERYWHERE

"We Do Our Part." Three unlikely spots for the display of the otherwise ubiquitous NRA eagle.

spending and encouraging the public to put savings back into banks reduced the amount of money in circulation, further deflating the economy. Roosevelt soon reversed course. In late April, he temporarily took the country off the gold standard, an inflationary measure. Simultaneously, he launched a major relief effort.

To provide funds for the unemployed, Congress, at the president's request, set up the Federal Emergency Relief Administration (FERA), which, over the next three years, spent about $1 billion a year—roughly 2 percent of the national income. The actual distribution of funds was left to the states, but Harry Hopkins, the head of FERA, established federal guidelines. Among other things he insisted that only public agencies receive federal funds, undercutting the leading role private charities historically had played in poor relief.

In spite of Hopkins's efforts, the relief system remained plagued by serious problems. Benefits varied greatly from state to state; monthly payments were ten times higher in New York than in Mississippi. In many localities relief funds were used to provide patronage jobs. Furthermore, although a FERA rule prohibited "discrimination because of race, religion, color, [or] noncitizenship"—an important break with past norms—many state and local agencies favored whites. In 1935 FDR received a letter from Reidville, Georgia, complaining that "they give . . . us black folks . . . nothing but a few cans of pickle meat and to white folks they give blankets, bolts of cloth and things like that." Still, even with its problems, FERA represented an enormous expansion of federal responsibility for the poor and unemployed.

Along with FERA, Congress approved one of Roosevelt's pet projects, the Civilian Conservation Corps (CCC). Like his distant cousin Teddy Roosevelt, FDR believed that outdoor living was morally and physically curative. Accordingly, the New Deal extolled small-town and rural life. The CCC provided temporary jobs to three million young unemployed men while exposing them to rustic living. Under the direction of army officers, CCC volunteers, living in semimilitary camps, constructed recreation facilities and carried out conservation projects. (At the insistence of African-American congressman Oscar DePriest of Chicago, the law establishing the CCC specified that black and white volunteers were to be paid and treated equally. In many southern states, however, whites were given preference for CCC openings, and many CCC camps were segregated.)

During the first hundred days, Congress also realized a longtime goal of Senator George Norris by setting up the Tennessee Valley Authority (TVA) to build dams and hydroelectric plants and promote economic development along the Tennessee River. Other measures provided loans to homeowners unable to pay their mortgages, established the Federal Deposit Insurance Corporation (FDIC) to insure savings accounts, and placed tighter regulations on the stock market and the banking industry. Finally, two laws authorized the administration's major recovery programs, the Agricultural Adjustment Act and the National Industrial Recovery Act.

The principal aim of New Deal agricultural policy was to raise the purchasing power of farmers by restoring "parity," the World War I–era relationship of farm prices to industrial prices. A system of payments was made to farmers who agreed to reduce the size of their crops. New Deal officials argued that just as major industrial companies kept up prices by lowering production, so a reduction in the amount of land under cultivation would force up agricultural prices. To finance farm payments, a tax was placed on food processors, who generally passed it on to consumers. The Agricultural Adjustment Administration (AAA) ran the main farm program. Separate agencies gave out loans at favorable rates to farmers who reduced their planted acreage and aided soil conservation efforts.

Since the planting season had already begun by the time Roosevelt's farm bill was passed, farmers seeking benefit payments had to destroy crops and livestock: 10 million acres of cotton were plowed under and 6 million baby pigs killed. This destruction amid want created a furor, and the whole crop-reduction policy remained highly controversial.

Overall, the AAA was quite successful in achieving its goals. By 1936 gross farm income had risen by one-half and crop prices were higher. (The drought also helped drive up prices.) Large commercial farmers benefited most, since they could make the greatest reductions in their crops and thereby receive the largest government payments. Many large farmers used money from the AAA to retire debts, expand their farms, and purchase new equipment. Smaller farmers did not benefit nearly as much. Still worse off were tenant farmers and sharecroppers.

Legally, landowners were obligated to share crop-reduction payments with tenants and sharecroppers, but they commonly evaded these AAA rules. Furthermore, as the amount of land being cultivated was reduced and cash became available through the crop-reduction program, many landowners stopped renting fields to tenants, forcing them to become sharecroppers or day laborers, or evicted them entirely. This violated AAA regulations, but local officials usually looked the other way.

The impact of the AAA on tenants and sharecroppers led to a new wave of farmer protest. In 1934, sharecroppers and laborers—black and white—working on cotton plantations on the Arkansas side of the Mississippi River organized the Southern Tenant Farmers' Union (STFU). The STFU sought to pressure landowners and Washington officials to stop the widespread eviction of tenants and croppers and give them their fair share of government parity payments. Through its ties to the Socialist Party, the STFU was able to generate considerable favorable national publicity for its policies of nonviolence and interracialism. At the end of its first year, the organization had 10,000 members.

As the STFU grew, planters and local authorities undertook a campaign of beatings, arrests, and shootings against its activists. This reign of terror forced the STFU underground. Nonetheless, in 1936 the union organized strikes of cotton pickers in five states. Black tenant farmers became the union's most ef-

"THE ROPE WAS TIED IN A HANGMAN'S KNOT. . . ."

Robert Reed, a young white Communist Party organizer for the Southern Tenant Farmers' Union, recounts what happened when he and a fellow organizer, Lucien Koch, visited a group of forty to fifty black sharecroppers in a church in Gilmore, Arkansas, in 1934. The union meeting had started with the sharecroppers singing the gospel song "We Shall Not Be Moved," when four armed white men burst in.

THEY started clubbing Lucien, and covered me with guns. They were drunk. . . . They had a rope with them which they dropped on the steps of the church. The rope was tied in a hangman's knot. . . . They took us to the county seat . . . into the offices of the county judge. . . . He was a kindly faced old gentleman, and as much of a racist as anyone I ever saw. They wanted to know our background, where we came from, and why we were in their county, and what were white men doing involved with blacks, though they didn't call them that—they called them "niggers." . . . The old judge questioned us. He told us about how they had a lot of black politicians in Arkansas up until about the turn of the century, and hundreds had been driven into the Mississippi River, and that a lot of lives were lost then, and the whole thing was likely to occur over again if we persisted in the sort of activities we were in. The judge finally said that they were going to escort us back to the Poinsett County line, and that if we came back again, we would be lucky to get off next time with our lives.

Organizing in Arkansas. Black and white farmworkers attend a Southern Tenant Farmers' Union meeting.

fective organizers, using their skill in underground action to counter the planters' repressive tactics.

Some federal officials were deeply sympathetic toward the plight of tenant farmers. But Roosevelt and many of his aides were more concerned about losing support for the New Deal among conservative southern Democrats. In 1935 the Department of Agriculture fired several officials who had sided with tenant farmers. At the same time, to provide some help for poor farmers and farm workers, a new agency was set up, the Resettlement Administration. But without sufficient funding it could do little. Meanwhile, lacking strong support from Washington, the STFU slowly began to buckle under the weight of the forces of repression. While the New Deal benefited well-established farmers, it proved at best a mixed blessing for the rural poor.

The administration's plan for industrial recovery was a compromise hammered out by Roosevelt's advisers after the president came out against a Senate-passed bill, backed by the AFL, that would have limited the workweek to thirty hours in factories producing goods for interstate sale. A shorter workweek, supporters of the bill argued, would create new jobs and give labor a larger share of the fruits of mechanization. Roosevelt's substitute, the National Industrial Recovery Act (NIRA), instead allowed businesses to regulate themselves while the government provided jobs for the unemployed.

One section of the NIRA set up a major public works program to increase employment and stimulate the economy. Over $3 billion was appropriated for the construction of bridges, roads, dams, and other projects, to be administered by the Public Works Administration (PWA). In 1930 the federal government had spent less than one-tenth that amount on public works. Another agency, the Civil Works Administration (CWA), provided immediate employment on short-term projects. Designed primarily to help the unemployed get through the winter of 1933–34, the CWA gave jobs to over four million people before being disbanded.

The other main section of the NIRA authorized what was, in effect, a government-sanctioned system of business self-regulation to be coordinated by the National Recovery Administration (NRA). For each industry, a detailed code would spell out permissible production and marketing practices in an effort to end cutthroat competition,

"... A REAL MOTHER TO THE NATION"

Millions of Americans felt a close personal bond with Franklin and Eleanor Roosevelt. In letters sent to the White House, they recounted their personal troubles and expressed their gratitude to the President and First Lady. Below are excerpts from letters addressed to Eleanor Roosevelt. The first correspondent begged for a loan to buy baby clothes; the others praised the Roosevelts in strikingly religious terms.

Jan. 2, 1935
Troy, New York

Dear Mrs. Roosevelt,

About a month ago I wrote you asking if you would buy some baby clothes for me with the understanding that I was to repay you as soon as my husband got enough work. Several weeks later I received a reply to apply to a Welfare Association so I might receive the aid I needed. Do you remember?

Please Mrs. Roosevelt, I do not want charity, only a chance from someone who will trust me until we can get enough money to repay the amount spent for the things I need. As a proof that I really am sincere, I am sending you two of my dearest possessions to keep as security, a ring my husband gave me before we were married, and a ring my mother used to wear. Perhaps the actual value of them is not high, but they are worth a lot to me. If you will consider buying the baby clothes, please keep them until I send you the money you spend. It is very hard to face bearing a baby we cannot afford to have, and the fact that it is due to arrive soon, and still there is no money for the hospital or clothing, does not make it any easier. . . .

eliminate overproduction, increase industrial efficiency, and raise prices, profits, and wages. The codes were to be written and administered largely by the affected businesses themselves through their trade associations. The government, consumers, and labor were also to be involved.

To win labor support, Section 7a of the NIRA required, at least in theory, that "employees shall have the right to organize and bargain collectively through representatives of their own choosing ... free from the interference, restraint, or coercion of employers." Employers were forbidden to require their employees to join company unions or sign yellow-dog contracts. In addition, individual industry codes or the president could set maximum working hours and minimum wages.

General Hugh Johnson, picked by Roosevelt to head the NRA, used many of the propaganda techniques developed during World War I to turn the recovery effort into a national crusade. Companies that agreed to cooperate with the NRA were allowed to display a blue eagle. Parades, speeches, and posters urged the public to spend money only where the blue eagle was displayed. Meanwhile, in industry after industry, code writing got under way.

Throughout the country, the impact of the New Deal was felt directly by millions of people. For some it meant a job or relief or farm benefit payments. For others it meant knowing that their savings were protected by federal insurance. Businesses, farmers, and homeowners all got access to badly needed credit through federal loan payments.

A "New Deal for Indians," centered around the Indian Reorganization Act of 1934, offered hope to Native American peoples. John Collier, FDR's newly appointed commissioner of Indian affairs, set out to transform the relationship between the federal government and Na-

---

Ridley Park, Pennsylvania
9/1/34

Dear Mrs. Roosevelt.

I was delighted but I dont believe I was very much surprised when I received your letter. Just to look at your picture and that of our President seems to me like looking at the picture of a saint. So when you answered my letter and promised to have some one help me it only proved you are our own Mrs. Roosevelt. I have told everyone what you done for me. I want them to know you are not too busy to answer our letters and give us what help and advice you can. You hold the highest place any woman can hold still you are not to[o] proud to befriend the poorer class. ... Thank you and God bless you both.

Nov. 25, 1934
Arkansas City, Kansas

Dear Madam:

I beg to inform you that I have been reading your writings in the Wichita *Beacon* and I must say that the whole nation should be enthused over them. I was especially carried away with the one on Old Age Pensions. It brought my mind back to the day of the Chicago Convention, when Mr. Roosevelt was nominated for the presidency.

In our little home in Arkansas City, my family and I were sitting around the radio ... and when he spoke it seems as though some Moses had come to alleviate us of our sufferings. Strange to say when he was speaking to see the moisten eyes and the deep feeling of emotions that gave vent to every word and when you spoke then we knew that the white house would be filled with a real mother to the nation.

tive Americans. Collier reversed the policy established by the 1887 Dawes Act of dividing up tribal lands and abolishing tribes as legal entities; over 7 million acres of tribal lands were ultimately restored to Native American control. Tribes were incorporated as federally recognized governments, with democratically elected leaders. Collier also pushed for the restoration of traditional Native American cultural expression, including ancient dances and religious practices that had been discouraged or banned under the Dawes Act. Despite such enlightened policies, many Indians, especially traditional tribal leaders, remained suspicious of the government's motives. Most Native American people remained poor and their tribal lands badly used, as they had been for decades.

This response notwithstanding, the tremendous popularity of the New Deal became evident in the 1934 congressional elections. In the Senate, the Democrats won nine new seats, giving them well over a two-thirds majority. In the House, the Republicans were left with less than a quarter of the seats, the lowest percentage since the party had been founded. Most of the newly elected Democratic senators and representatives were strong backers of the New Deal; if anything they sought more radical measures.

A modest economic recovery during the early years of the Roosevelt administration helped the Democrats. But the popularity of the New Deal had an important personal dimension as well: millions of Americans felt that FDR and his wife, Eleanor, truly cared about them. They wrote thousands of letters to the White House to recount their personal troubles or to express gratitude.

Roosevelt and the New Deal were not popular everywhere. By 1934 many businessmen were growing critical of Roosevelt, while movements demanding more drastic action were gaining strength. Communists, Socialists, and many liberals disapproved of the NRA, which they felt had handed far too much power to the very businessmen whose practices had led to the Depression. Some even feared that the Roosevelt administration was moving toward fascism. Still, after two years in office Roosevelt had won remarkably broad and deep backing.

THE REVIVAL OF ORGANIZED LABOR

Before the Depression, unions were clustered in a few industries: coalmining, construction, railroads, garment manufacturing, and public utilities. Open-shop drives, unfavorable court decisions, postwar prosperity, and company unionism had effectively blocked organizing efforts in other fields.

Labor's problems were compounded by the collapse of the economy. As unemployment rose, union membership dropped sharply; by early 1933 it had fallen below 3 million, to less than 10 percent of the national workforce—a situation comparable to the early years of the century. Even well-established unions were devastated. In 1933, for instance, there were only 583,000 unionized construction workers, down from 919,000 four years earlier. The number of walkouts also fell during the early Depression years, to the lowest level of the century. With unemployment so high, few workers were willing to risk their jobs by going on strike. Union leaders became extremely cautious.

In 1933, however, workers suddenly and dramatically turned toward collective action as the number of strikes jumped sharply and unions launched organizing drives in industry after industry. Anger had been building among workers since the Depression began. Pay cuts, hour reductions, speedups, and layoffs caused widespread discontent. Many workers particularly resented the tremendous power foremen and supervisors held over their lives. Often workers who had relatives or friends in management or who gave presents or kickbacks to supervisors kept their jobs while more senior employees were laid off. At the same time, many companies reduced or eliminated their benefit programs. GE, for example, stopped paying bonuses to workers with good attendance records, eliminated paid vacations for blue-collar workers, and stopped subsidizing home mortgages. "Welfare capitalism" had been promoted as an alternative to unionism. When companies eliminated benefits that their employees had come to see as their due, an implicit agreement between the workforce and management was broken.

The catalyst that turned discontent into action was Section 7a of the NIRA. Although Section 7a was only a vague statement of policy, it had enormous psychological and political impact. The NIRA enabled union organizers to portray joining a union as a patriotic contribution to the national recovery effort. This was important because during the 1920s unions often had been portrayed as un-American. Furthermore, many workers had experienced government repression of their unions after World War I; Section 7a gave workers confidence that they could organize without government interference.

Organizing efforts were aided by management hesitancy about instituting harsh antiunion measures. Confused and demoralized by the Depression, Roosevelt's election, and the tenor of Congress, businessmen were no longer sure that they could count on government backing. Although many companies continued to use scabs, spies, and wholesale firings to crush unions, others avoided provocative action. Sensing this change of mood, workers became less fearful of collective action.

One of the first signs of labor's revival was the virtual rebirth of the United Mine Workers of America, which had been decimated by

Steel strike, October 1933. Armed with shotguns and machine guns, steel company private police fire on pickets outside the Spang-Chalfant Tube factory in Ambridge, Pennsylvania. One striker was killed and fifteen were wounded.

the coal industry's chronic slump and the Depression. In February 1933, a UMWA member reported that "as far as West Kentucky is concerned there is no sign of organization . . . you could not organize a *baseball team*." But once it became clear that the NIRA would be passed, the miners' union gambled its remaining resources on a lightning organizing campaign, throwing a hundred organizers into the field. Organizers leaned heavily on patriotism and President Roosevelt's popularity. A circular distributed in Kentucky claimed that the NIRA "recommends that coal miners . . . organize in a union of their own choosing." Some leaflets stretched the truth even further, stating, "The President wants you to join the union."

The response was tremendous. By June 17, the day after Roosevelt signed the NIRA, 80 percent of Ohio miners had signed union cards. The miners "organized themselves for all practical purposes," UMWA veteran John Brophy observed. Backed by his swelling membership and the close ties he had carefully developed to the Roosevelt administration, UMWA chief John L. Lewis pressed the mine operators to accept the union's proposals for the NRA code covering the bituminous coal industry. A series of wildcat strikes added to the pressure. In September 1933 the operators gave in, accepting a code that raised wages, reduced variations in pay among different parts of the country, outlawed child labor, established the eight-hour day and the five-day week, gave miners the right to select their own check-weighman, and banned the use of scrip for wage payments. Almost overnight the UMWA had reversed the balance of power in the coal industry and achieved many of its long-standing goals.

The two principal garment unions, the Amalgamated Clothing Workers (ACW) and the International Ladies' Garment Workers' Union (ILGWU), which had fallen on hard times during the late 1920s, also rebuilt their memberships and won important employer concessions immediately following the passage of the NIRA. In the summer of 1933 the two unions launched a series of strikes designed to increase their influence in the NRA code-writing process, win back former members, and sign up new ones. The largest effort mobilized 60,000 New York dressmakers.

During World War I the ACW had benefited greatly from government regulation of the clothing industry. Sidney Hillman, the union's president, though critical of many aspects of the NIRA, saw it as a chance to repeat the ACW's previous success. Hillman used his connections to key New Deal officials (he served on the NRA Labor Advisory Board) to win favorable labor provisions in the NRA garment codes. Coupled with successful strikes and organizing drives, this brought more than 200,000 new members to the needle trade unions.

Other unions made more modest gains in the aftermath of the passage of the NIRA. For instance, leaders of the Pulp and Paperworkers' Union, an old-line AFL union, did not launch an all-out organizing crusade. Workers flocked to the union anyway. "I have so many calls for organizers," the union's president declared, "that I have neither the men nor the money to take care of all of them." By the end of 1933, the union's membership was double what it had been before FDR's inauguration.

At the same time that existing unions were taking on new life, workers were organizing new ones, especially in the basic manufacturing industries and in agriculture. The new unions usually were local units covering one plant or mill or city, but they soon formed ties with one another. Some were organized by local AFL officials or by rank-and-file workers themselves. Others were started by organizers from left-wing or nationalist groups.

Mexican agricultural workers in California, for example, did not wait for the NIRA or the AFL (which had systematically barred them from membership in the past) to begin to unionize. Mexican farm laborers, many born in the United States, were crucial to the dramatic post–World War I expansion of California's commercial agriculture. By 1930, three of every four of the state's 200,000 agricultural workers

Cotton strike, October 1933. After Pixley and Arvin, California, cotton growers opened fire on unarmed Mexican pickers, killing three, strikers demanded that local police take action. Instead, authorities issued additional gun permits to growers and appointed many as deputies. Eventually, several growers in the Pixley incident were prosecuted for murder (and later acquitted by a friendly jury), while a strike leader was charged with criminal syndicalism.

were Mexicans. As early as 1927, Mexican workers in Southern California had organized the Confederación de Uniones Obreros Mexicanos (CUOM), patterned after the union movement in Mexico and animated by anarchosyndicalist and socialist ideals.

Concerted efforts by California businessmen, politicians, and some craft unionists to deport Mexicans in response to growing unemployment failed to intimidate Mexican agricultural workers. Nearly 50,000 workers, the vast majority Mexican, undertook nearly forty strikes between April and December 1933, affecting almost all of the major crops in the state. In June, for example, 1,500 Mexican berry pickers employed by small Japanese ranchers in El Monte, a Los Angeles suburb, went out on strike for higher wages. Daily mass meetings and efforts to spread the strike to surrounding agricultural communities abounded, encouraged by Mexican and Anglo organizers from the Communist Party. The El Monte strikers were soon joined by 5,000 celery fieldworkers (including a sizable number of Japanese and Filipinos) in Santa Monica and Culver City, near Los Angeles. In July the strikers organized the Confederación de Uniones de Campesinos y Obreros Mexicanos (CUCOM), a nationalist union with ties to Mexico and the earlier CUOM. By the end of the year,

CUCOM boasted fifty member unions and as many as 10,000 members. Concerned about the growing influence of Communist organizers, California governor James Rolph and the Mexican and Japanese consuls encouraged the growers to settle with CUCOM. A July agreement called for a modest wage increase, although the growers refused to recognize the union.

The year 1934 brought a series of strikes in the fruit and vegetable fields across California, from the Imperial Valley on the Mexican border to Santa Clara Valley near San Francisco. These strikes were led by Mexican workers (but also involved Filipino, Anglo, and even some African-American farm laborers) organized into a series of local unions; Communist Party organizers for the Cannery and Agricultural Workers' Industrial Union also played a key role. Many strikes ended in violence and defeat. In the Imperial Valley, for example, local and state police tear-gassed union meetings, forcibly evicted over 2,000 strikers and their families, and burned workers' homes; two Mexican strikers (including a child) were killed; and many strike leaders, including several Communists, were arrested, tried, and sentenced to jail terms. It would be a generation before another unionizing drive succeeded in improving the lot of California agricultural workers.

Post-NIRA unionizing efforts among urban industrial workers generally enjoyed more lasting results. In Akron, Ohio, Wilmer Tate, the head of a small machinists' local, set out with several friends ten days after the passage of the NIRA to organize his city's rubber workers. Their leaflets proclaimed that "President Roosevelt has given you the chance to organize a union without interference from the rubber bosses." Five thousand rubber workers showed up at the first meeting Tate called. By November 1933, union membership in the Akron area had gone from 400 to 30,000.

In Akron and elsewhere, the workers flooding into the labor movement presented a problem for the leaders of the AFL. The skilled trades unions—the electricians, plumbers, and sheet metal workers, for example—wanted to enroll craftsmen in the large industrial plants. But what should they do with the much larger body of semi-skilled operatives? If the International Association of Machinists or the International Brotherhood of Electrical Workers were to admit all the operatives employed in the auto assembly or the radio manufacturing plants, their skilled memberships would be overwhelmed and might lose control of their organizations. But where else could the industrial workers be placed?

Many craft unions responded to this dilemma by simply not trying to organize the basic industries. For the basic industry workers who were signed up, the AFL formed federal locals to represent them on an industrial basis until they could be divided up among the craft unions. These federal locals were run directly by the AFL, with the federation making decisions on local union structures, constitutions, and even on whether to strike. The AFL opposed efforts by federal locals to assert their independence or to engage in broader industrial union struggles.

As a result, several new unions sprang up completely outside the AFL. In New York, for instance, a small group of Communist organizers and rank-and-file transit workers founded the independent Transport Workers' Union (TWU). In other cases, such as in the steel industry, union activists organized locals formally affiliated with AFL unions but that acted independently, defying national leaders. Also, many workers became increasingly active in company unions, trying, sometimes with considerable success, to turn them into bona fide labor organizations.

Many of those who helped organize the new unions were experienced, skilled workers who had had previous contact with the union movement either in the United States or the British Isles. The leading unionist at Cleveland's White Motor Company, for instance, was Wyndham Mortimer, who had begun working in Pennsylvania coalmines at age twelve; at various times he had joined the UMWA, and IWW, and a railroad brotherhood. A lathe operator long interested in socialism and close to the Communist Party, Mortimer, with a small group of fellow workers, launched a drive in 1932 to unionize their plant. Initially spurned by the AFL, they began signing up workers for the Auto Workers' Union, led by the Communist Party. When AFL leaders then became interested, Mortimer's group accepted an AFL federal charter. Union membership in the plant grew, and in the spring of 1934, after threatening a strike, the new union won a wage increase.

Clarence Irwin, the president of a new AFL local at the Brier Hill works of Youngstown Sheet and Tube Company, was forty-two years old in 1934. He had worked in the steel industry for twenty-eight years, had belonged to the AFL since 1910, and had been active in the 1919 strike. A skilled roller, he was married, had three children, and was a longtime Democrat. Most other leaders of new steel locals, he noted, were also "middle-aged family men, well paid, and of Anglo-Saxon origin."

Joining such older skilled workers at the forefront of the new unions were many young workers who had been forced into humble positions by the Depression. For instance, Douglas Lincoln Mac-Mahon, the son of a Brooklyn real-estate broker, lost his Wall Street job when the stock market crashed. After taking an unskilled maintenance job in the New York City subways, he began reading socialist literature, trying to understand what had happened to him and the country. Within a few years he joined the Communist Party and became a top officer of the TWU. Similarly, James Carey, the first president of the United Electrical Workers, had attended college at night, hoping to become an electrical engineer. But during the Depression he was transferred from a laboratory job at Philco Radio in Philadelphia to factory work. Soon he was leading a union group that successfully struck for company recognition.

Most of the new unions of the 1930s emerged in industries that employed few women. Electrical equipment manufacturing companies were an exception; they employed a large number of female workers. The pioneer male unionists in the industry tended to be highly skilled, relatively well-paid workers, many of whom had emigrated from the British Isles in the early 1920s. The women activists typically were less skilled and younger. Many came from union households, often the children of eastern or southern European immigrants.

Building new industrial unions, of course, required more than a core of able and enthusiastic activists; the mass of workers, historically divided along ethnic, racial, sexual, craft, and political lines, had to be won over. Several changes in American life since World War I facilitated this.

First, the working class had become more homogeneous. By the early 1930s, immigration had been slowed for nearly two decades; the proportion of foreign-born men and women in the workforce had declined, while their children had become an increasingly significant presence. Second-generation workers generally spoke English. Also, as a result of the impact of mass culture and the Americanization campaigns during and after World War I, they were less tied than their parents to their particular ethnic groups.

Second, Fordism, and mechanization generally, tended to narrow the range of industrial skills. Although tensions remained between skilled craftsmen and less skilled workers, they were not as sharp as earlier. Semiskilled machine operators played a particularly important role in the rise of the new unions.

Finally, both the corporate welfare plans of the 1920s and the Depression itself had strengthened workers' identification with particular companies. Workers had grown more reluctant than in the past to quit their jobs; when dissatisfied with conditions, they increasingly saw the solution not in looking for a better job but in improving the one they had.

By the middle of 1934, the industrial union movement was exploding. New unions were popping up across the country, and strikes were becoming more frequent. A temporary improvement in economic conditions contributed to unionists' growing confidence. Three dramatic strikes were a sign of how far things had come and how far they might go.

Toledo, Ohio, was a major center for automobile parts manufacturing. In the summer of 1933 workers from several parts plants were
swept up in a wave of enthusiasm for unionism, organizing an AFL
federal local. The next February, 4,000 Toledo autoworkers struck.
After six days the strike was settled with a modest wage hike and an
agreement to negotiate other issues. But when one large company,
Electric Auto-Lite, spurned negotiations, the walkout resumed. This
time the employers hired scabs and kept their plants operating.

Just as the strike began faltering, a local unemployed group, affiliated with the socialist American Workers' Party, joined the struggle,
throwing up mass picket lines in defiance of a court injunction. On
May 23, when the local sheriff and special deputies paid by Auto-Lite
arrested several picket leaders and beat an old man, the "Battle of
Toledo" erupted. For seven hours a crowd of 10,000 blockaded Auto-
Lite, preventing the strikebreakers inside from leaving. Deputies used
tear gas, water hoses, and occasional gunfire in an effort to clear the
crowd, which responded by stoning the plant and burning cars in its
parking lot.

The next day the National Guard was called in, but fighting resumed. Even the killing of two protesters by the National Guard
failed to break the strike. Finally, the troops' commander ordered the
plant shut. After two weeks of federal mediation, an agreement was
reached providing for recognition of the union, a higher minimum
wage, and the 5 percent pay hike.

Simultaneously, an even more dramatic struggle unfolded in Minneapolis. In February 1934, Teamsters' Union Local 574—several of
whose leaders were followers of the dissident, exiled Russian Communist leader Leon Trotsky—conducted a short, meticulously
planned strike, including efforts to involve the city's unemployed,
that won union contracts from most of the city's coal delivery companies. Seeing this, all kinds of truckers and warehousemen poured into
Local 574. On May 15, after their employers all but ignored the local's
demands, 5,000 truckdrivers and warehousemen walked off their jobs.

To prepare for the strike, the union rented a large garage equipped
with sleeping, meeting, and eating facilities, a makeshift hospital,
and a center for dispatching "cruising picket squads." The Ladies'
Auxiliary of unionists' relatives was set up to support the strikers. For
several days the walkout remained peaceful, but on May 19 the Citizens' Alliance (a secretive businessmen's group) and the police lured
a group of picketers into an alley and beat them with nightsticks and
leather saps.

Two days later the union sprang an ambush of its own. Over 1,500
pickets armed with clubs, pipes, and bats, converged on the city's central market, routing the assembled police and 1,000 deputies recruited by the Citizens' Alliance to transport food. The union

emerged victorious again the next day in another full-scale battle at the market in which two Citizens' Alliance supporters, including a prominent Minneapolis businessman, were killed.

Under pressure from Minnesota governor Floyd Olson, a compromise settlement was reached. But in July a dispute over the agreement led to another strike. This time it was the strikers who took the heaviest casualties: two strikers were killed and several dozen wounded by police gunfire. The National Guard was called out, but the union hung on. After five weeks and with federal pressure for a settlement increasing, the employers finally surrendered and signed a contract.

In Toledo and Minneapolis, unionists had talked about escalating their struggles into general strikes. In San Francisco such a mass walkout actually occurred, the outgrowth of a fierce battle on the city's waterfront. In the early 1930s a new local of the International Longshoremen's Association (ILA), led by Harry Bridges, an Australian-born longshoreman who worked closely with the Communist Party, rapidly signed many new members. From the start Bridges and his colleagues had to battle not only the employers but also the corrupt, conservative national leaders of the East Coast–based ILA.

In the spring of 1934, a threatened West Coast longshoremen's strike was called off at the request of FDR. Top ILA leaders then secretly negotiated an agreement with the employers. But the agree-

Tear-gas attack. Strikers battle police during the San Francisco general strike, July 1934.

ment fell far short of rank-and-file demands for a shorter workweek, higher pay, union recognition, and union-run hiring halls to replace the "shape-ups" by which individual dockworkers were hired. Defying the national ILA leadership, the San Francisco longshoremen struck on May 9. They were soon joined by dockworkers in every other West Coast port except Los Angeles. Sailors and waterfront truckers also stopped work. From Seattle to San Diego, 40,000 maritime workers walked out in the largest maritime strike the country had yet seen.

After nearly two months, the employers realized that the strike would not collapse on its own. So on July 3 they used police and scabs in an effort to resume work. A fierce battle resulted. On "Bloody Thursday," July 5, two strikers were shot and killed by police; scores more were seriously hurt.

Outraged, workers throughout San Francisco called for a general strike. Local union officials, worried that they were about to lose control of the city's labor movement to radicals, reluctantly went along. By July 16, San Francisco was at a virtual standstill, as 130,000 workers—including trolley drivers, construction workers, teamsters, bartenders, even entertainers—walked off their jobs. Oakland, Berkeley, and other nearby municipalities were shut down as well.

The general strike was short-lived. Local businessmen, newspapers, and government officials maneuvered furiously to split the ranks of labor, denouncing the longshoremen's leaders as dangerous radicals while egging on vigilante groups that destroyed the offices of the Communist Party and several allied organizations. The NRA's Hugh Johnson joined in, calling the strike a "bloody insurrection." Under this pressure, the General Strike Committee each day allowed more workers to return to work. On July 19, the committee called off the general strike. With their backing gone, the striking waterfront unions were forced to accept arbitration. But in October an arbitration decision granted the longshoremen

---

"... LABOR WAS IN CONTROL"

The following description of the San Francisco general strike was written by "rank-and-file journalist" Mike Quin.

THE paralysis was effective beyond all expectations. To all intents and purposes industry was at a complete standstill. The great factories were empty and deserted. No streetcars were running. Virtually all stores were closed. The giant apparatus of commerce was a lifeless, helpless hulk.

Labor had withdrawn its hand. The workers had drained out of the shops and plants like life-blood, leaving only a silent framework embodying millions of dollars worth of invested capital. In the absence of labor, the great machinery loomed as so much idle junk. . . .

Everything was there, all intact as the workers had left it—instruments, equipment, tools, machinery, raw materials and the buildings themselves. When the men walked out, they took only what belonged to them—their labor. And when they took that they might as well have taken everything, because all the elaborate apparatus they left behind was worthless and meaningless without their hand. The machinery was a mere extension of labor, created by and dependent upon labor.

Labor held the life-blood and energy. The oners remained in possession of the corpse.

Highways leading into the city bristled with picket lines. Nothing moved except by permission of the strike committee. Labor was in control. . . .

Popeye versus the Goon. During 1933–34, readers of E. C. Segar's comic strip were introduced to the Goons, powerful, mindless servants of the sailor's nemesis, the horrible Sea Hag. The name was soon applied to violent strikebreakers who patrolled the San Francisco waterfront.

union recognition, hiring halls that the union could effectively control, a thirty-hour workweek, and a pay increase.

The Toledo, Minneapolis, and San Francisco strikes had certain common features. In each case Socialists and Communists, defying conservative AFL leaders, played a key role in mobilizing thousands of working people in concerted, militant action. Workers developed innovative tactics and countered force with force. And when employers and police launched attacks, moderate unionists came to the aid of the strikers. The strikes ended in compromises, but each laid the bases for future gains: Toledo unionists soon played a major role in the creation of the United Automobile Workers' Union; the leaders of the Minneapolis strikes went on to organize long-distance truckers throughout the Midwest, contributing to the phenomenal growth of the Teamsters' Union; and the San Francisco strike led to the formation of the International Longshoremen and Warehousemen's Union and the growth of maritime unionism up and down the Pacific Coast.

Labor's accomplishments in Toledo, Minneapolis, and San Francisco were not the whole story by any means. After the employers' initial shock over Section 7a had worn off, executives in steel, auto, rubber, and a host of other industries followed a two-pronged strategy to forestall unionization: they established or revived company unions to channel worker discontent in nonthreatening directions, and they vigorously resisted organizing drives. The largest strike of 1934, which occurred in September, when 376,000 textile workers walked off their jobs, turned into a terrible defeat for labor.

The textile industry had been devastated by the Depression. Unemployment was widespread, and shortened workweeks were common. Wages were so low that malnutrition and disease were common in textile workers' families. Child labor was extensive, and thousands of families had to live in decaying company housing. But the millworkers' loudest complaint was of "stretch-outs," the assigning of more and more looms to each worker until the pace of work became unbearable.

After the NRA textile codes were written, wage rates were supposed to be higher, working hours shorter, and child labor prohibited. But because the board that enforced the code was controlled by the textile employers, workers' hopes for better lives were soon dashed. Some employers simply violated the code, while others further sped up work to compensate for higher wages. Furthermore, to eliminate overproduction, in late 1933 the NRA began ordering textile mills to operate only part-time, drastically cutting workers' earnings.

For textile workers, Section 7a also proved hollow. Soon after the passage of the NIRA, textile workers poured into the United Textile Workers' Union, which grew from 50,000 members in 1933 to

300,000 in mid-1934. But millowners fired some 4,000 union members while NRA officials looked the other way.

The 1934 textile strike was the millhands' protest against the betrayal of the millowners and New Deal officials. The strike, which stretched from Maine to Alabama, initially crippled production in every major textile center. But the employers—who saw the walkout as an opportunity to crush unionism once and for all—hired spies and thugs, and convinced local authorities to evict strikers from company housing and cut them off relief. In state after state, governors called up the National Guard to aid the millowners. Violent incidents were common, with the death toll of picketers quickly mounting.

To settle the strike, Roosevelt appointed a board of inquiry. The union was willing to accept arbitration, but the employers stood pat. By the second week of the strike, many southern mills, protected by troops, resumed production. After three weeks, the union leadership, without consulting the membership, called off the strike. Some 15,000 strikers were not rehired, and union membership plummeted.

The textile union never fully recovered. Later in the decade, when unions triumphed in industry after industry, southern textile mills remained largely nonunion. Textile workers continued to live in misery, while the growth of organized labor throughout the South was retarded. The entire labor movement was weakened as a result. Furthermore, southern politics remained largely unaffected by the liberal influence unionism had elsewhere, a fact that shaped national politics for decades to come.

THE COLLAPSE OF THE FIRST NEW DEAL

Between 1933 and 1934, as a result of the New Deal, national income rose by one-quarter, unemployment dropped by 2 million, and factory wages rose. Still, national income was only slightly more than half of what it had been in 1929, 10 million workers were without jobs, and almost twice that many people were at least partially dependent on relief. Furthermore, the recovery was stalled. Secretary of the Treasury Henry Morgenthau, Jr., frankly admitted that "we are not making any headway."

With the economy stagnating, criticism of the Roosevelt administration grew. Many businessmen feared growing government intervention in the economy. Labor leaders were disappointed by the administration's halfhearted support. And a series of mass movements were demanding radical action to end the Depression and redistribute the nation's wealth. The NRA came under particularly fierce attack; writing and enforcing industry codes had brought to the surface sharp conflicts among competing interests.

For labor, the NRA provided only limited benefits. Although Section 7a gave unionism a tremendous boost in morale, only a few unions won significant say in shaping specific industry codes. Furthermore, the implementation of Section 7a was much disputed. In August 1933, the tripartite National Labor Board (NLB) was set up under the NRA to help resolve labor conflicts. The board established an important precedent when it ruled that if employees so requested, employers were obligated to hold secret ballot elections to determine who would represent workers in negotiations; the organization that won a majority of votes would have the exclusive right to represent all employees.

This system of government-sponsored elections to determine exclusive bargaining agents, which unions hailed as a major step forward, was soon undermined in two ways. First, when various companies defied the National Labor Board, it became clear that the board had only limited authority to enforce its orders. Second, some industries, such as auto and textile, were not covered by the NLB but by special boards. These boards often refused to hold exclusive-representation elections. In resolving a dispute in the automobile industry, FDR himself ruled that if several organizations claimed to represent workers in an auto plant, each could have representatives on a committee that would bargain with the employer. Unionists bitterly resented this decision, which they felt would all but destroy collective bargaining. When New York senator Robert Wagner tried to shore up the National Labor Board by introducing a comprehensive labor bill, it failed to win administration support and died. By 1935, disgruntled workers were calling the NRA the "National Run Around."

Many farmers, small businessmen, and consumer groups were also disillusioned with the National Recovery Administration. NRA price and production controls, they argued, had been written primarily by and for large corporations; their effect was to keep up prices, stifle competition, and retard economic expansion. Even corporate leaders began to doubt the value of the NRA. Section 7a, weak as it was, added to their labor problems. Furthermore, they feared that the growing debate over corporate influence on the recovery agency might lead to revised regulations that would limit their freedom to act.

Business criticism of the NRA spilled over into general criticism of the New Deal. Most businessmen opposed federal deficit spending, fearing it would undermine the economy and lead to higher taxes. They also worried about the effects of government relief efforts. "Five Negroes on my place in South Carolina refused to work this spring," complained retired DuPont vice president R. R. M. Carpenter to his friend John J. Raskob, a DuPont executive and adviser to Al Smith. "A cook on my houseboat at Fort Myers," he continued, "quit because the government was paying him a dollar an hour as a painter."

As time went on, more and more business leaders blamed the economy's ills on government functionaries, labor leaders, and individual "chiselers." Government power and budgets, they insisted, had to be reduced drastically, while business should be given a greater voice in setting national policy. To promote this view, in the summer of 1934 Raskob, Pierre DuPont, and GM chairman Alfred P. Sloan resigned from Roosevelt's Business Advisory Council and founded the American Liberty League. The league represented the most reactionary, anti-Roosevelt wing of the business community. Although it attracted many corporate leaders, it failed miserably in its well-financed effort to become a mass movement that included farmers, workers, and other groups. Still, by mid-1934 even moderate businessmen were turning against Roosevelt.

At the very time that many businessmen were criticizing the government for doing too much, a variety of mass movements were winning wide support by attacking the government for doing too little. While promoting diverse ideologies and programs, these movements all tapped a growing sense among working-class and middle-class Americans that the New Deal had failed to confront the economic crisis successfully.

The most prominent southern critic of the New Deal was Louisiana senator Huey Long, who rose to power by attacking corporate interests and portraying himself as the champion of the common man. Elected governor in 1928, he completely dominated Louisiana's government. Under Long, Louisiana built hundreds of schools, hospitals, and bridges, paved thousands of miles of roads, distributed free textbooks and increased taxes on oil and gas interests.

Long supported FDR in 1932, when Long himself won election to the Senate, but he soon broke with the president. Long criticized the New Deal both for creating huge bureaucracies that interfered in local affairs and for failing to curb the power of the rich. In 1934 he proposed the "Share Our Wealth Plan," a system of confiscatory

"EV'RY MAN A KING . . ."

Like Roosevelt, Huey Long was a master of radio. He also saw the political possibilities of other popular media. In 1935 he teamed up with Louisiana State University band director Castro Carazo to write a song about sharing the nation's wealth. Long announced that if he ran for president "Every Man a King" would be one of his campaign songs, and he arranged to have it recorded for presentation on a national newsreel service by a well-known band, Ina Ray Hutton and Her All-Girl Orchestra.

Why weep or slumber America
Land of brave and true
With castles and clothing and food for all
All belongs to you
Ev'ry man a King, ev'ry man a King
For you can be a millionaire
But there's something belonging to others
There's enough for all people to share
When it's sunny June and December too
Or in the Winter time or Spring
There'll be peace without end
Ev'ry neighbor a friend
With ev'ry man a King

Inauguration. Huey Long takes the presidential oath of office in an illustration from his *My First Days in the White House*. In his fantasy, Long instituted a range of social and fiscal reforms, aided by a National Share Our Wealth Committee composed of cooperative bankers and industrialists, and assembled a distinguished cabinet—including Franklin Delano Roosevelt as secretary of the navy. The book was published in 1935, shortly after Long's assassination.

taxes on large fortunes and incomes that would enable the government to provide every family with "enough for a home, an automobile, a radio, and the ordinary conveniences" plus a guaranteed annual income. Setting up thousands of "Share Our Wealth Clubs," Long developed a large national following.

Other critics of the New Deal took their cues from Charles E. Coughlin, a Catholic priest from the suburbs of Detroit. Coughlin's weekly radio broadcasts reached an audience of 30 million to 45 million listeners. Like Long, Coughlin initially supported Roosevelt but then grew disillusioned. Though vehemently anticommunist, Coughlin blamed the Depression on "Wall Street" and "international bankers." Inflationary monetary policy, he believed, would lead to recovery. More broadly, Coughlin promoted "social Catholicism," a call for class harmony, "living wages," and social legislation to combat the evils of industrialism. Increasingly influenced by European fascism and anti-Semitism, Coughlin was soon calling for government control over production, profits, working conditions, and unions.

On the West Coast, Francis Townsend, an elderly doctor from Long Beach, California, proposed that every citizen over sixty who was not working receive $200 a month from the government "on the condition that they spend the money as they get it." These pensions, to be financed by a national sales tax, would pump money into the economy and, by encouraging retirements, open up jobs for the young. At least 10 million people signed petitions in support of Townsend's plan, and 2 million mostly elderly Americans joined 7,000 Townsend clubs.

Townsend, Coughlin, and Long capitalized on popular discontent with the Depression and the unequal distribution of wealth and power. But in spite of their attacks on the rich, they all firmly rejected social ownership of the means of production, the basic socialist tenet. Instead, they combined nostalgia for an older, more community-based way of life with simple plans that they claimed would solve all social ills. The possibility that the Long, Coughlin, and Townsend movements might join forces and enter national politics in 1936 deeply worried Roosevelt and his advisers.

Administration leaders also were concerned about the impressive electoral achievements of left-liberal alliances in several states. In California, the novelist Upton Sinclair resigned from the Socialist Party in 1933 to form the End-Poverty-In-California (EPIC) movement within the Democratic Party. Sinclair called for "Production for Use and Not for Profit," proposing that the state set up a network of factories and land colonies for the unemployed and impose higher taxes on corporations and the rich. Sinclair shocked the Democratic establishment by winning the party's nomination for governor in the 1934 primary. Many New Deal Democrats, including FDR, refused to back Sinclair in the general election. Attacked as a communist, Sinclair was defeated but received well over a third of the votes, helping twenty-three EPIC-backed candidates get elected to the state legislature.

In Washington State, EPIC backers succeeded in electing a U.S. senator and went on to help form the Washington Commonwealth Federation, a powerful force in the state's politics. In Minnesota, the leading party was the labor-backed, left-wing Farmer-Labor Party, which controlled the state's governorship for most of the decade. Behind the scenes, the Communist Party—which in 1935 adopted a "Popular Front" strategy of building broad alliances—gained considerable influence in both organizations. Meanwhile, in Wisconsin, Senator Robert M. LaFollette, Jr., and his brother Phil, a former governor, pulled out of the Republican Party and revived the old Progressive Party. The possibility that a national, left-leaning third party might form in time for the 1936 presidential election seemed plausible.

By the spring of 1935, then, the New Deal was under attack from all sides, while its main industrial recovery agency, the NRA, was falling apart. The final blow came on May 27, when the U.S. Supreme Court declared the NIRA unconstitutional; the Court said that Congress, in allowing the NRA to write legally enforceable codes, had unlawfully delegated its own legislative authority. This decision was correctly seen as an indication that the Court would strike down much of the first New Deal. FDR, whose first year in office had raised so many hopes, now faced an uncertain future with neither a strategy nor a well-defined constituency.

The 1930s were a time of national trauma. For the previous decade Americans had been told, and many had come to believe, that the economic and social ills of the country were being solved. Prosperity fostered the assumption that continual individual and social progress were certain. The devastating economic collapse shattered this confidence, permanently undermining an entire generation's sense of security. Many years later a sanitation worker said of himself, "There's a conditioning here by the Depression. I'm what I call a security cat. I don't dare switch [jobs]." Such personal conservatism was common among those who lived through the 1930s. For a half century afterward Americans measured their well-being against Depression era conditions.

For many, FDR, with his suave smile and his seemingly unending self-confidence, appeared as a savior. But though the first New Deal broadened the scope of federal action far beyond what it had ever been before in peacetime, it failed to put an end to hunger and misery, failed to spark a sustained recovery, failed to bring the Great Depression to an end. During the first half of the 1930s, the structures of government, politics, and labor relations had proved inadequate, as they had earlier during the Gilded Age, for dealing with the nation's profound economic and social crisis. By the middle of the decade, most Americans agreed that basic changes were necessary. The question that remained to be resolved was, What sort of changes, and in whose interest?

Just before the tear gas—
September 16, 1936. At the height
of the Salinas Valley lettuce strike,
members of the Fruit and Vegetable
Workers' Union block a downtown
Salinas, California, street to stop a
convoy of trucks carrying produce
harvested by strikebreakers.

8

LABOR DEMOCRATIZES AMERICA

THE YEAR 1934 had been one of fierce and unprecedented political and industrial rebellion. But labor's stunning organizing successes in the early New Deal years quickly evaporated. In Akron, Ohio, the victory of sit-down strikers at General Tire in the summer of 1934 was followed by a year of rapidly declining membership. In Michigan, auto executives repeatedly defied the Automobile Labor Board by discharging and blacklisting union activists. In Pittsburgh, steelmakers used company-dominated employee-representation plans to channel worker discontent within safe limits. Altogether, five hundred AFL local unions had disbanded by early 1935.

These defeats emboldened America's business leaders, who blamed misguided New Deal policies for encouraging unionism. At an annual meeting of the Chamber of Commerce in April 1935, Silas Strawn summarized the anger many businessmen felt toward FDR and the New Deal: "We have floundered along for two years without knowing whether we were going to be locked up or not. . . . Businessmen are tired of hearing promises to do constructive things, which turn out to be only attempts to Sovietize America."

Though he often joked about such attitudes, Roosevelt could not ignore businessmen's continued opposition to the New Deal. When the U.S. Supreme Court declared the National Industrial Recovery Act codes unconstitutional in May 1935, the administration decided to change course, confronting both business recalcitrance and increasing worker militancy. Roosevelt and his supporters orchestrated a new national political coalition that embraced workers and their labor organizations. The resulting change in the political environment encouraged working people to extend and consolidate the dramatic victories of 1934.

In a series of militant and largely successful organizing struggles between 1935 and 1938, U.S. workers brought to life a new, militant industrial union movement. The birth and rapid growth of the Congress of Industrial Organizations in these years augured a transformation in U.S. industrial relations. Not surprisingly, American businessmen did not accept this change without a fight.

THE SECOND NEW DEAL

The Second New Deal, launched in the spring of 1935, greatly expanded the role and authority of the federal government, as had Progressivism a quarter century earlier. New Deal laws attempted to address three major social problems created by an unfettered "free market" economy: poverty and unemployment; undemocratic concentrations of economic wealth and power; and the absence of rights and protections for workers interested in joining unions.

The Second New Deal confronted the problem of unemployment by securing passage of the $4.9 billion Emergency Relief Appropriations Act. Under the act, several federal agencies put millions of Americans back to work. The National Youth Administration initiated work projects for more than 4.5 million students and young workers. The Resettlement Administration attempted to aid the rural homeless, agricultural tenants, and owners of small farms. Another New Deal agency, the Rural Electrification Administration, hired the unemployed to run electric power lines to communities previously forced to do without.

The most important of the new government agencies dealing

with unemployment was the Works Progress Administration (WPA), established to provide jobs on public works projects. By 1943, when it went out of business, the WPA had given work to over 8 million people and financial aid to 30 million more at a cost of $11 billion.

Much more than the short-lived Civil Works Administration, the WPA constituted government-financed production and employment—a recurring demand of the jobless for nearly a century—on an unprecedented scale. No one could miss the significance of the measure, both as a valued aid to the needy and as a breakthrough in public policy. Equally impressive were the WPA's enduring fruits: thousands of schools, libraries, airports, parks and playgrounds, waterworks, sewage plants, hospitals, and roads. And thousands of painters, sculptors, writers, actors, singers, dancers, and puppeteers brought the arts to new and broader audiences.

The second program to combat poverty and economic insecurity was the Social Security Act, passed in June 1935. Funded by equal contributions from employers and employees, the act provided minimal payments to unemployed workers, the aged, and dependents of deceased breadwinners. Like the WPA, the Social Security Act represented a major step toward the government's assumption of responsibility for ameliorating social and economic ills. Government now acknowledged its obligation to provide a minimum standard of economic security for those least able to help themselves: the poor, the sick, the elderly, children, and the unemployed. The act represented a fundamental break with traditional elitist notions that blamed the poor and the unemployed for their condition; it became the foundation for a partial welfare state that protected all citizens. The criticism of conservative New Jersey senator A. Harry Moore was characteristic of upper-class responses. The Social Security Act, he complained, "would take all the romance out of life. We might as well take a child from the nursery, give him a nurse, and protect him from every experience that life affords."

Two other measures aimed at reducing concentrations of economic wealth and power. The first was FDR's 1935 Wealth Tax bill. Ironically, the First New Deal had increased the relative tax burden on low-income rather than high-income groups. Roosevelt now called on Congress to prevent greater concentration of wealth by distributing "the burden of taxes equitably." Accordingly, FDR proposed the taxation of large inheritances and gifts as well as a modest 3 percent rise in the corporate tax rate. Under fierce business pressure, Congress weakened the bill; nevertheless, the Wealth Tax Act of 1935 increased estate, gift, and capital-stock taxes and levied a new excess-profits tax. Altogether, the act increased federal revenues by a modest $250 million.

The second assault on concentrated economic power focused on utilities monopolies. Congress resisted an extremely intense lobbying campaign and passed the Public Utilities Holding Company Act in the summer of 1935. Within three years, most of the holding companies that controlled the nation's myriad utilities companies, especially water and electric power, were broken up. The act also authorized the Securities and Exchange Commission to supervise the financial transactions of utilities companies.

The creation of a federal apparatus to enforce workers' rights to organize unions had initially not been part of the Second New Deal. New York senator and liberal Democrat Robert F. Wagner had introduced his National Labor Relations bill in February 1935. "Men versed in the tenets of freedom become restive when not allowed to be free," he argued. "Until the promises made by [Section 7a] are given definite meaning . . . increasing unrest is inevitable." Proof of the inevitability of class conflict was plentiful, according to Wagner, in "the serious industrial disturbances of last summer, when blood ran freely in the streets and martial law was in the offing."

FDR, who still hoped to gain corporate compliance with his National Industrial Recovery Act, did not at first support Wagner's bill. "It ought to be on the record," his labor secretary noted, that the bill was "not a part of the President's program. It did not particularly appeal to him when it was described to him." But when the U.S. Supreme Court struck down the NIRA in May and Wagner's National Labor Relations bill was passed by one house of Congress, FDR finally endorsed the bill.

The Wagner Act was approved in June. It granted workers rights to select their own union by majority vote, and to strike, boycott, and picket. It enumerated a list of "unfair labor practices" by employers, including financing of company unions, arbitrary dismissal of activists, refusal to bargain, blacklisting, and employment of industrial spies. Under the law, when workers requested representation elections, a new National Labor Relations Board would conduct balloting. If workers chose to organize, their employer had to bargain exclusively with the union they selected. In 1938, the Fair Labor Standards Act prohibited child labor, set a minimum wage, and wrote the forty-hour workweek into federal law.

Although FDR's "Second Hundred Days" represented a broadening of his political base to include organized labor, each piece of legislation contained limitations. Federal work relief reached only about one-third of the millions of jobless, and even they suffered from frequent layoffs and poor pay. The Social Security Act was an insurance fund paid for equally by employers and employees and administered by state authorities. It established a national pension system, administered by the federal government; unemployment compensation, administered by the individual states; and aid for the disabled and dependent children, also administered by the states. The act covered only those employed for wages, which meant that it excluded half the population, particularly the neediest workers. Not only did it impose a heavy financial burden on low-paid workers, it provided inadequate benefits as well, particularly in southern states, whose political and business leaders were hostile to providing relief, even to those in dire need. The Wealth Tax Act did not significantly alter the distribution of personal or corporate wealth. The Utilities Holding Company Act did not put a dent in the concentration of corporate power.

Perhaps of greatest significance to working people, the Wagner Act and the Fair Labor Standards Act excluded agricultural and service workers, public employees, and anyone employed outside interstate commerce; this meant that African-Americans, Mexican-Americans, and women who were concentrated in agricultural, service, and domestic work benefited little from either act. One congressman facetiously proposed the following amendment: "Within 90 days after the appointment of the Administrator, she shall report to Congress whether anyone is subject to this bill." Nonetheless, the Wagner Act—and the rest of the legislation implemented under the Second New Deal—marked a decisive break with past government policies. The Roosevelt administration extended permanent benefits and protections for the first time to millions of ordinary Americans; in the process it created the basis for a partial welfare state that has endured for over half a century.

The New Deal's shift in political orientation in 1935 also presented both a challenge and an opportunity to those labor leaders anxious to harness the extraordinary militancy displayed by workers across the country in 1934. Events that year demonstrated that new unions organized on a broad, industrywide basis could succeed. This position was championed by several leaders of established industrial unions within the AFL, such as John L. Lewis of the United Mine Workers of America (UMWA) and Sidney Hillman of the Amalgamated Clothing Workers, as well as many up-and-coming leaders of AFL federal unions.

To Lewis and Hillman, passage of the Wagner Act and the increasingly antibusiness tenor of the White House meant that there would never be a better time to unionize industrial workers and to use workers' increasing militancy to push the New Deal forward. If the AFL could seize this opportunity, it would grow dramatically in members, economic power, and political clout. If not, others would assume the task of rebuilding the labor movement—very likely organizations on the left, such as the Communist and Socialist parties.

Events in the Camden, New Jersey, shipyards during the months following the Wagner Act's passage showed that the time for action was ripe. Camden shipyard workers had organized an industrial union in 1933–34 but had been unable to secure recognition from their employers. In the spring of 1935, Lewis agreed to donate UMWA funds to support a final organizing effort in the shipyards. Throughout the summer of 1935, shipyard workers led by Scottish-born Camden worker John Green and Philip Van Gelder, a left-wing activist from nearby Philadelphia, struck for recognition of their union, the United Marine and Shipyard Workers of America. Late in August, the owners of the shipyards capitulated.

In stark contrast to the shipyard workers' victory in Camden, halfhearted attempts by the AFL in 1935 to organize industrial workers made little headway. In steel, the bankrupt Amalgamated Association of Iron and Steelworkers continued to insist on control but provided no leadership. In auto, the determination of the craft unions to uphold their jurisdiction over maintenance and machine shop workers kept the AFL in constant conflict with leaders of the federal local unions that had emerged in auto parts plants. Meanwhile, few workers employed by the Big Three automakers had signed union cards. In the tire industry, membership in the federal locals was declining precipitously as rubberworkers tired of the AFL leadership's caution.

At the AFL's convention in Atlantic City in October 1935, advocates of industrial unionism voiced a new urgency. The big strikes of 1934 had made clear, as Charles Howard, president of the Typographers' Union argued, that "the workers of this country are going to organize, and if they are not permitted to organize under the banner of the American Federation of Labor they are going to organize under some other leadership."

But the majority of craft union leaders rejected resolutions calling for an all-out organizing effort, believing that industrial workers would not make good trade unionists. Teamsters' president Daniel Tobin betrayed this prejudice when he derided "the rubbish that have lately come into other organizations. We do not want the men today if they are going to strike tomorrow." William Collins, the AFL's New York State representative, joked, "My wife can always tell from the smell of my clothes what breed of foreigners I have been hanging out with."

As the AFL convention neared its end, John L. Lewis brought matters to a head. When William Hutcheson, president of the Carpenters' Brotherhood, tried to silence an advocate of industrial unionism by raising a point of order, Lewis shouted, "This thing of raising points of order all the time on minor delegates is rather small potatoes." Hutcheson rose to the bait, calling Lewis a "bastard." "Lewis jumped to his feet," one observer recalled. "Quick as a cat, he leaped over a row of chairs toward Hutcheson, jabbed out his right fist, and sent the carpenters' president sprawling. . . ." Hutcheson left the floor with blood on his face, while "Lewis casually adjusted his tie and collar, relit his cigar, and sauntered slowly through the crowded aisles."

Lewis was no radical. In the 1920s, he had been a Republican and a bitter opponent of left-wing unionism; he ran the UMWA with an autocratic hand. Nevertheless, he was determined to organize the labor movement by industry, not by craft. "Great combinations of capital," he argued, "have assembled to themselves tremendous power and influence, and they are almost 100 percent effective in opposing . . . the American Federation of Labor. . . . If you go in there with your craft union they will mow you down like the Italian machine guns will mow down Ethiopians in the war now going on in that country."

Lewis now called together leaders of the International Ladies' Garment Workers' Union, the Amalgamated Clothing Workers, the Mine Workers, and several other unions to plan a new organization. A month later, the group reassembled to establish the Committee for Industrial Organization (later the Congress of Industrial Organizations, or CIO) within the AFL "to encourage and promote organization of the workers in the mass production and unorganized industries of the nation."

The AFL leaders demanded that the CIO be dissolved. When that demand was rejected, all unions affiliated with the committee were suspended and later expelled from the AFL, including the UMWA; the Mine, Mill, and Smelter Workers; the Amalgamated Clothing Workers; and the Textile Workers.

"WE DONE IT!"

The CIO victory in the Akron, Ohio, rubber factories was made possible by the workers' use of a new tactic: the sit-down strike. Instead of walking out of the factory and picketing outside, the workers simply occupied the plant. Ruth McKinney, a novelist, graphically described the occupation of the Firestone tire plant in January 1936.

IT was 1:57 A.M. January 29, 1936.

The tire builders worked in smooth frenzy, sweat around their necks, under their arms. The belt clattered, the insufferable racket and din and rhythm. The clock on the south wall, a big plain clock, hesitated, its minute hand jumped to two. A tire builder at the end of the line looked up, saw the hand jump. The foreman was sitting quietly staring at the lines of men working under the vast pools of light. . . .

The tire builder at the end of the line gulped. His hands stopped their quick weaving motions. Every man on the line stiffened. All over the vast room, hands hesitated. The foreman saw the falter, felt it instantly. He jumped up . . . his eyes darting quickly from one line to another.

This was it, then. But what was happening? Where was it starting? He stood perfectly still, his heart beating furiously, his throat feeling dry, watching the hesitating hands, watching the broken rhythm.

Then the tire builder at the end of the line walked three steps to the master safety switch and, drawing a deep breath, he pulled up the heavy wooden handle. With this signal in perfect synchronization, with the rhythm they had learned in a great mass-production industry, the tire builders stepped back from their machines.

Instantly, noise stopped. The whole room lay in perfect silence. The tire builders stood in long lines, touching each other, perfectly motionless, deafened by the silence. . . .

Out of the terrifying quiet came the wondering voice of a big tire builder near the window: "Jesus Christ, it's like the end of the world."

He broke the spell, the magic moment of stillness. For now his awed words said the same thing to every man, "We done it! We stopped the belt! By God, we done it!" And men began to cheer hysterically, to shout and howl in the fresh silence. Men wrapped their long sinewy arms around their neighbors' shoulders, screaming, "We done it! We done it! . . ."

The CIO's first few months were difficult. There were some breakthroughs, especially the organization of the United Electrical and Radio Workers of America, an industrial union established in defiance of the AFL; the new union's first act was to affiliate with the CIO. And there were some organizing victories in Akron's rubber factories. But defeats were more common. Employers fired workers as if the Wagner Act had never been passed, asserting that the act, like parts of the NIRA before it, would be found unconstitutional. Union organizing drives stalled in the steel towns of western Pennsylvania; the milltowns of the Piedmont; and the mining towns of Arizona, Colorado, and Montana.

The tide turned late in 1936, in the midst of FDR's reelection campaign. John L. Lewis played a highly visible role in FDR's campaign; indeed, during the spring and summer, Lewis devoted himself fully to reelecting the man he now called "the greatest statesman of modern times." Without federal allies, Lewis believed, the CIO could not organize the mass production industries.

The AFL also lined up behind Roosevelt, if less energetically. Teamsters' president Dan Tobin served as head of the Democratic Party's Labor Committee. In April, Lewis, Sidney Hillman of the Amalgamated Clothing Workers, and George L. Berry of the AFL's printing pressmen's union founded Labor's Non-Partisan League to funnel labor energies and funds—$600,000 from the mineworkers alone—into Roosevelt's campaign. The president praised Non-Partisan League efforts and personally promised to support Lewis in the pending struggle to unionize the steelworkers.

To challenge Roosevelt for the presidency, the Republicans nominated Kansas governor Alfred M. Landon, whose campaign emphasized themes cherished by the American Liberty League, the U.S. Chamber of Commerce, and the National Association of Manufacturers. Landon blasted Roosevelt for swelling the federal deficit and for undermining the Constitution, the dollar, and the free market.

Leaders of the Coughlin, Long, and Townsend movements formed the Union Party, nominating North Dakota congressman William Lemke for the presidency (Huey Long, who would have been the obvious choice of the new party, had been assassinated in September 1935). But they were unable to bridge the cultural and ideological gaps that separated the three movements, and the Union Party quickly splintered.

Both the Socialist and Communist parties ran halfhearted campaigns, implicitly backing Roosevelt. "Nothing but socialism will save us," Socialist Party candidate Norman Thomas contended, but if "reform is the way out, better stick to the Roosevelt administration." Communist Party chairman Earl Browder recalled that he conducted an "ambiguous campaign in favor of 'my rival,' Roosevelt."

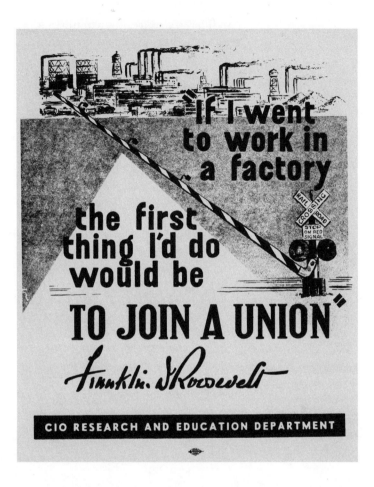

"If I went to work in a factory the first thing I'd do would be TO JOIN A UNION"

Franklin D. Roosevelt

CIO RESEARCH AND EDUCATION DEPARTMENT

Like the man says . . . A CIO recruiting poster quotes the president.

Roosevelt ignored the small parties, directing his fire against the Republicans and the "economic royalists" who took "other people's money" to "impose a new industrial dictatorship." He charged that the forces of "organized money are unanimous in their hate for me—and I welcome their hatred." "I should like to have it said of my first Administration," FDR concluded, "that in it the forces of selfishness and of lust for power met their match."

Stressing the Second New Deal's social welfare and union rights legislation and identifying himself with the aspirations of wage-earners and small property owners, FDR garnered 60 percent of the total popular vote and carried every state but Vermont and Maine. The Republicans lost twelve more seats in the House of Representatives, giving the Democrats three-quarters of the total. In the Senate, seven new Democrats were elected, giving the president's party nearly eight of every ten seats in that body. Democratic gubernatorial candidates also won in Michigan, Ohio, Pennsylvania, and New York, where the battles for union organization were sure to be fought. The largest third-party presidential vote, that of the Socialist Party's Norman Thomas, dropped from 800,000 in 1932 to only 187,000 votes. Franklin Roosevelt had managed to isolate electorally those to his left as well as those to his right.

Though the Roosevelt vote included traditionally Democratic strongholds in the West and the "Solid South," urban working people composed the core of the new Democratic electorate. Overwhelming support came from children of turn-of-the-century southern and eastern European immigrants and from the native-born millions, black and white, who left the land for the cities during the 1920s. The shift of African-American voters to the Democratic Party—loyal Republicans since they secured the franchise during Reconstruction—was especially dramatic.

Some found the turnaround in political allegiance of African-Americans puzzling. Roosevelt never added black equality to his legislative agenda, and many of his programs discriminated against African-Americans. The Agricultural Adjustment Act had enabled the landlords to dispossess so many African-American tenants and sharecroppers that the bill was often referred to as the "Negro Removal Act." Relief programs regularly shortchanged African-Americans, and work programs often assigned them to segregated units. The Tennessee Valley Authority (TVA) ran its construction, administration, and settlement programs on an openly discriminatory basis. "You can raise all the rumpus you like," confided one TVA official. "We just aren't going to mix Negroes and white folks in any village in TVA."

Nor had FDR thrown his

"PRESIDENT ROOSEVELT IS A FRIEND TO THE LABORIN' MEN . . ."

African-Americans wrote and sang many songs during the Depression to acknowledge the debt they felt to President Roosevelt or tell the story of how joining unions changed their lives. Many of these songs used the rhythms and style of old spirituals or prison work songs. The lyrics of one such song, "Union Dues," were written in a more modern musical idiom, the blues, which became popular in southern African-American communities in the 1920s. "Union Dues" was recorded by the folklorist George Korson during the 1940s.

President Roosevelt is a friend to the laborin' men,
Gives us the right to organize an' be real union men,
Union, union is all over the wide worl',
Back on the farm an' tobacco barns.
I'm glad I'm a union man; long may it live on,
The union will be livin' when I'm dead an' gone.

I got the union blues, don't care where I go,
I got the union blues, don't care where I be,
It's good for you an' good enough for me;
I'm goin' down the road feelin' mighty glad,
I'm goin' down the road feelin' mighty glad,
The union is the best friend that labor ever had.
I'm goin' to write a letter, goin' to mail it in the month o' May.
I'm goin' to write a letter, goin' to mail it this very day.
I'm goin' to thank the President for that seven-hour day.
I'm goin' to close my song, but won't close my mind,
I'm goin' to close my song, but won't close my mind—
That laborin' man was not left behind.

support behind the antilynching law proposed in November 1933 by the NAACP. In 1934, a dozen governors—including the governor of Florida—voiced support for the bill. But though Roosevelt publicly denounced lynching, he acceded to the power of the racists ensconced in the Democratic Party and refused to endorse the antilynching bill. "The Southerners . . . are chairmen or occupy strategic places on most of the Senate and House committees," FDR explained. "If I come out for the antilynching bill now, they will block every bill I ask Congress to pass to keep America from collapsing."

Nevertheless, African-American support for Roosevelt mushroomed midway through his first term. Part of the reason for the shift was that the Roosevelt administration had begun to respond to the needs of rural African-Americans when the disastrous impact of the Agricultural Assistance Act on tenant farmers became apparent. New Deal agencies gave loans to struggling black farmers, helped some tenants to buy land, and created agricultural settlements where displaced farmers could begin anew, aiding hundreds of thousands of poor rural families, black as well as white.

But the primary reason that African-Americans abandoned the party of Abraham Lincoln to support Roosevelt was that New Deal relief measures and employment projects rescued many blacks from the brink of starvation. On Chicago's South Side, one resident remembered when "the WPA came along and Roosevelt came to be a god. . . . You worked, you got a paycheck, and you had some dignity." In Columbia, South Carolina, a registrar of voters reported that black Americans "say Roosevelt saved them from starvation, gave them aid when they were in distress, and now they were going to vote for him." In September 1936, 16,000 Harlem residents attended an election rally for FDR in Madison Square Garden; similar rallies occurred in sixteen other cities. By 1936, the black vote for Roosevelt ranged from 56 percent in Knoxville, Tennessee, to 75 percent in Pittsburgh, to 81 percent in New York City.

LABOR'S UPSURGE

At a meeting of the CIO executive board just after Roosevelt's lopsided reelection, Lewis announced, "We . . . must capitalize on the election. The CIO was out fighting for Roosevelt, and every steel town showed a smashing victory for him. . . . We wanted a President who would hold the light for us while we went out and organized."

CIO unions targeted the steel industry, allocating almost $750,000 for the newly established Steel Workers' Organizing Committee (SWOC). Lewis placed the SWOC under the control of United Mine Workers' vice president Philip Murray and other officials on loan from the UMWA. Murray sent dozens of UMWA activists as well as seasoned Communist and Socialist organizers into steel towns. Asked if he was worried about the presence of so many "Reds," Lewis replied, "Who gets the bird? The hunter or the dog?"

Lewis was determined to bring millions of industrial workers into the union fold, he was willing to take unprecedented steps to realize this end, and he thought he had a perfect strategy to win the opening battle in the war for industrial unionism. But the automobile workers confounded the CIO's plans: they unleashed a massive strike wave before the campaign to organize the steel industry began. This proved to be typical of the era of industrial struggle that followed. For the rest of the decade, angry, impatient working people proved to be a militant force that could not be controlled by labor leaders, corporate executives, the police, or politicians.

In the fall of 1936, the fledgling United Automobile Workers (UAW) challenged the automakers' fierce anti-unionism. Several small unions had merged to establish the UAW as an affiliate of the American Federation of Labor in October 1935, but the autoworkers were never comfortable within the AFL hierarchy. AFL president Green's effort to select the UAW's leadership and dictate its organizing strategy provoked heated resistance, and by the summer of 1936 the autoworkers joined the new CIO.

Excited by the magnitude of FDR's reelection victory in November, the UAW immediately began planning a general organizing assault on the auto industry. The union decided to fight the first battle against General Motors, the nation's largest industrial employer, with more than a quarter-million workers, in 1936. The corporation's before-tax profit that year was $284 million. Prominent on the list of current and previous GM officers were the three principal founders of the antilabor, anti-Roosevelt American Liberty League.

Determined to avoid unionization at all costs, GM had spent close to $1 million between January 1934 and July 1936 to intimidate its workforce with what a U.S. Senate committee called "the most colossal super system of spies yet devised in any American corporation." "I have so many contacts" within the UAW's nucleus, one spy boasted, "that it would be impossible to organize the union; I know everything that is going on inside." This surveillance had devastated unionization efforts.

Throughout November and December 1936, as the UAW leaders formulated their plans, autoworkers jumped the gun: they began strikes in South Bend, Kansas City, Detroit, and Atlanta. Following the earlier example of Akron rubberworkers, these industrial actions by autoworkers took the form of "sit-down" strikes. Workers seized control of the plants where they worked, remaining inside rather than picketing outside, until management capitulated. This innovative

Someone didn't like the message. Union members repair damage to a Detroit billboard set up by the Ford Organizing Committee of the United Automobile Workers the day after arsonists tried to burn it down.

The billboard reads:

I Work in a Union Shop
OB SECURITY
UMANE MANAGEMENT
LIVING WAGE

I Toil in an Open Shop
DISCRIMINATION
DRIVING FOREMAN
HAUNTING FEAR

UNITED AUTO WORKERS OF AMERICA · NOW ·
FORD ORGANIZING COMMITTEE OF U.A.W.A.

8TH FLOOR
HOFFMAN BLDG.
DETROIT

tactic, which demonstrated the workers' willingness to violate owners' private-property rights to win their demands, prevented companies from replacing strikers with scabs. It also discouraged the use of violence against strikers, because deploying police, troops, or other armed groups against sit-downers risked destroying expensive company-owned buildings, machinery, and materials.

The UAW leadership, aware of the spreading auto "wildcats" (i.e., strikes called without official union sanction), decided to attack GM by striking the company's key Fisher Body plants in Cleveland and Flint. The strike was scheduled for right after New Year's Day, following the inauguration of New Dealer Frank Murphy as governor of Michigan.

But events raced ahead of the union leaders' plans. When workers in one department in the Cleveland Fisher Body plant sat down to protest wage cuts on December 28, the rest of the factory's 7,000 employees joined them. In Flint, an attempt by managers in Fisher Body Plant No. 2 to discipline three union members on December 30 led fifty workers to occupy that building. The next day, angry workers from Fisher No. 1 gathered at Flint's UAW hall, shouting at their leaders, "Shut her down! Shut the goddamn plant!" Streaming back into No. 1, between 500 and 1,000 workers took control of the factory in minutes, shutting down the assembly line.

The month-long sit-down strike in Flint that followed proved to be the pivotal labor struggle of the decade. If Flint autoworkers could beat General Motors—the largest producer of automobiles, parts, and accessories in the world—their victory would galvanize workers in auto and other basic industries. The Flint strike was emblematic of

Sit-down. Strikers in General Motors'
Fisher Body Plant No. 2 greet
friends and supporters gathered
outside.

countless other labor battles between 1936 and 1942 because it revealed rank-and-file workers' extraordinary creativity and bravery in
the struggle for industrial unions.

Located sixty miles northwest of Detroit, Flint was a virtual company town. The mayor, police chief, and three city commissioners—
as well as Flint's newspaper, radio station, and school officials—all
were or had been on the General Motors payroll. General Motors'
Chevrolet, Buick, Fisher Body, and AC Spark Plug plants employed
four of every five workers in the city. Overwhelmingly white and
male, most of these workers had migrated to Flint earlier in the decade from the Midwest and South.

Three grievances, typical of all auto plants, angered workers in all
of GM's Flint plants: frequent and prolonged layoffs; arbitrary actions
by management; and the killing speed of the work. Because of the
industry's seasonal production cycle, employees worked long, hard
hours in one period, only to be laid off for long stretches later the
same year. "The fear of being laid off," one journalist noted, "hangs
over the head of every worker. He does not know when the sword will
fall."

Second, GM management was free to discipline, fire, lay off, and
rehire at its own discretion, a power that foremen used to punish
"troublemakers" and reward pets. "If he happened to like you," a Chev-

rolet employee explained, "or if you sucked around him and did him favors . . . you might be picked to work a few weeks longer than the next guy."

Speed-up was the workers' deepest grievance. The foremen "treated us like a bunch of coolies," a Flint Chevrolet employee later remembered. " 'Get it out. If you cannot get it out, there are people outside who will get it out.' That was their whole theme." Genora Dollinger—a twenty-three-year-old mother of two, wife of sit-down leader Kermit Johnson, and Socialist Party activist—described the toll on her husband. Kermit was, she remembered, "a young man grown old from the speed-up. He has come home at night . . . so tired he couldn't eat. He was wakened the next morning with his hands so swollen he couldn't hold a fork." Autoworkers' powerlessness to change such oppressive conditions fueled an abiding anger toward the company.

This anger had led a thousand workers to seize control of Fisher Body plant No. 1 on December 31, 1936, and for thousands of their fellow GM workers to follow suit in other plants in Flint and elsewhere. Their demands were extensive: a thirty-hour week, a six-hour day, and time-and-a-half pay for overtime so that work would be spread more widely; a minimum pay rate "commensurate with an American standard of living"; seniority based on length of employment (to limit management's arbitrary power) and reinstatement of

Catching up on the news. Strikers occupying General Motors' Fisher Body Plant No. 1 during the sit-down strike.

"unjustly" fired employees; abolition of piecework; and establishment of joint control by management and the union over the speed of production in GM plants. To safeguard these and other gains from company and company-union tricks, the strikers demanded what the Wagner Act had only promised: recognition of the UAW as the "sole bargaining agency" for GM employees.

Seizing control of the plant and issuing a set of demands were only the first steps in winning the struggle with General Motors. The seized plants needed to be protected against company efforts to retake them, and the demands of the strikers had to be gotten out beyond the plant gates. To secure the plant from the inside and to supervise meals, sanitation, defense, education, and entertainment, a committee, which included representatives from each department in the plant, was formed.

Sit-downers lived up to a strict code of discipline. "We had guys patrol the plant, see that nobody got involved in anything they shouldn't," striker Bob Stinson recalled. "If anybody got careless with company property—such as sitting on an automobile cushion without putting burlap over it—he was talked to." Discipline was imposed

"SOLIDARITY FOREVER . . ."

Music played an important part in the Flint sit-down strike. All meetings of sit-down strikers were opened and closed with a verse from "Solidarity Forever," the old IWW anthem written by Ralph Chapin.

When the union's inspiration
Through the workers' blood shall run
There can be no power greater
Anywhere beneath the sun.
But what force on earth is weaker
Than the feeble strength of one?
For the union makes us strong
Solidarity forever
Solidarity forever
Solidarity forever
For the union makes us strong.

During the strike, those sitting down in the mill composed verses to popular tunes. These helped create a sense of unity and maintained the strikers' morale during the long separation from their families. The following verses were sung to the tune of "Gallagher and Shean." The two men referred to were Alfred Sloan, president of General Motors, and Bob Travis, the UAW leader in Flint who was close to the Communist Party.

by the workers themselves; each night, all those in the plant met to review the committee's decisions.

The shop committee's work was supported by a Women's Auxiliary, organized by fifty women, many of them Socialist and Communist Party activists. Its members were everywhere—on picket lines, speaking at forums, leafleting the public, providing food and first aid for strikers and childcare for female activists, raising money, and mobilizing outside support.

Genora Dollinger initiated a second women's organization: the Women's Emergency Brigade. The red-bereted brigade served as the female shock troops of the solidarity movement; its members carried two-by-fours when they joined in violent confrontations, placing themselves between strikers and police and militia.

General Motors depicted the strike as the work of a "small handful of workers" misled by "outside agitators" in the service of "a vast conspiracy to destroy all for which life is worth living." By occupying the plants, GM insisted, the UAW was "striking at the very heart of the right of the possession of private property," thereby endangering the property of every other company, businessman, and even homeowner in the land. GM found a judge to issue an injunction ordering strikers not only to leave the plants but also to refrain from picketing outside them. But when the CIO exposed the fact that the helpful judge owned over $200,000 worth of GM stock, this particular maneuver backfired.

Flint's large body of non-union autoworkers also played a key role. On the eve of the Flint sit-down, a local businessman with strong ties to General Motors had begun organizing a company union, the Flint Alliance. While the UAW repeatedly charged that GM workers were coerced into signing Flint Alliance membership cards, the truth is probably more complex: Flint had long been a company town dominated by a powerful, paternalistic employer to which many workers felt loyal. And the

Oh! Mr. Sloan! Oh! Mr. Sloan!
We have known for a long time you would atone,
For the wrongs that you have done
We all know, yes, everyone.
Absolutely, Mr. Travis!
Positively, Mr. Sloan!

Oh! Mr. Sloan! Oh! Mr. Sloan!
Everyone knows your heart was made of stone,
But the union is so strong
That we'll always carry on.
Absolutely, Mr. Travis!
Positively, Mr. Sloan!

Maurice Sugar, one of the UAW's lawyers, wrote the verse to "Sit Down!" another popular labor song, just after the strike against General Motors was won.

When they tie the can to a Union man
 Sit down! Sit down!
When they give 'im the sack, they'll take him back
 Sit down! Sit down!

Sit down, just take a seat
Sit down, and rest your feet
Sit down, you've got 'em beat
Sit down! Sit down!

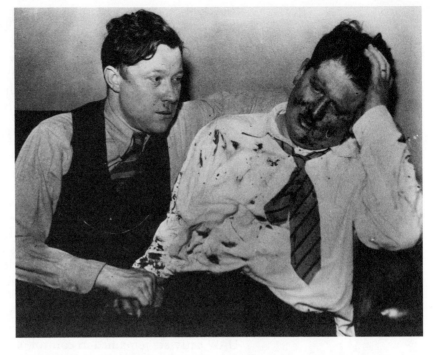

Friendly persuasion. On May 26, 1937, employees of Ford's Service Department demonstrate the company's willingness to use force to stop union organizing. As UAW organizers Robert Kantor, Walter Reuther, Richard Frankensteen, and J. J. Kennedy pose for press photographers on an overpass near the entrance to the Ford River Rouge plant (1), they are approached by Ford Service Department men (2). The Ford men attack, press cameras recording the assault on Frankensteen (3). Reuther and Frankensteen immediately after the incident (4).

sit-down strikers *were* a minority; the majority of Flint autoworkers were waiting to see whether the UAW had a chance to win before committing themselves.

In any case, the Flint Alliance's charges that the sit-down strikers were depriving loyal workers of their right to continue working did influence public opinion. Gallup polls taken during the sit-down strike indicated that a majority of Americans believed that the strikers should leave the plant but that GM should not use force to evict them.

After GM's attempt to get a court injunction failed, the company turned to more drastic tactics. Company guards turned off the heat inside the Chevrolet No. 2 plant (in 16-degree weather) and barred strike supporters from bringing in food. When sit-downers forced open the factory gates to allow the food in, GM called out the police. On January 11, sheriff's deputies and police, using tear gas, billy clubs, and guns, stormed the plant.

Strikers repelled the assault by turning on the plant's fire hoses and raining two-pound car hinges down on the police. Later that night the police returned. "We want peace!" shouted UAW leader Victor Reuther as the police charged again. "General Motors chose war! Give it to them!" The police were driven back a second time. Humiliated and angry, the cops opened fire, wounding several strikers. A third police charge, at midnight, also failed. Defeated, the police (known in the jargon of the day as "bulls") abandoned the field.

The "Battle of the Running Bulls" on January 11 galvanized GM workers dispirited by years of company intimidation. The next morning, Flint workers lined up two abreast at UAW headquarters to sign membership cards and pay dues. Ten thousand people gathered at the battle site, repeatedly singing "Solidarity Forever," the anthem first written by IWW balladeer Joe Hill.

Under pressure from GM officials, Michigan governor Frank Murphy ordered 1,500 National Guardsmen into Flint and tried to talk the unionists into leaving the plants with the promise of negotiations. GM was unwilling to compromise, however. Company agents, police, and vigilantes beat UAW pickets and organizers not only in Flint but also in Detroit, Saginaw, and Anderson, Michigan, and in other auto plants where sit-down strikes inspired by events in Flint had spread. And though John L. Lewis called on President Roosevelt to help the workers, FDR remained silent. Roosevelt wanted a negotiated end to the strike and opposed using troops to evict the strikers, though he labeled the strikers' tactics "wrong."

After a month, the situation at Flint reached a stalemate. While employees slowly returned to work at most of Flint's GM operations, UAW activists remained in control of two Fisher Body plants in defiance of General Motors, the Flint police, Governor Murphy, and President Roosevelt. GM's repeated efforts to oust the sit-downers failed; unless Governor Murphy ordered the National Guard to seize the two Flint plants, the world's largest corporation could only wait.

The UAW devised a ruse to break the stalemate. Union leaders decided they could win the strike if they could stop production at Flint's Chevy plant No. 4, the sole source of engines for Chevrolet's entire car line. But a frontal assault was out of the question: GM's armed guards were simply too strong; they had to be decoyed. At a secret meeting, UAW officials informed company spies who had infiltrated the strike's leadership that the union planned to seize control of a different plant, Chevy No. 9. As the UAW hoped, GM shifted most of its guards to the decoy plant. When a small contingent of strikers entered Chevy No. 9 on February 1, GM guards went in after them. A fierce battle raged inside No. 9; police used tear gas, which Women's Emergency Brigade members helped dissipate by breaking the plant's windows with wooden clubs. Meanwhile, union stalwarts marched into Chevy No. 4 and took over the plant without violence as women patrolled the gates outside. Half of the 4,000 workers in No. 4 immediately joined the sit-down; the other half left the plant. By the time GM officials realized what had happened, the UAW controlled the key factory in Flint.

GM finally caved in. With its car production at a near standstill, its share of the automobile market plummeting, and its tactics in Flint frustrated at every turn, General Motors agreed on February 3 to negotiate. A week later, the company conceded defeat on the key issue of union recognition at its struck plants, acknowledging the UAW as bargaining agent for its members in those plants and agreeing not to organize company unions for six months. GM also agreed to drop all related lawsuits and to refrain from disciplining the strikers. All the other UAW demands would be discussed in a national labor-management conference.

On paper, the battle remained unfinished, since most of the strike demands had yet to be won. In practice, however, the victory was enormous. Recognition by GM meant that UAW members could for the first time speak and act openly among their coworkers. "Even if we got not one damn thing out of it other than that," declared one GM employee in St. Louis, "we at least had a right to open our mouths without fear." More than this, GM's surrender boosted the spirit and self-confidence of the autoworkers and encouraged them to rely on militant, on-the-spot collective action to obtain and defend further gains.

Everybody's doing it. Employees of Detroit's Goody Nut Shops stage a sit-down strike in March 1937.

And that is what they did. Within three weeks, GM was hit by eighteen sit-down strikes. In March, the first formal contract between GM and the UAW established a multistage, legalistic procedure for processing specific grievances. But the sit-downs had taught the workers the power of organized, direct action. As a UAW member later recalled, "Every time a dispute came up the fellows would have a tendency to sit down and just stop working." Such tactics put teeth into thousands of local demands to raise pay, cease harassing union members, rein in tyrannical foremen, improve safety conditions, and decrease the speed of production. One Flint employee, who had earlier opposed the sit-down strike, exulted in early 1937 that "the inhuman high speed is *no more*. We now have a voice, and have slowed up the speed of the line. . . . The high pressure is taken off." Although often called without official UAW sanction and technically in violation of the GM contract, these sit-downs and "quickie" strikes were, as UAW leader Roy Reuther later noted, "the greatest organizers."

But the victory at Flint had a still wider impact. Having withstood everything thrown at them by the nation's largest and richest manufacturing corporation, the UAW proved itself to autoworkers across the country. Chrysler Corporation, hit by a sit-down of its own, came to terms with the UAW in early April. By October 1937, UAW membership neared 400,000—up from only 30,000 just one year earlier. Every major auto manufacturer except Ford had been brought to the bargaining table. Nor was Flint's impact limited to the automobile industry. The UAW established a general union, Local 156, that organized workers in all of Flint's industries. CIO forces working within the Democratic Party also quickly won control of the city government, ousting local politicians who had ruled with corporate support for decades.

The CIO's large investment in organizing the steel industry did not produce a breakthrough as dramatic as that at Flint. John L. Lewis and Philip Murray's Steel Workers' Organizing Committee (SWOC) differed dramatically from the UAW. In contrast to what *CIO News* editor Len DeCaux called the "tumultuous democracy" of the UAW, the SWOC was dominated by Murray and other officials of the UMWA. "Our union was created from the top down," recalled steelworker Ed Mann of Youngstown, Ohio, many years later. "It was financed by the Mine Workers, and the hierarchy and staff all came out of the Mine Workers. And they said, 'Here's a union. Now you get people to join it.'"

Nonetheless, the SWOC counted some successes. At the U.S. Steel Corporation South Works in Chicago, Mexican-American organizers held meetings and distributed literature in English, Spanish, and Polish to bring the union's message to the plant's ethnically diverse workforce. By 1936 they had succeeded in transforming the plant's long-standing company union into Local 65 of the SWOC. Mexican organizers in the Inland Steel and Youngstown Steel plants in East Chicago, Indiana, employed similar tactics to sign up a majority of steelworkers into the SWOC by early 1937.

These organizing successes notwithstanding, it was the victory of the Flint autoworkers against GM in March 1937 that finally pushed steel company officials to take action. U.S. Steel president Myron Taylor read GM's capitulation at Flint as a sign that "complete industrial organization was inevitable." To avoid a violent conflict with its own workers, U.S. Steel—the second-biggest manufacturing company in the world, the corporation that had smashed the old Amalgamated Association of Iron, Steel, and Tin Workers in 1901 and the nationwide steel strike in 1919—went directly to Lewis and Murray and consented to recognize the CIO's Steel Workers' Organizing Committee as sole bargaining agent for its employees. U.S. Steel also conceded a 10 percent wage increase, reduction of the standard workweek to forty hours, and payment of time and a half for overtime work.

This stunning if bloodless victory provided another spur to the SWOC and the CIO organizing drives. By April 1937, the SWOC claimed 280,000 members. Fully 4.7 million workers took part in some kind of strike action during 1937, more than twice as many as in the year before. This number included 400,000 workers who participated in sit-down strikes. On the whole, their efforts were successful, as CIO organizing drives in rubber, auto, meatpacking, electrical equipment, textiles, trucking, and on the docks gained union recognition. "Sitting down has replaced baseball as a national pastime," the Detroit *News* commented. *Time* magazine guessed Detroiters were "getting an idea of what a revolution feels like." By September 1937, the CIO boasted a membership of above 3.7 million.

Ironically, the AFL reaped many benefits from the upsurge of worker militancy and industrial unionization. Once AFL leaders such as Teamsters' president Dan Tobin and Carpenters' president William Hutcheson saw the CIO winning victories, they began organizing the same workers they had previously scorned. Outside the mass-production industries, in meatpacking, food processing, and the retail and service trades, the AFL's network of central labor bodies provided effective political, legal, and financial support to craft union organizers. In small and decentralized industries, AFL unions competed successfully with the CIO. Many anti-union employers, frightened by CIO successes, were now happy to negotiate with AFL unions to avoid having to deal with "Lewis's Reds."

The Teamsters were one of the AFL's success stories. Before the Depression, the Teamsters' ranks had been limited to truckdrivers hauling goods within the nation's urban areas. But after radicals in Minneapolis demonstrated that organizing warehousemen and other goods handlers could strengthen the union, Teamster locals throughout the nation began organizing workers they had previously ignored. The Teamsters also began signing up long-distance, intercity drivers. Within five years, the Teamsters had grown to 440,000 members and secured a powerful grip on the nation's economy. The AFL gained 1 million new members by September 1937, raising the total strength of the nation's unions to above 7 million.

DEMOCRATIC VISTAS

The Depression shattered millions of American lives and destroyed many people's sense of security. Depression era Americans experienced deep feelings of shame and personal inadequacy. In response to these desperate feelings, several political and cultural currents offered Americans a new sense of belonging, a growing consciousness of and pride in the nation's heritage. The first and most effective promoter of patriotism was Franklin Roosevelt, a master manipulator of the symbols of national pride and identity. His "fireside chats," broadcast live on the new national radio networks as soon as he took office in 1933, drew listeners into the Oval Office. There they were welcomed by a warm and caring president, who expressed absolute confidence in the ability of the American people to pull themselves out of the Depression. The early New Deal employed marching bands, parades, and the ubiquitous Blue Eagle symbol to heighten the feelings of national unity and national mobilization.

Like the New Deal, the movements associated with Father Coughlin and the American Liberty League employed patriotic rhetoric and symbols. But unlike FDR, the leaders of these political movements articulated a conservative ideology that appealed to many Americans' insecurities and fears of foreigners and "radicals."

Leaders of the industrial union movement (as well as the movements associated with Huey Long in Louisiana and the End Poverty In California campaign) also employed patriotic themes and issues with great success. From the early days of the NRA, when UMWA organizers told miners that "the president wants you to join the union," John L. Lewis and his organizers emphasized the union movement's ties to a popular government and political leader.

Working people's appreciation for such patriotic symbols was not simply the product of manipulation. When the victorious sit-down strikers emerged from occupied Flint GM plants in February 1937 proudly waving American flags, they said a lot about how they understood their struggle. They also passed on an important message to their fellow citizens, who saw every flourish of the Stars and Stripes on the weekly newsreel in movie theaters all across the country. A new kind of working-class patriotism thus emerged in working-class communities during the 1930s. This phenomenon had diverse historical origins. Some immigrant workers—Poles, Greeks, Italians, and Slavs whose primary identification had been with their own nationality—had served side-by-side in the U.S. Army during World War I. That common experience helped break down ethnic barriers. More importantly, immigrants on the home front—who far outnumbered those who went to war—had been subjected to a barrage of wartime propaganda, Americanization classes, and civics courses that stressed patriotic shared values. The postwar Red Scare, with its coercive efforts to Americanize the foreign-born, intensified such patriotic feelings among immigrant workers. And the mass culture of the 1920s—movies, radio, popular music, and advertising—further eroded ethnic identities, particularly among the sons and daughters of immigrant families. When early New Deal programs and the labor movement appealed to workers on the basis of their reverence for the country's democratic heritage, most American workers, whatever their nationality or race, were eager to respond.

The Roosevelt administration encouraged this enthusiasm, fostering support for its New Deal programs by helping to create and disseminate new forms of mass, democratic culture. The painting of thousands

---

"... MADE IN THE U.S.A."

Thomas Bell's 1941 novel Out of This Furnace *spans three generations in the life of a family of Slovak immigrants who toiled in Pittsburgh's steel mills. The story spans the years from the grandfather's arrival in 1881 to the grandson's participation in the CIO organizing drives of the late 1930s. In the closing pages of the novel, Dobie, the grandson, reflects on the sense of empowerment he and his fellow steelworkers now enjoy, concluding that, despite his ancestry, his participation in the formation of the Steelworkers' Union has made him feel as American as if his family had arrived with the Puritans.*

AND he realized now what it was that had once puzzled him about the CIO men. Whatever their ancestry, they had felt the same way about certain things; and because Dobie had been born and raised in a steel town, where the word meant people who were white, Protestant, middle-class Anglo-Saxons, it hadn't occurred to him that the CIO men were thinking and talking like Americans.

"Maybe not the kind of American that came over on the *Mayflower*," he reflected, "or the kind that's always shooting off their mouths about Americanism and patriotism, including some of the God damndest heels you'd ever want to see, but the kind that's got 'Made in U.S.A.' stamped all over them, from the kind of grub they like to the things they wouldn't do for all the money in the world."

He stared down at the sleeping town without really seeing it.

"Made in the U.S.A.," he thought, "made in the First Ward. Mikie was right; it's too bad a person can't pick their own place to be born in, considering what it does to you. I'm almost as much a product of that mill down there as any rail or ingot they ever turned out. And maybe that's been part of the trouble. If I'm anything at all I'm an American, only I'm not the kind you read about in history books or that they make speeches about on the Fourth of July; anyway, not yet. And a lot of people don't know what to make of it and don't like it. Which is tough on me but is liable to be still tougher on them, because I at least don't have to be told that Braddock [Pennsylvania] ain't Plymouth Rock and this ain't the year 1620."

... Made in the U.S.A., he thought, made in the First Ward. But it wasn't where you were born or how you spelled your name or where your father come from. It was the way you thought and felt about certain things. About freedom of speech and the equality of men and the importance of having one law—the same law—for rich and poor, for the people you liked and the people you didn't like.... About the uses to which wealth and power could honorably be put.... About human dignity, which helped a man live proudly and distinguished his death from an animal's; and, finally, about the value to be put on a human life, one's enemy's no less than one's own.

"The Corn Parade." Few of the post-office murals commissioned by the Treasury Department Section of Fine Arts displayed the humor of Orr C. Fisher's paean to corn. But the Iowa-born Fisher's work suggests the kind of regional boosterism and pride of place that characterized many murals painted by local artists.

of murals on post offices and other federal buildings was one example of this cultural flowering. The idea came from George Biddle, a socially prominent Philadelphian, who had studied painting with the great Mexican muralists. Biddle joined a group of prominent painters in calling for a "revival of mural painting" on the walls of government buildings. In December 1933, the federal government began a long involvement in the production and dissemination of public art. Over the next four years, thousands of artists produced more than 15,000 items, including murals, oils, watercolors, and prints. The subject matter was America, especially America at work. Most of the murals and paintings were done in a heroic style that celebrated ordinary people engaged in the daily struggle to survive.

An even larger public arts program—the Federal Art Project (FAP)—was begun in 1935 within the Works Progress Administration. The FAP built community art centers throughout the South and West, including over one hundred in Arizona alone. More important, the FAP employed as many as 6,000 artists, 90 percent of them on relief. Project artists depicted the human cost of the Depression through images of breadlines, derelicts, and "Hoovervilles." They painted murals for public buildings, made sculptures for public display, and produced prints, especially at the Graphic Arts Workshop in New York. The sensibility of the FAP work, like the WPA's murals, was decidedly populist, depicting the struggles of a multinational, multiracial working class. This approach reflected the left-wing politics of many artists, who found in the WPA a place that allowed them to produce politically engaged art at the same time as they received a modest paycheck.

Labor-oriented theater enjoyed a renaissance during the New Deal years as well. In Minnesota, Charles Walker organized the Theatre Union to produce plays dealing with "deep-going social conflicts, the economic, emotional and cultural problems that confront the majority of the people." In New York, Lee Strasberg and Harold Clurman organized the Group Theatre, which discovered such playwrights as Clifford Odets, William Saroyan, and Irwin Shaw; a number of its actors, such as Lee J. Cobb, later became Broadway and Hollywood stars. Also in New York, the International Ladies' Garment Workers' Union established the Labor Stage in 1935. Its production of *Pins and Needles* became a Broadway hit. Using actors from the garment shops, the show presented satirical sketches about workers' lives.

The most important theatrical development of the decade was the growth of the WPA's Federal Theatre Project, initiated by federal relief administrator Harry Hopkins in 1935 to produce plays about "American life" that working people could afford to attend. The Federal Theatre Project was national in scope and was an important form of popular education; when Sinclair Lewis's play about a possible dic-

"Pocahontas Rescuing Captain John Smith." At times, local tastes clashed with individual artists' expression, particularly when murals portrayed American society, past and present, in a critical light. In the case of Paul Cadmus's mural for Richmond's Parcel Post Building, however, it was male nudity that aroused concern. Although Pocahontas's breast remained bared, along with the foreground Indian brave's buttocks, Cadmus had to retouch a suggestive foxhead that he had mischievously placed over another brave's groin.

One-third of a Nation. Taking the title from FDR's Second Inaugural Address, the 1938 Federal Theatre Project production played to packed houses in New York and ten other cities. Arthur Arent's "living newspaper" play combined documentation and drama—and an imposing four-story tenement set—to convey the causes of and solutions to America's housing crisis.

tatorship in the United States, *It Can't Happen Here,* opened, there were simultaneous productions in twenty-eight theaters around the country, with African-American, Spanish, and Yiddish versions and casts. Among the Federal Theatre's successes were "living newspapers," which presented commentaries on political events; *One-third of a Nation,* a play about the housing crisis, played for almost a year in New York and then moved to ten other cities. In addition to supporting new playwrights and plays on contemporary subjects, the Federal Theatre also sponsored the traditional theatrical repertoire, including plays by Shakespeare, Molière, and George Bernard Shaw. Children's plays, circuses, and vaudeville were also presented across the country.

Other aspects of democratic culture benefited as well from the New Deal's involvement. Thousands of unemployed writers and teachers—including famous authors such as James Agee, Richard Wright, and John Cheever—were hired by the WPA to rediscover the nation's heritage and to preserve the written and oral record of the past. They scoured the nation's backwoods and mountain hollows, collecting folk songs and oral histories of former slaves. They also did exhaustive research on communities across the country, preserving documents and writing guidebooks to and histories of hundreds of towns and cities. The voluminous material collected and written by WPA workers formed the basis of some of the best histories ever written on the nation's diverse communities. It also provided many of the

---

"THE ULTIMATE ARBITER IS THE PEOPLE ..."

The Federal Theatre Project developed "living newspapers" as a vehicle for conveying news and commenting on contemporary political and social issues for a broad popular audience. In the following selection from The Triple A Plowed Under, *FTP writers and actors criticize the U.S. Supreme Court's 1936 decision to declare the Agricultural Adjustment Act (the "Triple A") unconstitutional.*

VOICE OF LIVING NEWSPAPER *(over loudspeaker):* January 6, 1936. . . . Supreme Court invalidates AAA in Hoosac Mills case.
VOICE *(also over loudspeaker):* The majority opinion—Justice Roberts.

> *(As travelers [curtains] open from rear, projection of Constitution is thrown on glass curtain. Discovered in shadow against projection are* JUSTICE STONE, *three other justices, then* JUSTICE ROBERTS, *and the four remaining justices, right.* ROBERTS *rises to one-foot platform directly in front of him. Five justices who concurred in his opinion, turn in profile as he begins to speak.)*

JUSTICE ROBERTS: . . . The Constitution is the supreme law of the land, ordained

insights as well as much of the data used by social historians who thirty years later rewrote the history of ordinary Americans.

The painters, sculptors, playwrights, actors, and writers who participated in New Deal projects reflected and helped to create a public concern about what was happening to America in the midst of the Depression. That public concern was also intensified by still other cultural forms and institutions that emerged during the New Deal, particularly the dramatic rise in government-sponsored documentary photography. The Roosevelt administration, to build broad public support for its programs, encouraged New Deal agencies to document the human suffering that resulted from the economic downturn. The WPA, the Department of Agriculture, and especially the Farm Security Administration (FSA)—the reorganized Resettlement Administration—hired some of that time's most accomplished photographers to travel across America and record the lives of ordinary people. FSA photographers alone shot over 250,000 images of rural and urban life. Some of these photos—particularly Dorothea Lange's haunting evocations of poor farm women, Arthur Rothstein's shots of dust storms, and Walker Evans's depictions of the desperate lives of sharecroppers—became visual icons of the Depression decade. They were widely circulated in the popular magazines of the era, including *Time*, *Look*, and *Life*, and were featured in major museum exhibits and in a number of best-selling books; they helped communicate the human tragedy of the Depression to all Americans.

Movies during the Depression also played a significant role in communicating the changing moral, social, and political values of the New Deal period. Despite the sharp reduction in disposable income, Americans of all classes went to the movies in record numbers during the 1930s. In part, it was because of the introduction of sound after 1927; "talkies" made the movies that period's most popular form of entertainment. But Americans also responded to the changing content of motion pictures. Among the more memorable pictures were those that dealt with social and moral themes, including *Little Caesar* (1930) and *Public Enemy* (1931),

and established by the people. All legislation must conform to the principles it lays down. The power to confer or withhold unlimited benefits is the power to coerce or destroy. This [the AAA] is coercion by economic pressure. The judgment is affirmed. . . .

THOMAS JEFFERSON: There must be an arbiter somewhere. True, there must. But does that prove it is either the Congress or the Supreme Court? The ultimate arbiter is the people of the Union, assembled by their deputies in convention at the call of Congress or two-thirds of the States.

(Travelers slowly close, with JEFFERSON *remaining standing on platform, center.)*

VOICE OVER LOUDSPEAKER: Farmers voted, by more than 6 to 1, for continuance of Triple-A.

(Men start crossing stage in front of travelers, from right to left.)

FIRST MAN: The AAA is dead. . . . *(Exits left.)*

SECOND MAN: No more allotment checks. . . . *(Exits left.)*

THIRD MAN: What the hell're we agoin' to do this winter? *(Exits left.)*

A WOMAN: How're we goin' t' get coal? *(Exits left.)*

FOURTH MAN: They say the people wrote the Constitution. . . . *(Exits left.)*

FIFTH MAN: Them people have been dead a long time. . . . *(Also exits.)*

Blackout

The Fields family, Hale County, Alabama, summer 1936. From 1935 to 1943, photographers working for several government agencies, principally the Farm Security Administration, produced the most enduring images of the Great Depression. This Walker Evans picture of rural poor, like Dorothea Lange's photographs in the previous chapter, was part of that massive documentation effort. Wishing to convey both suffering and dignity, FSA photographers searingly presented conditions to the American public, selecting effective compositions and poses influenced by advertising and mass-market magazine formats.

a look at the human pathos that led to criminality; *I Am a Fugitive from a Chain Gang* (1932), which explored the social origins of crime and the inhumanity of punishment; and *The Grapes of Wrath* (1940), based on the best-selling novel by John Steinbeck, which offered a sympathetic portrait of "Okies" forced by the drought and dust storms to abandon their Oklahoma farms for the cruel fate of migratory laborers in California. Also popular were the comedies of the Marx Brothers, W. C. Fields, and Mae West, all of whose films lampooned the social pretensions of the wealthy, and the social messages implicit in Frank Capra's *Mr. Deeds Goes to Town* (1936) and *Mr. Smith Goes to Washington* (1939), in which the hero, played by James Stewart, overcomes the corrupt practices of a powerful U.S. senator and wins a victory for "the little guy." Of course, pure fantasy films were also very popular: Busby Berkeley's extravagant production numbers in such films as *Gold Diggers of 1933* offered moviegoers escape from the dreary circumstances of America in the Depression. But many 1930s movies communicated the message that poverty had dire consequences and that ordinary citizens had to play a part in solving the nation's deepening economic and political problems.

As the New Deal era's cultural nationalism deepened, American radicals sought to adapt their politics to fit the changing American scene. The growing popularity of FDR and his programs led many leftists to turn away from the radical identities and theories out of which their parties and ideas had emerged. Socialist Party leader Norman Thomas, for example, began to talk of "industrial democracy"

I Am a Fugitive from a Chain Gang, Mervyn LeRoy's 1932 film, starring Paul Muni as a wrongly imprisoned World War I veteran, exposed the abuses of the southern penal system.

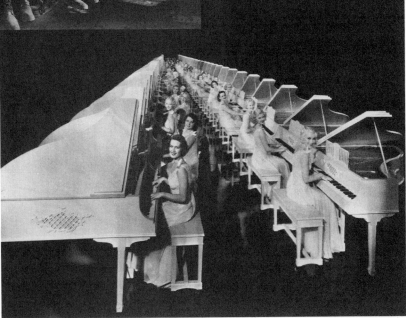

Gold Diggers of 1933. One of dance director Busby Berkeley's extravagant musical numbers in Mervyn LeRoy's sunnier treatment of "making it" in the Depression era theater world.

rather than socialism. "Democracy," Thomas wrote, "means, in Lincoln's phrase, government of the people, by the people, and for the people. . . . [I]ndustrial democracy is the application of that same idea to our economic life."

Communist Party leaders followed a similar path. Instructed in 1936 by leaders of the Communist International to create a broad alliance against "fascism" in the United States, American Communists formulated a strategy for escaping their isolation on America's revolutionary fringe. The party's "Popular Front" strategy, which involved establishing mass organizations devoted to broad popular issues such as public housing, worker benefits, and peace, led to a spurt in membership to 80,000 in the late 1930s, with hundreds of thousands more sympathizers. Popular Front organizations, which brought together middle-class and working-class citizens, embraced Americanism, displaying pictures of Lincoln and Jefferson, writing and singing folk songs about America's greatness, and giving speeches about the dignity of labor and the decency of the common man. The Communist Party's version of patriotism stressed a broad cultural pluralism that defined the nation's greatness as residing in the people in all their diversity.

The works of popular writers, such as John Dos Passos's *U.S.A.* and John Steinbeck's *The Grapes of Wrath*, and popular entertainers, such as singer-songwriter Woody Guthrie and actor and singer Paul Robeson (all of whom were close to the Communist Party), further popularized this notion of cultural democracy. Popular music written and performed by Communists and other radicals drew on the nation's musical inheritance. Woody Guthrie's "This Land Is Your Land"; the old Wobbly tune "Solidarity Forever" (sung to the tune of "The Battle Hymn of the Republic"); and "Roll the Union On," the Southern Tenant Farmers' Union's organizing song, played an important role in creating a sense of America's working people as bearers of the nation's democratic heritage at the same time as they allowed the Communist Party to bask in the warm glow of American values. While this change in political and cultural direction resulted in sub-

---

"I AM HANGING ON TO THE PRINCIPLES OF THE NEW DEAL . . ."

In his classic 1941 study of rubberworkers in Akron, Ohio, the sociologist Alfred Winslow Jones painted a complex picture of workers' political consciousness at the close of the New Deal era. Jones's study revealed that despite participating in various industrial actions (including the 1936 sit-down strike) and their anger at the abuses of banks, bosses, and corrupt policemen, a large majority of Akron's unionized rubberworkers continued to accept the basic right of capitalists to use their property as they saw fit. This belief was tempered, however, by a strong sense of social justice growing out of the workers' own experiences in fighting to organize a union.

The following interview with James Hunt, a tirebuilder whose family had been coalminers in Ohio for four generations and who had moved to Akron to work in the rubber plants twenty years earlier, typified the attitudes of many Akron workers and unionists. Hunt's comments suggest that while American workers might be angry about the way employers and political leaders denied them the right to a decent job and fair wages, they still believed that they would win those rights within the framework of the existing political and economic order.

ALL my spare time I devote to the union—to meetings and activities. That's my

stantial increases in party membership, the Popular Front strategy also diluted the Communist Party's distinct political identity as the largest and most important group fighting for revolutionary socialism and for a distinct class-based culture.

Nonetheless, as the New Deal and the labor and radical movements reached high tide in 1937, there were signs that many American workers felt, perhaps for the first time, that they were a political, organizational, and cultural force to be reckoned with. The fragmentation and divisions that earlier had plagued the labor movement seemed to give way to a larger sense of unity in which differences could be accepted. That labor unity, for the first time in nearly half a century, encompassed African-American, Mexican-American, and women workers as well.

AFRICAN-AMERICAN WORKERS

Blacks suffered more deeply than other Americans the ravages of poverty in the Depression. New Deal public works programs did alleviate some African-American destitution. In Cleveland, for example, by the mid-1930s the federal government had become the largest employer of African-Americans, whose jobless rate fell from 50 to 30 percent. New Deal agencies also built over 3,000 slum clearance units that were made available to the city's African-American residents. This total represented nearly half the public housing units built in Cleveland under the New Deal.

Yet racism continued in the city's public works and housing programs. Although federal officials had committed their agencies to hire skilled blacks in proportion to their representation in Cleveland's total labor force, African-Americans were hired almost exclusively as unskilled laborers on public works projects. And Cleveland's public housing reinforced segregation; blacks were barred from projects built in mostly white or all-white areas.

President Roosevelt and his cabinet officers received hundreds of letters complaining of

social enjoyment. I want to see the union eventually a sound and steady organization. I am not at all satisfied with it the way it works at present.... Don't get me wrong. I'm a hundred per cent for unions and I think we are twice as well off since the union was organized.... Since the union was organized we have had more freedom, security, dependability, and stability in wages. The union has sprung up as a sort of social change in the face of the present fast speed-up system. In the beginning the union grew so fast that ... anybody and everybody just jumped in and went along. Socialism has crept in and I'm no socialist so I greatly disapprove of that. I want to see majority rule in a union as well as in our government, but that is not true in either at present.... We must build a constructive organization instead of a destructive one.

... The big trouble with the New Deal is that a few people run the country instead of the majority like they should. Although I have been non-partisan all my life, I am hanging on to the principles of the New Deal, but I really know that it won't solve our problems.

... Every worker should make more than just living expenses, but the average one certainly does not. There ought to be a limit on how much the rich can earn and on the profits of any factory or corporation. There ought also to be a minimum for everybody. There is no sense in one man making a dollar an hour and another working twice as hard and making fifty cents. But I don't contend that everyone should make equal wages for that would be wrong too.

Public housing. Legislators and real-estate lobbyists tried to keep expenditures for public housing low, contributing to the drab uniformity of many government-sponsored projects. But some public housing offered inexpensive homes with the style and amenities of a locality's private residences. With their tall windows and cast-iron balconies, New Orleans' St. Thomas Houses, for example, fit comfortably into the city's traditional architectural design.

the discriminatory actions of local relief officials. From Chicago came an anonymous letter asking, "We would like to know do the government insist on Jim Crow on the W.P.A. projects." From Vicksburg, Mississippi, another anonymous letter claimed: "The way they are treating the Darkies here is a Shame. They wont give them food nor Cloths nor Work too do[.] When they Ask for Any thing they drive them away as they were dogs."

The limitations in New Deal efforts to relieve African-American poverty convinced many black leaders of the necessity of allying with the labor movement. As early as 1933, the president of the Brotherhood of Sleeping Car Porters (BSCP), A. Philip Randolph, had urged the annual AFL convention to mount an active unionizing campaign among black workers spearheaded by African-American organizers. Only by making the labor movement truly interracial, he argued, could the unions achieve labor unity, avoid racially motivated strikebreaking, and "remove from the hands of the employing class the weapon of race prejudice." Randolph's resolution was quashed. The following year Randolph proposed that the AFL repudiate the exclusion of African-American workers from any trade union and expel any affiliate that persisted in such discrimination. That resolution, too, was rejected, just as it was each time Randolph reintroduced it in the next few years. The practical result of this refusal could be sharply felt by African-American workers. In 1940, for example, when the AFL's lily-white International Brotherhood of Boilermakers successfully struck the Tampa (Florida) Shipbuilding Corporation for union recognition, six hundred black employees who had supported the strike swiftly found themselves frozen out of their jobs as well as the union.

In the early 1930s, the 35,000 members of the BSCP contained nearly half of all the African-American trade unionists in the nation. Nevertheless, the AFL withheld an international charter from the BSCP for seven years. Finally, in July 1935 an overwhelming vote by Pullman porters compelled a federal mediation board to certify the BSCP as "duly designated and authorized" to represent the porters and maids of the Pullman Company. A year later the BSCP finally won full rights as an independent AFL union. In 1937 a third milestone was passed when the BSCP forced the Pullman Company to the bargaining table, winning for its employees higher wages, greater job security, and reductions in hours.

These achievements catapulted Randolph into a position of major influence. In February 1936 he helped found and became president of the National Negro Congress (NNC), a federation of existing organizations, including the Sleeping Car Porters, the Communist Party, the Urban League, and some sections of the NAACP. Although the NNC did not begin as a Communist-dominated organization, the Communist Party played a big role within it, treating it as its Popular Front organization among African-Americans.

The NNC's first convention, in Chicago, attracted more than 5,000 observers and delegates from 585 organizations. Randolph's keynote address proclaimed: "The Negro should not place his problems for solution . . . at the feet of his white sympathizers and allies . . . for in the final analysis, the salvation of the Negro . . . must come from within." John P. Davis, an attorney, was selected to direct the NNC's day-to-day operations.

In 1936–37, the NNC's main work took place on the local level, initiated and coordinated by seventy regional councils. The councils' efforts focused first on local instances of discrimination. The Chicago council, for example, emphasized jobs, housing (it conducted rent strikes on the South Side), and public relief. It forced the addition of black motormen to the previously all-white workforce on city streetcars. It also mobilized 10,000 people in defense of a public housing project under attack from real-estate interests. The Boston council exposed and won withdrawal of racist school textbooks and fought discrimination in hiring. In Detroit, the NNC fought the fascist Black Legion. The Washington, D.C., council collected 24,000 signatures on a petition protesting police brutality, winning the creation of a civilian trial board. In New York, the NNC-backed Greater New York Coordinating Committee for Employment, led by the Reverend Adam Clayton Powell, Jr., induced the Uptown Chamber of Commerce in 1938 to fill a third of all retail jobs with African-Americans and to hire blacks preferentially until that goal was reached.

Much of the NNC's work focused on what Randolph called "the movement to draw Negro workers into labor organizations and break down the color bar in the trade unions that now have it." Nationally, the NCC campaigned in support of Randolph's fight against the AFL's Jim Crow policies. The Richmond, Virginia, council led thousands of black tobacco workers in the first strikes in that industry in three decades. In Chicago, the council worked with the International Ladies' Garment Workers' Union to enroll 3,000 African-American women employed in South Side clothing factories. The Washington, D.C., council helped the Hotel and Restaurant Workers' Union win labor contracts.

The drive to unionize the steel industry was central to the NNC's work. By 1936 the country's 85,000 black steelworkers constituted 20 percent of all laborers in the industry. "There is no effort in which the National Negro Congress could possibly engage at this time more helpful to large numbers of Negro workers," John Davis wrote, "than the organization of Negro steel workers." This was true because "85,000 Negro steel workers with union cards will signal the beginning of the organization of all Negro workers." The steel drive, Davis believed, offered the opportunity "to write a Magna Carta for black labor." Davis persuaded the CIO leaders to appoint a dozen African-Americans as SWOC organizers, many of them local leaders of the National Negro Congress. The NCC's regional councils also helped win support for SWOC in the African-American community.

Long experience with the AFL left most African-American workers and community leaders with a deep-seated suspicion, if not outright hostility, toward the labor movement. Heeding Randolph's calls for unity between black and white workers and drawing upon the mineworkers' positive experience in creating

---

"... NOTHING BUT GOOD TO SAY ABOUT THE CIO"

Jim Cole, an African-American packinghouse worker from Chicago, describes the CIO's commitment to organizing interracial industrial unions. The Packinghouse Workers' Union was the CIO's most integrated union.

■I'M working in the Beef Kill section. Butcher on the chain. Been in the place twenty years, I believe. You got to have a certain amount of skill to do the job I'm doing. Long ago, I wanted to join the AFL union, the Amalgamated Butchers and Meat Cutters.... They wouldn't let me in. Never said it to my face, the reason of it was plain, Negro. Just didn't want a Negro man to have what he should. That's wrong—you know that's wrong.

Long about 1937 the CIO came. Well, I tell you, we Negroes were glad to see it come. Sometimes the bosses or the company stooges try to keep the white boys from joining the union. They say, "You don't want to belong to a black man's organization. That's all the CIO is." Don't fool nobody, but they got to lie, spread lying words around....

I don't care if the union don't do another lick of work raising our pay, or settling grievances about anything. I'll always believe they done the greatest thing in the world getting everybody who works in the yards together, and breaking up the hate and bad feelings that used to be held against the Negro. We all doing our work now, nothing but good to say about the CIO.

In my own local, we elected our officers, and it's the same all over. We try to get every people represented. President of the local, he's Negro. First vice president, he's Polish. Second vice president, he's Irish. Other officers: Scotchman, Lithuanian, Negro, German. Many different people can't understand English very well and we have to have union interpreters for lots of our members. But that don't make no mind; they all friends in the union, even if they can't say nothing except "Brother" and shake hands.

interracial unions, the CIO strove to bridge the color chasm. The pressure of black and radical white workers considerably strengthened that commitment. In 1936, Philip Murray promised that in the CIO unions "there shall be no discrimination under any circumstances, regardless of creed, color, or nationalities."

The campaign to unionize the steel industry put such promises to the test. Black-white conflict had helped kill the nationwide steel strike of 1919. In the 1930s, by contrast, the presence of black SWOC organizers and local officers helped reassure skeptical African-American steelworkers that their interests would be taken seriously by the union. Indeed, during the 1930s, the SWOC had a larger proportion of black officers than black members.

In Baltimore, employers had long used "divide and rule" tactics to inflame race relations. The CIO succeeded in overcoming deep and long-lived African-American suspicions of white-dominated unions, especially in the city's steel mills, garment shops, and shipyards, which had a large black workforce. Edward Lewis, head of the city's most active civil rights organization, the Urban League, was deeply committed to interracial unionism. He persuaded the city's African-American churches to open their doors to the CIO, and these congregations heard news about strikes and rallies from their ministers. The Interdenominational Ministers' Alliance endorsed CIO campaigns and sponsored boycotts; some CIO organizers joined African-American churches and sang in their choirs. Despite the fact that the publishers of Baltimore's black newspaper, the *Afro-American*, were notoriously anti-union, the paper covered strikes and union meetings, publicized rallies, and allowed Edward Lewis to spread his pro-labor message in its pages.

When the SWOC began organizing Bethlehem Steel's Sparrows Point mill in 1936, it appealed to African-American workers through their community organizations. Arthur Murray, a veteran black steelworker and an organizer for the National Negro Congress, came to Baltimore as soon as the SWOC was organized; he walked door-to-door through East Baltimore, pleading with blacks to trust the white leadership of the CIO. It took five years for the SWOC to organize the Sparrows Point plant, and African-American workers played a major role in the victory.

SWOC victories during the 1930s brought an end to some of the most glaring discriminatory practices in the steel industry and an easing of previously deep racial divisions among steelworkers. "Well, you know, I'll tell you what the CIO has done," one Chicago black worker noted. "Before, everyone used to make remarks about, 'That dirty Jew,' 'that stinkin' black bastard,' 'that low-life Bohunk,' but you know I never hear that kind of stuff anymore. I don't like to brag, but I'm one of the best-liked men in my department. If there is ever any trouble, the men usually come to me." "I can say this," the white financial secretary of one steel local suggested, "the union has done a lot in the mills to overcome and educate white workers and break down the barriers of discrimination. . . . Through union activity, white and colored . . . are drawn closer together on the job. This is not peculiar to the relation of Negroes and whites but true of all national groups."

Others put these changes more cautiously. Asked whether "the white union men are sincere, this time, in urging Negroes to join" the union, an African-American steelworker replied: "They're sincere enough, because it's the only way out, or else they'd have the same thing as in 1919. They realize this, so whether they like it or not, they have to include Negroes. We know it, and they know it. They're sincere, if you can call that sincereness."

As these words indicate, the legacy of racial antagonism and suspicion in the industry was not easily or quickly overcome. For example, cooperation between white and black workers on the job and in unions did not automatically bring personal friendships or easy social mixing. "If you ask them to your dances, they'll come and they won't just dance with each other," the white president of a SWOC women's auxiliary complained, "but some of them will try to dance with white people. If they do, the white women will just stop going to dances. There's something about colored men that just makes you afraid." UAW locals sometimes capitulated to such fears, canceling union-sponsored social affairs.

Also, rigid seniority rules (designed to block company favoritism in promotions, layoffs, and recalls) helped perpetuate existing discriminatory employment patterns that relegated African-Americans to the most dangerous, unhealthy, and poorly paid jobs. And in the South, at U.S. Steel's Birmingham complex, for example, the SWOC did not even try to overcome the segregationist attitudes of the majority of white steelworkers. Despite these weaknesses, however, the CIO attitude toward African-Americans in the SWOC, the UAW, the National Maritime Union, and the Packinghouse Workers constituted a significant advance for interracial unionism.

WOMEN WORKERS ORGANIZE

Hundreds of thousands of women flocked to the union banner during the New Deal era. While the CIO said and did little about the particular problems facing working women, women nonetheless played an important role in building the CIO. The number of female unionists tripled during the decade, reaching 800,000 by 1940. In addition, CIO unions encouraged the formation of women's auxiliaries, continuing to draw relatives of union members into active support of the labor movement. And in specific cases, the CIO made special efforts to deal with women's particular concerns, notably the still unaddressed demand for equal pay for equal work.

Major union drives occurred in industries with large numbers of female workers, notably in garments, textiles, and electrical assembly. As a result of these campaigns, the CIO's new Textile Workers' Union grew from 20,000 in 1936 to 120,000 in 1943. The Amalgamated Clothing Workers of America (ACWA) went from about 60,000 members in 1932 to over 300,000 a decade later. The membership of the International Ladies' Garment Workers' Union (ILGWU) swelled from 40,000 to 200,000, and wages in the New York City dress industry increased 35 to 65 percent. In just the first nine months of 1937, membership in the United Electrical and Radio Workers of America (UE) grew from 33,000 to 120,000. The UE's constitution sought the unity of "all workers in our industry on an industrial basis, and rank and file control, regardless of craft, age, sex, nationality, race, creed, or political belief."

In 1937 and 1938, thousands of women in manufacturing and service jobs engaged in sit-down strikes and other militant actions. Philadelphia's Pennstate Tobacco Company responded to a sit-down by 250 of its female employees by trying to relocate its shop and equipment; the women then placed their bodies in the path of the moving trucks. In San Antonio, Texas, in the spring of 1937, Mexican-American women garment workers, organized into an ILGWU local, won a three-month strike against a local dress company despite the arrest of 50 pickets and a harsh court injunction. In Detroit, 200 young women employed by two F. W. Woolworth stores sat down at work one Saturday afternoon in early March 1937. They demanded a 10-cent-per-hour pay

---

"ALMOST EVERYBODY WAS THERE . . ."

Women dominated the workforce in a number of industries, including mechanized laundry work. Evelyn Macon, a laundry worker in New York City, describes how the CIO organized the United Laundry Workers' Union in her plant in 1937. All told, the union signed up 14,000 New York laundry workers that year.

I worked as a press operator before we unionized. Slavery is the only word that could describe our conditions under which we worked. At least fifty-four hours a week it was speed-up, speed-up . . . for almost ten hours per day. . . .

The toilet at our place wasn't fit for animals. . . . When I complained, the boss said, "There ain't many places paying ten dollars a week now, Evie." That ended my protests, because I didn't want to get fired. . . .

One day a fellow got a job at our place as a sorter. He certainly did not speed up like the rest of us. The boss told him he would have to work faster. He laughed at the boss and told him that a man was a fool to rush during the first hour when he had seventeen more staring him in the face. . . . But the boss hit the ceiling when lunch hour came. He came out and yelled, "On the fly," which meant for us not to stop for lunch, but to eat while we worked. . . .

"Bruiser," the new fellow, picked up his lunch and went out. . . . In exactly one hour Bruiser was back. . . . The boss charged up to him demanding, "What the hell do you mean by going out to lunch during a rush?" Bruiser laughed at him and said he always ate his meals on time. . . . [T]he boss paid him and fired him.

That night when I got off . . . Bruiser . . . said he was a CIO organizer and he gave me a leaflet . . . [about] a meeting the following night. I don't have to tell you that I was the first one to reach the meeting. Almost everybody was there. . . .

The boss was frantic. . . . He fired some of us and the rest walked out. We threw a picket line around the place. We had the one scab and the boss imported others. . . . They [the scabs] messed up so that the boss called us back to work at union hours, union wages, and better conditions.

"Hello, Mama. We're makin' history." Denys Wortman's cartoon in the March 25, 1937, New York *World-Telegram* captures the excitement and sense of power felt by many working men and working women when they participated in militant labor action.

increase (on salaries as low as $10 a week), a forty-hour workweek, and collective-bargaining rights. After seven days, they won major concessions from Woolworth's management, including union recognition. Incorporating new ideas into a World War I army song, the women strikers ridiculed romantic notions about their lives, contrasting the situation of working women with that of Woolworth heiress Barbara Hutton.

> *Barbara Hutton has the dough, parlez-vous*
> *Where she gets it, sure we know, parlez-vous*
> *We slave at Woolworth's five-and-dime*
> *The pay we get is sure a crime.*
> *Hinkey-dinkey parlez-vous.*

Working women also joined in solidarity actions in key industrial conflicts. The Flint UAW Women's Auxiliary and Women's Emergency Brigade provided models for similar groups in Cleveland, Toledo, Detroit, Lansing, and elsewhere. In Akron, Ohio, the United Rubber Workers' Women's Auxiliary worked to counter employer pressure on strikers' family members. When the Akron strikers were victorious, the Akron *Beacon Journal* reported, "Shoulder to shoulder with their men, the wives, daughters, and sisters of strikers marched through the business district to strike headquarters in a great victory parade." The Chicago steelworkers, the Kansas City Packinghouse Workers' Organizing Committee, and New York's Transport Workers' Union all boasted active women's auxiliaries as well.

The role played by women inside the CIO brought about some changes in the way union leaders treated women members. In May 1936, for example, the United Electrical and Radio Workers of America won a 10 percent wage increase for men and a 15 percent increase for women employed at Philco in Philadelphia. "The purpose of this demand," a union representative explained, "is to close up the gap in wages between men and women workers." The East Pittsburgh UE local required lower dues from its female than from its male workers until wage differentials could be eliminated.

Nevertheless, the CIO, like the AFL, remained overwhelmingly male in leadership and made little attempt to place women in leadership positions. Only one woman sat on the ILGWU's twenty-four-person executive board, although three-quarters of the membership was female. Nor did many male union leaders devote much time or energy to women's concerns. Stella Nowicki, a Communist Party member and Packinghouse Union activist, noted that the male union officials "didn't take up the problems women had" and that "the union didn't encourage women to come to meetings." And despite the UE's example, little was done in the CIO to fight sex discrimination at work. Some CIO unions—including the almost half-female Amalgamated Clothing Workers—tolerated sex-segregated pay scales and seniority lists. Other unions organized their members into sex-segregated locals.

Those women who played leading roles in labor organizing during the 1930s tended to be people living in unusual circumstances—divorcées, widows, political radicals, or members of union-conscious households. For example, Margaret Darin, a leading member of the UE's East Pittsburgh local, came from a trade-union and socialist family.

Most working women were young and unmarried and lived at home with their parents. They tended to question their social subordination only after the mass movement got under way. "No girl would say anything or even complain, because she was afraid she would lose her job," garment worker Anna Weinstein recalled:

> The boss would do everything in his power to rob the girl of her self-confidence, and in a short period of time she became nothing more than a robot. With the coming of the union all these things changed. Now the girls have a power stronger than the bosses to back them. We are no longer

robots. We are independent. We are strong. No longer can a boss cheat us out of pay. We now have the courage to tell him he is doing wrong and he must stop.

Not only wage-earning women experienced a sense of empowerment and purpose. A woman married to a Cadillac striker and eventually drawn into UAW support work reported: "I found a common understanding and unselfishness I'd never known in my life. I'm living for the first time with a definite goal. I want a decent living for not only my family but for everyone. Just being a woman isn't enough anymore. I want to be a human being." "A new type of woman was born in the strike," a female UAW activist from Flint believed. "Women who only yesterday were horrified at unionism, who felt inferior to the task of organizing, speaking, leading, have, as if overnight, become the spearhead in the battle of unionism." Labor journalist Mary Heaton Vorse described a meeting of these women: "The hall was packed with women, the men standing in a fringe at the back. The chairwoman of the meeting was in command." As she watched, "women from different towns got up and talked about the many activities in which they were engaged, what they did for their children, of the classes formed, how their committees worked, how they made little plays about the episodes of the strike." Vorse concluded, "All of the women were finding in themselves new powers and new strength and they had found each other."

"... A LARGE GROUP OF GIRLS IN THIS OFFICE VERY MUCH INTERESTED IN HAVING THE UNION"

In this selection from an oral interview, Florence Luscomb recalls the CIO drive to organize women officeworkers, an increasingly important occupational category, into industrial unions. Luscomb had a long and distinguished career as a Progressive reformer, suffragist, trade unionist, and peace activist. Educated as an architect at MIT, Luscomb was an officer in the NAACP, an organizer for the International Ladies Garment Workers' Union, and, as she recalls, president of the Boston local of the CIO's United Professional and Office Workers of America.

I joined the American Federation of Labor, what they called, the Stenographers, Typewriters, Bookkeepers, and Accountants Union. Not typists, but typewriters. I joined it in the early thirties, because I believed in labor unions, and so I wanted to be a member. And it was really just a fake union. There was just this one public stenographers' office in Boston, and that was a union office.... When I became president in 1936, I wanted to put on big campaign to unionize more office workers. And they [the AFL union] wouldn't do it.... When the Congress of Industrial Organizations came along and started to establish a United Office and Professional Workers Union ... we set up local No. 3 of the UOPWA in the CIO. I was the president for several years, and we did a lot of very active work without getting a very large union.

For example, there was one big firm which had quite a large office staff, and they paid very low wages. We used to go around and find one girl in the office who would think that they ought to be organized, and she'd give us the names and addresses of all the office workers. We'd go and visit them in their homes, and talk union with them. And we got a large group of girls in this office who were very much interested in having the union there. The firm got wind of it, that they were probably going to have a strike on their hands. So they raised their girls' pay, whereupon the girls lost all interest in joining the union! And that happened various times. We got more stenographers with pay raises than we got members of the union, but we did gradually build up the union. It was a new idea for office workers to organize—it was a very unusual idea. They felt themselves socially superior to the person working in a factory, although they might get much less pay than the girls who were working in the factory. The CIO didn't give much assistance in having secretaries organized; they'd be too busy trying to organize the textile workers, and the railroad workers, and large "important" bodies of the working class.

THE BUSINESS COUNTERATTACK

The working-class upsurge after 1935 resulted in extraordinary gains for the labor movement. But in 1937, just months after the UAW breakthrough at General Motors, it became clear that business leaders were readying a massive counterattack.

Several developments emboldened business. First, the CIO unionization drive and the New Deal were increasingly attacked by conservative politicians, the antilabor press, business organizations, and the AFL. Second, FDR miscalculated in announcing plans to pack the U.S. Supreme Court. Finally, a sharp decline in the economy in 1937 further sapped the president's popularity and stalled the CIO organizing campaigns.

The counterattack against the CIO and the Second New Deal took many forms. Emblematic was the House Committee on Un-American Activities, chaired by Texas Democrat Martin Dies, which held hearings in 1938 that suggested that many of America's problems were caused by Communist agitators. From the CIO's standpoint, the most damaging witness was John P. Frey, head of the AFL Metal Trades Department, who charged that "there are more than 145 well-known members of the Communist Party who are on the payroll of the CIO." John L. Lewis, he added, was a frequent guest at the Russian embassy, where Lewis "has been dined [and] . . . wined." Lewis had never covered up his employment of radical organizers in CIO unionization struggles. But Frey's words, no matter how absurd, planted seeds of suspicion in the minds of many citizens.

The public also began to weary of the sit-down strikes that spread throughout industry following the UAW's dramatic triumph in Flint. The public mood, shaped by the press, began to turn, not against employers who openly violated the Wagner Act, nor against the police forces and militia who refused to carry out the act's intent, but against unionists. Politicians who had supported organized labor out of respect for its political clout were quick to note the shifting winds.

The CIO–New Deal coalition was also weakened by a major miscalculation by FDR. After his landslide victory in November 1936, the president decided to move against his strongest surviving opponent: the U.S. Supreme Court. Fearful that the Court would invalidate the legislation of his Second New Deal as it had the NRA, Roosevelt proposed in the winter of 1937 to add four new justices to the Court as a means of ensuring a pro–New Deal majority.

FDR's decision to "pack the Court" proved a political disaster. Outrage at what many considered to be "changing the rules" in midgame turned many New Deal congressmen against the president. The largely anti-Roosevelt press opposed the "dictatorial" design. Popular sentiment, so fervent for the president in November, began to turn.

The president, unused to defeat in the halls of Congress, slowly and ungraciously retreated.

The sorry fate of Philip Murray's plan to quickly organize the rest of the steel industry after U.S. Steel's capitulation to the SWOC in March 1937 epitomized the success of the right-wing counterattack. During May and June 1937, the SWOC confronted a coalition of steel corporations, including Bethlehem, Republic, Inland, and Youngstown, that together employed nearly 200,000 workers. Only in comparison with the gigantic U.S. Steel Corporation did this group merit its nickname "Little Steel."

When the Little Steel strike began in late May, the Youngstown and Inland plants in East Chicago, Indiana, were immediately shut down by well-organized picketers, 75 percent of whom were Mexicans, according to one SWOC official. These initial union successes did not particularly faze steel company officials, who displayed planning, determination, and sheer ruthlessness that caught SWOC leaders such as Philip Murray—with his sunny expectations of a simple "mopping-up operation"—quite unprepared. For example, Republic Steel managers had spent nearly $50,000 during May to reequip the company's private police force with an arsenal of billy clubs and nightsticks, pistols, rifles, shotguns, tear gas grenades, and gas guns. The steel companies also organized anti-union "citizens' alliances" in each of the steel towns. These alliances, though mostly creatures of the corporations, gave the anti-union efforts popular legitimacy. The press depicted the SWOC as a dictatorial force trying to coerce workers to join unions against their will. As a result, the steel corporations, backed by their business allies, and state and local governments were prepared to launch a relentless and bloody onslaught against the SWOC. Although rank-and-file steelworkers demonstrated great courage, their meetings and picket lines were repeatedly broken up by armed strikebreakers, vigilantes, police, and the National Guard.

The mobilization of the antilabor forces had immediate political ramifications as well. In Illinois, Pennsylvania, and Ohio, three states that were central battlegrounds for the CIO organizing campaigns, prominent Democratic politicians—Mayor Edward Kelly of Chicago, Governor Martin Davey of Ohio, and Governor George Earle, Jr., of Pennsylvania—turned the power of government against the unions. The role played by Chicago's police in the suppression of the SWOC strike at Republic Steel on Memorial Day in 1937 was emblematic of both the dramatic shift in the political winds and the naked savagery of the employer-government counterattack.

That afternoon, an American-flag-bearing crowd of over one thousand steelworkers, their families (including children), and supporters marched to the main gate of Republic Steel on Chicago's South Side.

"The Memorial Day Massacre." One of the many photographs taken of the May 29, 1937, incident outside the gates of the Republic Steel Company's South Chicago factory. During the subsequent investigation by the Senate's LaFollette Committee, these images—including motion-picture newsreel footage—proved that the brutal suppression was unprovoked by the unarmed strikers. Only two words were audible on the newsreel sound track: "God Almighty!"

The demonstrators represented a cross section of the ethnically diverse workforce in the Chicago steel industry, including southern Europeans, who probably constituted a majority, and smaller numbers of African-Americans and Mexican-Americans. Max Guzmán, a Mexican worker at Republic Steel, was one of the two flag-bearers at the head of the crowd. The mood of the marchers was peaceful; Mayor Kelly had promised to respect the union's right to picket at the plant. Two blocks north of the plant gate, the first ranks of the crowd encountered a force of two hundred Chicago police.

For a few minutes, individual marchers talked with the police, asking to be allowed to set up a picket line; the police refused. From the ranks of the strikers, several rocks were thrown. Immediately, the police opened fire on the crowd. As men, women, and children ran for their lives, policemen shot the fleeing figures in the back, killing ten. Police bullets struck thirty others, including three children, permanently disabling nine people. Another twenty-eight were hospitalized with injuries inflicted by police clubs and ax handles.

The headlines in one of Chicago's newspapers the next day read: "Reds Riot at Steel Mill." A graphic Paramount Pictures newsreel of the bloody conflict was never shown in Chicago for fear of "inciting riots." And a coroner's jury pronounced the killings "justifiable homicide." On June 2, the SWOC gave the ten slain marchers a mass funeral.

The Memorial Day Massacre, as it came to be known, set the tone for what followed. Across the Midwest, eight more strikers were killed in June, another 160 were seriously wounded, and many more were subjected to tear-gassing and arrest. In Monroe, Michigan, an anti-union crowd brutally beat black SWOC organizer Leonidies McDonald. Afterward, Republic Steel's private police tear-gassed union pickets and burned the SWOC's Monroe headquarters. In Youngstown, Ohio, deputies shot two strikers outside Republic's gates; another forty-two men and women were injured. The National Guard—sent in by Ohio governor Davey and at first welcomed by SWOC leaders—jailed all the union's organizers and hundreds of its members.

Davey's betrayal of the CIO forces that had helped him win election testified to the impact of the business counterattack. Elected on President Roosevelt's coattails, with strong support by the CIO, Davey sensed that the mobilization of anti-union elements in his state combined with fierce press attacks on "violent" and "radical" union activists had turned many of his constituents against labor. Though unionists had seemed underdogs during the dark years of the Depression, now many people saw them more as bullies. And so Davey, declaring that the "right to work is no less sacred than the right to strike," ordered the National Guard to protect and escort strikebreakers into the struck steel plants. Picketing and union meetings were also forbidden. Ohio National Guardsmen killed and wounded dozens of strikers and jailed hundreds more in the confrontations that followed.

Staggered, Philip Murray called on President Roosevelt to aid the steelworkers, who had

---

". . . A BLOODSTAINED FIELD OF BATTLE"

The novelist Howard Fast describes the Memorial Day Massacre. Although he was not present in Chicago, Fast based his dramatic description on the extensive newsreel footage and still photographs entered into evidence at the U.S. Senate Committee on Education and Labor investigation of the Republic Steel violence.

MEMORIAL Day in Chicago in 1937 was hot, humid, and sunny; it was the right kind of day for the parade and the holiday.

. . . Most of the strikers felt good. . . . The strike was less than a week old; the strikers had not yet felt the pinch of hunger, and there was a good sense of solidarity everywhere.

. . . Republic Steel stood abrupt out of the flat prairie. Snakelike, the line of pickets crossed the meadowland, singing at first: "Solidarity forever! The union makes us strong," but then the song died, as the sun-drenched plain turned ominous, as five hundred blue-coated policemen took up stations between the strikers and the plant.

. . . About two hundred and fifty yards from the plant, the police closed in on the strikers. Billies and clubs were out already, prodding, striking, nightsticks edging into women's breasts and groins. But the cops were also somewhat afraid, and they began to jerk guns out of holsters.

"Stand fast! Stand fast!" the line leaders cried. "We got our rights! We got our legal rights to picket!"

The cops said, "You got no rights. You red bastards, you got no rights."

. . . [Tear gas] grenades began to sail now; tear gas settled like an ugly cloud. Children suddenly cried with panic, and the whole picket line gave back, men stumbling, cursing, gasping for breath. Here and there a cop tore out his pistol and began to fire; it was pop, pop at first, like toy favors at some horrible party, and then as the strikers broke under the gunfire and began to run, the contagion of killing ran like fire through the police.

They began to shoot in volleys at these unarmed men and women and children who could not strike back or fight back.

. . . And so it went, on and on, until seven [actually, ten] were dead and more than a hundred wounded. And the field a bloodstained field of battle.

The Hilo Massacre. Demonstrators are driven into Hawaii's Hilo Harbor trying to escape police gunfire on the morning of August 1, 1938. In support of striking Honolulu workers, more than two hundred Hilo trade unionists had peacefully gathered to protest the unloading of the SS *Waialeale*.

supported him loyally at the last election. But Roosevelt, weakened by his Supreme Court defeat, considered the strike "a real headache" and replied to Murray's plea at a public press conference. "The majority of the people are saying just one thing," FDR declared: " 'A plague on both your houses.' " John L. Lewis pointedly observed: "It ill behooves one who has supped at labor's table and who has been sheltered in labor's house to curse with equal fervor and fine impartiality both labor and its adversaries when they become locked in deadly embrace."

The SWOC's stunning defeat in 1937 at the hands of the Little Steel companies, the police, and the National Guard slowed the CIO's momentum. Even more important was the drastic change in the economic climate that followed. In 1937 FDR began cutting government spending as a way to balance the federal budget. These budget cuts helped throw the country into a new phase of the Depression in the fall in which 5 million additional workers lost their jobs. Official figures now showed a total of 11 million Americans without work; no one knows how many other jobless went uncounted. Basic industry, where some unions had just won recognition, announced big layoffs.

The automobile workers' union alone lost 90,000 members. Roosevelt responded to this new economic downturn by making overtures of friendship to corporate heads in the hope of stimulating investment. By early 1938, the nation found itself back in the deepest valley of the Depression.

Having taken credit for the earlier economic upturn, the Democrats bore the political burden of the "Roosevelt recession." The Democrats lost a total of eighty-one seats in the House, eight seats in the Senate, and thirteen governorships in the 1938 elections.

For Roosevelt, the 1938 congressional defeat was far worse than these totals would indicate. In the spring of 1938, FDR had put his prestige on the line with a campaign to "realign" the Democratic Party. He supported Democratic primary candidates who backed the Second New Deal against those conservative Democrats who opposed his program. The president's targets included conservatives such as Kentucky governor Albert "Happy" Chandler, who was challenging an FDR stalwart, Senator Alben Barkley; Senators Connally and Adams of Texas and Colorado, respectively, who had opposed FDR on the Court-packing plan; and Senator Walter George of Georgia, one of the South's leading conservatives. The CIO supported Roosevelt's realignment campaign but could contribute little in the South, where most of the battles were fought: the

---

"... THE CHARGE HAS BEEN MADE THAT THIS ARTICLE OF YOURS IS ENTIRELY COMMUNISTIC"

The election of a large number of new conservative congressmen and senators in 1938 and the subsequent attack on and rollback of federal programs had ominous implications for the New Deal coalition. In 1938, congressional conservatives established the House Committee on Un-American Activities (HUAC) to investigate Communist influence both in and out of government. Among those called to testify in December was Hallie Flanagan, director of the Federal Theatre Project, who was questioned by Democratic representative Joseph Starnes of Alabama about an article on workers' theater she had written seven years earlier. Despite its ridiculous qualities, the exchange between Starnes and Flanagan reveals the lengths to which conservative Democratic and Republican politicians would go to use the taint of communism to discredit progressive institutions and individuals.

MR. Starnes: I want to quote finally from your article "A Theater Is Born" ... "The power of these theaters springing up everywhere throughout the country lies in the fact that they know what they want. Their purpose—restricted, some will call it, though it is open to question whether any theater which attempts to create a class culture can be called restricted—is clear. This is important because there are only two theaters in the country today that are clear as to aim: one is the commercial theater which wants to make money; the other is the workers' theater which wants to make a new social order. The workers' theaters are neither infirm nor divided in purpose. Unlike any art form existing in America today, the workers' theaters intend to shape the life of this country, socially, politically, and industrially. They intend to remake a social structure without the help of money—and this ambition alone invests their undertaking with a certain Marlowesque madness." You are quoting from this Marlowe. Is he a Communist?

Mrs. Flanagan: I am very sorry. I was quoting from Christopher Marlowe.

Mr. Starnes: Tell us who Marlowe is, so we can get the proper reference, because that is all that we want to do.

Mrs. Flanagan: Put in the record that he was the greatest dramatist in the period immediately preceding Shakespeare.

Mr. Starnes: Put that in the record because the charge has been made that this article of yours is entirely Communistic, and we want to help you. ... Of course, we had what some people call Communists back in the days of the [ancient] Greek theater.

Mrs. Flanagan: Quite true.

Mr. Starnes: And I believe Mr. Euripides was guilty of teaching class consciousness also, wasn't he?

Mrs. Flanagan: I believe that was alleged against all of the Greek dramatists.

Mr. Starnes: So we cannot say when it began.

textile workers' defeat in 1934 cast a long shadow over the CIO's role in the 1938 primaries. Once again, FDR's plans backfired, with conservative Democrats retaining their congressional seats.

The southern conservatives who survived the attempted purge went on to play a crucial role in American politics. For the next forty years, these "Dixiecrats," as they were known, formed a coalition with conservative Republicans to frustrate liberals' efforts to complete the welfare state that New Dealers had begun to build.

The CIO suffered with the decline in Democratic fortunes. Fewer strikes were called and fewer workers took part in them. Early in 1938, union organizing committees in the textile and steel industries reduced their staffs by three-quarters. In 1939, total CIO membership was only 400,000 larger than in 1937. The CIO's loss of momentum had one clear-cut result: the AFL organized more workers than the CIO in the years between 1937 and 1941.

Just as important, CIO defeats affected the character of the industrial unionism that emerged from the Depression. Once the CIO found its attempts to organize basic industries through mass action stymied by local police and antilabor politicians, it increasingly relied on the regulatory mechanisms of the National Labor Relations Board to win its unionization battles. Soon the federal government through the NLRB, rather than the workers through their sit-down strikes and pickets, was defining the scope of bargaining units, deciding which issues were proper subjects for collective bargaining, and determining which strike tactics were appropriate.

In sum, the success of the conservative mobilization made organized labor more dependent on government than ever before. Labor leaders now looked increasingly to legalistic procedures to win representation elections rather than the mass action that had led to labor's great breakthroughs earlier in the decade.

THE DEMOCRATIZATION OF AMERICA

In the last half of the 1930s, working people made America a more democratic nation. By organizing, protesting, sitting-in, and voting as a progressive bloc, they forced the federal government to begin acting as a guarantor of workers' rights to organize, bargain collectively, and earn a decent wage, as well as of citizens' rights to livable housing and a secure retirement.

The New Deal's dramatic transformation of the federal government's role can partly be attributed to the devastating impact of the Depression: traditional, free-market-oriented cures had failed to stimulate an economic recovery. Growing popular anger toward big business was another key reason for the Roosevelt administration's

The Depression continues. Migrants camp along U.S. Route 99 in Kern County, California, in November 1938.

reorientation. But the dramatic gains of the New Deal era would have been unimaginable had not workers themselves arisen in a storm of angry protest to organize new industrial unions. In the 1930s, racial, sexual, and skill divisions among the workforce in basic industry began to diminish. To be sure, employers tried to play one ethnic group against another, sowing the seeds of suspicion and discord, using spies and informers to spread rumors of betrayal and bigotry. But this time, in the crucible of the Depression, workers tended to support one another. Solidarity, once a radical's dream, became a shop-floor reality in the 1930s.

By challenging big business's political and economic domination, workers extended the formal democracy of America's political system into their workplaces and communities. For the next forty years, in many industrial communities throughout America, in places such as Johnstown, Flint, and Chicago, working people exercised real power in their local governments and cultural institutions. At the same time, a partial welfare state, with its commitment to providing a minimum standard of comfort and security for those who could not help themselves—the poor, the sick, the elderly, children, and the unemployed—put down deep roots in the subsoil of American politics.

But by 1938, the labor movement's momentum began to ebb, well before it had succeeded in organizing the entire industrial sector. The success of the conservative counterattack halted the New Deal and the labor movement before a realignment of American politics and the construction of a full welfare state could be completed. As 1939 dawned, many Americans shifted their gaze to what was happening on the other side of the Atlantic Ocean.

9

A NATION TRANSFORMED

THE SECOND WORLD WAR AND ITS AFTERMATH

PROSPECTS FOR the New Deal looked grim in 1938. Despite federal recovery programs, U.S. unemployment shot up to levels near that of 1932. FDR's unsuccessful attempt to pack the U.S. Supreme Court shattered the political coalition that had pushed for a strong federal role in solving social and economic problems. The president's difficulties emboldened business conservatives and the right, who launched a headline-grabbing attack on labor, the left, and the New Deal.

The New Deal faced this political counterattack before it could complete the construction of a welfare state. Social Security promised retirement benefits for millions, but a quarter of the population, including most farmers, domestic servants, and hospital

War production and victory. Belching defense industry smokestacks resemble cannonfire in this Office of War Information poster urging higher industrial production.

workers, were excluded. The Fair Labor Standards Act set maximum hours and minimum wages across the nation but left unprotected millions of the most exploited workers. The health and housing needs of "one-third of a nation" remained largely unmet. Fierce business resistance to organized labor had left large sectors of the U.S. economy untouched by unionization. In Congress, a coalition of conservative southern Democrats and anti–New Deal Republicans vetoed any new initiatives put forward by the urban, liberal majority that had dominated American politics from 1934 to 1938.

We will never know how the struggle between these political forces would have been resolved, for in 1938 war loomed over both the Atlantic and the Pacific. Before the end of President Roosevelt's second term, war engulfed both Europe and Asia and decisively recast the politics and economy of the United States.

FROM PREPAREDNESS TO PEARL HARBOR

Just as the Depression of the 1930s sharpened antagonisms within the United States, it also bred international conflicts. Advanced industrial nations responded to the widespread decline in consumer buying power and commodity price levels by shutting foreign competitors out of their home markets while scrambling for additional customers abroad. "Foreign markets must be regained if America's producers are to rebuild a full and enduring domestic prosperity for our people," FDR had warned during his third year in office.

Such concerns were even stronger among latecomers to greatpower status such as Germany, Japan, and Italy, whose domestic markets and resources were relatively limited. The militaristic leaders of those countries saw the existing world order as functioning solely to maintain the supremacy and privileges of Great Britain, France, and the United States. Hitler sought *Lebensraum* (living space) for Germany through "the reorganization of Europe." Mussolini dreamed of a new Roman Empire on the Mediterranean. In Asia, Japan's rulers set out to replace European colonial empires with an "East Asian Coprosperity Sphere."

The first big guns sounded in Asia. In 1931, Japanese troops occupied the Chinese province of Manchuria, and six years later invaded China proper. In 1935, Italy invaded Abyssinia (Ethiopia), in northeastern Africa. Successful there despite valiant resistance by the Ethiopian people, Mussolini next turned to Europe, conquering Albania in 1939. In 1936, Hitler broke the Treaty of Versailles by taking back and rearming the Rhineland in western Germany. In that same year, Japan, Italy, and Germany signed pacts with one another, giving birth to the Axis military alliance. And fascist forces led by Generalissimo Francisco Franco and aided by Hitler and Mussolini crushed

Just before the battle. Members of the Abraham Lincoln Battalion march in the streets of Barcelona in January 1937, shortly after their arrival in Spain. Within a month they would face their first action against Franco's rebels in the ten-day Battle of Jarama. Sustaining heavy losses (295 of 450 killed or wounded), the Lincoln Battalion, along with other International and Spanish Republican forces, succeeded in preventing the rebels from severing the strategic Madrid–Valencia road.

the democratically elected Republican government of Spain in a brutal civil war, despite the participation of thousands of international socialists and communists (including Americans in the Abraham Lincoln Battalion) who fought on the side of the Spanish Republicans.

By 1938, Germany was ready to move against Austria and then Czechoslovakia. The Soviet Union, fearing German attack and unable to draw England, France, or the United States into an alliance against Hitler, chose to sign a nonaggression pact with Germany in August 1939. Hitler's armies invaded Poland on September 1 of that year, swallowing its western regions while Stalin's troops occupied the eastern part of the country.

Two days after the invasion of Poland began, England and France declared war on Germany. Germany proved stronger and the Allies weaker than expected. The spring of 1940 saw German troops sweep through Denmark, Norway, Belgium, and the Netherlands. The French army collapsed in mid-June and the Germans swept into Paris.

Hitler next turned his attention across the English Channel, launching a bomber offensive against London. As the semifascist governments of Hungary, Romania, and Bulgaria joined the Axis, German troops also moved into Yugoslavia and Greece the next year. Finally, on June 22, 1941, Hitler, ignoring the nonaggression pact, invaded the USSR, where his huge armies took millions of Soviet prisoners and reached the gates of Moscow and Leningrad.

The United States tried for some time to avoid direct participation in the European bloodletting. Many Americans now recalled World War I as a time of purposeless slaughter and arms-merchant superprofits; conservatives feared that after a decade of worldwide social crisis a new war would open the door to even greater radical social and economic changes. "It is fairly certain," asserted a corporate leader active in the isolationist America First Committee, "that capitalism cannot survive American participation in this war." These

"ALWAYS THE WAVES FROM EUROPE BREAK LIKE THUNDER . . ."

Nebraska-born poet Helene Margaret wrote this poem, titled "Tomorrow, America," to commemorate the 1939 World's Fair in New York City. Rather than celebrating the fair's futuristic wonders, its "World of Tomorrow," Margaret conveys the feeling that the United States stood like a beacon of hope for a world poised at the brink of war.

From the chill winds and samphire-covered rocks
Of Maine, where dancing sea-mews breast the tide,
To the sun-favored palmettos and flocks
Of pink flamingoes stalking down the wide
White sands of Florida . . . along our shore
Always the waves from Europe break like thunder,
Always the haunting death . . .

    . . . Here is the nation's gain.
Stronger than battleships and guns are these
Cascades of color marking the end of pain
And the long heroic fight against disease,
Matter made into life, and industry
Transformed to beauty by the curving span
Of a steel bridge, an iron doorway, a free
Range for the all-creating mind of man.
The lamp in the chemist's laboratory burns
All night; the blue prints of the engineer
Lie open on the desk; a piston turns
The giant wheel against another year.

concerns had led Congress to pass the 1935 Neutrality Act, which discouraged American citizens from traveling into a war zone and imposed an embargo on arms sales to belligerent nations.

During the first year of the Axis's existence, most of official Washington believed it possible to work out a compromise. But after Japan invaded China, the United States qualified its neutrality, sending both loans and military equipment to Chinese president Chiang Kai-shek. Two years later the German invasion of Poland pushed policymakers still farther from formal neutrality. A Germany-dominated Europe and a Japan-dominated Asia, the White House recognized, would endanger U.S. interests. As John J. McCloy, a key figure in the War Department, warned in the summer of 1941, "With German control of the buyers of Europe and her practice of government control of all trade, it would be well within her power as well as the pattern she has thus far displayed to shut off our trade with Europe, with South America, and with the Far East."

Meanwhile, isolationist sentiment in the United States declined. In 1939, the United States repealed its arms embargo and agreed to sell weapons to Britain and France on a cash-and-carry basis. After the fall of France, Congress tripled the War Department's budget, voted the nation's first peacetime draft law, and in March 1941 agreed to lend or lease war matériel to anti-Axis powers (chiefly Great Britain; later, also the Soviet Union). In August 1941, Roosevelt and Churchill met on a battleship off the Canadian coast, where they issued a joint declaration of war aims, the "Atlantic Charter," which called for the destruction of "Nazi tyranny" and projected a postwar world in which "all men in all the lands may live out their lives in freedom from fear and want."

... What of the steadfast, hard-faced pioneers
Drinking from sulphur pools, the men who dug
Graves for their kind among the prickly pears
And marked the place with a knife or a whiskey jug?
And what of those who crossed an alien hill,
Jingling the coins that said "In God We Trust,"
The dreamers wandering back from Sutter's Mill
After the golden nuggets turned to dust?
Their covered wagons shall turn west no more.
But now, holding the world's sun from decline,
We cleave the mountains for a richer ore,
And hail with hope a better "forty-nine."
This is our gift: the healing touch to allay
Hungers of flesh and spirit. The hearts of men
Shall sing like meadowlarks against the day
We teach a crippled world to walk again.

Here in these halls of science,
  Here in these towers of art
We have built the true defiance
  And girded the nation's heart,
Not with enduring stone
  Or muscles that twist with pain,
But with the fires that burn
  A vision in the brain.
The tri-colored flag was cut
  For us with subtle shears.
No doors we open can shut
  In a hundred thousand years.

"The World of Tomorrow." The 1939 New York World's Fair opened in the shadow of approaching war, yet its theme and exhibits optimistically predicted a prosperous, pollution-free future based on the technological expertise provided by American corporations. Among its many attractions was Elektro, a seven-foot "moto-man" in Westinghouse's "Singing Tower of Light." Elektro—who "talks, sees, smells, sings, and counts with his fingers"—represented the benefits of electrical power.

The U.S. Navy was soon patrolling the North Atlantic. From there it was but a short step to outright—if undeclared and unreported—naval warfare between Germany and the United States. U.S. leaders adopted a parallel policy in the Pacific. Japan's invasion of the French colonies in Indochina provoked Congress to freeze all Japanese assets in the United States. Britain and Holland followed suit, thereby making it impossible for Japan to purchase oil, steel, and other essential materials. Between August and November 1941, U.S. and Japanese diplomats exchanged a series of fruitless peace proposals. When those talks collapsed, U.S. secretary of state Cordell Hull declared, "I have washed my hands of the Japanese situation, and it is now in the hands of . . . the Army and Navy." The problem remaining, Secretary of War Henry Stimson confided in his diary at the end of November, only days before Japan bombed Pearl Harbor, "was how we should maneuver [Japan] into . . . firing the first shot without allowing too much danger to ourselves."

LABOR MOBILIZES

With the approach of war, the New Deal era of social reform came to an end. In 1940, with his liberal-labor coalition in eclipse and his attention increasingly focused on the international situation, FDR directed special adviser and campaign organizer Thomas (Tommy the Cork) Corcoran to ". . . cut out this New Deal stuff. It's tough to win a war." Roosevelt, Corcoran later explained, had "heard complaints from the people who could produce the tanks and other war stuff. As a payoff, they required an end to what they called New Deal nonsense."

In July, Roosevelt appointed conservative advocates of U.S. intervention—including Henry Stimson, who had served in Herbert Hoover's cabinet, and Frank Knox, Alf Landon's 1936 running mate—to influential government posts. These men recognized that it would be impossible to repeal the New Deal laws or to roll back labor's organizing victories. But they aimed to block a new round of social reforms and to stop the decline in power and prestige of big business.

For most trade unionists, the administration's renewed alliance with business conservatives proved dispiriting. Trade union leaders were unanimous in their condemnation of fascism, but many labor officials feared and opposed U.S. entry into the war. They shared the belief, widespread during the 1930s, that the same businessmen and politicians responsible for the Depression had earlier plunged the country into World War I merely to defend their power and expand their profits. These were the "merchants of death" attacked in films, novels, and congressional investigations of the interwar years.

Many trade unionists remembered how the government had turned against labor and reform forces during the Red Scare following World War I, and they feared that such repression would again accompany U.S. participation in a new world war. "War has always been the device of the politically despairing and intellectually sterile statesman," announced CIO head John L. Lewis soon after Nazi armies rolled across Poland. Anti-intervention sentiment was especially strong among Americans of German, Italian, and Japanese descent, who did not want to fight against relatives and compatriots in the old country, and among Irish-Americans, for whom Britain was a hated enemy.

In the months that followed the German defeat of France in June 1940, the main body of American trade unionists gradually swung over to support Franklin Roosevelt's program of active U.S. involve-

THE YANKS ARE **NOT** COMING

Published by
THE YANKS ARE NOT COMING COMMITTEE
District Council No. 2, Maritime Federation of the Pacific
Price 3c

Communists originated the slogan, organized labor adopted it.

No, thanks. Antiwar sentiment in the labor movement as indicated by a pamphlet distributed by the Maritime Federation of the Pacific.

ment in the world conflict. Few unionists could see any alternative to the president's defense program. Although John L. Lewis realistically forecast the conservative economic and social consequences of total war, his efforts to project an isolationist defense against European fascism seemed both politically naïve and militarily impractical. Meanwhile, the U.S. Communist Party moved from a policy of encouraging U.S. preparedness to one that discouraged American intervention after the Soviet Union and Germany signed the 1939 nonaggression pact. But once Germany invaded the Soviet Union in June 1941, the Communists demanded outright American belligerency and close trade union cooperation with Roosevelt's defense buildup. Finally, the idea of opposition to the war on either pacifist or revolutionary grounds seemed virtually nonexistent, a sharp contrast to the situation during the First World War, when large sections of the working class had been influenced by such views.

Indeed, unionists such as Sidney Hillman of the heavily Jewish Amalgamated Clothing Workers' Union saw American participation in the war as both morally right and politically advantageous to liberal-labor forces. Roosevelt recognized Hillman as an ally and sympathetic spokesman within the labor movement. In 1940, the president appointed him to an important defense mobilization post, from which the CIO founder worked to make unions full partners in the development of government economic and social policy. During the presidential campaign of that year, John L. Lewis denounced Roosevelt, criticized Hillman's activities, and endorsed FDR's Republican opponent, utility executive Wendell Willkie. But despite Lewis's continuing prestige in labor circles, the overwhelming majority of American workers supported the president for an unprecedented and highly controversial third term, which he won in November 1940.

The defense employment boom that began in 1940 offered organized labor an opportunity to rebuild and expand the industrial union movement so gravely damaged by the defeat in the Little Steel strike and the "Roosevelt recession" of 1937–38. CIO unions launched a wave of strikes in the period of rising defense production between June 1940 and December 1941. In those fifteen months the AFL and the CIO enrolled 1.5 million new members. Almost 2.5 million men and women engaged in work stoppages, over two-thirds of them under CIO leadership. Because the U.S. Supreme Court had already outlawed sit-downs, many strikers resorted to another militant tactic: mass picketing, which kept out scabs—and police—by surrounding plants with huge, densely packed, moving picket lines. These strikes clearly demonstrated the unions' renewed power and won wage increases for workers in the southern Appalachian coalfields as well as at General Motors, U.S. Steel, and General Electric.

Many of these work stoppages were strikes for union recognition

Guns make butter. July 1941 listings of available industrial jobs clutter a Detroit labor-exchange blackboard, showing the automatic effect of the war in Europe on the American economy.

directed against the nation's most reactionary, anti-union employers. The most dramatic such strike came at the Ford Motor Company, which had been the only large automaker to resist the UAW's 1937–38 organizing drive successfully. On April 1, 1941, tens of thousands of Ford workers poured out of the gigantic River Rouge complex in support of the union. Using their personal automobiles as a mobile barricade, the Ford strikers established a "picket line" that stretched for miles around the Dearborn plant. Within a few weeks, more than 100,000 new workers were enrolled in the United Auto Workers under a union-shop contract that overnight turned the pioneering auto firm into a bastion of militant unionism.

But this conflict-plagued organizing drive finally foundered on the shoals of national politics. In January 1941, Roosevelt declared that "Whatever stands in the way of speed and efficiency in defense preparations must give way to the national need." He added, "We shall not stop work for a single day. If any dispute arises we shall keep on working while the dispute is solved by mediation, conciliation, or arbitration—until the war is won." Building on that premise, defense contractors, congressional conservatives, the military, and the White House demanded an end to the industrial disputes that the War Department now called "an unpredictable drain on defense production." At Sidney Hillman's urging, a number of CIO unions called off strikes in progress and the AFL agreed to curtail work stoppages on defense-related construction sites.

But neither Hillman nor the president could guarantee compliance at the local level. When union-busting tactics at a Milwaukee defense plant triggered a violent strike early in 1941, the Roosevelt administration set up the National Defense Mediation Board. The new board, which included representatives of organized labor, management, and the government, established a system of government-supervised wage agreements and voluntary arbitration of industrial disputes. Though new CIO director Philip Murray (John L. Lewis had resigned) recognized that a war-oriented labor-relations system would

"The ideal picket." In 1941, trade union activism reached the workplace where some of the nation's favorite fantasies were produced. After Walt Disney fired union organizers on his art staff, his studio cartoonists went on strike. This cartoon from a newspaper report indicates how Disney strikers brought new skills to labor organizing. "There are mighty few labor disputes," the caption states, "in which just about every striker can make his own picket signs. Consequently, the signs are bright and lively . . . attracting the passerby and winning friends for the Screen Cartoon Guild."

automatically "find its attention directed against labor in order to maintain the status quo as much as possible," the CIO agreed to cooperate; Murray became one of the board's labor members.

Two June 1941 strikes demonstrated the extent to which the federal government would use the defense emergency to throw its weight against union militancy and political radicalism. Wages were low and profits enormous at the booming North American Aviation plant at Inglewood, California, which supplied vitally needed training planes to the Army Air Corps. However, when a strike erupted in early June, Sidney Hillman and the National Defense Mediation Board cooperated with the army's top brass to persuade UAW officials to declare the strike a "wildcat" (a work stoppage unauthorized by union headquarters) motivated by Communist opposition to the war. Southern California strike leaders, a few of whom were indeed identified with the Communist Party, resisted orders from national UAW officials to return to work. President Roosevelt then dispatched 2,500 active-duty troops to disperse pickets and ban all gatherings within a one-mile radius of the factory. Within a few days the strike was broken.

Government intervention also had a decisive impact in a Minneapolis Teamsters' Union dispute two weeks later. Here a fast-growing unit of this important AFL union sought to disaffiliate from its parent organization and join the more militant CIO. But this was no ordinary inner union squabble, for Teamsters' Local 544 was heavily influenced by Trotskyist radicals of the Socialist Workers Party (SWP), who had helped lead the militant citywide strikes that rocked Minneapolis in 1934. The radicals opposed U.S. involvement in a war they considered one of imperialist rivalry. They also rejected the union's conservative national president, Daniel Tobin, who was one of FDR's key trade union supporters. At Tobin's urging, FBI agents raided the offices of Local 544 and the SWP, charging several of the radical leaders with violations of the Smith Act. Passed the year before, the act penalized individuals who advocated the overthrow of the U.S. government by force. Meanwhile, Tobin sent a squad of thugs to recapture Local 544 physically. The group was led by a youthful Jimmy Hoffa, who would later become the celebrated and corrupt president of the Teamsters' Union.

These episodes demonstrate the extent to which the federal government, in concert with politically cooperative union leaders, imposed new limits on labor's freedom during World War II. But in contrast to other moments of political repression—such as those in 1886, 1894, and 1920—government authorities did not seek to smash trade unionism outright, only to tame and contain it. In Minneapolis, Hoffa successfully reorganized Local 544 into a new union loyal to Tobin and the war effort. And in California, the army pressured the

National Defense Mediation Board to give the workers at North American Aviation a big wage increase, thus helping national UAW leaders reclaim the loyalty of the workforce there. When wages were finally boosted in July 1941, a UAW paper greeted news of the award with the triumphant headline "Responsible Unionism Wins at Inglewood."

GI'S AT WAR

The United States was well on its way toward full wartime mobilization by December 7, 1941, when the Japanese launched a surprise attack on U.S. forces in Hawaii and the Philippines and on British forces in Malaya. At Pearl Harbor, Japanese planes sank or disabled several of the heaviest ships in the U.S. Pacific Fleet and killed 2,400 American soldiers and sailors. The following day, Britain and the United States declared war on Japan. Three days later, Germany declared war on the United States.

In the next six months, the Allies took a terrible beating in the Pacific. By May 1942, Japan had taken Indonesia from the Dutch, Indochina from the French, the Philippines from the Americans, and Malaya and Burma from the British. Japan also occupied most of eastern China.

In Europe, the USSR bore the blunt of the fighting. Facing almost 200 German divisions along a huge front, Soviet military and civilian defenders stopped, drove back, and then encircled 300,000 German troops in a dramatic victory at the year-long Battle of Stalingrad. When the German Sixth Army finally surrendered to the Red Army at the end of January 1943, fewer than half of the Sixth Army's troops were still alive. This was the turning point of the titanic conflict in eastern Europe, where military and civilian deaths rose well above 25 million.

Throughout this period, Stalin repeatedly called on Britain and the United States to invade occupied France and thereby open a second battlefront in Europe, which would force Hitler to divert some of his forces from the Eastern Front. But during 1942 and 1943, the English and Americans concentrated their forces on the Mediterranean or southern periphery of Hitler's European fortress, confronting a total of just twenty German divisions. Between October 1942 and September 1943, the Allies regained control of North Africa, conquered Sicily, and then slowly fought their way up the Italian peninsula toward Rome.

But until the final year of the war only a small fraction of the 16 million Americans who served in the armed forces actually saw combat. For most soldiers and sailors the war was one of training and supply for a vast and complex organization. They learned to march

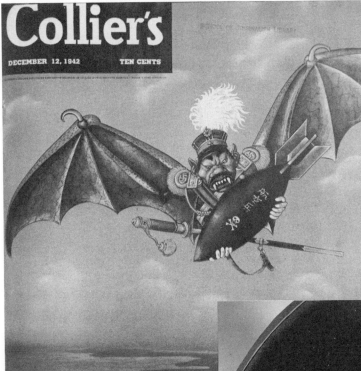

The cover of a December 1942 issue of *Collier's* commemorates the first anniversary of the Japanese attack on Pearl Harbor. The vampire-bat portrayal of Prime Minister Hideki Tojo indicates one way in which the Japanese were presented in the American popular media and war propaganda. Unlike images of the European enemy, the Japanese were depicted as vicious animals, most often taking the form of apes or parasitic insects.

A 1942 poster depicting the Nazi enemy uses a stereotype of the monocled Prussian officer that dated back to the war-propaganda images of World War I.

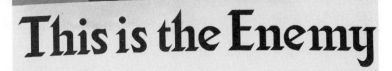

KOEHLER
ANCONA

This is the Enemy

and shoot straight, but also to drive a truck, repair a radio, type, and keep accurate records. For almost all soldiers, what had been true in the Civil War and World War I was true in this war, too: life in uniform broadened horizons. Wartime service introduced provincial Americans to Europeans, North Africans, and Asians. And because the World War II draft proved more egalitarian than that of any other U.S. conflict, many GI's were thrown together with Americans up and down the class structure and from different parts of the country. "The first time I ever heard a New England accent," a midwesterner

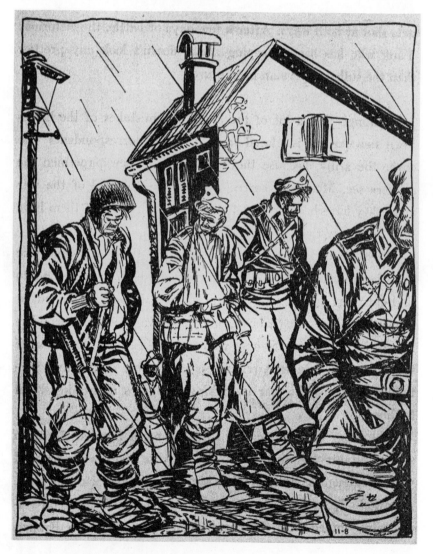

" 'Fresh, spirited American troops, flushed with victory, are bringing in thousands of hungry, ragged, battle-weary prisoners ...' (News item)." Sergeant Bill Mauldin's cartoons in *Stars and Stripes*, the Army newspaper distributed to troops, contradicted the American press's upbeat and sanitized coverage of the war. Mauldin's unromantic and biting cartoons, often celebrating the insubordinate spirit of American soldiers, were reviled by officers such as General George S. Patton (who personally reprimanded the cartoonist for "undermining the morale of the army"). But Mauldin's work, featuring the weary and cynical archetypal GI's Willie and Joe, was eagerly read by the troops.

"WE WERE FIGHTING AND SLEEPING IN ONE VAST CESSPOOL . . ."

The historian William Manchester served as a marine in the Pacific Theater. He described the horror of hand-to-hand combat in the Battle of Okinawa, as U.S. troops neared Japan in the war's final months.

ALL greenery had vanished; as far as one could see, heavy shellfire had denuded the scene of shrubbery. What was left resembled a cratered moonscape. But the craters were vanishing, because the rain had transformed the earth into a thin porridge—too thin even to dig foxholes. At night you lay on a poncho as a precaution against drowning during the barrages. All night, every night, shells erupted close enough to shake the mud beneath you at the rate of five or six a minute. You could hear the cries of the dying but could do nothing. Japanese infiltration was always imminent, so the order was to stay put. Any man who stood up was cut in half by machine guns manned by fellow Marines.

By day, the mud was hip-deep; no vehicles could reach us. As you moved up the slope of the hill, artillery and mortar shells were bursting all around you, and if you were fortunate enough to reach the top, you encountered the Japanese defenders, almost face to face, a few feet away. To me, they looked like badly wrapped brown paper parcels someone had soaked in a tub. Their eyes seemed glazed. So, I suppose, did ours.

Japanese bayonets were fixed; ours weren't. We used the knives, or, in my case, a .45 revolver and M1 carbine. The mud beneath our feet was deeply veined with blood. It was slippery. Blood is very slippery. So you skidded around, in deep shock, fighting as best you could until one side outnumbered the other. The outnumbered side would withdraw for reinforcements and then counterattack.

During those 10 days I ate half a candy bar. I couldn't keep anything down. Everyone had dysentery, and this brings up an aspect of war even Robert Graves, Siegfried Sassoon, Edmund Blunden and Ernest Hemingway avoided. If you put more than a quarter million men in a line for three weeks, with no facilities for the disposal of human waste, you are going to confront a disgusting problem. We were fighting and sleeping in one vast cesspool. Mingled with that stench was another—the corrupt and corrupting odor of rotting human flesh. . . .

After my evacuation from Okinawa, I had the enormous pleasure of seeing [John] Wayne humiliated in person at Aiea Heights Naval Hospital in Hawaii. Only the most gravely wounded, the litter cases, were sent there. . . . Each evening Navy corpsmen would carry litters down to the hospital theater so the men could watch a movie. One night they had a surprise for us. Before the film the curtains parted and out stepped John Wayne, wearing a cowboy outfit—and 10-gallon hat, bandanna, checkered shirt, two pistols, chaps, boots and spurs. He grinned his aw-shucks grin, passed a hand over his face and said, "Hi ya, guys!" He was greeted by a stony silence. Then somebody booed. Suddenly everyone was booing.

This man was a symbol of the fake machismo we had come to hate, and we weren't going to listen to him. He tried and tried to make himself heard, but we drowned him out, and eventually he quit and left. If you liked [John Wayne's film] *Sands of Iwo Jima,* I suggest you be careful. Don't tell it to the Marines.

recalled, "was at Fort Benning." For white youth in particular, service in the military helped reduce the ethnic and regional differences that had so long divided the American working class.

Those who experienced combat entered a nightmarish world of violence and death. The combatants in World War II possessed far greater firepower than ever before, and within those units actually fighting the enemy, the incidence of death and mutilation was extremely high, sometimes one in three. Not surprisingly, the majority of the 405,000 combat deaths suffered by U.S. forces came in the war's final year, when American armies spearheaded the assault against the German and Japanese forces. War correspondent Ernie Pyle spent a great deal of time talking and living with the average soldier in uniform. Pyle wrote, "We see from the worm's-eye view, and our segment of the picture consists only of tired and dirty soldiers who are alive and don't want to die . . . of shocked men wandering back down the hill from battle . . . of smelly bed rolls and C rations . . . and of graves and graves and graves."

Thrown together with strangers (in contrast to the Civil War, where men fought side by side with their neighbors), soldiers nonetheless quickly formed strong bonds that enabled them to survive and fight. "The reason you storm the beaches is not patriotism or bravery," one ex-GI explained. "It's that sense of not wanting to fail your buddies. That's sort of a special sense of kinship."

Men (and women) who lived close together in same-sex facilities—under the shadow of death, and dependent on each other for survival—often formed intense emotional attachments. This camaraderie provided the basis for lifelong friendships sometimes institutionalized in the veterans' organizations and unit reunions that proved so popular after the war.

Life in the armed services also had a long-lasting impact on America's homosexual population. Far from home, many gay military men and women felt less social pressure to conform to heterosexual norms and more freedom to express their sexuality than they had in civilian life. On the front lines and in military bases and hospitals throughout Europe and the Pacific, gays and lesbians were able to create a sense of identity and community. Bob Ruffing, a naval officer, remembered his early experiences in the navy:

> When I first got into the Navy—in the recreation hall, for instance—there'd be eye contact, and pretty soon you'd get to know one or two people and kept branching out. All of a sudden you have a vast network of friends, usually through this eye contact thing, some through outright cruising. They could get away with it in that atmosphere.

Many who expressed their sexual orientation during the war became pioneers in the latter-day movement to build gay and lesbian organizations in postwar America.

But the relative freedom from conventional constraints and mores made possible by military life also engendered outbursts of antisocial behavior. One soldier reported that four of every five members of his company took part in looting. The death of buddies, accounts of Axis brutality, racist propaganda, and simple terror all combined to produce a frightful bloodthirstiness in many American soldiers. A huge billboard over Tulagi Harbor in the Solomon Islands read: "Kill Japs; kill more Japs; you will be doing your part if you help to kill those yellow bastards."

For African-American servicemen, wartime life presented a unique set of experiences and problems. The patterns of discrimination that beset black civilians also confronted black soldiers, despite the battlefield valor demonstrated by African-American troops in the Civil War, the Spanish-American War, and World War I. In 1940, African-Americans were excluded from the marines, the Coast Guard, and the Army Air Corps; in the navy, blacks at first saw service only in the ships' mess, though by the spring of 1942 African-American sailors were allowed to perform general labor.

The army accepted blacks—700,000 of them by 1944—only on a segregated basis. "The policy of the War Department," Washington announced, "is not to intermingle colored and white enlisted personnel in the same regimental organizations." Black enlistees and draftees trained in segregated camps. Dempsey Travis, an African-American soldier who trained at Camp Shenango, in Pennsylvania, remembers:

> The troop train was Jim Crow. They had a car for black soldiers and a car for whites. They went to their part and sent us to the ghetto. It seems the army always arranged to have black soldiers back up against the woods someplace. Isolated. We were never near the main gate. If you went through camp as a visitor, you'd never know black soldiers were there, unless they happened to be working on some menial detail. . . .

General George C. Marshall, chairman of the Joint Chiefs of Staff, justified the policy by explaining that "the War Department cannot ignore the social relationships between negroes and whites which have been established by the American people through custom and habit." Early in the war, African-American GI's found themselves restricted to duty in transportation, construction, and other support units. A black ex-sergeant in the Quartermaster Corps recalled bitterly, "We serviced the service. We handled food, clothing, equipage. We loaded ammunition, too. We were really stevedores and servants."

Racial conflict was not uncommon. In and around the training camps, white soldiers and civilians regularly abused black GI's. In response, some African-American servicemen retaliated. In one incident at Pennsylvania's Camp Shenango, white army police shot into a crowd of African-American GI's protesting segregated and inferior movie theaters; the ensuing riot lasted seventy-two hours. Dempsey Travis remembered that when the Red Cross medics "got to me, they said, 'He'll live. He just seems to be shot in several places.' I was shot three times. Then they looked at my friend. They threw a flashlight on him. They said, 'He'll make it. Niggers don't die when you shoot 'em in the head.' "

Such conflicts and protests, combined with the rising manpower needs of the military, eventually lowered some racial barriers. Although as late as 1943 white air force officers continued to dismiss "the Negro type" as lacking "the proper reflexes to make a first-class fighter pilot," President Roosevelt agreed to establish an all-black fighter squadron. Known as the Tuskegee Airmen and led by Colonel Benjamin Davis, a black man, the 99th Fighter Squadron won accolades in the January 1944 Allied offensive in Italy, shooting down twelve German fighters on two successive days. African-American pilots went on to distinguish themselves in the remaining months of the European campaign.

"YOU CAN'T FIGHT ALL OF THEM . . ."

The African-American novelist, photographer, and filmmaker Gordon Parks served as a reporter-writer assigned to an all-black air force unit during the war. He recalls a small but telling racial incident that occurred in Virginia.

●UR plane took off in a blinding rainstorm—and it landed in another one at Norfolk, Virginia. A taxi took me to the ferry landing where I would cross over into Newport News. I sat there in the waiting room for an hour on top of my battle gear among a boisterous group of white enlisted men. Four Negro soldiers were huddled in a nearby corner. Two of them were propped against each other, sleeping. . . .

We filed out when the ferry whistled. It was still raining and we stood near the edge of the dock watching the boat fasten into the slip. Through the wetness I noticed a sign reading COLORED PASSENGERS and another one reading WHITES ONLY. The four black soldiers moved automatically to the colored side, and so did I. How ironic, I thought; such nonsense would not stop until we were in enemy territory.

After all the outgoing passengers were off and the trucks and cars had rumbled past, we started forward. Then I saw a Negro girl step from the ferry. She . . . was in the direct line of the white enlisted men, who stampeded to the boat screaming at the tops of their voices. I saw the girl fall beneath them into the mud and water. The four Negro soldiers also saw her go down. The five of us rushed to her rescue. She was knocked down several times before we could get to her and pull her out of the scrambling mob.

"You lousy white bastards!" one of the Negro soldiers yelled. "If I only had a gun!" Tears were in his eyes, hysteria in his voice. A long knife was glistening in his hand.

"Soldier!" I shouted above the noise, letting him get a look at my officer's cap. "Put that knife away!"

He glared at me fiercely for a second. "But you saw what they did!"

"Yes, I saw, but we're outnumbered ten to one! You can't fight all of them. Get on the boat!" He looked at me sullenly for another moment, then moved off. We cleaned the mud from the girl's coat and she walked away without a word. Only proud anger glistened on her black face. Then the four of us joined the soldier I had ordered away. He was standing still tense beneath the sign reading COLORED PASSENGERS.

"Sorry soldier," I said. "We wouldn't have had a chance against a mob like that. You realize that, don't you?"

"If I gotta die, I'd just as soon do it where I got real cause to." His tone was resolute. I had to answer. I was tempted to hand him the bit about the future and all that, but the future was too uncertain. The yelling was even louder now on the other side of the boat. "Sons-of-bitches," he muttered under his breath.

Further progress occurred in January 1945 at the Battle of the Bulge, when the Germans broke through Allied lines, killing or capturing thousands of Americans. The 2,500 African-Americans who volunteered as replacements were assigned initially to segregated platoons officered by whites. "Leadership is not embedded in the Negro race yet," Henry Stimson explained; trying to make blacks into combat officers would produce only "disaster." Despite such attitudes, black soldiers fought hard to repel the final Nazi counteroffensive of the war.

The military experience of Mexican-Americans contrasted sharply with that of African-Americans, in large part because Latino soldiers were never officially segregated. Mexican-Americans were usually welcomed into combat units, and the army encouraged publicity about their outstanding records under fire. By the war's end, seventeen Mexican-Americans had earned the Congressional Medal of Honor. Still, Mexican-American soldiers suffered casualties disproportionate to their numbers in the general population. Texas political leader Alonso Perales asked the U.S. government why Mexican-Americans from southern Texas suffered between 50 and 75 percent of the area's total casualties in the war while constituting less than 10 percent of the state's total population: "We are quite proud of the opportunity afforded us to defend our country on the firing line; but we want to ascertain for sure whether . . . there are not sufficient soldiers of other [ethnic] extractions."

Such complaints notwithstanding, the heightened self-confidence that the military experience produced among Mexican-Americans contributed to the formation of new organizations at the end of the war, including the Mexican-American Political Association, the American GI Forum, the Community Service Organization, and the Political Association of Spanish-Speaking Organizations.

HOME-FRONT MOBILIZATION

At home, the Japanese attack on Pearl Harbor swept away nearly all popular resistance to U.S. involvement in the war. An explosion of patriotic sentiment and an all-but-universal striving for national unity helped smooth over many prewar social and political conflicts. A prominent member of Congress experienced "a feeling of real relief, that at last we are a united people. . . . The atmosphere has cleared."

Government propaganda and coordination reinforced spontaneous feelings of patriotism. Civilians volunteered to collect scrap metal and old newspapers, donate blood, and serve on local defense and ration committees. Twenty million families planted "victory gardens," producing more than a third of the nation's vegetables. Millions more bought low-denomination "Liberty Bonds" during a series of morale-building Treasury Department campaigns that relied on the promotional efforts of Hollywood movie stars.

World War II ended the Depression with a massive dose of government-stimulated demand. With the military taking about 47 percent of all production and services at the peak of the war, the gross national product doubled during the four wartime years. But because of chronic shortages in machinery, raw materials, and labor, the government could not let the free play of the market determine the cost and pace of either military or civilian production. This became clear in 1941. Detroit's automakers, then enjoying their best year since 1929, dragged their heels in the conversion of their factories to the production of military matériel; production of tanks and aircraft thus got off to a slow start. Government officials concluded that the whole economy would have to be centrally planned and controls put in place to determine the distribution and cost of virtually everything: steel and machine tools, of course, but also chickens, chocolate, and clothing.

FDR assigned primary responsibility for mobilizing American industry to the military and to corporate executives. The armed ser-

To buy is patriotic. From smoking to skin care, after the United States entered the conflict advertisers rushed to identify their products with the war effort.

vices set the overall production requirements, and big businessmen, now serving as "dollar-a-year men" still on the payroll of their old companies, staffed the key posts in the mobilization agencies that sprang up in Washington. They established what Donald Nelson, a vice president of Sears who became chairman of the War Production Board, called "a set of rules under which the game could be played the way industry said it had to be played." The government suspended the antitrust laws, paid most of the costs involved in building new defense plants, and loaned much of the rest at low rates of interest. "Cost-plus" contracts guaranteed a profit on the production of military goods.

To fight inflation, other government agencies regulated wages, prices, and the kind of jobs people could take. After Pearl Harbor, FDR set up a new War Labor Board to arbitrate labor-management disputes and set wage rates for all workers. The Office of Price Administration (OPA) began the complicated and controversial task of setting price ceilings for almost all consumer goods and distributing ration books for those items in short supply. Because most Americans fully endorsed the war effort, OPA regulations were generally obeyed, but after 1943 "black markets" sprang up for gasoline, meat products, and cigarettes. Finally, the Selective Service and the War Manpower Commission largely determined who would serve in the military, whose work was vital to the production effort, and when a worker could transfer from one job to another.

The transformation of the rubber industry demonstrated the impact of mobilization policies on one vital sector of the economy. With the rubber plantations of Southeast Asia in Japanese hands, the War Production Board halted tire production for civilians, and the Office of Price Administration began to ration gasoline (five gallons a week for most people). At a cost of $700 million, the government perfected the manufacture of synthetic rubber and built fifty-one new plants, leasing them cheaply to manufacturers holding cost-plus defense contracts.

Governmental planning of this sort fostered further concentration of the U.S. economy. In 1940, the top one hundred companies turned out 30 percent of total manufactured goods. By the end of the war, those same one hundred companies held 70 percent of all civilian and military manufacturing contracts. Corporate political connections with key military procurement officers helped bring the prime contracts and obtain the matériel and labor needed to meet the military's production requirements. Small businesses were pushed aside. If they went under, commented one War Production Board official, that was "the process of natural selection in the business world."

Not unexpectedly, military officials and big business "dollar-a-year men" came to share much the same political and economic vision. Lieutenant General Brehon Somervell, the chief of supply for the U.S. Army, established a quasi-secret school at Fort Leavenworth, Kansas, where business leaders participated in seminars and classes that explained and defended the military's new role in running so much of U.S. economic life. General Electric president Charles E. Wilson, the powerful number-two man at the War Production Board, proposed that business executives receive reserve commissions so that when the war ended close cooperation between defense contractors and the military might continue on intimate terms. The postwar relationship that came to be known as the "military-industrial complex" was born.

World War II was a metal-turning, engine-building, multiyear conflict that required an enormous amount of manual labor; thus unemployment, which had stood as high as 14 percent in 1940, virtually disappeared by early 1943. World War II–era factories were gigantic, not only because of the great production requirements but also because the technology of the assembly-line era massed together huge numbers of men, women, and machines. In the aircraft industry, for example, 100,000 worked at the Douglas Aviation plants in El Segundo and Long Beach, California; 50,000 at Curtiss-Wright in New Jersey;

A 1942 poster issued by the Office for Emergency Management uses design conventions perfected in commercial advertising to motivate war-production workers.

and 40,000 at Ford's bomber plant in Ypsilanti, Michigan. The Kaiser shipyards employed 60,000 in Portland, Oregon, and another 30,000 in Richmond, California. Forty-three percent of all American workers outside farming were now blue-collar workers, the highest proportion ever in U.S. history.

Full employment had a radical impact on the lives of ordinary Americans. Fifteen million workers—a third of the prewar work-force—used their new labor power to change and upgrade their jobs. Some shifted from one factory department or office to another; at least 4 million, triple the prewar total, crossed state lines for better employment opportunities. The rural South experienced the largest outmigration, California and Michigan the greatest influx. Factory work, especially in defense facilities, grew in prestige and earning power; office and service employment declined in both.

Real wages grew by 27 percent between 1939 and 1945. Indeed, the wages of those at the bottom of the social scale grew more rapidly than did the highly taxed incomes of those at the top, generating the most progressive redistribution of American wealth to take place in the twentieth century. George Peabody, who worked at Lockheed as a machinist, remembered the fat paychecks of those years:

> My income increased very rapidly because of the number of hours I worked. By 1944 . . . it was eight hours a day on Saturdays and Sundays and ten to twelve hours a day all during the week. We didn't have a day off. Even though the wages per hour didn't increase a great deal, the take-home pay was tremendous by comparison.

Most servicemen and urban workers enjoyed an unprecedented expansion in their "social wage." The military "socialized" medical and educational benefits for a substantial portion of the male military population, while a larger proportion of the working class could now afford to take advantage of schools, hospitals, and clinics. After remaining stagnant for a decade, life expectancy increased by three years for the white population and by five years for African-Americans. Infant mortality declined by more than a third during the years 1939–45.

In just five years, the total population of the ten largest war production centers grew by a fifth. Aircraft worker Don McFadden remembered that Los Angeles "was just like a beehive. . . . The defense plants were moving full-time. . . . Downtown movies were staying open twenty-four hours a day." To reduce absenteeism, the federal government also funded workplace amenities such as in-plant training, child-care centers, and good cafeterias. "For the majority of workers the war was an experience of opportunity rather than limitation," observed Katherine Archibald of her fellow shipyard workers in Oakland, California. "It was like a social," Peggy Terry of Paducah, Kentucky, said, remembering her first months in a defense plant. "Now we'd have money to buy shoes and a dress and pay rent and get some food on the table. We were just happy to have work."

Unlike the anti-immigrant "Americanization" campaigns of World War I, propaganda in this war helped advance a culturally pluralist but fundamentally unified sense of American national identity. The *Detroit News* praised the nearly spotless attendance records of six workers at the GM Ternstedt Division in Detroit whose names were Kowalski, Netowski, Bugai, Lugari, Bauer, and Pavolik. "Look at the names . . . the sort of names one finds on an All-American football team . . . and at Ternstedt's, management and workers alike are hailing them as the plant's All-American production team."

As a result of these developments, the institutions that bound working-class immigrants to their native cultures, such as foreign-language radio programs and newspapers, fell on hard times. Fraternal organizations of the foreign-born also lost thousands of members, and American Catholics—Polish and Italians as well as Irish—lost much of what remained of their defensive mentality. In many factories and mills they used the newly powerful industrial unions to break the Protestant/Masonic job trust that had once controlled access to skilled work and first-line supervision.

World War II–era pluralism had its limits, of course. Despite the fact that Nazi Germany was one of the nation's principal enemies, anti-Semitism in the United States remained barely hidden. This fact accounts in part for the failure of the State Department and other government officials to take the energetic steps necessary to rescue more than a handful of the millions of Jews who eventually perished in Europe. In one 1940 incident, the ship *St. Louis*, filled with nine hundred German Jewish refugees, sailed from one U.S. port to another, begging that her passengers be disembarked; all doors were barred, and the passengers were forced to return to Hamburg. Most ended up in Nazi death camps.

Conscientious objectors (CO's)—above all, Jehovah's Witnesses—had an extremely difficult time in World War II. The government sent at least six thousand CO's to prison; their sentences averaged five years, and beatings by guards and other prisoners were common. When drafted into the army, Jehovah's Witnesses refused to salute the flag, in accordance with their understanding of the Bible. They were then court-martialed and kept in solitary confinement for many months, often on a ration of bread and water.

U.S. treatment of Japanese-Americans proved the most egregious and racist wartime abridgement of civil liberties. Portrayals of the

C IS DULL BRONZE IN COLOR — WHILE J IS LIGHTER — MORE ON THE LEMON-YELLOW SIDE. C'S EYES ARE SET LIKE ANY EUROPEAN'S OR AMERICAN'S — BUT HAVE A MARKED SQUINT.... J HAS EYES SLANTED TOWARD HIS NOSE...

THE CHINESE HAS A SMOOTH FACE...THE JAP RUNS TO HAIR....LOOK AT THEIR PROFILES AND TEETH... C USUALLY HAS EVENLY SET CHOPPERS — J HAS BUCK TEETH... THE CHINESE SMILES EASILY — THE JAP USUALLY EXPECTS TO BE SHOT... AND IS VERY UNHAPPY ABOUT THE WHOLE THING...ESPECIALLY IF HE IS AN OFFICER!

THE CHINESE AND OTHER ASIATICS HAVE FAIRLY NORMAL FEET... THE JAP WORE A WOODEN SANDAL ("GETA") BEFORE HE WAS ISSUED ARMY SHOES... HE WILL USUALLY HAVE A WIDE SPACE BETWEEN THE FIRST AND SECOND TOES... OFTEN CALLOUSED FROM THE LEATHER STRAP THAT HELD THE "GETA" TO HIS FOOT...

How to Tell a Chinese from a "Jap." Three panels from the *Pocket Guide to China*, a U.S. Army pamphlet distributed to soldiers and illustrated by cartoonist Milton Caniff (best known for the comic strips *Terry and the Pirates* and, after the war, *Steve Canyon*), show how outrageous racial stereotypes were used to distinguish between friend and foe in official publications during the war.

German and Italian enemy usually condemned the fascist leadership and officer corps, but American magazine articles and films set in the Pacific commonly depicted the Japanese people as cruel, devious, and inhuman. "The Japs don't understand the love we have for our women," Cary Grant explained in the film *Destination: Tokyo*. "They don't even have a word for it in their language."

Unlike German-Americans or Italian-Americans, Japanese-Americans were presumed disloyal simply by virtue of their national origin. General John L. DeWitt, chief of the West Coast Defense Command, held that "the Japanese race is an enemy race. It makes no difference whether he is an American citizen or not." Secretary of War Stimson considered the "racial characteristics" of Japanese-Americans sufficient justification for their summary incarceration.

Beginning in March 1942, the government began rounding up all West Coast Japanese-Americans, citizens and noncitizens alike. Enthusiastic support for Japanese relocation and detention came from nativists and racists in California, who had long resented successful Japanese merchants, fishermen, and fruit and vegetable farmers. But many who claimed liberal or radical credentials joined in the anti-Japanese chorus. America's leading journalist, Walter Lippmann, supported the deportations, as did California attorney general (and later chief justice of the United States) Earl Warren. Many union leaders in California stood in the forefront of the anti-Japanese clamor, as did the now-ultrapatriotic Communist Party, which endorsed the policy as "a necessary war measure."

By the fall of 1942, over 100,000 Japanese were forced to abandon their jobs, businesses, and homes for a life in one of ten concentration camps throughout the West. Set in isolated, barren locations, surrounded by barbed wire and armed guards, inmates lived in overcrowded barracks barely divided into one-room enclosures furnished only with cots, blankets, and bare light bulbs. Exemption from internment was granted to those few Japanese-Americans who could find jobs far from the West Coast in a community where they would be accepted. But by the end of 1944, less than a third of all camp inmates had met such requirements.

Initially, Japanese-Americans, like other first- and second-generation Americans, were overwhelmingly loyal to the United States. But among a sizable minority, the detention camps bred precisely the hostility and resistance that U.S. government officials assumed had always existed. Some young Japanese-Americans actively resisted the suffocating camp regimen. In California's Camp Manzanar, a group of inmates beat up a fellow detainee suspected of being a government informer. When guards arrested one of the attackers, a mass protest followed. Soldiers hurled tear gas grenades and fired into the crowd, killing two young men.

Manzanar Relocation Center, April 1942. Japanese-Americans in the newly opened California internment camp gather to watch the arrival of fellow internees.

In 1943, more than one of every four Japanese-American males born in this country refused to pledge loyalty to the United States. Only 1,200 detainees accepted a government offer to leave the camps (with their families) and enlist in the U.S. armed forces. They formed the "Fighting 442nd" Division, which became the most decorated U.S. unit in the European Theater. A larger number of uncooperative Japanese-Americans, over 18,000 in all, were relocated to a camp at Tule Lake, California, where conditions were even more brutal. Riots and collective acts of resistance resulted, and open identification with Japan grew stronger among these detainees.

In December 1944, most inmates were finally allowed to leave the relocation camps, though five thousand were still barred from returning to the West Coast. Approximately eight thousand Japanese-Americans chose to move to Japan, but more than half the evacuees attempted to return to their West Coast homes. For the most part they discovered their jobs and property had been taken by others. Legal action and public protest over the course of decades eventually induced the U.S. government to offer the surviving Japanese-Americans modest financial restitution and a formal apology, which finally came in 1989.

African-Americans experienced their full share of victimization and discrimination during the war years, but the early 1940s also saw the first flowering of the modern civil rights movement. A surge of activism coincided with a dramatic shift in the social structure of black America. African-Americans now possessed the collective resources to inaugurate a liberation movement of nationwide scope and impressive political impact. Almost 10 percent of the southern black population moved to the urban North during the war, while an approximately equal number migrated within the South from farm to city. The number of African-Americans who held industrial jobs almost doubled, and their earnings soared from 40 percent of the average white wage in 1939 to nearly 60 percent after the war.

Life was far from easy in overcrowded war production centers such as Detroit and Los Angeles, but African-Americans made their growing numbers felt and aspirations heard in an unprecedented fashion. "The characteristic movements among Negroes are now for the first time becoming proletarian," asserted one philanthropic study of the black community in 1942. NAACP membership increased ninefold during World War II, and voting participation more than doubled during the war and the years immediately after. The

---

"I'M AS LOYAL AS ANYONE IN THIS COUNTRY ..."

In July 1943, government investigator Morris Opler interviewed a Japanese man, identified only as "an Older Nisei" (the first generation of Japanese-Americans born in the United States), who was interned at Camp Manzanar. The man was indignant at having to sign a formal declaration of loyalty to the United States.

... IF this country doesn't want me they can throw me out. What do they know about loyalty? I'm as loyal as anyone in this country. Maybe I'm as loyal as President Roosevelt. What business did they have asking me a question like that?

I was born in Hawaii. I worked most of my life on the west coast. I have never been to Japan. We would have done anything to show our loyalty. All we wanted to do was to be left alone on the coast.... My wife and I lost $10,000 in that evacuation. She had a beauty parlor and had to give that up. I had a good position worked up as a gardener, and was taken away from that. We had a little home and that's gone now....

What kind of Americanism do you call that? That's not democracy. That's not the American way, taking everything away from people.... Where are the Germans? Where are the Italians? Do they ask them questions about loyalty? ...

Nobody had to ask us about our loyalty when we lived on the coast. You didn't find us on relief.... We were first when there was any civic drive. We were fist with the money for the Red Cross and the Community Chest or whatever it was. Why didn't that kind of loyalty count? Now they're trying to push us to the east. It's always "further inland, further inland." I say, "To hell with it!" Either they let me go to the coast and prove my loyalty there or they can do what they want with me. If they don't want me in this country, they can throw me out....

Evacuation was a mistake, there was no need for it. The government knows this. Why don't they have enough courage to come out and say so, so that these people won't be pushed around? ...

I've tried to cooperate. Last year I went out on furlough and worked on the best fields in Idaho. There was a contract which said that we would be brought back here at the end of the work. Instead we just sat there.... We had to spend our own money. The farmers won't do anything for you. They treat you all right while you're working hard for them but as soon as your time is up, you can starve.... When I got back to Manzanar, nearly all my money that I had earned was gone....

industrial areas of Texas, Louisiana, North Carolina, and Georgia generated tens of thousands of African-American voters.

As they gained access to better jobs and higher incomes, blacks began to use the democratic and egalitarian cast of American war propaganda to legitimize their aspirations and demands. In 1943, for example, when the War Labor Board ordered an end to wage differentials based on race, it explained that "whether as vigorous fighting men or for production of food and munitions, *America needs the Negro.*" Removal of racial barriers at home, it added, "is a test of our sincerity in the cause for which we are fighting." The African-American-owned *Pittsburgh Courier* responded by popularizing the "double-V" slogan, which stood for victory over fascism abroad and victory over discrimination at home.

The CIO's wartime organizing efforts contributed to a growing consciousness about civil rights among African-Americans. Despite the racism still rife among white workers and its institutionalization in corporate hiring practices and union seniority rules, the CIO's campaign to organize a multiracial workforce into plantwide industrial unions gave black workers enormous leverage to press their grievances and aspirations. Thus an NAACP journalist found the CIO a "lamp of democracy" throughout the old Confederacy. "The South has not known such a force since the historic Union Leagues in the great days of the Reconstruction era."

But if wartime conditions made African-American advancement possible, forceful and well-organized protests of black workers were still required to make the unions and the federal government act against discrimination in jobs, housing, and political life. The first, and in many ways the most dramatic, protest movement began in 1940, when A. Philip Randolph and other leaders of the Brotherhood of Sleeping Car Porters decided that only a show of strength would compel equal treatment for blacks working in the new defense plants. Randolph's March on Washington movement promised that thousands of African-Americans would descend on the still-segregated capital city unless the federal government took vigorous steps to end racial discrimination in defense plants and the military. Throughout the country, the chance to act stirred thousands of black Americans never before touched by a civil rights organization. By the summer of 1941, Randolph was predicting that one hundred thousand would march.

Fearing the politically explosive consequences of such a demonstration, Roosevelt urged Randolph to cancel the march. Randolph refused, but entered into negotiations with White House emissaries in June. A presidential aide soon instructed Labor Department lawyer Joseph Rauh to get involved. Rauh remembers being told, "Some guy named Randolph is going to march on Washington unless we put out a fair employment practices order. . . . We got defense factories goin' up all over this goddamn country, but no blacks are bein' hired. Go down to the Budget Bureau and work something out." Roosevelt quickly issued Executive Order 8802, which directed that government agencies, job-training programs, and contractors must avoid racial and religious discrimination; it also set up the Fair Employment Practices Committee (FEPC). In return, Randolph canceled the march.

Neither the executive order nor the FEPC changed very much. Neither addressed segregation in the armed forces; in the South, federal nondiscrimination policy was nothing more than a legal fiction. In the Galveston shipyards, for example, African-Americans worked at skilled jobs for the pay of unskilled helpers. When the FEPC filed three cases against the shipyard and one against a Boilermakers' Union local, other federal agencies declined to cooperate, and FEPC intervention proved ineffectual. Likewise in Baltimore, black workers were treated unfairly by the Maryland State Employment Service, a branch of the U.S. Employment Service. Alexander Allen, who worked for the Baltimore Urban League, remembered that "Blacks were sent around the corner to the annex on Lombard Street, where they handled common labor and unskilled work. Even if you had a graduate degree in electronics, you would still be sent to the black entrance. And there were police to enforce it."

On the other hand, the federal government could be compelled to act more forcefully, especially if war-related production or services were at stake. In Philadelphia, which was second only to Detroit as a center of defense production, the FEPC and the War Manpower Commission ordered the city's transit system to promote eight African-Americans to positions as streetcar drivers. When the system's white employees responded with a protest strike, closing down Philadelphia's entire transit system and paralyzing the city's wartime industries, the federal government sent in eight thousand armed soldiers to break the strike and enforce FEPC orders. Afterward, Philadelphia employers opened more good jobs for the city's African-Americans.

Even more important, both Roosevelt's executive order and the FEPC's public hearings stimulated more direct and forceful forms of shop-floor and community action by black workers and their allies. For example, in Detroit—where hundreds of thousands of southern migrants of both races had moved during the war—African-American employees at Chrysler's Dodge Division walked out three times during 1941 to protest racial discrimination by management and the United Auto Workers. The following year, the NAACP organized two busloads of black female job-seekers to occupy the personnel office at Ford's new Willow Run factory and demand the jobs for which they had previously been excluded; and in 1943 three thousand black foundrymen quit work for three days over issues of job discrimination at Ford's River Rouge complex. Shortly thereafter, an integrated crowd of ten thousand, carrying banners that proclaimed "Jim Crow Must Go" and "Bullets and Bombs Are Colorblind," marched to Detroit's Cadillac Square, where union and NAACP leaders joined together to declare that "full and equal participation of all citizens is fair, just, and necessary for victory and an enduring peace. . . ."

Just as the latter-day civil rights movement of the late 1950s would face massive and sometimes violent opposition, so, too, did African-American assertiveness in the early 1940s generate white resistance, especially in the urban factories and neighborhoods where the races were in direct contact and competition for jobs and housing. Among the most spectacular manifestations of this tension were the "hate" strikes that flared when blacks entered formerly all-white workplaces or occupations. Hate strikes sometimes had the informal support of management, the local union leadership, or racist groups such as the Ku Klux Klan. They increased in number after 1941, reaching a climax in June 1943, when 25,000 white workers at Detroit's Packard engine factory walked out over the transfer of two African-American workers to jobs previously held only by whites.

Black workers were not intimidated. Supported by more seasoned and union-conscious white workers, they insisted that top union leaders and the government take vigorous steps to contain these explosive work stoppages. To face down one hate strike at Hudson Motors, UAW president R. J. Thomas wired local leaders that the strikers' "display of vicious race prejudice" violated the union constitution. He asserted that these strikers "face expulsion from the union unless they return to work at once."

United Electrical Workers' organizer Henry Fielding remembered North Canton, Ohio, as "a lily-white community; they wouldn't even permit a black into town. But as soon as a black worker entered the shop, the three thousand other white employees shut down the plant. . . ."

> There was a mass meeting during working hours, and I took them on. I remember to this day a screaming, hysterical audience of three thousand people calling me everything under the sun and threatening me. . . . It took a couple of hours, and although I did not convince the workers that it was right, I did persuade them to go back to work, that there was no alternative.

Racial conflicts were not confined to workplaces. In Detroit, fights broke out wherever large numbers of blacks and whites mixed. In early 1942, a crowd of working-class whites, led by second-

The Detroit riot, June 21, 1943. While police stand by, white crowds terrorize African-Americans on Detroit's Woodward Avenue. As shown here, African-American motorists were pursued and beaten, their cars destroyed. Shortly after this photo was taken, the victim's car (halted in front of the bus) was overturned and set on fire.

generation Polish-Americans and supported by the Klan, attacked African-Americans attempting to move into the new federally financed Sojourner Truth housing project, located in a predominantly white area. When both City Hall and Washington moved to bar occupancy by blacks, a coalition of African-American civic groups and CIO members (black and white) forced an about-face. By the end of April, African-Americans moved into the project.

Racial violence peaked in 1943 with 250 incidents in forty-seven cities. The worst riot broke out in Detroit, where a fight at the Belle Isle amusement park on the evening of June 20 ignited thirty hours of violence. Angry blacks struck back at police and at white motorists and passersby. White crowds roamed the city, assaulting African-Americans; blacks were dragged out of local movie theaters and pulled from streetcars. The Detroit police sided openly with the white rioters. Thirty-six hours later, nine whites and twenty-five blacks lay dead, three-quarters of the African-Americans killed by the police; more than seven hundred Detroiters were injured. Only the UAW and the Michigan CIO defended the African-American population, demanding an investigation of police conduct. African-American New Deal official Robert Weaver recalled that the UAW's action served to "impress the Negro community with the significance of a strong labor organization as an ally."

Race riots broke out in wartime Los Angeles as well, but with a difference: there, white rioters targeted not only young blacks but also Mexican-American males. Resentment against Mexican-

Zoot suit riot. In the weeks preceding the riots, a nationally syndicated comic strip satirically skewered the zoot suiters. Li'l Abner Yokum, cartoonist Al Capp's good-natured and dullwitted hero, becomes the pawn of zoot-suit manufacturers. As "Zoot-Suit Yokum," he performs heroic deeds that prompt a nationwide fashion fad—much to the horror, as this panel shows, of more levelheaded citizens. Capp's treatment reflected general hostility toward the defiant style favored by many young Mexican-Americans. After the riots, the Los Angeles City Council passed a law that made wearing a zoot suit a misdemeanor.

Americans—especially those who defied mainstream society by wearing the distinctive, loose-fitting "zoot suits" then in vogue—mushroomed as discriminatory employment barriers fell. In early June 1943, local newspapers played up a story that Mexicans had beaten up a group of Anglo sailors. In response, thousands of marines, sailors, soldiers, and civilians imposed a reign of terror on Mexican-American neighborhoods in Los Angeles, beating up young zoot suiters, stripping off their clothes, and cutting their long hair. More than one hundred were injured. Only when the Mexican ambassador interceded—and the fear grew that the Axis would make effective propaganda use of the riots—did the U.S. government declare downtown Los Angeles off-limits to naval personnel. Meanwhile, the Los Angeles rioters inspired anti-Mexican activity in seven other cities.

The wartime mobilization also transformed the roles played by women in the workplace. Shortly after America entered the war, the War Manpower Commission mounted a special campaign to recruit women, especially previously nonwage-

"WE'RE LOOKING FOR ZOOT-SUITS TO BURN . . ."

Al Waxman, editor of the Eastside Journal, *an East Los Angeles community newspaper, describes the brutality of soldiers and the Los Angeles police during the 1943 anti-Mexican riot.*

AT Twelfth and Central I came upon a scene that will long live in my memory. Police were swinging clubs and servicemen were fighting with civilians. Wholesale arrests were being made by the officers.

Four boys came out of a pool hall. They were wearing the zoot-suits that have become the symbol of a fighting flag. Police ordered them into arrest cars. One refused. He asked: "Why am I being arrested?" The police officer answered with three swift blows of the night-stick across the boy's head and he went down. As he sprawled, he was kicked in the face. Police had difficulty loading his body into the vehicle because he was one-legged and wore a wooden limb. Maybe the officer didn't know he was attacking a cripple.

At the next corner a Mexican mother cried out, "Don't take my boy, he did nothing. He's only fifteen years old. Don't take him." She was struck across the jaw with a night-stick and almost dropped the two and a half year old baby that was clinging in her arms. . . .

Rushing back to the east side to make sure that things were quiet here, I came upon a band of servicemen making a systematic tour of East First Street. They had just come out of a cocktail bar where four men were nursing bruises. Three autos loaded with Los Angeles policemen were on the scene but the soldiers were not molested. Farther down the street the men stopped a streetcar, forcing the motorman to open the door and proceeded to inspect the clothing of the male passengers. "We're looking for zoot-suits to burn," they shouted. Again the police did not interfere. . . . Half a block away . . . I pleaded with the men of the local police sub-station to put a stop to these activities. "It is a matter for the military police," they said.

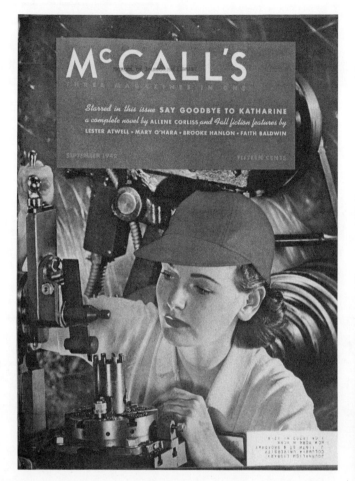

MᶜCALL'S

THREE MAGAZINES IN ONE

Starred in this issue SAY GOODBYE TO KATHARINE
a complete novel by ALLENE CORLISS *and* Fall fiction features by
LESTER ATWELL • MARY O'HARA • BROOKE HANLON • FAITH BALDWIN

SEPTEMBER 1942   FIFTEEN CENTS

Industrial chic. Though she now operates a drill press, her lipstick is still unsmeared. The September 1942 cover of *McCall's* imbues the new female industrial worker with the same kind of clean, unruffled glamor that the magazine had previously conferred on women's household work before the war.

earning married women, into the defense industry workforce. Government propaganda suggested that war work was little different from traditional housework. *Glamour Girls of '43*, a government-produced newsreel, announced, "Instead of cutting the lines of a dress, this woman cuts the pattern of aircraft parts. Instead of baking a cake, this woman is 'cooking' gears to reduce the tension in the gears after use. . . ."

But, of course, work in a factory represented an enormous transition from the kitchen, one that enhanced the self-confidence and expanded the horizons of millions of American women. War worker Delle Hahne remembered:

> The seeds of my liberation and many other women's started with the war. The first intimation I had that it was taking place came when I was invited to a friend's house

for Sunday dinner and I heard his mother and grandmother talk about which drill would bite into a piece of metal at the factory. . . . My God, this was Sunday dinner in Middle America, and to hear, instead of a discussion of the church service, a conversation about how to sharpen tools—it was a marvelous thing.

A popular song frequently heard on the radio celebrated a young defense worker named "Rosie the Riveter," who kept

> *a sharp lookout for sabotage,*
> *sitting up there on the fuselage.*
> *That little frail can do*
> *more than a male can do.*
> *Rosie—(brrr) the riveter.*

Women responded eagerly to new opportunities. The number of employed women rose from 11 million to nearly 20 million during the war; perhaps 5 million were completely new to wage labor. A large proportion were married women with children. The biggest

After work. Men and women workers begin to unwind as they finish their shift in a Richmond, California, shipyard.

change was that women moved from low-paying jobs to higher-paying industrial work. In the auto industry, one of every twenty production workers was a female in 1940, but by 1944, that proportion had grown to one in five. And in electrical manufacturing, the influx of women grew to fully one-half. African-American women, who had been largely confined to agricultural labor and domestic work before the war, made a dramatic, and in some instances bitterly resisted, entry into higher-paying and more dignified factory, clerical, and sales work. Women's proportion of total union membership doubled—to 20 percent—by war's end.

Unlike black workers, whose expanded ranks reinforced a nascent civil rights consciousness in the United States, the growth of female employment in the war did not generate such a radical transformation in the way most Americans defined the rights and proper role of American women. Many male workers retained a profound prejudice against the working woman, often greeting "Rosie" with a barrage of hisses and whistles when she made her way through formerly all-male workplaces. Moreover, most employers, unions, and government officials insisted that "Rosie" would be "the Riveter" for the duration of the war only.

Women workers were therefore denied more specialized kinds of training, and employers and government agencies operated on the assumption that women would gratefully turn their jobs over to returning veterans and other men in need of factory work once the war was over. Indeed, a strict system of job segregation by sex persisted in virtually all factories. Although the War Labor Board insisted on "equal pay for equal work," employers frequently assigned women to jobs such as inspection or small assembly, or to work simply labeled "light"; they remained segregated in a low-wage ghetto.

"... WE WERE DETERMINED TO STAY"

Celia Saparsteen Yanish, who worked as a machinist in New York City, recalls the trials and tribulations of breaking into "men's work" during the war.

BEFORE the war I worked in metal shops, assembling locks and doing other assembly work, until 1941 when the government set up a defense training school where they taught you to operate a bench lathe and drill press.... I was one of three girls in the school.

When the class was over we were sent to the machine shop. I was very happy. For the first time in my life I was going to be able to do skilled work.... I didn't know what it was, but I knew that until then only men had done this work.

[The men] were afraid we women were taking away jobs and they resented us. They complained they wouldn't be able to undress in the shop and work half nude like they did before. They said the women would interfere with their work, would distract them....

I was about 24 at the time and I knew how to handle myself. I didn't laugh at the men's dirty jokes. But another girl who was only 17 did laugh and so the men got more and more brazen. They would be looking up her skirt until she would start to cry.

We worked on a competitive system. You had to keep up with the man standing next to you because he made more money if he could increase his production. If you slowed down, they would say, "we knew these women would be no damn good." We were exhausted all the time. The men would go home and sit down to a prepared meal, but when the women came home they had to get the meal ready for their family....

It was very rough for a while, but we were determined to stay, and eventually, the majority of the men learned to accept us and respect us as co-workers and union sisters.

Working wives and mothers bore the double burden of homework and wagework. Housing was cramped and ration-restricted foods were more difficult to prepare in the overcrowded war centers to which so many women were drawn. The government did build hundreds of child-care facilities during the war—far more than had ever been built in this country before. By 1943, more than 50,000 children attended such centers. But federal day-care programs were inadequate, and large numbers of women refused to send their children to the centers because of their inaccessibility, high cost, low quality, and restricted hours.

Unions responded ambiguously to the needs of their female members. Trade unions staunchly supported "equal pay for equal work" policies, if only to protect their male members who might otherwise find their jobs eliminated or pay reduced by the tide of women workers. The United Electrical Workers' Union (UE), which had a substantial number of female members, aggressively petitioned the War Labor Board to eliminate the pay gap not only between men and women doing the same work, but also between those doing comparable work in sex-segregated jobs. In 1945, the UE won its case, but with the end of the war, Westinghouse and General Electric refused to comply with the board's order. The problem of unequal pay for equal work would live on: in the 1970s, women filing suit against these same companies would use data gathered in World War II to document their charges of continuing bias.

Most unions were apathetic or even hostile to issues such as maternity leave without loss of seniority, improved child care, and nondiscriminatory unemployment benefits. A 1944 UAW conference of women workers endorsed such demands, but as Millie Jeffrey, first head of the auto union's Women's Bureau recalled, "The policies of the UAW were always very good. Getting them implemented was another story." When management began to fire women workers at the end of the war, unions such as the UAW raised few objections.

LABOR'S WAR AT HOME

The war brought permanent changes in the relationship between labor and capital, both at the point of production and in the corridors of power in Washington. Most labor leaders had quickly agreed to a "no-strike pledge" at the outset of the conflict. The resulting decline in shop-floor strife pleased the Roosevelt administration and business leaders alike. But patriotic unionism had its problems. In arbitrating wages for millions of workers, the War Labor Board (WLB) gave priority to increasing production and resisting inflation, not dealing with workers' grievances about low wages. The keystone of the WLB's policy was its July 1942 decision in the "Little Steel" case to raise workers' wages only 15 percent above the level of January 1, 1941. Since most union workers had already won a negotiated wage increase in the spring of 1941, the board's ruling meant that few workers could expect a wage boost for the duration of the war.

Board officials and even some employers recognized the dilemma this created for trade union leaders. If the unions could not strike or bargain for higher wages, then why should workers join them? As a major West Coast shipper asked, "Can union leaders be held accountable for labor troubles if because of a falling off in membership they find they control a minority rather than a majority in the plants where they are the bargaining agents?" "Too often," a government official agreed, "members of unions do not maintain their membership because they resent the discipline of a responsible [union] leadership."

To counter this, the War Labor Board enacted a "maintenance of membership" policy virtually mandating that any employee at a unionized workplace had to join and pay dues to the union. From that point, expansion of war production led almost automatically to an expansion of union membership and a swelling of union treasuries. Trade union membership jumped from less than 10 million to nearly 15 million. UE organizer Henry Fielding recalled, "We'd circulate membership cards in front of the management and dare the management to do something about it. . . . I remember a two-year period, 1942–43, where we went through some sixty-six or sixty-eight plants, organized them, and held elections. We lost one!"

But union growth hardly eliminated the problems defense workers faced every day. Although take-home pay was higher than ever, wages represented more than money to most workers. Wages also symbolized a worker's social worth, and in years past the paycheck had often been an explicit indicator marking the social status of men and women, blacks and whites, recent immigrants, and those born in the United States. Thus, in a war in which patriotic egalitarianism was a pervasive homefront ideology and workers' pay was a product of government fiat, wage-rate inequalities proved to be among the most vexing and persistent causes of shop-floor discontent. "A man at the blast furnace does the same work another fellow does at the open hearth, but gets a few cents an hour less," reported a United Steelworkers' official in 1942. "Now frankly it's not a question of starving, much as he could use the money. It's just not right. A man does not see any sense in it and gets pretty mad."

Workers also clashed with managers and government officials over control of work on the shop floor. Foremen and managers often took advantage of labor's "no-strike pledge" to regain some of the power unions had wrested from them in the turbulent prewar years. And the wartime demand for more and more production also generated conflicts over speed-up and safety. Edward Osberg, who worked for Chrysler during the war, remembers:

> We were making airplane engines. . . . They had to go, go, go. Whenever engineers and general superintendents devised a new process to make something faster or better, they went ahead and did it. They didn't care if it killed someone or if the fumes and dust were dangerous. . . . One of the worst accidents I remember involved one of our maintenance men. He was oiling the gears of the hundred-ton sand mixer in the aluminum foundry, and he got his fingers in too far. Little by little the machine pulled in his fingers and hand until finally his arm was jerked off at the shoulder girdle.

Workers challenged management over the right to set production standards and piece rates, assign work, and discipline employees. A production manager at Packard Motors recalled that for two years during the war "the [union shop] stewards at the plant objected every time we went in. A number of times they told the time-study man to get out, so he got out." Unauthorized strikes over such issues mounted steadily from 1942 until the end of the war, when the number of workers who stopped work exceeded the level sustained in 1937. Most of these "quickie" stoppages or "wildcats" involved half a dozen to a few hundred employees who halted work for a single shift or less. Managers often responded by firing the "ringleaders," frequently generating larger, factorywide stoppages.

Such "wildcat" strikes were often denounced as unpatriotic, but rank-and-file pressure soon forced many shop stewards and local union leaders to champion these industrial actions, against the wishes of top union officials. The president of a UAW local in Ohio explained, "The only time I have ever had respect from the membership is when I finally had guts enough to stand up and face the people we had directing things in [UAW] Region 2A and tell them I didn't give a damn what they done, I was sticking with my membership."

Politically aware union leaders also used rights-conscious, working-class patriotism to legitimate wartime strikes. Mike Novak, a second-generation Pole who became the first president of the UAW's giant Dodge Local 3 in Detroit, justified a massive 1945 wildcat in the following terms: "We strike because we can't relax our principles. We've got to keep them as high as they were just before the war, so veterans can come back to good working conditions. Servicemen are fighting against what we're fighting against. We are against speed-ups. We are against racial discrimination."

The largest wartime labor confrontation took place in the coal industry. John L. Lewis had never thought the War Labor Board's Little Steel wage formula just or equitable. During 1942, he came under increasing pressure from hard-pressed miners to boost their pay. By December, a wave of wildcat strikes in eastern Pennsylvania stopped production and undermined Lewis's authority.

Lewis soon challenged the board, the "no strike" pledge, and the implicit alliance that existed between Roosevelt and most trade-union leaders. Lewis understood that although the New Deal had been enormously helpful at the birth of the new industrial unions, the unprecedented power now wielded by the wartime government represented a real threat to an independent labor movement. He sought a return to prewar—indeed, to pre-Wagner Act—collective bargaining norms. So estranged did he feel from both the Roosevelt administration and the CIO that in mid-1943 Lewis led the UMWA out of the organization he had founded and took it back into the AFL. To break the "Little Steel formula," Lewis called 500,000 miners out on strike four times in 1943 alone.

These mine strikes generated a storm of protest. All major newspapers denounced John L. Lewis, and public-opinion polls turned decisively against the strikes. Roosevelt had the Interior Department seize the mines and the Selective Service threaten to draft those who "strike against the government." Lewis's old CIO comrades blasted their former chief as "this man [who] has consistently schemed to undermine duly established wartime agencies." The Communist Party denounced Lewis as a traitor; War Labor Board member Wayne Morse, usually considered prolabor, explained that "in time of war, when a union seeks to defy the government of the United States, I am in favor of breaking that union."

In June 1943, Congress passed the Smith-Connally War Labor Disputes Act, which broadened presidential power to seize strikebound plants involved in war production, made it a crime to advocate strikes in such workplaces, and forbade

---

"IS THAT GIVING LABOR A SQUARE DEAL?"

In 1942, the Michigan CIO Council formally endorsed the no-strike pledge, but the employer attack on wages the following year caused the council to reconsider its actions. At the 1943 annual meeting, delegates debated a resolution recommending that "unless the assurances that were made to labor at the time we gave up our right to strike" were honored, the pledge should be nullified.

DELEGATE Washington (Local 600, UAW): We are hurting ourselves. We are taking things away from our boys who are on the battle lines the products of labor that they need to protect themselves and win this war. And I want to urge all of you who are Americans, who are with the allied nations, who are sincere in wanting to see this war won that you vote down this resolution and continue to give your support to the administration. Delegate Lucas: Some time ago labor made a very noble gesture. That was a matter of giving a no-strike pledge. Arguments to the contrary notwithstanding, there were certain commitments that were made to labor at that particular time. Does anyone in the hall question that these commitments have not been lived up to by the administration? . . .

When it comes to the question of giving labor its just due, it seems that the administration seems to not be able to find any money to do anything with but when it comes to the question of building plants for corporations who have already more than they need, they can find billions of dollars to do that with. Is that giving labor a square deal? I don't think so. My personal sentiments are on this question that the no-strike pledge should be revoked here and now.

union contributions to electoral campaigns. It was the first anti-union measure passed by Congress since the early 1930s, and it fore-shadowed the more conservative legislative climate of the postwar years. FDR vetoed the measure as unworkable and counterproductive, but a coalition of Republicans and southern Democrats mustered the strength to override the president's veto. *Time* magazine called this episode "the most stinging rebuke of [FDR's] entire career."

But Lewis and the miners were not entirely isolated. UMWA work stoppages generated considerable support among other industrial workers, especially those in cities such as Akron, Youngstown, and Canton, Ohio; Detroit; and Pittsburgh, where many were recent migrants from the coalfields. "Many workers in the plant," reported UAW president R. J. Thomas, "say to me John L. Lewis has the right program." In 1943, one of every four members of the UAW participated in a work stoppage, and the next year more than *half* did so.

Throughout this conflict Lewis had maintained that "bayonets cannot mine coal," that government coercion could not force union workers into the mines against their will. Ultimately, the Roosevelt administration agreed, and in November 1943, Lewis and Secretary of the Interior Harold Ickes signed a contract that effectively broke the Little Steel formula. Every other major union soon petitioned the War Labor Board for a general wage increase, thus setting the stage for the great postwar strikes that would determine the new American standard of living.

ALLIED VICTORY

Despite the turmoil in the nation's defense plants, American arms production far outstripped that of any other nation. With planes, tanks, and guns pouring across two oceans, the Allied war effort eventually ground down German, Italian, and Japanese resistance.

On June 6, 1944, the long-awaited Anglo-American invasion of western Europe began. A total of 176,000 troops landed on the beaches of Normandy, France. Reinforcements soon swelled the Allied forces to 2 million, under the command of U.S. general Dwight David Eisenhower. By September, the Allies had retaken most of France and Belgium; they reached the Rhine River, on Germany's western border, in November. The German Army staged a desperate counterattack in December—the Battle of the Bulge—pushing across the Rhine into France. But this final German offensive stalled when German tanks ran out of fuel and American soldiers were able to slow the forward march of Hitler's elite troops.

General Eisenhower's army crossed the Rhine in March 1945, entering southern Germany in the early spring. They soon encountered horrifying evidence that the Nazis had been exterminating millions

On the road to Rome, 1944. A sketch by Fifth Army, 88th Division, Corporal Ben Hurwitz shows GIs and their mules pausing in a hill town north of Naples. Mules were the only means of transport for American troops who had to cross the steep and narrow paths of the Apennine Mountains toward Rome.

of Jews and other eastern Europeans in a string of concentration camps that spread from Buchenwald in Germany to Auschwitz in Poland. Much later, the world discovered that leaders of the Roosevelt administration had known about the Nazi genocide but had failed to appreciate or act against the enormity of this crime.

Roosevelt, whose physical condition deteriorated rapidly following his reelection to a fourth term in November 1944, died on April 12, 1945. The vice president, Harry S. Truman, a former Missouri senator, took over.

Meanwhile, three huge Soviet armies blasted their way into the heart of Germany from the east. On April 26, Anglo-American and Soviet troops linked up at the Elbe River in central Germany. Ten days after Hitler's suicide, Germany surrendered unconditionally on May 4, 1945; the war in Europe was over.

In the Far East, the Allied counterattack generally avoided direct confrontation with the main body of the Japanese Army on the Asian mainland. Instead, the United States closed in on Japan by island-hopping

"... THE WALKING DEAD"

Leon Bass, an African-American soldier, recalls what he felt as a nineteen-year-old with the 183rd Combat Engineers when he helped liberate the Buchenwald concentration camp.

WE had gone through the Bulge, we had seen the horrors of war: death, people who were wounded. Many of us came very close to losing our lives during that period. But we had no knowledge, and our first encounter came one day when we were asked to go to a place outside of Weimar, Germany. It wasn't a mission of battle, it was just to go. And we came to this place, which was somewhat like a security place, a place you might see in any urban center that was a prison. But we were totally unprepared—at least I was, for what I encountered when I went into Buchenwald. The outside was very beautiful . . . the grass was well-manicured and cared for. And then you go inside, and then all of a sudden the stark horror of it all strikes you. And that's the way I encountered it at the age of 19. When I walked in I saw what should be considered to be human beings, that had been reduced to the point where they were just merely surviving. I called them the walking dead, because I felt they had reached the point of no return. The malnutrition had set in and it was just a matter of time. . . .

I didn't speak to anyone else that day. The shock was just too much. . . . No, I didn't encounter anyone to share feelings with at that time. I only know that after I got there it became a part of me; and as much as didn't want to deal with it, I couldn't get rid of it. . . .

Death camps. When American soldiers liberated the concentration camp in Nordhausen, Germany, in April 1945, they found thousands of unburied dead. The residents of the adjacent town, who claimed ignorance about what went on in the camp, were forced to bury the bodies. The systematic extermination of almost 6 million European Jews during World War Two was part of an overall death toll that claimed at least 55 million lives.

across the Pacific. Savage, hand-to-hand combat on Tarawa, Saipan, and Guam yielded great gains by late 1944. U.S. forces began the re-conquest of the Philippines, devastating the Japanese Navy at the Battle of Leyte Gulf in October. The next spring, after ferocious fighting, the United States took the islands of Iwo Jima and Okinawa, near the Japanese homeland. In early May 1945, British, Indian, and Nationalist Chinese troops retook Burma in South Asia.

By the middle of 1945, Japan had lost most of its navy and much of its air force, along with its holdings in the Pacific. Her still-intact army retained control of Korea, Manchuria, and much of China and Southeast Asia. But massive and continuous bombing raids on civilian as well as military targets terrorized and demoralized the population, smashed Japanese industry, and further isolated its military forces on the Asian mainland from the home islands. During June

The Battle of Pelellu Island, September 1944. Oppressed by 115-degree heat and trapped by withering Japanese fire, marines take cover in the sandy terrain of the small Central Pacific island.

and July, high Japanese officials in a "peace" faction of the government made repeated efforts to open negotiations with both the Soviets and the Americans. Allied leaders agreed that when Japan surrendered, they would allow the emperor to retain his throne and that the nation would eventually regain self-rule. The end of the war was in sight.

When Germany surrendered in May, British and American intelligence agencies expected that Japan would also stop fighting, especially if the Soviet Union finally entered the war in the Far East. Therefore, Britain and the United States pushed for the earliest possible Soviet entry into the fighting in Asia. The Soviets agreed to declare war on Japan on or about August 8, three months after Germany's surrender. "Fini Japs when that comes about," President Truman wrote in his diary.

But Truman did not wait. On August 6 and 8, U.S. planes dropped atomic bombs on the Japanese cities of Hiroshima and Nagasaki, respectively. "Fat Man" and "Little Boy"—the names of the weapons were taken from their design and shape—were the products of an enormous wartime mobilization of scientific talent, engineering skill, and the money and muscle available in a virtually unlimited military budget. The Manhattan Project, the U.S. effort to produce an atomic bomb, inaugurated not just a new age of weaponry but also the era of bureaucratically organized and government-funded big science that would prove so influential in the postwar era.

The atomic blast in Hiroshima leveled nearly five square miles and instantly vaporized nearly 80,000 people. Tens of thousands more died soon afterward from injuries, burns, and radiation. In Nagasaki, where poor visibility resulted in faulty targeting, about one and a half square miles were destroyed, 35,000 people were killed immediately, and another 60,000 were injured. In less than a week, Japan agreed to surrender, doing so formally on September 2.

President Truman explained that the bombings of Hiroshima and Nagasaki had been necessary to compel Japan's surrender without the enormous loss of life that would have resulted if Allied forces had invaded the Japanese home islands. Most Americans accepted that explanation. After the devastating bombing raids by both sides on civilian targets, two more bombs, even though they were atomic bombs, did not seem particularly excessive. "We're sitting on the pier in Seattle," one GI remembered, "sharpening our bayonets, when Harry [Truman] dropped that beautiful bomb. The greatest thing that ever happened."

Others raised pointed questions. Hadn't the Japanese already signaled their readiness to surrender months earlier? What was the rush? The Americans had no major military operations planned for the next three months—until November 1— and the projected full-scale invasion of Japan was not to occur in any case before spring 1946. Why couldn't Truman wait for the Soviet Union to enter the war? Questions like these led General Eisenhower to conclude that "it wasn't necessary to hit them with that awful thing." Admiral William Leahy, head of the U.S. joint chiefs of staff, concurred: "The use of this barba-

"... THEY WERE DEALING WITH A NEW SICKNESS"

The novelist John Hersey describes in graphic detail the suffering of thousands of Hiroshima citizens in the days following the detonation of the atomic bomb above the city.

DR. Sasaki and his colleagues at the Red Cross Hospital watched the unprecedented disease unfold and at last evolved a theory about its nature. It had, they decided, three stages. The first stage had been all over before the doctors even knew they were dealing with a new sickness; it was the direct reaction to the bombardment of the body, at the moment when the bomb went off, by neutrons, beta particles, and gamma rays. The apparently uninjured people who had died so mysteriously in the first few hours or days had succumbed in this first stage. It killed ninety-five per cent of the people within a half mile of the center, and many thousands who were farther away. The doctors realized in retrospect that even though most of these dead had also suffered from burns and blast effects, they had absorbed enough radiation to kill them. The rays simply destroyed body cells.... The second stage set in ten or fifteen days after the bombing. Its first symptom was falling hair. Diarrhea and fever, which in some cases went as high as 106, came next. Twenty-five to thirty days after the explosion, blood disorders appeared: gums bled, the white-blood-cell count dropped sharply, and *petechiae* [eruptions] appeared on the skin and mucous membranes.... The third stage was the reaction that came when the body struggled to compensate for its ills—when, for instance, the white count not only returned to normal but increased to much higher than normal levels. In this stage, many patients died of complications, such as infection in the chest cavity....

As the symptoms revealed themselves ... the doctors ... gave victims liver extract, blood transfusions, and vitamins, especially B1. The shortage of supplies and instruments hampered them ... the disease had some baffling quirks. Not all the patients exhibited all the main symptoms. People who suffered flash burns were protected, to a considerable extent, from radiation sickness. Those who had lain quietly for days or even hours after the bombing were much less liable to get sick than those who had been active. Gray hair seldom fell out. And, as if nature were protecting man against his own ingenuity, the reproductive processes were affected for a time; men became sterile, women had miscarriages, menstruation stopped....

Miyuki Bridge, Hiroshima, August 6, 1945. Three hours after the atomic bomb detonation, shocked and wounded survivors wander near a bridge a little over a mile from ground zero.

rous weapon at Hiroshima and Nagasaki was of no material assistance in our war against Japan. The Japanese were already defeated and ready to surrender."

John Grove, who worked at the University of California Radiation Laboratory developing the A-bomb, remembers hearing of the bombing of Hiroshima:

> My immediate reaction was, Thank God we really were successful. That proves that all the money that was spent on the [Manhattan] project was worthwhile. That was my first thought. About two seconds later it struck home. "O my God, Hiroshima. They dropped the atomic bomb on a city." I went to my superior and then I got another stunning blow. I said, "You heard the news?"
>
> He said, "Yes."
>
> I said, "Why a city? Why didn't they drop it on the great naval base at Truk, or some other military installation? God knows how many people they've killed. Maybe a hundred thousand, maybe five hundred thousand." And this man, who was Jewish, said, "What the hell difference does it make? They're only Japs."

Why, then, were atomic bombs dropped? Less for military than for political reasons, it seems. With victory in sight by mid-1945, tensions were quickly rising between the Anglo-American forces and their Soviet allies over the shape of the postwar world. President Truman decided that it was important to avoid extensive Soviet participation in the war against Japan. If the Soviet Army moved into northern China, they would be in a position to aid the Chinese Communists against the Nationalists. It could also entitle Stalin to participate in the occupation and administration of postwar Japan. The White House wanted to ensure America's supremacy in postwar Asia.

American officials expected the bomb's immense destructive power to intimidate the Soviet Union and give the United States the upper hand in shaping the postwar world. One atomic scientist recalled that Secretary of State Byrnes "did not argue that it was necessary to use the bomb against the cities of Japan in order to win the war Mr. Byrnes' view [was] that our possessing and demonstrating the bomb would make Russia more manageable." Byrnes later recalled the widely shared hope in Washington that the bomb's use would enable the United States "to dictate our own terms at the end of the war."

CONVERSION TO A PEACETIME ECONOMY

During the war, the federal government had become a giant planning apparatus, coordinating the production, pricing, and distribution decisions of thousands of corporations. Large planning bureaucracies—the Office of Price Administration alone had 73,000 paid employees and 200,000 volunteers—had the capacity to monitor and restructure the entire economic life of the nation. As the war drew to a close, the nation had to decide whether to dismantle this governmental apparatus or use it in the conversion to a peacetime economy.

Americans felt they had made heavy sacrifices during the war and now deserved a higher living standard. All the idealism of the New Deal and the war against fascism encouraged many workers to demand more equitable treatment by bosses and government officials. Perhaps never before did the mass of Americans feel such a strong sense of entitlement.

Detroit's 1945 mayoral election demonstrated the forces at work. Richard Frankensteen, a UAW vice president, entered the race, announcing, "Our boys are now coming back. Shall they come back to a city torn by hatred? Or shall we go to work and build a better city with opportunity for all to work at a decent wage, to live in decent homes, and to live in unity?" Labor's candidate promised to use the city's tax revenues to modernize the trolley system, clear slums, and build new schools and housing. He endorsed fair employment laws, then at the heart of the civil rights agenda. A biracial, working-class electorate gave Frankensteen first place in the April 1945 nonpartisan primary. He won 42 percent of the city vote.

But Detroit business leaders soon counterattacked. The city's three daily newspapers warned that business would close numerous plants if labor's candidate were elected. Right-wing papers warned of "white neighborhoods in peril," charging that a Frankensteen victory would boost "the attempts of Communist-inspired Negroes to penetrate white residential areas." "Concerned property owners" organized a telephone campaign to inflame fears that a CIO triumph would "destroy property values."

These racist appeals worked. Voters in wards that were strongly middle class or composed of recent white migrants from the South went two-to-one for incumbent Mayor Edward Jeffries in the election, overwhelming Frankensteen's support among African-Americans, Poles, Italians, and Jews.

As this electoral campaign demonstrated, America's transition to a peacetime economy would take place in a highly charged atmosphere. Haunting all the debates about the future were memories of the past: the economic collapse after World War I; the bitter labor wars of 1919–23; and the bread lines and Hoovervilles of the Great Depression. The war economy had generated millions of new jobs. What would happen when the defense plants shut down and 12 million GI's came home? Could a return to relatively "free markets" successfully reemploy these workers, keep inflation under control, and raise the standard of living? Or should the nation retain and expand its seemingly successful wartime arrangements, which made prices, wages, and the deployment of capital subject to direct political control by Washington?

At this critical juncture, the U.S. trade union movement and their many liberal allies put forward a social and economic agenda that was broad, ambitious, and had a chance to succeed. Most unions, especially those in the CIO, believed that the welfare of the working class would be advanced not only, or even primarily, by postwar collective bargaining but by labor's growing influence on economic and business decisions, both public and private. Thus, in the early years of the war the CIO's Philip Murray urged the creation of a series of "industry councils" that would fuse economic and political bargaining: "a program for democratic economic planning and for participation by the people in the key decision of the big corporations."

Organized labor and their liberal supporters thought such a democratic reconversion of the war economy might be possible. The labor movement had increased its numbers by half during the war, and in 1944 the industrial unions had organized a pioneering political action committee that played a key role in reelecting Roosevelt to a fourth term. Nine months later, progressives in the United States took heart from the Labor Party's smashing victory in Great Britain's first postwar election. As one observer characterized labor's general outlook:

Welcome back. During the war, housing construction came to a virtual standstill. The return of millions of servicemen to civilian life in 1945 set off a national housing crisis.

"Union leaders no longer regard themselves as a force merely reacting to managerial decisions . . . but as a force which itself can influence the whole range of industrial economic activity."

The UAW's Walter Reuther, a union pioneer and former socialist, embodied this outlook most forcefully in the mid-1940s. Reuther was a trade unionist equally at ease among the shop-floor militants of Detroit and the policy-making bureaucrats of Washington. He called on the government to convert taxpayer-financed war plants to the mass production of badly needed housing and railroad equipment under the authority of a New Deal–style agency. Most strikingly, Reuther demanded a 30 percent wage increase for autoworkers, which would just about make up for the income lost when the postwar workweek shifted from sixty to forty hours. But Reuther did not limit his argument to a narrow consideration of wages. Instead he also challenged management to keep car prices at prewar levels. Directed toward General Motors, the world's largest corporation and pacesetter for all American industry, Reuther's program sought to stave off an inflationary surge, increase working-class purchasing power, and enlist middle-class consumers on the side of organized labor's struggle with capital.

The federal government seemed an ally in this fight when President Truman spelled out his reconversion policy before a special session of Congress just after the Japanese surrender in September 1945. Truman had none of Roosevelt's immense self-confidence and commanded little of the loyalty or hatred generated by a man elected four times to the presidency. But Truman did seek to continue New Deal traditions, and his postwar program reflected the heightened expectations of America's working people. Truman proposed to continue rationing to hold inflation in check, to increase the minimum wage, to federalize and increase unemployment compensation, to enact a fair employment practices law, and to appropriate billions of dollars for a nationwide housing program. Key members of his administration, including Secretary of Commerce Henry Wallace and Office of Price Administration chief Chester Bowles, endorsed most of labor's program, including its contention that industry could afford to give an inflation-free increase in workers' wages.

But the business community envisioned a very different postwar future. Unlike their counterparts in continental Europe or Great Britain, who had been tarred with the brush of collaboration with or appeasement of the Nazis and were less powerful as a result, American business leaders found the wartime experience both commercially successful and politically advantageous. While they and their companies had profited handsomely from their involvement with the government, the close state-sponsored labor-management collaboration that helped legitimize a postwar capitalist economy in Western Europe held little attraction for U.S. businessmen. Indeed, they remained intensely suspicious of the kind of New Deal social engineering favored by organized labor, and they wanted to be free of government or union interference in determining wage-price relationships in each industry. As GM's Alfred P. Sloan put it, "It took fourteen years to rid this country of prohibition. It is going to take a good while to rid the country of the New Deal, but sooner or later the ax falls and we get a change."

A labor-management conference convened by President Truman in November 1945 collapsed when no accord proved possible on either the shop-floor prerogatives of management or labor's right to negotiate a postwar wage formula that held prices in check. The National Association of Manufacturers and the U.S. Chamber of Commerce cranked out graphs and charts demonstrating that free enterprise was doomed unless Congress eliminated price controls. Corporate public-relations people coordinated public testimony by hundreds of doctors, ministers, newspaperboys, and Rotarians. There was even a group of bankrupt businessmen who blamed their failure on government bureaucrats.

This debate over the government's role was overwhelmed by events. In the same month that the labor-management conference failed, the UAW's Walter Reuther endorsed a companywide strike against General Motors as necessary to win more pay for GM's 320,000 workers. Reuther wanted the walkout to harness the anger of workers long denied the right to strike because of the war effort; he also hoped to advance his own standing in the bitterly factional politics of the autoworkers' union. Reuther directly challenged GM's tightly held management prerogatives, insisting that the company "open the books" to prove that high wartime profits justified the UAW's demand for a wage increase with no jump in car prices.

Speaking for all American industry, GM rejected the UAW demands out of hand. "We don't even let our stockholders look at the books," one GM executive argued. The company's counteroffer was a 10 percent wage increase, tied to a formula for obtaining higher prices from the still-functioning Office of Price Administration. After the UAW's GM council rejected this offer, Reuther proposed submitting the dispute to government arbitration. GM dismissed this counterproposal, warning, "America is at the crossroads! It must preserve the freedom of each unit of American business to determine its own destiny. . . ." In newspaper editorials and pamphlets, the corporation argued that "A look at the books is a clever catchphrase. . . . The UAW-CIO is reaching for power. . . . It leads surely toward the day when union bosses . . . will seek to tell us what we can make, when we can make it, where we can make it, and how much we can charge. . . ."

In the end, forces outside the control of GM and the UAW resolved the conflict. Two months after the GM strike began, the United States entered the most strike-torn year in its history, except for 1919. The nation was brought to a virtual standstill during 1946 as millions of American workers undertook a rolling wave of walkouts, protests, and other job actions. These actions climaxed in a series of well-planned general strikes that shut down a number of small and midsize industrial cities across the country, including Stamford and Hartford, Connecticut; Lancaster, Pennsylvania; Houston, Texas; Rochester, New York; Camden, New Jersey; and Oakland, California. More than 1 million unionists in the steel, meatpacking, and electrical industries joined the massive strike wave, launching a series of walkouts unsurpassed in their massive solidarity and peaceful character.

Like Reuther's GM strike, these industrywide stoppages and city-wide general strikes had a twofold purpose: to win substantial wage

"IT IS NONE OF YOUR DAMNED BUSINESS ..."

UAW president Walter Reuther distributed the transcripts of the UAW-GM negotiations to the press as part of the union's campaign to enlist public support for the UAW's bargaining position and its campaign to "open the books."

HARRY COEN (GM assistant director of personnel): Is the UAW fighting the fight of the whole world?

REUTHER: We have been fighting to hold prices and increase purchasing power. We are making our little contribution in that respect.

COEN: Why don't you get down to your size and get down to the type of job you are supposed to be doing as a trade-union leader, and talk about money you would like to have for your people, and let the labor statesmanship go to hell for a while." ...

ELWIN CORBIN (UAW official): Do you mean if we came in here with a 30 percent wage demand and offered to join with you in going before OPA [the Office of Price Administration] for a 30 percent increase in the price of your cars, you would talk business?

COEN: We don't ask you to join with us on the price of cars. It is none of your damned business what OPA does about prices.

CORBIN: The hell it isn't. I intend to buy a car. . . .

REUTHER: But don't you think it is constructive for us to relate our wage question to prices?

COEN: Nobody else is doing that but you. You are the fellow that wants to get the publicity out of this whole thing. You want to enhance your personal political position. That is what the whole show is about. . . .

REUTHER: [I]f I came in here and said we want 30 percent and we don't care about prices, we don't care about profits, that is your business . . . then you would say Reuther is being a trade unionist and not trying to build himself up politically. But when Reuther comes and there is what you say is an attempt to be a statesman, you think that is bad. I think if I didn't do it that way, it would be bad. I think if we came in here on a selfish basis and said, "We want ours and the world be damned," then you should take our pants off.

COEN: . . . None of the other labor leaders have been taking the position you are taking.

REUTHER: . . . They don't care what happens to prices?

COEN: I don't know whether they care or not. They haven't coupled it up with their demand. . . . I don't think the people out on the picket lines care anything about wage theories, too. . . . What does he care about GM books?

REUTHER: He doesn't care anything about GM books providing you . . . give him a satisfactory wage increase.

COEN: That is right.

REUTHER: But if you say, "No dice, we can't give you a wage increase," he says, "Let's see your books to see why you can't."

increases that would set the pattern for all American wageworkers in the immediate postwar years; and to preserve government-mandated price ceilings so that inflation would not ravage working-class living standards. President Truman soon appointed high-level "fact-finding" boards that ruled that employers in the major industries could indeed afford pay hikes—the government recommended about 20 percent— without raising prices.

But steel industry leaders flatly announced that "until [the Office of Price Administration] authorizes fair prices, nothing can be settled through collective bargaining." Thus the great strikes in the winter of 1946 took on a fundamentally political character: a struggle over the fate of the Truman administration's program to sustain price controls and plan economic reconversion along lines that gave noncorporate voices a full hearing. Facing unemployment and economic dislocation, Truman finally caved in, announcing that in return for a wage increase of about eighteen cents per hour, he would permit the steel corporations to raise the price of steel by five dollars a ton.

Although Reuther and the GM strikers insisted that they were determined to hold out for an inflation-free wage boost, most union leaders concluded that political realities had now shifted. AFL unions such as the carpenters and the teamsters had never subscribed to the CIO's brand of social unionism. CIO president Philip Murray, who also led the steelworkers, made it clear that his organization had little stomach for a long and bitter strike that might well turn into a political confrontation with the Truman administration. And even within the ranks of the autoworkers, union leaders at Ford and Chrysler abandoned the goals of the GM strike. After nearly four months, Reuther finally called off the strike.

The great strikes of 1946 therefore ended in something of a Pyrrhic victory for organized labor. Unlike 1919, every major corporation agreed to negotiate with the union that represented its employees; the 1946 strikes demonstrated the permanence of the new industrial unions built during the 1930s and expanded during the war. But businessmen also insisted that postwar contracts include a "management rights" clause that gave them more power to set production standards and limit the authority of shop stewards and local union officials. The wage increases won during the walkouts finally evaporated under the galloping inflation let loose when government price controls were drastically weakened a few months later.

Unions that sought to break the wage pattern negotiated that winter, such as the railroad brotherhoods and the mineworkers, found that the government now considered their goals incompatible with the national welfare. In the late spring of 1946, both the miners and railway workers were involved in major confrontations with the Truman administration; both unions shut down their respective industries in a vain effort to raise wages. Truman now concluded that labor strife had become unpopular and that the unions presented an easy target. He adopted a tough, uncompromising attitude toward these two strikes, briefly putting both the railroads and the coalmines under government control. In private he railed against the work stoppages, at one point announcing to his attorney general his plan for ending a rail strike: "We'll draft 'em first and think about the law later."

Because of the inevitable postwar inflation, most of the big unions had to return to the bargaining table for another round of wage negotiations in the fall of 1946. All settled without stopping work, most for a fifteen-cent hourly wage advance. Businessmen then used such pay boosts, which were often accompanied by work stoppages, to justify raising retail prices. They typically blamed "Big Labor" for the inflationary spiral that gripped the economy. This analysis shaped the conservative, antilabor political environment that increasingly characterized the postwar years.

Congress began selling off government-financed war plants during 1946 to private industry at fire-sale prices. The great steel mills in Pittsburgh; Southern California; Geneva, Utah; East Chicago, Indiana; and Buffalo, New York, paid for with hundreds of millions of tax dollars, were claimed by the major steel corporations at a fraction of their real cost. And the huge aircraft plants that Walter Reuther envisioned as publicly owned factories building mass-produced housing for war veterans and mass-transit equipment for a new nationwide rail network were quickly sold to the auto companies.

"PEOPLE WERE LITERALLY DANCING IN THE STREETS . . ."

Autoworker Stan Weir, an enthusiastic participant in the 1946 general strike in Oakland, California, describes the workers' jubilant mood in the early hours of the strike and the way they took control of the city for more than two days.

THE Oakland general strike was called by no leader. It was unique, I think, in general strikes in this country. There was a strike of women who were the clerks at Kahn's and Hastings' department stores and it had been going on for months. The Teamsters had begun to refuse to make deliveries to those department stores and the department stores needed commodities badly.

Not many people had cars right after the war and you took public transportation to work in the morning. You had to go downtown to the center of Oakland and then out in the direction of your workplace. So thousands and thousands of people traveled through the heart of town every morning on the way to work, on public transportation. Very early one morning, here were the policemen of Oakland herding in a string of trucks, operated by a scab trucking firm in Los Angeles, with supplies for these department stores. Some truck driver or some bus driver or street car conductor asked some policeman about the trucks. . . . Well, that truck driver, that bus driver, or that street car conductor didn't get back on his vehicle . . . and that increased till those trucks and those buses and those street cars just piled up and thousands of people were stranded in town.

In a small way it was a holiday. The normal criteria for what was acceptable conduct disappeared. No one knew what to do and there were no leaders. No one called it. Pretty soon the strikers began forming into committees on the street corners. Certain shopkeepers were told to shut down and drug stores to stay open. Bars could stay open if they didn't serve hard liquor, and they had to put their juke boxes out on the sidewalk. People were literally dancing in the streets in anticipation of some kind of new day. Soon the strikers began to direct traffic and only let union people into town and keep out those who it was feared might be against the strike. It lasted fifty-four hours.

The New Deal was over, and with it a cycle of union growth and working-class recomposition that had transformed the structures of American society during the Depression and World War II. To be sure, unions were established participants in America's political and economic life in the postwar period. And the federal government continued to exercise far greater power than it had a generation earlier. But perhaps the most profound transformation derived from the immense influence the United States now exercised over the economic and political affairs of the rest of the world. None of the issues raised by the Depression, the New Deal, or World War II—the degree of government involvement in the economy, the future of social welfare legislation, the fate of the labor and nascent civil rights movements, even the future of gender politics—could be considered without reference to America's new power and responsibility in a world increasingly divided along ideological and economic lines.

PART THREE

THE RISE AND FALL OF THE "AMERICAN CENTURY"

1945–1991

AS AMERICANS surveyed the world in the aftermath of World War II, magazine publisher Henry Luce's 1940 prophecy of the "American Century" seemed to have come true. The United States was the world's preeminent military power in 1945 with nearly twelve million soldiers under arms and sole possession of the horrifying power of nuclear weapons. The economies of Europe and much of Asia lay in ruins, while America's industrial and agricultural might remained untouched by the ravages of war. The result of this fundamental difference in wartime experiences was striking: by the end of the 1940s the average American enjoyed an income fifteen times greater than that of the average foreigner.

But for all their prosperity, Americans did not feel secure. In 1945, the planet quickly divided into two armed and hostile camps, embodying different social and ideological systems: one composed of nations allied to or occupied by the Soviet Union; the other, a slightly looser network of states led by the United States. This military and ideological rivalry—dubbed the "Cold War"—generated an expensive and dangerous arms race and armed conflicts in China, Greece, Korea, Cuba, and Vietnam.

America's protracted conflict with the Soviet Union mobilized economic resources and regimented social, political, and intellectual life at home. The postwar arms race helped sustain the economic boom begun during World War II. The U.S. obsession with communism also generated a sharp turn to the right and a drastic narrowing of what the government and many ordinary Americans considered acceptable political ideas and social behavior. "McCarthyism"— named for the senatorial investigations of "subversives" conducted by Wisconsin senator Joseph McCarthy—provided a convenient label for political and intellectual repression during the 1950s.

The civil rights movement of the late 1950s and 1960s broke the stalemate that gripped domestic American politics. An amazingly creative biracial movement led by African-Americans swept aside the structures of legal segregation and discrimination that for almost one hundred years had mocked the North's victory in the Civil War. This great crusade made all Americans more "rights" conscious, giving rise to a series of social movements modeled on the civil rights revolution. These movements transformed the expectations and aspirations of many Americans: students, women, homosexuals, other ethnic and racial groups, and the many men and women who sought to extend to the office and factory the fundamental citizenship rights that they enjoyed in the larger society. These diverse social movements provided the pivot upon which postwar U.S. history would turn.

The civil rights revolution also helped inaugurate a new burst of reform that reached its peak during the presidency of Lyndon Johnson. Great Society legislation fulfilled many of the promises—for medical care, welfare rights, and access to education—first raised during the New Deal. But Johnson's reform initiative was derailed by the war in Vietnam. The war generated a military stalemate in Southeast Asia, a massive antiwar movement at home, and a constitutional crisis that thwarted the Johnson and Nixon presidencies. The United States lost the war in Vietnam because the American people no longer had the political will to wage it.

In Vietnam's aftermath, America's economic and political preeminence came to an end. Beginning in the early 1970s, higher oil prices, a flood of imported goods, and rising interest rates generated increased levels of unemployment and a decline in U.S. living standards. For many business and political leaders, but also for many ordinary Americans, increased demands for higher wages and social services and the cultural and personal "excesses" of the 1960s had precipitated this economic stagnation and political decline. A veritable cultural and political war erupted in the late 1970s between a New Right intent on rolling back the social and cultural changes of the 1960s, and those women, African-Americans, and others intent on defending their new sense of empowerment. U.S. politics swung markedly to the right in these years. Military and law-enforcement spending expanded, social spending was cut, and tax rates were slashed. Republican presidents Ronald Reagan and George Bush took advantage of the rightward political tilt to undertake military interventions in Grenada, Panama, and the Persian Gulf.

The half-century since the end of World War II thus witnessed a fundamental transformation of American life. Today, as in 1945, the United States is the world's leading military power. But the nation's economic strength has diminished, even as the Cold War has ended and the Soviet Union has collapsed. Although the U.S. economy is still the largest and most powerful in the world, its creativity and dynamism have languished, superseded by capitalist innovators in Japan and Germany.

The American working class also was fundamentally transformed in the postwar era. The incomes of the vast majority of working Americans have stagnated for two decades. The typical American worker of 1950—a male "breadwinner" in a blue-collar union job supporting a family—has virtually ceased to exist. The doubling in the proportion of women in the paid labor force has forever transformed family and work life. The wave of suburbanization during the 1950s and 1960s, followed by significant loss of millions of factory jobs, has eroded the nation's old industrial base and virtually destroyed traditional urban working-class neighborhoods. The labor movement has lost half its strength since its high point immediately after World War II and has seen its political and social influence wither. And the relatively homogeneous makeup of the American workforce evident at midcentury has changed. A new geography of racial, ethnic, and economic stratification now defines the United States, as millions of new immigrants, most from Asia and Latin America, poured into the United States during the 1970s and 1980s.

As the United States enters the last decade of the twentieth century, Americans must contend with a faltering economy, an increasingly fragmented social structure, and a nagging feeling of uncertainty fundamentally at odds with its great moment of triumph at the outset of the "American Century."

10

THE POSTWAR ERA

Smile when you say that. Despite the calm demeanor of this anti-Rosenberg picketer at a 1953 Washington, D.C., demonstration, the message on his sign suggests the intensity of anti-Communist hysteria in the period.

"**AMERICA AT** this moment stands at the summit of the world," announced Winston Churchill in August 1945. The former British prime minister stood in awe for good reason. During World War II the United States had mobilized an army of twelve million and bankrolled or equipped an equal number among its allies. It had assembled the world's largest navy and air force and built the atomic bombs that wiped out two Japanese cities. But the most impressive thing to observers such as Churchill was the extraordinary strength of the U.S. economy. In four wartime years national income, wealth, and industrial production all doubled or more. By 1947, the United States produced half the world's manufactures: 57 percent of the steel; 43 percent of the electricity; and 62 percent of the oil. And

CITIES FROM COAST TO COAST
adopt identification necklaces of Bead Chain for students

From New York City to Redwood, California, many cities across the country are ordering Identification Necklaces as a safeguard for their school children. Each student is being issued a necklace carrying a tag on which is stamped the student's identity and other information necessary for civilian defense.

For this purpose, Bead Chain has long been accepted as standard by our Armed Forces, for whom we have made identification necklaces for many years.

So flexible that it can't kink . . . economical, attractive, comfortable and very strong . . . Bead Chain is also preferred for religious chains and many other products made for personal wear. Write for catalog and complete information.

The BEAD CHAIN® Mfg. Co.
26 Mountain Grove St., Bridgeport, Conn.

Better safe than sorry. An advertisement in a 1951 edition of the professional periodical *School Executive* sells "dog tag" necklaces for children to help identify their presumably mutilated remains after nuclear war. New York City's public-school system issued tags during that year.

America dominated precisely those industries, including aviation, chemical engineering, and electronics, that spelled victory in modern war.

This enormous military and industrial power enabled the United States to become the guardian of a postwar *Pax Americana*, restructuring international politics and world capitalism to make them more responsive to American interests. However, in playing the role of the world's police force, Americans soon found themselves entangled in a series of small and sometimes bloody wars in far-off lands, and in a lengthy "Cold War" with the Soviet Union. The nuclear arms race began, casting a shadow of horror and insecurity into everyday life. Fear of communism led to repression and conformity at home and encouraged the resurgence of conservative business and military influence. The reform momentum of the New Deal and wartime years was halted, and American politics settled into an uneasy stalemate.

At the same time, America's global economic dominance, together with its technological advances, contributed to a period of unrivaled affluence at home. Reforms won in previous years helped open postwar prosperity to a growing number of Americans. Swelling families, new suburban homes, televisions, and above all, big, powerful, shiny automobiles symbolized the hopes and possibilities of the era. Seemingly limitless material abundance and the apparent decline of class and ethnic divisions led many contemporary observers to conclude that American society had managed to solve all its significant conflicts and problems.

In fact, postwar American society was not a seamless, harmonious whole. While traditional social divisions, such as religious and ethnic differences, were declining in importance, new rifts appeared: political conflicts over the meaning of Americanism and generational tensions over sexual and cultural norms. And some older problems, such as racial antagonism and the subordination of women, persisted in new forms. For a time, material affluence and the popular celebration of the "American way of life" obscured these tensions in the emerging postwar society, but eventually the discrepancy between rhetoric and social reality would become obvious.

PAX AMERICANA

As the postwar era dawned, Americans looked forward hopefully to a period of peace and domesticity. An entire generation had grown up in a period racked by depression and war. Now they wanted to focus on their personal lives, on jobs, homes, and families. In a somewhat similar period at the end of World War I, the country had voted for a "return to normalcy," turning away from European affairs in favor of domesticity and isolation. Though many Americans may have wished for a similar development in the late 1940s, it was not to be. World War II had confirmed America's role as a leading world power, its interests closely linked to an emerging global order. In the postwar years, more than ever before, the everyday lives of American women and men were shaped by international developments.

At the end of World War II, Americans surveyed a world marked by reconstruction and potentially radical change. In western Europe, depression and war had so discredited the old elites that capitalism itself was badly shaken. In France, the Communists and Socialists who had led anti-Nazi resistance were far more popular than business leaders, and many French voters supported nationalization of banks and manufacturing firms. In Britain, the Labour Party swept to power, raising the possibility that America's closest ally might go socialist. And in Greece, Italy, and Yugoslavia, Communist parties seemed on the verge of taking power. Meanwhile, as powerful independence movements emerged in Asia and Africa, the colonial empires built by France, Germany, and Britain began to crumble.

In this moment of uncertainty, only two states—the United States and the Soviet Union—had the political dynamism, ideological confidence, and military strength to construct a new world order. Promoting what the leaders of each superpower considered their own vital interests, these nations clashed in a protracted conflict whose ideological debate was as important as its military and diplomatic rivalry. Though Soviet dictator Joseph Stalin had betrayed the ideals of the Russian Revolution and established a regime of systematic brutality, millions of people throughout the world still looked to the Soviet Union as an alternative to capitalism, which they identified with the chaos of the Great Depression and World War II. Soviet foreign policy combined traditional Russian interest in creating a buffer zone of friendly states along its European border with an opportunistic probing of Western political and social weakness. In wartime conferences at Teheran and Yalta, American policy-makers had seemed to accept a Soviet sphere of influence in eastern Europe, if only as compensation for Russia's wartime sacrifices. After mid-1945, however, President Truman grew uncomfortable with this arrangement. Although Stalin showed little interest in invading western Europe, the Soviet Union's links with anticapitalist and anticolonial movements worldwide led Western leaders to see the USSR as an inherently expansionist power.

Meanwhile, flush from their wartime victory, American military and political elites felt they had the right and the duty to shape a new global political and economic order. Henry Luce, the influential publisher of *Time*, *Life*, and *Fortune*, thought an "American century" was in the making. In 1947, Luce confidently told his readers, "Go over the earth, as investors and managers and engineers, as makers of mutual prosperity, as missionaries of capitalism and democracy." When other nations resisted American hegemony, conflict was inevitable. At the Bretton Woods Conference in 1944, several European nations had opposed U.S. efforts to make the dollar the basis for international monetary transactions; eventually, however, most acquiesced to secure U.S. loans for their faltering economies. The Soviets balked and later refused to join such United States-dominated institutions as the

"Number 1, 1948." The postwar movement of Abstract Expressionism, exemplified in Jackson Pollack's work, marked a sharp break from earlier representative painting. Unlike the previous generation of artists, the Abstract Expressionists rejected explicitly political themes, developing techniques that reflected the irrationality of Cold War hostilities and potential nuclear annihilation. But these paintings' obscurity made them malleable propaganda tools in U.S. government–sponsored cultural festivals and exhibits. Ironically, Abstract Expressionism became a symbol of America's postwar power.

World Bank and the International Monetary Fund. Torn by suspicion and conflicting goals and interests, the wartime alliance between the two giants quickly unraveled.

The conflict came to a head in 1947, when the United States began supporting conservative Greek monarchists against Communist guerrillas (the former leaders of popular anti-Nazi resistance). Although Stalin provided no aid to these guerrillas, Truman interpreted the conflict as a battle in a larger war between the "free world" and the "Communist bloc." Requesting $400 million in economic and military aid for Greece and Turkey, the president framed American goals in sweeping terms: "At the present moment in world history, nearly every nation must choose between alternative ways of life," he declared in a speech later dubbed the Truman Doctrine. "I believe that it must be the policy of the United States to support free peoples who are resisting attempted subjugation by armed minorities or by outside pressures. . . . If Greece should fall under the control of an armed minority ... confusion and disorder might well spread throughout the entire Middle East."

The Truman Doctrine initially succeeded in Greece, where the insurgency was wiped out. At home, it helped mobilize popular sentiment for a "Cold War" against communism. A fiscally conservative Congress appropriated huge sums ($16 billion) for the reconstruction of western Europe. The new plan, put forward in a June 1947 speech by Secretary of State George Marshall, offered aid to even the Communist regimes of eastern Europe, but only under conditions that would compromise the socialist nature of their economies. When the Soviets forced these nations to reject Marshall Plan assistance, the economic division of Europe was confirmed.

The militarization of American foreign policy soon followed. In 1949, the United States was the prime mover in the creation of the North Atlantic Treaty Organization (NATO), which looked to the eventual rearmament of West Germany as the cornerstone of a Western military alliance. The Soviets soon replied with their own European alliance, the Warsaw Pact, which rearmed East Germany. Europe was now polarized into two mutually hostile camps. In the East, Communist governments suppressed all opposition political parties and institutions; in western Europe, the new alliance system put a halt to the political and economic experimentation of the early postwar years.

If a frozen stability settled over Europe by the end of the 1940s, upheaval continued in the rest of the world. From Africa to Iran, from India through Southeast Asia to China, World War II had undermined Western colonial power and unleashed a great wave of nationalism. Burma, Indonesia, India, and the Philippines soon achieved their independence, followed a decade later by most of the colonies of Africa. Often, anticolonial nationalism was linked to revolutionary social movements. In Vietnam and China, Communists under the leadership of Ho Chi Minh and Mao Zedong, respectively, championed the land hunger of peasants and the nationalism of urban intellectuals to build powerful military insurgencies.

During the war, the United States had looked with some favor on Asian anticolonial movements, especially if they fought against Japan. American foreign service officers who visited Chinese Communists during the war praised them as "land reformers"; and in September 1945, U.S. intelligence agents were honored guests when Ho Chi Minh borrowed language from America's Declaration of Independence to declare Vietnam's freedom from France.

The Cold War transformed U.S. policy, however, especially after 1949, when Mao's Communist army overthrew the government of the corrupt but pro-Western Chinese dictator Chiang Kai-shek. The "loss" of this giant nation led many American policy-makers to dis-

An Ex-Soviet Officer Tells:

HOW RUSSIA BUILT THE NORTH KOREAN ARMY

The Reporter

September 26, 1950   25c

Cold War illusions. The September 26, 1950, issue of *The Reporter,* an influential liberal weekly, featured an article by a Russian colonel who had defected to the United States in 1949. Kyril Kalinov's "How Russia Built the North Korean Army" was presented as proof of Soviet treachery. Kalinov, however, did not exist; the article was written by a Central Intelligence Agency operative.

trust the nationalist and reform movements growing in Asia, Africa, and Latin America. Nations and leaders whose actions did not serve American interests were increasingly seen as elements in a vast pattern of Soviet-inspired subversion.

The Cold War grew bloodier as it took on a global dimension. In June 1950, the instability and nationalism of postwar Korea exploded as Communist North Korea invaded South Korea. Despite evidence that the Russians were caught off-guard by the North Korean move, Truman saw the invasion as a Soviet attack on *Pax Americana*. South Korea had previously not been considered vital to U.S. security, but Truman sent troops right away. His administration used the war to triple U.S. military spending and dispatch arms and advisers to help France hold on to Vietnam. After Chinese troops confronted the Americans in November 1950, the Korean War settled into a three-year stalemate. In July 1953, after 34,000 American deaths and 100,000 Americans wounded, the United States settled for a truce that left the Communists in control of North Korea. But a precedent of global confrontation had been set. Henceforth the United States was determined to project its power on every continent. By 1955, the United States had hundreds of military bases in thirty-six countries.

The United States established alliance systems throughout the world, keeping many Asian and Latin American states friendly through a combination of diplomacy, foreign aid, and covert manipulation of foreign newspapers, politicians, and trade unions. In Korea, Spain, and the Philippines, the mere presence of large U.S. military bases bolstered authoritarian governments; but on occasion more forceful methods were employed. The U.S. Central Intelligence Agency supported internal military coups in Iran (1953), Guatemala (1954), Brazil (1964), and Chile (1973), in each case removing popularly elected liberal and leftist leaders who had sought to nationalize Western property. U.S. troops intervened directly in conflicts in Vietnam, the Congo, and the Dominican Republic. Filled with what J. William Fulbright, chairman of the Senate Foreign Relations Committee, later called "the arrogance of power," American policymakers had little patience with or respect for nations that refused to enlist in the fight against Soviet power and international communism.

POLITICAL STALEMATE AT HOME

As *Pax Americana* and the Cold War transformed America's international role, domestic politics became more conservative. In addition to international tension, there were three important sources of this shift: first, a rekindling of business self-confidence; second, an internal split within American liberalism; and third, the manipulation of anti-Communist sentiment by opponents of social reform, as a weapon to defeat the left and narrow the scope of legitimate political debate.

Although economic failure in the Great Depression years had discredited business leaders, the World War II "miracle of production" sped the relegitimization of capitalism as a system and individual businessmen as influential public figures. Corporate executives emerged from the war firmly identified with a robust American patriotism. Their experience as wartime administrators and their service in the Truman and Eisenhower administrations made clear that state regulation could enhance rather than threaten business interests. When President Eisenhower's new secretary of defense, Charles E. Wilson, formerly of General Motors, was asked whether he foresaw a conflict between his official role and his ties to his former company, which did substantial business with the military, he confidently remarked that "what is good for our country is good for General Motors, and vice versa."

Armed with this renewed self-confidence, and the labor movement's failure to win dramatic gains during the 1946 strike wave, business leaders took the offensive. They knew that higher wages might have to be paid to organized workers, but the idea of democratic power-sharing in shops and offices had to be resisted at all costs. "In industry as in government or anywhere else, there are two classes of people," argued one businessman. "There are those who decide and those who carry out." Executives complained that the new industrial unions had deprived them of their rightful power to assign work as they saw fit, to fire unsuitable employees, and to speed up production. "We recognize that in some of our shops the union committeeman exercises greater authority than the foreman," acknowledged the industrial relations director of a big rubber firm, while an auto executive was even more angry and blunt: "If any manager in this industry tells you he has control of his plant he is a damn liar."

The situation, which executives had reluctantly accepted during World War II, now seemed intolerable, especially since the political winds had begun to shift in 1946. Employers now counterattacked, both in Washington and in their own companies. Unlike those of the 1920s, most business leaders did not seek to destroy the unions but to contain their power, to channel their demands toward issues that could be safely negotiated on a routine basis, and to transform unions, as much as possible, into disciplinarians of the workforce.

Employers sought to make the state an active ally in this campaign. In the eighteen months after the Japanese surrender, over seventy antilabor bills were introduced in the House alone. "During the New Deal, labor unions were coddled, nursed, and pampered," argued Republican congressman Fred Hartley of New Jersey. Business leaders, especially those heading labor-intensive manufacturing firms, called for a sweeping revision of the Wagner Act. Their chance came after the 1946 congressional elections, when Republicans gained control of both legislative houses and, with their like-minded southern Democratic allies, secured a commanding majority. Their victory was a product of the anti-union, anti–Democratic Party sentiment generated by the 1946 strike wave and the rapid inflation brought on by the end of wartime price controls.

Over President Truman's veto, Congress passed the landmark 1947 Taft-Hartley Act, which deprived foremen of the protections afforded workers under the Wagner Act, made sympathy strikes and boycotts more difficult, and allowed states (in practice those in the South and West, with weak union movements) to ban the union shop. The law also gave the federal government a veto over union politics and strike strategy. Labor leaders had to declare themselves non-Communists if they wanted their unions to participate in NLRB elections. And if they led a big union, they now had to bargain knowing that the president could postpone for eighty days any strike he deemed a "national emergency" (a power Truman used thirty-seven times during the remainder of his term). None of these restrictions made Taft-Hartley into the "slave labor law" denounced by unionists, but taken together they advanced the managerial effort to deradicalize the union movement, curb interunion solidarity, and confine the labor movement to its existing geographical and demographic terrain. The law signaled a major shift in the tenor of class relations in the United States. To survive, the unions would have to function less as a social movement and more as interest groups protecting their own turf.

If the tide of public sentiment, congressional votes, and administration policy were all shifting against unions, the labor movement was not without resources to mount a counterattack. There were two elements in the unions' postwar political strategy: first, Operation Dixie, a concerted union campaign to organize the South; and second, a political comeback in 1948, based on the reform and realignment of the Democratic Party.

In Operation Dixie, the CIO sought to break the political power of the reactionary landlords and employers in the South by striking at the racial discrimination and low-wage labor that sustained this conservative elite. During World War II, unions had organized more than 800,000 southern workers, one-third of them black. African-American voting registration doubled in the 1940s. In Winston-Salem, North Carolina, wartime organization of the Reynolds Tobacco Company put 3,000 African-Americans on the polling lists and opened local politics to black participation for the first time since the Populist era. Along the Gulf Coast, the CIO mobilized war workers into a progressive political force that ended the political career of two archconservative congressmen. Black veterans, often in uniform, marched boldly into rural courthouses in the deep South, demanding the right to register and vote.

Beginning in 1946, Operation Dixie sought to repeat these local breakthroughs on a larger scale, mobilizing an interracial electorate that could reshape southern politics. Northern unions, especially in the CIO, hired hundreds of organizers, opened scores of offices, and began vigorous organizing campaigns in textiles, lumber, tobacco processing, and other southern industries. "When Georgia is organized," predicted a leader of the union drive, "you will find our old friend Gene Talmadge [the conservative governor of the state] trying to break into the doors of the CIO conventions and tell our people that he has always been misunderstood."

Operation Dixie was a thorough failure, however. Resistance from the political and industrial leadership of the white South proved overwhelming, and the proportion of southern workers organized into unions actually declined during the next few years. Textile and lumber mills were usually located in tightly controlled company towns where city officials, churches, and police were bitterly hostile to "outside" labor organizers. Black workers proved exceptionally union-conscious, but many southern whites rejected interracial union solidarity. Union organizers found that "mixed" meetings could only be held outdoors, interracial handshakes were taboo, and African-American participation had to be downplayed. But most important, Operation Dixie organizers faced the same sort of physical

---

"WHITE PEOPLE WAKE UP . . ."

Conservatives played upon southern whites' racist fears in battling postwar efforts to end Jim Crow and unionize workers. Propaganda such as this 1950 North Carolina election flyer helped defeat southern liberals like Frank Graham, a former member of President Harry Truman's Civil Rights Commission.

WHITE PEOPLE
WAKE UP

Before it's too late
You may not have another chance

DO YOU WANT?

NEGROES   working beside you, your wife and daughters in your mills and factories?

NEGROES   eating beside you in public eating places?

NEGROES   riding beside you, your wife and your daughters in buses, cabs and trains?

NEGROES   sleeping in the same hotels and rooming houses?

NEGROES   teaching and disciplining your children in school?

NEGROES   sitting with you and your family at all public meetings?

NEGROES   going to white schools and white children going to Negro schools?

NEGROES   to occupy the same hospital rooms with you and your wife and daughters?

NEGROES   as your foremen and overseers in the mills?

NEGROES   using your toilet facilities?

Northern political labor leaders have recently ordered that all doors be opened to Negroes on union property. This will lead to whites and Negroes working and living together in the South as they do in the North. Do you want that?

FRANK GRAHAM FAVORS MINGLING OF THE RACES

He admits that he favors mixing Negroes and whites—he says so in the report he signed (For proof of this, read page 167, Civil Rights Report)

DO YOU FAVOR THIS—WANT SOME MORE OF IT?
IF YOU DO, VOTE FOR FRANK GRAHAM

But if you don't
VOTE FOR AND HELP ELECT
WILLIS SMITH for SENATOR

He will uphold the traditions of the South

****

Know the truth committee

intimidation that civil rights workers would confront in the 1960s. A Louisiana organizer recalled the dangers of organizing African-Americans in a company town. "We went over and had a meeting down the railroad tracks with the blacks that worked in the plant. . . . And someone rode around the street there and shot the meeting up. They just shot the little wooden church full of holes."

Organizing the South in the late 1940s would have required a massive, socially disruptive interracial campaign and a militant CIO leadership. But the national labor movement had lost much of its élan, and its ranks were increasingly divided over the role Communists and other radicals could play. Labor's ambivalence proved particularly damaging in the South, where some of the most dynamic unionists, such as the tobacco workers of North Carolina and the boatmen of Memphis, were African-Americans hospitable to radical ideas, even those of the Communists. The crisis came to a head in Alabama, when war broke out between the United Steel Workers and a local of the Mine, Mill, and Smelter Workers' Union that represented African-American iron miners around Birmingham. Recruiting from elements close to the KKK, the USW blended anti-communism with overt racism to raid the Mine, Mill, and Smelter local and destroy one of the black community's most progressive institutions. The legacy of this conflict extended into the 1960s, when Birmingham became synonymous with brutal white resistance to the civil rights movement.

The failure of Operation Dixie meant that unions would not transform southern politics. But the labor movement still hoped to "realign" America's two-party system, either by building the power of labor, small farmers, and African-Americans within the Democratic Party, or by creating an entirely new third party, based on a liberal labor coalition. Until the spring of 1948, most union leaders repudiated Harry Truman as their presidential candidate, and many expressed interest in forming a third party. Indeed, more than half of all CIO union officials favored such a political initiative.

In 1948, a coalition of progressives and Communists ran former vice president Henry Wallace for president at the head of a new Progressive Party. But this initiative hardly realigned American politics; instead, it rapidly brought an end to political experimentation and wedded labor even more closely to the Democrats.

At the end of World War II, Henry Wallace's vision of an expanded New Deal and peaceful coexistence with the Soviet Union coincided closely with that of many progressives and CIO leaders. The most liberal elements in the New Deal coalition, including members of the Communist Party, saw the Progressive Party as an opportunity to halt the drift into a Cold War with the Soviet Union and advance domestic reform and racial equality. But Wallace supporters were sharply chal-

'Jim Crow Must Go'

WALLACE SHOWS IT CAN BE DONE

HENRY WALLACE

Wins Battle Against Segregation

See story on page 3

KKK "SCARE" FAILED! — Crowds gathered to hear former Vice President Henry Wallace speak to non-segregated audiences in the deep South. This definitely mixed audience reflects the keen feeling and interest aroused by Mr. Wallace's words. In Atlanta, despite KKK threats, never in the city's history did so many white photographers and writers seek entry to an affair at a Negro institution. The rally was held in the Wheat Street Baptist Church. Above, the New Orleans' audience was typical of the mixed crowds which came from far and near to hear Wallace.

Picture and caption courtesy Pittsburgh Courier

The Wallace campaign. A Progressive Party flyer promotes integration in the deep South.

lenged by more centrist liberals such as Eleanor Roosevelt, Walter Reuther, and the young Minneapolis mayor, Hubert Humphrey, who joined together to form the Americans for Democratic Action (ADA). The ADA considered itself a staunchly liberal, prolabor, pro–civil rights organization, but its leaders denounced Wallace as a Communist dupe, sought the elimination of Communist influence in all liberal and labor organizations, and defended Truman's tough stance toward the Soviet Union.

In 1947–48, conflict over the Wallace candidacy divided both liberals and the labor movement. Though the vision of a vital, independent third party held out attractive prospects, support for the Progressives went against two key tenets of the emerging Cold War consensus: alignment with the government in the global Cold War, and exclusion of Communists from domestic politics. Thus AFL and CIO officials denounced the Progressive Party and quickly endorsed Truman.

This support proved crucial in the 1948 election. Most observers assumed the presidential contest would put Republican Thomas Dewey, the financially well-connected New York governor, in the White House. But Truman surprised everyone. Denouncing "Wall Street" Republicans at nearly every stop of his frenetic whistle-stop campaign, Truman reminded voters that he had opposed the Taft-Hartley Act and favored a system of national health insurance. The president lost the Deep South to a "Dixiecrat" fourth party, but thwarted Wallace and Dewey by galvanizing the old Roosevelt coalition among midwestern farmers and urban workers. Voters in big industrial states cast their ballots along class lines to a greater degree than ever before in the twentieth century; as Truman excitedly told the press, "Labor did it!"

Truman's victory helped put Democrats back in control of Congress, but a strategic defense was all they could achieve. When Truman sought to push through Congress a "Fair Deal" program, including national health insurance, public housing, repeal of Taft-Hartley, and an agricultural subsidy scheme for small farmers, he could not find sufficient votes. Without a sense of general crisis to mobilize the electorate, such powerful interests as the National Association of Real-Estate Boards (representing the private housing market), the Farm Bureau Federation (large farmers), and the American Medical Association (doctors) were able to defeat Truman's legislative initiatives.

The stalemate continued through the administration of Republican president Dwight D. Eisenhower. A World War II hero and a reassuring symbol of America's small-town past, Eisenhower's personal popularity helped him win election to two terms, in 1952 and 1956. Eisenhower appointed eight millionaires to his first cabinet; one of them, Secretary of Commerce Sinclair Weeks, told the National Association of Manufacturers in 1953 that "a climate favorable to business has most definitely been substituted for the socialism of recent years." Eisenhower's administration was not one of conservative reaction, however. A self-styled "modern Republican," Eisenhower kept the right wing of his party in check, and his aloofness from partisan politics ensured that the White House would not launch an assault on the welfare state. By the mid-1950s, American politics had settled into a holding pattern; New Deal reforms were locked into place, but the reform momentum of the 1930s and early 1940s was spent.

THE USES OF ANTICOMMUNISM

One of the most dramatic factors in the rightward shift in postwar American politics was the widespread obsession with domestic communism. Antiradicalism had long been a staple of American politics, and the 1917 Russian Revolution had directed conservative passions against communism. Communists and other radicals had gained some acceptance during the 1930s, but the Cold War brought anticommunism roaring back: first spurred by the government's need to mobilize support for U.S. foreign policy, then sustained by interparty political battles and antilabor campaigns led by business.

Anticommunism was part of a redefinition of civic life in postwar America that narrowed political debate and chilled the democratic process for almost a generation. The most prominent anti-Communist campaigns were led by national politicians who turned the issue into an obsessive quest for "internal security." In 1947, fearing that he might be outflanked by the Republicans, Truman had set up a loyalty program for federal employees, asked the attorney general to draw up a list of subversive organizations, and allowed the FBI to expand rapidly. Meanwhile, between 1945 and 1952, eighty-four hearings were conducted by congressional committees; the most infamous were those held by the House Committee on Un-American Activities (HUAC), investigating Communist subversion in the entertainment industry, higher education, unions, and the federal government.

HUAC demanded that witnesses not only affirm that their views were now orthodox, but also that they prove their loyalty by publicly naming former Communist associates. "Don't present me with the choice of either being in contempt of this committee and going to jail," pleaded Hollywood actor Larry Parks, "or forcing me to really crawl through the mud to be an informer." Parks informed but, like those of many others grilled by HUAC, his career was ruined by "blacklists" maintained by employers. Even the threat of a HUAC probe could breed tragedy. When Stanford University biochemist William Sherwood received a HUAC summons in 1957, he took poison and killed himself. "The Committee's trail," he wrote in a suicide note, "is strewn with blasted lives, the wreckage of useful careers. . . .

The scientific mind cannot flourish in an atmosphere of fear, timidity and imposed conformity."

Republican senator Joseph McCarthy of Wisconsin perfected the techniques used by HUAC and turned them against "respectable" targets, including the State Department, Ivy League universities, and the U.S. Army. McCarthy achieved national stature in early 1950 by exploiting Cold War frustrations over the "loss" of China and the Soviet consolidation of power in eastern Europe. To McCarthy and his followers these were not just diplomatic setbacks. "The reason why we find ourselves in a position of impotency," he told a Republican audience, "is not because our only powerful potential enemy has sent men to invade our shores, but rather, because of the traitorous actions of those who have been treated so well by this nation. . . ." At one point, McCarthy claimed to have a list of 205 Communists employed by the State Department. In McCarthy's eyes, Secretary of State Dean Acheson was the "Red Dean . . . Russian as to heart, British as to manner"; while Adlai Stevenson, the 1952 Democratic presidential candidate, "endorsed and could continue the suicidal Kremlin-directed policies of the nation."

McCarthy, journalist Richard Rovere remarked, "was a political speculator who found his oil gusher in Communism." Using his chairmanship of a minor Senate subcommittee as a bully pulpit, McCarthy conducted wide-ranging and often crudely partisan investigations, charging that in the high-

"NEVER TALK . . . ABOUT CONTROVERSIAL ISSUES"

As the Cold War deepened in the late 1940s, the government established an array of "loyalty boards" to screen federal employees. These administrative tribunals often paid little attention to the usual rules of evidence. Thousands of employees lost their jobs because of mere suspicion that they held unorthodox ideas or associated with former leftists. Thurman Arnold, a prominent liberal attorney in Washington, satirized these boards in Harper's Magazine in 1948.

1. Do not attend any social gathering, no matter how large, at which a "subversive" may also be present. This includes dances.

2. Never talk, even to your neighbors or at social gatherings, about controversial issues. If your views offend someone, they may show up in a report in a distorted fashion and you will never even know who gave the information.

3. Do not subscribe to the *New Republic* or the *Nation*, or any other liberal publication. Maybe it's communist and you don't know it. Don't read any books about Russia even out of curiosity, because you can never prove that it was only curiosity. You will be safer if you can honestly swear that you do not know where Russia is or what it is like.

4. If anyone sends you as a gift a publication of the sort described in the foregoing Commandment, cancel it at once, with an indignant letter. . . .

5. Do not ever attend the large annual reception at the Russian Embassy. . . . I recently advised a friend of mine not to attend a party at the Polish consulate in New York City.

6. Do not contribute any money for the legal defense of some old acquaintance or college classmate charged with disloyalty, for even if he is found innocent, you may be charged because of your contribution.

7. Do not marry anyone who, however many years before, had radical associations in college. Avoid, if you can, marriage with anyone who has ever visited Russia, read Karl Marx, or contributed to war relief drives for the Spanish Loyalists.

8. Be particularly careful never to ride in an automobile in which a "subversive" may be another rider. The car pool is a favorite object of suspicion.

9. Do not yourself be unduly critical of Fascists or Nazis, and carefully avoid the company of those who have been outspoken on these subjects.

10. If any relative of yours, no matter how distant and no matter how much you disagree with him, has ever been a "radical," do not take a government position at all. The salary can't possibly be worth the effort it may take to defend yourself.

est reaches of government, Communist sympathizers were shielding Soviet spies. His charges were largely nonsense, but his manipulation of the press and the new medium of television (which broadcast many of his hearings) proved so masterful that he became one of the most feared political figures of the 1950s.

Anticommunism did not victimize only the well-known office-holders, actors, and scientists hauled before congressional commit-tees. HUAC furnished data on 60,000 people to inquiring employers. At least 15,000 federal employees were fired or forced to resign as a result of investigations by government loyalty boards. Hundreds of high-school teachers, community college instructors, and municipal librarians were forced out of their posts, either because they failed a security review or because they refused to sign the loyalty oath that most cities and states instituted. In San Francisco, as many as a fifth of all seamen and longshoremen were denied clearance to work on vessels owned or chartered by the government. By one estimate, 13.5 million Americans came within the scope of various federal, state, and private loyalty programs. Roughly one of five working people had to take an oath or receive clearance as a condition of employment.

Government and private investigations uncovered remarkably few active Communists, but they did disrupt the lives and activities

The informer as hero. *I Led Three Lives*, a syndicated series about the infiltration of the Communist Party by an FBI informer, ran on television from 1953 to 1956. Starring Richard Carlson (best known for roles in low-budget science-fiction movies) as Herbert Philbrick (who actually testified at the 1949 Smith Act trial of eleven Communist Party leaders), the series depicted the informer as intrepid hero. In the series, while leading an ordinary life (Philbrick was an advertising manager of a Boston movie theater), he consistently foiled the party's attempts at espionage and murder.

of many non-Communist Americans. Liberals, non-Communist radicals, labor activists, and others who questioned the direction of postwar society were often the real targets of "anti-Communist" probes. As the head of one government loyalty board noted, "The fact that a person believes in racial equality doesn't prove he's a Communist, but it certainly makes you look twice, doesn't it?" Republic Aviation reported that by 1954 at least 250 workers had been fired as security risks. "We may get information on a man through anonymous letters, phone calls, or personal visits," reported the company's security director. "Several years ago we encouraged employees up and down the line to report suspicious activities of fellow workers. . . . We're alert to which men are becoming prominent in plant organizations, ranging from hobby and sport to religious and political groups."

From the earliest days of the Cold War, labor unions were attacked in the name of anticommunism. After the militant strikes of 1945–46, many businessmen found Communist subversion a convenient explanation for labor conflict. "Whoever stirs up needless strife in American trade unions advances the cause of Communism," asserted the *Nation's Business* late in 1946. For some businessmen, the popular obsession with Communists served as a tool to restore the old social and economic order that had been disrupted during the New Deal years. Employers worked closely with congressional investigators who were happy to "Red-bait" union officials when a strike or certification election was imminent. In 1954, for example, HUAC came to Seattle to undercut the International Woodworkers' Union, which was about to strike major lumber companies. Employers also joined forces with state investigative agencies, such as the Massachusetts Special Commission on Communism, and private anti-Communist groups such as the American Security Council and the American Legion.

Meanwhile, anticommunism polarized the labor movement. In the industrial union drives of the late 1930s and early 1940s, Communists and other radicals had played important if usually subordinate roles. Many unionists thought of Communists as "liberals in a hurry" who mistakenly looked to the Soviet Union as a model society. Communists led several important trade unions, including the CIO's third-largest, the United Electrical, Radio, and Machine Workers. All this changed with the Cold War. While sparking the battle over the Progressive Party, anticommunism ignited a civil war in the labor movement, and fierce leadership contests erupted in many CIO unions.

The battles in the labor movement were not merely about politics and leadership jobs but also about the ways working people defined themselves. In the late 1940s, millions of workers were still first- or second-generation immigrants whose sense of "Americanism" had only recently been affirmed by the patriotism that surged through workers' communities during the New Deal years and World War II. Although many immigrants, especially in the German, Finnish, and Russian Jewish communities, had once sought to combine socialist politics with an American identity, the Cold War forced them to choose. To be a radical, let alone a Communist, now seemed "un-American."

Ironically, the Communists had been among the most zealous missionaries of patriotism during World War II. Their lockstep support of the war effort helped disarm left criticism and twist wartime antifascism into a celebration of anything labeled "American." After the war, this resurgent nationalism was turned against the Communists. In the million-member UAW, Walter Reuther denounced the wartime antistrike activities of his Communist-backed opponents and appealed to workers' reawakened sense of patriotism. "UAW Americanism for Us" read the slogan many local union officers now propped on their desks. Not all left-wingers were ejected from their unions; those who were effective trade unionists sometimes retained rank-and-file support. But a virulent anticommunism became official policy. In 1949 the CIO expelled nine unions, representing 900,000 workers, for refusing to purge themselves of Communist leaders and support government policies such as the Marshall Plan.

Are you now or have you ever been . . . ? Autoworker Basil Gordon kneels on the sidewalk outside a Los Angeles Chrysler Corporation plant in July 1950 after receiving a beating from fellow workers. Gordon and two other workers were attacked when they refused to say whether they belonged to the Communist Party.

The enemy within. Hollywood producers, cowed by the House Committee on Un-American Activities' witch hunts, strove to prove their loyalty. *The Red Menace* (1949) was but one of a flurry of films that melodramatically "exposed" a gangsterlike network of Communists subverting America. Audiences, however, seemed to prefer science-fiction fantasies that portrayed malevolent intergalactic creatures infiltrating American society.

Anticommunism not only split individual unions and weakened campaigns such as Operation Dixie. It also undercut the idea that trade unionism was part of an inclusive social movement that welcomed unconventional proposals about how to reshape the entire society. Along with its broad social vision, labor lost some of its boldness. For example, in the early 1950s the union movement backed off its historic quest for shorter hours, in part because such demands were equated by business leaders with a Communist drive to hamper U.S. production during the Korean War.

Working Americans had a range of responses to anticommunism. Catholics, especially those of Irish or East European extraction, who in the 1920s had been the subject of nativist prejudice, formed the backbone of popular anticommunism in the union movement. The Red Army's occupation of eastern Europe had an electrifying impact on millions of Slavs and Hungarians, who made up perhaps half of the CIO membership. When the Soviets arrested church leaders in Poland, the American Catholic Church mobilized tens of thousands of its adherents to protest what it called "Satan-inspired Communist crimes." Priests from working-class parishes played an aggressive role in the effort to oust Communists from the leadership of such unions as the United Electrical Workers, which enrolled many second-generation Slavs, and New York's heavily Irish Transport Workers' Union. Catholics tended to back Joseph McCarthy by a margin considerably greater than that of either Jews or Protestants.

In contrast, relatively few African-Americans joined in the anti-Communist crusade. In part this reflected the Communist Party's long commitment to civil rights and its active recruitment of black workers. More important, the discrimination African-Americans endured meant they looked with a skeptical eye on white efforts to define what constituted an "American" attitude. Coleman Young, once a Ford worker and later the first African-American mayor of Detroit, denounced a congressional investigating committee that questioned his loyalty:

> I am a part of the Negro people. I fought in the last war and . . . I am now in process of fighting against what I consider to be attacks and discrimination against my people. I am fighting against un-American activities such as lynchings and denial of the vote. I am dedicated to that fight, and I don't have to apologize or explain it to anybody.

Of all ethnic groups, American Jews were most divided and devastated by McCarthyism. By the late 1940s, anti-Semitism seemed on the wane and the prospects for assimilation attractive: Second- and third-generation Jewish-Americans were entering the middle class more rapidly than any other ethnic group. Yet American Jews had been solid Roosevelt partisans, and they had provided a large share of the support Henry Wallace won in cities such as New York and Los Angeles. Jews were often victims of the anti-Communist witch hunt. In New York City 90 percent of all teachers fired by the Board of Education were Jewish, while in Detroit and Flint, Michigan, Communists "run out" of auto plants were often taunted with anti-Semitic as well as antiradical epithets.

The Rosenberg case accentuated Jewish fears about renewed anti-Semitism. In 1950 Julius and Ethel Rosenberg, both active Communists and the children of Jewish immigrants, were charged with delivering atomic secrets to the Soviet Union. They were convicted the next year and, despite worldwide protests, executed in June 1953. They were the first American citizens executed for treason in peacetime, and this brutal punishment so frightened some Jewish progressives that they abandoned as dangerous their longtime participation in liberal and radical causes.

The Rosenberg executions notwithstanding, McCarthyism was on the wane. The election of the Republican Eisenhower as president in 1952 lessened its political usefulness, while the end of the Korean War the following year eased Cold War tensions and national anxieties. Meanwhile, McCarthy's attacks on other politicians and well-placed officeholders created a set of powerful enemies. In November 1954, the Senate voted to condemn his methods; thereafter he rapidly lost most of his influence. But anticommunism's legacy lingered, and until a new political generation appeared in the mid-1960s, American politics remained largely frozen within the orthodoxy of the early Cold War years.

THE POSTWAR BOOM

Anticommunism, the Cold War, and the specter of nuclear devastation cast deep shadows across postwar America; yet life in the postwar years was far from totally grim. From the end of World War II until the early 1970s, a period of more than a quarter century, the United States enjoyed an unprecedented era of sustained economic growth. Even with this period's five short recessions, production of goods and services doubled while unemployment and inflation stayed below 5 percent each year. This material affluence deeply affected life on the job and at home and helped reshape the ways Americans thought of themselves and their society.

Nothing symbolized this boom so well as the automobile. Production of civilian vehicles had been halted during World War II; for nearly a decade afterward, car-starved Americans bought whatever Detroit turned out. In the late 1940s and early 1950s, hundreds of thousands of people flocked to annual events in New York where major automakers unveiled their new models. A near-riot took place in 1949 when Ford displayed its first all-new postwar model in the grand ballroom of the Waldorf-Astoria Hotel. That year five million cars were sold and sales finally surpassed the banner year of 1929. Afterward, auto production rarely flagged, and by the early 1970s there were two cars on the road for every three adult citizens.

The auto industry stood at the center of American society. Auto manufacturing represented the epitome of postwar production technology, providing secure, high-wage jobs for more than a million members of the UAW, the nation's most prominent union. The industry spurred the growth of suburbs, the spread of interstate highways, and the emergence of "drive-in" movies and restaurants and other elements of a booming car culture. Bigger and more powerful each year, with tail fins, bold colors, and automatic transmissions, these postwar station wagons, hot rods, sports cars, and sedans embodied an exciting sense of personal identity, individual mobility, and material gratification.

The automobile industry's success was possible only because the economic boom put real money in the average citizen's pocket. The income of the average family almost doubled between 1941 and 1969. Moreover, Americans not only earned more money, they also spent more money on a wider range of goods and services. In 1952, the Department of Commerce reported, Americans spent $255

"IF YOU HAD A FAST CAR . . . YOU WERE A BIG MAN"

In the 1950s tens of thousands of Americans, most of them white working-class men, transformed the standardized consumer automobiles coming out of Detroit into personalized masterpieces. Among them were Ed Schafer and Boyd Pennington of St. Louis. Interviewed in the late 1970s, they recalled their teenage passion for "hot rods."

ED SCHAFER: I had my first car when I was 14 in 1953. I was the only guy in the 8th grade that drove to school. I lived in the country and drove to school on the back roads. I had a 1940 Chevrolet that you had to tie the doors shut, but I could tear the engine down and put it back together. I bought it for $25, a piece of junk, but it ran and I could keep it running. . . . You had to have fender skirts and you had to have the rear end of the car dropped almost to the axle. . . . I think what we tried to do was make it as different as possible to what Detroit put out and it was neat to watch Detroit follow us; decking, cleaning the chrome and the ornaments off, lowering the silhouette, lowering the entire car.

BOYD PENNINGTON: If two guys had exactly the same color car within two days somebody had something different. There was quite a lot of rivalry between cars even though they were old cars, of course some of it was show; terrycloth seat covers and mud flaps.

ED SCHAFER: Our interest was stimulated by California, by the news we got from there and by the movies and songs that were prevalent then.

BOYD PENNINGTON: The West Coast always led. You could travel out to California and it would take a year for that trend to move to the Midwest. In the early 1950s there was *Honk, Hot Rod, Rod and Custom, Car and Custom*, just a whole stack of West Coast magazines.

BOYD PENNINGTON: There are some things I'm not too proud of. We did steal from other people; we did make regular trips into South St. Louis because it was so easy to steal fender skirts, hubcaps, tail-lights or whatever was big at the time. . . . People knew what we were doing, I mean it's hard to conceal from your parents that you have, probably four, five thousand dollars of equipment in your garage. . . .

ED SCHAFER: We had a fairly large group of people, 15, 16 guys, and the camaraderie was unbelievable. There was no way one guy would rat on another. . . . Your importance in the club increased by your performance on the dragstrip. It didn't matter if you were a nerd; if you had a fast car and could make it down a quarter mile faster than anyone else, you were a big man.

million on chewing gum, $235 million on greeting cards, and $23 million on mouthwash. The flood of new consumer items, both practical and frivolous, seemed to help many Americans take their minds off the fearful complexities of the Cold War.

Millions of Americans also turned their attention to home and family. The postwar "baby boom" was a worldwide phenomenon, but it was more marked in the United States than elsewhere. The birth rate, which had fallen to nineteen per thousand in the mid-1930s, leaped upward by 25 percent at the end of the war and stayed there throughout the 1950s. "It seems to me," wrote a British visitor in 1958, "that every other young housewife I see is pregnant."

Economic growth fed the baby boom in at least two ways. First, because Americans felt more economically secure, they went ahead with marriages and pregnancies that had been postponed during the Depression and war years. Second, increased affluence improved the general health of the population. Americans ate better, lived in less crowded homes, and could afford to see doctors more often. In addition to boosting the number of successful pregnancies, these improvements also meant that people lived longer. For white Americans, life expectancy increased from sixty-three to sixty-seven years during the 1940s; for African-Americans it rose from fifty-three to sixty-one years.

Though it initially took many Americans by surprise, the affluence of the postwar period was no accident; it was constructed out of New Deal politics, the experience of World War II, and America's new role in the world. To many, the great lesson of World War II was that federal money and political will power could vanquish unemployment. Congress passed the Employment Act of 1946, which committed the federal government to promote "maximum employment, production, and purchasing power" and set up a Council of Economic Advisers charged with developing "national economic policies."

During the next quarter century, government policy was based largely on theories developed by British economist John Maynard Keynes. Keynes argued that in modern capitalist societies business slumps could be avoided if governments used their taxing and spending power to regulate public demand for goods and services. Liberals wanted to sustain public purchasing power through government spending on public works, schools, housing, Social Security, and unemployment insurance. Conservatives, who feared such programs would erode market incentives and open the door to government planning, instead favored tax reductions for business as the best way to keep the money flowing. Throughout the 1950s, liberals and conservatives fought to a standoff on these economic issues. Business taxes remained at the high levels established during World War II, but government social spending grew only slowly.

Nevertheless, America's political economy functioned within a "Keynesian" mold in this era because of two new factors: a strong union movement and an enormous peacetime military establishment. The 1947 Taft-Hartley Act and the failure of Operation Dixie signaled the end of labor's challenge to the basic hegemony of American capitalism, but large unions still constituted a major force that negotiated higher wages and pushed for increased government spending. The labor movement enrolled more workers than at any other time in U.S. history, reaching a high point in 1946 of nearly 40 percent of the labor force. In cities such as Pittsburgh and Detroit, 60 percent of all households contained a union member. For the first time, American unions had a social weight comparable to that of organized labor in western Europe. Key unions such as the Steelworkers or the United Auto Workers negotiated wage increases that set the standard for millions of other workers, union and nonunion alike. Wages increased independently of market pressures, meaning that in the periodic recessions of the postwar era, workers' purchasing power remained intact and the economy could rebound quickly.

The second pillar of the postwar boom was military spending. By 1950, more than 10 percent of all goods and services consumed in the United States (or about half the federal budget) went to the armed services. Because of the Cold War, massive government outlays in the form of military spending were welcomed by most citizens, including conservatives otherwise hostile to high taxes and large federal expenditures. "Government planners figure they have found the magic formula for almost endless good times," reported conservative columnist David Lawrence in 1950. "Cold war is the catalyst. Cold war is an automatic pump primer. Turn a spigot, and the public clamors for more arms spending. Turn another and the clamor ceases."

Arms production helped fuel the growth of such key sectors of the economy as aircraft manufacturing and electronics. It fostered economic growth and urbanization in the South, where many military bases were built, and in Southern California, in Seattle, and on Long Island, where military dollars for the aviation industry sustained a vibrant postwar sprawl.

Military spending acquired a permanent economic constituency in these regions, with powerful political spokesmen such as Senator Henry Jackson of Washington (dubbed the "senator from Boeing") and Congressman L. Mendel Rivers of South Carolina. Moreover, the political consensus on military spending allowed the federal government to fund otherwise controversial social programs. Educational, medical, housing, and pension benefits for veterans all expanded in the late 1940s. In 1956, Congress used the military's ostensible need for an improved transportation system to vote funds for the multibillion-dollar Interstate and Defense Highway Program, which became the largest public works project in the nation's history.

Together, the unions and the military helped boost employment and wage levels. Rising levels of consumption spurred increased production, which in turn generated new jobs. The whole system seemed to form a never-ending spiral of growth and abundance. Many contemporary observers concluded that American capitalism had found the solution to all economic problems. "The world revolution of our times is 'Made in the USA,'" wrote business consultant Peter Drucker in 1949. "The true revolutionary principle is the idea of mass production."

The boom had a profound impact on the way Americans thought about economic and social problems. In the 1930s, many New Dealers thought the U.S. economy was permanently crippled. Its strength, they believed, could be restored only by breaking up big corporations and redistributing wealth and income. The postwar boom made this political agenda seem irrelevant. Postwar economic growth appeared to reduce class tensions over the distribution of power and resources in American society. The distribution of income was actually frozen in the postwar years (the top tenth of the population consistently took home almost 40 percent of the national income), but the economic pie was getting bigger, so there seemed to be no need to con-

Television dreams. Enacting the peculiarly American fantasy of achieving instantaneous fame and fortune, television quiz shows were wildly popular in the 1950s. A Columbia University English instructor, Charles Van Doren (left), was the most renowned quiz-show celebrity, going on from his triumph on NBC's *Twenty-one* to become one of the stars of the network's *Today* show. However, a 1959 congressional investigation revealed that many of the big-money game shows were rigged. Van Doren was implicated in the scandal, which led to fraud indictments and his disappearance from television.

sider redividing it. Had the "labor problem" now been solved? Many influential Americans clearly thought so. "The union," wrote the editors of *Fortune*, "has made the worker, to an amazing degree, a middle class member of a middle class society." It is significant, pointed out *Life* magazine, that "of all the great industrial nations, the one that clings most tenaciously to private capitalism has come closest to the socialist goal of providing abundance for all in a classless society."

Of course, these were not new ideas; from the Revolution onward, many Americans—especially those who enjoyed a measure of economic security—wanted to believe that the United States was a nation in which class was unimportant, wealth widely shared, and social conflict muted. In the postwar era, however, this vision became remarkably pervasive—among conservatives certainly, but also on college campuses and in union halls, newsrooms, and television studios.

In retrospect, it is clear that economic growth did not solve all the problems of American society. Nor were all Americans members of a unified middle class. The lines dividing American society did not disappear in the 1950s; rather, they were redrawn. Affluence united white, male, adult working-class and middle-class Americans, who became more homogeneous. At the same time, however, new rifts became apparent: the division between unionized workers earning high wages and nonunion workers in low-wage industries; between young and old; between city dwellers and suburbanites. And, of course, there were the nation's historic divisions as well: between men and women; and between Americans with white skins and those whose skins were black, brown, or yellow. Increasingly, these were the fault lines upon which political debate and social conflict would center in the postwar years.

THE LABOR-MANAGEMENT ACCORD

Beginning in the late 1940s, the union movement groped its way toward a less confrontational relationship with management. Labor organizations had more members than at any other time in American history, but the failure to realign the party system or forestall the rise of McCarthyism drastically narrowed the union movement's range of strategic options.

The labor-management accord that resulted guaranteed high wages to union members and insulated well-established unions from direct corporate assault. At the same time, it protected management's right to organize production on the shop floor and decide business strategy in the boardroom. The main elements of this accord, which would last for more than a quarter century, were put into place by big unions negotiating with such major employers as General Motors and

U.S. Steel. But the pattern spread to many other firms, union and nonunion alike.

There were two main elements of the postwar settlement. First, corporations in the same industry agreed not to compete over labor costs. This meant that once a leading firm such as Goodyear or Boeing reached agreement with the union representing its workers, then other major companies in rubber or aircraft would copy that settlement, meeting the new costs of the contract by a general price increase. This system removed wages from competition, but it was possible only because of the overall health of the economy and the oligopolistic structure of major industries.

Second, workers were protected against inflation. A cost-of-living adjustment (COLA) clause was first suggested by General Motors in its 1948 negotiations with the United Automobile Workers. GM had staved off UAW efforts to link company pricing policy to a negotiated wage package in 1946, but corporation head Charles Wilson realized that disruptive strikes and contentious wage negotiations, especially if couched as part of a broad offensive against corporate power, would embitter shop-floor labor relations and hamper the company's long-range planning. In 1948, GM offered the UAW a contract that included two pillars of the postwar accord: an automatic COLA keyed to the general price index; and a 2 percent "annual improvement factor" wage increase designed to give workers a share of GM's productivity gains.

The 1948 GM-UAW agreement was a dramatic departure from past union-management practice. It was premised on the emergence of a new era of prosperity and social peace—a development that at first seemed unlikely to veterans of the Great Depression. But when a 1949 recession turned out to be milder than expected and economic growth quickly resumed, the door was opened to broad ac-

"UAW AMERICANISM FOR US"

As industrial unions' relationship to corporations changed, so did life within the union. The journalist Samuel Lubell visited a UAW local in 1948, and he found it "hard to believe it was the same place" he had visited in 1940.

When I first visited Chrysler Local Seven of the United Automobile Workers a few days after Franklin Roosevelt's third term victory [in 1940], the scene was one of belligerent activity. Bulletin boards bristled with photographs of police clubbing strikers and of tear gas riotings. When the union's educational director heard that I was analyzing the election ... he [had] stiffened suspiciously and seemed about to have me thrown out. Then, he began boasting freely of how class conscious the auto workers were and how ready they were to vote Roosevelt a fourth or a fifth term. He wore a lumber jacket. With his feet on his desk and a buzzer by his hand, he looked the very picture of newly arrived power.

Returning eight years later, after Truman's victory, the whole atmosphere of the local had changed. The strike photographs had come down from the bulletin boards and had been replaced by idyllic snapshots of the union's annual outings and sporting events. An honor roll listed fifty-nine union members who had been killed in the war. Nearby stood a cabinet filled with loving cups and other trophies won in city-wide UAW tournaments. The "class-conscious" educational director was gone—ousted in the UAW-wide fight against Communists which Walter Reuther led. On their desks, the new officers had propped the slogan, "UAW Americanism for Us."

In 1940 the flavor of the local was one of street barricades and sit-down strikes; eight years later it was almost like a lodge hall.

commodation between big unions and major corporations. Again the UAW pioneered, with a new agreement in 1950, a five-year "Treaty of Detroit" providing pensions and a COLA on top of a wage increase. *Fortune* hailed the new contract as "the first that unmistakably accepts the existing distribution of income between wages and profits as 'normal' if not as 'fair' . . . thus throwing overboard all theories of wages as determined by political power and of profits as 'surplus value.'" By the end of the 1950s, the COLA principle had been incorporated in more than 50 percent of all major union contracts. Non-union firms such as IBM and DuPont, anxious to keep unions out, followed the pattern by paying top wages, matching union benefits, and establishing employee grievance systems.

This economic settlement had a steep price, however: the decline of democracy and activism within the unions and in the workplace. "This kind of collective bargaining," wrote Frederick Harberson, "calls for intelligent trading rather than table pounding . . . for internal union discipline rather than grass roots rank-and-file activity." In return for acceptance of unions and high wage contracts, corporate management insisted that wildcat strikes must stop, that long-term contracts were essential, and that all disputes must be handled through official channels (in most cases a multistep grievance procedure). Shop stewards were often replaced by full-time committeemen who functioned less as shop-floor leaders than as contract police.

Despite this accord, strikes continued in the 1950s, and at a level scarcely less than in the tumultuous years of the Depression. Workers were delighted to receive higher pay, but many did not accept the "trade-off" between more money and less shop-floor power. One-third of all strikes in the 1950s were "wildcat" stoppages that arose when workers balked at a "speed-up" or contested efforts to erode established workplace rights. During the Korean War, workers led thousands of such strikes and forced several big firms to reopen their contracts. In 1959, rank-and-file steelworkers pressured UAW officials into a 119-day strike and forestalled management efforts to increase crew size and eliminate work rules won in the 1930s and 1940s.

These strikes did not disrupt the overall pattern of labor-management accord, however. Most companywide strikes aimed to adjust the wage and benefits package, not to change the distribution of power at the workplace. And wildcat strikes, which were almost always called over shop issues, had little long-range effect, even when they proved temporarily successful. "We're moving rapidly away from the crusading spirit of the thirties," admitted a Buffalo aircraft union shop steward at the end of the decade.

> In 1953 we had one of the most militant unions in the labor movement. We had wildcat strikes, direct job action,

and the contract permitted us to refuse work if we thought the jobs were unsafe. Today there is much less of this. People no longer file grievances because they think it is no use.

The merger of the AFL and the CIO in 1955 ratified the changes in the union movement. With the CIO's expulsion of Communist-dominated unions, few substantial political differences remained between the two labor federations. Controlled by construction trades and business unionists, the AFL was almost twice the size of the CIO, so it was fitting that the chief of the new AFL-CIO would not be UAW and CIO president Walter Reuther but George Meany, a Bronx plumber who had risen to command the AFL in the early 1950s. Meany, who would later boast he had never led a strike, represented a tradition of unionism that won high wages for its members by adapting itself to the existing contours of American capitalism. "We do not seek to recast American society in any particular doctrinaire or ideological image," Meany asserted. "We seek an ever rising standard of living."

Some observers hoped the AFL-CIO merger would open a dynamic era for American trade unionism. But the merger proved, in the words of economist Richard Lester, a "sleepy monopoly." Most union officials preferred ease and routine to conflict and innovation. The primary obligation of these leaders became to preserve and protect their own organizations. Unions came to function less as a social

"SWEETHEART DEAL"

Trade-union corruption became big news in the 1950s, after Senate investigating committees found Mafia influence at the highest levels of the Teamsters, the International Longshoremen's Association, and the Hotel and Restaurant Workers. Allen Friedman, a Teamster strongarm man in Cleveland in the 1950s, later described how he had worked with a local attorney to "organize" the workers at local Italian restaurants while "shaking down" the restaurant owners.

The attorney's idea was for me to go to each of the restaurants he represented, signing up the members so that he would have to be called in to negotiate the contracts. In exchange for his giving me the list of names of the restaurants involved, I would negotiate a "sweetheart deal" which wouldn't cost the restaurant owners very much more than they were already paying. It was a good arrangement for everyone....

The idea that unions organize workers isn't always true. With big places we had to work hard to sign people to pledge cards, then present enough pledge cards to the boss to show that the workers were behind us.... With smaller places we didn't always bother to organize. We'd just tell the boss we had the members pledged to join, flashing phony cards, not all of which were even filled out by the employees. Sometimes we'd have two or three signatures. Sometimes we'd have none. It didn't matter. If we could bluff our way through, we would.

I worked with a partner from Local 10, which was created from the combined unions serving restaurant and hotel workers. We walked into the restaurant ... and demanded that the union be recognized. The owner would yell at us and throw us out of the restaurant. Then we could go to the car, pull out the picket signs, and start walking back and forth in front of the business.

John Felice, an acquaintance of mine, headed the local that controlled the beer truck drivers. When the beer arrived, I'd tell the driver that he wasn't supposed to deliver the beer that day because John Felice sanctioned the strike. The driver would go on to his next stop.... It was easy to organize those places. Stop the supplying of essential services and they're out of business.

Generally the meetings would be similar. The restaurant owner would start yelling, the attorney talking with him in his native language, quieting him. He then would explain that the owner should slip me a few hundred dollars and I would give him a sweetheart contract. The owner understood the bribe, paid it, and got a good deal. The employees didn't care because they kept their jobs and got a little better deal than they had had.

movement and more as an interest group. And a few union leaders, notably those who held certain top offices in the Teamsters and the East Coast longshoremen's unions, were little more than corrupt businessmen who undercut the price of the labor they "sold" for kickbacks and payoffs from the employers. The proportion of American workers who were AFL-CIO members declined steadily, from about 35 percent at the time of the merger in 1955 to little more than one-fifth of the workforce two decades later.

The labor-management accord and the maturation of the union movement helped ensure a wider dispersal of the benefits of postwar affluence. And it encouraged those who wished to believe that class divisions and social conflict had been permanently eliminated from American life. What most contemporary observers failed to recognize, however, was that the accord was only temporary, and that even at its height in the mid-1950s, many working Americans were excluded from its protection.

CHANGING JOBS, CHANGING WORKERS

Postwar capitalism in America generated two sorts of jobs. The core of the economy—big firms, government bureaucracy, and the military—expanded modestly in the quarter century after the war. Corporations were making money, governments hired more teachers and policemen, and unions improved many formerly unstable jobs. Jobs in this sector, both white- and blue-collar, provided relatively well-paid, virtually lifetime employment.

However, millions of jobs—perhaps as many as 40 percent—shared none of these characteristics. Farm laborers, cabdrivers, cannery workers, and dime-store clerks were poorly paid and lacked job security. Many economists have come to see such jobs as part of a distinct, "secondary" labor market, segregated from the more secure work of the core economy but essential to the functioning of the system. Casual employment has long been part of the American working-class experience, but in the postwar era the secondary labor market changed from manual labor to clerical and service employment. And most of these workers came from "marginal" groups: racial minorities, teenagers, and women.

In the postwar years the growth of this secondary labor market was spurred on by three dramatic changes in the composition of the American workforce: the flight from agriculture; a big rise in service, sales, and clerical work; and the increasing employment of women. The biggest change came in traditional sectors such as mining and agriculture, which together had supported one in four American families before World War II. Consolidation and mechanization eliminated 15 million rural jobs in one generation. The country's postwar agricultural population fell from one in five to one in twenty. In midwestern states such as Iowa and Ohio, rural migrants—mainly whites with some education—were readily absorbed into the factories and offices of the regional urban economy. But the depopulation of the rural South, Puerto Rico, and the Mexican borderlands was more traumatic.

In the American South, more than 4 million farmers and farm laborers lost their livelihoods, as cotton farming became mechanized. African-Americans were the hardest hit. By 1960, less than 10 percent of all African-Americans worked on the land. The great black migration out of the South—under way since the early twentieth century— grew to enormous proportions. Between 1910 and 1970, more than 6.5 million African-Americans moved from the South to the North; 5 million of them came after 1940. Their destination was overwhelmingly urban. At one point in the 1950s, the black population of Chicago was swelled by more than 2,200 new arrivals each week.

The South Side neighborhood of Chicago emerged in the postwar years to replace Harlem as the cultural capital of black America. New arrivals swelled a community that was home to the renowned boxing champion Joe Louis; America's only black member of Congress, William Dawson; the gospel singer Mahalia Jackson; and the nation's largest black congregation, the Mount Olivet Baptist Church. The South Side had substantial homes and apartment complexes, access to Lake Michigan beaches, and famous nightclubs where the world's finest jazz and blues artists played. It also had crowded slums, with decaying tenements, storefront churches, and the familiar urban problems of prostitution, crime, and alcoholism.

Economic transformation also drove Puerto Ricans off their island farms and into mainland cities. During the 1940s, the U.S. government's "Operation Bootstrap" encouraged the mechanization of the island's sugarcane economy and the growth of tax-free, low-wage industries in cities such as San Juan, the island's capital. As a consequence, rural employment plunged and the island's urban population tripled. Despite "Operation Bootstrap," Puerto Rico's overall unemployment remained among the highest in the Caribbean.

These conditions encouraged a large Puerto Rican migration to the mainland. A small but steady stream of Puerto Ricans had been migrating to New York and other eastern cities since the 1920s; now cheap airfares, previously established family and community connections, and the hope of urban jobs lured 40 percent of all islanders make the move. By the end of the 1960s, New York City claimed a larger Puerto Rican population than San Juan. While Puerto Rican neighborhoods sprouted around the city, the center of Puerto Rican life in the city was El Barrio, in East Harlem. El Barrio came to be known as the home of *salsa* music, Puerto Rican social clubs, and hundreds of small grocery stores, or *bodegas*, which served as centers of social and economic life. Like Italian immigrants of the early twentieth century, many Puerto Ricans came hoping to earn money and then return home to buy a piece of land on the island.

Mexican immigrants escaping the poverty of their homeland also poured into American cities. While many crossed the border illegally, a government-sponsored *bracero* program in the 1950s brought hundreds of thousands of Mexicans to the Southwest, where they joined long-established Mexican-American communities. Some of the new immigrants found employment on vast factory farms that dominated California and Arizona agriculture. But many came to the growing urban centers of California and the Southwest. From 1950 to 1960, the Chicano (Mexican-American) population in Los Angeles County doubled, going from 300,000 to more than 600,000. By 1968, the Los Angeles Chicano community, centered in East Los Angeles, was ap-

"... WE CONSIDER THIS PART OF THE CITY TO BE OURS"

When Puerto Ricans began arriving in New York City in massive numbers in the late 1940s, they found already established Latino communities. In this excerpt from Guillermo Cotto-Thorner's autobiographical novel, Trópico en Manhattan *(Tropic in Manhattan), Juan Marcos, a new arrival, travels with his friend Antonio, a seasoned New Yorker, from the airport to El Barrio, the Puerto Rican community in uptown Manhattan.*

• • • The plane prepared for a graceful landing in the mysterious city of hope. Off in the distance, Juan Marcos saw the vertical zig-zag of the Manhattan skyline. The streets seemed so wide to him; he hadn't yet adapted to the dimensions of the metropolis. . . .

In a few minutes he found himself "walking underground" for the first time in his life. The subway captivated him. He began to feel that sensation of mystery and splendor that the city instills. . . . Their car of the subway filled up at the first stop, and the newly arrived greenhorn saw a beautiful blonde balanced before him clinging to one of the stiff, enameled handles that hung from the ceiling. Juan Marcos thought he was in Puerto Rico where courtesy hasn't suffered the sad fate that it has in New York. He stood up and in broken English said to the woman: "Lady, dis is a sit for yu." The girl looked him up and down and said in a rude, contemptuous tone, "Don't be a sucker."

Juan Marcos felt as though he'd been slapped across the face. . . . Juan Marcos thought: "What a shameless girl. Are all the women here like that?" He was extremely agitated. He felt like giving the girl a piece of his mind, but how, if his

proaching 1 million. In that same year, 85 percent of the Chicano population nationwide was living in urban areas.

The postwar era thus marked a watershed in the history of American cities. The arrival of millions of Mexican-American immigrants and black and Puerto Rican migrants reshaped the contours of the nation's urban centers, increasing the diversity of an already complex racial and ethnic mixture.

In some ways, the lives of these postwar migrants and immigrants resembled those of earlier immigrants, such as the Irish of the 1850s or the Jews, Italians, and eastern Europeans of the early twentieth century. They faced a similar process of making the change from rural to urban life, figuring out the city's ways, and, in some cases, learning a new language. Much like earlier immigrants, Chicanos, Puerto Ricans, and African-Americans drew on their traditional cultures as they adapted to the new urban world.

In other ways, however, postwar arrivals confronted new challenges. Perhaps the biggest change affecting the lives of urban African-Americans, Puerto Ricans, and Chicanos was economic. Although the American economy grew in the postwar years, it no longer generated an ever-increasing number of the unskilled and semiskilled construction and manufacturing jobs that had been the mainstay of previous immigrant groups. By the late 1950s, many industries had moved out of the inner cities. In Chicago, such changes helped eliminate more than 90,000 jobs, many in such high-wage, unionized industries as meatpacking and steel manufacturing. As urban unemployment rose, many postwar migrants and immigrants were forced into low-wage, insecure positions at the bottom of the job market.

Racial discrimination added to this problem. In many cities, the job market remained rigidly divided in the 1950s. In Chicago, African-Americans could get

English wasn't even good enough to sell a bag of tomatoes? . . .

Juan Marcos had read and heard so much about El Barrio, the Puerto Rican colony in Manhattan scattered all over lower Harlem. Leaving the subway station, he stopped instinctively to look it over, while Antonio carried his suitcase as a gesture of courtesy. . . . On both sides of the wide street, the newly arrived friend could only distinguish two large buildings which stretched from corner to corner. Parallel windows, identical stairs reaching down to the sidewalk from six floors above the street. No, they weren't two buildings: they were many apartment buildings stuck together. . . . Hundreds, thousands of fellow Puerto Ricans lived there who, like him, had left the Island to try their luck in New York. . . .

Two men were playing checkers on a little table they had brought out onto the sidewalk, while two others watched. They were in front of "The Cave," a Puerto Rican "greasy spoon," which exuded the delicious aromas of fried pork rinds, *pasteles*, and fried codfish. Next to the table where the two men were playing, there was a wooden box full of coconuts and pieces of ice. The players spoke not a word, their concentration was total in spite of the hustle and bustle around them. . . .

"This," [said] Antonio, "is our neighborhood, El Barrio. It's said that we Latins run things here. And that's how we see ourselves. While the Americans take most of the money that circulates around here, we consider this part of the city to be ours. Notice the store signs—'La Fe' (The Faith), 'La Mallorquina' (The Mallorcan), 'El Nuevo Gardel' (The New Gardel), 'El Atómico' (The Atomic), 'Las Tres Marías' (The Three Marys) and that's not all. The stores, barbershops, restaurants, butcher shops, churches, funeral parlors, greasy spoons, pool halls, everything is all Latino. Every now and then you see a business run by a Jew or an Irishman or an Italian, but you'll also see that even these people know a little Spanish."

jobs in big mail-order houses and post offices, but insurance companies and construction unions kept them out. Puerto Ricans, including many women, found work in New York's garment industry, but were generally kept at the bottom of the job hierarchy. Others found work as janitors, doormen, or hospital service workers. Both Puerto Ricans and Chicanos had to overcome language barriers; many Chicanos faced the added problem of being illegal immigrants, which meant that they had few legal rights and had to be constantly alert to avoid deportation.

To be sure, earlier immigrant groups had faced prejudice and discrimination in America, but African-Americans, Puerto Ricans, and Chicanos confronted the additional problem of what W. E. B. DuBois had called "the color line." Though these three groups possessed distinct cultures and histories, and often did not get along with each other, most white Americans saw them as a single, unsettling, dark-skinned mass. Puerto Ricans, Chicanos, and African-Americans faced discrimination not only in hiring but also in housing, schooling, and social services. Many were forced to live in the poorest housing and attend the worst city schools. When they tried to move into traditionally white neighborhoods, they were blocked by realtors, landlords, and violent mobs of angry white homeowners.

White Americans' racial fears and prejudices also manifested themselves in the treatment handed out by urban police forces, which were overwhelmingly white through the 1950s and 1960s. Young African-Americans, Puerto Ricans, and Chicanos found that most police officers automatically treated them as criminals. The Chicano community, for example, charged the Los Angeles Police Department with a string of police-brutality incidents. On Christmas night in 1951, L.A. police dragged six Chicano youths out of a bar and began beating one of them; when the other youths protested, they were all arrested for assaulting an officer and taken to the central jail, where gangs of officers took turns beating the youths so severely that they had to be hospitalized. Police Chief William Parker refused to discipline the officers involved. In 1960, Parker publicly suggested that Chicanos were genetically inclined toward crime and violence.

Political remedies for such problems were not easily available to Chicanos, African-Americans, and Puerto Ricans. Since many Chicanos were not American citizens and thus could not vote, they had few political representatives. Although all Puerto Ricans were granted full U.S. citizenship in 1917, in New York City most Puerto Ricans were prevented from registering to vote by means of literacy tests. This situation continued until 1964, when the passage of the federal Civil Rights Act ended the practice. Urbanized African-Americans could and did vote in the 1950s, and this gave them slightly greater leverage. But urban political machines, such as the

Integration, peanuts, and Cracker Jacks. Jackie Robinson steals home plate during the fifth inning of a Braves-Dodgers game at Ebbets Field, August 22, 1948. Robinson broke baseball's race barrier, but major-league teams continued to resist desegregation. By 1953, only six teams had African-American players.

Chicago Democratic machine headed by Richard Daley, managed to largely contain African-Americans' social and political demands.

Throughout the 1950s, most African-Americans, Puerto Ricans, and Chicanos lived in relatively segregated and culturally isolated communities, even in America's most cosmopolitan cities. Symbolic changes, such as the integration of major-league baseball, which followed Jackie Robinson's joining the Brooklyn Dodgers in 1947, did not change the realities of everyday life. Each group mounted limited protests against job discrimination and police brutality; but until the late 1950s and the rise of the African-American civil rights movement in the South, these campaigns did not generate mass involvement or media attention. For the most part, these communities remained inwardly focused, sustained by distinct cultures of survival. Their impact on the broader American society would be more powerfully felt in the decades to come.

The second great change in the American workforce came with the rapid rise in the number of jobs in government, services, and retail trades. In the two decades after 1950, 9 million jobs opened up for secondary-school teachers, hospital support staff, and local govern-

"... MODERN MUSIC SHOULD BE FAST AND COMPLICATED"

In the late 1940s, jazz musicians experimented with new forms that expressed the spirit of their growing African-American urban communities. The most significant style to emerge was "bebop," or "bop." The modernist sounds of bebop reached a creative and popular peak with the work of musicians such as Dizzy Gillespie and Charlie "Yardbird" Parker. Richard Boyer's 1948 New Yorker article surveys this new music scene.

Bebop, according to its pioneer practitioners, is a manifestation of revolt. Eight or ten years ago, many Negro jazz musicians ... began to feel, rightly or wrongly, that the white world wanted them to keep to the old-time jazz. They held the opinion that the old jazz, which they called "Uncle Tom music," was an art form representative of a meeker generation than theirs.... "That old stuff was like Mother Goose rhymes," [says Dizzy Gillespie]. "It was all right for its time. We couldn't really blow on our jobs—not the way we wanted to. They made us do that two-beat stuff. They made us do that syrupy stuff. We began sayin', 'Man, this is gettin' awful sticky.' We began gettin' together after hours at Minton's Playhouse, on a Hundred and Eighteenth Street." Another who attended the after hours sessions at Minton's was Thelonious Monk, a somber scholarly twenty-one-year-old Negro with a bebop beard, who played the piano with a sacerdotal air, as if the keyboard were an altar and he an acolyte. "We liked Ravel, Stravinsky, Debussy, Prokofieff, Schoenberg," he says, "and maybe we were a little influenced by them." ... Perhaps the strongest influence, though, was Yardbird Parker, who had never heard of Schoenberg and says that he developed most of his ideas about bebop on his saxophone in his mother's woodshed in Kansas City. "Bebop is what I brought from Kansas City," he says. [Gil] Fuller's comments on the new music are more general. "Modern life is fast and complicated, and modern music should be fast and complicated," he says. "We're tired of that old New Orleans beat-beat, I-got-the-blues pap." It was at Minton's that the word "bebop" came into being. Dizzy was trying to show a bass player how the last two notes of a phrase should sound. The bass player tried it again and again, but he couldn't get the two notes. "Bebop! Be-bop!" Dizzy finally sang.

ment office workers. The growing demand for consumer goods spurred the creation of new department stores and supermarkets staffed by 3 million additional employees. Meanwhile, new white-collar jobs were created in almost every large corporation. Hundreds of thousands of supervisors and personnel managers were hired to control workers and keep unions out of these workplaces. Millions more were assigned to planning, advertising, sales, and public relations. Finance, real estate, and insurance companies added 4 million new workers in the twenty years after 1950.

In 1956, for the first time in U.S. history, white-collar workers outnumbered blue-collar workers. Professional, managerial, clerical, and sales workers, who composed less than a third of the workforce in 1940, swelled to almost half by 1970. Meanwhile, blue-collar employment declined steadily as a proportion of the workforce, down to 35 percent by 1970. Declared one journalist, "Increasingly, the representative wage earner became a pencil pusher working for a large, impersonal entity."

The growth of the service industry reinforced the notion that the United States had become a classless, "postindustrial" society. But there were two things wrong with this idea. First, blue-collar work did not disappear in the 1950s and 1960s. Although they were a declining proportion of the workforce, factory workers actually increased their numbers, from 22 million to 26 million, between 1950 and 1970. Despite the deployment of highly publicized automation machinery, factory work still required an army of manual workers.

Moreover, half of all service jobs involved manual labor: trash collection, maintenance, and food preparation, for example. The greatest growth in so-called white-collar employment came in the categories labeled sales and clerical work. These jobs might be white collar in the sense that a typist did not spot-weld body joints. But most clerical and sales jobs had little creative or autonomous content. "My job doesn't have prestige," bank teller Nancy Rodgers noted. "It's a service job. Whether you're a waitress, salesperson, anything like that . . . you are there to serve them. They are not there to serve you."

Most of the half-million women who worked for the telephone company were classified as service or clerical staff, but their work was as routinized as any factory job. AT&T employees were rigidly divided between an all-male craft unit, whose unionized staff repaired and installed equipment, and the largely female departments that handled long-distance calls and took sales and installation orders. Operators were closely monitored, confined to their consoles, and expected to meet a daily work quota. "You've got a clock next to you that times every second," reported a Chicago operator. "They do keep track. How many calls you take, how well you mark your tickets, how many errors you make. You're constantly being pushed. It's hectic." These operators shared many characteristics of workers in the casual labor market: turnover was high; pay was low; and, in the big cities, workers were increasingly African-American or Latino.

The American economy's shift to service and clerical work would have been impossible without the third great change: the influx of 20 million women into the postwar workforce. In 1950, a total of 31 percent of all women were employed;

". . . ONE CAN NEVER BE CERTAIN WHERE THE OBSERVATION STOPS"

The journalist Elinor Langer spent several months in 1969 working for the New York Telephone Company, a part of the AT&T system, then the largest employer of women workers in the nation. Within the company, she found a well-established system of workplace management that tightly controlled the actions of the nonunionized women workers.

Observers at the phone company are everywhere. I became aware of a new layer of Observation every day. The system works like this. For every five or six women there is . . . a Supervisor who can at any moment listen in from the phone set on her desk to any of her Representatives' contacts with a customer. For an hour every day, the Supervisor goes to a private room off the main floor where she can listen (herself unobserved) to the conversations of any of her "girls" she chooses. The women know, naturally, when she is doing this but not whose contact she is observing.

Further off the main floor is a still more secret Observing Room staffed by women whose title and function is, specifically, Observer. These women "jack in" at random to any contact between any Representative and a customer: their job is basically to make sure that the Representatives are giving out correct information. Furthermore, these Observers are themselves observed from a central telephone company location elsewhere in the city to make sure that they are not reporting as incorrect information which is actually correct. In addition the Observers make "access calls" by which they check to see that the telephone lines are open for the customers to make their connections. This entire structure of observation is, of course, apart from the formal representative-supervisor-manager-district supervisor-division head chain of managerial command. They are, in effect, parallel hierarchical structures.

One result of the constant observation (the technology being unbounded) is that one can never be certain where the observation stops. It is company policy to stress its finite character, but no one ever knows for sure.... This system coexists with the most righteous official attitude toward wiretapping. Only supervisors and managers can deal with wiretap complaints; Federal regulations about the sanctity of communications are posted; and the overt position toward taps, in the lower managerial echelons, is that they are simply illegal....

twenty years later, 42 percent worked outside the home. Unlike women workers during World War II, those in the postwar workforce were confined to a female job ghetto. Ninety-five percent of all women worked in just four job categories: light manufacturing (i.e., home appliances and clothing); retail trade; clerical work; and health and education. And within these categories, high-status work was usually male, low-status work female. In 1960, for example, high-school principals were 90 percent male, while elementary-school teachers were 85 percent female.

Job segregation helped keep women's work low-paid and dead-end. During World War II, women's wages in manufacturing had risen to about two-thirds of those earned by men, but within a few years of the war's end, women's median earnings dropped to only 53 percent of men's. In Baltimore, women clerical employees were allowed to stay on the job after the war, but those women who worked in high-wage aircraft assembly were forced to leave and take lower-paying jobs

Young mother. New Rochelle, New York, 1955.

as waitresses or service workers. Women's average weekly wages there fell from $50 to $37. The same process of exclusion took place in other types of work. Because professional schools discouraged female enrollment and because World War II veterans monopolized so many student slots, there were actually fewer women doctors and lawyers in the 1950s than two decades before.

The relegation of women to the secondary labor market was sustained by the sexual ideology of the early postwar years, which Betty Friedan called the "feminine mystique" in her 1963 best-selling book. The wartime self-confidence and workplace equality symbolized by "Rosie the Riveter" gave way to a definition of gender roles—for both men and women—that took on the rigid distinctions reminiscent of the mid-nineteenth century. Experts now celebrated women's submissive domesticity and saw sexual freedom as potentially subversive, even pro-Communist. In the popular media, women were increasingly portrayed as incompetent and vulnerable, sexually fulfilled only in the context of a stable and secure marriage. By the late 1940s, women's magazines such as the *Ladies' Home Journal* and *Redbook* were full of articles such as "What's Wrong with American Women?"; "Isn't a Woman's Place in the Home?"; and "Really a Man's World, Politics." African-American women did not escape, as *Jet* advanced a similar view of women's proper role in a 1951 article, "What's Wrong with Negro Women?"

American men were also subject to a new sexual orthodoxy, which equated masculinity with rationality and rigid control over one's emotions. To be a "family man," even in late adolescence, was considered a sign of maturity and political reliability. Men still single in their thirties were considered suspect by many employers, while homosexuality was a criminal offense that was said to sap the moral fiber of the individual and the nation. Indeed, the anti-Communist movement of the postwar years engendered a wave of officially sponsored homophobia, and the persecution of male and female "perverts" became more intense than ever before. The FBI mounted an all-out effort to discover the personal sexual habits of those under suspicion of subversive behavior. Gay-baiting rivaled Red-baiting in its ferocity, destroying careers, encouraging harassment, and forcing those who "confessed their guilt" to name others with whom they associated. Meanwhile, the postwar era gave birth to the materialistic and sexually permissive (at least for men) philosophy of *Playboy* magazine, which was first published in 1953. Lust, *Playboy* demonstrated, could be channeled in socially acceptable directions.

Despite the social emphasis placed on being a "family man" in the 1950s, most American men saw cooking, cleaning, and changing the baby's diapers as "women's work." Consequently, women who did work outside the home were usually left with the burden of house-

CIVIL DEFENSE GROUPS

Men	Women
FIRE-FIGHTING	MEDICAL TEAMS
RESCUE WORK	CAR-DRIVING
MEDICAL TEAMS	AIR-RAID WARDEN
GEIGER CREW	GEIGER CREW
STREET CLEARING	CHILD CARE
POLICE AUXILIARY	HOSPITAL WORK
AIR-RAID WARDEN	SOCIAL WORK
REBUILDING	EMERGENCY FEEDING

Holocaust or no holocaust, a woman's place is in ... An illustration in the widely circulated 1950 book *How to Survive an Atomic Bomb* designates "appropriate" civil-defense jobs for men and women.

work and childrearing. Although American homes were filling up with dishwashers, vacuum cleaners, and other "labor-saving appliances," the intensification of this domestic ideology meant that the average woman's housework demanded as much time as it had thirty years earlier. Half of all service and blue-collar working women surveyed in the 1950s said that they had no leisure time whatsoever.

The gender orthodoxy of the period also justified low pay and employment practices that discriminated against women. Many working women came to see themselves as "temporary" workers whose income was directed toward a specific goal: school clothes for the kids, a new refrigerator, or a larger house. A 1968 supervisor's handbook argued that sex discrimination at work made sense because "the role of achievers still belongs to men. . . . Women as a rule don't seek job promotion—their emotions are secure in a limited job."

Women workers learned to make the best of a bad situation. In workplaces large and small, postwar women, like their mothers before them, created a rich work culture that both accommodated and resisted the sexist system. With ample opportunities for talk, clerical workers and saleswomen created a social world of birthdays, bridal showers, and shopping trips that provided some compensation for unrewarding paper-shuffling and order-taking. Large firms sometimes took advantage of such social networks to generate group competition and *esprit de corps*, but more often women and men found in friendships and office rituals a source of worklife satisfaction and resistance to management.

CULTURAL COHESION AND DIVISION IN THE WORKING CLASS

The experiences and problems of women, blacks, and others who worked in the secondary labor market went largely unrecognized in the 1950s. Most contemporary observers focused on the growth of affluence, the swelling middle class, and unionized industrial workers. This selective focus bolstered the enthusiastic celebration of "the American way of life," but it limited widespread understanding of the complex changes occurring at the workplace and elsewhere in society.

In the 1950s and 1960s ethnic and religious divisions were growing less important to white Americans. Almost two generations had passed since the end of mass European immigration, and there were only half as many foreign-born in the United States as in the Depression years. Ethnic differences diminished in part because they were increasingly irrelevant to the functioning of such institutions as the church, the military, and the high school. Although church and synagogue attendance increased in the 1950s, religious belief seemed increasingly homogenized into a vague "civic religion" that validated the "American way of life." Catholic schools, especially those organized along ethnic lines, began a long-term decline. Perhaps President Eisenhower put it best when he affirmed, "Our government makes no sense unless it is founded in a deeply religious faith—and I don't care what it is."

The postwar military draft, which lasted from 1948 until 1971, diluted ethnic, religious, and regional parochialism for millions of working-class young people who came to see "the service" as part of their rite of passage from adolescence to adulthood. The growth of the comprehensive high school had some of the same effect. After the war, secondary-school enrollment rose to 80 percent of its potential constituency. Virtually all white Americans now spent three or four of their formative years in an institution whose official ideology was one of classless homogeneity. Elaborate sports contests and the emergence of a distinct teen culture in the 1950s eclipsed the ethnic antagonisms that had bitterly divided white American youth since the late nineteenth century.

The explosive growth of college and university enrollments contributed to this process as well. Wartime enactment of the G.I. Bill (officially known as the Servicemen's Readjustment Act of 1944) helped democratize higher education by making it broadly available for the first time in U.S. history. Surpassing all expectations, World War II veterans took advantage of generous government payments to jam classrooms and hastily expanded living facilities of state universities and older elite colleges. "Everybody went to college," remembered a Sicilian-born architect who had spent his childhood in the Bronx, where his father kept a wine press in the apartment basement. "Suddenly we looked up, we owned property. Italians could buy. The G.I. Bill, the American dream. Guys my age had really become Americanized."

Of course, such upward mobility still took place along a pathway clearly structured along class and racial lines. In high school the "tracking" of students into academic or vocational courses usually replicated class divisions in the local community; and many of the white, working-class young men who found higher education now within their reach enrolled in community colleges and technical schools, not the prestigious liberal arts colleges that were still the gateway to managerial and professional jobs. Until the late 1960s, African-Americans found such career ladders largely blocked.

Postwar changes in housing patterns also helped reshape American society. Depression and war had virtually halted residential construction, but after the war millions of veterans and cash-rich workers needed homes for themselves and their growing families. By 1945, the United States was in the grip of a first-class crisis: Chicago

Suburban development, 1957. An aerial view of Levittown, Pennsylvania, under construction.

put 250 old streetcars up for sale as potential homes; an ad in an Omaha newspaper read, "Big Ice Box, 7 × 17 feet, could be fixed up to live in." Something had to be done to address this problem.

In the early postwar years, the construction of new suburbs was only one of a range of possible solutions to the housing crisis. Before World War II, suburbs had been largely reserved for the well-to-do; working-class Americans lived near their work, often in ethnic neighborhoods, in apartments or cramped row houses. Most workers rented (except in the Midwest), for purchasing a house required as much as a 50 percent down payment on a ten- or fifteen-year mortgage.

Reformers had experimented with a variety of housing programs in the 1930s and 1940s. During the New Deal, the government helped plan and construct several "greenbelt" towns that clustered garden apartments close to workplaces and recreation facilities. The desperate need to house wartime defense employees led the government to finance construction of thousands of new rental units, many convenient to public transportation and some designed with the needs of single workers or working mothers in mind. Vanport City, Oregon, which housed 40,000 shipyard workers during the war, included childcare, restaurants, and recreational facilities as part of the original city plan.

In the postwar era, however, such experimentation quickly gave way to the single-family house in a suburban tract, best symbolized by the three huge Levittowns that sprouted amid potato fields on the fringes of New York and Philadelphia. William Levitt's wartime experience constructing family quarters on a navy base convinced him that if financing were available, a contractor could make millions housing veterans and their families. Prodding the Veterans Administration and Federal Housing Administration, builders convinced these New Deal agencies to guarantee low-interest, minimal-down-payment loans that would make owning a suburban tract home cheaper than renting. Assured of a mass market, Levitt adapted assembly-line methods to put up thousands of identical Cape Cod–style homes. Sold at a modest $6,990, each small house was a self-contained world, with a white picket fence, a green lawn, and a well-equipped kitchen. Buyers snapped up 1,400 houses in the first three hours after sales began in March 1949, though Levitt permitted neither blacks nor single women to sign a mortgage.

By 1960, home ownership had become the norm for the first time in U.S. history, with three of five families owning their dwelling. Some thought Levittowns heralded a new society in which feisty urban ethnics were transformed into middle-class suburban homeowners chiefly concerned with keeping the crab grass at bay. "No man who owns his own house and lot can be a Communist," Levitt asserted. "He has too much to do." The folk singer Malvina Reynolds agreed in her 1962 ballad satirizing the conformist life-style of suburbanites who lived in "little boxes made of ticky-tacky" that all looked "the same."

Even in the suburbs, however, blue-collar workers remained in a working-class world. Although they might own a home nearly identical to that of their middle-class neighbors, they were unlikely to vote Republican or repudiate their union. Autoworkers who followed a Ford plant from urban Richmond, California, to a new tract near Milpitas liked the spaciousness of their new homes, but most did not believe they had left the working class. Blue-collar families still valued security more than mobility. In a suburban community, one sociologist reported, "the people of working-class culture stay close to home and make the house a haven against a hostile, outside world."

Married women found the new suburban world ambiguous at best. Although millions of married women were entering the labor market, suburban housing patterns were designed for a family in which Mom stayed home, Dad worked in the city, and other relatives

Public housing. In the years following World War II, as many middle-class families moved to the suburbs, inner-city public housing increasingly became identified with poor Americans. Living in public housing was viewed by many as a stigma, and the newer, high-rise projects took on a harsh and regimented appearance.

remained at a distance. The early housing tracts contained few of the social institutions—the corner grocery store, the nearby grandparent, or the convenient streetcar—that women had long relied on to ease the burden of shopping, housework, or childrearing. By making work outside the home more difficult for women and cutting them off from traditional support networks, the insular character of suburban life enforced the polarization of gender roles in postwar society.

Meanwhile, government housing policies deepened some racial and class divisions. The FHA, which financed about 30 percent of all new homes in the 1950s, advised developers to concentrate on a particular housing market based on age, income, and race. The FHA endorsed anti-Jewish and antiblack "restrictive covenants" to ensure neighborhood homogeneity and preserve "property values." Central-city housing stock deteriorated in the 1950s because federal housing agencies followed private lenders in "red-lining"—refusing to write mortgage loans—where millions of working Americans still lived. Such neglect slowly turned these wards into slums. Millions of African-American and Puerto Rican migrants found that their race and low income barred them from what was left of the decent urban housing stock. As minority ghettos pressed against the boundaries of traditionally white neighborhoods, racial tensions flared. In cities such as Chicago, Philadelphia, and Buffalo, housing integration failed as white families fled for the suburbs within a few years of the appearance of the first African-American family on their block. Northern housing became more rigidly segregated than at any time since the Civil War.

America's public housing failure added to the problem. Because of resistance from realtors, mortgage bankers, and home builders, only 320,000 units were funded in the decade after Congress passed Truman's 1949 public housing bill. It might have been better had no new units been built, however, since the program led to the bulldozing of acres of old housing stock and its reconstruction in the most brutal and utilitarian style. In the new public housing projects, closets were left without doors (to ensure tenants' neatness) and cinder blocks were left exposed in hallways. To save on land costs, most projects were built in massive blocks. Apartments were cramped, and many mothers found the barren play areas, wedged between highrises, too unpleasant or dangerous for their children. "You feel like you can't breathe," reported a St. Louis public housing resident in the mid-1960s. "People are everywhere. Children are in the bathroom when you are using the toilet, somebody is sitting in every chair in the house, you've got to eat in shifts."

Unlike tax subsidies for single-family, suburban homes, public housing was thought of as welfare, so local governments usually imposed income restrictions on project residents. Families with rising incomes had to leave, ensuring economic segregation for those who remained. In the end, no one liked American-style public housing— not the taxpayers, not the housing industry, not urban politicians, and not even the people who lived there. As one resident explained, government bureaucrats had been "trying to get rid of the slum, but they didn't accomplish too much. Inside the apartment they did, but not outside."

Adding insult to injury were the massive expressways that slashed through urban neighborhoods in the late 1950s. Replacing more accessible trolleys and interurban trams, the new superhighways often disrupted stable working-class communities. When residents protested, they were told that "you can't stop progress." Like low mortgage rates for single-family home dwellers, the government-sponsored freeway boom represented a massive subsidy for suburban commuters and a tax, both fiscal and social, on urban dwellers.

Together with housing and education, the union movement sped the homogenization of one group of workers, at the same time separating it from the remainder of the working class. Unions greatly reduced wage differences between skilled and unskilled work. By 1958, skilled tool and die makers made only 20 percent more than unskilled assembly-line workers. Through grievance and seniority systems, unions also reduced the influence of personal or ethnic favoritism in blue-collar workplaces. In many steel mills, eastern European Catholic workers, who had labored for three generations at heavy, sweaty jobs, finally got a shot at skilled work. At Ford, managers admitted that the old saying "It's not what you know but who you know" was laid to rest once UAW committeemen could challenge the foreman's ability to assign work.

But the stagnation of the union movement created a context in which other, sharp divisions reappeared within the working class. Race and gender prejudice had separated American workers for many years. Now, in the context of the postwar consolidation of the AFL-CIO, the defeat of Operation Dixie and the labor movement's failure to organize women, African-Americans, and other members of the growing "secondary" labor force contributed to the further division of the working class.

Union policy on two key issues of the period—automation and employee fringe benefits—also helped divide workers. In the 1930s, unions had often sought to spread the burden of unemployment by reducing the length of the workweek, even if this meant smaller paychecks for all. In the 1950s, massive unemployment was less of a problem, but workers now confronted rapid technological change that threatened jobs by automating and reorganizing some work processes. In the hosiery industry, for example, new high-speed knitting machines destroyed the skilled jobs of highly paid, unionized workers; likewise, in telephone offices the introduction of direct local dialing eliminated the work of many operators.

Instead of meeting this challenge with calls for retraining or a reduced workweek, or demands for a voice in decisions about new technology, most unions focused on trying to protect the interests of their longtime members. On the West Coast docks, for example, Harry Bridges, president of the International Longshoremen's and Warehousemen's Union, agreed to employers' plans to eliminate safety rules and install the new technology necessary to "containerize" cargo handling. In return, Bridges won a fat pension benefit for older longshoremen. On the docks, accident rates took off; employers began hiring nonunion "temporary" workers; and as "containerization" became a reality, unemployment soared.

A subtle but more pervasive redivision of the working class took place when unions focused their energy on bargaining over health and pension schemes and cost-of-living adjustments, which came to constitute a sort of "private welfare state" for union members. By the late 1940s, as political efforts to expand Social Security and inaugurate national health insurance stalled, unionists turned to the bargaining table to secure equivalent benefits for their own members. After John

Robots. During the 1950s, science-fiction stories and films became increasingly popular, although their vision of the future was often pessimistic. Besides alien invasions and atomic disasters (including devastating destruction wrought by gigantic monsters created or awakened by nuclear experiments), another favorite theme was the mixed blessing of automation: the robot as a labor-saving device that all too easily could turn against humankind.

L. Lewis and the United Mine Workers won a health and pension fund from mine owners in 1947, other big unions followed. By the end of the 1960s, pension plans amounting to nearly $1 trillion covered more than 30 million unionized workers.

Union success in these efforts had unforeseen consequences, however. In the inflationary postwar environment, COLAs and hefty benefit packages gave unionized industrial workers a tremendous financial advantage over unorganized, poorly paid service and clerical workers. The relatively egalitarian wage pattern of the mid-1940s eroded steadily over the next two decades. Soon high-wage workers came to resent the taxes they paid to fund those on state-supported welfare, especially when the tax structure became more regressive in the 1960s and 1970s. Thus, the weakness of the postwar welfare state and the creation of a privatized substitute for organized labor sped the redivision of the American working class into a relatively secure segment and a growing stratum—predominantly young, minority, and female—left out in the cold.

THE WORLD OF *FATHER KNOWS BEST*

Television reinforced the family-oriented privatization of American social life in the postwar era. TV was a fixture in 90 percent of all American homes by 1960, and its TV programming mirrored, often in exaggerated form, the larger social and cultural landscape. In the early days of television, just after the end of World War II, radio-inspired situation comedies had offered the new TV audience a sympathetic glimpse of urban, working-class families enmeshed in an ethnic world of tenements, street-corner stickball, and manual labor. The most successful of these comedy series was *The Goldbergs*, which made the transition from radio to television in 1948. Each episode in the life of this Jewish working-class family began as Molly Goldberg leaned out the window of her Bronx tenement to "schmooze" with her neighbors. Played by Gertrude Berg (later the victim of anti-Communist blacklisting), Molly was a strong, sharp-witted woman with opinions about everything. Along with the show's other adult characters, she spoke with an accent and used Yiddish phrases. Her teenage kids were being Americanized, and many episodes explored the comic possibilities of their hybrid culture. Though working class and Jewish, the Goldberg family offered the TV audience a warm humanism that dignified and made universal their trying encounters with urban, workaday life.

During the 1950s, however, series such as *The Goldbergs* and *The Life of Riley* (about the travails of an aircraft worker and his family) were replaced by situation comedies and westerns that bleached ethnicity, class, and social comment out of their story lines. Introduced in 1953, *Father Knows Best* exemplified the new world of suburban respectability. The Andersons lived in a large house on Maple Street in "Springfield." Robert Young, who played Jim Anderson, the father, would never dream of going to work carrying a lunchpail with two bologna sandwiches, as William Bendix had on *The Life of Riley*. Anderson's work as an insurance executive remained always offscreen. He had no politics, few strongly held opinions, and never a bad day at the office. All the action in *Father Knows Best* took place at home, where the middle-class father exercised a benevolent despotism over three not particularly rebellious children. Jane Wyatt, who played the Anderson mother, maintained perfect order in her house. In contrast to Molly Goldberg, she kept her opinions to herself. TV viewers sensed that *Father Knows Best* was hardly a realistic portrayal of the average American family, but this insular, classless world seemed the appropriate model of contemporary life, and they tuned in faithfully.

Though clearly the dominant cultural ideal, the placid world of *Father Knows Best* was challenged from unexpected quarters. Emerging in the mid-1950s, a small group of intellectual rebels used poetry and literature to mock the values of the American mainstream. Led by Allen Ginsberg and Jack Kerouac, the "beat" poets idolized African-Americans, especially jazz musicians, and denounced what they saw as the materialism, sexual repression, and spiritual emptiness of middle-class life. "These have been years of conformity and depression," wrote Norman Mailer in 1957, voicing a critique common among intellectuals sympathetic to the beats. "A stench of fear has come out of every pore of American life, and we suffer from a collective failure of nerve."

Though the beats attracted only a small following, they stirred wide controversy and comment. Newspaper and magazine reports sneered at the "beatnik" style of dress and talk, and hinted darkly about racial mixing and sexual "immorality" at beat parties. *Life* magazine derided the beats as a group of "sick little bums" and "hostile little chicks." Writing in *Esquire,* critic Norman Podhoretz claimed that the beats represented a "conspiracy" to replace Western civilization with "the world of the adolescent street gangs."

Beats—by way of Hollywood. A publicity still from the 1959 film *The Rebel Set* displays some of the stereotyped characteristics ascribed to "beatniks." Dressed in black, wearing sandals, and sporting distinctive hair styles (goatees for men; severe yet flamboyant ponytails for women), the two beats crouch on a bare mattress and "groove" on poetry. The paintings arranged in the background display drug-induced nightmare themes.

The pulp threat. A 1954 montage that appeared in newspapers presents what many Americans saw as a new danger threatening the nation's youth. In Senate committee hearings and other forums, parents, social scientists, and public officials called for censorship laws, claiming that crime and horror comic books, along with other sensational publications, contributed to the growing problem of juvenile delinquency.

This comparison of the beats to juvenile delinquents was no coincidence. At the same time that the beats were writing their poems and books, a separate culture of rebellious adolescence was emerging, highlighted by a nationwide debate over juvenile delinquency. The near-hysterical attention focused on "JDs" by the FBI, the mass media, and Hollywood did not arise out of any significant growth in youthful criminality. Instead, it reflected underlying fears about the stability of the family and more vocal alarm at the growing assimilation by some middle-class youth of the cultural values of the black ghetto and the urban working class: disrespect for teachers and the police; underage drinking; "hot-rodding"; rock-'n'-roll music; "going steady"; and the distinctive clothing, hair styles, and slang that gave 1950s teenagers a new, self-protective identity. The growth of a distinct teenage culture was shaped not only by the vitality of African-American music in the postwar years but also by the cross-class fertilization taking place in big-city high schools and the discovery and exploitation of a multibillion-dollar teenage market.

Rock-'n'-roll, one of the most prominent features of the new teenage life-style, originated in the music that dominated black working-class communities during and after World War II. Its leading artists were usually newly urbanized migrants from the rural South. Among the most important was blues singer Muddy Waters, who moved from rural Mississippi to Chicago in 1941. Waters and his band introduced the pulse and energy of the electric guitar to the traditional country blues form. By the mid-1950s, Waters and other black singers such as Ray Charles, who performed throughout the South, Big Joe Turner in Kansas City, and Chuck Berry in St. Louis had created and refined a new musical form, rhythm-and-blues, that anticipated the rock-'n'-roll revolution that followed. Charles's gospel-inspired piano-playing on "I Got a Woman" launched the revolution in 1954. Turner's 1954 rhythm-and-blues hit "Shake, Rattle, and Roll" was the first rhythm-and-blues tune "covered" (copied) by a major white artist. And Chuck Berry's distinctive guitar playing and upbeat performance on songs such as "Johnny B. Goode" inspired rock-'n'-roll's subsequent sound and style.

But it would be a white Memphis truck driver not yet out of his teens named Elvis Presley who combined the drive of African-American rhythm-and-blues with the lyrics and sentiments of southern white "country music" to launch the national rock-'n'-roll craze. Flaunting his sexuality and his working-class style, Presley created a national scandal when he appeared on television in 1956. His songs became rock-'n'-roll anthems because they offered millions of young fans a sense of generational solidarity based on a rejection of proper dress, "refined" music, and other middle-class norms. African-American

"... THEY BEHAVE AS IF DRUGGED"

Many middle-class American adults were disturbed by the nature of the adolescent culture that emerged in the 1950s. Some parents sought advice from "experts" such as the psychiatrist Fredric Wertham, who gained fame as a critic of comic books. This letter from a middle-class mother expresses a range of common concerns.

Dear Dr. Wertham:

We have two boys, 7 and 13, with unusually high intelligence and excellent ability in school and in sports . . . . They have a library of fine books of their own, and read library books almost daily, yet in the presence of comic books they behave as if drugged, and will not lift their eyes or speak when spoken to . . . . What we would like to know is, what can be done about it before it is too late? My boys fight with each other in a manner that is unbelievable in a home where both parents are university graduates and perfectly mated. We attribute the so-called "hatred" that they profess for each other to be harmful influence of these books, plus movies and radio. . . .

We consider the situation to be as serious as an invasion of the enemy in war time, with as far reaching consequences as the atom bomb. If we cannot stop the wicked men who are poisoning our children's minds, what chance is there for mankind to survive longer than one generation, or half of one?

Fear of teenagers. Teenagers exhibit behavior many adults thought bordered on the criminal. From dancing to grooming to just "hanging out," teenage popular culture seemed to undermine notions of innocence and propriety.

artists also used rock as a way of expressing social frustrations. Little Richard composed one of his first songs after a long day washing dishes in a Georgia bus station. "I couldn't talk back to my boss man. He would bring all those pots back for me to wash, and one day I said, 'I've got to do something to stop that man . . .' and I said, 'Awop bop-a-lop bop-a-wop bam boom, take 'em out!' and that's how I came to write 'Tutti Frutti.' "

While some parents and conservative social critics denounced rock-'n'-roll as an evil influence on the young, Hollywood quickly discovered that money could be made from the rebellious youth culture. Films such as *The Wild One*; *Rebel Without a Cause*; and *The Blackboard Jungle*, which featured Bill Haley's classic recording of "Rock Around the Clock," offered sympathetic portraits of teenage "delinquents" trapped in a crass adult society that neither understood nor cared about them. Brilliant acting performances by the young Marlon Brando and James Dean embodied the personal alienation of a generation. Partly as a result of the popularization of such attitudes, millions of Americans would, within a decade, come to see the rejection of middle-class life not as semicriminal but as a "counterculture," an alternative way of looking at and perhaps changing an unhappy world.

EMERGENCE OF THE CIVIL RIGHTS MOVEMENT

The sharpest exception to America's celebration of an affluent, classless social order was the racism prevalent in both North and South. Shaped by the legacy of slavery and the failure of Reconstruction, race relations constituted a glaring failure, the "American dilemma" that the Swedish sociologist Gunnar Myrdal exhaustively surveyed in an influential 1944 book. As an economic structure, a public policy, and a private belief system, racism was on the defensive by the end of World War II, but this did not mean that segregation was vanquished. African-Americans, Puerto Ricans, Mexican-Americans, and Asian-Americans continued to face discrimination in virtually every aspect of life, from housing to jobs, education, politics, and legal rights.

African-Americans took the lead in challenging racial inequality. The mass migration of African-Americans out of agriculture and into urban industrial society helped move the problem of racism to center stage. The migration process had been taking place throughout the twentieth century, but rapid urbanization in the 1940s and 1950s created the conditions that would support an effective protest movement: a growing black electorate and an integrated union movement in the North; and an increasingly assertive black church in the South.

Civil rights for African-Americans had already become a national issue by the end of President Harry Truman's first term. A border state politician with a traditional racial outlook, Truman found that his reelection in 1948 would hinge, in the words of adviser Clark Clifford, on winning the support of "labor and the urban minorities." Fearful that Henry Wallace's Progressive Party would steal these votes, Truman made civil rights a major presidential priority for the first time in seventy-five years. In early 1948, he called on Congress to pass a Fair Employment Practices Act that would end employment discrimination; in July, he capitulated to the protest campaign led by African-American union leader A. Philip Randolph and signed an executive order desegregating the armed forces.

Although Truman sought to moderate his gestures enough to retain the loyalty of the white South, the Democratic Party cracked under the strain. At its 1948 nominating convention in Philadelphia, a coalition of delegates from unions, the Americans for Democratic Action, and northern urban political machines pushed through a civil rights plank calling for the federal government to guarantee equal

Jim Crow, 1951.

voting and employment rights. "To those who say the civil rights program is an infringement of states' rights," Hubert Humphrey told the convention, "I say this, that the time has come for the Democratic Party to get out of the shadow of states' rights and to walk forthrightly into the bright sunshine of human rights." Waving the battle flag of the Confederacy, Mississippi and Alabama delegates marched out in protest, and three days later a convention of "Dixiecrats" chose South Carolina governor Strom Thurmond as their own party's presidential nominee.

With this fracture in Democratic Party ranks, African-Americans seemed on the verge of a major breakthrough. But the Democratic Party victory in the November national election actually diminished the pressure on Truman and other politicians to take forthright action. With the Progressive Party smashed, most Democratic leaders sought to regain the loyalty of the white South. Truman's commitment to black equality became largely rhetorical during his second term, and the 1952 Democratic presidential nominee, Adlai Stevenson, downplayed the civil rights issue even further, choosing as his running mate an Alabama senator who stood for the maintenance of the racial status quo. Republicans also stood aloof: many hoped to build a southern base for their party among that region's growing number of suburban, conservative whites.

Southern politicians and business leaders soon mobilized against the extension of federal power, the spread of unions, and the demand for civil rights. Truman's civil rights program was blocked in Congress; African-Americans were beaten when they sought to register to vote; union organizers were harassed; and legal stratagems were employed to keep schools segregated. In the early 1950s the growth in the number of black voters came to a halt, and southern election campaigns were increasingly characterized by xenophobic anticommunism and outright appeals to white supremacy. "Northern political labor leaders have recently ordered that all doors be opened to Negroes on union property," declared one election flyer. "This will lead to whites and Negroes working and living together. . . . Do you want that?"

Even the U.S. Supreme Court's landmark 1954 decision, *Brown* v. *Board of Education*, did little to thwart southern white militancy. The *Brown* case represented the climax of an extended legal campaign by the NAACP that, year after year, had chipped away at the "separate but equal" façade of legalized "Jim Crow." Basing his opinion on the Fourteenth Amendment, adopted at the height of the Reconstruction era, and new evidence on the psychological impact of segregation, Chief Justice Earl Warren declared segregated public schools unconstitutional. African-Americans and others favoring integration celebrated, but their hopes for rapid change were tempered the next year by the Court's plan to implement the *Brown* decision. Seeking to avoid offense to the white South, the Court called for desegregation not at once but with "all deliberate speed," a confusing and cautious phrase. Meanwhile, President Eisenhower expressed distaste for the *Brown* decision, asserting, "It's all very well to talk about

Back of the bus, 1951. Segregated seating on a southern streetcar.

school integration—if you remember that we may also be talking about social *dis*integration."

Federal ambivalence encouraged white segregationists. In their 1956 "Southern Manifesto," 101 congressmen and senators vowed opposition to the Court's order, while a quarter million of their constituents joined local White Citizens' Councils to defend segregation. African-Americans pushing for the implementation of *Brown* were met with harassment and intimidation. Southern politicians, led by Virginia governor Harry F. Byrd, called for "massive resistance" to school integration, African-American voting rights, and social reform.

The 1957 battle to integrate Central High School in Little Rock, Arkansas, dramatized the political conflict. Although local school officials were prepared to desegregate, Governor Orville Faubus (who was in the midst of a tight reelection battle) created a crisis by sending National Guardsmen to block the entry of black schoolchildren and preserve "order" at Central High. After stirring local emotion on the issue, Faubus withdrew the troops and let a shrieking crowd chase six black teenagers from the school. President Eisenhower reluctantly federalized the Arkansas Guard and sent a thousand paratroopers to Little Rock. In response, Faubus prevented integration by closing the city's public high schools for the entire year, a strategy also adopted in many Virginia counties. Across the South, the number of school districts engaging in even token desegregation fell from 712 in the first three years after the *Brown* decision to just 49 between 1957 and 1960.

It took a new, decade-long campaign of mass protest and civil disobedience to break the back of white supremacy in the South. Inspired in part by the rise of anticolonial movements in Africa and elsewhere, the second phase of the modern civil rights movement mobilized blacks throughout the South as well as in the urban North, and replaced the trade unions with the black church as the key institution around which the movement would coalesce.

The new movement was born in the heart of Dixie—Montgomery, Alabama, where the Confederate flag still flew over the state capitol building. Montgomery had felt the stirrings of postwar social change: The African-American population had doubled; nearby Maxwell Air Force Base was largely integrated; and the city had even begun to build a new sports stadium without separate entrances for white and "colored." But the city's theaters, schools, parks, and restaurants remained segregated. And nothing rankled Montgomery's black community more than the segregated bus system. It was a twice-daily humiliation. Blacks had to pay their fare in the front, then get off the bus and reenter in the back. If the bus began to fill with

Montgomery, Alabama, 1956.
Evidence of the effectiveness of the
year-long bus boycott.

whites they had to give up their seat. White drivers would often shout "Niggers get back!" when the bus got crowded.

On a cold December afternoon in 1955, Rosa Parks, a longtime NAACP activist, refused to cooperate with this humiliating ritual. Tired from a long day at the department store where she worked as a seamstress, she kept her seat as whites crowded into the bus. "I felt it was just something I had to do," she later recalled. She was taken to jail and charged with violating a city segregation ordinance. Word of her arrest spread through the community, and within hours, African-American leaders decided to boycott the city bus system in protest. E. D. Nixon, president of the Alabama NAACP and head of the local Brotherhood of Sleeping Car Porters, knew that the black community would rally around Rosa Parks, for she was no ordinary seamstress. For twelve years she had worked as NAACP secretary. "She was decent, and she was committed," Nixon remembered, "so when she stood up to talk, people'd shut up and listen. And when she did something people just figured it was the right thing to do."

While Nixon and a host of churchwomen organized black-owned taxis and church vans to replace the buses, Montgomery's African-American ministers chose as their spokesperson the Rev. Dr. Martin Luther King, Jr., a twenty-six year old whose inspiring speeches helped sustain the pioneering protesters. King told more than five thousand blacks on the first night of the boycott:

> There comes a time when people get tired. We are here this
> evening to say to those who have mistreated us so long that
> we are tired—tired of being segregated and humiliated,

tired of being kicked about by the brutal feet of oppression. . . . If you will protest courageously and yet with dignity and Christian love, in the history books that are written in future generations, historians will have to pause and say "there lived a great people—a black people—who injected new meaning and dignity into the veins of civilization."

The thirteen-month-long boycott demonstrated how a social movement creates its own momentum. African-American demands were initially modest: greater courtesy toward black passengers; employment of African-American drivers in black neighborhoods; and an easing—but not an end to—segregated seating on the buses. However, as week after week passed, Montgomery's black citizens grew more confident of their ability to stick together and resist white in-

"WE WERE PREPARED . . ."

Groups in Montgomery's African-American community had organized against segregationist laws for many years before Rosa Parks refused to give up her seat on the bus. The Women's Political Council, an organization of black working-class and middle-class women formed in 1946, had vigorously protested the segregated bus system. Jo Ann Robinson, president of the WPC and an English teacher at the all-black Alabama State College, describes what her organization did to help organize the bus boycott.

Fred Gray told me Rosa Parks was arrested. Her case would be on Monday. He said to me, "Jo Ann, if you have ever planned to do anything with the council, now is your time." I called all the officers of the three chapters, I called as many of the men who had supported us as I could reach, and I told them that Rosa Parks had been arrested and she would be tried. They said, "You have the plans, put them into operation." We had worked for at least three years getting that thing organized.

The Women's Political Council had begun in 1946, after just dozens of black people had been arrested on the buses for segregation purposes. By 1955, we had members in every elementary, junior high, and senior high school, and in federal, state, and local jobs. Wherever there were more than ten blacks employed, we had a member there. We were prepared to the point that we knew that in a matter of hours, we could corral the whole city.

I didn't go to bed that night. I cut stencils and took them to the college. . . . We ran off thirty-five thousand copies. After I had talked with every WPC member in the elementary, junior high, and senior high schools to have somebody on the campus during the day so I could deliver them, I took them to school with me in

timidation. Eventually they decided they would be satisfied with nothing short of complete integration.

By the time the U.S. Supreme Court ruled that Montgomery buses must integrate, a new civil rights movement had been born. Although black ministers and later black college students were the organizing cadre of this movement, its real strength came from its capacity to mobilize tens of thousands of African-American working people. A strategy of nonviolent civil disobedience proved particularly effective in exposing the hypocrisy of legally segregated institutions and generating support from the northern liberal-labor community, although it did little to dampen the violence of white vigilantes. By its example, the civil rights movement helped create a new mood in America, which slowly dissolved the frozen politics of the early 1950s and opened the way to a civic culture that became increasingly democratic and participatory in the 1960s.

my car. I taught my classes from eight o'clock to ten o'clock. When my ten o'clock class was over, I took two senior students with me and I had the flyers in my car, bundled and ready to be given out. I would drive to the place of dissemination, and a kid would be there to grab them. I was on the campus and off before anybody knew that I was there.

Most of the people got the message, but there were outlying areas that didn't. And one lone black woman, who was so faithful to her white lady, as she called it, went back to work and took one of the circulars to this woman so she would know what the blacks had planned. When the woman got it, she immediately called the media. After that, the television, the radio, and the evening newspapers told those persons whom we had not reached that there would be a boycott. So the die was cast.

Monday morning, December the fifth, 1955, I shall never forget because many of us had not gone to bed that night. It was the day of the boycott. We had been up waiting for the first buses to pass to see if any riders were on them. It was a cold morning, cloudy, there was a threat of rain, and we were afraid that if it rained the people would get on the bus. But as the buses began to roll, and there were one or two on some of them, none on some of them, then we began to realize that the people were cooperating and that they were going to stay off the bus that first day. What helped us to keep them off, too, was that the police department had decided that they would put a police on a motorcycle with a white cap who would accompany the buses and any of the blacks who wanted to get on. They would help them to get on without what they called "the goon squads" keeping them from riding. And that helped out the cause because those few blacks who were going to ride were afraid that the police who were following the buses would hurt them. So they didn't ride. As a result, a very negligible number of riders rode that first day.

Birmingham, Alabama, 1963.

THE RIGHTS-CONSCIOUS 1960s

AS THE 1960s opened, America seemed to many observers to be on the verge of a golden age. The presidency of the youthful John F. Kennedy, elected in 1960, seemed to give Americans a feeling of success, matching imperial splendor abroad with prosperity, harmony, and progress at home. By the end of the 1960s, however, these assumptions were no longer self-evident. Using mass protests to mobilize public opinion, the civil rights movement shook the country and sparked a broad wave of popular activism that called for the full realization of America's democratic promise. And just as the African-American freedom struggle reached its peak, the Vietnam War brought to the surface of national life the political contradictions of the Cold War.

During the 1960s and early 1970s, millions of ordinary Americans came to feel that they could make their collective weight felt on issues once handled behind the closed doors of the county courthouse or the corporate boardroom. This growing sense of "rights consciousness" brought to public attention the heretofore unfocused grievances of group after group in American society: those defined by ethnicity, such as Latinos and Native Americans, and also those defined by age, gender, and sexual orientation.

The labor movement played an ambiguous role in the diverse social movements of this period. Many working people took part, especially in movements such as the civil rights movement, which was powered by the actions of poor and working-class African-Americans. And some unions supported aspects of the civil rights struggle. But most movements of the 1960s did not focus on economic issues; and, in contrast to the movements of the 1930s, unions did not play a significant leadership role.

Social activism in the 1960s had its ideological roots in a sense that all things were finally possible in affluent, postwar America; and that hypocrisy, of either a personal or a social sort, would no longer be tolerated. This earthly "perfectionism," like that which had motivated abolitionists William Lloyd Garrison and John Brown before the Civil War and socialist Eugene Debs and reformer Jane Addams in the nineteenth and early twentieth centuries, gave enormous spirit and energy to the social movements around which so much of the politics of the 1960s revolved.

And like the antebellum reformers who linked temperance and abolition, social reform and salvation, many activists of the 1960s also affirmed that "the personal is political." Through the politicized spiritualism of the African-American church, the counterculture of the New Left, and the consciousness-raising groups of the women's movement, this spirit of personal liberation laid the basis for a strong sense of movement culture, which partially compensated for activists' failure to build strong institutions that could sustain their influence. "In most basic terms," a student activist of the mid-1960s remembered, "what the Movement provided for me was a sense of purpose and a feeling of community which had been missing from my life before then."

By the early 1970s, the spread of new social values had begun to transform the workplace as well, creating new demands: for a fair shake in hiring and promotion; for a healthy and safe environment; and for personal recognition and dignity where none had existed before. Although trade unions played a relatively limited role in the progressive political changes of the period, the social movements of the 1960s at least partially revived the grass-roots militancy that had once been part of the culture of the American working class.

THE SIT-IN MOVEMENT

On February 1, 1960, four neatly dressed African-American students from North Carolina A&T College violated a municipal ordinance by taking seats at a Greensboro Woolworth's lunch counter to demand the service traditionally denied them. While Franklin McCain, Ezell Blair, Joe McNeil, and David Richmond had only decided to "sit in" a few days before, the whole of their lives had prepared them for this struggle. Barely teenagers when the U.S. Supreme Court declared public school segregation unconstitutional, they had ruefully attended segregated schools, followed news of the Montgomery bus boycott, and joined the activist NAACP Youth Council. Once in college they discussed civil rights constantly in class and in the local churches they attended.

"All of us were afraid," recalled David Richmond, "but we went and did it." When the four freshmen took seats at the lunch counter, a nervous waitress refused them service. The four stayed in their seats, saying they would sit at the counter until served.

Woolworth sit-in, May 28, 1963. White youths shower abuse and food on a Tougaloo College professor and students staging a sit-in at a segregated lunch counter in Jackson, Mississippi. After soda, ketchup, mustard, and sugar failed to deter them, the civil rights demonstraters were doused with spray paint and beaten.

The sit-in galvanized other A&T students. Several dozen returned to Woolworth's the next day, followed by hundreds more each afternoon until the city closed the store a week later. By then, a network of church and student activists had begun leading sit-ins throughout the upper South. At least 70,000 persons, most of them African-Americans, participated in sit-ins in more than a hundred cities in the winter and spring of 1960. "I felt at the time it was like a crusade," Nashville sit-in leader John Lewis remembered. Gangs of white youths often taunted the students, poured ketchup on their hair, and knocked them to the floor.

The sit-ins pumped new life into the civil rights movement. They demonstrated that mass civil disobedience and nonviolent confrontation were effective tactics with a powerful appeal to young black men and women. In April, at a conference called by the Rev. Dr. Martin Luther King, Jr., sit-in activists organized the Student Nonviolent Coordinating Committee (SNCC), which would serve for the next several years as the vanguard of the movement. SNCC was never a large organization, but its members, predominantly young African-Americans, were creative and dedicated: "commando raiders," one observer called them, "on the more dangerous and exposed fronts of the racial struggle."

Civil rights activism operated on several levels in the early 1960s. At one level, activists launched sit-ins and demonstrations to demand desegregation and respect from city politicians and the owners of downtown businesses. In these confrontations with local white elites, civil rights activists proved partly successful. Many lunch counters were desegregated, but others were not. SNCC voting registration drives proved dangerous and difficult in Mississippi and Alabama; and despite numerous demonstrations and jailings, white officials in Albany, Georgia, and St. Augustine, Florida, refused to open up jobs or beaches to the black community.

In addition to their immediate impact, civil rights protests were designed to draw national attention to racial injustice and prompt the federal government to take a more active role in the struggle. In May 1961, the Congress of Racial Equality (CORE), a civil rights group based primarily in the North, organized a series of "Freedom Rides" to test recent court orders mandating the integration of southern bus terminals. "Our intention," CORE leader James Farmer later explained, "was to provoke the southern authorities into arresting us and thereby prod the Justice Department into enforcing the law. . . ." When the integrated group of Freedom Riders reached Alabama, white mobs burned one of their buses and, with the tacit approval of local police, savagely attacked the riders. But SNCC bolstered the Freedom Riders with new volunteers, who soon filled Mississippi's jails. Federal marshals finally had to stop the mob violence, and the

Kennedy administration was forced to ensure compliance with the desegregation orders.

While attacking local instances of segregation and seeking action from the federal government, civil rights strategy also aimed to create grass-roots organizations to serve as vehicles of empowerment for African-American communities. Most participants in the early sit-ins and Freedom Rides were students, but local organizing helped enlist all segments of the black community. African-American maids, farm tenants, and laborers who worked for white employers had traditionally been more cautious than ministers and businessmen, who derived their income from the black community. But the sit-ins and Freedom Rides opened the way for broader activity and organization. This change became clear during a year-long series of demonstrations in the town of Albany, Georgia, in 1961 and 1962.

"THEY SHOT THE TIRES OUT . . ."

Volunteers from all over the country arrived in the South to integrate the segregated southern buses on a series of "Freedom Rides" organized by the Congress for Racial Equality. One Freedom Rider, Hank Thomas, recalls the destruction of an integrated bus by a white mob in Anniston, Alabama, on May 14, 1961.

The Freedom Ride didn't really get rough until we got down in the Deep South. Needless to say, Anniston, Alabama, I'm never gonna forget that. When I was on the bus they [whites] threw some kind of incendiary device on. I got real scared then. You know, I was thinking—I'm looking out the window there, and people are out there yelling and screaming. They [whites] just about broke every window out of the bus.... I really thought that that was going to be the end of me. They shot the tires out, and the bus driver was forced to stop.... And we were trapped on the bus.

It wasn't until the thing [smoke bomb] was shot on the bus and the bus caught afire that everything got out of control.... First they [whites] closed the doors and wouldn't let us off. But then I'm pretty sure ... that somebody said, "Hey, the bus is gonna explode ..." and so they started scattering, and I guess that's the way we got off the bus. Otherwise, we probably all would have been succumbed by the smoke.... I got whacked over the head with a rock or I think a stick as I was coming off the bus.

The bus started exploding, and a lot of people were cut by flying glass.... Took us to the hospital, and it was incredible. The people at the hospital would not do anything for us. They would not. And I was saying "You're doctors, you're medical personnel." They wouldn't.... But strangely enough, even those bad things don't stick in my mind that much. Not that I'm full of love and goodwill for everybody in my heart, but I chalk it off to part of the things that I'm going to be able to sit on my front porch in my rocking chair and tell my young'uns about, my grandchildren about.

SNCC activists met with high-school and college students, farmers, day laborers, and ordinary churchwomen in Albany, as well as with local African-American leaders. Soon a coalition organization emerged to mobilize the entire community for a precedent-setting civil disobedience campaign. Demanding integration of stores, restaurants, bus stations, and schools, protesters filled Albany's jails week after week. Children as young as eleven and twelve were prominent in these demonstrations. Going to jail, which for southern African-Americans had been a shameful as well as a dangerous experience, now became a badge of courage. One of twenty Albany blacks spent time behind bars.

African-American women formed the backbone of the Albany movement and other community organizations built by the civil rights movement. "There is always a 'mama,'" commented SNCC's Georgia project director, Charles Sher-

Mississippi, 1963. Volunteers visit a Ruleville, Mississippi, home during a SNCC voter registration drive.

rod. "She is usually a militant woman in the community, outspoken, understanding, and willing to catch Hell, having already caught her share." These women were often the largest and most dynamic element within the black church, sometimes forcing ministers to open their churches to civil rights workers.

In Ruleville, Mississippi, Fanny Lou Hamer emerged as the determined leader of a voter registration drive launched by SNCC in early 1962. A tenant farmer, Hamer was forced off her land after she refused her landlord's demand that she take her name off the voter registration list. Repeatedly arrested and beaten, Hamer was not intimidated. "The only thing they could do to me was kill me, and it seemed like they'd been trying to do that a little bit at a time ever since I could remember." Hamer's courageous spirit soon made her a leader of the statewide movement.

Television broadcasts and magazines kept the civil rights movement's message before millions of people, and it soon captured the attention of thousands of white students from northern colleges. Rennie Davis, son of a Truman administration economist, was at Oberlin College when news of the sit-ins hit campus. "Here were four students from Greensboro who were suddenly all over *Life* maga-

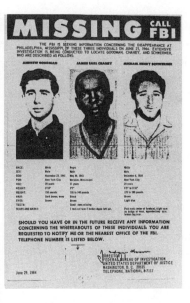

Missing. The notice issued by the FBI in June 1964 for missing civil rights workers Andrew Goodman, James Chaney, and Michael Schwerner.

zine," he remembered. "There was a feeling that they were us and we were them, and a recognition that they were expressing something we were feeling as well, and they'd won the attention of the country."

The southern civil rights movement was overwhelmingly black, except during the Freedom Summer campaign of 1964, when SNCC and CORE organized hundreds of northern student volunteers to help register black voters in Mississippi. Civil rights leaders expected the presence of white students to focus the nation's attention on Deep South racism. The strategy worked, all too tragically. In mid-June, three civil rights workers were reported missing: James Chaney, an African-American activist from Meridian, Mississippi; Michael Schwerner, a white CORE activist from New York City; and Andrew Goodman, a summer volunteer from Queens College in New York City. Federal agents eventually uncovered their mangled bodies: Klansmen and Mississippi police had kidnapped the activists and beaten them to death with clubs and chains. The deaths, together with the Freedom Summer campaign, helped northerners grasp the ferocity of southern white resistance and the necessity of federal action.

Civil rights activity put federal officials on the spot. In the early 1960s, President John F. Kennedy found the movement divisive and embarrassing. By revealing America's racism, the movement made it more difficult for Kennedy to woo the newly independent nations of Africa and Asia. And the growing civil rights battle also made it harder for Kennedy to retain the support of the all-white southern congressional delegation, which held veto power over his legislative agenda. The president and his brother Robert, the attorney general, supported integration, but they also wanted political stability. During the Freedom Rides, the Kennedys called on southern governors to suppress white violence, but they also urged CORE and SNCC to end the rides and focus instead on voter registration. In 1962, the president mobilized federal troops to guarantee the admission of James Meredith to the all-white University of Mississippi. But the Kennedys still tried to prevent the civil rights struggle from becoming a dominant national issue.

In the spring of 1963, the battle to desegregate Birmingham, Alabama, made headlines throughout America and the world. Using the model of organization and mobilization SNCC had pioneered in Albany, Dr. King's Southern Christian Leadership Conference (SCLC) and Birmingham blacks forged a tightly knit community of struggle. In Birmingham's largest Baptist church, mass meetings were held for sixty-five consecutive nights, often followed by downtown marches that ended in arrest or police attack. The Birmingham police, under command of Eugene "Bull" Connor, used fire hoses and police dogs to disperse marchers. Thousands of high-school students singing "freedom songs" joined the protests, as did hundreds of African-American workers from the city's steel mills and coke ovens. "I have stood in a meeting with hundreds of youngsters and joined in while they sang 'Ain't Gonna Let Nobody Turn Me 'Round,'" explained King to a northern audience. "It is not just a song, it is a resolve. . . . These songs bind us together, give us courage together, help us to march together."

After masses of black teenagers peacefully but repeatedly disrupted downtown Birmingham, the city's economic elite decided that maintaining segregation was not worth the price they would have to pay. Birmingham officials agreed to desegregate municipal facilities and open downtown businesses to African-American patronage and employment. By then, the Birmingham protests had sent a shock wave throughout the nation. Two things were happening at the same time. First, the Birmingham demonstrations signaled the transition from a protest movement seeking desegregation to a mass movement demanding fundamental economic and social change. King embodied this new focus when, on one key march, he replaced his suit and tie with the bib overalls of the farm laborer.

Second, Birmingham helped the civil rights movement reach out to northerners. The televised image of Birmingham police dogs attacking defenseless marchers helped swing northern public opinion massively against segregation. Northern civil rights activists seized the moment to point out that racism was a nationwide problem. In 1963, there were actually more demonstrations and marches above the Mason-Dixon line than below it. In San Francisco, Detroit, and New York City, hundreds of thousands of blacks and whites marched side by side. Scores more demonstrations followed: construction-site protests demanding more jobs for minority youth; school boycotts designed to end segregation and increase funding at inner-city schools; picket lines protesting police brutality. There were an amazing 758 demonstrations during the summer of 1963. More than half of all African-Americans polled by a national newsmagazine reported a sense of "personal obligation" to get involved.

A. Philip Randolph, the African-American trade unionist whose threat of a 1941 march on Washington had helped integrate World War II war plants, now unveiled plans for a new mass demonstration in the capital to demand jobs, housing, and higher wages for blacks. Backed by the United Auto Workers and other liberal trade unions, the August 1963 "March on Washington for Jobs and Freedom" brought to the capital a crowd of almost a quarter million, at that time the largest political gathering in U.S. history. Defying conservative's predictions of a drunken riot, the racially integrated march was peaceful and dignified. On the steps of the Lincoln Memorial, Dr.

King delivered a speech that articulated a broad moral vision of the civil rights movement, a singular synthesis of Christian idealism and appeals to America's highest principles of freedom and equality. "I have a dream," he declared, "that one day this nation will rise up and live out the true meaning of its creed . . . when the sons of former slaves and the sons of former slaveowners will be able to sit together at the table of brotherhood."

Skillfully defining themselves within America's mainstream reform tradition, King and other civil rights leaders rode a massive wave of public support. President Kennedy and other Democratic Party leaders were forced to respond. Kennedy declared racial segregation a powerful "moral issue" that required tough new laws outlawing segregation in public places, integrating public schools, and prohibiting discrimination wherever federal money was spent. Kennedy was still concerned about how to control the movement and limit its possible repercussions; he secretly approved FBI plans to tap the telephones of movement leaders, including King. Outwardly, however, Kennedy and his administration embraced the March on Washington. The vision and determination of civil rights activists and "ordinary" African-American working people had generated a nationwide outpouring too powerful for even a president to ignore.

THE LIBERAL HOUR

The civil rights movement reopened the door to reform in American politics, a door that had been shut tight since the waning years of the Great Depression. For more than a generation, the conservative alliance between the white South and northern business had successfully resisted extension of the welfare state. The civil rights movement broke this stalemate by isolating southern conservatives and breathing new life into the liberal-labor coalition that had backed New Deal reforms a generation earlier.

After Kennedy's November 1963 assassination in Dallas, the new president, Texan Lyndon Johnson, championed the reform impulse, both as a way to legitimate his unexpected assumption of presidential power and to accommodate growing pressure from the African-American community. In January 1964 Johnson declared an "unconditional War on Poverty" in his State of the Union address, and then in the spring and summer used his persuasive political skills to win passage of Kennedy's long-delayed Civil Rights Act.

The presidential elections of 1964 ratified this great shift in the political balance. In a polarized contest, Johnson won 61 percent of the electorate, defeating Republican conservative Barry Goldwater, whose Senate vote against the Civil Rights Act attracted heavy support from white southerners but alienated Republican moderates. Riding on Johnson's coattails, the Democrats won staggering majorities in both the House (295 to 140) and Senate (68 to 32). This landslide ushered in a brief era of liberal politics during which almost all of Lyndon Johnson's "Great Society" legislation was written into law.

At the heart of the Great Society was the legal revolution in civil rights. The federal government put its moral and legal weight behind the black movement, insisting for a few years that traditional elites in business and politics must conform to a national standard mandating legal equality for minorities and women. The Equal Employment Opportunity Commission, set up under the 1964 Civil Rights Act, championed demands for equitable hiring and promotion practices in private employment. Newspaper help-wanted columns, which for years had listed jobs for "white" and "colored" as well as for "men" and "women," abolished these distinctions.

In a similar fashion, the Voting Rights Act of 1965, passed after Alabama authorities violently resisted a drive to register African-Americans to vote, gave the attorney general the right to supervise registration in areas where less than half of all eligible voters were registered. The new law sent thousands of federal voter registrars into the "Black Belt" counties of the South, and within a decade put two million additional African-Americans on the voting rolls. As a result the South underwent its greatest political transformation since the end of Reconstruction. By the 1970s, there were thousands of black elected officials in the South, from mayors and sheriffs to state legislators and congressional representatives.

The newly energized reform forces also allowed President Johnson to secure congressional enactment of his broader Great Society program. In five years, Congress dramatically increased federal aid to public schools, enacted new programs of federal health insurance for the elderly (Medicare) and the poor (Medicaid), and liberalized the immigration laws to eliminate the racist quota system that had been in effect since 1924.

Great Society programs doubled the proportion of the nation's total income going to pay for the social welfare of its people. The bulk of this spending went for "entitlement programs" available to the middle class as well as the poor—Social Security, Medicare, and unemployment compensation. Because these programs benefited a wide spectrum of the population, they were largely free of controversy. At the same time, Johnson launched his highly publicized War on Poverty. In the early 1960s, socialist Michael Harrington's *The Other America* had called national attention to the existence of pervasive poverty amid growing affluence. President Kennedy responded by asking advisers to draft a "War on Poverty." After Kennedy's death, Johnson made the project his own.

In the postwar era, most Americans believed that the national economy offered unlimited opportunity; therefore the poor must be responsible for their own plight. Most federal officials who planned the War on Poverty shared this belief; their proposals assumed that poverty could be eliminated by teaching the poor to take advantage of the opportunities open to them. The War on Poverty included some financial aid to poor people, in the form of the Food Stamps and Aid to Families with Dependent Children programs; but most of the attention of poverty officials went to programs of job training, drug rehabilitation, and work counseling. As one New Jersey antipoverty official later recalled, "The antipoverty program was premised on the assumption that poverty existed primarily in the heads of the poor."

The War on Poverty achieved limited gains. As a result of government programs and a strong economy, total poverty declined in the United States, but inequalities of power and income remained. The number of poor people, as defined by the U.S. government, decreased from 23 percent of the population in 1962 to 11 percent in 1973. Nevertheless, the increase in welfare spending that began in the mid-1960s hardly made a dent in the class structure or the general distribution of income. Furthermore, from 1965 to 1975, taxpayers at the bottom fifth of the income ladder saw their tax rate more than double, while the one-tenth of taxpayers with the highest incomes saw their burden drop by 16 percent.

Why did the War on Poverty fail to have a deeper and more enduring effect? Part of the reason was that federal officials failed to address one of the root causes of postwar poverty: the structural changes in the postwar economy that made it increasingly difficult for poor people to earn a decent living. The decline of the Appalachian coal industry in the 1950s had thrown more than half a million miners out of work. The mechanization of southern cotton production had pushed millions of African-Americans off the land. Economic changes in both Puerto Rico and Mexico had crippled labor-intensive agriculture, forcing millions of Latinos with few economic resources into northern cities. These massive population movements took place at precisely the time that industry was fleeing to the suburbs, stripping central cities of more than a million blue-collar jobs. These structural changes doomed millions of Americans, especially minorities and women, to a "secondary labor market" characterized by low-paying, insecure, nonunion jobs.

In some cases it was outright discrimination that forced African-Americans, Mexican-Americans, Puerto Ricans, and women to stay in low-paying, nonunion jobs. In the late 1950s and early 1960s, such jobs as trash collector, hospital orderly, janitor, and office clerk fit this description. Yet when the civil rights laws of the 1960s were implemented, this secondary labor market did not disappear. Low-paying jobs, and the poverty that went with them, proliferated along with the growth of the service sector.

"... WE ARE POOR BUT WE KNOW WHAT WE WANT"

The War on Poverty was supposed to be conducted with "maximum feasible participation" on the part of the poor communities being served. But those who tried to act upon this mandate came into conflict with established bureaucracies and political machines. The Woodlawn Organization, a community group representing a poor Chicago neighborhood, sought to help shape local War on Poverty policy. Testifying before Congress in April 1965, the organization's president, the Rev. Lynward Stevenson, expressed his frustration.

Why haven't we, the Woodlawn Organization, a grassroots neighborhood community organization representing the Greater Woodlawn Community, been allowed to fight the War on Poverty? Is it that we are too stupid, that we are poor, that we are Negroes, that we are like children who must be planned for? . . .

The Organization which elected me its President has said to the city of Chicago, "All right, we are poor, but we know what we want and we will fight in the great American tradition to get it." We have told the city of Chicago we will fight for jobs, for an end of slumlord exploitation, for an end to dead-end ghetto schools, for security from "Negro removal" via the bulldozer. This is SELF-DETERMINATION. That is what drove this nation into its birth, and brought forth every historical advance since.

. . . We took hope when Congress and President Johnson proposed to the nation the War on Poverty. It meant to us that this can be our great leap forward into an open, integrated, equal country. In Chicago, [however,] there is no War on Poverty. There is only more of the ancient, galling war *against* the poor.

It is a war against the poor when only the rich benefit from public funds. It is a war against the poor when the white-shirted social workers, the bankers who run the powerful charities, the ward committeemen get fat off money appropriated to help the poor lift themselves off the bottom.

It is a war against the poor when we are told by the President and Congress that we can plan for ourselves, but then find that we can only stand in the waiting rooms of Chicago's city hall, while plans are made for us. It is a war against the poor when the Chicago Committee deals out its money to people whose knowledge of the poor comes from the television set. Oh, it is not a war of guns and explosives. It is an undeclared war by the rich and by the local politicians. What they want to do is to destroy our dignity. That is why they insist on planning for us.

I am here to tell you that we want the Federal law on maximum feasible local participation enforced in Chicago. My people want it. The 40,000 poor of Greater Woodlawn who make up the Woodlawn Organization want it. . . .

Before we will be shorn of our dignity we will go into the streets. For the rich of this land must understand this is our dignity, our place in America that we are struggling for. And our dignity can no longer be bought for a pittance, or decided by others.

The War on Poverty refrained from attacking the structural causes of poverty because to do so would have required a far greater commitment—political as well as financial—than the president and Congress were willing to make. The collapse of one federal government initiative, the Community Action Program (CAP), revealed the limits of the War on Poverty. The CAP segment of the antipoverty legislation ordered that residents of impoverished areas be allowed "maximum feasible participation" in running the programs that affected their communities. Within two years more than a thousand Community Action agencies had sprung up across the nation, many infused with the spirit of the civil rights movement. Taking the Johnson administration at its word, the new agencies challenged the ways local officials used federal antipoverty funds. Often this involved mobilizing the poor to picket City Hall and filing lawsuits against city and state officials. "The mood of applicants in welfare waiting rooms had changed," reported two observers. "They were no longer as humble, as self-effacing, as pleading. They were indignant, angrier, more demanding."

The local elites who had long controlled federal largess were naturally outraged. "We are experiencing a class struggle in the traditional Karl Marx style," asserted one city official in Syracuse, New York. This was an exaggeration, but it did point to very real conflict. Those who were troubled by agitation, one political activist warned, "should bear in mind that poverty is a reflection of class differentials in power."

When local elites demanded an end to this federally sponsored challenge to their power, the White House pulled back. After 1966, funding for experimental antipoverty programs declined, and governors and mayors assumed the right to take over any community-based agency they did not like. Unwilling to back programs that challenged local political bosses, administration officials never even considered undertaking the struggle with major corporations that would have been necessary to address the structural causes of poverty. As a result, Johnson's "unconditional War on Poverty" turned out to be not much more than a skirmish.

BLACK POWER

Just as Great Society liberalism failed to shift the structures of power in American society, so, too, did it prove inadequate to the new mood that swept black America. At the time of the March on Washington, the civil rights movement seemed to be the culminating affirmation of a liberal faith in the harmonious perfectibility of American institutions. In a passionate speech calling for the passage of the 1965 Voting Rights Act, President Johnson himself declared that "we shall overcome." Yet at the moment of its greatest triumph, the movement revealed that dignity and freedom for African-Americans could not be won without a fundamental challenge to the existing distribution of power in the United States.

This process began as early as the summer of 1964, when civil rights forces in Mississippi challenged the legitimacy of the segregationist white Democrats who composed the state delegation to the Democratic National Convention in Atlantic City. Calling itself the Mississippi Freedom Democratic Party (MFDP), this largely African-American group hoped the convention would throw out the segregationists and seat the MFDP instead. The MFDP took the moral high ground when Fannie Lou Hamer told convention delegates of her efforts to vote in Mississippi. "I was beaten until I was exhausted," she told a national TV audience. "All of this on account we wanted to register, to become first-class citizens. [If] the Freedom Democratic Party is not seated now, I question America."

This was Lyndon Johnson's convention, however, and he would brook no challenges to his authority. Johnson wanted to sweep the fall elections, and to do so he felt he needed votes from the white South, votes that would be lost if the MFDP challenge were sustained. The president ordered Minnesota senator Hubert Humphrey, his prospective running mate and one of the party's foremost liberals, to turn back the MFDP challenge. Humphrey recruited other key liberals, including the UAW's Walter Reuther. Humphrey and his allies forged a "compromise" plan that seated the white Mississippians, gave the MFDP two delegate slots, and mandated racially integrated state delegations in future years.

The MFDP angrily rejected this plan. "We want much more than 'token' positions," explained SNCC's Charles Sherrod. "We want power for our people." The MFDP experience convinced many activists that "white liberals" such as Humphrey and Reuther could not be trusted and that a radical break with mainstream politics was necessary. "We are a country of racists, with a racist heritage, [and] a racist economy," thundered the normally soft-spoken Sherrod, "and we need a naked confrontation with ourselves."

In the years that followed the Atlantic City debacle, the battle against racial injustice took on an increasingly bitter tone. Beginning in the summer of 1965, Los Angeles, Cleveland, Newark, and other cities were swept by fierce street battles and massive fires as urban African-Americans fought police and focused the national spotlight on racial tensions in the North. Hundreds were killed, thousands injured, and millions of dollars' worth of property destroyed as upheavals scarred more than two hundred American cities.

Urban racial violence was hardly new in American history: in 1919 and 1943, race riots had churned through Chicago and Detroit

Bayonets on Linwood and Hazelwood. African-American residents gaze at a Michigan National Guard patrol on the second day of the Detroit riot.

with murderous result. But until the end of World War II such disturbances had largely consisted of white vigilante attacks on African-American city dwellers. The riots of the 1960s were different: in response to incidents of police hostility and discrimination, blacks took angry action against white-owned ghetto property. Fires and looting erupted. Police and National Guardsmen escalated the violence with mass arrests, brutal beatings, and murderous, indiscriminate gunfire. Tanks and armored troop carriers rumbled through city streets, raking apartment houses with heavy machine-gun fire. America's cities were transformed into deadly combat zones.

Newspaper headlines blamed the violence and bloodshed on small groups of radical agitators and heavily armed black snipers. Later investigations revealed that the vast majority of casualties were African-Americans shot by government forces. In Detroit, where newspapers' sniping claims were shrill, reporters later admitted that such gunmen had caused at most three of the city's forty-three riot-related deaths and that two of those were doubtful cases. A presidential commission found that the riots were not the work of a small group; large numbers of African-Americans had taken part, including many who held steady jobs and helped support their families. Property destruction was targeted, not indiscriminate. Much like the patriot crowds who had stormed the houses of Tory officials during the American Revolution, rioters demonstrated a rough sense of social justice. Looting and arson was generally directed against stores that charged excessive prices or sold inferior goods. Homes, churches, and schools usually were spared.

Investigators also spotlighted the social problems that lay behind the upheavals. Detroit, for example, had long been a mecca for black migrants; but in the 1950s and early 1960s the auto companies built new manufacturing plants in all-white suburbs such as Livonia and Wyandotte, leaving the central city with outmoded factories and a decaying downtown shopping district. Although manufacturing boomed in Michigan during most of the 1960s, Detroit's unemployment rate rarely dropped below 10 percent. As a result, the median income of African-Americans remained at about 55 percent that of whites. As the city's tax base dwindled, schools were understaffed and poorly maintained, and social services began to unravel. The civil rights movement brought hope that something could be done to end these problems, but the persistence of rats, rapacious landlords, and racial prejudice fed bitterness and anger.

In the Watts ghetto of Los Angeles the situation was even worse: unemployment remained stuck at 20 percent; three of every five Watts residents received some sort of welfare benefit. On the street, teenagers bitterly resented the treatment handed out by the nearly all-white Los Angeles Police Department (LAPD), which many saw as an alien, occupying army. The LAPD seemed to make arrests less to enforce the law than to intimidate young African-Americans. One study showed that 90 percent of juveniles arrested never had charges filed against them. Meanwhile, Watts residents confronted other reminders that they lived in a racist society. In 1964, a huge majority of white Californians voted to repeal a state law banning racial discrimination in the sale and rental of housing. "Everyone was angry that it had even come up," said a black teacher active in the election. "Everybody in Watts was aware that they were being rejected by somebody, by somebody white."

Blacks' frustrations were heightened by the sense that other Americans were enjoying growing affluence. When the Watts riot erupted, involving as many as 80,000 people, one Los Angeles resident explained that it was as if the community were saying, "We're hungry. Our schools stink. We're getting the shit beat out of us. We've tried the integration route. It's obvious the integration route ain't going to work. Now we've got to go another way."

Many white Americans saw the riots as fearsome outbreaks of criminal insanity. White suburbanites rushed to gun stores to arm themselves, and the police lobbied for military hardware. Some civil rights activists, on the other hand, saw the riots as compelling evidence that the movement had to turn its attention to the North. Not only did the riots highlight the racism and poverty endemic to northern cities, they also suggested to some observers that urban African-Americans were ready to take action and force nationwide social change.

As the movement shifted North, however, it encountered fewer successes. Activists found the problems of poverty and the types of discrimination practiced in the North harder to confront than the formalized segregation of the South. Northern white liberals, once eager to condemn southern racism, were less willing to address problems in their own local governments, corporations, or unions. Moreover, activists learned that urban ghettos were fragmented and difficult to organize, in part because the black church was less of a community center in the urban North than in the rural South.

Even the movement's most prominent leaders found this new terrain difficult. Rev. Dr. Martin Luther King, Jr., tried to bring the movement's moral fervor and church-based organization to bear on the housing and employment problems of African-Americans in Chicago, where Mayor Richard Daley headed a corrupt and racially divisive political order. King's campaign met fierce resistance from hostile policemen and angry white homeowners, who heaped torrents of abuse (and a few bricks) on civil rights marchers intent on housing integration. King was forced to withdraw with relatively little to show for his efforts.

As Dr. King and his allies seemed to stumble, new African-American leaders emerged with alternative visions. For many young urban blacks, the most inspiring figure was a charismatic Black Muslim named Malcolm X. Orphaned in childhood by a Ku Klux Klan murder, a dope peddler and pimp in his teenage years, Malcolm converted to Islam during a long term in prison. Critical of the nonviolent tactics of the civil rights movement, Malcolm saw integration as an illusory solution to black problems. "The system in this country cannot produce freedom for an Afro-American," he argued. "It is impossible for this system, this economic system, this political system, this social system . . . to produce freedom right now for the black man. . . ."

Articulate, dramatic, and controversial, Malcolm contended that massive, nationwide change was necessary. And he advocated black pride and unity as key elements of his strategy. "The worst crime of the white man has been to teach us to hate ourselves," Malcolm declared. "We hated our head, we hated the shape of our nose. . . . Yeah, we hated the color of our skin." Malcolm broke with more traditional

Black Muslims such as Elijah Muhammad and Louis Farrakhan, and then was assassinated in the spring of 1965. But his ideas lived on to become widely popular among urban African-Americans.

Radical young activists such as SNCC leader Stokely Carmichael tried to pick up Malcolm's mantle. Hoping to harness the energy of northern ghettos, Carmichael called for a militant black assertiveness, symbolized by the slogan "Black Power." Carmichael stirred African-American crowds with the impatient declaration "It's time we stand up and take over; move on over, or we'll move on over you." In 1966, some SNCC Black Power advocates, who felt that only blacks could lead the freedom struggle, forced white activists to leave the organization.

"... FIGHT THEM AND YOU'LL GET YOUR FREEDOM"

In December 1964, less than two months before his assassination, Malcolm X spoke with a group of African-American teenagers from McComb, Mississippi. The group, composed of youthful activists, had come to New York City under the auspices of SNCC. When they visited Malcolm, he applauded their efforts and urged them toward an even bolder stance.

One of the first things I think young people, especially nowadays, should learn, is how to see for yourself and listen for yourself and think for yourself. Then you can come to an intelligent decision for yourself. This generation, especially of our people, has a burden, more so than any other time in history. The most important thing that we can learn to do today is think for ourselves. . . .

My experience has been that in many instances where you find Negroes talking about nonviolence, they are not nonviolent with each other, and they're not loving with each other, or forgiving with each other. Usually when they say they're nonviolent, they mean they're nonviolent with somebody else. I think you understand what I mean. They are nonviolent with the enemy. A person can come to your home, and if he's white and wants to heap some kind of brutality on you, you're nonviolent; or he can come to take your father and put a rope around his neck, and you're nonviolent. But if another Negro just stomps his foot, you'll rumble with him in a minute. Which shows you that there's an inconsistency there.

I myself would go for nonviolence if it was consistent, if everybody was going to be nonviolent all the time. I'd say, okay, let's get with it, we'll all be nonviolent. But I don't go along with any kind of nonviolent unless everybody's going to be nonviolent. If they make the Ku Klux Klan nonviolent, I'll be nonviolent. If they make the White Citizens' Council nonviolent, I'll be nonviolent. But as long as you've got somebody else not being nonviolent, I don't want anybody coming to me talking any nonviolent talk. . . .

I think in 1965, whether you like it, or I like it, or they like it or not, you will see that there is a generation of black people becoming mature to the point where they feel that they have no more business being asked to take a peaceful

First in Oakland, California, and then in other cities, such as Chicago, the Black Panther Party linked Black Power with a class analysis of American social injustice, insisting that African-Americans be in the vanguard of a socialist revolution in America. Urging blacks to defend themselves against police brutality, the Panthers presented a vivid image of armed and disciplined black youth. They drew police attacks and heavy media attention, and briefly overshadowed most other forms of African-American political activity.

Although Black Power was denounced by moderate African-American leaders and used by many whites as an excuse to turn against civil rights reforms, the phrase captured much that was stirring in black America. Black Power encouraged African-Americans to take increased pride and interest in their African roots, and in their history of struggle and cultural innovation in America. For some it meant building black institutions and communities that depended as little as possible on whites. Many blacks began to explore and extend the African-American heritage of values and life-styles, food and fashions, poetry and prose, theater, dance, and music. Within little more than a decade, black voters united to elect a score of black mayors in cities such as Newark, Detroit, and Oakland. Though the movement could not dismantle the structures of inequality in the larger society, African-American political activists gained a certain degree of control over their immediate environments.

THE SPREAD OF CIVIL RIGHTS CONSCIOUSNESS

Civil rights activism, urban strife, and demands for Black Power indicated that African-Americans could no longer be easily relegated to the bottom

approach than anybody else takes, unless everybody's going to take a peaceful approach.

So we here in the Organization of Afro-American Unity are with the struggle in Mississippi one thousand per cent. We're with the efforts to register our people in Mississippi to vote one thousand per cent. But we do not go along with anybody telling us to help nonviolently. We think that if the government says that Negroes have a right to vote, and then some Negroes come out to vote and some kind of Ku Klux Klan is going to put them in the river, and the government doesn't do anything about it, it's time for us to organize and band together and equip ourself and qualify ourselves to protect ourselves. And when you can protect yourself, you don't have to worry about being hurt. . . .

I hope you don't think I'm trying to incite you. Just look here: look at yourselves. Some of you are teenagers and students. How do you think I feel—and I belong to a generation ahead of you—how do you think I feel to have to tell you, "We, my generation, sat around like a knot on a wall while the whole world was fighting for its human rights—and you've got to be born into a society where you still have that fight." What did we do, who preceded you? I'll tell you what we did: nothing. And don't you make the same mistake we did. . . .

You get freedom by letting your enemy know that you'll do anything to get your freedom; then you'll get it. It's the only way you'll get it. When you get that kind of attitude, they'll label you as a "crazy Negro," or they'll call you a "crazy nigger"—they don't say Negro. Or they'll call you an extremist or a subversive, or seditious, or a red or a radical. But when you stay radical long enough, and get enough people to be like you, you'll get your freedom. . . .

So don't you run around here trying to make friends with somebody who's depriving you of your rights. They're not your friends, no, they're your enemies. Treat them like that and fight them, and you'll get your freedom; and after you get your freedom, your enemy will respect you. And we'll respect you. And I say that with no hate. I don't have any hate in me. I have no hate at all. I don't have any hate. I've got some sense. I'm not going to let somebody who hates me tell me to love him. I'm not that way-out. And you, young as you are, and because you start thinking, are not going to do it either. . . .

Oakland, California, September 1968. The Black Panther Party's headquarters after two police officers fired into the unoccupied storefront.

of the labor market. After the 1964 Civil Rights Act forbade employment discrimination on the basis of race or gender, the government developed "affirmative action" guidelines requiring large corporations, public agencies, and craft unions to compensate for past patterns of discrimination. Some giant employers, including AT&T, U.S. Steel, and the Bank of America, were pressured to recruit black and Latino workers and promote women out of the female occupational ghettos to which they had long been consigned.

Inspired by the civil rights movement, African-American workers in the textile industry, restaurants, and janitorial services began to reject second-class treatment. In Los Angeles, unionized African-American janitors launched a successful campaign to upgrade their poorly paid, part-time jobs and win the kinds of hours and fringe benefits enjoyed by other organized blue-collar workers. When owners of southern textile mills hired thousands of rural blacks to fill "white" job slots, they expected a docile and grateful workforce. But they found that paternalism was no longer effective. African-American workers provided the backbone for union drives across the South. "Back in the late 1960s," remembered one union organizer, "whenever you went into one plant the first thing you looked to was how many blacks are there working. . . . And if there were forty blacks you could count on forty votes."

Some unions linked themselves directly to the civil rights struggle. Seeking to organize New York City's hospital service workers, such as orderlies and cafeteria workers, the leaders of Local 1199, the Drug and Hospital Employees' Union, proclaimed that their campaign ran on "union power plus soul power." The workforce in the city's private, nonprofit hospitals—predominantly African-American, Puerto Rican, and female—had remained largely nonunion through the 1950s. But by the early 1960s, according to African-American hospital worker Doris Turner, workers came to see a link between their own struggle and the movement in the South: "Really and truthfully, they were one [struggle], just being waged in different places." Local 1199 encouraged this perception. It sent contingents to civil rights marches, such as the 1963 March on Washington. And during a 1965 strike in Bronxville, New York, picketing workers car-

XIXth Olympiad protest. As "The Star-Spangled Banner" is played during the 1968 Mexico City Olympics, the American gold and bronze medalists in the 200-meter dash raise their fists in the Black Power salute. Outraged by this silent tribute to black dignity and protest against racial discrimination in sports, the International Olympics Committee ejected Tommie Smith (center) and Juan Carlos (right) from the Olympic Village.

Union rights and civil rights. Malcolm X and trade union leader A. Philip Randolph share a platform during a 1962 rally celebrating a successful hospital workers' strike.

ried signs that read: "Freedom Now!" and "Bronxville, Mississippi" and "Lincoln Freed the Slaves, but Bronxville Hasn't." By the end of the 1960s, Local 1199 had won union recognition and concrete improvements for workers at hospitals around the metropolitan area, and was reaching out to workers in places as far away as Charleston, South Carolina.

Two thousand miles away, in California's Central Valley, a farm labor workforce composed largely of Chicano (Mexican-American) and Filipino workers also adopted the tactics and ideas pioneered by the civil rights movement. Unionization efforts among workers on giant commercial farms had a long, bitter history going back to the Mexican Revolution–inspired unions of fruit and vegetable pickers of the 1920s and the organizing drives of the Communist-led Commercial and Agricultural Workers' Industrial Unions in the early 1930s. In the postwar years, Mexican workers made up the vast majority of California's agricultural workforce, and as with southern blacks, their poverty and powerlessness were products of a hierarchical and discriminatory social structure dominated by a powerful elite.

Led by César Chávez, a charismatic organizer who had spent his childhood as a migrant laborer, California farmworkers struck the Delano vineyards early in 1965. Had these desperately poor workers

La Huelga. The Aztec eagle was adopted as the symbol for the United Farm Workers.

relied only on their own resources, their union would have been smashed like other agricultural labor unions before them. Farmworkers were not covered by federal labor laws, and the growers controlled the local police, enabling them to import thousands of strikebreakers across the Mexican border.

The United Farm Workers (UFW) held on for five years by presenting their strike not as a simple union-management conflict but rather as *la causa*, an awakening of the Mexican-American community to its ethnic heritage and full American citizenship. UFW rallies, marches, and picket lines featured huge, blood-red banners imprinted with a black Aztec eagle symbolizing Mexican pride and power. Their strikes took on the feel of a Chicano civil rights movement and religious convocation. During a three-hundred-mile march to the state capital, strikers sang "We Shall Overcome" in Spanish and English and held aloft the banner of Our Lady of Guadalupe. "Since this is both a religious pilgrimage and a plea for social change for the farmworker," Chavez declared, "we hope that the people of God will respond to our call and join us for part of the walk just as they did with our Negro brothers in Selma."

Chavez won a large national following, which was essential to the success of a national boycott launched by the UFW against California grape growers. Incorporating thousands of student volunteers into his boycott organization and winning solid backing from the Catholic Church and the United Automobile Workers, the UFW challenged the growers in supermarkets and freight yards across America. "We got to the point where we could track a grape shipment from California to Appleton, Wisconsin, and have pickets waiting for them at the loading docks at two o'clock in the morning," remembered one organizer.

The UFW strategy not only won formal recognition from many growers but also soon made the union an important political force in the Southwest. With broad support in the Chicano community and on college campuses, the UFW could mobilize more campaign workers than the entire California AFL-CIO. In Arizona, where the union led a recall campaign against an antiunion governor, the UFW registered 100,000 new Mexican-American voters. Adapting the tactics of the civil rights movement, Chicanos in the Southwest gained new respect as well as increased political clout.

Welfare recipients, largely female, also took inspiration from the civil rights movement and acted to take control of their lives. Despite the War on Poverty, welfare grants in the mid-1960s were often inadequate, providing as little as one-third of the amount necessary to maintain a family at the federal poverty line. And many families eligible for assistance stayed away from the welfare offices, in part be-

Live like a dog Dec.1-7.

Test President Nixon's welfare plan.

19¢ Breakfast   19¢ Lunch   19¢ Dinner

National Welfare Rights Organization.

"Zap FAP!" As part of the campaign against the Nixon administration's Family Assistance Plan, a National Welfare Rights Organization poster shows the limited daily diet supported by the welfare-reform proposal. The complicated and controversial reform plan provided federal assistance to states and cities to relieve the burden of rising welfare expenses. Many critics argued, however, that FAP's real aim was to cut welfare rolls.

cause of the arrogant treatment they often received and in part because they were ashamed of themselves for being poor. The National Welfare Rights Organization (NWRO), founded in 1966 by civil rights activists, tried to address this situation by urging poor people to take advantage of their legal rights within the welfare system and by showing them that poverty was caused not by individual weakness but by the structure of the economy.

In the activist atmosphere of the middle and late 1960s, poor urban residents, especially African-American women, responded eagerly to the welfare rights message. NWRO chapters sprouted in forty-five cities; welfare recipients led demonstrations for better treatment and special grants for housing, food, and children's school cloth-

"THE WOMEN HAVE TO BE INVOLVED"

Jessie Lopez De La Cruz came from a family of migrant farmworkers living in California's San Joaquin Valley. Her experiences as a farmworker and a mother of six children helped her effectively organize for the UFW. Her ability to relate to the workers in the field and to involve the women in the unionization struggle were important contributions to the battle for farmworkers' rights. Here she tells of her experiences as an organizer.

Growing up, I could see all the injustices and I would think, "If only I could do something about it! If only there was somebody who could do something about it!" That was always in the back of my mind. And after I was married, I cared about what was going on, but felt I couldn't do anything. So I went to work, and I came home to clean the house, and I fixed the food for the next day, took care of the children and the next day went back to work. The whole thing over and over again. Politics to me was something foreign, something I didn't know about. I didn't even listen to the news. I didn't read newspapers hardly at all. *True Romance* was my thing!

But then late one night in 1962, there was a knock at the door and there were three men. One of them was Cesar Chavez. And the next thing I knew, they were sitting around our table talking about a union. I made coffee. Arnold had already told me about a union for the farmworkers. He was attending their meetings in Fresno, but I didn't. I'd either stay home or stay outside in the car. But then Cesar said, "The women have to be involved. They're the ones working out in the fields with their husbands. If you can take the women out to the fields, you can certainly take them to meetings." So I sat up straight and said to myself, "*That's what I want!*"

When I became involved with the union, I felt I had to get other women involved. Women have been behind men all the time, always. Just waiting to see what the men decide to do, and tell us what to do.... I'd hear [women] scolding their kids and fighting their husbands and I'd say, "Gosh! Why don't you go after

ing. In part because of such activity, increased numbers of poor people eligible for welfare began requesting assistance. In 1960, only 745,000 families had applied for AFDC grants; by 1972, more than 3 million families were applying. Such activity did not eliminate the underlying causes of poverty, but it did ameliorate its worst effects for millions of Americans.

THE ROAD TO VIETNAM

If the civil rights movement and its related movements revealed the domestic problems of postwar society, the Vietnam War brought to the surface the tensions inherent in the U.S. effort to manage the global political economy. The road to Vietnam was paved with the arrogance of American Cold War liberalism. President Kennedy, Secretary of Defense Robert McNamara, and other American leaders of the early 1960s wanted the United States to appear strong, to command respect from foe and friend, and thereby maintain the international balance of power. Anything less, they thought, would invite instability, especially in the Third World, where American policy-makers wanted to control the pace and direction of change. But the Kennedy administration suffered humiliation during its first months in office. In April 1961, a CIA-organized invasion of Cuba failed to overthrow Fidel Castro's new revolutionary regime. In August, East German Communists erected a brutal concrete wall across Berlin, hoping to stop the flow of refugees to the West. Then a pro-Western government in the Southeast Asian kingdom of Laos collapsed. None of these setbacks was of overriding importance, but they suggested to

the people that have you living like this? Why don't you go after the growers that have you tired from working out in the fields at low wages and keep us poor all the time? Let's go after them! *They're the cause of our misery!*" Then I would say we had to take a part in the things going on around us. Women can no longer be taken for granted—that we're just going to stay home and do the cooking and cleaning. It's way past the time when our husbands could say, "You stay home! You have to take care of the children! You have to do as I say!"

I think I was made an organizer because in the first place I could relate to the farmworkers, being a lifelong farmworker. I was well-known in the small towns around Fresno. Wherever I went to speak to them, they listened. I told them about how we were excluded from the NLRB in 1935, how we had no benefits, no minimum wage, nothing out in the fields—no restrooms, nothing. I would talk about how we were paid what the grower wanted to pay us, and how we couldn't set a price on our work. I explained that we could do something about these things by joining a union, by working together.

It was very hard being a woman organizer. Many of our people my age and older were raised with the old customs in Mexico: where the husband rules, he is king of his house. The wife obeys, and the children, too. So when we first started it was very, very hard. Men gave us the most trouble. . . . They were for the union, but they were not taking orders from women, they said. When [the union] formed the ranch committee [to represent workers' grievances to management] at Christian Brothers [a large wine company], the ranch committee was all men. . . .

That year, we'd have a union meeting every week. Men, women, and children would come. Women would ask questions and the men would just stand back. I guess they'd say to themselves, "I'll wait for someone to say something before I do." The women were more aggressive than the men. And I'd get up and say, "Let's go on, let's do it."

When the first contract was up, we talked about there being no women on the ranch committee. I suggested they be on it, and the men went along with this. And so women were elected.

the Kennedy administration that it would have to demonstrate its will to stand up to the Communists somewhere.

Toughness seemed to pay off in the fall of 1962, when the Soviets installed intermediate-range ballistic missiles in Cuba. Kennedy responded with a U.S. naval blockade around the island. For a brief moment, the world seemed to be poised on the brink of nuclear war. The crisis ended when the Soviet Union agreed to remove the missiles. Kennedy's victory won him much support at home and gave him the political strength to negotiate a treaty with the USSR limiting the testing of nuclear weapons. But long-term consequences of the Cuban missile crisis were ambiguous. Determined never to be outgunned again by the United States, the Soviets built up their naval and long-range missile forces and ended a five-year period of internal reforms. Kennedy and his successors, meanwhile, concluded that the controlled escalation of military force was an effective tool of statecraft.

This reasoning helped lead the United States into a tragic war in Vietnam. A Communist movement led by Ho Chi Minh had won substantial support among Vietnamese peasants and intellectuals who sought to end years of French colonial rule. By 1954, Ho's forces had defeated the French and won independence for the northern half of Vietnam. The United States quickly stepped in to replace France as the dominant power in the southern part of the country. The United States backed a Catholic aristocrat, Ngo Dinh Diem, in a vain effort to build up a viable political alternative, but his support never spread much beyond the army and a narrow circle of landlords and urban Catholics.

Kennedy and his advisers were aware of Diem's weaknesses. But Kennedy was determined to demonstrate U.S. power and steadfastness. Vietnam would be the place, not so much because of its strategic or economic value but because the president chose it as the site to prove, in the words of one Pentagon analyst, that the United States was "willing to keep promises to its allies, to be tough, to take risks, get bloodied, and hurt the enemy badly." Kennedy steadily increased the number of U.S. military "advisers" in Vietnam; upon his death in November 1963, they numbered more than 16,000.

Lyndon Johnson was equally convinced that Vietnam was a proving ground for U.S. global power. On the basis of a spurious naval clash in the Gulf of Tonkin near North Vietnam in August 1964, Johnson secured from Congress the "Tonkin Gulf Resolution," a virtual blank check to conduct the war in any way he saw fit. This opened the way for a sustained bombing campaign against North Vietnam, and for the introduction of large numbers of U.S. ground combat troops, beginning in the summer of 1965.

With the introduction of combat troops, the military system began organizing the flow of American teenagers, most of them working-class, toward Vietnam. In the first years of the war, most soldiers were actually enlistees rather than conscripts, but for high-school males this was not much of a distinction. Most working-class young men thought of "the service" as an event like measles or graduation, something that was part of growing up in America. At first, few young men gave much thought to the politics of the war. "I didn't have any feelings one way or the other," one draftee remembered. "I figured it was more or less right, because why would I be going if it wasn't right?"

The military draft, or Selective Service system, was indeed selective. Because college students initially enjoyed deferments, most escaped the first years of the draft. If they did end up in the army, they usually served as officers, or in noncombat posts. Of all the graduates of Harvard, Princeton, and Yale during the 1960s, precisely two had been drafted and killed in Vietnam as of June 1970. In contrast, poor Americans, white as well as black and Latino, were far more likely to be drafted and assigned to combat. Draftees, only about a quarter of the army, represented 88 percent of infantry riflemen in 1970 and two-thirds of all battle deaths. A Veterans Administration survey concluded that "while minority Americans may have suffered a disproportionate share of the exposure to combat and combat fatalities, their suffering was the product not of racial discrimination, but of discrimination against the poor, the uneducated, and the young." This was a big change from World War II, when the draft had reached deep into the middle class, and when GIs had averaged twenty-six years of age, almost seven years older than those who served in Vietnam.

Politics and new technology helped shape U.S. military strategy in Vietnam. Since World War II, the navy and air force had dominated

Operation Barrel Roll, 1982. The Plain of Jars in northern Laos, pockmarked with bomb craters nine years after the United States ended its aerial campaign there.

the American military: big ships, fast planes, and lots of bombs could hold the peace or win a war, or so it was thought. Vietnam-era strategy assumed that expensive technology and sophisticated organization would substitute for the blood and sweat of ground combat. In practice this meant that day after day, U.S. bombers piloted by college-educated young officers took off from Southeast Asian air bases and U.S. Navy aircraft carriers to bomb Vietnam, Laos, and after 1970, Cambodia as well. More than seven hundred U.S. planes were eventually shot down in Southeast Asia, but the air war had a bureaucratic routine about it that belied both its destructiveness and its futility. A B-52 run from Guam had the feel of an interstate haul in a big truck, except that the cargo consisted of more than two hundred bombs unloaded by computer decision from an elevation of 30,000 feet. Eventually the United States dropped more than four times as many bombs on Southeast Asia as were dropped in all of World War II.

But the air war neither stopped the infiltration of personnel and supplies from North Vietnam nor destroyed the southern bases of the insurgent National Liberation Front (NLF, or "Viet Cong"). The Vietnam War would have to be fought by individual soldiers operating in small units in unfamiliar and dangerous jungle terrain. At first the United States used marines to guard the air bases it had constructed in South Vietnam, but after July 1965 U.S. troops sought out the enemy in a series of "search and destroy" opera-

"BUT WE ARE NOT ALONE . . ."

This poem, written by Corporal William Ehrhart in the early 1970s and entitled "A Relative Thing," expresses the sense of futility experienced by many American foot soldiers during the Vietnam War.

We are the ones you sent to fight a war
You didn't know a thing about.

It didn't take us long to realize
The only thing that we controlled
Was covered by the bottom of our boots.

When the newsmen said that naval ships
Had shelled a VC staging point,
We saw a breastless woman
And her stillborn child.

We watched ourselves becoming insensitive.
We laughed at old men stumbling in the dust
In frenzied terror to avoid our three-ton trucks.

We fought outnumbered in Hue City
While the ARVN soldiers looted bodies
In the safety of the rear.
The cookies from the wives of Local 104
Did not soften our awareness. . . .

We are the ones who have to live
With the memory that we were the instruments
Of your pigeon-breasted fantasies.
We are inextricable accomplices
In this travesty of dreams;
But we are not alone. . . .

Just because we will not fit
Into the uniforms of photographs
Of you at twenty-one
Does not mean you can disown us.

We are your sons, America,
And you cannot change that.
When you awake,
We will still be here.

tions. The enemy proved elusive; neither the NLF nor regular units of the North Vietnamese Army wanted to fight pitched battles with U.S. forces. Frustrated, U.S. military leaders came to define victory, not by the seizure of land or even the defeat of enemy battalions, but by the physical annihilation of individual enemy soldiers.

The war of attrition led to a bureaucratic fixation with the daily "body count." U.S. soldiers were soon reporting as an enemy fatality any Vietnamese killed by U.S. firepower. To American soldiers, the distinctions between civilians and combatants became hopelessly confused, not only because of ignorance of the Vietnamese language and customs but also because the nature of the war made such distinctions meaningless. As a guerrilla army, the NLF relied on its ability to blend in with the rest of the population. U.S. soldiers came to fear that the street urchins who asked for candy doubled as NLF couriers and that the "friendlies" who washed your clothes in the morning might take part in a deadly ambush that night. A T-shirt worn by some U.S. soldiers expressed their response: "KILL THEM ALL! LET GOD SORT THEM OUT!"

The ultimate consequence of such attitudes came in the village of My Lai, where an American platoon landed one morning in 1968. "When the attack started," one sergeant recalled, "it couldn't have been stopped by anyone. We were mad and had been told that the enemy was there and we were going in there to give them a fight for what they had done to our dead buddies." No enemy fire was received, but within a matter of minutes the village exploded with American

The My Lai Massacre, Quang Ngai
Province, March 16, 1968.

grenades and machine-gun bursts. "People began coming out of their hooches and the guys shot them and burned the hooches—or burned the hooches and then shot the people when they came out," another soldier recalled. That day more than 350 Vietnamese villagers were murdered. There was one American casualty, a GI who shot himself in the foot out of disgust at what he was witnessing.

THE NEW LEFT

The Vietnam War was fought on two fronts: at home and abroad. U.S. policy-makers conducted the war with one eye always focused on national opinion. Neither Kennedy nor Johnson was confident that the American public would support another large military conflict in Asia. The escalation of the war therefore took place step by step: Johnson never formally declared that U.S. ground troops would fight in Vietnam; and although U.S. troop strength would climb to 550,000 by 1968, the military reserves were never called up, nor was a general war tax imposed.

Most Americans initially supported the war, but a small corps of critics grew steadily. By 1968, Washington policy-makers faced widespread domestic opposition in the streets, in congressional hearing rooms, and at the ballot box. This antiwar movement, which deprived the nation's elite of the exclusive right to set the foreign policy agenda, was part of an even broader social movement, often labeled the "New Left," that emerged from the civil rights movement to challenge American policy-makers on a wide range of issues.

The New Left came to life on college and university campuses in the early 1960s, when few contemporary observers expected U.S. students to be interested in radical social activism. College students in the 1960s were children of the baby boom, products of America's postwar economic growth and affluence, young people who could look forward to comfortable, middle-class futures. Yet it was at places like Stanford, Oberlin, and the Universities of Michigan and California, which drew the smartest and often the most affluent young Americans, that students rediscovered a radical critique of American society, and it was from these campuses that the antiwar movement drew its initial strength.

Despite the emphasis on being "new," the New Left was linked in many ways to previous radical movements, including the Communist-dominated left of the 1930s. The early New Left differed from the 1930s left primarily in its rejection of Marxist ideology and Stalinist party discipline. It sought to build a movement based on a radical interpretation of American values of democracy and equality. Activists identified with the civil rights movement, which promised to restore moral vision to American life, and with the university, which seemed a place where ideas could have immediate and beneficial consequences. Unlike most working-class students, whose social outlook was often shaped by a felt need to find a secure job, middle-class students in the prosperous 1960s were "free" for a few crucial years to reflect skeptically on the gap between the liberal promise of American life and social reality.

The 1962 Port Huron Statement, a founding manifesto of the leading New Left organization, Students for a Democratic Society (SDS), called on America to live up to its highest democratic ideals. SDS urged activists to respond not only to issues of poverty but also to the problems of modern life, from alienation and bureaucratic impersonality to the threat of nuclear war. "A new left," SDS proclaimed, "must give form to the feelings of helplessness and indifference, so that people may see the political, social, and economic source of their personal troubles and organize to change society."

Early SDSers such as Michigan student Tom Hayden hoped that organized labor might regain its "missing idealism," and they thought a revitalized labor movement essential to the new America they envisioned. Such sentiments won SDS the warm regard of many labor liberals in the early 1960s. UAW leaders, for example, thought SDS might help the labor movement get its message across on college campuses and among unorganized white-collar workers, and it provided the college group with funds for some of its early organizing activities. But early New Leftists did not see labor as the sole engine of progressive social change. Instead, they saw the civil rights movement as proof that other groups, including students, intellectuals, and African-Americans, could pick up the mantle of leadership.

The student movement of the early 1960s was in many ways a stepchild of the civil rights movement. Across the North and West, students supported civil rights sit-ins with money and with picket lines at stores and businesses that refused to integrate their southern branches. SDS leaders traveled south to observe and work with SNCC, and as they built their own movement they emulated SNCC's rhetoric, strategy, and loose organizational style. "SDS seemed hip and bold," recalled Jeremy Brecher, an Oregon student in the early 1960s. "It had an enthusiasm for direct action, an attitude of defiance towards the establishment, and a constant looking for points where change could be stimulated and supported."

In the early 1960s, New Left activists experimented with ways to use the civil rights model of activism to build movements around other issues. From 1963 to 1966, SDS sent groups of students to Chicago, Newark, and elsewhere to organize "interracial movements of the poor." Though students mobilized some poor city-dwellers and helped spur the welfare rights movement, these projects collapsed in a few years. But they taught hundreds of activists valuable lessons about organizing and about the inequalities of American politics.

Student activists at the huge Berkeley campus of the University of California pioneered a different way to adapt the civil rights model: the student power movement. In the early 1960s, influenced by the radical politics of the northern California labor movement and the cultural dissidence that radiated from San Francisco's "beat" community, California students made Berkeley a stronghold of northern civil rights activity. Scores of Berkeley students went south, and thousands joined civil rights demonstrations in the Bay Area. In September 1964, after local politicians and businessmen demanded that university officials crack down on such activism, the school issued new rules prohibiting the collection of funds or distribution of political literature on campus. Activists responded with a "Free-Speech Movement" (FSM), using civil rights–style tactics to wage a nonviolent but highly disruptive struggle against university officials.

Though it began with a committed minority, the movement swept into its ranks many more who were radicalized in the struggle, especially after eight hundred students were arrested during a December sit-in at a university administration building. As the struggle mounted, some FSM activists developed a critique of the impersonal university and the way it trained students to serve the corporate, bureaucratic order. Many came to agree with FSM leader Mario Savio, a Freedom Summer veteran who compared the university bureaucracy, with its "sophisticated powers of manipulation," to Mississippi's white segregationists. "The same rights are at stake in both places," he told Berkeley students, "the right to participate as citizens in democratic society and the right to due process of law."

Student power campaigns continued throughout the decade, as activists on hundreds of campuses sought a voice in university policies. But campus reform issues were often overshadowed and, in some cases, swallowed up by the growth of a new issue. In February 1965, one month after the Free-Speech Movement concluded its successful campaign, President Johnson escalated the war in Southeast Asia by ordering the daily bombing of North Vietnam. Armed with organizing skills and a skepticism about authority gained through civil rights, community organizing, and campus reform activism, the New Left led American students into the forefront of the antiwar movement.

Activists' reasons for opposing the war varied. A few were pacifists, who rejected all violence and war. Others came to sympathize with and even glorify the NLF as heroic nationalists. Most agreed that the war—and America's role as global policeman—violated the ideals of democracy and freedom. "We'd been brought up to believe in our

"... ASSEMBLY LINES IN THE UNIVERSITIES"

Student activists of the 1960s campaigned for university reform, improved education, and greater student involvement in university decision-making. In this 1966 speech, SDS leader Carl Davidson described universities as "knowledge factories" and tried to link the university reform movement to an analysis of changing economic and class structures.

SDS has named the existing system in this country "corporate liberalism." And, if we bother to look, its penetration into the campus community is awesome. Its elite are trained in our colleges of business administration. Its defenders are trained in our law schools. Its apologists can be found in the political science departments. The colleges of social sciences produce its manipulators. For propagandists, it relies on the schools of journalism. It insures its own future growth in the colleges of education. If some of us don't quite fit in, we are brainwashed in the divisions of counseling. And we all know only too well what goes on in the classrooms of the military science buildings.

What we must see clearly is the relation between the university and corporate liberal society at large. Most of us are outraged when our university administrators or their student government lackeys liken our universities and colleges to corporations. We bitterly respond with talk about a "community of scholars." However, the fact of the matter is that they are correct. Our educational institutions *are* corporations and knowledge factories. What we have failed to see in the past is how absolutely vital these factories are to the corporate liberal state.

What do these factories produce? What are their commodities? The most obvious answer is "knowledge." Our factories produce the know-how that enables the corporate state to expand, to grow, and to exploit people more efficiently and extensively both in our own country and in the third world. But knowledge is perhaps too abstract to be viewed as a commodity. Concretely, the commodities of our factories are the *knowledgeable.* AID officials, Peace Corpsmen, military officers, CIA officials, segregationist judges, corporation lawyers, politicians of all sorts, welfare workers, managers of industry, labor bureaucrats (I could go on and on): Where do they come from? They are products of the factories we live and work in.

It is on our assembly lines in the universities that they are molded into what they are. As integral parts of the knowledge factory system, we are both the exploiters and the exploited. As both the managers and the managed, we produce and become the most vital product of corporate liberalism: bureaucratic man. In short, we are a new kind of scab.

Finally, perhaps we can see the vital connections that our factories have with the present conditions of corporate liberalism when we ask ourselves what would happen if the military found itself without ROTC students, the CIA found itself without recruits, paternalistic welfare departments found themselves without social workers, or the Democratic Party found itself without young liberal apologists and campaign workers? In short, what would happen to a manipulative society if its means of creating *manipulable* people were done away with?

The answer is that we might then have a fighting chance to change that system.

hearts that America stood for fighting on the side of justice," remembered one student of the mid-1960s. "World War II was ingrained in us—my father had volunteered. So there was this feeling of personal betrayal."

The antiwar movement grew rapidly. Antiwar marches, which had drawn but a few thousand in 1965, grew in size until they could put a million marchers in the streets of New York, San Francisco, and Washington, D.C., two years later. SDS membership mushroomed. In addition to national protest marches, activists organized local demonstrations, targeting napalm (highly incendiary jellied petroleum) manufacturer Dow Chemical and universities that conducted war-related research. Activists held vigils, tried to block troop trains, went door-to-door with petitions, and supported "peace candidates" for public office.

For young Americans, the draft stood as a prime symbol of the war. Millions of young men tried to evade the draft: some fled to Canada; many feigned insanity or disability in hopes of winning deferments; others used family connections to gain safe berths in the military reserve. A few thousand took public stands as draft resisters, burning their draft cards and challenging the government to imprison them. Inspired by the actions of Catholic priests Philip and Daniel Berrigan, small activist groups organized

"From Protest to Resistance."
Confronted by a phalanx of soldiers,
federal marshals, and police, antiwar
demonstrators block the Pentagon
on October 21, 1967.

hundreds of clandestine strikes against local draft boards, burning
files or drenching them with blood. By the late 1960s, draft resistance—organized and unorganized, overt and covert—was so widespread that the nation's legal system could no longer effectively
handle the flood of cases.

Although the antiwar movement was initially based in the
middle class, it won thousands of working-class recruits after 1968.
By then, nonelite universities such as Wayne State in Detroit; Kent
State in Ohio; Boston University; and all-black Southern University,
in Baton Rouge, Louisiana, had become centers of movement activity.
Long hair, marijuana, and rock music, which had first symbolized
campus political and social alienation, soon spread to factory night
shifts, construction sites, and mailrooms staffed by young workers.

The radicalization of working-class youth had a direct effect on
the military, where internal conflict undermined the morale of many
Vietnam combat units. After 1967, drug use soared, desertions quad-
rupled, and hostility toward officers took on a political coloration.
Peace symbols and Black Power fists appeared on GIs' helmets. "Almost to a man, the members of my platoon oppose the war," explained one sergeant in 1971. "There is a great deal of pressure on
leaders at the small-unit level to conduct what are popularly referred
to as 'search and avoid' missions, and to do so as safely and cautiously
as possible." Officers who failed to accommodate their men might

find a live grenade rolled under their bunk—more than a thousand such "fragging" incidents were recorded after 1969. As thousands of bitter Vietnam veterans joined peace marches, antiwar and antiauthority sentiment spread Stateside, to European bases, and to naval vessels, undermining U.S. military strength around the globe.

Political and social radicalism in the United States also helped spark an international student movement that challenged leaders on both sides of the Cold War. As in the United States, the first generation to come of age in postwar Europe felt stifled by the rigid social structures of the Cold War era. Young people in France, Germany, and Italy campaigned against the Vietnam War and helped revitalize socialist traditions, and even in Poland and Czechoslovakia many glimpsed the possibility that Soviet control might be weakened and communism given a human face.

The international New Left reached a peak of sorts in the spring of 1968, when student demonstrations and university occupations at the Sorbonne in Paris, at Columbia University in New York, and at the Free University of Berlin seemed to shake the structures of world politics. In the "Prague Spring," students were in the vanguard of the effort to humanize East European communism. In France, university protests initially directed against the rigidities of the centralized educational system struck a nerve in the whole society, touching off factory occupations and strikes involving almost 10 million workers.

In the United States, however, the relationship between the New Left and the labor movement had gone sour. By the late 1960s, many

Operation Dewey Canyon III. Facing a barricade erected to keep them off the steps of the Capitol, hundreds of veterans—many in wheelchairs and on crutches—return medals they received during tours of duty in Vietnam. Perhaps the most moving antiwar demonstration, this ceremony was the culmination of a week-long campaign during April 1971 organized by the Vietnam Veterans Against the War (VVAW) to publicize dramatically atrocities committed by the United States. The VVAW named the protest after secret American invasions of Laos in 1969 and early 1971.

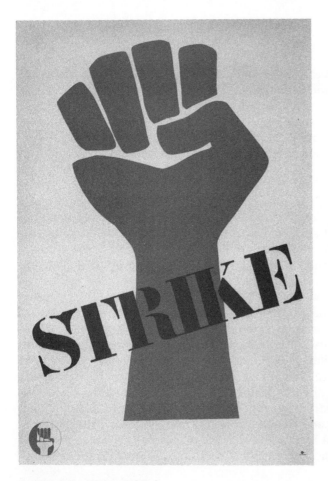

Student strike. Posters printed during the spring 1969 Harvard strike. Inspired by the political posters produced by students and workers at the Paris School of Fine Arts during May 1968, the Harvard posters boldly conveyed the student movement's demands for political and personal liberation.

New Leftists felt that unions had no role to play in transforming American society. The AFL-CIO leadership continued to support the Vietnam War; and, in the eyes of many activists, the "affluent" white working class had bargained away its radical potential. "The next time some $3.90-an-hour AFL-type workers go on strike for a 50-cent raise," exploded Berkeley activist Marvin Garson in 1967, "I'll remember the day they chanted 'Burn Hanoi, not our flag,' and so help me, I'll cross their picket line."

Many activists looked instead for models in the Black Power movement, or the Cuban and Vietnamese revolutions. Their critique of American society grew bitter, as some repudiated the ideology of anticommunism and the justness of America's basic institutions and social arrangements. Frustrated by the failure of massive, peaceful protests to halt the war, some New Leftists sought to emulate urban rioters or the guerrilla warriors led by the Latin American revolutionary Che Guevara.

Repressive police activity encouraged this shift toward confrontation. While state and local police attacked marchers and harassed demonstrators, the federal government assigned thousands of undercover agents to infiltrate and manipulate activist groups. Initiated by Presidents Kennedy and Johnson and greatly expanded by President Richard Nixon after 1968, the FBI's counterintelligence program (COINTELPRO) spearheaded a nationwide effort to "expose, disrupt, and otherwise neutralize" civil rights and antiwar activity. In addition to putting tens of thousands of activists under surveillance, intelligence agents posed as radicals, disrupting meetings and urging movement groups toward violence in order to discredit them. A 1976 U.S. Senate report condemned COINTELPRO and other domestic intelligence programs as "unworthy of a democracy and occasionally reminiscent of the tactics of totalitarian regimes."

Angry, confused about strategy, and destabilized by police agents, SDS self-destructed in the summer of 1969. One SDS splinter group, the Weathermen, identified themselves as urban guerrillas waging underground warfare as part of the global struggle against the "Amerikkkan" empire. Although hundreds of thousands of activists still turned out for protests after 1969, the New Left fragmented at the very moment when broad layers of the American people might have been most receptive to its political and moral arguments.

In part, the New Left grew as large as it did because activists struck a chord that echoed long and loud throughout American society. Like antebellum reformers in the 1830s and the Populists of the 1890s, New Left radicals generated a multifaceted "counterculture" that expressed itself in the values and rituals of daily life. Activists and their

Comix! In the spirit of the counterculture, underground cartoonists rejected the style and substance of commercial comics and enthusiastically embraced every taboo. The starched suburban antics of "Archie" were replaced by the slovenly inner-city iconoclasm of Gilbert Shelton's "Fabulous Furry Freak Brothers" (represented here by brother Fat Freddy). The standard paternal and patriotic superheroes were rearranged into Shelton's sadistic and superpatriotic "Wonder Wart Hog," or Spain Rodriguez's vengeful guerrilla-fighter "Trashman." Meanwhile, Robert Crumb and S. Clay Wilson delved into the darker recesses of consciousness, producing a range of characters who reveled in the violent excesses of "sex, drugs, and rock-'n'-roll."

"hippie" fellow travelers questioned traditional forms of monogamy and family, suburban life, the headlong pursuit of material possessions, and the value placed on scientific rationality and emotional repression. Unconsciously following earlier American dissenters, they sought new forms of meaningful community life. As the availability of oral contraceptives sparked a "sexual revolution," young people helped lead an assault on taboos against premarital sex. Use of marijuana and psychedelic drugs, together with rock music, accompanied many young people on their search for personal and spiritual fulfillment.

Music was central to the 1960s counterculture. Early in the decade, folk musicians such as Bob Dylan set the tone for the era's political idealism by reviving such songs as Woody Guthrie's "This Land Is Your Land," which celebrated a democratic, populist America. By 1963, however, the year of the Birmingham demonstrations and President Kennedy's death, Dylan's "Blowin' in the Wind" reflected impatience with a liberalism turning sour. Soul singers such as Otis Redding and Aretha Franklin, Motown stars such as Marvin Gaye, and British rock-'n'-roll groups such as the Beatles and the Rolling Stones soon emerged, renewing rock-'n'-roll's connection to its vital African-American roots. After 1965, San Francisco bands such as the Grateful Dead, who performed routinely at protest rallies, enlivened the robust Bay Area radical culture. Popular music now seemed to spread the messages of social criticism and possibility. "The music and the world it created," recalled one former activist, "helped give us a sense that we were defining the culture, and the whole society was following."

Mainstream newspapers and television initially ignored or denounced the New Left and its counterculture, so the movement needed its own voice. Hundreds of "underground" community newspapers sprang up in the late 1960s. Their very names—*Los Angeles Free Press, Berkeley Barb, Austin Rag*—announced their viewpoint. These newspapers celebrated rock music and the drug scene, publicized movement protests, and experimented with a journalistic style that was intensely personal and committed to radical perspectives. With the decline of New Left movements, most of these papers collapsed, but before they disappeared they profoundly influenced what defined "news" and helped open the doors to a new generation of investigative journalists.

American culture seems to have an endless capacity to absorb and transform what is new and different. Such was the fate of the counter-culture, especially after it became divorced from the radical movement that gave it direction. Record companies, clothing manufacturers, and other purveyors of consumer goods quickly recognized a new market. Soon rock albums accounted for two-thirds of

If you can't beat 'em, absorb 'em. Columbia Records denounces the "Establishment" in an advertisement placed in underground newspapers during December 1968. Abbie Hoffman later commented that such corporations "were taking the energy from the streets and using it for a commercial value, saying, 'If you are in the revolution, what you got to do is buy our records,' while we were saying, 'You got to burn your draft card, you can't go to Vietnam, you have to come to the demonstrations and the protests. . . .' It was a conflict and we called their process cooptation: . . . They were able to turn a historic civil clash in our society into a fad, then the fad could be sold."

the sales of large record companies. Expensive stereo systems sold briskly, and advertisers renamed youth the "Pepsi Generation." Long hair, stylish informal clothes, rock music, and "recreational" drug use would, by the 1970s, become part of mainstream American culture.

While the counterculture was not as revolutionary as its adherents had hoped, the cultural currents sweeping the country contributed to broad change, reaching even bastions of social conservatism. American Catholicism, for instance, underwent a surprising transformation during the 1960s, in response both to the 1962 Second Vatican Council and to the new social movements. Among the laity, obedience to church authority declined. As popular mores changed, millions of Catholics came to ignore church teachings on sexual matters. By the mid-1970s, three-quarters of all Catholics polled indicated that they would have an abortion or advise their wives to do so, and in Chicago two-thirds of those Catholics under thirty who considered themselves pious approved of premarital sex. A small but growing group of Catholics plunged into civil rights and farmworker support activities and opposition to the Vietnam War. A daring corps of radical nuns and priests, including Daniel and Philip Berrigan, took nonviolent action against the draft and helped push the American Catholic Church toward an increasingly liberal stand on issues of war, peace, and nuclear weapons.

1968

There are some years in American history that schoolchildren come to know as important: 1776, 1861, 1929. The year 1968 joins this short list, not only because it was full of dramatic and unexpected events but also because the United States faced a turning point in its history. On the all-consuming issue of Vietnam, the Cold War consensus broke apart. Americans were no longer willing to pay the price of defeating communism and maintaining control of Vietnam. Though the war dragged on for seven more years, Johnson's presidency suddenly disintegrated, and modern American liberalism went into sharp decline.

Beginning in January, during Tet, the Vietnamese New Year, a massive NLF offensive overwhelmed cities and towns across South Vietnam. The nightly news brought pictures of NLF troops infiltrating the American embassy compound in Saigon, undermining the Johnson administration's stance that there was "light at the end of the tunnel" in Vietnam. The bitter fighting, which raged through February and March, left NLF forces militarily weakened. But the Tet offensive dealt Johnson's Vietnam policy a political deathblow by revealing to the American public the limits of U.S. power and the difficulty of achieving victory in Vietnam.

Tet forced a general reassessment of U.S. policy. Until then, media coverage of the war and the antiwar movement was largely favorable to the U.S. government. The news media were themselves big businesses that framed the news in ways that legitimated social order at home and U.S. interests abroad. Moreover, the most respected correspondents, such as CBS anchorman Walter Cronkite, had learned about combat journalism in World War II, when newsmen proudly saw their job as telling the army's story to the folks back home.

Tet shattered the optimistic story line. "To say that we are mired in a stalemate seems the only realistic, if unsatisfactory, conclusion," reported Cronkite from Vietnam. Thereafter, the news media greeted official government pronouncements with skepticism and gave antiwar activity increased coverage and respect. *Life* magazine demonstrated how far this shift had gone in June 1969, when it underlined the human cost of the war by publishing on its front cover the youthful pictures of the 247 American servicemen killed in the fighting that week.

The NLF offensive shook the Democratic Party as well. Until Tet, party liberals hesitated to criticize President Johnson; in late 1967, when antiwar senator Eugene McCarthy of Minnesota announced he would challenge the incumbent president for the 1968 Democratic nomination, his prospects seemed marginal. After Tet, however, the media spotlighted McCarthy's effort, student volunteers poured into his campaign, and he startled Johnson with a near-upset in the New Hampshire primary. New York senator Robert Kennedy sensed Johnson's vulnerability and declared his own presidential candidacy, calling for a halt to the bombing and a revival of the War on Poverty.

In the next three months, McCarthy and Kennedy demonstrated that, if given the choice, Democratic Party voters would choose a candidate committed to deescalation of the war. McCarthy was an inept campaigner, but his willingness to challenge Johnson won him the fierce loyalty of many antiwar activists. In contrast, Kennedy was a more traditional liberal and a latecomer to the antiwar cause. Nevertheless, Kennedy had become a passionate advocate of social justice, and he won the hearts of many Latinos and African-Americans as well as a substantial portion of the white working class. His ties to established urban politicians also helped propel him to the front of the race.

Meanwhile, Tet precipitated a revaluation of the war by the elite lawyers, bankers, and State Department officials who had presided over U.S. foreign policy since World War II. The war had generated disquiet on Wall Street and complaints from America's allies in Europe. To men such as Dean Acheson, a corporate lawyer and former secretary of state, and Clark Clifford, a powerful lawyer whom Johnson had just appointed secretary of defense, the war was an open wound that weakened the nation and sapped America's global strength. Acheson told Lyndon Johnson: "We need to stand back and get our priorities right. Enemy number one is Russia. Enemy number two is China. The vital strategic areas in their proper order are Western Europe (particularly Germany), Japan, the Middle East, Latin America—and only then Southeast Asia. The most crucial priority of all, of course, is the home front."

Johnson caved in. On March 31 he announced that he would stop bombing North Vietnam, cancel a planned troop increase, and end his reelection campaign. The antiwar movement had split the Democratic Party and forced a powerful president to repudiate his own foreign policy and virtually withdraw from office. This could have opened the way for America to make a decisive turn to the left, toward a more radical reform program. Yet 1968 proved a turning point that did not turn. Within two months, the two most visible opposition figures in American politics, Robert Kennedy and Martin Luther King, Jr., lay dead, struck down by assassins' bullets. Soon after, the movement for fundamental change began to fragment.

King was the first to fall. Convinced that the black movement had to take up the demand for economic as well as political justice, King had gone to Tennessee to help organize support for striking Memphis garbage collectors. Led by the American Federation of State, County, and Municipal Employees, the strike lasted for two months. Marches, demonstrations, and arrests gave the strike much of the flavor of the early civil rights movement; the slogan boldly printed on their picket signs, "I AM A MAN," spoke as clearly to the real meaning of the conflict as did the union's demand for higher wages and a contract. On April 4, hours before King was to lead another mass march on City Hall, a white ex-convict shot him from ambush. After King's death, ghettos across the United States exploded in riots, signaling the bitter end of the once-hopeful civil rights era.

After helping to lead the mourning for King, Robert Kennedy returned to the primary campaign. In June, he celebrated his growing support by winning the California primary, thus positioning himself to capture the Democratic candidacy. But after making a triumphant speech to his California campaign workers, Kennedy was shot down by an assassin as he returned to his hotel room. "I won't vote," one black New Yorker told a pollster. "Every good man we get they kill."

The killings of King and Kennedy left liberals dazed and uncertain, creating a political vacuum soon filled by the right. Student-led

"Identify Them by Their Garb." As Democratic National Convention delegates and protesters arrived in Chicago in late August 1968, the Chicago *American* published a guide to the "cast of characters" converging on the city. Illustrating student supporters of Eugene McCarthy, activists identified with the National Mobilization Against the War (the "Mobe"), liberal Democrats opposed to the Johnson administration, hippies, Yippies, apolitical greasers, and outlaw bikers, the guide identified political attitudes through stereotypes of dress and hair style. The *American* failed to note any African-Americans among the dissenting delegates and demonstrators.

Here's Cast of Characters in Drama of Streets

CLEAN GENES   THE MOB   OPEN CONVENTIONERS   HIPPIES   YIPPIES   GREASERS   BIKERS

upheaval in France and campus rebellions at Columbia University and hundreds of other U.S. colleges added to the sense of confusion and social instability. In August, as Chicago police brutally beat antiwar demonstrators gathered outside the convention hall, Vice President Hubert Humphrey captured the Democratic presidential nomination with solid backing from urban political bosses and organized labor. However, burdened by nationwide revulsion over the Chicago violence and his support of an unpopular war, Humphrey could not unite Democratic voters. Humphrey's chief opponent was Republican Richard Nixon, a former vice president. Nixon aimed his campaign at white southerners and at what he called the "silent majority" of "forgotten Americans, the nonshouters, the nondemonstrators." But Nixon also went after the "peace vote," declaring he had a "secret plan" to end the war. By the time Humphrey pledged to halt the bombing of North Vietnam, it was too late to forestall Nixon's narrow victory in November.

Humphrey's difficulties were compounded by third-party candidate George Wallace, who stepped into the void created by liberalism's disarray. Wallace was a Vietnam hawk and a racist who had learned to substitute new code words, such as "law and order," for the old segregationist language. At the end of September, polls gave Wallace 21 percent of the national vote, with his greatest strength among traditionally Democratic voters in the white South, in the lower middle class, and among blue-collar workers in the industrial Midwest.

Northern white workers' support for Wallace did not necessarily mean that they were

". . . HE WAS JUST A PERSON"

In August 1968 a few thousand antiwar activists and "Yippies"—a flamboyant group led by Abbie Hoffman and Jerry Rubin—gathered in Chicago to protest the Democratic National Convention. The activists' presence—and, in some cases, their acts of provocation—spurred a stunning display of police violence. The Chicago police broke up protests with tear gas and billy clubs, beating hundreds of activists, bystanders, and reporters. Vivid reports of the battle fed a widespread sense that American society was being torn apart. Barry Edmonds, a prize-winning photographer for the Booth Newspaper chain, covered the demonstrations. Here, he describes what he saw one night as he drove down Wells Street in Chicago.

After about two blocks, a running mob of people—about fifty—burst out of an alley in front of our station wagon. I stopped to avoid running over them. There were police chasing them with billy clubs.

A young man in a tan summer suit—he was well-dressed and carried one camera—ran in front of our vehicle. A cop yelled, "Get out of here with that camera." The man ran to the sidewalk, but one cop circled a parked car to cut him off, and another cop was just five feet behind him with a raised club.

The young man raised his hands when he saw the cop in front, like he was surrendering, but both cops grabbed him, one on each side. A third cop came up behind him with a billy club and made a running swing at the man's head. It didn't knock him out. He began screaming in a high pitched voice, like a girl, it sounded. He dropped to the sidewalk, and the two cops turned away, but the cop who had clubbed him from behind—he was a short, stocky man—was still clubbing the man, who lay on the pavement, still screaming. Then the cop left, and "Yippie medics" came up, wearing white smocks. . . .

I drove on, slowly. . . . Some more "Yippies" in their white smocks with crude red crosses sewn on the sleeves were kneeling by another man down on the sidewalk. The man's face was bloody. . . . I heard somebody ask, "Can you take this man to the hospital? . . ." They laid the man across the back seat of our station wagon. He had a bandage around the crown of his head. . . .

There were police all over, and we told the man to stay down. He kept saying, "I'm sorry. I'm sorry. Gee, my wife is really going to be worried." He didn't look like a Yippie or a hippie or a newsman—he was just a person.

more racist or prowar than the rest of the population. Surveys taken in the late 1960s showed that racial hostility was as prevalent in upper-middle-class suburbs as in white ethnic neighborhoods and that opposition to the war was greatest in workers' communities. Rather, Wallace attracted northern supporters by tapping a deep vein of alienation and social resentment among working Americans. He appealed, in his own words, to the "average man," the "steelworker, paperworker, small businessman, the cabdriver" who was "sick and tired of theoreticians in both national parties and in some of our colleges and some of our courts telling us how to go to bed at night and get up in the morning."

Wallace attracted support from two kinds of northern workers: older skilled workers, often of Polish or Italian extraction, who feared African-American encroachment in their neighborhoods; and rebellious young production workers alienated from their union and the established order. As one young autoworker noted, if "[UAW President Walter] Reuther was for Wallace, we'd be for Humphrey." Frightened by the Wallace phenomenon, the AFL-CIO and the UAW deluged their members with leaflets and pamphlets pointing out Wallace's antiunion, proemployer record. This appeal worked, and Humphrey picked up many votes from northern workers who had once favored Wallace.

Nixon's narrow victory in November set the stage for four years of political stalemate. His "peace plan" turned out to mean seven more years of war and United States–led invasions of Cambodia and Laos, but a slow reduction in combat roles for U.S. troops. On domestic issues, Nixon sought to encourage the conservative mood in the electorate. He nominated conservative judges, escalated the government's clandestine war against political activists, and inaugurated a series of well-publicized but unsuccessful prosecutions of prominent radicals. At the same time, Nixon was forced to make concessions to the liberals: he proposed linking Social Security benefits to the cost-of-living index; he continued the desegregation of southern public schools; and he pioneered occupational health and safety legislation. The Democratic Party, which dominated Congress, remained split on the Vietnam War but managed to defend most of the previously passed civil rights and Great Society legislation.

FROM RIGHTS-CONSCIOUSNESS TO LIBERATION

While America's elected politicians were mired in stalemate after 1968, popular upheavals continued to reshape the social and political landscape. The giant Woodstock rock festival of August 1969 and massive antiwar protests in November 1969 and May 1971 demonstrated that the culture of dissent had spread far beyond the campuses

Wearing your politics. Political buttons adorn the sleeve of an antiwar demonstrator in the fall of 1968. During the 1960s, political buttons were produced in the millions, providing people with an inexpensive and stylish way to express their beliefs and commitments publicly.

that gave them birth. Though most New Left organizations had fragmented, and some veteran activists were exhausted, the late 1960s and early 1970s saw the emergence of new movements addressing a range of issues.

One of the largest movements to emerge in these years was the ecology movement. On April 22, 1970, hundreds of thousands of Americans nationwide signaled their growing concern over pollution and the degradation of the environment by taking part in the first "Earth Day" demonstrations. Activists held rallies and teach-ins in hundreds of communities in an effort to inform and mobilize others. The naturalist René Dubos suggested that Earth Day demonstrated a widespread conviction that "Gross National Product and technological efficiency are less important than the quality of the organic world and the suitability of the environment for a truly human life."

The ecology movement, which grew to become a major political force in the 1970s and 1980s, had its roots in the conservation movement of the early twentieth century that had helped establish the national parks system. However, this movement dwindled until the 1960s, when the proliferation of automobiles and the spread of an affluent, high-consumption, "throwaway" economy combined to generate new levels of pollution and concerns about its consequences. "We are beginning to realize," wrote one group of environmental activists, "that our life-styles, our industries, and our population growth are leading to the extinction of more and more species, to the poisoning of our air, water, and food, and to the exhaustion of resources on earth. This growing destruction threatens the continued existence of the human species."

The ecology movement borrowed direct-action tactics from the civil rights movement and resonated with the "back to nature" ethic of the counterculture. Ecology groups held sit-ins and demonstrations; one Chicago activist dumped polluted sludge and garbage in the executive suite of a polluting company. But most ecology activists shunned heated confrontation in favor of a gentle, healing image. Their movement gained wide support among middle-class, white Americans who saw pollution as a threat to their right to health and security for their families and communities.

Other movements of the Nixon era drew support from different groups. In California and the southwestern states, the growing Mexican-American community began to take a new activist stance. In the spring of 1968, inspired by the farmworkers' campaign and the civil rights movement, Chicano students in Los Angeles and other cities held a series of school boycotts or "blowouts." Poor-quality education was a spark-plug issue for the whole community, according to participant Carlos Vasquez. "Chicano students became radicalized," he recalled, "when they asked, 'Why are our schools the way they are?'" The student protests spurred a broader movement seeking increased power for the Mexican-American community and an end to social, economic, and political discrimination.

Meanwhile, across the continent, in Chicago and New York City, a similar movement emerged in the Puerto Rican community. There the catalyst was the Young Lords, an organization that drew members from urban street gangs as well as from college campuses. The Lords protested police violence, created a Black Panther–style free breakfast program for children, and took over an East Harlem hospital in an effort to force officials to act to end lead poisoning among inner-city children. The key to the group's success, according to Pablo Guzman, a New York leader, was its ability to draw on the cultural traditions and community ties of El Barrio (the neighborhood). "At one rally we used a Puerto Rican flag. The people turned out by the hundreds and the rally turned into a huge march," he recalled. "We tapped an in-

Wounded Knee, 1973. An American Indian Movement activist rejoices after hearing that the federal government has agreed to extend a cease-fire and negotiations at the Pine Ridge Reservation in South Dakota. The three-month confrontation between AIM and federal marshals began in February 1973, when AIM seized hostages at a reservation trading post to dramatize their protest against Bureau of Indian Affairs policy and conservative tribal leadership.

tense nationalistic fervor among Puerto Rican people. In this way we were able to cut across all ages and types and reach a broad segment of the population."

In March 1969, the Young Lords joined Chicano activists at a conference of *La Raza* (The Race), held in Denver. More than fifteen hundred participants signed a declaration reaffirming the heritage of the Latin American cultures and the Spanish language, calling for community control of Latino neighborhoods, and promising support for working-class and anti-imperialist struggles. The unity ended, however, when the conference voted to bar African-Americans from the movement, and the Puerto Rican contingent walked out in protest.

The era's climate of dissent also encouraged Native Americans to create a protest movement. Native Americans had been largely ignored by white society over the past century. But the 1960s brought signs that some Native Americans would no longer suffer in silence. In 1964, the Puyallup in the state of Washington held "fish-ins" to protest state court decisions that denied them their treaty-guaranteed fishing rights. In the spring of 1969, the Navajo and Hopi began protesting against the strip-mining operations of the Peabody Coal Company on Hopi lands in the Southwest. One Navajo woman, a tribal elder and protest organizer, explained, "Peabody's monsters are digging up the heart of the earth, our sacred mountain, and we also feel the pain."

In November 1969, a group of seventy-eight Native Americans, calling themselves "Indians of All Tribes," drew nationwide media attention by taking over the San Francisco Bay island of Alcatraz (which had previously housed a notorious federal prison) and turning it into a liberated area free from federal control. The Alcatraz occupation lasted eighteen months before federal forces finally brought it to an end.

Native American activists chose another historic site for an even more dramatic confrontation in 1973. In March, roughly three hundred Oglala Sioux and their allies returned to Wounded Knee in North Dakota, where U.S. troops had massacred hundreds of Indian men, women, and children in 1890. Calling themselves the American Indian Movement (AIM), these activists occupied Wounded Knee and declared it liberated territory. Responding swiftly, more than two hundred FBI agents and other federal forces, armed with automatic rifles, armored cars, and grenade launchers, set up a blockade around the village. Despite blazing gun battles, the AIM activists held out for seventy-one days before negotiating a truce. Together with the Alcatraz takeover, Wounded Knee became a symbol of growing Native American activism and consciousness.

Grass-roots activity spread in countless directions in the early 1970s. Asian-Americans became increasingly assertive about their rights, calling for extension of the legal and moral struggle against discrimination to encompass the growing numbers of Asians in the United States. Modeling themselves on the Black Panther Party, a group of senior citizens organized the Gray Panthers, which employed direct-action tactics drawn from the labor and civil rights movements to secure better treatment for elderly Americans. And following a riot between New York City police and gay patrons of the Stonewall Inn in June 1969, homosexual men and women began calling for "Gay Power," consciously linking their grass-roots struggle to those of African-Americans and other "oppressed minorities." Throwing off years of secrecy during which homosexuality had been treated by the dominant society as a sickness and a crime, gays and lesbians moved aggressively into the open, holding marches, pushing legislation to end decades of bias and discrimination, and calling for "gay liberation."

But the largest and most striking of all the movements of the early 1970s was the women's liberation movement, which mobilized millions of American women and fundamentally reshaped American society. The stunning rebirth of American feminism emerged in part from the New Left's probing of the political dimension of personal life. As an ideology and social movement, feminism had flourished in the years before World War I and faded in the 1920s and 1930s; it was reborn in the late 1960s as a result of the creative merger between the self-emancipatory impulse of the New Left and the political agenda long put forward by an older generation of women reformers.

Beginning in the late 1950s, a small group of well-placed American women sought to assure equality between the sexes in much the

After Stonewall I. In the months following the June 1969 Stonewall Rebellion, New York police continued to raid bars where lesbians and gay men gathered. In the early morning hours of March 9, 1970, police raided the Snake Pit, a Greenwich Village bar, arresting all 167 employees and patrons. After the "suspects" were taken to a local station house, Alfredo Vinales, an illegal alien afraid of being deported if his homosexuality was discovered, tried to escape. Leaping from a second-floor window, he was impaled on an iron picket fence.

After Stonewall II. Vinales's act of desperation graphically articulated the oppression of gays. "No matter how you look at it," as one gay activist slogan went, "Vinales was pushed." The horror of the Snake Pit incident helped mobilize hundreds of gays to join the new movement. In June 1970, the first march commemorating the anniversary of the Stonewall Rebellion was organized—an event now observed every June by hundreds of thousands of gays and lesbians around the world.

same way that the NAACP used the courts and Congress to fight racial discrimination. Prodded by such veteran liberals as Eleanor Roosevelt, President Kennedy appointed a Commission on the Status of Women in 1961, but women's issues won popular notice only with the 1963 publication of Betty Friedan's best-selling book *The Feminine Mystique,* which offered an incisive critique of the postwar status of women. In 1966, Friedan and twenty-seven other professional women established the National Organization for Women (NOW) "to take action to bring American women into full participation in the mainstream of American society *now.*" Inspired by the victories won by African-Americans, NOW prodded the federal government to enforce the ban on sex discrimination in employment and public accommodations included in the 1964 Civil Rights Act (a provision inserted by conservatives hoping to discredit the whole bill).

"WE ARE INSIDE YOU . . ."

The Gay Liberation Movement celebrated the first anniversary of the Stonewall riot with a New York City march. Participant Fran Winant wrote this poem, entitled "Christopher Street Liberation Day, June 28, 1970."

With banners and our smiles
we're being photographed
by tourists police and leering men
we fill their cameras
with 10,000 faces
bearing witness
to our own existence
in sunlight
from Washington Maryland
Massachusetts Pennsylvania
Connecticut Ohio
Iowa Minnesota
from Harlem and the suburbs
the universities and the world
we are women who love women
we are men who love men
we are lesbians and homosexuals
we cannot apologize
for knowing
what others refuse to know
for affirming
what they deny
we might have been

The feminist impulse might have remained confined to these relatively elite women had their ideas not been given a dynamic moral vision and intense personal meaning by the explosion of feminist consciousness within the New Left. Young women had joined the political movements of the 1960s with fervor and dedication. But many were dismayed to discover that their male comrades did not think of them as equals. At SDS meetings, remembered one participant, "Women made peanut butter sandwiches, waited on tables, cleaned up, got laid. That was their role." This gap between radical vision and discriminatory practice drove tens of thousands of young women out of the antiwar and student movements. Bringing with them skills, networks, tactics, and a language for describing their oppression, these young women built an explosive and ultimately massive movement for women's liberation. As one woman remembered, "In the black movement I had been fighting someone else's oppression. Now there was a way I could fight for my own freedom, and I was going to be much stronger than I ever was."

Flowering in the early 1970s and continuing to grow throughout the decade, the women's movement shook first the radical community and then sent shock waves into every recess of American society. NOW membership multiplied rapidly; and *Ms.* magazine, which first appeared in 1971, sold out its first 300,000 copies in little more than a week. Hundreds of thousands of women took part in "consciousness-raising groups," where women discussed every aspect of their lives, ranging from discrimination on the job, to the destructive results of competition over men, to failed sexual relationships with boyfriends and husbands.

These consciousness-raising groups served as springboards for action. For example, in the

the women and men
who watched us and waved
and made fists
and gave us victory signs
and stood there after we had passed
thinking of all they had to lose
and of how society punishes
its victims
who are all of us
in the end
but we are sisters and sisters
brothers and brothers
workers and lovers
we are together
we are marching
past the crumbling old world
that leans toward us
in anguish from the pavement
our banners are sails
pulling us through the streets
where we have always been
as ghosts
now we are shouting our own words
we are a community
we are a society
we are everyone
we are inside you
remember
all you were taught to forget
we are part of the new world . . .

CR. A consciousness-raising group meets at the New York Women's Center in December 1970.

"... PERSONAL PROBLEMS ARE POLITICAL PROBLEMS"

Consciousness-raising groups, a common feature of the women's liberation movement, helped women discover the social roots of their individual problems. These quotations suggest the diverse ways that different "CR" groups grappled with the link between the personal and the political. The first quotation is from a woman talking in 1970 about her ongoing group. The other statements were made by women in the 1980s, recalling their experiences in the late 1960s and early 1970s.

CAROL H: So the reason I participate in these meetings is not to solve any personal problem. One of the first things we discover in these groups is that personal problems are political problems. There are no personal solutions at this time. There is only collective action for a collective solution. I went, and I continue to go to these meetings because I have gotten a political understanding which all my reading, all my "political discussions," all my "political action," all my four-odd years in the movement never gave me.... I believe at this point, and maybe for a long time to come, that these analytical sessions are a form of political action....

ARLENE S.: Our group was very different, nonpolitical. Other groups seemed to have a harshness to them. The message was you had to move forward, you had to deal with issues. There was a sense of confrontation and judgment. Our group, I feel, accomplished so much more, but in a different

course of discussing their lives, many married women articulated for the first time their feelings about being "trapped" in the traditional role of housewife, spending all day, every day, doing housework and taking care of children. Frustrated at having no choices and angry at the unfair division of household labor, they explored ways to change their lives. Individually, many women confronted their husbands and partners, pushing for new attitudes and arrangements. Collectively, feminists fought for the creation of childcare centers across the country. Initially seen as a radical innovation, childcare soon gained popular acceptance as feminists pushed corporations, universities, and local and state governments to establish childcare centers.

In the economic arena, women demanded greater wage parity. In 1968, women's wages were, on average, less than 60 percent of men's. And because of systematic discrimination, less than 10 percent of the nation's doctors, lawyers, college professors, business executives, and architects were women in 1970. Feminists used petitions, picketing, and legal action to push employers to increase wages and open upper-level jobs to women. The Women's Equity Action League brought class-action suits against nearly three hundred colleges and universities, forcing them to agree to change their employment patterns. One woman surgeon confronted a male colleague who had publicly stated that women were incapable of doing surgery. "I said, 'Doctor, I want to watch you work. I want to see what part of your anatomy you use in performing surgery that I am not equipped with.'"

The new feminists also acted to change the ways that women were perceived and represented in American culture. In August 1968, a group of women startled the nation by disrupting the Miss America pageant, charging that beauty contests encouraged the notion that women were not whole people but rather objects for men's sexual pleasure. Believing that language was crucial to the formation of attitudes, feminists attacked the use of such demeaning labels as "chicks" and urged women who married to keep their own surnames as

way. We just talked about ourselves, and it was very warm.

FRANCES H.: It was a time of tremendous turmoil. And I think the turmoil may have preceded our understanding of what was really going on. It was like being a little boat on a rocky sea, and you think it's your fault that you are rocking the boat. But in fact you are on this tremendously disturbed social ocean. So that's how I think of CR [consciousness-raising] now. We were this little boat battering around, having our conversations, but, now, as I look back, in fact, I see a much larger panorama.

ABBY T.: When I first joined consciousness-raising, I was aware of its being part of large political ferment. There were the civil rights movement, the assassinations, the antiwar stuff, the SDS organizations on campus. The Women's Movement just seemed to flow out of all of this, and so right from the beginning I thought of it as political.

PHYLLIS F.: We perpetuate sexism until we become conscious of the part that we play. That's what women's groups were meant to do because they were really well thought out. They were actually political groups. They really got me. You know, if you said politics to me back then, I would have left the room. I came from the dead 1950s, and I didn't know from radical politics. But in the group, they just said, well, the personal is political. Just work on yourself, that's politics. Okay, I could deal with that. And you know, it works. Not immediately that minute, maybe, but over time. There are battered women's shelters and rape crisis services across the state of New York that did not exist in the early 1970s. These came out of CR groups.

symbols of their individuality. Feminists challenged television producers to begin portraying women in more diverse and realistic fashion, and pushed newspapers and magazines to address women's social and economic concerns. Arguing that traditional scholarship ignored women, feminists researched the role of women in history and demanded an end to gender stereotyping in educational materials.

Health care was another major area of concern to feminists. They charged that medical schools excluded women and taught male doctors to treat women patients condescendingly. As a result, feminists felt, women received poor care and often were pushed into unnecessary hysterectomies and radical breast surgery. While some activists pressured medical schools to reform, others created independent health-care clinics run by and for women.

Linked to feminists' health-care concerns was the campaign for the legalization of abortion. Before 1970, abortion was illegal in virtually every state in the country. Women seeking to end unwanted pregnancies were forced to seek out illegal abortions or to self-induce miscarriages; thousands of women died each year as the result of botched operations. Arguing that women had a right to control their bodies, feminists mounted abortion rights rallies and joined clergy and population-control advocates in lobbying state legislatures for more liberal legislation. They made slow, state-by-state progress until 1973, when the U.S. Supreme Court's landmark *Roe* v. *Wade* decision guaranteed women access to abortions in the early stages of pregnancy.

The feminist challenge to traditional sex roles also encouraged the growth of the lesbian movement. Some feminists endorsed sexual relationships with women, hoping they would be less oppressive and more fulfilling than relationships with men. Many lesbians who had long hidden or denied their sexual orientation found that the women's movement provided them with a broader community in which they could openly profess their sexuality.

The women's movement was highly controversial, and many Americans resisted its ideas and demands. Through the early 1970s, however, opinion polls recorded a steady shift in public opinion toward feminist positions on such issues as pay equity, childcare, and abortion. By 1976, the *Reader's Digest* conceded: "Women's Liberation has changed the lives of many Americans and the ways they look at family, job and sexual equality." Many working-class women did not identify with feminism, but they embraced the transformations it had wrought. As one secretary put it, "I'm no women's libber, but I believe women should get equal pay." Millions of women office workers changed their work culture by refusing to serve coffee, by wearing slacks to work, and by insisting on being addressed as adults.

The rights-conscious spirit of these diverse movements touched other aspects of working-class life as well. In the early 1970s, a democratic sensibility surged through the nation's factories. "The worker wants the same rights he has on the street after he walks in the plant door," asserted Jim Babbs, a twenty-four-year-old white worker at a Ford plant outside Detroit. "This is a general feeling of this generation, whether it's a guy in a plant or a student on campus, not wanting to be an IBM number."

For a brief moment, even the U.S. government acknowledged the desire for change in the structure of American work life. "All authority in our society is being challenged," announced a Department of Health, Education, and Welfare report, "professional athletes challenge owners, journalists challenge editors, consumers challenge manufacturers . . . and young blue-collar workers, who have grown up in an environment in which equality is called for in all institutions, are demanding the same rights and expressing the same values as university graduates."

Most major industrial unions faced significant internal challenges to the leadership at some time between 1963 and 1973. Contract rejections, a rarity before 1962, soared in 1968; unauthorized "wildcat" strikes reached a postwar high. Opposition movements demanded aggressive strike action to raise wages, combat speed-ups, and ensure dignity on the job. Top union leaders who seemed too complacent were denied reelection in the steelworkers', miners', teachers', and postal employees' unions. There was no unionwide challenge to UAW head Walter Reuther, but between 1961 and 1973 every national auto contract signed by the UAW generated at least a score of local strikes by workers determined to force plant managers to "humanize" working conditions.

This new working-class mood had its greatest impact among public employees, especially those who worked for the eighty thousand units of state and local government. Before World War II, public employment meant secure, high-status jobs, often reserved for those with close ties to the city machine or the local ethnic political club. By the 1960s, civil service employees' wages had fallen well behind those of organized labor, while overcrowded classrooms, deteriorating public transit systems, and teeming welfare offices reduced the quality of public employees' work life.

Strikes among public employees, for years virtually unheard of, punctuated the late 1960s. Work stoppages grew from 42 in 1965 to 382 in 1974. Because many of these strikes were illegal, public-sector unionism had the flavor of an underground movement, a consciousness-changing social crusade. In Hamtramck, Michigan, junior-high teachers defied state law in 1965 to stage a twenty-four-hour-a-day "prolonged teachers' meeting" to force the local school board to recognize their union. Leaders of the American Federation of Teachers were frequently jailed during the still-illegal teachers' strikes of the late 1960s.

The American Federation of State, County, and Municipal Employees (AFSCME) tripled its membership in the late 1960s and early 1970s. AFSCME grew as Great Society aid to states and cities generated new jobs and programs designed to serve African-American and Latino youth. Minority workers wanted rights that unionization could provide, and AFSCME wanted to organize new workers in order to protect longtime employees. In the 1960s, most AFSCME members were blue-collar employees or low-level clericals, but there was also a sizable minority of old-line employees who transformed their "professional" associations into organizations affiliated with the trade-union movement.

The most startling expression of the new militancy erupted in the postal system in March 1970, when 200,000 workers struck urban postal facilities across the North and West. Postal employees had once been mostly older white males, but by the late 1960s the number of blacks and white females had risen, and many young hippies with shaggy hair were delivering the mail. Many of the half-million postal workers found themselves subject to factorylike discipline as the Post Office Department mechanized their jobs. Postal unions had existed since 1962, but strikes were illegal, and union leaders functioned more as lobbyists than as labor spokesmen. Thus, when postal workers walked out in March 1970, their strike amounted to a revolt against their leaders as well as their federal employer. President Nixon countered by sending troops to sort the mail, but the strike succeeded in forcing Congress to raise wages and reorganize the postal system.

Workers also became increasingly conscious of their right to a safe and healthy workplace in the early 1970s. During these years, industrial accident rates and health problems jumped almost 50 percent. The rising industrial output of the 1960s meant injuries, as managers pushed workers and machines to the limits of their capacities. By the end of the decade, the Labor Department estimated that 2.2 million workers were disabled each year from job-related health problems, proportionately far more than in western Europe or Japan.

Before the early 1970s, neither workers nor their unions made health and safety top issues. "In the past," noted one labor official, "the union practice . . . was to trade and barter its safety and health demands for a couple of cents an hour in wages." For many workers, a combination of fatalism and masculine stoicism had forestalled earlier action on safety and health issues. "When it came to safety, the older guys would say 'If you die, you die,'" recalled one construction worker. For other workers, including utility linemen and hard-rock miners, the dangers of the work sustained their pride in the skill needed to do the job. But these sentiments changed in the 1960s, especially when it came to dangers generated by chemicals and air pollution. Male workers could find little "manliness" in being exposed to lead and mercury poisoning, asbestos, cotton and coal dust, pesticides, and radiation.

In the late 1960s, unions in steel, coal, and oil pressured Congress for health and safety laws. In response, Congress passed the 1970 Occupational Safety and Health Act (OSHA), which created a new set of workplace rights and, like the U.S. Supreme Court's 1954 *Brown* v. *Board of Education* decision, helped legitimate a grass-roots struggle. OSHA was a compromise, but it offered union activists an organizing tool. At the Olin Corporation's Film Division works in North Carolina, unionist James Reese used his chairmanship of the plant safety committee to confront management over the safe use of many chemicals. Proudly, he memorized the OSHA standards for each. "For once," he explained, "I had something that they had to listen to. I finally had a law to back me up."

More than a thousand miles away, Karen Silkwood felt the same. The new consciousness about safety issues motivated her to become a union activist for the Oil, Chemical, and Atomic Workers' Union (OCAW) at Kerr-McGee's plutonium processing plant in Oklahoma. Silkwood had never taken much interest in activism until she discovered that Kerr-McGee policies often exposed her and her fellow workers to radioactive hazards. Her death in a mysterious auto accident followed months of harassment at the hands of company personnel. Silkwood became a martyr for the growing safety and health movement; her story dramatized a new social issue.

Industrialists were caught unaware when OSHA became law, but once they saw how it empowered workers, they lobbied Congress for cuts in inspection funds, exemptions for small firms, and delays in implementation of health standards. Governmental action to assure safe working conditions proved to be dependent on the extent to which workers in each industry forcefully pressed their claims. In the coalfields, a dynamic "black lung" movement led by miners, antipoverty activists, and liberal doctors forced Congress to establish the Mine Safety and Health Agency, better funded and more sympathetic to workers than OSHA; accident rates in the coalfields declined. In contrast, workers in the largely nonunion textile industry gained little from OSHA. Their employers, contemptuous of the claim that "brown lung" disease was a serious malady, were able to dominate the debate over health and safety in the mills. OSHA failed in its efforts to force the industry to reduce factory cotton dust, and "brown lung" went largely uncompensated by insurance companies and local workmen's compensation boards.

THE STATE OF THE UNIONS

American unions had many things going for them in the 1960s. The AFL-CIO had a cordial relationship with Presidents Kennedy and Johnson, and its leaders supported the Great Society programs of the mid-1960s and the occupational health and safety legislation of the early 1970s. The unions enjoyed the longest era of sustained high employment since World War II. Protected by cost-of-living adjustments written into their contracts, many blue-collar workers won real wage increases even in the inflationary years after 1966. Most big unions won employer-funded health insurance, higher pensions, and increased vacation pay.

Despite such favorable circumstances, the labor movement did not hold its own in the 1960s. Unions recruited 2 million additional members in the decade, largely in public employment, but the proportion of all workers who belonged to unions declined from 29 percent in 1960 to 23 percent fifteen years later.

American unions had an uneasy relationship with the social changes of the 1960s. On one hand they benefited from the new rights-conscious mood sweeping large sections of the working class. By the mid-1970s, unions were notably more female and interracial than they had been fifteen years before. The UAW, AFSCME, and the AFL-CIO contributed hundreds of thousands of dollars to organize black workers in Memphis and Chicano farmworkers in California. In the early 1970s, OCAW and the International Association of Machinists were highly active in the effort to establish health and safety rights on the job.

But on the two great issues of the 1960s—race and Vietnam— unions stood divided and hesitant, no longer in the vanguard of social change and sometimes, as on the issue of Vietnam, allied with the most conservative forces in the land. Standing outside the main reform currents of the decade, the unions were unable to take advantage of the idealism and energy of civil rights and antiwar activists. No major trade union leader was prepared to enroll the radicals of the 1960s in an effort to revitalize the labor movement, as John L. Lewis had once invited the communists and socialists to help build the industrial unions in the 1930s. Although many 1960s radicals eventually found their way into the union movement in the 1970s and 1980s, they did so only after the dynamic force of their own social movements was largely spent.

The United Farm Workers' success in attracting the support of student activists pointed up the opportunities that other unions were missing. At college campuses across the country, the UFW recruited students to picket stores selling boycotted farm products. Hundreds of students dropped out of school to work full-time on the boycott campaign, and the resulting decline in sales forced growers to sign union contracts. Furthermore, the grape and lettuce boycotts taught the values of trade unionism to thousands of students who might otherwise have dismissed labor organizations as tools of the establishment. Despite these advantages, most unions kept their distance from the campus movements of the late 1960s and early 1970s.

When it came to civil rights, unions were both part of the problem and part of the solution. Since the 1940s, the trade union movement had been the most integrated major institution in American life. In the early 1960s, black and minority workers made up about a quarter of total union membership, a far higher proportion than in most suburban churches or college faculties. Yet many civil rights activists found the union movement a disappointing ally. Unlike other American institutions, the unions claimed to represent a tradition of justice and struggle in which African-Americans could enter fully. Civil rights activists therefore judged the unions by a higher standard than they did universities or corporations.

During the 1950s and early 1960s the AFL-CIO maintained a split personality on civil rights issues. The labor federation forbade discrimination in its new constitution, backed U.S. Supreme Court desegregation rulings, and worked hard for passage of civil rights laws. But the federation seemed to lack the will to fight racial discrimination within its union affiliates, many of which excluded minority workers. AFL-CIO head George Meany was an organization man, not a racist, but the net effect was much the same. Along with other top union officials, Meany disliked socially disruptive civil rights demonstrations, including the 1963 March on Washington. And he resented efforts by A. Philip Randolph of the Sleeping Car Porters to organize a black caucus within the AFL-CIO. "Who the hell appointed you the guardian of all the Negroes in America?" Meany once shouted at the venerable civil rights leader across a union convention floor.

Although segregationist locals of big industrial unions were eventually forced to integrate lodge halls and seniority lists, the construction trades remained almost all-white, in part because their power rested on the ability to restrict membership and limit competition for jobs. "We don't take any new members, regardless of color," said one building trades leader. When apprenticeships did open up, many construction workers felt union cards should go to their sons and relatives as a sort of patrimony, much like a family-run business.

Such exclusionary practices were offensive to urban African-Americans, who saw white workers from the suburbs earning good pay on construction projects only a few blocks from the ghetto. By the end of the decade, white craft unionists were regularly embroiled in street conflicts with black activists, and courts were ordering the unions to recruit minority members. In 1969 the federal government endorsed the Philadelphia Plan, which established affirmative action goals for six building trades. With construction stalled by a recession, the unions resisted fiercely; the next year they struck a deal by which the Nixon administration backed off on enforcement in exchange for the unions' active support for the president's Vietnam policies.

Since the construction trades had always been in the most conservative wing of the union movement, racial tensions there were less damaging to the maintenance of a labor-black alliance than in traditionally progressive sectors of the movement. For example, the ILGWU had once been a crusading union, embodying the hopes of its Jewish and Italian immigrant membership. But as the post–World War II garment industry recruited African-American and Puerto Rican workers, the old union leadership grew isolated from its members. Meanwhile, union locals composed of skilled and well-paid Jewish and Italian "cutters" opposed federal job training programs and offered blacks and Puerto Ricans only token representation in union offices. The ILGWU soon came under attack by the NAACP, CORE, and local antipoverty agencies.

An even more ominous conflict emerged in 1968 as the New York City local of the American Federation of Teachers (AFT) fought a decentralization plan that offered parents a limited form of "community control" of the schools. The AFT claimed that some local school boards were dominated by black nationalists hostile to Jewish teachers, and that the new plan would give these activists the power to gut seniority rights and grievance procedures. Community-control advocates, on the other hand, argued that the AFT was unwilling to share power with African-American and Puerto Rican parents and their increasingly assertive leaders. This bitter conflict, which began in the Ocean Hill–Brownsville school district, generated four strikes in the fall of 1968 and drove a wedge between groups that had long been allies in the fight against discrimination.

Even the UAW, whose progressive leaders put money and muscle behind the civil rights movement, found itself at odds with black activists. By 1960, 300,000 African-American workers made up more than a quarter of total UAW membership, but they were largely confined to the most grueling work in the most dangerous and dirty departments. Black UAW staffers organized an opposition group, the Trade Union Leadership Conference, to push civil rights issues. The conference soon became a mass organization of 7,000 unionists. It proved decisive in putting African-Americans on the UAW executive board and in paving the way for the 1973 election of Coleman Young as mayor of Detroit; his career had begun as a foundry worker and UAW organizer at Ford's River Rouge complex.

The Trade Union Leadership Conference had little impact on conditions in the auto plants, however. In the late 1960s, production speed-ups, combined with black workers' growing racial militancy, generated explosive social tensions in many urban plants. In the aftermath of the 1967 Detroit riot, African-American workers organized the Dodge Revolutionary Union Movement (DRUM) at Chrysler's Dodge Main factory in Hamtramck. Similar groups quickly sprang up in other Detroit plants. Combining Black Power nationalism and workplace militancy, these young militants compared their factories to plantations and called white foremen brutal overseers. Shutting down inner-city plants in more than a dozen wildcat strikes, they criticized both the seniority system and grievance procedures as ineffective or racist. UAW leaders quickly denounced the protests. UAW secretary-treasurer Emil Mazey, once a fiery union militant, branded the dissidents "black fascists."

Though these revolutionary groups collapsed in the 1970s, they left a permanent imprint on the Detroit labor movement. Because of pressure from DRUM and other groups, Chrysler hired more African-American foremen, the UAW hired more African-American staff, and the more obvious forms of racial discrimination were reduced, if not eliminated, in most plants. Most inner-city UAW locals were soon headed by African-Americans, some of them veterans of the DRUM insurgency.

Vietnam proved to be equally problematic for the labor movement. Under the leadership of George Meany, the AFL-CIO steadfastly defended U.S. conduct of the war, even after big-business leaders had begun to waver. Because many top AFL-CIO leaders had won their posts in battles with Communist opponents two or three decades before, Meany had little difficulty winning support for his conservative foreign policy. Meany called opponents of the war a "coalition of retreat," and he used secret files supplied to him by the FBI to discredit antiwar forces in the union movement.

Meanwhile, the AFL-CIO received millions of dollars from the U.S. government, some from the CIA, to undermine Asian, African, and Latin American trade unions that appeared anti-American or Communist-led. In their stead, AFL-CIO operatives supported pro-U.S. unions that were often less representative of their country's working class. The conservative and corrupt International Longshoremen's Association (ILA) worked directly with U.S. military authorities to resolve waterfront labor problems in Vietnam and to keep American military equipment flowing there. And in Guyana, Brazil, and Chile, the AFL-CIO cooperated with the CIA to topple populist political leaders that the U.S. government considered hostile to its interests.

Not all trade union leaders supported the Vietnam War. In traditionally liberal unions such as the UAW, the Packinghouse Workers' Union, Local 1199, and AFSCME, union officials criticized the war and Meany's hawkish politics. In New York, San Francisco, and Los Angeles, local unions participated in mass antiwar marches; and in 1968 Walter Reuther, who had grown frustrated with Meany's knee-jerk anticommunism, pulled the UAW out of the AFL-CIO. With the Teamsters, the UAW formed the Alliance for Labor Action (ALA), which Reuther hoped would "revitalize" the labor movement. But the ALA disintegrated in the early 1970s, after the Teamsters raided the farmworkers' union in California and endorsed President Nixon for reelection in 1972. Slow in responding to the social problems of the 1960s, the union movement was divided and disorganized as it turned to face the economic challenges of the 1970s.

THE WHITE BACKLASH

Conflict between the social movements of the 1960s and organized labor was not confined to top-level disputes over foreign policy or civil rights legislation. In his 1968 campaign, George Wallace demonstrated the extent to which white working-class discontent—with high taxes, declining neighborhoods, black militancy, and student radicalism—could be turned toward a populism of the right. In the years that followed, most workers remained liberals when it came to such welfare-state programs as Social Security, unemployment compensation, aid for dependent children, and job training, and they grew increasingly hostile to the war, as polls and referendums demonstrated. But on other "social issues" of the era—affirmative action, school busing to achieve racial balance, a woman's right to an abortion, and the rejection of the traditional symbols of American patriotism—white working-class men grew increasingly willing to attack the New Left and its allies.

This became clear in New York City on May 8, 1970. Antiwar demonstrators had gathered at a federal building near Wall Street to protest the U.S. invasion of Cambodia and the Ohio National Guard's murderous attack on a Kent State University antiwar protest. Suddenly a shining wave of yellow and orange surged through the crowd. A contingent of two hundred construction workers wearing bright plastic hard hats and armed with pliers and hammers pounced on the "longhairs." To the chant of "All the way with the USA" the "hard-hats" roughly elbowed the young protesters aside and returned the flag, put at half mast in homage to the four students slain at Kent State, back to full height.

Although the hard-hat demonstration had been carefully orchestrated by the White House and the conservative leaders of the New York building trades, it created a new social stereotype: the tough, prowar, blue-collar worker; a hardworking taxpayer hostile to blacks on welfare; a family man who spurned marijuana and the liberation of women. The "hard-hats" seemed to stand for working-class anger and resentment against all the social changes and political innovations of the 1960s. When construction trades officials presented Nixon with an honorary hard hat, the latter described the gift "as a symbol, along with our great flag, for freedom and patriotism to our beloved country."

The popular TV comedy series *All in the Family* captured this mood. Built around the character of Archie Bunker, a gruff and opinionated Queens warehouse foreman, the show broadcast the language of racial and political insult. Caught in a world he had not made, Archie lashed out against the forces of change, revealing an undisguised hatred for imagined enemies. "If your spics and spades want their rightful share of the American dream," Archie told his liberal son-in-law, "let 'em go and hustle for it just like I done." *All in the Family* had been created by the liberal producer Norman Lear to poke fun at what he saw as blue-collar parochialism, but its popularity reflected the genuine anger that existed within sections of the white working class.

Yet Archie Bunker was more myth than reality. In the early 1970s, white workers were not the reactionaries portrayed on television. On the Vietnam War issue, for example, opinion polls indicated that rank-and-file workers were substantially less hawkish than the college-educated. "The whole goddamn country of South Vietnam is not worth the life of one American boy," declared a construction worker, "no matter what the hell our politicians tell us."

But precisely because a disproportionate number of working-class men were drafted and sent to Vietnam, blue-collar Americans resented the college students who led antiwar protests. At issue was not a difference over foreign policy, but class antagonism. Working-class opponents of the Vietnam War hated antiwar demonstrators even more than they disliked the war. One worker whose son was serving in Vietnam lamented the inability of poorer boys to "get the same breaks as the college kids. We can't understand," he added, "how all of those rich kids—the kids with beards from the fancy suburbs—how they get off when my son has to go over there and maybe get his head shot off."

The women's liberation movement sparked similar patterns of reaction and resentment. Many Americans, male and female, felt threatened by the renewal of the women's movement and its challenge to cherished traditional values. Though increasing numbers of women were entering the paid labor force, most held unglamorous jobs that offered few psychic or emotional rewards. To many such women, the role of mother in the traditional family seemed more likely to provide a sense of security and dignity. Seeing "women's libbers" as privileged professionals, many working-class women interpreted feminist criticism of traditional women's roles as a threat to their own sense of self-worth. President Nixon appealed to this antifeminist reaction in 1971 when he vetoed federal support for daycare centers, arguing that they would undermine the nation's "family-centered traditions" and "commit the vast moral authority of the national government to . . . communal approaches to childrearing."

The backlash against New Left radicalism fed an already strong conservative movement. While the 1960s are generally remembered for the spread of liberal and New Left activism, ultraconservative groups such as Young Americans for Freedom and the John Birch Society were also organizing. Politicians such as 1964 presidential candidate Barry Goldwater and actor Ronald Reagan, elected governor of California in 1966, symbolized the power of conservatives within the Republican Party.

President Nixon drew on the energy of all streams of conservatism in his 1972 reelection campaign, which targeted radicals, hippies, black activists, and welfare mothers as the causes of America's problems. The Democrats, still reeling from the debacle of 1968 and subsequent attempts to provide representation for blacks, women, and antiwar activists, nominated South Dakota senator George McGovern. An antiwar liberal, McGovern proved inept at running a presidential campaign. Nixon swept the election, winning southern and blue-collar voters away from the Democrats.

Nixon's reelection seemed to mark the consolidation of conservative power. But his second term unraveled around the Watergate constitutional crisis, which revealed the widespread use of illegal surveillance and "dirty tricks" by the White House. During his first term, the Nixon administration had not only escalated covert police activity against black and antiwar activists, it had also begun using government spies against an "enemies list" of elite journalists, Democrats, and even "dovish" Republicans. The June 1972 break-in at the Watergate offices of the Democratic National Committee was one of many such actions; this time, however, a security guard caught the intruders, two of whom had been White House security consultants. Nixon's press secretary dismissed the break-in as a "caper," but the subsequent effort by the White House to cover up the burglary and other illegal activities was Nixon's undoing.

As the Watergate crisis grew, first the press and then a congressional investigation revealed the White House role in the world of political deceit and unconstitutional governance. Faced with certain

"I am not a crook." In 1973, as the Watergate scandal grew, political cartoonist Edward Sorel likened the Nixon administration to a band of trapped gangsters.

congressional impeachment for "high crimes and misdemeanors" and a possible constitutional crisis, Nixon resigned the presidency on August 7, 1974. Although Nixon was soon pardoned by his hand-picked successor, Gerald Ford (Nixon's vice president, Spiro Agnew, had been forced out of office in October 1973 in a bribery scandal), twenty-five other members of the Nixon administration, including several top advisers and the attorney general, served time in prison. With the conservative triumph stalled, liberalism in disarray, and the post–New Left social movements heading off in disparate directions, mid-1970s America settled into an uneasy stalemate.

The Nintendo war. Americans largely glimpsed the Persian Gulf war through television, often seeing images that were in fact composed of other video images. In this case, a video display aboard a Stealth F-117 bomber locks a Glide "smart" bomb's infrared guidance camera onto a target in Baghdad. The accuracy and glamour of such "high-tech" weapons were highlighted in news coverage heavily censored by the military. Only after the war did the military reveal that "smart" weapons constituted only 7 percent of the 81,980 tons of bombs dropped on Iraq and Kuwait—and of that total figure, 70 percent, or 62,137 tons, missed their targets.

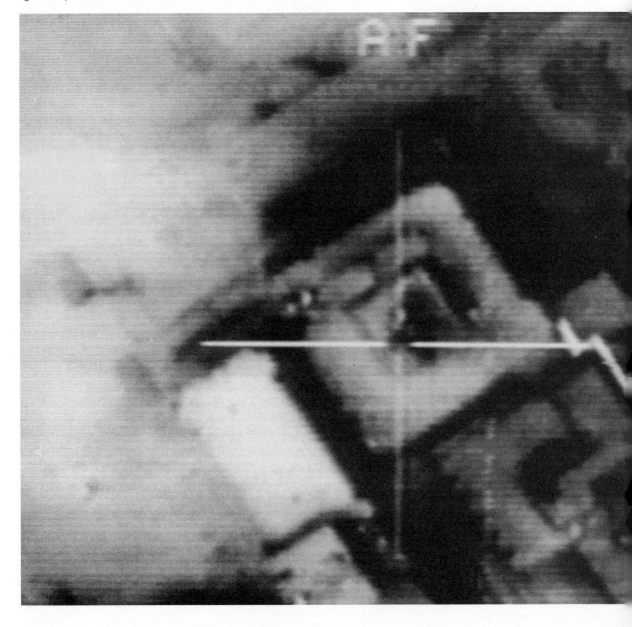

12

THE UNITED STATES AND THE GLOBAL ECONOMY

IN THE EARLY 1970s the U.S. defeat in Vietnam, political outrage over the Watergate revelations, and the most severe economic downturn since the Great Depression plunged America into crisis. Over the next two decades competing regions, groups, and ideologies— the "Rustbelt" and the "Sunbelt"; capital and labor; blacks and whites; Americans and foreigners; feminists and advocates of the "traditional" family; "straights" and "gays"—clashed over the nation's declining resources and its political and cultural ideals. Americans, regardless of identity, struggled in these years to understand a rapidly changing world in which assumptions about U.S. political dominance and economic prosperity no longer seemed certain.

THE END OF THE "AMERICAN CENTURY"

On the eve of the U.S. entry into World War II, Henry Luce, publisher of *Life* and *Time* magazines, proclaimed the "American Century," confident that American values and institutions would dominate the postwar international order. The United States indeed became the world's most powerful nation in the quarter-century following the war, a status built on U.S. military preeminence and the dynamic growth of the American economy. American policy-makers set the terms after 1945 for world capitalism's operation, not only determining the West's Cold War priorities but also establishing the dollar as the basis for international exchange.

Major cracks in this American-designed international edifice appeared in the late 1960s. The Vietnam War's spiraling costs set off the first of several great waves of inflation. America's postwar prosperity and its vaunted standard of living began to ebb. By the early 1970s, U.S. policy-makers, facing defeat in Vietnam and a raft of domestic problems, could no longer dominate the world economy.

In August 1971, President Richard Nixon devalued the U.S. dollar against foreign currencies and allowed its previously fixed value to "float" according to changing economic conditions. By year's end, monies paid to foreign producers for imported goods exceeded those paid for U.S. exports, the first time in this century that the United States had registered such a balance-of-payments deficit.

Other indications of the end of the American Century soon followed. In October 1973, in the midst of the "Yom Kippur" war between Israel and its Arab neighbors, Arab oil producers declared an embargo on oil shipments to the United States and Western Europe. The disruption of energy supplies and the dramatic rise in the price of oil led to federally mandated gasoline rationing in 1974. Panicked motorists across the country began lining up at gas stations, looking for a tank of gas. Some enraged Americans even wielded tire irons in defense of their right to buy a commodity most had taken for granted only a few weeks before.

The dollar's devaluation and the oil "shock" reverberated through the U.S. economy. The rising price of gas and oil forced many energy-reliant industries to close. American consumers, fearing the worst, drastically reduced their purchases of gas-guzzling, U.S.-made automobiles as well as American-manufactured goods. Factory output fell 10 percent in 1974 alone, and unemployment nearly doubled; at the same time, inflation more than doubled. Economists coined a new term—"stagflation"—to describe an unprecedented mix of economic problems: low levels of economic growth combined with high levels of unemployment and inflation led to falling real incomes and declining investment.

The U.S. economy continued to falter over the next ten years. The fast-growing economies of Japan and Western Europe, especially West Germany, now posed a direct competitive challenge to the United States. Steel, automobiles, machine tools, and home electronics equipment produced in Western Europe and Asia poured into the United States during the 1970s, undercutting the prices and often surpassing the quality of American-made products. The value of imported manufactured goods skyrocketed from less than 14 percent of U.S. domestic production in 1970 to nearly 40 percent in 1979. With annual inflation levels reaching double digits and the unemployment rate rarely below 7 percent, the ten years after 1973 brought the post–World War II boom in the United States to an unsettling end.

Why had the U.S. economy encountered such severe difficulties? Higher oil prices and growing competition from foreign producers were only part of the explanation. The militarization of the American economy also contributed to the nation's economic difficulties.

The Cold War with the Soviet Union profoundly shaped U.S. economic priorities. Encouraged by huge government military contracts, American businesses—especially electronics and aviation—focused their capital resources and technological know-how on producing armaments. Nearly one of every two federal dollars expended in the 1950s went to the military. Such massive spending provided employment for large numbers of defense industry workers in the postwar years. But ultimately the nation's substantial military budget—on a proportionate basis twice as great as Germany's and seven times that of Japan—sapped America's overall productive strength and diverted resources from the development of commercially (as opposed to militarily) strategic products.

Although America's defense industry was the most advanced in the world, the expertise that made possible "high-tech" military products was not readily transferable to the increasingly competitive consumer market. One writer noted that while American electronics manufacturers were profitably engrossed in building " 'smart bombs,' people sniffers, and other warlike wizardry," they lost the ability to produce televisions, stereos, and videocassette recorders.

The fate of the Singer Sewing Machine Company symbolized the consequences of America's post–World War II commitment to military production. For a century Singer had stood for Yankee ingenuity in every hamlet from Spain to Suriname. But Singer's share of the world market spiraled downward in the 1970s as a succession of managers shifted the company away from manufacturing sewing machines and into the less competitive and more profitable production of guidance systems for missiles and airplanes. Singer failed to retool its American sewing machine factories and lost its reputation for high-quality production. Sewing machines from Sweden and Korea took over the U.S. market, forcing Singer to close its flagship New Jersey factory in 1979. The once legendary American company virtually disappeared in the "leveraged buyout" mania of the 1980s.

The rise in popular expectations associated with the social movements of the 1960s—the civil rights and antiwar movements and the remarkable renaissance of American feminism—also profoundly affected American economic life in the 1970s. Workers in factories and offices demonstrated a growing "rights consciousness." The elderly, the sick, and those who received government assistance also argued for an extension of the democratic promise of the 1960s. These Americans asserted their rights to health care, government entitlements, a safe workplace, and access to jobs and public accommodations. And they demanded that federal and state governments enact expanded protective and welfare legislation as well as environmental, pension, and health and safety programs.

Union leaders and rank-and-file workers used the Occupational Safety and Health Administration, created in 1970, to push the federal government to improve unsafe conditions in the workplace. The United Mine Workers of America and the Oil, Chemical, and Atomic Workers' Union took the lead in seeking protective legislation for their industries in the 1970s. Though OSHA and federal mine inspectors did not always uphold workers' or unions' claims, there was a dramatic increase in the 1970s in government regulation of workplace-related health and safety problems, especially in the chemical, nuclear, mining, and electrical industries.

These efforts contributed to the dramatic rise in the 1970s of a new ecological awareness among the American people. The environmental movement grew dramatically, building on the initial success of the first Earth Day, in 1970. In the same year, Congress passed the National Environmental Policy Act, which required federal agencies to consider the environmental impact of government policies and programs. Passage of the federal Clean Air and Clear Water acts soon followed.

Rather than rely on often spotty enforcement by federal agencies, middle-class and working-class Americans established local organizations that fought toxic dumping, destruction of forests, nuclear power, and water pollution. Oil spills off the California and Massachusetts coasts in the 1970s, for example, mobilized local citizens to demand that the federal and state governments halt offshore oil drilling. The evacuation of the Love Canal neighborhood near Niagara, New York, following the uncovering of a hazardous waste dump in 1978 alerted Americans to environmental problems literally in their own backyards. And growing opposition to the destructive consequences of nuclear power—which peaked after the near calamity at the Three Mile Island nuclear plant in Pennsylvania in 1979—coa-

No nukes! A broad-based movement against the proliferation of nuclear weapons and nuclear-power facilities emerged during the late 1970s and early 1980s. Many activists used "direct action" tactics to forestall the building of reactors; on May Day 1977, thousands of demonstrators affiliated with the Clamshell Alliance blocked construction of a nuclear plant in Seabrook, New Hampshire. Almost 1,500 were arrested and jailed in armories around the state. After two weeks, the armories were still filled because many demonstrators refused to leave until all "clams" were unconditionally released. Governor Meldrim Thomson, Jr., who had hoped to stem protest with mass arrests, relented.

lesced into a nationwide antinuclear coalition that helped stop the proliferation of nuclear power plants.

The women's movement also grew in the early 1970s, building on the early personal and organizational successes of feminism. Women's organizations secured passage of a series of federal laws that banned discrimination against women in federal employment and federally supported educational programs and expanded the jurisdiction of the federal Equal Employment Opportunity Commission to include discrimination against women. Similarly, welfare rights advocates, especially those organized by the National Welfare Rights Organization, fought for increases in basic welfare benefits and entitlement programs for dependent women and children. So, too, did advocates for the medically and mentally ill and the handicapped, who pushed state and federal governments to increase access to health care for the elderly, the poor, and the disfranchised and to public accommodations for the disabled.

While these diverse demands and movements did not fully succeed, they reflected one of the lasting legacies of the 1960s: a sense of democratic empowerment. The civil rights movement had yielded tangible gains: voting rights laws passed by Congress helped make possible the election of almost seven thousand African-Americans to public office nationwide (mostly in the South) by the end of the 1970s, twelve times greater than the number who held office in the early 1960s. The antiwar movement enjoyed a similar sense of empowerment, successfully unseating a popular sitting president and helping transform public opinion about the Vietnam War. And the cultural openness of the 1960s gave ordinary Americans a sense of individual possibility, a notion that they could make a difference in their own and other people's lives if they acted in concert.

The spread of rights consciousness helped millions of ordinary Americans to improve their lives. But their sense of empowerment posed problems for government and business. In an influential 1975 study titled *The Crisis of Democracy*, Harvard political scientist Samuel Huntington concluded that the democratic "surge" of the 1960s had in fact led to an "excess of democracy." The assertion of democratic rights by women, African-Americans, environmentalists, and others had, according to Huntington, raised "expectations which it is impossible for government to meet." By 1974, federal and state spending on defense was down and welfare and Social Security benefits already amounted to 27 percent of the gross national product, a sharp increase from the previous decade.

Federal education, welfare, environmental, and regulatory pro-

"... DISABLED WOMEN CAN LEARN FROM THE WOMEN'S MOVEMENT"

Participation in the women's movement during the 1970s empowered many individuals. A group of disabled women speak about how feminism helped them in their struggle to change the ways differently abled Americans were perceived and treated by the larger society.

CONNIE L.: At first, though I've always considered myself a supporter of the feminist movement, I felt rather isolated from it. I could not understand their outrage at being judged wholly or primarily on the basis of their sex, but my problem was having people recognize that I had a sex.

As time went on, though, I felt disabled women fit well into the women's movement. The need to fit into a particular mold in order to be considered a "real woman" was lessened by the movement.... A sensitizing of men, a reevaluation of what they considered important in a woman and a relationship, couldn't help but make life better for disabled women. And, of course, the more wide open the choice of life styles, the better it is for us highly "irregular" types; so I think disabled women could not only benefit from the changes but have a lot to offer in helping to bring them about.

MAE EVANS: Before I was disabled, I had a comfortable identity as a wife,

grams enacted in the late 1960s and early 1970s also translated into higher labor costs and taxes for businesses. Such costs—along with increasing energy prices, foreign competition, rising wages, and the failure of American business leaders to develop effective strategies to deal with these problems—seriously undermined corporate profits, which declined sharply in the 1970s. By the end of the decade, profits were approximately one-third less than they had been a generation earlier; in manufacturing, only about one-half what they had been. Policy-makers in government and business agreed that the rising costs of government and declining corporate profits had to be brought under control.

THE CORPORATE POLITICS OF THE 1970s

Beginning in the early 1970s, prominent business leaders and politicians began calling for "pain" and "sacrifice" to save the economy and keep America competitive internationally. A 1974 *Business Week* editorial, for example, frankly asserted that "it will be a hard pill for many Americans to swallow—the idea of doing with less so that big business can have more." American corporations, supported by sympathetic federal officials, both Democratic and Republican, adopted a twofold strategy to realize this end. They searched for ways to lower their production costs and to attack the high wages and benefits enjoyed by workers in older, unionized industries.

For generations, American firms had periodically moved their production facilities throughout the United States to take advantage of cheap labor and cheap land. In the 1920s, for example, New England textile manufacturers transferred mills to the South. In the 1960s and 1970s this shift of manufacturing accelerated, as firms moved their operations to a broad "Sunbelt" stretching from Virginia south to Florida and west through Texas to Southern California. A federally funded superhighway grid and a more efficient telecommunications

mother, and community leader. . . . I thought "women's rights" were for others who had not lucked into a good life situation. After paraplegia, things were different. I lost my comfortable identity because I could no longer function in that role. I had to find some other way to operate, but there was no other way because I was no longer able to do the things that a female person "does" to be worthwhile. When I went into therapy for post-paraplegia depression, I became angry that the depression was not caused by the leg loss; it was caused by my original low self-esteem which prevented me from accepting leg loss. I discovered that I had been a victim of cultural attitudes on women and didn't even know it.

YVONNE DUFFY: Disabled women can learn from the women's movement how they have been held back by things other than their own disabilities. We may not be able to improve our personal physical situation, but we can change how we and others feel about our being women. My ideal person will do whatever is necessary to help me function independently, then, will forget about my specific physical condition and treat me as me—lover, friend, writer, or whatever. . . . When WE can forget about being Differently Abled, I am convinced that it helps others to do so. Forgetting about it does not mean being passive or giving up the fight for accessible buildings and transportation, equal opportunities for employment, and legal rights. On the contrary, we must become ever more assertive about obtaining these; having them will render us more independent and, thus, make it easier to concentrate on others rather than on ourselves and our limitations.

network linked this vast southern region to the older metropolitan centers in the Midwest and Northeast. The widespread introduction of air conditioning also made the move to the South more palatable. And a massive influx into Florida, Texas, and California of Latin American and Southeast Asian workers, beginning in the 1970s, opened up a large pool of cheap, nonunion labor. These new immigrants had the added virtue, from the employers' point of view, of being untouched by the social values of the 1960s that had intensified the demands of American workers.

By the late 1970s the South, including Texas, gained more than a million manufacturing jobs, while the Northeast and Midwest lost nearly two million. Formerly rural North Carolina had the highest percentage of manufacturing workers of any state in the 1980s; it also had the lowest blue-collar wages and the lowest unionization rate in the country.

The Northeast lost more than traditional manufacturing jobs. Computerization of clerical work also made it possible for big firms such as Merrill Lynch, American Express, and Citibank to shift many of their operations to the South and the West. According to the *Wall Street Journal*, these companies targeted "low-cost Sun Belt areas for future growth, such as industrial companies did decades ago when they moved from the Northeast to the South. They seek places where labor, land, electricity and taxes are cheap."

If jobs could be moved to Texas they could also be shifted to Mexico and Singapore in American business's unrelenting search for low-wage labor. Until the 1960s, U.S. investment in Latin America and what was called the Pacific Rim (the countries, east and west, that bordered the Pacific Ocean) focused largely on the extraction and processing of raw materials mined or grown in those regions. But beginning in the 1970s, a number of American firms bought or produced some of their most sophisticated component parts in low-wage foreign factories: between 1971 and 1976 American color TV manufacturers shifted more than 90 percent of their subassembly production to Asia; similarly, the Ford Motor Company built its most advanced automobile manufacturing complex in Hermosillo, Mexico. The foreign "outsourcing" of such high-value goods and parts sustained the profitability of many "American" product lines. But in the long run such policies further eroded America's manufacturing base and the technical expertise of its workers, managers, and engineers.

Federal officials tried to assist corporations throughout the 1970s by implementing policies they hoped would bolster the relative strength of American capitalism internationally and lower the overall cost of doing business. In August 1971, for example, when the Nixon administration devalued the dollar, it also froze wages and prices and slapped a tariff on Japanese-made cars. In addition, Nixon's "New

Economic Policy" was designed to keep a lid on wage increases and rein in organized labor. The implementation of these policies gave Nixon enough inflation-free breathing space in which to win the 1972 election. But the president's program proved unequal to the profound shift in the U.S. economy. Inflation continued unabated in 1973 and 1974, fueled by sharp increases in the prices of grain, oil, lumber, and other internationally traded commodities.

The fiscal pain the federal government could not successfully impose at the national level was administered locally, however, in one of the most liberally governed of all American political jurisdictions: New York City. Along with many other large cities in the East and Midwest, many of New York's traditional industries—including garment manufacturing, printing, and electrical products—had declined,

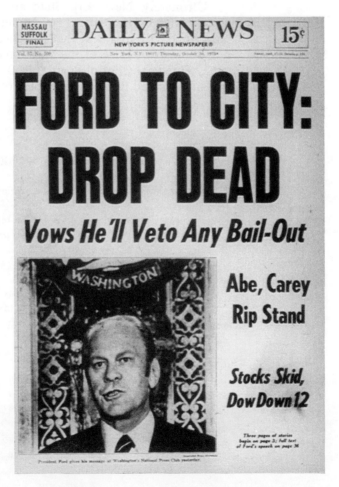

Fiscal crisis, federal neglect. The front page of the October 30, 1975, New York *Daily News* the morning after President Gerald Ford opposed federal aid to the nearly bankrupt city.

mainly as a consequence of foreign competition and the corporate search for a cheaper labor force. But the city remained a mecca for unskilled immigrants from the American South, Puerto Rico and other Caribbean nations, Latin America, and Asia. Social programs had also expanded the city payroll in the 1960s and 1970s, while aggressive unions such as Local 1199, the hospital workers' union, and AFSCME District Council 37, the municipal workers' union, kept wages rising at or above the inflation rate.

With city revenues stagnant and social welfare expenditures rising each year, New York City borrowed heavily to pay its bills. In 1975, New York's leading banks, suffering their own serious economic problems, precipitated a fiscal crisis by announcing that they would no longer buy New York's municipal bonds. New York's mayor Abraham Beame appealed to President Gerald Ford for federal aid, but the U.S. government refused assistance.

Ultimately, New York State and the city's municipal unions (joined later by the federal government) provided funds to bail out New York City in a deal that included concessions on wages and a reduction in the size of the workforce. A banker-dominated Emergency Financial Control Board (EFCB) demanded increases in public transit fares and firings of tens of thousands of teachers, police, and

"A WAR AGAINST WORKING PEOPLE. . ."

The Labor-Management Group, a nongovernmental committee of eight corporate executives and eight labor leaders, met regularly in the late 1970s to discuss cooperative approaches to resolving labor-management conflicts. United Auto Workers president Douglas Fraser resigned from the group in July 1978, arguing that business leaders sought confrontation, not cooperation, in their dealings with working people.

I believe leaders of the business community, with few exceptions, have chosen to wage a one-sided class war today in this country—a war against working people, the unemployed, the poor, the minorities, the very young and the very old, and even many in the middle class of our society. The leaders of industry, commerce and finance in the United States have broken and discarded the fragile, unwritten compact previously existing during a past period of growth and progress.

For a considerable time, the leaders of business and labor have sat at the Labor-Management Group's table—recognizing differences, but seeking consensus where it existed. That worked because the business community in the U.S. succeeded in advocating a general loyalty to an allegedly benign capitalism that emphasized private property, independence and self-regulation along with an allegiance to free, democratic politics.

sanitation workers. The EFCB cut back health services and welfare support for the poor and forced the closure of several municipal hospitals and many city libraries and the virtual abandonment of several city parks. One cutback seemed particularly symbolic: for more than a century the City University of New York had offered the city's overwhelmingly immigrant working class a tuition-free higher education. Since the 1960s, CUNY also had maintained an "open admissions" program that further increased educational opportunities for the city's working-class and poor high-school graduates. Both of these policies were curtailed after 1976.

Such austerity measures barely dented the soaring inflation rate, however. And by the time Democrat Jimmy Carter, a former governor of Georgia, was inaugurated as president in 1977, economic stagnation again bedeviled government policy-makers. Carter had few ties to organized labor. He had won the White House by appealing to the anti-Washington, anti-incumbent mood that had been so pronounced in the years following Watergate and President Ford's unpopular pardon of ex-president Richard Nixon. Moreover, Congress contained dozens of suburban Democrats who owed their election to the temporary defection of the Republican electorate after Watergate, not to any surge in support for increased spending on social welfare programs.

Carter's personal rectitude, his efforts to make human rights an important element in American foreign policy, and his administration's vigorous enforcement of civil rights laws were significant departures from recent Republican policies. But these important steps did not mean that Carter was about to increase government expenditures dramatically or resurrect the coalition of liberals, labor, and African-Americans. Carter rejected any efforts to renew the social-welfare initiatives of the 1960s, including progressive Democratic proposals for national health insurance, a federal program to achieve full employment, and federal payment of

That system has worked best, of course, for the "haves" in our society rather than the "have-nots." Yet it survived in part because of an unspoken foundation: that when things got bad enough for a segment of society, the business elite "gave" a little bit—enabling government or interest groups to better conditions somewhat for that segment. That give usually came only after sustained struggle, such as that waged by the labor movement in the 1930's and the civil rights movement in the 1960's. . . .

But today, I am convinced there has been a shift on the part of the business community toward confrontation, rather than cooperation. Now, business groups are tightening their control over American society. . . . The rise of multinational corporations that know neither patriotism nor morality but only self-interest, has made accountability almost non-existent. At virtually every level, I discern a demand by business for docile government and unrestrained corporate individualism. Where industry once yearned for subservient unions, it now wants no unions at all. . . .

Business blames inflation on workers, the poor, the consumer, and uses it as a club against them. Price hikes and profit increases are ignored while corporate representatives tell us we can't afford to stop killing and maiming workers in unsafe factories. . . .

I have concluded there is no point to continue sitting down at Labor-Management Group meetings and philosophizing about the future of the country and the world when we on the labor side have so little in common with those across the table. I cannot sit there seeking unity with leaders of American industry, while they try to destroy us and ruin the lives of the people I represent.

abortion services for poor women. And he refused to support the labor movement's political agenda, which included a bill to reform and expand the National Labor Relations Board. Influential business groups lobbied against passage of the bill, which would have made employer resistance to union organizing drives more difficult. Without support from the White House, labor law reform died in 1978.

The Carter administration evinced far more sympathy for the plight of big business. In 1979, the Chrysler Corporation stood on the verge of bankruptcy. Japanese imports had savaged its market, while Chrysler's products were outmoded and its aging plants inefficient. The nation's third-largest automaker needed billions of dollars to retool, but the big banks would not extend credit to the financially troubled corporation. Only a government loan guarantee—a federal bailout—could save the company and thousands of jobs.

Such loan guarantees were not new: in 1971, the Lockheed Corporation, one of America's major defense contractors, had secured federal help of this sort. But the conditions under which Washington guaranteed the Chrysler loan opened the door to a further decline in the standard of living of millions of American workers. Working closely with the big banks, federal officials demanded that Chrysler workers offer hundreds of millions of dollars in wage concessions as part of the bailout package. As Chrysler president Lee Iacocca explained in the midst of the crisis, "It's freeze time, boys. I've got plenty of jobs at seventeen dollars an hour; I don't have any at twenty."

The UAW convinced auto workers that such concessions were the only way to save jobs. Chrysler went on to earn record profits in the mid-1980s, although it did so only by cutting its workforce in half and shutting most of its inner-city factories. The Chrysler bailout also proved to be the first in a long wave of concession contracts and wage rollbacks that swept through almost every unionized industry.

The Carter administration heeded other conservative business voices as well. In the same year as the Chrysler bailout and shortly after a sharp increase in oil prices in 1979, the president appointed Paul Volcker to the powerful chairmanship of the Federal Reserve Board. Volcker quickly slammed on the economic brakes, adopting a "monetarist" policy that restricted the growth of the money supply, curbed inflation, and pushed interest rates toward 20 percent—their highest level since the Civil War.

The results were predictable. Automobiles, houses, and other big-ticket items became far more expensive for consumers; high interest rates at home pushed up the value of the dollar against foreign currencies, which made American cars, steel, and electronic products even less competitive overseas. The United States plunged into another recession, this one more severe than the 1974 downturn. Thousands of businesses shut down. The nation's unemployment rate soared to over 9 percent; in states such as Michigan, Illinois, and Pennsylvania it rivaled the double-digit levels of the Great Depression. This government-engineered recession continued almost unabated for the next three years. Eventually the recession halted inflation, but at the social and economic cost of devastated cities, thousands of bankrupt firms, and millions of lost jobs.

AMERICAN POLITICS TURNS RIGHT

American politics sharply turned right in the late 1970s, encouraged by economic, social, and political changes in postwar America. A decline in electoral participation that had begun in the late 1960s and continued through the next two decades provided the first push toward conservatism. Barely half of all potential voters actually cast ballots in the post-1968 presidential elections, about one-third less than in the heyday of the New Deal coalition and in the early 1960s.

This withdrawal from the electoral process was concentrated among working people and the poor. In 1976, the two congressional districts with the lowest voter turnout in the United States were overwhelmingly poor, African-American, and Latino: Bedford-Stuyvesant and the South Bronx, both in New York City. Only about one-fifth of all those eligible there cast ballots, in sharp contrast to the 70 percent who voted in the districts with the highest turnout, wealthy suburbs outside Chicago and Minneapolis. The disappearance of poor and working-class voters had enormous political consequences: it skewed election returns to the right. Had voter turnout in 1976 equaled that of a decade earlier, Jimmy Carter would have defeated Gerald Ford in a landslide rather than a squeaker, and the Congress would have been overwhelmingly Democratic.

The decline in voter turnout had many sources, but two stand out. Institutions that traditionally linked individual voters to national politics—such as trade unions and urban political machines—became far less influential after 1972, especially after the Democratic Party changed its delegate rules that year. In their place came the professionally crafted thirty-second television clip and the computer-generated direct-mail letter. These political tools were simply not as effective in mobilizing those at the bottom of the social ladder.

Second, political participation declined among poor and working-class voters because the Democratic Party failed to offer alternative policies around which these voters, once its most loyal supporters, might be mobilized. Although African-Americans continued to vote Democratic more than nine to one, their turnout declined sharply in the 1970s. The Democratic Party had moved so forcefully toward conservative positions on economic issues that it no longer appealed to inner-city ghetto dwellers or blue-collar workers. Thus in California, Jerry Brown, an otherwise liberal Democratic governor, declared that the state had entered a new "era of limits," and in the White House President Jimmy Carter publicly doubted the ability of the government to resolve the nation's pressing social and economic problems.

Such attitudes gave rise in the 1970s to a feeling that electoral politics, especially at the national level, was a spectator sport and that government would not respond to citizens' needs and aspirations. "Why don't people vote?" one welfare worker asked rhetorically. "Because it doesn't make a difference." Between the end of the 1960s and the end of the 1970s, the number of Americans polled who agreed that government will "do what is right most of the time" fell from 56 to 29 percent, and those who affirmed that the "people running the country don't really care what happens to you" shot up from 26 percent to 60 percent.

At the same time as this political demobilization occurred among once-stalwart supporters of the Democratic Party, a "New Right" made a powerful bid for their allegiance. For most of the twentieth century, American political conservatism, the "Old Right," had been linked with old money, the Anglo-Saxon "heritage," and distaste for "foreigners," blacks, and labor unions. This brand of conservative politics mistrusted activist and reformist government, denounced international communism, and defended laissez-faire economic policies. The Old Right did not disappear in the 1970s, but its elite spokesmen lost much of their influence to a New Right, which relied on an array of economic, political, and cultural issues to mobilize American voters in support of conservative causes.

The New Right grew in response to a widely recognized decline in popular confidence in American institutions. The Vietnam War and the Watergate crisis, along with the economic turmoil of the post-Vietnam era, led many Americans to worry that the United States had lost its position of world leadership and the American Dream was in jeopardy. The movements of the 1960s had further challenged traditional values and social hierarchies; and many Americans eagerly exercised new choices about how to live and how to define one's family and community identities. But other Americans found these changes threatening. They felt that their traditional values—family, religion, patriotism—were under attack and might collapse, leading to moral and social chaos. The New Right successfully spoke to this sense of unease.

Race was the most immediate and compelling issue that pushed white voters to the right. The increased political visibility of African-Americans in politics during the late 1960s and early 1970s—particularly in cities that elected black mayors, such as Carl Stokes in Cleveland and Richard Hatcher in Gary, Indiana, in 1967, and Maynard Jackson in Atlanta and Coleman Young in Detroit in 1973—spurred white opposition. As important were the profound legal and social changes wrought by the civil rights revolution, which affected not only African-Americans but also the urban white working class—the Irish of Boston, the Slavs of South Chicago, the Italians of Brooklyn—as well as once-poor southern whites. It was the schools, jobs, and neighborhoods of white workers that were to be integrated and in which the resulting social frictions were most difficult to resolve. As long as cities were prosperous and schools well funded it seemed possible that integration might benefit all. But the economic hard times of the 1970s and the resulting cutbacks in urban social services made it virtually certain that racial conflict would erupt and white working-class politics would shift to the right.

This shift became evident in the early 1970s controversy over the busing of children to achieve racial balance in the schools. Public education had been a racial battlefield since the *Brown* v. *Board of Education* decision in 1954. Most African-American parents saw busing as an important step toward racial equality. They also were quite pragmatic in hoping that attendance at better schools in white neighborhoods would enhance black children's chances for advancement. Most white parents vehemently opposed busing. In Pontiac, Michigan; Louisville, Kentucky; and Kansas City, Missouri, busing programs quickly generated organized opposition and some violence. But the most spectacular clash over school busing came in Boston, the city that spawned the nineteenth-century movements for free public education and the abolition of slavery.

For years the Boston school board—controlled for more than half a century by Irish politicians who used the educational system as part of their patronage machine—had kept the city's schools racially segregated. After a long, NAACP-initiated battle in the courts, a federal district court issued a sweeping integration order in 1975, mandating, among other remedies, the court-ordered busing of pupils from all-black Roxbury to Charlestown, a declining Irish working-class section of the city. The burden of the busing plan fell almost entirely on the children of the urban working class, both black and white. Federal courts in Massachusetts, as elsewhere, excluded from integration plans the white, middle-class suburbs that surrounded Boston and most other American cities.

The stage was set in September 1975 for an ugly confrontation when the first black students were bused into Charlestown and other predominantly white school districts. For the next three years, Boston police were required to protect black children from angry crowds of local residents screaming "Nigger go home!" Boston's inflamed ra-

South Boston backlash. The Boston busing controversy turned violent in spring 1976. On April 5, a group of white high-school students from South Boston and Charlestown opposed to busing visited City Hall to meet with a councilwoman who supported their boycott of classes. Outside the building, the teenagers encountered and then assaulted labor lawyer Theodore Landsmark. The attack sparked a series of violent racial incidents that extended into the summer.

cial climate was finally alleviated somewhat in the 1980s when several of the city's white and African-American politicians constructed grass-roots, populist electoral campaigns that helped defuse racial tensions. The busing controversy also faded nationally in the early 1980s, largely because more conservative judges backed away from the busing idea and because the overwhelmingly African-American and Latino makeup of most big-city school systems made integration of any sort moot.

Racial issues continued nonetheless as a staple of American politics. Direct appeals to racial intolerance were no longer possible in American politics, largely because of the enfranchisement of millions of African-American voters, the enactment of a large body of civil rights legislation, and the election of thousands of African-American officials nationwide. But American political life in the 1970s and 1980s remained saturated with an array of code words and phrases and substitute issues that spoke indirectly to racial issues. Attacks on welfare "chiselers," fear of "crime in the streets," and even the militarization of the campaign against inner-city drugs gave American politics a barely submerged racial edge that helped propel a majority of white southerners out of the Democratic Party and divided the loyalties of the northern white working class.

The New Right also made political gains after 1978 by addressing the increasing economic difficulties facing large numbers of American working-class and middle-class families. In states such as California, housing prices were shooting skyward, putting the purchase of a first house (a central part of the American Dream) beyond the reach of many young couples. Huge property tax bills shocked hundreds of thousands of middle-class and working-class citizens fortunate enough to own their homes. Substantial increases in the Social Security payroll tax, enacted in the 1960s and early 1970s, added to these burdens. The tax system was regressive and unfair, and getting more so all the time.

A series of antigovernment "tax revolts" swept the nation in the late 1970s. California voters inaugurated the nationwide revolt in 1978 when they approved Proposition 13, a ballot initiative that capped property taxes and slashed local government revenues. As in California, many populist-sounding campaigns elsewhere were organized by longtime conservative activists who argued that the issue was less the fairness of the tax system than wasteful big government expenditures for education, welfare, and other social programs. Surveys taken at the time showed that most of those who voted for such tax limitations did not actually reject these government programs. Antitaxation campaigns nonetheless had a profound impact on civic life. Combined with the stale taste left by the Watergate revelations, they helped mobilize sentiment against government responsibility for social problems and encouraged many Americans to change their self-image from concerned "citizen" to self-interested "taxpayer."

Race and taxes were not the only issues exploited by the New Right in the 1970s. Explosive moral and cultural questions about the role of women and the status of homosexuals proved as powerful in the New Right's rise. For members of the New Right animated by Protestant fundamentalism or Catholic doctrine, these gender and sexual issues took on the air of a religious war.

The New Right threw many soldiers into these battles. Evangelical Christianity enjoyed an extraordinary renaissance in the 1970s among black and white Americans. While membership in liberal Protestant churches declined, the conservative Southern Baptists, America's largest Protestant denomination, gained 3 million members between 1965 and 1985. More than 45 million Americans considered themselves fundamentalists at the start of the 1980s. The New Right drew many of its converts from this broad evangelical base. Dozens of conservative fundamentalist ministers had moved to the suburbs and built huge new churches in the 1970s, often with

Heritage USA. A scene in the Baptism Pool in Jim and Tammy Bakker's 2,300-acre revivalist theme park and campground, on the border between North and South Carolina. By 1986, Heritage USA was one of the nation's top tourist attractions, drawing over six million visitors a year to its rides, water park, petting zoo, hotel, and shopping mall.

money donated by the Sunbelt's energy, real estate, and banking entrepreneurs. These ministers, such as the fundamentalist preacher Jerry Falwell, used the latest television marketing techniques to spread their conservative message well beyond the South's old "Bible Belt."

Three issues, each the result of the gains of the 1960s social movements, served as the New Right's cultural and religious lightning rods: the 1973 U.S. Supreme Court *Roe* v. *Wade* decision legalizing abortion; the feminist-backed effort to pass the Equal Rights Amendment (ERA) to the U.S. Constitution; and the increasing visibility and assertion of rights by gay Americans.

Even before its 1973 legalization, abortion was an option exercised primarily by young, unmarried women, many of whom were of the working class, unemployed or students. Though women who sought abortions were not necessarily feminists or New Leftists, New Right leaders directly linked the abortion issue to what they perceived as the sexual licentiousness of the 1960s. They denounced the

1973 U.S. Supreme Court decision legalizing abortion as murder of the unborn, a spur to sexual promiscuity, and, as one activist put it, an attack on "the right of a husband to protect the life of the child he has fathered in his wife's womb."

Antiabortion forces quickly rallied across the country. In the North, Catholic Church leaders organized the first antiabortion demonstrations immediately after the *Roe* v. *Wade* decision. Among many Catholics, as among evangelical Protestants, the depth of one's religious convictions was now closely aligned with opposition to abortion and defense of what many saw as the sanctity of the male-dominated family and a respect for "God-given" gender roles.

The rise of "pro-life" groups and their use of mass picketing and occasional civil disobedience to shut down abortion clinics brought the antiabortion movement to national prominence in the late 1970s. Across the picket lines they faced an equally fervent feminist "pro-choice" movement that argued for women's right to control their bodies and to exercise their option to choose abortion.

Pro-life props. Antiabortion demonstrators brandish fetal images as they protest outside a New Jersey abortion clinic in February 1990. Pictures play a significant role in promoting the "pro-life" cause, reducing a complex debate over women's rights and the development of life into a single figure, "the unborn child." Ignoring developmental stages in the womb, their images either present full-term babylike "fetuses" (like the rubber doll here), or focus on the most developed parts of the fetal anatomy (such as the head, hands, and feet) while avoiding those that are less identifiably "human."

"Operation Rescue." Pro-choice advocates demonstrate in opposition to an antiabortion sit-in at a clinic in 1988. Much to the consternation of the women's movement and its allies, "Operation Rescue," a radical antiabortion activist group, appropriated many civil disobedience tactics devised by the civil rights movement.

The ERA, which both houses of Congress approved in 1972, was also high on the political agenda of the women's movement. Both the amendment itself and feminists' commitment to its passage further mobilized the New Right. The proposed ERA stated simply that "equality of rights under the law shall not be denied or abridged by the United States or by any State on account of sex."

As each state legislature debated passage of the proposed constitutional amendment, New Right leaders such as Phyllis Schlafly and Jerry Falwell, a founder of the politically influential "Moral Majority," organized thousands of activists against this assertion of women's basic legal equality. As Falwell told his large television audience, "The Equal Rights Amendment is a delusion. In families and in nations where the Bible is believed, Christian women are honored above men. . . . The Equal Rights Amendment strikes at the foundation of our entire social structure." Although twenty-eight of the required thirty-eight state legislatures approved the ERA within one year of its passage by Congress, Schlafly, Falwell, and their allies turned public opinion against the amendment.

The key to the New Right's success lay in the very different meaning that ideas about women's equality held for men and women divided by age, class, and economic expectations. Many working-class men feared that passage of the ERA would undercut whatever control they still possessed over their work and family lives. Many working-class women, even those who were union members, failed to identify with predominantly middle-class feminist leaders who had so successfully injected the ERA into national politics. One activist in the Service Employees' International Union explained her dislike for *Ms.* magazine publisher Gloria Steinem: "Maybe I have my own stereotype of her, but I think maybe she looks above us. I feel she's fighting for women like herself, professional women. . . . So I don't consider myself part of her movement." And a number of working-class and middle-class women feared that the spread of feminist ideas about equality would undermine the implicit bargain upon which traditional marriage and family life were based. Though the legally mandated time period for state legislative approval of the ERA finally expired in the early 1980s, the amendment's prospects for passage had ended several years earlier.

The new visibility and political rights enjoyed by gay Americans in the 1970s also engendered fierce resistance from the New Right. In the surge of "gay pride" that followed the 1969 Stonewall Inn riot in New York City, many homosexuals expressed their sexual orientation with an openness denied previous generations. They built a new kind of urban "counterculture," which included gay and lesbian bars, newspapers, and magazines, as well as community groups dedicated to uncovering the previously buried history of gay Americans. Local politicians acknowledged for the first time a very real and definable gay vote. The victorious mayoral campaigns of George Moscone in San Francisco and Edward Koch in New York City in the mid-1970s benefited from the endorsements of gay political groups and the high turnout

". . . KEEPERS AT HOME"

Teddi Holt, a full-time homemaker from Georgia with three sons, helped found "Mothers on the March (MOM)" in the late 1970s, a New Right organization dedicated to "preserv[ing] and strengthen[ing] the home."

I am pleased that God blessed me with the privilege of being a woman. I have never been envious of the role of men but have had respect for both sexes. There's no doubt that there has been discrimination against women, but that is past history, just as discrimination against blacks is past history in the US. . . .

NOW's [The National Organization for Women's] primary goal was to pass the Equal Rights Amendment (ERA) without amendment. Second, it included as a secondary goal—"right to abortion on demand." And third, it supported "a woman's right to . . . express her own sexuality and to choose her lifestyle. . . ." Such goals were foreign to me. I could not imagine any woman with my background having such goals, because they did not hold to traditional values and/or Judeo-Christian ethics on which the Constitution and our laws are based. . . .

It was obvious to me that ERA was certainly not a protection of women's rights. In fact, it would remove many protections and exemptions that were specifically placed in our laws, recognizing the fact that our Creator had most certainly created us male and female: two separate, very different, equally important human beings. . . .

Just what were we women to be liberated from? These women [feminists] were calling for liberation from the things women like me love most—our husbands, our children, our homes. My cry became: "God, liberate us from the Liberators!" . . .

We believe that the mothers of this and other nations must stand up for the protection of our homes and our children. In no way are we extremists, unless we be guilty of extreme devotion to our husbands, our children, and our homes. It is our sincere belief that if we do not unite against the threats to the home, if we retire to the convenience and security of our houses and do not speak out, then it will not be long until we, the "keepers at home" (Titus 2:5) will not have a home to keep!

of gay voters. And like feminists who fought for the ERA, homosexual Americans successfully struggled on a local level for passage of laws that forbade discrimination based on sexual orientation.

Evangelical Protestant and Catholic leaders attacked homosexuality as blasphemous. The Christian fundamentalist and popular singer Anita Bryant, for example, raised the specter of "militant" homosexuals corrupting young students in Florida's public schools in 1977. Bryant spearheaded a successful campaign to repeal a recently passed Dade County antidiscrimination ordinance that covered homosexuals.

Bryant's success in Florida took place in a climate of growing hostility toward homosexuals, in large part in response to growing openness about their sexual orientation. The number of physical attacks on gay men and lesbians increased in the mid-1970s. These attacks reached an ugly crescendo in 1978. In San Francisco, home of one of the country's largest and best-organized gay communities, Mayor George Moscone and City Councilman Harvey Milk, an openly gay political leader, were assassinated by Dan White, a disgruntled former policeman who had served on the City Council. White's plea at his murder trial (he said he was made temporarily insane by consuming too much "junk" food) enraged the San Francisco gay community, which erupted in violence on the night White was found not guilty by reason of insanity.

The New Right's hostility toward homosexuals intensified rapidly in the early 1980s when AIDS, the deadly Acquired Immune Deficiency Syndrome, began to ravage the male homosexual communities of San Francisco, New York, Los Angeles, and other big cities. To many heterosexual Americans, not only those in the New Right, AIDS seemed less a disease than a moral judgment on the gay life-style. A wave of homophobia, including a sharp increase in physical assaults, swept the nation's cities in the mid-1980s.

THE REAGAN REVOLUTION

The cultural and economic issues that propelled the New Right to political prominence during the 1970s coincided with domestic and international changes wrought by America's unprecedented defeat in Vietnam. Many Americans responded to the nation's humiliation in Indochina and the economic malaise that followed by calling for a forceful U.S. military presence internationally. To those who had opposed the war, or saw its costs as too great, defeat in Vietnam offered the United States the opportunity to rethink its militarized foreign policy and inaugurate an era of détente and arms control that would lower America's profile abroad.

Outside the United States, the American defeat in Vietnam inspired the growth of revolutionary movements or regimes throughout the Third World. Revolutions in Angola and Rhodesia (soon renamed Zimbabwe) overturned white minority rule. In Central America, mass revolutionary upsurges of peasants, intellectuals, and urban workers fought brutal regimes that had exercised power for generations with the support and complicity of the U.S. government. In 1979, following a bloody civil war, Sandinista-led forces in Nicaragua succeeded in toppling the Somoza regime. While reaching out to the United States for aid, the Sandinista leadership also began implementing a land redistribution program and a partially socialized economy.

The Nicaraguan revolution was overshadowed for a time by events in Iran. The Islamic-led revolution there helped precipitate a second oil "shock" in 1979, which further strained the already weakened American economy. Adding insult to injury, Islamic militants seized the U.S. embassy in November 1979 and refused to release fifty-two hostages in protest of America's sheltering of the deposed shah. The nightly televised hostage crisis, which lasted 444 days in 1979 and 1980, focused popular American anger on foreign revolutions in general and the Iranian leader, the Ayatollah Khomeini, in particular. In turn, the crisis generated widespread public sentiment for increased arms expenditures, a get-tough foreign policy, and a surge of intense patriotism that further bolstered the American conservative agenda.

This worldwide revolutionary upsurge corresponded with the collapse of the post-Vietnam era of détente with the Soviet Union. The Soviets supported Third World revolutions both to secure their political and military influence and to blunt the projection of U.S. power. In December 1979, for example, the Soviets airlifted thousands of troops into Afghanistan, a traditionally neutral country on the Soviet Union's southern border. Soviet leaders hoped their troops would shore up a pro-Communist regime that seemed on the verge of collapse.

In response, President Jimmy Carter, who had shaped a more open and conciliatory foreign policy in the initial two years of his term, decided to get tough with the Soviet Union. He suspended grain sales to the Soviets, orchestrated a Western boycott of the 1980 Summer Olympics in Moscow, and shelved SALT II, the nuclear missile treaty just negotiated with the Soviet Union. Shifting gears, Carter called for a big increase in the military budget and urged America's NATO allies to do likewise. Carter's U-turn intensified political divisions in the Democratic Party and opened the way for Ronald Reagan.

Photo op. Press photographers take pictures of Ronald Reagan during a "photo opportunity." These formal photography sessions scheduled by the White House staff dated back to the 1930s, when FDR's press secretary instructed photographers to avoid showing the polio-afflicted president in a wheelchair. Under the Reagan administration, however, photographic access to the president was controlled and orchestrated to virtually guarantee that *no* unflattering or negative picture would be recorded. Believing that the "look" was more important than the meaning of an event, the White House staff dictated the time, the place, and even the angle of vision of "photo ops." The resulting pictures helped shape a positive, upbeat image of Reagan for the public.

In the 1940s, Reagan, a Hollywood actor, had been a prolabor liberal who served as president of the Screen Actors' Guild. But in the 1950s, as a corporate spokesperson for General Electric, Reagan became a militant anti-Communist. Elected California governor in 1967, Reagan served two terms, during which he cut state spending for health, education, and welfare. He used his substantial political visibility during the 1970s to turn the national Republican Party to the right.

In the 1980 presidential campaign, Reagan emphasized the need to revive American power abroad, appealing to the late-1970s resurgence of patriotism. He also exploited the national economic problems that dogged the Carter presidency. Reagan attacked big government and championed the New Right's social agenda. Perhaps more important than the particular policies he espoused, Reagan offered voters a reassuring father figure who would stand up for America in a way that Carter had not. Reagan was able to communicate that image because substantial financial support from the business community gave his campaign virtually unlimited access to television. Reagan easily defeated Jimmy Carter, who could not escape the perception that he was a vacillating leader who had failed to solve the Iranian hostage crisis. Despite military and diplomatic efforts by the Carter administration, the hostages were not finally freed until a few hours after Ronald Reagan was sworn in as president.

Reagan won the 1980 election by retaking the white South from the Democrats and by increasing the already large majorities Republican presidential candidates enjoyed among middle-class voters. Most strikingly, Reagan captured the votes of half of all blue-collar workers and more than 40 percent of union households. Only African-Americans voted solidly Democratic. The Reagan victory allowed the Republicans to overturn more than a generation of Democratic control of the U.S. Senate.

Reagan and the Republicans promised to reorganize American politics in a fashion just as sweeping as that inaugurated by the New Deal nearly fifty years earlier. The Reagan Revolution began by dramatically expanding the U.S. military machine and by willingly employing military force throughout the world. The administration proposed a 40 percent increase in arms spending that included expensive new weapons systems such as the B-1 bomber and the "Star Wars" antimissile shield. They also unveiled a "rollback" strategy toward revolutionary movements. Reagan labeled the Vietnam War a "noble effort" while declaring the Soviet Union an "evil empire." Reaganite intellectuals such as U.N. ambassador Jeane Kirkpatrick and State Department official Elliot Abrams defined most Third World insurgencies as Soviet-inspired and Soviet-supported "terrorism." The Reagan administration also sought to overcome the "Viet-

Fantasies of invasion. Hollywood exploits the New Cold War in John Milius's *Red Dawn*, a 1984 film about a Soviet takeover of the United States. Such fantasies, however, failed to anticipate the direction that invasion would actually take: six years later, McDonald's opened its first fast-food franchise in Moscow.

nam syndrome," which it defined as Americans' lingering skepticism about committing U.S. military forces abroad. To this end, the new administration increased U.S. military support for the Afghan rebels, organized and armed a group of counterrevolutionary Nicaraguans, sent the Marines into the Lebanese civil war, and finally launched a military invasion in 1983 of the tiny Caribbean island of Grenada, where a radical government held power.

The Reagan administration funded the massive military buildup by reversing the trajectory followed by American politics since the New Deal: federal social spending, business regulation, and taxation would be cut sharply, thereby "getting the government off the backs" of the American people. Reagan's approach promised to unleash a tide of entrepreneurial energy that would sustain high levels of employment and generate new tax revenues. Commentators called this "supply-side economics," or "Reaganomics."

Such was the theory. Reaganomics did cut taxes sharply for corporations and the wealthy, reducing the top individual tax rate from 70 percent in the 1970s to 28 percent in 1986. A family with an income between $100,000 and $200,000 gained $8,400 in extra income from the Reagan tax cuts, while families whose total income was less than $10,000 paid just $58 less in federal taxes. But since state and local governments increased their taxes to make up for reductions in federal aid and because Social Security taxes had risen sharply over the previous few years, working-class Americans now paid a far higher proportion of their income in taxes than did the rich.

The Reagan tax policy had an additional long-range consequence, which its architects understood from the outset. Federal income-tax receipts plummeted by $750 billion between 1981 and 1986. This loss of income, combined with huge increases in military spending, resulted in a staggering federal budget deficit of some $150 billion to $200 billion a year. Because the government now had to borrow so much to cover the deficit, interest rates remained high and economic growth stayed sluggish. Reaganomics helped assure that regardless of which party controlled Congress or the White House, and however great the social need, the continuing budget deficit would make it virtually impossible for the federal government to initiate new programs.

Reaganomics also promised to make deep cuts in welfare spending. The social programs inaugurated or expanded in the late 1960s had helped reduce poverty in the United States, particularly among the elderly. But inflation and the 1970s recessions undermined these gains. During the 1980s, conservative ideologues such as Charles Murray and George Gilder argued that poverty was the product of liberal social policy itself, which had generated a dependent "underclass" enmeshed in a self-perpetuating welfare pathology. Reagan administration policy-makers, ideologically hostile to such social spending, declared these programs a failure and set out to destroy them. They made big cuts in food-stamp, child-nutrition, and job-training programs; aid to families with dependent children; public service employment; and low-income housing. Half a million working families, all headed by women, lost child-assistance benefits, while 70 percent of the savings in the food-stamp program came from families already living below the poverty line.

But not all welfare programs were cut so drastically. Those social programs and tax policies—Social Security, Medicare, and the tax deduction for interest on home mortgages—that provided benefits for both middle-class and working-class Americans were far more likely to be immune from deep cuts than welfare programs targeted at the poor alone. There was no stigma attached to these middle-income entitlement programs. Most Americans considered them a "right" rather than a handout. Even conservative Republicans in Congress gave in to pressure from a broad constituency that relied on these programs or expected to do so.

Reagan-era economic policies had another consequence. By instituting the high interest rates necessary to curb inflation and fund the growing federal deficit, Reaganomics made U.S. government bonds and notes attractive to foreign investors. High interest rates also meant the dollar's value increased against foreign currencies, making imported goods such as cars and electronic equipment relatively cheap for Americans to buy. The result was an explosion of foreign imports and another sharp recession in 1982.

Smokestack America was devastated as wave after wave of plant closings swept through the Midwest and the Middle Atlantic States. In 1982, 2,700 mass layoffs and plant shutdowns eliminated over 1.25 million industrial jobs. In the steel industry, employment fell by

Plant closing, fall 1988. A northern California lumber company auctions off its works and equipment.

150,000 between 1979 and 1982. Youngstown, Ohio; South Chicago, Illinois; Buffalo, New York; and Bethlehem, Pennsylvania, once crown jewels of America's industrial heartland, now were part of a declining "Rustbelt." Tens of thousands of jobs in unionized industries disappeared in the 1982 downturn. Almost 11 percent of the total U.S. workforce was unemployed at the recession's peak, the highest rate since 1940.

Behind the abstraction of these numbers was acute human suffering. Workers, particularly older male breadwinners, often felt as if the factory where they had worked was the center of their world; when the plant closed, they experienced a deep sense of loss. During the long months of unemployment that typically followed a shutdown, it was common for workers to become depressed, or to turn to alcohol for solace. Many laid-off men felt that their inability to "bring home the bacon" reflected badly on their masculinity. Some fought with their wives; others abandoned their families altogether. Few blue-collar workers over age forty were able to "retool" themselves; most

"YOU KNOW YOU GET DESPERATE ..."

The decline of the steel industry in the 1970s left unemployed steelworkers with few options. Mary Morgan, an African-American steelworker laid off from U.S. Steel's South Works in early 1983, and Carl Stezco, who worked at the Wisconsin Steel mill for thirty years until the plant shut down in 1980, describe what it felt like to lose a job and be unable to find another one.

MARY MORGAN: I started in at South Works in 1973. I had two kids still at home and was just separated from my husband. He died a few months later.

I really liked that job. By me being a widow, I could support myself. I didn't have to go out and ask somebody for money. I didn't have to go on Aid [Family Assistance]. I could support my own self. That's very important to me.

I've been off work for [one and one-half years]. I haven't been able to find anything else. And all my benefits is ran out, even my little savings. My children help a little. I have six—all grown now. They're all unemployed. Three of them worked at one company that was sort of like the mill. It's all but closed down now. They had been going on unemployment and trying to find a job, but that has ran out now. I have my youngest son, my oldest daughter and one little grandchild living with me. Altogether, I have ten grandchildren. That's what makes it rough....

I've been looking for other jobs. I've been to Sweetheart, Tootsie Roll, Sure-Plus, Libby's, Soft Sheen.... Most of them just say they're not hiring. It gets discouraging.

would find new work, but rarely with the same high levels of pay or benefits.

Not all blue-collar workers gave up without a fight. Laid-off steelworkers in the Monongahela Valley outside Pittsburgh created an organization of the unemployed in the 1980s that lobbied for increased unemployment benefits and government assistance and that picketed corporate headquarters and business leaders' homes. They also founded a community newspaper, the *Mill Hunk Herald*, which spread the word about their collective actions to blunt deindustrialization's effects.

The same economic policies that devastated the country's industrial heartland generated regional booms that gave the United States an aura of prosperity throughout most of the 1980s. Defense spending, foreign investment, and the maturation of the "baby boom" generation helped send real-estate values soaring in California and New England. In such financial centers as New York, Dallas, Los Angeles, and Miami, the Reagan administration's deregulation of the banking industry and the stock market set off a wave of speculation. New York, home of Wall Street and most of the large banks, recovered from its mid-1970s fiscal crisis to become an international financial and real-estate center for the superrich. Mammoth new skyscrapers now dotted Chicago's Loop—just fifteen miles from decaying steel mills—as the Windy City joined the highly speculative world of stock, bond, and commodity-futures trading.

The dramatic growth in real estate, finance, retail trade, and high-tech manufacturing also became visible in the new suburban and exurban centers that overnight threatened the very existence of downtown office and shopping districts. Tysons Corner, Virginia; Plainsboro, New Jersey; Clayton, Missouri; Newport Beach, California; the Route 580 corridor just east of the Oakland hills in northern

I have very little hope—very, very little. I'm praying that I can find me a job somewhere. But if they don't open up something where people can get a job, it don't look very good at all. I guess they just want us all to dig a hole and get in it.

CARL STEZCO: I've been every place [to] look for a job. . . . I went to Jay's Potato Chips. They gave me a test and said, "You're overqualified." I said, "I'll tell you what, you said you're paying $5 an hour, well I'll work for $3." They still wouldn't take me. I'm a skilled electrician, plumber, a pipe fitter. But they ain't gonna hire a guy like me. I still go out every day and look.

My wife isn't healthy. She can't work. We have a two-flat, but the mortgage isn't paid off. I get $160 in rent on the other apartment. I'm paying $200 on the mortgage and $160 in gas bills. So you can't make ends meet. I only eat one meal a day. Food stamps turned me down. I don't know where to turn. I'm ashamed to ask for anything. I always swore I'd never go on pension—I'd work till the day I died.

I did go to the alderman for a year and a half trying to get a job. I was begging, pleading. I saw him at least twenty times. They kept telling me, "You're at the top of the list." You know you get desperate: one day I approached him in the parking lot to ask him about the job. The next time I saw him, he really went after me, just about spit on me 'cause I did that. You're never supposed to come up to him about something like that outside of his office. I just had to sit there and take it. I'm a big guy. Fifteen years ago, maybe I would have knocked him down. But when you got nothing, you've got to take that kind of stuff. Maybe the good Lord will come down and help me. I pray every day. That's all I have faith in anymore.

California; and Rockville Pike, Maryland—these were not the bedroom suburbs of the 1950s, but new towns composed of gleaming new office towers, huge shopping malls, and high-priced homes and condominiums. Here was another American workforce, one segregated by race and class as well as by personal expectations from the struggling industries and declining cities they had left behind. Here was the physical manifestation of the great social divisions generated by Reaganite capitalism in the 1980s.

"BACK TO THE FUTURE": AMERICA'S NEW GILDED AGE

Reaganomics helped create a new American class structure. This new social order reflected deep changes in the distribution of economic wealth, nationally and internationally; the recomposition of the American population; and the reordering of political power, particularly the decline of the New Deal coalition.

Though far less egalitarian than in other industrial democracies, including Japan and West Germany, income distribution in the United States had remained fairly stable for a quarter-century after the end of World War II. But by the early 1980s the United States, in the words of the economists Barry Bluestone and Bennett Harrison, took a "Great U-Turn." "The economic distance between rich and poor, between well paid and poorly paid, is higher today," they wrote, "than at any point in the lifetimes of all but our most senior citizens, the veterans of the Great Depression."

Between 1977 and 1990 the income of the richest fifth of the population rose by one-third, while that of the top 1 percent almost doubled. The net worth of the richest 400 Americans nearly tripled in these years. The richest 2.5 million Americans received nearly as much income after taxes in 1990 as the 100 million Americans with the lowest incomes. The total income of the bottom 60 percent, in fact, fell in real dollar terms, with the income of those living below the official poverty level established by the federal government dropping most sharply. Most strikingly, one of every three *working* Americans had an annual income that fell below the poverty line.

The beneficiaries of these changes in the distribution of wealth spent with an abandon not seen since the Gilded Age a century earlier. Greed and extravagance became the stuff of popular culture. Television dramas such as *Dallas* and *Dynasty* profiled the stylish and ruthless men and women of the new wealth who reveled in a seemingly endless array of luxury homes, yachts, cars, jet airplanes, and designer clothes. Their real-life counterparts paraded across the fashion and society pages of glossy magazines, daily newspapers, and an

Haves. The ostentatious display of self and wealth became a hallmark of 1980s America. In this case, a "yuppie" couple pose in their high-rise apartment for a magazine photograph—unself-consciously displaying the "nanny" as one of their possessions.

aptly named television "documentary" series, *Lifestyles of the Rich and Famous.*

Financial speculation generated hundreds of thousands of extremely well-paid jobs. Young lawyers, bankers, MBA's, and stockbrokers—neatly summarized (and parodied) as "Yuppies" (young urban professionals)—flocked to thriving financial districts in New York, Los Angeles, and Chicago. Here they sought to win their share of the vast fortunes created by the corporate consolidations and leveraged buyouts that *Business Week* dubbed the "Casino Economy." Their heroes were "junk bond" king Michael Milken, who earned $550 million in fees in one extraordinary year; Ivan Boesky, a stock market arbitrageur who made hundreds of millions of dollars in corporate mergers; and Donald Trump, who parlayed his father's substantial real-estate business into an empire of prestige hotels and gambling casinos.

Standing well below these high rollers on America's sharply inclined income pyramid were millions of white-collar professionals, constituting perhaps 30 percent of the working population. The salaries of these white-collar workers increased modestly in the tumultuous economy of the Reagan era. Many lived, worked, and shopped in new suburban and exurban town houses, tract-home communities, office parks, and shopping malls that spread out along an expanded highway system from almost every major metropolitan area. This slice of the middle class seemed to bask in the glow of the Reagan Revolution: their income taxes were lower; they voted Republican in overwhelming numbers; and they managed to remove themselves from the urban blight and racial conflict that all too often typified even such Sunbelt cities as Miami, Houston, New Orleans, and Atlanta.

This seemingly prosperous middle stratum was not immune, however, from the economic and social difficulties of the 1980s. Since the end of World War II, white-collar workers had received job stability in return for their loyalty to corporate employers. While large firms routinely hired and laid off blue-collar workers with the ebb and flow of sales, white-collar workers expected largely uninterrupted employment. But the heavy debt assumed by corporations through mergers and leveraged buyouts and the squeeze on profits from domestic and international competition led corporate leaders to implement a "lean and mean" strategy. During a typical eighteen-month period in 1985 and 1986, DuPont dismissed or pushed into retirement 11 percent of its white-collar workforce; Exxon, 17 percent; General Electric, 8 percent; and AT&T, 10 percent. When another downturn struck at the end of the decade, a new wave of reorganization and layoffs swept through the middle layers of the banking, stock brokerage, and real-estate industries.

"I was hurt," remembered a middle manager nudged into retirement by a big drug firm. "After thirty-four years with the company, I was surprised that it came down to an economic relationship between the two of us. I thought I was in—a family kind of thing." For the millions of professionals, managers, and white-collar technicians who remained after "downsizing," such incidents worked a sea change in their expectations.

The advances in income and life-style made by the middle class in the 1970s and 1980s had been made possible by enlisting the paid labor of various family members. The most important additions to the workforce were women, primarily wives, whose labor force participation increased from about 40 to nearly 60 percent between 1970 and 1990. In the latter year, paid work was virtually universal among middle-class and working-class women under age forty; indeed, their labor represented the difference between comfort and hardship for the broad middle stratum of the U.S. population. Virtually all of the income gain among white, two-parent families in the years after 1967 can be accounted for by the wages of wives and daughters.

American middle-class family life changed dramatically as a result. "Traditional" families—husband and wife with children, with the father as sole breadwinner and the mother as homemaker—now represented only one of every ten American households. Nearly 60 percent of all women with children under age six worked outside the home in 1990. Likewise, teenage employment, even among middle-class families, increased dramatically in the 1970s and 1980s. The spiraling cost of a middle-class teenage life-style—a college education, a car of one's own, a well-stocked wardrobe—combined with the pull of a booming service sector to draw millions of teenagers into the workforce.

The relative affluence of the American middle class in the 1980s was also sustained by what can only be called family speed-up. To the surprise of optimistic social forecasters, the growth of office automation and the deployment of a wide array of "labor-saving" gadgets—from personal computers to faxes and car phones—did not reduce working time for professionals and office workers. About one-third of all professionals and managers worked more than forty-nine hours a week at the end of the 1980s, and on average Americans had nearly ten fewer hours of leisure time weekly in 1987 than they enjoyed in 1973.

Of course, most Americans were not part of the salaried middle class. For these working Americans, even a two-paycheck income could not prevent stagnation or actual reduction in their standard of living during the 1980s. For at least two-thirds of all American workers, the 1980s were years in which their taxes went up and their standard of living declined. The decline of basic industries and corporate consolidations between 1975 and 1990, as we have seen, dramatically transformed the income and job prospects of blue-collar working men.

The children of blue-collar workers were even more profoundly affected. The average real income of a twenty-five-year-old male stood about one-quarter lower than that of his blue-collar father two decades before. Given the sharp jump in housing costs in the 1970s and 1980s, many young people were forced to remain at home after finishing high school or college. Only about 15 percent of all twenty-five-year-old Americans could afford to buy a home in 1989, down from 25 percent only seventeen years before. Many could not even afford to rent a big-city apartment. Such statistics reflected the experience of young men such as "Rick," the twenty-two-year-old son of a Long Island machinist, sleeping each night in the same bedroom he had occupied since the third grade. Blocked from the kind of manufacturing job that had propelled his parents into home ownership during the 1960s, Rick got by on little more than spending money from his two service industry jobs: parking cars during the day, and working as a bouncer all night.

Profound changes in the economy also led to a fundamental remaking of the American working class. Jewish, Italian, and Polish immigrants had entered the U.S. job market after 1900 to fill millions of semiskilled and unskilled factory jobs. In the 1970s and 1980s, huge numbers of Asian and Latino immigrants flocked to U.S. shores for the millions of new service, retail, clerical, and light manufacturing jobs that now opened up.

"Roundup." U.S. Border Patrol agents "herd" a group of Mexicans arrested after illegally crossing into the United States near San Diego, California. The growing presence of "undocumented" workers, especially Latinos, stimulated an immigration restriction movement in the 1990s. The Immigration Restriction and Control Act of 1987, popularly called "Simpson-Mazzoli," offered some long-term illegals an amnesty leading to eventual citizenship. But it set further restrictions on employment for more recent immigrants and extended the threat of deportation if they were apprehended by the Immigration and Naturalization Service. Despite passage of the law, over 1 million immigrants were arrested while crossing the border between Mexico and the United States in 1990; 400,000 were caught and deported in the San Diego area alone.

This contemporary wave of immigrants rivaled in sheer numbers the great transatlantic flows that made the U.S. working class so ethnically diverse a century earlier. In the 1970s, 4.5 million legal immigrants arrived in the United States; that number increased to nearly 6 million during the 1980s. Estimates indicate that an equal number of undocumented (or "illegal") immigrants (the largest percentage from Mexico) also entered the United States in these two decades. Over 40 percent of the newcomers were from numerous Asian countries, especially the Philippines, China, South Korea, and Vietnam; about 35 percent arrived from Latin America and the Caribbean.

One of every three new immigrants entered the United States through California, making the nation's most populous state its unofficial Ellis Island as well. By 1990, the population of Los Angeles, the nation's second-largest city, was one-third foreign-born. It was also the second-largest Spanish-speaking city (after Mexico City) on the North American continent. Hundreds of thousands of Mexicans and Central Americans streamed into poor neighborhoods and communities in East Los Angeles and the San Gabriel Valley. At the same time, several hundred thousand Koreans settled in an old working-class neighborhood just west of Los Angeles's downtown, while an equal number of immigrants from Taiwan, Hong Kong, and Vietnam transformed the old Chinatown neighborhood near City Hall and San Gabriel Valley towns such as Monterey Park. Demographers estimate that Asians and Latinos will make up more than half the workforce in Los Angeles and California as a whole by early in the twenty-first century.

New York's foreign-born population, like Los Angeles's, also approached 35 percent of its total populace in 1990, a level the city last reached in 1910, at the height of southern and eastern European immigration. In addition to growth of the long-established Puerto Rican community, other New York neighborhoods were transformed during the 1980s as hundreds of thousands of Haitian, Dominican, Colombian, East Indian, Chinese, and Russian immigrants settled in the city's poor and working-class communities. The newest additions to New York's incredible ethnic diversity were nearly 200,000 Mexican immigrants, who arrived after 1986. Mostly undocumented, they traveled thousands of miles by truck and car from some of the poorest rural regions of Mexico to find work. "We came to New York because we are poor farmers and our parents did not have enough resources to send us to school," explained a young food deliverer.

New immigrants transformed cities and towns other than New York and Los Angeles. Miami had the highest percentage of foreign-born residents of any U.S. city by the 1980s, spurred by the influx of nearly

---

"THERE IS BLOOD IN EVERY DOLLAR I MAKE . . ."

Mr. Ji (not his real name) was a quality control officer in a pharmaceutical factory in Canton, China; his wife worked in a factory day-care center. The Jis decided to come to the United States in the early 1980s in order to get better medical care for their twelve-year-old daughter. The Ji family bags and tags garments in a New York City sweatshop, working long hours at below minimum wage. Mr. Ji, age sixty-two, recounts the difficulties he and his family have had to endure in coming to America.

It was very crowded with over ten people living in [his brother-in-law's] apartment. There's no room for our luggage and we were sleeping in the living room. This is a complete surprise for us. We thought in the U.S. there are all high rises and big apartments. We started searching for the apartment right away. We found a one bedroom apartment on 56th St., Brooklyn, from the classified ads in the Chinese newspapers. It's two blocks from my father-in-law. The rent was $480 and the landlord is very nasty. . . .

I was disappointed with my relatives. . . . The first thing people ask you here is "How much money do you make?" They measure you by how much you can make. My circle of friends are too busy. It's not like China. Here they don't have time to see you at all. They just ask you to call. My in-laws put me down. They said, "You are a college graduate. See how much you are making. What good is going to school?" They said I'm lazy, that I don't work hard enough. . . .

I don't understand America's policy. They let you come. But once you are here, they don't care at all. They don't care if you can get a job or what you do. You are all on your own. It's one thing to let immigrants in. But once they are here, you have to digest them. We get below minimum wages. This is the tenth factory we worked in. It's all the same. Finally we decided to stop hopping around. There is no labor law here. The government is acting like an idiot who doesn't know what's going on. The minimum wages are not for real. . . . In China, I just do desk work, giving people ideas. Now I'm doing this totally meaningless work. America is a world where the strong devours the meek.

I am at a point of no return. If I go back, I'll be looked down on by everybody. They'll think I'm such a failure. . . . I can't go back empty-handed. It'll be so embarrassing. . . . I want to learn English, I felt handicapped. I feel I'm without my limbs. I don't want to be dependent on other people. But I don't have any time at all. . . . Now I'm so tired when I get home, sometimes I don't even cook, just make some instant noodles. . . .

We have to work so hard for so little money. Last Saturday we worked from 9 until 10:30 p.m. Between us we made eighty dollars. It's the best day since I came to the U.S. . . . I am tied down to my job. I feel like a slave. I can't go anywhere. Even if there is gold out there, I won't have time to pick them up. . . . There is blood in every dollar I make. . . . We all thought U.S. is such an advanced country. I don't see too much personal freedom here. You are free if you have money.

600,000 Cubans, many of them well-to-do, who arrived after the 1959 Cuban revolution. Tens of thousands of refugees from Haiti, Guatemala, El Salvador, and Nicaragua also came to Miami during the 1980s to escape political and economic turmoil in their countries. Miami's huge number of Latino immigrants changed the face of the city, displacing the long-resident African-American population and increasingly making Spanish the language of commerce and government. Similarly, in many old industrial cities in New Jersey such as Passaic, Paterson, and Union City, Latinos—primarily from Cuba, Chile, Colombia, Ecuador, and Guatemala—now outnumber both Anglos and African-Americans. Latino-owned businesses, including restaurants, nightclubs, fruit stands, clothing stores, and even shops selling hand-rolled cigars have transformed the look, sound, and texture of the main shopping areas in these New Jersey municipalities. One Union City resident noted that a few years ago many shops "used to [have] signs saying, 'We speak Spanish.' Now the signs say, 'We speak English.'"

New immigrants came from a range of economic situations. Some arrived with significant economic resources. Among the most visible were Koreans, many of whom owned and managed fruit and vegetable markets that sprang up in Los Angeles, New York, and other cities. In addition to hard work, especially of family members, these small businesses were built with family funds brought from Korea. These new businesses also relied on ethnic networks that supplied additional capital and organizational resources. The new wave of immigrants included a small number of wealthy elites from places such as Hong Kong, who were able to make substantial investments in real estate and factories.

Most of the new immigrants were more typically of the working class. They came because even minimum-wage work in the United States paid five or ten times more than they could earn in the large cities, barrios, and villages of their homelands. Many came to the United States with the hope of saving enough and returning to their native countries to buy a farm or open a small business. Most did not succeed. "We came with illusions of earning a little money, investing it, and doing something in Mexico," noted one undocumented immigrant in New York City. "But those who get $180 for working seven days, what can they do? They return defeated to Mexico."

Many undocumented workers ended up working in sweatshops, ironically manufacturing goods that compete with cheap imported products manufactured by their fellow countrymen and countrywomen in Asia and Latin America. In New York, for example, recent Latino and Asian immigrants work in hundreds of garment sweatshops that sprang up in lower Manhattan and Brooklyn in the 1980s. "Industrial homework"—whole families living and working in

Sweatshop 1991. Asian workers labor in a garment shop in lower Manhattan, a setting reminiscent of sweatshop working conditions in the clothing industry earlier in the twentieth century.

cramped and unhealthy tenement apartments—also reappeared in New York and Los Angeles under conditions strikingly similar to those that Progressive Era reformers had fought to abolish.

Even where the work is "high-tech" and entirely legal, job hierarchies resembled those of the pre–New Deal era. Thus, many of California's most successful new computer firms maintained a pyramid job structure: a few optimistic professionals with an innovative concept at the top; English-speaking clerical, sales, and "development" workers in the front office; while in the shop in back, scores of Asian and Latino women are building chips or stuffing circuit boards. Seventy percent of all electronics manufacturing jobs in the computer-oriented Silicon Valley in northern California are held by women, half of whom are Latino and Asian immigrants.

At the very bottom of the American social hierarchy stood the one in eight Americans the U.S. government counted as officially below the 1990 poverty line—about $13,000 for a family of four. As a result of Great Society welfare programs, the proportion of all Americans considered poor reached its postwar low in 1973, when it stood at one in nine Americans. Stagflation drove this number upward in the 1970s until it peaked at 15 percent in the early Reagan years; then it declined slowly to about 13 percent, or 32 million, at the end of the 1980s. About one-tenth of all whites were poor; one-third of the nation's African-Americans; and one-quarter of all Latinos.

Low pay, structural changes in the economy, and institutional racism were the chief causes of continuing poverty in late-twentieth-century America. During the 1980s, American business generated some 20 million new jobs. But few of these jobs paid the wages, or provided the full-time employment, to keep even a two-paycheck family much above the poverty line. Between 1979 and 1984, six of

"IT'S THE FREON . . ."

Silicon Valley production workers not only labor in tedious and low-paying jobs (often at or just above the minimum wage); they are also frequently exposed to an array of toxic chemicals. At Q.E.S., where the journalist Diana Hembree worked in the early 1980s, production workers were exposed to freon 113, which caused skin rashes, drowsiness, nausea, giddiness, and nervous-system depression.

From the outside, the plant looked more like a real estate office than a factory. Along with hundreds of other "board shops" in the area, it makes printed circuit boards—the brains and memory banks of computers—for other high-tech firms. . . .

At first I was so pleased to have persuaded Q.E.S. to hire me that I clipped the tiny wires with unfeigned enthusiasm. But as the morning wore on, my neck and shoulders ached from craning over the boards, my eyes smarted, and I felt drowsy. After what seemed like interminable hours clipping boards, I stole a glance at the clock: only 9:45. I could smell a peculiar odor, but had no idea what it was.

"Sleepy?" asked the older woman beside me when I tried to stifle a yawn. "It's the freon," she said confidentially, nodding at a machine a few feet away. "Go to the bathroom and splash cold water on your face and arms; that helps a little. Or, if you can't keep your eyes open a second longer, drop something on the floor and take your time picking it up. That's what I do. . . ."

Since [Angel, a co-worker had] been working with the freon, he had broken

ten jobs added to the U.S. labor market paid $7,000 a year or less. Most were in the service sector, as home health-care attendants, salesclerks, food servers, janitors, or office clerks. Besides low pay, these jobs offered few pension or health-care benefits, were often part-time or temporary, and had few opportunities for promotion. Thus McDonald's, the largest employer of black youth in the nation, hired almost all of its workers on a part-time, minimum-wage basis, which virtually assured a turnover rate of more than 100 percent per year. "You make minimum wage," complained one Baltimore resident, "and there are so many people applying that the jobs are snapped right up."

Government welfare programs and wage standards, designed to compensate for the economy's inability to generate enough high-paying jobs, were cut back or abandoned during the Reagan era. By 1989, state and local welfare payments dropped by an average of 40 percent from their 1973 level. Job-training programs were also sharply curtailed, and the minimum wage (frozen by the Reagan administration at 1981 levels) lost some 44 percent of its real value because of inflation. The U.S. Labor Department admitted that a full-time minimum-wage worker could not keep a family of four out of poverty.

Single mothers, especially African-American and Latino women, were hit hardest by the decline in social services and by the absence of high-paying jobs. A marked jump in out-of-wedlock births and female-headed households, which doubled in the years between 1970 and 1989, contributed to what analysts called the "feminization of poverty." Abandoned by her husband, twenty-four-year-old Donna Keyes supported three children on her welfare check. "How do I go on?" she asked. "We either pay the rent, we pay all the bills, or we eat. We don't do all three." Given such choices, it was not surprising that every day one of eight American children went hungry in 1990.

out in a rash and he had painful, recurring stomach aches.... Richard, a friendly, awkward twenty-year-old who was clipping beside Angel, said he didn't know if freon could actually hurt him, but washing circuit boards made him feel dizzy and disoriented. "The last time I did it," Richard said, "I felt like I was in a white cloud...."

Gloria Luna, Angel's twenty-four-year-old sister, worked in the assembly room next door. Having learned English as a teenager, she served as unofficial translator for the other Mexican women. She was two-and-a-half months pregnant with her second child....

[The] new floor supervisor, Ray Burks, told me ... : "Worrying about chemicals is fine if you have money and options, but compared to being evicted tomorrow if you can't pay the rent, chemical fumes and skin rashes seem pretty minor...."

At the back of the assembly room stands a large machine in which circuit boards are coated with molten tin-and-lead solder. For the past three weeks, the machine has blanketed the room with noxious fumes, causing dizziness among the work force and sending several women to the bathroom to vomit....

"I've never been sick so much in my life," Laura, a single mother in her twenties, told me today. "Since I've been here, I've been sick at least once a week...."

Supervisors traced the problem to a new kind of oil used in the machine, but some employees were not satisfied with the explanation. Worried, I called OSHA [Occupation Safety and Health Administration] and asked that an inspector do air sampling for lead.

At least three other employees have called OSHA to ask for an investigation of the foul-smelling fumes; they talk about it daily in excited whispers. But so far, no inspectors have shown up.

Growing numbers of Americans virtually fell out of the world of work. The decline in the values of unemployment compensation and welfare, sharp hikes in urban rents, and the elimination of federally supported housing programs generated a new, or at least vastly more visible, phenomenon: homeless Americans, who numbered between one million and three million during the 1980s. When homeless people first appeared in large numbers in the late 1970s, many Americans thought of them as primarily "bag ladies, winos, and junkies," or people released from mental hospitals. But within a few years it

"YOU DON'T HAVE TO KNOW HOW TO COOK . . ."

Eight million Americans have found work at McDonald's; most are paid the minimum wage. In the name of efficiency and profitability, McDonald's has reduced formerly semiskilled jobs such as short-order cook to unskilled and mindless grill-tending. A teenager describes cooking hamburgers on a computerized grill in the allotted ninety seconds.

They called us the Green Machine 'cause the crew had green uniforms then. And that's what it is, a machine. You don't have to know how to cook, you don't have to know how to think. There's a procedure for everything and you just follow the procedures. . . .

You're on the ten-in-one grill, ten patties in a pound. Your basic burger. The guy on the bin calls, "Six hamburgers." So you lay your six pieces of meat on the grill and set the timer. Beep-beep, beep-beep, beep-beep. That's the beeper to sear 'em. It goes off in twenty seconds. [Then press the patties down with a spatula.] Sup, sup, sup, sup, sup, sup. Now you turn off the sear beeper, put the buns in the oven, set the oven timer and then the next beeper is to turn the meat. This one goes beep-beep-beep, beep-beep-beep. So you turn your patties, and then you drop your re-cons [handfuls of reconstituted onions] on the meat, t-con, t-con, t-con. Now the bun oven buzzes. This one turns itself off when you open the oven door so you just take out your crowns [tops of buns], line 'em up and give 'em each a squirt of mustard and a squirt of ketchup.

Now, you get to put on the pickles. Two if they're regular, three if they're small. That's the creative part. Then the lettuce, then you ask for a cheese count ("cheese on four please"). Finally the last beep goes off and you lay your burger on the crowns. . . .

Then scoop up the heels [the bun bottoms] which are on top of the bun warmer, take the heels with one hand and push the tray out from underneath and they land (plip) one on each burger, right on top of the re-cons, neat and perfect. It's like I told you. The procedures makes the burgers. You don't have to know a thing. . . .

You follow the beepers, you follow the buzzers and you turn your meat as fast as you can. . . . To work at McDonald's you don't need a face, you don't need a brain. You need to have two hands and two legs and move 'em as fast as you can. That's the whole system. I wouldn't go back there again for anything.

ONE PENN PLAZA

ESCALATORS TO STREET and SHOPPING MALL

Have-nots. Homeless people spend a night during January 1990 in New York's Pennsylvania Station.

became clear that for millions of working Americans trapped at the bottom of the income pyramid, homelessness was only a layoff or severe family illness away. In fact, one of every five homeless people held a full-time or part-time job. On cold winter nights whole families, not just single men, searched for shelter and food at the crowded and often squalid shelters that opened in almost every American city. By the end of the 1980s, families with children constituted one-third of the urban homeless population.

Unlike the poverty of the Great Depression, which was widespread, today's poor, especially African-Americans, are often economically and racially isolated in ghetto communities. The 1960s civil rights revolution helped expand the small black middle class to perhaps as many as one in four African-Americans by the end of the 1980s. But new fair employment and housing laws passed during the civil rights era also generated an exodus of middle-class and stable working-class families from traditionally black inner-city neighborhoods. African-American poverty, as the sociologist William Julius Wilson has pointed out, has become geographically concentrated, thus depriving ghetto residents of a historically important "social buffer" that provides community leadership and socially positive role models for black youth.

Endemic poverty and social isolation contributed to a fearful wave of criminality and violence that washed over the youthful, largely black and Latino populations of urban America in the 1980s. Exacerbated by a wave of hard drugs, especially inexpensive "crack" cocaine, inner-city neighborhoods were overwhelmed by a violent anarcho-feudal world of well-armed drug lords and street-corner salesmen, whose fate was likely prison or death. By the 1980s, homicide was the leading cause of death among urban black males age fifteen to twenty-four, a rate six times greater than for other Americans. In New York City, one of every four African-American men in their twenties (and one of every eight Latino men of similar age) was in prison, on probation, or on parole.

"... I FEAR FOR MY CHILDREN"

Deborah M., a homeless single mother in New York City, speaks about trying to raise her children while shifting from one dormitory-style public shelter to another. Early in 1991, a city agency finally placed her and her children in their own apartment.

This could happen to anyone. As for me, I finished high school, I've done a year and a half of college, I'm a certified nurse's aid and a bank teller, and I'm homeless. . . . I have four children: fourteen, thirteen, nine, and the baby was two. . . . I had teenage girls so we had to sleep in [our] clothes. . . . You don't have locks on your doors. . . . The worst part of being there is that I fear for my children. . . . Whatever place we moved, I took them to [school in] Queens. We had to get up at five. It took us in traveling time an hour and a half to an hour and forty-five minutes. . . .

From the little timid children that they were, they're not that anymore. . . . My oldest daughter had to stop her cheer leading, swim meets, her gymnastics because we didn't know where we would be living day by day. I have a lot of problems with her now. . . . There is a lot of bad kids in the shelter. I don't blame the mothers or nothing. A year from now I see her not in school, pregnant. . . . She thinks that she's so much older and wiser now . . . like nobody can tell her anything.

My son said that he is tired of moving around, he's sleepy: "Do we have to move tomorrow again?" We moved to six different shelters, most of them was overnight. My children changed drastically, they got hostile, disrespectful, angry, they just got the attitude that they just didn't care anymore. . . . Like they lost their self-identity. . . . My children lost all sense of security.

When they just saw the place [temporary apartment-style shelter] they ran through the whole apartment. "This is going to be my room. Oh, we have a bathroom!" The first thing my daughter said is, "I'm just going to love it here, I'm so glad that we're not in the shelters anymore." My children have improved greatly since we moved here. They have found me an apartment back in Queens, it's a whole house, and hopefully in the next two or three weeks, we'll be out of here.

Prisons were in fact one of the great growth industries of the 1980s. Politicians poured a large proportion of declining government revenues into building new jails, which allowed for a doubling (to nearly 700,000) of the nation's prison population. By 1990, the ratio of prisoners to the general U.S. population was among the highest of any nation in the world. The United States was also one of the few Western nations that used the death penalty. After the U.S. Supreme Court affirmed its legality in 1975, southern and western states carried out executions with increasing frequency.

THE LABOR MOVEMENT IN DECLINE

Reaganite policies and the profound transformation of the nation's class structure proved disastrous for American trade unions during the 1980s. Organized labor lost more than 3 million members over the course of the decade. By 1990, unions represented but 16 percent of the nation's 101 million workers, less than half the percentage in their heyday right after World War II. The number of strikes declined dramatically during the 1980s. The proportion of workers who stopped work was less than 20 percent of the level in the previous decade.

What accounts for this debacle? The plant closings and layoffs that swept through so many heavily unionized industries provide one answer. For example, U.S. Steel, which had once employed a unionized workforce of 200,000, transformed itself in the early 1980s into USX Corporation, shut scores of steel mills, and acquired Marathon Oil, from which it soon derived the bulk of its sales and profits. The United Steelworkers of America lost almost half its members in the process, as imports and corporate reorganization drastically cut the number of jobs in the steel industry. When the union undertook a strike against USX in 1986, only 20,000 steelworkers were idled. The United Auto Workers also lost half a million members when the automakers and their supplier plants slashed payrolls after 1978 in an effort to compete with foreign imports.

In some old industrial cities—Youngstown, Ohio, and Hamtramck, Michigan, for example—the only active unionists left were retirees, who waged a new battle against their old employers to make sure their health benefits and pension checks were not cut back. In the 1980s, union strongholds such as Chicago, Detroit, Baltimore, and Philadelphia lost overall population, while such anti-union Sunbelt centers as San Diego, Phoenix, and Dallas gained hundreds of thousands of new residents. These three cities were now the sixth-, seventh-, and eighth-largest, respectively, in the nation.

Beginning in the 1970s, many employers aggressively sought a "union-free environment," especially in new plants in the Sunbelt.

Some argued that unions were unnecessary and offered their new non-union employees profit sharing, pay incentive schemes, and sometimes even rudimentary grievance procedures. Others relied on the union-busting stick rather than the paternalistic carrot. Management consultants hired by a group of New Jersey hospitals, for example, advised their clients to figure out "who is going to be most vulnerable if the union knocks," and then "weed 'em out. Get rid of anyone who's not going to be a team player." Such tactics violated the 1935 Wagner Act, designed to protect workers against anti-union employers. But management saw the mild penalties imposed by the National Labor Relations Board for such "unfair labor practices" as merely an additional cost of doing business. Pro-union workers soon were routinely fired during organizing drives; by 1984 the rate of such firings was four times that of 1960.

Newfangled anti-union tactics went hand in hand with an old-fashioned management strategy: cutting wages. The 1980s witnessed employer efforts to slash wages in industries facing foreign competition—auto, steel, and garment manufacturing—as well as in profitable industries whose only competition was domestic. U.S. meatpackers, for example, began shifting their operations away from unionized packinghouse districts in Chicago and Omaha to save money; by the 1970s a string of low-wage, nonunion meatpacking plants flourished in Iowa, Illinois, and Nebraska. Wages in this once thoroughly organized industry varied by as much as $3 an hour from one plant to another in the early 1980s. A business spokesperson neatly summed up the situation nationwide: "An abundant supply of labor makes it more possible than ever before to operate during a strike. This possibility constrains union demands." American workers lost about $500 billion in wage givebacks and other concessions during the first half of the 1980s.

In the midst of this wave of "concession bargaining," President Reagan's destruction of a trade union of government employees, the Professional Air Traffic Controllers' Organization (PATCO), immeasurably strengthened business's hand against organized labor. Ironically, PATCO had been one of the few unions to support the Republican presidential candidate in 1980. The union hoped that Reagan would endorse their call for reform and restaffing of the Federal Aviation Administration (FAA), the agency that employed most PATCO members. These well-educated, well-paid workers, many of them U.S. Air Force veterans, complained of the crushing mental and physical strain of air traffic control work. Mental burnout forced the average controller to retire by age thirty-five.

When the FAA did little to ameliorate these problems, PATCO struck in August 1981. Reagan quickly fired more than ten thousand

An illustration from a leaflet distributed during the summer and fall of 1981 by the Los Angeles local of the Professional Air Traffic Controllers' Organization. The leaflet urged other airline and airport workers to support PATCO, warning that the Reagan administration's suppression of the union would permit the airline companies to force layoffs and contract concessions from all workers in the industry.

striking air controllers and filled their jobs with supervisors, military personnel, and inadequately trained replacements. Not since Massachusetts governor Calvin Coolidge broke the 1919 Boston police strike had the government so thoroughly smashed a union of its own employees.

The labor movement had trouble developing an adequate response to this assault. Some labor officials, such as AFL-CIO president Lane Kirkland, who took over in 1979, had abandoned the self-serving complacency that characterized the last years of George Meany's tenure. In September 1981, the federation brought 400,000 unionists and supporters to Washington, D.C., for "Solidarity Day." The huge gathering revealed the loyalty and support the trade-union idea still enjoyed among working people, even at the height of Ronald Reagan's popularity. But the impulse generated by Solidarity Day quickly dissipated. AFL-CIO leaders sought to channel rank-and-file energy away from such mass actions toward traditional support for the Democratic Party, which ironically was increasingly reticent to defend organized labor or attack Reagan's economic policies.

Though some national union leaders initiated innovative collective bargaining and organizing strategies, particularly in the steel and coal industries, most union officials refused to consider building a broad-based movement during the 1980s to confront the intensifying attacks on unions and working-class living standards. Many old-style industrial union leaders, though nostalgic for the CIO struggles of the 1930s, were ambivalent about or even hostile toward linking up with the era's democratic social movements—linkages that might have offered a way to bolster the labor movement's declining fortunes and image. Some labor officials, especially former 1960s activists working in education, organizing, and political action departments, successfully pushed their unions toward broader racial, gender, and political alliances. But most key industrial unions, especially ones facing strong rank-and-file insurgencies (such as the Teamsters and the UAW), focused on quashing insurgent challenges in the 1980s rather than on redefining their union's and the labor movement's larger social role. More damagingly, some craft unions, especially in the construction trades, continued to limit African-American and female membership, contributing to lingering divisions among working people.

Given the inability of the larger labor movement to build bridges or offer an encompassing alternative to Reaganism, employers had little trouble during the early 1980s finding unemployed or underpaid workers willing to "scab" on union strikers. Most replacement workers usually were driven to scab by economic necessity, especially given the era's declining working-class living standards and high unemployment. But worker solidarity could hardly be expected to flourish in an era that celebrated flashy entrepreneurs and leveraged buyouts that destroyed thousands of jobs. This shift in public perception was graphically revealed during the 1984 professional football players' strike. Thousands of fans flocked to stadiums, jeered picket lines manned by players they thought too well paid, and then cheered on football teams of less talented strikebreakers or "replacement players," as they were called by television announcers.

Corporate attacks on unions were especially vicious in industries "deregulated" during the Carter and Reagan administrations. Democrats and Republicans agreed in the early 1980s to deregulate financial markets, trucking, airlines, and communications—industries traditionally regulated by the government. In the airline industry, for example, deregulation eliminated most guidelines that governed fares, schedules, and mergers. A fiercely competitive environment briefly flourished in which new, nonunion airlines—such as People Express—won a large slice of the market by offering low fares and no-frills service.

Airline managers, led by Frank Lorenzo, head of Texas Air, took advantage of deregulation to slash the wages of pilots, machinists, and flight attendants. In 1983, after selling hundreds of millions of dollars' worth of high-interest "junk bonds," Lorenzo bought Continental Airlines and declared the airline bankrupt in order to break its longstanding union contracts. He then offered to rehire the fired Continental workers at about half their old pay. When the workers struck, Lorenzo broke their unions by hiring replacement workers from among the tens of thousands of unemployed pilots and machinists laid off during the recession of the early 1980s.

Lorenzo then moved on to Eastern Airlines, which he added to his empire in 1986. Using the same tactics employed at Continental, Lorenzo demanded major wage reductions and precipitated a strike. But this time, well-paid airline pilots joined machinists and flight attendants in a highly effective strike that won sympathy from passengers, solidarity from the labor movement, and even grudging admiration from Wall Street. The multiyear strike grounded most Eastern planes, threw the airline into bankruptcy, and eventually forced Lorenzo out of the airline business.

In the 1980s, unions and their members were clearly on the defensive. Even when they went out on strike, workers were usually trying to maintain jobs, wage levels, and health benefits in the face of forced concessions, or "givebacks," demanded by employers. The battleground for these struggles was often a single factory, employer, or community where embattled unionists tried to mobilize families, neighbors, and community activists in defense of a whole way of life. In the coalfields of Appalachia, in the Arizona copper mines, in California's factory farms, in midwestern manufacturing towns, and in New England toolmaking factories, union members and rank-and-file leaders demonstrated that they could still organize for long, bitter social struggles reminiscent of the last quarter of the nineteenth century.

In Austin, Minnesota, a Hormel packinghouse workers' union, Local P-9, organized retirees, high-school students, family members, and sympathetic unionists in a battle against major wage conces-

Austin, Minnesota. Local P-9 strikers and National Guard troops outside the Hormel plant, January 1986.

sions. Through the bone-chilling winter of 1986, the Austin working-class community, "P-9 Proud," staffed spirited picket lines, sent organizers to nearby packing plants, and mobilized tens of thousands of supporters throughout the upper Midwest. The inspiring militancy of the P-9 workers and their families and national publicity generated widespread support for the strike. Despite this extraordinary effort, the Austin local could not win the long war against the combined weight of a multiplant company, strikebreakers recruited from Minnesota's depressed local farming communities, and National Guard troops sent in by the governor. P-9 also had to fight the national leadership of its own union, the United Food and Commercial Workers, which sought a new national agreement with the meatpackers that included wage reductions. The strike ended finally in 1986, with the Austin community divided, P-9 defeated, and Hormel victorious.

Not all labor-community mobilizations during the 1980s failed. At several of the nation's most prestigious universities—including Yale, Harvard, New York University, and the University of California—clerical workers and support staff fought protracted and successful organizing campaigns. University clerical workers, overwhelmingly women, worked for meager wages in an environment in which the largely male faculty and administration afforded them little dignity or respect. Campus organizers, many of them former activists in the civil rights and women's movements, successfully used feminist language to speak to the needs of clerical workers at these institutions. Such issues as "comparable worth"—equal pay for white-collar work that

"IT IS AGAINST THIS DENIAL OF YALE'S OWN VALUES THAT WE WITNESS"

Striking Yale University clerical and technical workers, overwhelmingly women, employed a number of innovative tactics—from mass civil disobedience to pressure exerted by supportive alumni—to get a recalcitrant university administration to negotiate a contract. In October 1984, nearly two hundred striking members of Local 34 decided to peacefully block access to the Yale president's house. The union issued this leaflet to explain its actions.

The membership of Local 34 has voted, by secret ballot, to join together in a Nonviolent Witness for Equality at the house of Yale President A. Bartlett Giamatti. As part of that Nonviolent Witness, some of us will submit to peaceful arrest, symbolic of our commitment, in the tradition of Gandhi and Martin Luther King.

We have joined in this Witness because Yale's announced intention to starve us into abandoning our 4-year struggle for equality leaves us no honorable alternative....

We believe that we have been patient beyond any reasonable call. We have negotiated in 73 meetings over a full year, and continue to seek further negotiation....

Yale has responded to our patience by massive distortion of our position, and of its own.... The University has knowingly concealed and distorted the statistical evidence supporting our [wage and sexual] discrimination charges....

We are mindful, too, that Yale University has no constructive approach to labor relations, beyond using its great wealth and power to try to dictate a contract....

We are, finally, painfully aware of the campaign of threats and harassment Yale has directed against our brothers and sisters in Local 35 [the union representing Yale's service and maintenance workers] because they have felt compelled not to cross a picket line made up of their wives, daughters, friends, neighbors, and co-workers.

Yale has told us, and the community, that it will never bend or compromise, but will merely wait until we—and our children—starve.

That is not what has made Yale a great university. It is against this denial of Yale's own values that we witness.

required equal or superior skills to traditional blue-collar jobs—struck a responsive chord among white-collar workers not known for their identification with traditional trade union ideals. These university union drives also enjoyed broad support from students, progressive faculty, and even campus craft unionists, such as stationary engineers, who staffed picket lines, published newsletters, and pressured university administrators to sign contracts.

The Eastern Airlines, P-9, and university clerical strikes, despite their mixed outcomes, demonstrated that worker solidarity and militancy were not dead, despite extraordinary government and corporate efforts throughout the 1980s to destroy unions.

THE END OF REAGANISM

Although the slow growth and fiscal austerity of the 1970s and 1980s shifted the terrain of American politics far to the right, Reaganism in fact reached an impasse long before the fortieth president left office. With the Democrats disorganized and intimidated by the Reagan Revolution and the New Right upsurge, the 1984 presidential campaign was a landslide for the Republicans. Employing hollow rhetoric ("It's morning in America") and boasting about his get-tough foreign policy, Reagan easily crushed Democratic nominee Walter Mondale.

The Reagan campaign rhetoric neatly ignored the severe economic problems and continuing social and cultural divisions that plagued the nation in the mid-1980s, as well as the spread of political protest. As we have seen, these years witnessed the stirrings of a revived labor movement. Protest also revived at college campuses. Opposing the Reagan administration's policy of "constructive engagement" with white South Africa, a broad national movement, spearheaded by university students, called for financial divestment in companies that continued to do business in South Africa. A similarly broad movement in opposition to U.S. government intervention in the civil wars in Nicaragua and El Salvador also gained nationwide momentum on college campuses as well as in churches and trade unions.

These grass-roots protests helped undercut Reaganism's seeming political consensus. In 1986 the ground gave way. The nation was stunned to learn that year that a network of White House officials had organized a covert and illegal government apparatus. These officials had sought to win the release of American hostages held captive in Lebanon by selling millions of dollars in military equipment to Iran, a regime the United States publicly denounced as terrorist. The profits from this trade, along with other money secretly raised from foreign governments, were then used to fund the CIA-backed "contra" war against Nicaragua's radical Sandinista government. These actions were in direct defiance of congressional directives that placed strict limits on covert operations and forbade under-the-table support for the contras. The need to provide covert funds to finance the contra war was a measure of the political impact of the mass protests of American citizens opposed to Reagan's pro-contra policies and revealed the administration's failure to convince a majority of Americans to support direct military intervention in Nicaragua.

Throughout the unfolding scandal, Ronald Reagan was never in danger of impeachment; the Democrats quickly shrank from such a momentous confrontation. But the televised Watergate-like hearings into the "Iran-contra" affair—which brought Colonel Oliver North, who had headed the White House operation, to political prominence—nonetheless deprived Reagan of the ability to set the national political agenda. In the 1986 elections the Democrats recaptured control of the U.S. Senate.

The weakening of Reaganism became more evident in 1987, when a remobilized liberal coalition, including feminists, civil libertarians, trade unionists, and civil rights activists successfully prevented U.S. Senate approval of Reagan's nominee to the U.S. Supreme

Symbols speak louder than words. Oliver North appears before the House Foreign Affairs Committee on December 9, 1986, to testify about his role in the Iran-contra scandal. Dressed in his Marine uniform, North presented himself as a symbol of American patriotism, hoping this appearance would counterbalance his refusal (citing his Fifth Amendment rights) to discuss his illegal activities in the basement of the White House.

Court, Robert Bork. Bork was an ideologue whom conservatives sought to elevate to the Court as a crucial step toward institutionalizing the right-wing swing in American politics begun ten years earlier.

The 1984 campaign for the Democratic Party presidential nomination waged by Jesse Jackson, a nationally prominent civil rights leader, contributed to the liberals' defeat of Bork. In Alabama, Louisiana, and other southern states with large African-American populations, the Jackson campaign boosted voter turnout and energized African-American activists and elected officials, whose influence helped sway the votes of several key southern senators against Bork. In 1988 Jackson again ran for the Democratic presidential nomination, with a program that directly challenged Reagan's economic and social policies. A wide range of 1960s radicals and liberals, some working-class and rural whites, and most African-American voters mobilized behind Jackson, demonstrating the continuing attraction of integrationist, populist politics.

The defeat of the Bork nomination was followed by another setback for Reaganism. In October 1987 the stock market crashed. The Dow Jones index dropped more than five hundred points in one day, proportionally a greater drop than that of "Black Thursday," which marked the beginning of the 1929 crash. No general economic collapse followed this stock market tumble; but the speculative boom of the 1980s was over. Soon real-estate and junk-bond prices plummeted, followed thereafter by a recession that began on both coasts and spread to the Midwest and South.

At almost the same time, several of the most celebrated Reagan-era financial wizards were charged and ultimately found guilty of illegal stock-market manipulation. Ivan Boesky, Michael Milken, and a score of other Wall Streeters ultimately went to jail, while the flashy real-estate empires of Donald Trump and other developers were diminished or dissolved.

Perhaps the most glaring example of financial chicanery during the Reagan era was revealed in the furor over the nation's savings and loan (S&L) industry. The deregulation of S&Ls during the Carter administration as well as lax federal supervision in the Reagan years transformed thousands of cautiously managed home-mortgage institutions into speculative enterprises that gambled federally insured deposits on questionable real estate and junk bonds and fueled the personal profligacy of S&L executives. One group of Beverly Hills S&L officials paid themselves well enough to enjoy the use of two $17 million jets on which they flew family and friends to vacation condominiums bought with depositors' money. They also spent several hundred thousand dollars to turn their executive bathroom into a bombproof bunker stocked with submachine guns and its own independent air and food supplies. The boom in southwestern oil, suburban office parks, and Sunbelt defense production that made such largess possible finally ended after 1987, plunging hundreds of savings institutions into bankruptcy and sending some S&L executives to jail, convicted of fraud and embezzlement. Because of federal guarantees on S&L deposits, U.S. taxpayers were left holding a bill approaching $500 billion.

Conservative cultural influences faded as well. In 1987 and 1988 several fundamentalist television evangelists, including Jimmy Swaggart and Jim Bakker, became embroiled in messy sex and money scandals. Enthusiasm for "televangelism" waned, prompting Jerry Falwell to disband his Moral Majority organization, which had had such an impact a decade before.

On network television, the glitzy celebrations of wealth and ruthless entrepreneurship that helped define the Reagan era in *Dallas* and *Falcon Crest* were canceled in the late 1980s. They were replaced by successful situation comedies such as *Roseanne, Married . . . with Children,* and *The Simpsons,* which revolved around the many frustrations and occasional joys of hard-pressed working families. These 1990s television families are descendants of the Kramdens in the 1950s *Honeymooners* and the Bunkers in the 1970s *All in the Family* series, though the class experience depicted on the contemporary programs has changed. Roseanne's husband is an independent construction contractor, while Homer Simpson is a "technical supervisor." They live in suburban houses and might well be considered middle class. But their lives hardly embody the security or stability that once seemed intrinsic to the American middle class. Parents and children battle each other and just about all outsiders as they struggle to survive in a world of declining expectations.

Popular music also changed dramatically. While rock-'n'-roll continued to account for most record sales, a compelling new musical form, rap (or hip-hop), emerged from the African-American community in New York City in the early 1980s and then spread to Washington, D.C., Los Angeles, and the rest of the country. Combining rhythmic poetry with a driving beat derived from "scratching" the surface of a record and "sampling" the music of other rhythm-and-blues and rock-'n'-roll artists, rap spoke to the daily experiences of black inner-city youth facing gang violence, the crack epidemic, police brutality, and the failure of the economic and educational systems. Early 1980s examples, such as Grandmaster Flash's "The Message," offered positive messages of pride and self-reliance, including warnings against drug use. Later in the decade, some rappers reveled in male bravado, the sexual mistreatment of women, and even criminality, as evidenced by the controversial recordings of 2 Live

Scratching. DJs work out "scratch" rhythms on records at a Bronx playground party in 1984.

Crew and N.W.A. ("Niggahs With Attitude"). Several women rappers, such as Queen Latifah, pronounced themselves feminists and directly confronted these macho attitudes in their own rap compositions.

Rap's immediacy and power spoke to the alienation many young people felt during the 1980s, much as early rock-'n'-roll did in the 1950s. By the end of the decade, other poor and working-class youths, particularly Chicanos (who introduced bilingual lyrics) and white suburban teenagers, enthusiastically embraced the music, the accompanying "hip-hop" style in fashion, and rap's outlaw image. But so, too, did advertisers interested in reaching the 1980s "youth market."

Rap also stimulated the resurgence of black nationalist (now called Afrocentric) politics and culture in the late 1980s. Rap groups such as Public Enemy, whose "Fight the Power" was an openly Afrocentric anthem, and KRS-One, who preached a more inclusive "edutainment" message, moved the music onto political terrain. So, too, did Spike Lee's hip-hop–inspired 1989 film *Do the Right Thing*, which depicted escalating racial violence and misunderstanding in American cities, concluding with long quotations from Martin Luther King, Jr., and Malcolm X calling for political action and armed self-defense.

The late 1980s also witnessed the reemergence of other political struggles. Abortion rights once again generated controversy. The abortion issue had simmered for most of the decade, with pro- and antiabortion demonstrators continuing tense confrontations at local abortion clinics. While a solid majority of American voters supported a woman's right to choose abortion, and while politicians of both parties boasted of their pro-choice credentials when seeking women's votes, abortion remained a volatile political issue.

In 1990, several U.S. Supreme Court decisions that gave individual states more authority to set abortion guidelines transformed the debate and escalated the political confrontations. Women's movement activists used the Court's rulings to marshal pro-choice forces locally and on a statewide level to influence elections, as they did in helping Douglas Wilder, a moderate African-American politician, win the Virginia governorship in 1989. But not all states were responsive to the pro-choice message. In 1991, Louisiana passed the nation's most restrictive antiabortion law. The state's conservative and largely male legislators hoped that their law would give the now solidly conservative U.S. Supreme Court the legal occasion to overturn the *Roe* v. *Wade* decision. Despite the Bork defeat, the Republicans succeeded in gaining four conservative appointments to the Court between 1986 and 1991 to replace retiring moderate and liberal justices. The last appointment—that of Clarence Thomas, who was narrowly confirmed in October 1991 after a sensational nationally televised Senate hearing that featured charges of sexual harassment—intensified already sharp conflicts over gender and racial questions and helped assure that issues such as abortion would remain at the top of the nation's political agenda in the 1990s.

Gay Americans had not remained passive during the Reagan era, either, despite the twin scourges—AIDS and homophobic violence—facing their community. Gay advocacy groups such as Gay Men's Health Crisis demanded and won faster government approval of several beneficial AIDS drugs and increased federal and state resources to fight the disease. And, recalling the self-defense tactics of the Black Panthers in the 1960s, even more militant gay and lesbian groups such as ACT-UP (AIDS Coalition to Unleash Power), Pink Panthers, and Queer Nation began aggressively confronting local politicians and employers and patrolling their own neighborhoods to protect against attacks of "gay-bashing." Perhaps the most visible collective expression of gay pride and the deep concern over the AIDS crisis was the huge march on Washington in October 1987. Taking a page from the civil rights movement, nearly half a million gay Americans and their heterosexual supporters massed to express their outrage over the rising tide of homophobia and the ravages of AIDS. The rally was among the largest political demonstrations ever held in the nation's capital.

Finally, the labor movement also helped demonstrate that American capitalism's era of unfettered control had reached its limits as

News-breaking. An ACT-UP protester, shouting "Fight AIDS, not Arabs," interrupts anchor Dan Rather during the January 22, 1991, broadcast of the *CBS Evening News.*

well. In several important conflicts fought after 1989, trade unionists were able to combine innovative tactics with old-fashioned labor solidarity and militancy to stop continued union-busting assaults.

The most clear-cut union victory came in southwestern Virginia in 1989–90. The United Mine Workers of America, led by a dynamic president, Richard Trumka, waged an eleven-month struggle against the Pittston Coal Company in defense of miners' health care benefits and pension rights. The strike featured the arrest of some three thousand miners and UMW supporters during a campaign that resurrected the sit-down tactics and mass, nonviolent demonstrations characteristic of the union and civil rights movements in their formative years. The union's "Camp Solidarity" in southwestern Virginia drew tens of thousands of trade unionists and other supporters from around the country. UMW leaders also mounted a nationwide corporate campaign that pressured Pittston management to settle. Following a long

Independence Day 1989. Four thousand miners, their families, and their supporters rally in St. Paul, Virginia, on July 4, 1989, to support the strike by the United Mine Workers of America against the Pittston Coal Company. Many of the demonstraters wore military camouflage to signify that the strike was a war to defend their way of life.

stalemate, with the national union facing devastating court-imposed fines, the strike was finally settled early in the spring of 1990 with a contract that restored the miners' health and pension benefits. "This was the classic David beats Goliath story," asserted Mary Blue, a Denver unionist who had made the long trip to Virginia to Camp Solidarity. "The victory at Pittston sends a clear message to corporate America: If you want to push us, we're willing to take a stand for what we believe."

The Pittston victory inspired unionized workers across the country. In New York City, for example, a bitter struggle in late 1990 at the venerable New York tabloid the *Daily News* revealed the gains to be won through labor solidarity. The *Daily News*'s owners forced a strike and brought in strikebreakers in an effort to destroy the paper's long-time craft unions. But the New York labor movement quickly rose to the challenge. Thousands of strikers and union sympathizers picketed, pressured local and state politicians, and prevented newsstand

"... I'M A DAUGHTER OF MOTHER JONES #14"

The active participation of the wives and daughters of striking miners was crucial in the United Mine Workers' victory at Pittston. When strikers were forced by a court-ordered injunction to stop picketing, a new organization, the Daughters of Mother Jones, took up the challenge. In a television documentary on the strike, several of the organization's members described their tactics and why they embraced Mother Jones, the fiery labor organizer who stood with the West Virginia miners during their epic struggles to unionize earlier in the century.

DELLA MULLINS: ... I joined the [UMW's] Ladies Auxiliary and we got out and we let the community be aware of what was coming. We delivered posters to stores saying "This Establishment Supports the UMW." We went to churches and got them involved. We went to the stores, we even went to the doctors and clinics. So when the strike came down the community already knew what they were up against.

SHIRLEY JOHNSON: I was a housewife. I didn't get out and get into nothin' until this. You learn a lot about different things if you're in a union—all the injustice and causes there are in this world. I say get out and get involved in 'em.

COSBY TOTTEN: I used to work in the coalmines and I got laid off and I heard that Pittston Coal Company had taken its health care away from the elderly workers. My first reaction was: they can't do that, can they? But they did and it made me angry so I got involved in this struggle.... Besides bein' on up there in front of the office picketing, we did take over the corporation office for 32 hours—we had fun.

BRENDA WALLACE: We went in at 9:00 one morning and didn't come out till 4:00 the next evening. When one of the women from the office came in and said, "Is this a sit-in?" we didn't say anything, we just started singin'.

EDNA SAULS: We didn't tell our names when we went into the Pittston building. 'Cause we had in mind that if we were arrested we'd tell 'em we were Daughters of Mother Jones. There were 39 women who went in there and we had numbers. I was #14. Reporters would ask me, "What's your name?" and I'd say, "I'm a Daughter of Mother Jones #14." Lots of reporters didn't even know who she was. She was a strong union leader. She stood up for the UMW and anywhere people needed help Mother Jones was there.... We're doin' civil disobedience and they don't know what to do about it. Our government was against us, our troopers, judges, their lawyers, we were really standin' alone until the *people* came in to help us, to stand with us.... I think we can go down in history on this thing....

CATHERINE TOMPA: I truly believe in fightin' for what you believe in. If it's right, fight for it, 'cause that's the only way you're gonna win anymore, is to fight. And I believe this old sayin' of Mother Jones, "Pray for the dead and fight like hell for the living."

"WHICH SIDE WAS I ON?"

Martha Southgate recalls the ambivalence that she and other Daily News *reporters felt when they were asked to join the strike.*

I had been a features reporter at the *News* for eleven months and had been dreading this day from the minute I took the job. By that cold October night, the paper had already been through ten months of bitter negotiations. All agreed that the paper's survival hinged on the outcome. Now the question had to be answered: Which side was I on? . . .

A white-collar union like the Newspaper Guild initially seemed anachronistic to me. We were all—blue and white collar alike—making decent salaries, and in the newsroom at least, day-to-day conditions were pretty good. Because of this, I had a hard time understanding our contract disputes. It wasn't until later that I understood that the debate wasn't about wages or benefits, but about one overwhelming question: Do unions have a right to exist? . . .

From the start, management had been extremely antagonistic—it hired the law firm that helped break the unions at the *Chicago Tribune* five years ago and set up heavily guarded alternative printing plants. . . .

Unfortunately, the union representatives didn't inspire a great deal of confidence either. They were out of touch with the rank-and-file and seemed dismissive of people's legitimate misgivings. They didn't seem to realize that very few of us were willing to follow a cry of "Solidarity Forever" straight to the unemployment line without knowing why.

And they were all men. The *Daily News* is a rough-and-tumble street tabloid largely run and written by white males. So it's not surprising that union leadership, like management, is mostly white men—some of whom specialize in macho rhetoric. As a black woman, I felt little common ground with the guys yelling . . . at our union meetings.

The week after the strike started was extraordinarily difficult. Many of my co-workers did cross the picket line. I was on the phone for twenty-four hours a day in a constant round of "should I or shouldn't I?" with friends, relatives and acquaintances. . . .

Finally a co-worker, to whom I'm eternally grateful, cut to the heart of the issue. He said, "If I go back to work, I'd be saying that unions have no right to exist, that union-busting is okay by me. I can't say that." Ultimately, neither could I. So I became one of the 2,300 workers on strike against the *Daily News*.

I realize that unions are not perfect—and that many of them are in need of reform. But I see now that that's what solidarity is all about. I don't have to love everyone in every union. I just have to stand with them for our right to stand together. More and more, people who work in the most difficult, dangerous and tedious jobs in our society—often women—are finding that without that right, they don't get a living wage, or decent health benefits, or a healthy work environment. Just ask any data processor or light-industry worker or K-Mart clerk. . . . I've found that having your values tested isn't easy. But I know that five or ten or fifty years from now, I won't be ashamed of what I've done. And that's worth more than any paycheck.

operators from carrying the scab-produced newspaper. After a long and sometimes violent strike, management finally sold the *Daily News* early in 1991 to newspaper mogul Robert Maxwell, who signed a compromise agreement with the unions.

The Pittston and *Daily News* strikes indicated that labor solidarity and mass rank-and-file actions, combined with innovative tactics and sophisticated use of the media, could win significant gains for the labor movement, even under difficult circumstances.

A NEW WORLD ORDER?

As the final decade of the twentieth century dawned, the fate of American working people was increasingly tied to the fortunes of workers and industries throughout the world. Transnational corporations, almost stateless in their loyalties and ownership, constantly searched for the best profit centers and most cost-efficient labor forces, regardless of national boundaries. IBM assembled and sold computers on every continent, while foreign-based companies, notably Japanese automakers, invested hundreds of billions of dollars in U.S. real estate and built state-of-the-art factories in the American heartland.

Capital's extraordinary mobility created profound dislocations in the international economy in the 1970s and 1980s. Nations throughout the world tried to solve their economic crises by holding down internal consumption while spurring the growth of exports. Global markets were soon glutted with manufactured goods and raw materials. The world economy of the 1980s suffered a crisis of overproduction and underconsumption similar to what occurred in the 1920s and 1930s. As rising energy costs and declining export prices squeezed the life out of many Third World economies during these decades, driving down already marginal living standards and disrupting traditional subsistence agriculture, millions of people were forced to seek better lives by immigrating to America or Western Europe. Political conflict, especially bloody civil wars in Southeast Asia and Central America, also contributed to this latest worldwide wave of immigration. But most ordinary people outside the United States and Western Europe did not choose to leave. Those who stayed also made dramatic and decisive changes in their personal lives and in the life of their homelands.

Beginning in the mid-1970s, popular social movements, sometimes amounting to outright revolutions, toppled dictatorships in Portugal, Spain, Iran, Nicaragua, Argentina, Brazil, Chile, the Philippines, and Korea. Not all of these nations ended up with democratic or progressive governments, but in almost every case the movement for social and political change had its greatest strength in poor and

Africa for USA! On February 28, 1986, the day after the 3M Company began to close its New Jersey plant, the entire black workforce of the company's factory in Elandsfontein, South Africa, walked off their jobs. In this unusual gesture of international solidarity, the Commercial Catering and Allied Workers Union of South Africa staged the half-day walkout to protest 3M's disregard for the fate of its 450 employees, members of the Oil, Chemical, and Atomic Workers' Local 8-760, in the Freehold audio and videotape production facility.

working-class neighborhoods where, as in the Philippines, "People Power" movements toppled corrupt regimes. In Korea, a rolling wave of strikes and workplace occupations, especially by the half-million-member metalworkers' union, paved the way for a turn toward a more democratic internal politics in 1987. In South Africa, black trade unionists were the key element in the broad democratic political coalition that forced the release of African National Congress (ANC) leader Nelson Mandela in 1990 after twenty-seven years of imprisonment, thus dooming the *apartheid* system and opening talks between the white government and the heretofore illegal opposition.

Even more dramatic were the world-transforming events taking place in Eastern Europe and the Soviet Union. The downfall of Communist governments began in 1980 when striking Polish workers organized Solidarity, an independent trade union of nearly ten million. Solidarity demonstrated how a working-class movement could offer an entire nation moral and political leadership and a program of economic revitalization. After nearly a decade of struggle with the Polish government, Solidarity won a smashing victory in Poland's first free elections in more than half a century.

Solidarity's efforts had an impact throughout Eastern Europe and in the Soviet Union. Under its new leader, Mikhail Gorbachev, the Soviet Union undertook a series of reforms after 1985 that dismantled much of the Stalinist political system. Soon there were strikes and demonstrations all over the country, and independent unions were formed among coalminers and electrical and railroad workers that called on the Gorbachev government to quicken the pace of political and economic reform.

Then came the revolution. Beginning in September 1989, a wave of huge demonstrations shook Communist regimes across Eastern Europe. On the night of November 9, demonstrators poured through the Berlin Wall, symbol of Communist repression and the Cold War division of Europe. The East German regime quickly fell, and by the end of 1990 East Germany had been incorporated into a reunited, capitalist Germany. The Communist government in Czechoslovakia also tumbled, and reformers took over in Hungary and Bulgaria. In Rumania, political change required a week of bloody street battles between ordinary citizens and security police, who defended the old order to the bitter end.

Radical change finally reached the Soviet heartland in August 1991 when thousands of Russian citizens poured into the streets to defeat a reactionary *coup d'état* by elements in the Communist Party, the military, and the secret police. The Communist Party quickly collapsed and the Soviet Union began the painful and uncertain process of reorganizing itself as a looser confederation of independent republics.

The Cold War was over, defeated not by the missiles and tanks of the principal protagonists but by the collective courage and willpower of ordinary men and women. New governments in the Soviet Union and Eastern Europe now sought to transform their economies, opening them to the capitalist West, selling off state-owned enterprises, and even establishing stock markets.

Had the United States "won" the Cold War? Republican president George Bush, elected to succeed Ronald Reagan in 1989, felt sufficiently emboldened by the collapse of communism to announce an American-dominated "new world order." Bush began by dispatching U.S. troops to Panama in December 1989 to oust a corrupt, drug-running dictator, Manuel Noriega, in an overt display of U.S. military power that echoed America's early-twentieth-century interventions in Latin America. Despite a short and bloody war that ended with Noriega's capture and extradition to the United States, Panama remains one of the major transshipment points for drugs in the western hemisphere.

Little more than a year later an even more massive use of U.S. military might confronted the armies of the Iraqi dictator, Saddam

Hussein, whose invasion and annexation of the oil-rich emirate of Kuwait threatened to destabilize U.S. allies in the Persian Gulf. The Bush administration dispatched nearly 300,000 troops to the region by the end of 1990 and in January launched a massive air assault against Iraq. The bombing lasted over a month, killing and wounding tens of thousands of Iraqi citizens and soldiers and destroying much of Iraq's infrastructure and military hardware. A coalition military force of half a million—dominated by U.S. soldiers and bankrolled by Saudi Arabia, Germany, and Japan—launched a ground assault in February that quickly reclaimed Kuwait and occupied large portions of Iraq. Despite the efforts of a small but vocal antiwar movement in the United States, the swift victory and light U.S. casualties (fewer than one hundred U.S. soldiers died in combat), aided by a cooperative press, generated a national wave of patriotic fervor. Though the situation in the Persian Gulf remained uncertain in the war's aftermath, the U.S. military victory did succeed in shattering the "Vietnam syndrome" and seemingly assuring George Bush's reelection in 1992. Notwithstanding these short-term political gains, the domestic political euphoria following the United States–led victory proved transitory. Americans and their political leaders were brought back to the grim reality of endemic social and economic problems that continued to plague the nation in 1991.

CONCLUSION

THE UPHEAVALS in Europe, Asia, and Latin America demonstrate that the democratic idea remains a powerful and contagious impulse as the end of the twentieth century nears. Can the sea change in the international order make its weight felt in the United States, where political stalemate and economic stagnation have put popular social movements, especially the labor movement, on the defensive for more than a generation? History offers no blueprint, but it does suggest that fundamental changes most frequently come in sudden and dramatic fashion. The liberation of African-Americans came in two great forward leaps: the first during and immediately following the Civil War; the second, a hundred years later in the civil rights revolution of the 1950s and 1960s. Likewise, many American women thrust the issue of their rights on the national agenda in a burst of self-activity, first in the decades before World War I, and then half a century later in an even more profound exploration of their personal and political consciousness. And finally, American workers have repeatedly discovered their voice and their organized power in a series of unexpected popular insurgencies that have invigorated the republic over the course of the last two centuries.

We cannot foretell the future. But we can be certain that in a globally integrated workplace where men and women still must labor for their livelihoods, working people will play a central role in shaping this new world. In new immigrant communities on the East and West coasts, in the old factory towns in the Midwest, in urban ghettos and suburban office parks, America's working people, in all their extraordinary diversity, will press their claims for dignity and economic and social justice. And, in the process, they will continue to build America.

SOURCES

These references indicate some of our intellectual debts to colleagues in the profession and point readers toward some of the most important work in U.S. history published during the past three decades and earlier.

Introduction

Brown, Dee, *The Year of the Century: 1876* (1966).

Bruce, Robert V., *1877: Year of Violence* (1959).

Cawelti, John G., "America on Display: The World's Fairs of 1876, 1893, 1933" in Frederic Cople Jaher, ed., *The Age of Industrialism in America: Essays in Social Structure and Cultural Values* (1968).

Foner, Philip S., *The Great Labor Uprising of 1877* (1977).

Post, Robert C., ed., *1876: A Centennial Exhibition* (1976).

Rydell, Robert W., *All the World's a Fair: Visions of Empire at American International Expositions, 1876–1916* (1984).

Weymouth, Lally, *America in 1876: The Way We Were* (1976)

Chapter 1: Progress and Poverty: The Growth of Industrial Capitalism

Banner, Lois W., *American Beauty* (1983).

Bensman, David, *The Practice of Solidarity: American Hat Finishers in the Nineteenth Century* (1985).

Billington, Ray Allen, and Martin Ridge, *Westward Expansion: A History of the American Frontier* (1982).

Blumin, Stuart M., "The Hypothesis of Middle-Class Formation in Nineteenth-Century America," *American Historical Review*, 90 (1985), pp. 299–338.

Brandes, Stuart D., *American Welfare Capitalism, 1880–1940* (1984).

Braverman, Harry, *Labor and Monopoly Capital: The Degradation of Work in the Twentieth Century* (1974).

Bremner, Robert H., *Children and Youth in America: A Documentary History; Vol. II: 1866–1932* (1971).

Brier, Stephen, "The Political Economy of Asian Labor," unpublished manuscript (1968).

Brody, David, *Steelworkers in America: The Nonunion Era* (1969).

Brown, Dee, *Bury My Heart at Wounded Knee: An Indian History of the American West* (1972).

Brownlee, W. Elliot, *Dynamics of Ascent: A History of the American Economy* (1979).

Bruchey, Stuart, *Growth of the Modern American Economy* (1975).

Burg, David F., *White City* (1976).

Cawelti, John G., "America on Display: The World's Fairs of 1876, 1893, 1933," in Frederic Cople Jaher, ed., *The Age of Industrialism in America: Essays in Social Structure and Cultural Values* (1968).

Chandler, Alfred D., *The Visible Hand: The Managerial Revolution in American Business* (1977).

Chudacoff, Howard P., *The Evolution of American Urban Society* (1981).

Cochran, Thomas C., and William Miller, *The Age of Enterprise: A Social History of Industrial America* (1965).

Degler, Carl N., *Out of Our Past: The Forces That Shaped Modern America* (1984).

Diamond, Sigmund, ed., *The Nation Transformed* (1963).

Dick, Everett, *The Sod-House Frontier, 1854–1890* (1937).

Diner, Hasia R., *Erin's Daughters in America: Irish Immigrant Women in the Nineteenth Century* (1983).

Dubofsky, Melvyn, *Industrialism and the American Worker, 1865–1920* (1985).

Dykstra, Robert, *The Cattle Towns* (1968).

Faragher, John Mack, *Women and Men on the Overland Trail* (1979).

———, and Christine Stansell, "Women and Their Families on the Overland Trail to California and Oregon, 1842–1867," *Feminist Studies*, 2 (1975), pp. 150–66.

Fel, Rendigs, *American Business Cycles, 1865–1897* (1959).

Fine, Sidney, *Laissez-Faire and the General-Welfare State: A Study of Conflict in American Thought, 1865–1901* (1956).

Fink, Leon, *Workingmen's Democracy: The Knights of Labor and American Politics* (1983).

Fite, Gilbert C., *The Farmer's Frontier, 1865–1900* (1966).

Foner, Eric, *Reconstruction: America's Unfinished Revolution, 1863–1877* (1988).

Foner, Philip S., *History of the Labor Movement in the United States; Vol. II: From the Founding of the AFL to the Emergence of American Imperialism* (1955).

Fox, Stephen, *The Mirror Makers: A History of American Advertising and Its Creators* (1985).

Garlock, Jonathan, *Guide to the Local Assemblies of the Knights of Labor* (1982).

Garraty, John A., *The New Commonwealth, 1877–1890* (1963).

———, ed., *Labor and Capital in the Gilded Age* (1968).

Gilman, Carolyn, and Mary Jane Schneider, *The Way to Independence: Memories of a Hidatsa Indian Family, 1840–1920* (1987).

Ginger, Ray, *The Age of Excess: The United States from 1877 to 1914* (1975).

Goodwyn, Lawrence, *Democratic Promise: The Populist Moment in America* (1976).

Gorn, Elliott J., " 'Glimpses of Gotham': The *National Police Gazette* and the Democracy of Pleasure," unpublished paper (1988).

Gutman, Herbert G., *Work, Culture, and Society in Industrializing America: Essays in America's Working Class and Social History* (1977).

———, *Power and Culture: Essays on the American Working Class* (1987).

Hahn, Steven, *The Roots of Southern Populism: Yeoman Farmers and the Transformation of the Georgia Upcountry, 1850–1890* (1984).

Hays, Samuel P., *The Response to Industrialism, 1885–1914* (1957).

Higgs, Robert, *The Transformation of the American Economy, 1865–1914* (1971).

Higham, John, *Strangers in the Land: Patterns of American Nativism, 1860–1925* (1971).

Hofstadter, Richard, *Social Darwinism in American Thought* (1944; 1955).

Jameson, Elizabeth, "Imperfect Unions: Class and Gender in Cripple Creek, 1894–1904," in Milton Cantor and Bruce Laurie, eds., *Class, Sex, and the Woman Worker* (1977).

Jeffrey, Julie Roy, *Frontier Women: The Trans-Mississippi West, 1840–1880* (1979).

Jones, Jacqueline, *Labor of Love, Labor of Sorrow: Black Women, Work, and the Family from Slavery to the Present* (1985).

Jones, Maldwyn A., *American Immigration* (1960).

Josephson, Matthew, *The Robber Barons: The Great American Capitalists, 1861–1901* (1914).

———, *The Politicos, 1865–1896* (1938).

Jussim, Estelle, *Frederic Remington, the Camera, and the Old West* (1983).

Kessler-Harris, Alice, *Out to Work: A History of Wage-Earning Women in the United States* (1982).

Kidwell, Claudia B., and Margaret C. Christman, *Suiting Everyone: The Democratization of Clothing in America* (1974).

Kirkland, Edward Chase, *Industry Comes of Age: Business, Labor, and Public Policy, 1860–1897* (1961).

Labor Bulletin of Massachusetts, 5 (1898).

Lamar, Howard, "From Bondage to Contract: Ethnic Labor in the American West, 1600–1890," in Steven Hahn and Jonathan Prude, eds., *The Countryside in the Age of Capitalist Transformation: Essays in the Social History of Rural America* (1985).

Lindsey, Almont, *The Pullman Strike: The Story of a*

Unique Experiment and of a Great Labor Upheaval (1942).

McCloskey, Robert, *American Conservatism in the Age of Enterprise, 1865–1910* (1951).

McMath, Robert C., Jr., *Populist Vanguard: A History of the Southern Farmers' Alliance* (1977).

———, "Sandy Land and Hogs in the Timber: (Agri)cultural Origins of the Farmers' Alliance in Texas," in Steven Hahn and Jonathan Prude, eds., *The Countryside in the Age of Capitalist Transformation: Essays in the Social History of Rural America* (1985).

Meier, August, and Elliot Rudwick, "Black Man and the 'White City': Negroes and the Columbian Exposition, 1893," *Phylon*, 26 (1965), pp. 354–61.

Miller, Kerby A., *Emigrants and Exiles: Ireland and the Irish Exodus to North America* (1985).

Mohl, Raymond A., *The New City: Urban America in the Industrial Age, 1860–1920* (1985).

Montgomery, David, "Labor in the Industrial Era," in Richard R. Morris, ed., *The U.S. Department of Labor History of the American Worker* (1976).

———, *Workers' Control in America: Studies in the History of Work, Technology, and Labor Struggles* (1979).

———, *The Fall of the House of Labor: The Workplace, the State, and American Labor Activism, 1865–1925* (1987).

Nelson, Daniel, *Managers and Workers: Origins of the New Factory System in the United States, 1880–1920* (1975).

Ozanne, Robert, *A Century of Labor-Management Relations at McCormick and International Harvester* (1967).

Paul, Rodman Wilson, *Mining Frontiers of the Far West, 1848–1880* (1963).

Pauly, Thomas H., "American Art and Labor: The Case of Anshutz's *The Ironworkers' Noontime*," *American Quarterly*, 40 (1988), pp. 333–58.

Porter, Glenn, *The Rise of Big Business, 1860–1910* (1973).

———, ed., *Encyclopedia of American Economic History* (1980).

Prucha, Francis Paul, *American Indian Policy in Crisis: Christian Reformers and the Indian, 1865–1900* (1976).

Rosenzweig, Roy, *Eight Hours for What We Will: Workers and Leisure in an Industrial City, 1870–1920* (1983).

Rothman, David, *Politics and Power: The United States Senate, 1869–1901* (1966).

Rydell, Robert W., *All the World's a Fair: Visions of Empire at American International Expositions, 1876–1916* (1984).

Scranton, Philip B., "The Politics of Production: Technology, Markets, and the Two Cultures of American Industry," paper delivered at the Woodrow Wilson Center, The Smithsonian Institution (1990).

Shannon, Fred A., *The Farmer's Last Frontier: Agriculture, 1860–1897* (1945).

Stansell, Christine, "Women on the Great Plains, 1865–1890," *Women's Studies*, 4 (1976), pp. 87–98.

Strasser, Susan, *Never Done: A History of American Housework* (1982).

Takaki, Ronald T., *Iron Cages: Race and Culture in Nineteenth-Century America* (1979).

Trachtenberg, Alan, *The Incorporation of America: Culture and Society in the Gilded Age* (1982).

Utley, Robert M., *The Indian Frontier of the American West, 1846–1890* (1984).

Ward, David, *Cities and Immigrants: A Geography of Change in Nineteenth-Century America* (1971).

Warner, Sam Bass, Jr., *Streetcar Suburbs: The Process of Growth in Boston, 1870–1900* (1962).

———, *The Urban Wilderness: A History of the American City* (1972).

Webb, Walter Prescott, *The Great Plains* (1931).

West, Richard Samuel, *Satire on Stone: The Political Cartoons of Joseph Keppler* (1988).

Woodman, Harold D., "Sequel to Slavery: The New History Views the Postbellum South," *Journal of Southern History*, 43 (1977), pp. 523–53.

Woodward, C. Vann, *The Origins of the New South, 1877–1913* (1966).

Wright, James E., *The Politics of Populism: Dissent in Colorado* (1974).

Yans-McLaughlin, Virginia, *Family and Community: Italian Immigrants in Buffalo, 1880–1930* (1977).

Chapter 2: The Emergence of Working-Class Collectivity

Ahlstrom, Sydney E., *A Religious History of the American People* (1972).

Ameringer, Oscar, *If You Don't Weaken: The Autobiography of Oscar Ameringer* (1940).

Ashbaugh, Carolyn, *Lucy Parsons: American Revolutionary* (1976).

Avrich, Paul, *The Haymarket Tragedy* (1983).

Ayers, Edward L., *Vengeance and Justice: Crime and Punishment in the Nineteenth-Century South* (1984).

Bean, Walter, *Boss Ruef's San Francisco: The Story of the Union Labor Party, Big Business, and the Graft Prosecution* (1967).

Bensman, David, *The Practice of Solidarity* (1985).

Berlin, Ira, and Herbert G. Gutman, "Class Composition and the Development of the American Working Class, 1840–1890," in Herbert G. Gutman, *Power and Culture: Essays on the American Working Class* (1987).

Brier, Stephen, "The Career of R. L. Davis Reconsidered: Unpublished Correspondence from the *National Labor Tribune*," *Labor History*, 23 (1982), pp. 420–29.

Burton, Orville, "The Rise and Fall of Afro-American Town Life: Town and Country in Reconstruction Edgefield, South Carolina," in Orville Burton and Robert C. McMath, Jr., eds., *Toward a New South* (1982).

Coleman, McAlister, *Men and Coal* (1943).

Conlin, Joseph R., *Big Bill Haywood and the Radical Union Movement* (1969).

Couvares, Francis G., *The Remaking of Pittsburgh: Class and Culture in an Industrializing City, 1877–1919* (1984).

D'Emilio, John, and Estelle B. Freedman, *Intimate Matters: A History of Sexuality in America* (1988).

Deutsch, Sarah, *No Separate Refuge: Culture, Class, and Gender on an Anglo-Hispanic Frontier in the American Southwest, 1880–1940* (1987).

Dubofsky, Melvyn, *We Shall Be All: A History of the Industrial Workers of the World* (1969).

Duis, Perry R., *The Saloon: Public Drinking in Chicago and Boston, 1880–1920* (1983).

Fink, Leon, "The Uses of Political Power: Toward a Theory of the Labor Movement in the Era of the Knights of Labor," in Michael H. Frisch and Daniel J. Walkowitz, eds., *Working Class America: Labor, Community, and American Society* (1983).

Foner, Philip S., *Mark Twain: Social Critic* (1958).

Garraty, John A., *The New Commonwealth, 1877–1890* (1968).

Goodwyn, Lawrence, *Democratic Promise: The Populist Moment in America* (1976).

Gorn, Elliott J., "'Glimpses of Gotham': The *National Police Gazette* and the Democracy of Pleasure," unpublished paper (1988).

Gutman, Herbert G., "The Negro and the United Mine Workers of America: The Career and Letters of Richard L. Davis and Something of Their Meaning, 1890–1900," in Julius Jacobson, ed., *The Negro and the American Labor Movement* (1968).

———, *Work, Culture, and Society in Industrializing America: Essays in America's Working Class and Social History* (1977).

Hahn, Steven, "Common Right and Commonwealth: The Stock-Law Struggle and the Roots of Southern Populism," in J. Morgan Kousser and James M. McPherson, eds., *Region, Race, and Reconstruction: Essays in Honor of C. Vann Woodward* (1982).

———, and Jonathan Prude, ed., *The Countryside in the Age of Capitalist Transformation: Essays in the Social History of Rural America* (1985).

Hales, Peter Bacon, *Silver Cities: The Photography of American Urbanization, 1839–1915* (1984).

Hayden, Dolores, *The Grand Domestic Revolution* (1983).

Hofstadter, Richard, *Social Darwinism in American Thought* (1944; 1955).

Jeffrey, Julie Roy, *Frontier Women: The Trans-Mississippi West, 1840–1880* (1979).

Kasson, John F., *Rudeness and Civility: Manners in Nineteenth-Century Urban America* (1990).

Kazin, Michael, *Barons of Labor: The San Francisco Building Trades and Union Power in the Progressive Era* (1987).

Keil, Hartmut, and John B. Jedntz, eds., *German Workers in Industrial Chicago, 1850–1910: A Comparative Perspective* (1983).

Keller, Morton, *The Art and Politics of Thomas Nast* (1968).

Lears, Jackson, *No Place of Grace: Antimodernism and the Transformation of American Culture, 1880–1920* (1981).

Leonard, Thomas C., *The Power of the Press: The Birth of American Political Reporting* (1986).

Levine, Lawrence W., *Highbrow/Lowbrow: The Emergence of Cultural Hierarchy in America* (1988).

Levine, Susan, *Labor's True Woman: Carpet Weavers, Industrialization, and Labor Reform in the Gilded Age* (1984).

McMath, Robert C., Jr., "Sandy Land and Hogs in the Timber: (Agri)cultural Origins of the Farmers' Alliance in Texas," in Steven Hahn and Jonathan Prude, eds., *The Countryside in the Age of Capitalist Transformation: Essays in the Social History of Rural America* (1985).

McNeill, George, ed., *The Labor Movement: The Problem of Today* (1887).

Miller, Kerby A., *Emigrants and Exiles: Ireland and the Irish Exodus to North America* (1985).

Montgomery, David, "Labor in the Industrial Era," in Richard R. Morris, ed., *The U.S. Department of La-*

bor History of the American Worker (1976).

——, "Labor and the Republic in Industrial America, 1860–1890," Le Mouvement Social, 111 (1980), pp. 201–15.

——, Workers' Control in America: Studies in the History of Work (1982).

Moquin, Wayne, and Charles Van Doren, eds., A Documentary History of the Mexican-Americans (1971).

Nash, Michael, Conflict and Accommodation: Coal Miners, Steel Workers, and Socialism, 1890–1920 (1980).

Palmer, Bryan D., "Discordant Music: Charivaris and Whitecapping in Nineteenth-Century North America," Labour/Le Travailleur, 3 (1978), pp. 5–62.

Riordan, William L., ed., Plunkitt of Tammany Hall (1963).

Rosengarten, Theodore, All God's Dangers: The Autobiography of Nate Shaw (1974).

Rosenzweig, Roy, Eight Hours for What We Will: Workers and Leisure in an Industrial City, 1870–1920 (1983).

Stange, Maren, Symbols of Ideal Life: Social Documentary Photography in America, 1890–1920 (1989).

Stein, Sally, "Making Connections with the Camera: Photography and Social Mobility in the Career of Jacob Riis," Afterimage, 10 (1983), pp. 9–16.

Stratton, Joanna L., Pioneer Women: Voices from the Kansas Frontier (1981).

Swinton, John A., Momentous Question: The Respective Attitudes of Labor and Capital (1895).

Taft, Robert, Artists and Illustrators of the Old West, 1850–1900 (1953).

Tchen, John Kuo Wei, Genthe's Photographs of San Francisco's Old Chinatown (1984).

Thernstrom, Stephan, Poverty and Progress: Social Mobility in a Nineteenth-Century City (1968).

Walkowitz, Daniel J., Worker City, Company Town: Iron and Cotton-Worker Protest in Troy and Cohoes, New York, 1855–1884 (1978).

Waller, Altina L., Reverend Beecher and Mrs. Tilton: Sex and Class in Victorian America (1982).

Washington, Booker T., Up from Slavery (1900; 1965).

Wright, Carroll D., Industrial Evolution of the United States (1895).

Chapter 3: Great Upheavals: The 1880s and 1890s

Amsden, Jon, and Stephen Brier, "Coal Miners on Strike: The Transformation of Strike Demands and the Formation of a National Union," The Journal of Interdisciplinary History, 7 (1977), pp. 583–616.

Avrich, Paul, The Haymarket Tragedy (1984).

Brecher, Jeremy, Strike! (1972).

Brier, Stephen, "Interracial Organizing in the West Virginia Coal Industry: The Participation of Black Mine Workers in the Knights of Labor and the United Mine Workers of America, 1880–1894," in Gary Fink, ed., Essays in Southern Labor History (1977).

Brown, Thomas N., Irish-American Nationalism, 1870–1890 (1966).

Brundage, David, "The Producing Classes and the Saloon: Denver in the 1880s," Labor History, 26 (1985), pp. 29–52.

Buchanan, Joseph R., The Story of a Labor Agitator (1903).

Burns, Sarah, Pastoral Inventions: Rural Life in Nineteenth-Century American Art and Culture (1989).

Cassity, Michael J., "Modernization and Social Crisis: The Knights of Labor and a Midwest Community, 1885–1886," Journal of American History, 66 (1979), pp. 41–61.

Cell, John W., The Highest Stage of White Supremacy: The Origins of Segregation in South Africa and the American South (1982).

Commons, John R., et al., History of Labor in the United States; Vols. I–IV (1918–1935).

Cooper, Jerry M., "The Army as Strikebreaker: The Railroad Strikes of 1877 and 1894," Labor History, 18 (1977), pp. 179–96.

David, Henry, The History of the Haymarket Affair (1963).

Degler, Carl N., Out of Our Past: The Forces That Shaped Modern America (1959).

Destler, Chester McArthur, American Radicalism, 1865–1901 (1966).

Dick, William M., Labor and Socialism in America: The Gompers Era (1972).

Dubofsky, Melvyn, Industrialism and the American Worker, 1865–1920 (1985).

Dulles, Foster Rhea, and Melvyn Dubofsky, eds., Labor in America: A History (1984).

Erlich, Mark, "Peter J. McGuire's Trade Unionism: Socialism of a Trades Union Kind," Labor History, 24 (1983), pp. 165–97.

Faulkner, Harold U., Politics, Reform, and Expansion, 1890–1900 (1959).

Filippelli, Ronald L., Labor in the USA: A History (1984).

Fink, Leon, *Workingmen's Democracy: The Knights of Labor and American Politics* (1983).

Foner, Eric, "Class, Ethnicity, and Radicalism in the United States: The Land League and Irish America," *Marxist Perspectives*, 1 (1978), pp. 6–55.

Foner, Philip S., *Organized Labor and the Black Worker, 1619–1981* (1982).

Garraty, John A., *The New Commonwealth, 1877–1890* (1968).

Goodwyn, Lawrence, *Democratic Promise: The Populist Moment in America* (1976).

Gordon, Michael A., "The Labor Boycott in New York City, 1880–1886," *Labor History*, 16 (1975), pp. 184–229.

Gorn, Elliott J., "'Glimpses of Gotham': The *National Police Gazette* and the Democracy of Pleasure," unpublished paper (1988).

Gutman, Herbert G., *Work, Culture, and Society in Industrializing America: Essays in America's Working Class and Social History* (1977).

———, *Power and Culture: Essays on the American Working Class* (1987).

Hart, Patricia, and Ivar Nelson, *Mining Town: The Photographic Record of T. N. Barnard and Nellie Stockbridge from the Coeur d'Alenes* (1984).

Higham, John, *Strangers in the Land: Patterns of American Nativism, 1860–1925* (1973).

Hoerder, Dirk, ed., *"Struggle a Hard Battle": Essays on Working-Class Immigrants* (1986).

Kaufman, Stuart B., *Samuel Gompers and the Origin of the American Federation of Labor, 1848–1896* (1973).

Kealey, Gregory S., and Bryan D. Palmer, *Dreaming of What Might Be: The Knights of Labor in Ontario, 1880–1900* (1983).

Kinzer, Donald L., *An Episode in Anti-Catholicism: The American Protective Association* (1964).

Kleppner, Paul, *The Cross of Culture: A Social Analysis of Midwestern Politics, 1850–1900* (1970).

———, *The Third Electoral System, 1853–1892* (1979).

Kousser, J. Morgan, *The Shaping of Southern Politics: Suffrage Restriction and the Establishment of the One-Party South* (1974).

———, and James M. McPherson, eds., *Region, Race, and Reconstruction: Essays in Honor of C. Vann Woodward* (1982).

Krause, Paul, "Labor Republicanism and 'Za Chlebom': Anglo-Americans and Slavic Solidarity in Homestead," in Dirk Hoerder, ed., *"Struggle a Hard Battle": Essays on Working-Class Immigrants* (1986).

Lazerow, Jama, "The Workingman's Hour: The 1886 Labor Uprising in Boston," *Labor History*, 21 (1980), pp. 200–220.

Leonard, Henry B., "Ethnic Cleavage and Industrial Conflict in Late-19th-Century America: The Cleveland Rolling Mill Company Strikes of 1882 and 1885," *Labor History*, 20 (1979), pp. 524–48.

Levine, Susan, "Labor's True Woman: Domesticity and Equal Rights in the Knights of Labor," *Journal of American History*, 70 (1983), pp. 323–39.

———, *Labor's True Woman: Carpet Weavers, Industrialization, and Labor Reform in the Gilded Age* (1984).

Lindsey, Altmont, *The Pullman Strike: The Story of a Unique Experiment and of a Great Labor Upheaval* (1942).

McLaurin, Melton A., *The Knights of Labor in the South* (1978).

McMath, Robert C., Jr., *Populist Vanguard: A History of the Southern Farmers' Alliance* (1977).

McMurray, Donald L., *Coxey's Army: A Study of the Industrial Army Movement of 1894* (1929).

Montgomery, David, "Labor in the Industrial Era," in Richard R. Morris, ed., *The U.S. Department of Labor History of the American Worker* (1976).

———, *Workers' Control in America: Studies in the History of Work, Technology, and Labor Struggles* (1979).

———, "Labor and the Republic in Industrial America, 1860–1890," *Le Mouvement Social*, 111 (1980), pp. 201–15.

———, "Strikes in Nineteenth-Century America," *Social Science History*, 4 (1980), pp. 81–104.

———, *The Fall of the House of Labor: The Workplace, the State, and American Labor Activism, 1865–1925* (1987).

Oestreicher, Richard Jules, *Solidarity and Fragmentation: Working People and Class Consciousness in Detroit, 1875–1900* (1986).

Painter, Nell Irvin, *Standing at Armageddon: The United States, 1877–1919* (1987).

Palmer, Bruce, *"Man Over Money": The Southern Populist Critique of American Capitalism* (1980).

Palmer, Bryan D., "Social Formation and Class Formation in North America, 1800–1900," in David Levine, ed., *Proletarianization and Family History* (1984).

Pollack, Norman, ed., *The Populist Mind* (1967).

Rezneck, Samuel, "Unemployment, Unrest, and Relief in the United States During the Depression of

1893–1897," *Journal of Political Economy*, 61 (1953), pp. 324–45.

Roediger, Dave, and Franklin Rosemont, *Haymarket Scrapbook* (1986).

Rosenzweig, Roy, *Eight Hours for What We Will: Workers and Leisure in an Industrial City, 1870–1920* (1983).

Ross, Steven J., *Workers on the Edge: Work, Leisure, and Politics in Industrializing Cincinnati, 1788–1890* (1985).

Salvatore, Nick, *Eugene V. Debs: Citizen and Socialist* (1982).

Samuels, Peggy, and Harold Samuels, *Frederic Remington: A Biography* (1982).

Saxton, Alexander, *The Indisputable Enemy: Labor and the Anti-Chinese Movement in California* (1971).

Schwantes, Carlos A., *Coxey's Army: An American Odyssey* (1985).

Scobey, David, "Boycotting the Politics Factory: Labor Radicalism and the New York City Election of 1884," *Radical History Review*, 28–30 (1984), pp. 280–326.

Sekula, Allan, "The Body in the Archive," *October*, 39 (1986), pp. 3–64.

Stromquist, Shelton, *A Generation of Boomers: The Pattern of Railroad Labor Conflict in Nineteenth-Century America* (1987).

Walker, Samuel, "Terence V. Powderly, Machinist: 1866–1877," *Labor History*, 19 (1978), pp. 165–84.

Ware, Norman, *The Labor Movement in the United States, 1860–1890: A Study in Democracy* (1929).

West, Richard Samuel, *Satire on Stone: The Political Cartoons of Joseph Keppler* (1988).

Williams, R. Hal, *Years of Decision: American Politics in the 1890s* (1978).

Williamson, Joel, *A Rage for Order: Black/White Relations in the American South Since Emancipation* (1986).

Woodward, C. Vann, *Tom Watson: Agrarian Rebel* (1963).

——, *The Strange Career of Jim Crow* (1974).

Worthman, Paul B., and James R. Green, "Black Workers in the New South, 1865–1915," in Nathan I. Huggins, Martin Kilson, and Daniel M. Fox, eds., *Key Issues in the Afro-American Experience* (1971).

Wright, James Edward, *The Politics of Populism: Dissent in Colorado* (1974).

Chapter 4: Working People and Reform

Almaguer, Tomas, "Racial Domination and Class Conflict in Capitalist Agriculture: The Oxnard Sugar Beet Workers' Strike of 1903," *Labor History*, 25 (1984), pp. 325–50.

America and Lewis Hine: Photographs 1904–1940, Foreword by Walter Rosenblum, Biographical Notes by Naomi Rosenblum, Essay by Alan Trachtenberg (1977).

Baker, Paula, "The Domestication of Politics: Women and American Political Society," *American Historical Review*, 89 (June 1984), pp. 620–47.

Baxandall, Rosalyn, Linda Gordon, and Susan Reverby, *America's Working Women: A Documentary History from 1600 to the Present* (1976).

Benson, Susan Porter, *Counter Cultures: Saleswomen, Managers, and Customers in American Department Stores, 1890–1940* (1986).

Bordin, Ruth, *Women and Temperance: The Quest for Power and Liberty, 1873–1900* (1981).

Blackbeard, Bill, and Martin Williams, eds., *The Smithsonian Collection of Newspaper Comics* (1977).

Braverman, Harry, *Labor and Monopoly Capital: The Degradation of Work in the Twentieth Century* (1974).

Brody, David, *Steelworkers in America: The Nonunion Era* (1960).

——, *Workers in Industrial America: Essays on the Twentieth-Century Struggle* (1980).

Buhle, Mari Jo, *Women and American Socialism, 1870–1920* (1981).

Cameron, Ardis, "Bread and Roses Revisited: Women's Culture and Working-Class Activism in the Lawrence Strike of 1912," in Ruth Milkman, ed., *Women, Work, and Protest: A Century of U.S. Women's Labor History* (1985).

Chandler, Alfred D., Jr., *The Visible Hand: The Managerial Revolution in American Business* (1977).

Couvares, Francis G., "The Triumph of Commerce: Class Culture and Mass Culture in Pittsburgh," in Michael H. Frisch and Daniel J. Walkowitz, eds., *Working-Class America: Labor, Community, and American Society* (1983).

Davis, Allen, *Spearheads of Reform: The Settlements and the Progressive Movement, 1890–1914* (1967).

Dubofsky, Melvyn, *When Workers Organize: New York in the Progressive Era* (1968).

——, *We Shall Be All: A History of the Industrial Workers of the World* (1969).

———, *Industrialism and the American Worker, 1865–1920* (1985).

DuBois, Ellen Carol, "Working Women, Class Relations, and Suffrage Militance: Harriot Stanton Blatch and the New York Woman Suffrage Movement, 1894–1909," *Journal of American History*, 74 (1987), pp. 34–58.

Dulles, Foster Rhea, and Melvyn Dubofsky, *Labor in America: A History* (1984).

Dye, Nancy Schrom, *As Equals and as Sisters: Feminism, Unionism, and the Women's Trade Union League of New York* (1980).

Ewen, Elizabeth, *Immigrant Women in the Land of Dollars: Life and Culture on the Lower East Side, 1890–1925* (1985).

Faulkner, Harold U., *The Decline of Laissez-Faire, 1897–1917* (1951).

———, *American Economic History* (1960).

Flexner, Eleanor, *Century of Struggle: The Woman's Rights Movement in the United States* (1975).

Foner, Philip S., *History of the Labor Movement in the United States; Vol. III: The Policies and Practices of the American Federation of Labor, 1900–1909* (1964).

———, *History of the Labor Movement in the United States; Vol. V: The AFL in the Progressive Era, 1910–1915* (1980).

———, *Organized Labor and the Black Worker, 1619–1981* (1982).

Fraser, Steven, "Combined and Uneven Development in the Men's Clothing Industry," *Business History Review*, 57 (1983), pp. 522–47.

———, "Dress Rehearsal for the New Deal: Shop-Floor Insurgents, Political Elites, and Industrial Democracy in the Amalgamated Clothing Workers," in Michael H. Frisch and Daniel J. Walkowitz, eds., *Working-Class America: Labor, Community, and American Society* (1983).

Glaab, Charles N., and Theodore A. Brown, *A History of Urban America* (1976).

Glenn, Susan A., *Daughters of the Shtetl: Life and Labor in the Immigrant Generation* (1990).

Gordon, David, Richard Edwards, and Michael Reich, *Segmented Work, Divided Workers: The Historical Transformation of Labor in the United States* (1982).

Green, James R., *Grass-roots Socialism: Radical Movements in the Southwest, 1895–1943* (1978).

———, *The World of the Worker: Labor in Twentieth-Century America* (1980).

Greene, Victor, *The Slavic Community on Strike: Immigrant Labor in Pennsylvania Anthracite* (1968).

Gutman, Judith Mara, *Lewis Hine and the American Social Conscience* (1967).

Hareven, Tamara K., *Family Time and Industrial Time* (1982).

Harris, William H., *The Harder We Run: Black Workers Since the Civil War* (1982).

Hays, Samuel P., *The Response to Industrialism, 1885–1914* (1957).

Hooker, Richard J., *Food and Drink in America: A History* (1981).

Hounsell, David A., *From the American System to Mass Production, 1800–1932: The Development of Manufacturing Technology in the United States* (1984).

Howe, Irving (with Kenneth Libo), *The World of Our Fathers* (1976).

Karson, Marc, *American Labor Unions and Politics, 1900–1918* (1958).

Kasson, John, *Amusing the Millions: Coney Island at the Turn of the Century* (1978).

Katzman, David M., *Seven Days a Week: Women and Domestic Service in Industrializing America* (1978).

Kazin, Michael, *Barons of Labor: The San Francisco Building Trades and Union Power in the Progressive Era* (1987).

Kessler-Harris, Alice, *Out to Work: A History of Wage-Earning Women in the United States* (1982).

Kleppner, Paul, *Who Voted? The Dynamics of Electoral Turnout, 1870–1980* (1984).

Kolko, Gabriel, *The Triumph of Conservatism: A Reinterpretation of American History, 1900–1916* (1967).

———, *Main Currents in Modern American History* (1976).

Lane, A. T., "American Trade Unions, Mass Immigration, and the Literacy Test: 1900–1917," *Labor History*, 25 (1984), pp. 5–25.

Lasch, Christopher, "The Moral and Intellectual Rehabilitation of the Ruling Class," in Christopher Lasch, *The World of Nations: Reflections on American History, Politics, and Culture* (1973).

Laslett, John, *Labor and the Left: A Study of Socialist and Radical Influences in the American Labor Movement, 1881–1924* (1974).

———, and Seymour Lipset, eds., *Failure of a Dream? Essays in the History of American Socialism* (1974).

LeFeber, Walter, *Inevitable Revolutions: The United States in Central America* (1983).

Link, Arthur S., and Richard L. McCormick, *Progressivism* (1983).

McCormick, Richard L., *The Party Period and Public Policy: American Politics from the Age of Jackson to the Progressive Era* (1986).

McGerr, Michael, *The Decline of Popular Politics: The American North, 1865–1928* (1986).

Melosh, Barbara, *"The Physician's Hand": Work Culture and Conflict in American Nursing* (1982).

Milkman, Ruth, ed., *Women, Work, and Protest: A Century of U.S. Women's Labor History* (1985).

Montgomery, David, *Workers' Control in America: Studies in the History of Work, Technology, and Labor Struggles* (1979).

———, "To Study the People: The American Working Class," *Labor History*, 21 (1980), pp. 485–512.

———, "The Irish Influence in the American Labor Movement," lecture reprint, Cushwa Center for the Study of American Catholicism, University of Notre Dame (1984).

———, *The Fall of the House of Labor: The Workplace, the State, and American Labor Activism, 1865–1925* (1987).

Nasaw, Daniel, *Children of the City: At Work and at Play* (1985).

Nelson, Daniel, *Managers and Workers: Origins of the New Factory System in the United States, 1880–1920* (1975).

Peiss, Kathy, *Cheap Amusements: Working Women and Leisure in Turn-of-the-Century New York* (1986).

Perlman, Selig, and Philip Taft, *History of Labor in the United States, 1896–1932; Vol. IV: Labor Movements* (1935).

Porter, Glenn, *The Rise of Big Business, 1860–1910* (1973).

Ramirez, Bruno, *When Workers Fight: The Politics of Industrial Relations in the Progressive Era, 1898–1916* (1978).

Riebe, Ernest, *Mr. Block: Twenty-four IWW Cartoons* (1913; 1984).

Rodgers, Daniel T., "In Search of Progressivism," in Stanley I. Kutler and Stanley N. Katz, eds., *The Promise of American History: Progress and Prospects* (1982).

Rosen, Ruth, *The Lost Sisterhood: Prostitution in America, 1900–1918* (1982).

Rosenzweig, Roy, *Eight Hours for What We Will: Workers and Leisure in an Industrial City, 1870–1920* (1983).

Rothman, David J., and Sheila M. Rothman, eds., *Sources of the American Social Tradition; Vol. II* (1975).

Salvatore, Nick, *Eugene V. Debs: Citizen and Socialist* (1982).

Seller, Maxine Schwartz, *Immigrant Women* (1981).

Shergold, Peter R., "Wage Differentials Based on Skill in the United States, 1889–1914: A Case Study," *Labor History*, 18 (1977), pp. 485–508.

Sklar, Robert, *Movie-Made America: A Cultural History of American Movies* (1976).

Skowronek, Stephen, *Building a New American State: The Expansion of National Administrative Capacities, 1877–1920* (1982).

Takaki, Ronald, *Strangers from a Distant Shore: A History of Asian-Americans* (1989).

Tax, Meredith, *The Rising of the Women: Feminist Solidarity and Class Conflict, 1880–1917* (1980).

Taylor, Philip, *The Distant Magnet: European Emigration to the U.S.A.* (1971).

Taylor, William R., "The Launching of a Commercial Culture: New York City, 1860–1930," in John Mollenkopf, ed., *Power, Culture, and Place: Essays on New York City* (1988).

Thelen, David, *The New Citizenship: The Origins of Progressivism in Wisconsin, 1885–1900* (1972).

Thernstrom, Stephan, Ann Orlov, and Oscar Handlin, eds., *Harvard Encyclopedia of American Ethnic Groups* (1980).

Trachtenberg, Alan, *Reading American Photographs: Images as History, Mathew Brady to Walker Evans* (1989).

U.S. Department of Commerce, Bureau of the Census, *1910 Census*.

———, *Historical Statistics of the United States: Colonial Times to 1970* (1975).

Vecoli, Rudolph J., "*Contadini* in Chicago: A Critique of *The Uprooted*," *Journal of American History*, 51 (1964), pp. 404–17.

Waldinger, Roger, "Another Look at the International Ladies' Garment Workers' Union: Women, Industry Structure, and Collective Action," in Ruth Milkman, ed., *Women, Work, and Protest: A Century of U.S. Women's Labor History* (1985).

Weinstein, James, *The Decline of Socialism in America, 1912–1925* (1967).

———, *The Corporate Ideal in the Liberal State, 1900–1918* (1968).

Wiebe, Robert H., *The Search for Order, 1877–1920* (1966).

Williams, William Appleman, *The Tragedy of American Diplomacy* (1972).

———, *The Contours of American History* (1988).

Worthman, Paul B., and James R. Green, "Black Workers in the New South, 1865–1915," in Nathan I. Huggins, Martin Kilson, and Daniel M. Fox, eds., *Key Issues in the Afro-American Experience* (1971).

Yans-McLaughlin, Virginia, "Patterns of Work and Family Organization: Buffalo's Italians," *Journal of Interdisciplinary History*, 2 (1971), pp. 299–314.

Zurier, Rebecca, *Art for the Masses: A Radical Magazine and Its Graphics, 1911–1917* (1988).

Chapter 5: Wars for Democracy

Adams, Graham, Jr., *Age of Industrial Violence, 1910–1915: Activities and Finding of the United States Commission on Industrial Relations* (1966).

Babson, Steve, et al., *Working Detroit: The Making of a Union Town* (1984).

Bing, Alexander M., *War-Time Strikes and Their Adjustment* (1921).

Brody, David, *Steelworkers in America: The Nonunion Era* (1960).

———, *Workers in Industrial America: Essays on the Twentieth-Century Struggle* (1980).

Bucki, Cecelia F., "Dilution and the Craft Tradition: Bridgeport, Connecticut, Munitions Workers, 1915–1919," *Social Science History*, 4 (1980), pp. 105–24.

Bukowczyk, John J., "The Transformation of Ethnicity: Corporate Control, Americanization, and the Polish Immigrant Middle Class in Bayonne, New Jersey," *Labor History*, 25 (1984), pp. 53–82.

Cardoso, Lawrence A., "Labor Emigration to the Southwest, 1916 to 1920: Mexican Attitudes and Policy," *Southwestern Historical Quarterly*, 79 (1976), pp. 400–416.

Chandler, Alfred D., Jr., *The Visible Hand: The Managerial Revolution in American Business* (1977).

Cochran, Thomas C., and William Miller, *The Age of Enterprise: A Social History of Industrial America* (1961).

Conner, Valerie Jean, *The National War Labor Board: Stability, Social Justice, and the Voluntary State in World War I* (1983).

Cronin, James E., and Carmen Sirianni, eds., *Work, Community, and Power: The Experience of Labor in Europe and America, 1900–1925* (1983).

Dawley, Alan, "The State Made Visible: Policing Work and Loyalty in the United States, 1917–1922," unpublished paper (1984).

Degler, Carl, *At Odds: Women and the Family in America from the Revolution to the Present* (1980).

Dubofsky, Melvyn, *We Shall Be All: A History of the Industrial Workers of the World* (1969).

———, *Industrialism and the American Worker, 1865–1920* (1975).

Edsforth, Ronald William, "A Second Industrial Revolution: The Transformation of Class, Culture, and Society in Twentieth-Century Flint, Michigan," Ph.D. dissertation, Michigan State University (1982).

Ewen, Elizabeth, *Immigrant Women in the Land of Dollars: Life and Culture on the Lower East Side, 1890–1925* (1985).

Faulkner, Harold U., *The Decline of Laissez-Faire, 1897–1917* (1951).

Flexner, Eleanor, *Century of Struggle: The Woman's Rights Movement in the United States* (1975).

Foner, Philip S., *History of the Labor Movement in the United States; Vol. VI: On the Eve of America's Entrance into World War I, 1915–1916* (1982).

———, *Organized Labor and the Black Worker, 1619–1981* (1982).

Freiburger, William, "War Prosperity and Hunger: The New York Food Riots of 1917," *Labor History*, 25 (1984), pp. 217–39.

Gardner, Lloyd C., *Safe for Democracy: The Anglo-American Response to Revolution, 1913–1923* (1984).

Garrison, Dee, ed., *Rebel Pen: The Writings of Mary Heaton Vorse* (1985).

Ginger, Ray, *Eugene V. Debs: A Biography* (1962).

Gompers, Samuel, *Labor and the Common Welfare* (1919).

Gould, Stephen Jay, *The Mismeasure of Man* (1981).

Green, James R., *Grass-roots Socialism: Radical Movements in the Southwest, 1895–1943* (1978).

———, *The World of the Worker: Labor in Twentieth-Century America* (1980).

Greenwald, Maurice W., *Women, War, and Work: The Impact of World War I on Women Workers in the U.S.* (1980).

Grubbs, Frank L., Jr., *Samuel Gompers and the Great War: Protecting Labor's Standards* (1982).

Harris, William H., *The Harder We Run: Black Workers Since the Civil War* (1982).

Hawley, Ellis W., *The Great War and the Search for Modern Order: A History of the American People and Their Institutions, 1917–1933* (1979).

Hess, Stephen, and Milton Kaplan, *The Ungentlemanly Art: A History of American Political Cartoons* (rev. ed., 1975).

Historical Committee of the General Strike Committee, *The Seattle General Strike* (1919).

Hofstadter, Richard, *The American Political Tradition*

and the Men Who Made it (1948).

Karson, Marc, *American Labor Unions and Politics 1900–1918* (1958).

Kazin, Michael, *Barons of Labor: The San Francisco Building Trades and Union Power in the Progressive Era* (1987).

Kennedy, David M., *Over Here: The First World War and American Society* (1980).

Kennedy, Susan E., *If All We Did Was to Weep at Home: A History of White Working-Class Women in America* (1979).

Kessler-Harris, Alice, *Out to Work: A History of Wage-Earning Women in the United States* (1982).

Kirby, Jack Temple, "The Southern Exodus, 1910–1960: A Primer for Historians," *Journal of Southern History*, 49 (1983), pp. 585–600.

Kiser, George C., "Mexican-American Labor Before World War II," *The Journal of Mexican American History*, 2 (1972), pp. 122–42.

Link, Arthur S., *Woodrow Wilson and the Progressive Era, 1910–1917* (1954).

Meyer, Stephen, III, *The Five-Dollar Day: Labor Management and Social Control in the Ford Motor Company, 1908–1921* (1981).

Monroy, Douglas, "Anarquismo y Comunismo: Mexican Radicalism and the Communist Party in Los Angeles During the 1930s," *Labor History*, 24 (1983), pp. 34–59.

Montgomery, David, *Workers' Control in America: Studies in the History of Work, Technology, and Labor Struggles* (1979).

———, *The Fall of the House of Labor: The Workplace, the State, and American Labor Activism, 1865–1925* (1987).

Perlman, Selig, and Philip Taft, *History of Labor in the United States, 1896–1932; Vol. IV: Labor Movements* (1935).

Peterson, Joyce Shaw, *American Automobile Workers, 1900–1933* (1987).

Radosh, Ronald, and Murray N. Rothbard, eds., *A New History of Leviathan: Essays on the Rise of the American Corporate State* (1972).

Ricardo, Romo, "Responses to Mexican Immigration, 1910–1930," *Aztlan-International Journal of Chicano Studies Research*, 6 (1975), pp. 173–94.

Scheiber, Jane Lang, and Harry N. Scheiber, "The Wilson Administration and the Wartime Mobilization of Black Americans, 1917–1918," *Labor History*, 10 (1969), pp. 433–58.

Scott, Emmett J., *Negro Migration During the War* (1920).

Smith, T. Lynn, "The Redistribution of the Negro Population of the United States, 1910–1960," *Journal of Negro History*, 51 (1966), pp. 155–73.

Soule, George, *Prosperity Decade: From War to Depression, 1917–1929* (1964).

Tax, Meredith, *The Rising of the Women: Feminist Solidarity and Class Conflict, 1880–1970* (1980).

Thelen, David P., *Robert M. La Follette and the Insurgent Spirit* (1976).

Thernstrom, Stephan, Ann Orlov, and Oscar Handlin, eds., *Harvard Encyclopedia of American Ethnic Groups* (1980).

Tuttle, William M., Jr., *Race Riot: Chicago in the Red Summer of 1919* (1970).

U.S. Bureau of Labor Statistics, "Bulletin of U.S. Bureau of Labor Statistics #339," (1923).

Weinstein, James, *The Decline of Socialism in America, 1912–1925* (1967).

———, *The Corporate Ideal in the Liberal State: 1900–1918* (1968).

Williams, William Appleman, *The Tragedy of American Diplomacy* (1972).

Zamora, Emilio, Jr., "Chicano Socialist Labor Activity in Texas, 1900–1920," *Aztlan-International Journal of Chicano Studies Research*, 6 (1975), pp. 221–36.

Zurier, Rebecca, *Art for the Masses: A Radical Magazine and Its Graphics, 1911–1917* (1988).

Chapter 6: "The New Era": Mass Society and Business Triumph

Anderson, Jervis, *This Was Harlem, 1900–1950* (1982).

Babson, Steve, et al., *Working Detroit: The Making of a Union Town* (1984).

Bernstein, Irving, *The Lean Years: A History of the American Worker, 1920–1933* (1960).

Black, George, *The Good Neighbor: How the United States Wrote the History of Central America and the Caribbean* (1988).

Braverman, Harry, *Labor and Monopoly Capital: The Degradation of Work in the Twentieth Century* (1974).

Burner, David, *The Politics of Provincialism: The Democratic Party in Transition, 1918–1932* (1968).

Chafe, William H., *The American Woman: Her Changing Social, Economic, and Political Roles, 1920–1970* (1972).

Chandler, Alfred D., Jr., *The Visible Hand: The Managerial Revolution in American Business* (1977).

Cohen, Lizabeth, *Making a New Deal: Industrial Workers in Chicago, 1919–1939* (1990).

Corey, Lewis, *The Decline of American Capitalism* (1934).

Cott, Nancy F., *The Grounding of Modern Feminism* (1987).

Dubofsky, Melvyn, and Warren Van Tine, *John L. Lewis: A Biography* (1977).

Edsforth, Ronald William, *Class Conflict and Cultural Consensus: The Making of a Mass Consumer Society in Flint, Michigan* (1987).

Ewen, Elizabeth, "City Lights: Immigrant Women and the Rise of the Movies," *Signs*, 5 (1980), pp. 545–65.

———, *Immigrant Women in the Land of Dollars: Life and Culture on the Lower East Side, 1890–1925* (1985).

Ewen, Stuart, *Captains of Consciousness: Advertising and the Social Roots of Consumer Culture* (1976).

Fite, Gilbert C., "The Farmers' Dilemma, 1919–1929," in John Braeman, Robert H. Bremner and David Brody, eds., *Change and Continuity in Twentieth-Century America: The 1920s* (1968).

Flint, J. Wayne, *Dixie's Forgotten People: The South's Poor Whites* (1980).

Foner, Philip S., *American Socialism and Black Americans: From the Age of Jackson to World War II* (1978).

———, *Organized Labor and the Black Worker, 1619–1981* (1982).

Ginger, Ray, *Eugene V. Debs: A Biography* (1962).

Gordon, David, Richard Edwards, and Michael Reich, *Segmented Work, Divided Workers: The Historical Transformation of Labor in the United States* (1982).

Gordon, Linda, *Woman's Body, Woman's Right* (1976).

Gosnell, Harold F., *Negro Politicians: The Rise of Negro Politics in Chicago* (1935).

Hall, Jacquelyn Dowd, et al., *Like a Family: The Making of a Southern Cotton Mill World* (1987).

Hareven, Tamara K., *Amoskeag: Life and Work in an American Factory City* (1978).

Harris, William H., *The Harder We Run: Black Workers Since the Civil War* (1982).

Hicks, John D., *The Republican Ascendancy, 1921–1933* (1960).

Hill, Robert A., ed., *The Marcus Garvey and Universal Negro Improvement Association Papers; Vol. I* (1983).

Hounsell, David A., *From the American System to Mass Production, 1800–1932: The Development of Manufacturing Technology in the United States* (1984).

Jackson, Kenneth T., *The Ku Klux Klan in the City, 1915–1930* (1967).

———, *The Crabgrass Frontier: The Suburbanization of the United States* (1985).

Katzman, David M., *Seven Days a Week: Women and Domestic Service in Industrializing America* (1981).

Kazin, Michael, *Barons of Labor: The San Francisco Building Trades and Union Power in the Progressive Era* (1987).

Kessler-Harris, Alice, *Out to Work: A History of Wage-Earning Women in the United States* (1982).

Kirby, Jack Temple, "The Southern Exodus, 1910–1960: A Primer for Historians," *The Journal of Southern History*, 49 (1983), pp. 585–600.

———, "Black and White in the Rural South," *Agricultural History*, 58 (1984), pp. 411–22.

Kirschner, Don S., *City and Country: Rural Responses to Urbanization in the 1920s* (1970).

Kobler, John, *Capone: The Life and World of Al Capone* (1971).

Lender, Mark Edward, and James Martin Kirby, *Drinking in America: A History* (1982).

Lens, Sidney, *The Labor Wars: From the Molly Maguires to the Sitdowns* (1973).

Leuchtenberg, William, *The Perils of Prosperity, 1914–1932* (1958).

Lowitt, Richard, *George Norris: The Persistence of a Progressive, 1913–1933* (1971).

Marchand, Roland, *Advertising the American Dream: Making Way for Modernity, 1920–1940* (1985).

Meier, August, and Elliot Rudwick, *Black Detroit and the Rise of the UAW* (1979).

Meyer, Stephen, III, *The Five-Dollar Day: Labor Management and Social Control in the Ford Motor Company, 1908–1921* (1981).

Milkman, Ruth, *Gender at Work: The Dynamics of Job Segregation by Sex During World War II* (1987).

Naison, Mark, *Communists in Harlem During the Depression* (1983).

Nelson, Daniel, "The Company Union Movement, 1900–1937: A Reexamination," *Business History Review*, 56 (1982), pp. 335–57.

Osofsky, Gilbert, *Harlem: The Making of a Ghetto* (1971).

Perlman, Selig, and Philip Taft, *History of Labor in the United States, 1896–1932; Vol. IV: Labor Movements* (1935).

Peterson, Joyce Shaw, *American Automobile Workers, 1900–1933* (1987).

Philippe, Robert, *Political Graphics: Art as a Weapon* (1980).

President's Research Committee on Social Trends, *Recent Social Trends in the United States* (1933).

Preston, William, Jr., *Aliens and Dissenters: Federal Suppression of Radicals, 1903–33* (1963).

Radford, Gail Ellen, "Modern Community Housing: New Responses to the Shelter Problem in the 1920s and 1930s," Ph.D. dissertation, Columbia University (1989).

Reisler, Mark, *By the Sweat of Their Brow: Mexican Immigrant Labor in the United States, 1900–1940* (1976).

Rosengarten, Theodore, *All God's Dangers: The Life of Nate Shaw* (1975).

Rudwick, Elliot, and August Meier, *From Plantation to Ghetto* (1976).

Schacht, John N., *The Making of Telephone Unionism, 1920–1947* (1985).

Schatz, Ronald W., *The Electrical Workers: A History of Labor at General Electric and Westinghouse, 1923–1960* (1983).

Sklar, Robert, *Movie-Made America: A Cultural History of American Movies* (1976).

———, ed., *The Plastic Age, 1917–1930* (1970).

Slosson, Preston W., *The Great Crusade and After, 1914–1928* (1971).

Smith, T. Lynn, "The Redistribution of the Negro Population of the United States, 1910–1960," *Journal of Negro History*, LI (1966), pp. 155–73.

Soule, George, *Prosperity Decade: From War to Depression, 1917–1929* (1964).

Stein, Judith, *The World of Marcus Garvey: Race and Class in Modern Society* (1985).

Stricker, Frank, "Affluence for Whom?—Another Look at Prosperity and the Working Classes in the 1920s," *Labor History*, 24 (1983), pp. 5–33.

Strom, Sharon Hartman, "'Light Manufacturing': The Feminization of American Office Work, 1900–1930," *Industrial and Labor Relations Review*, 43 (1989), pp. 53–71.

Thernstrom, Stephan, *A History of the American People; Vol. 2: Since 1865* (1984).

Trotter, Joe William, Jr., *Black Milwaukee: The Making of an Industrial Proletariat, 1915–1945* (1985).

Vincent, Theodore, *Black Power and the Garvey Movement* (1971).

Weiss, Nancy J., *Farewell to the Party of Lincoln* (1983).

Wik, Reynold M., "The Radio in Rural America During the 1920s," *Agricultural History*, 55 (1981), pp. 339–50.

Wollenberg, Charles, "*Huelga*, 1928 Style: The Imperial Valley Cantaloupe Workers' Strike," *Pacific Historical Review*, 38 (1969), pp. 45–58.

Wright, Gwendolyn, *Building the American Dream: A Social History of Housing in America* (1981).

Chapter 7: The Great Depression and the First New Deal

Bernstein, Irving, *The Lean Years: A History of the American Worker, 1920–1933* (1966).

———, *Turbulent Years: A History of the American Worker, 1933–1941* (1969).

———, *A Caring Society: The New Deal, the Worker, and the Great Depression: A History of the American Worker, 1933–1941* (1985).

Braeman, John, Robert H. Bremner, and David Brody, eds., *The New Deal; Vol. I: The National Level* (1975).

Brinkley, Alan, *Voices of Protest: Huey Long, Father Coughlin, and the Great Depression* (1982).

Brody, David, *Workers in Industrial America: Essays on the Twentieth-Century Struggle* (1980).

Corey, Lewis, *The Decline of American Capitalism* (1934).

Daniel, Cletus E., *Bitter Harvest: A History of California Farmworkers, 1870–1941* (1981).

Denby, Charles, *Indignant Heart: A Black Worker's Journal* (1978).

Dubofsky, Melvyn, and Warren Van Tine, *John L. Lewis: A Biography* (1977).

Edsforth, Ronald William, *Class Conflict and Cultural Consensus: The Making of a Mass Consumer Society in Flint, Michigan* (1986).

Foner, Philip S., *Organized Labor and the Black Worker, 1619–1981* (1982).

Fraser, Steve, "From the 'New Unionism' to the New Deal," *Labor History*, 25 (1984), pp. 405–30.

Freeman, Joshua B., *In Transit: The Transport Workers Union in New York City, 1933–1966* (1989).

Gonzalez, Rosalinda M. "Chicanas and Mexican Immigrant Families 1920–1940: Women's Subordination and Family Exploitation," in Lois Scharf and John M. Jensen, eds., *Decades of Discontent: The Women's Movement, 1920–1940* (1983).

Grubbs, Donald H., *The Cry from the Cotton: The Southern Tenant Farmers' Union and the New Deal* (1971).

Harris, William H., *The Harder We Run: Black Workers Since the Civil War* (1982).

Hawley, Ellis W., *The New Deal and the Problem of*

Monopoly: A Study in Economic Ambivalence (1966).

Hinckle, Warren, and Lisa Rubens, *The Big Strike: A Pictorial History of the 1934 San Francisco General Strike* (1985).

Kiser, George C., and Marthy Woody Kiser, eds., *Mexican Workers in the United States: Historical and Political Perspectives* (1979).

Klehr, Harvey, *The Heyday of American Communism: The Depression Decade* (1984).

Kushner, Sam, *Long Road to Delano* (1975).

Kwong, Peter, *Chinatown, N.Y.: Labor and Politics, 1930–1950* (1979).

LaFeber, Walter, Richard Polenberg, and Nancy Woloch, *The American Century: A History of the United States Since the 1890s* (1986).

Lasky, Majorie Penn, " 'When I Was a Person': The Ladies' Auxiliary in the 1934 Minneapolis Teamsters' Strikes," in Ruth Milkman, ed., *Women, Work, and Protest: A Century of U.S. Women's Labor History* (1985).

Lens, Sidney, *The Labor Wars: From the Molly Maguires to the Sitdowns* (1973).

Leuchtenberg, William E., *Franklin D. Roosevelt and the New Deal, 1932–1940* (1963).

Levine, Lawrence W., "American Culture and the Great Depression," *The Yale Review*, 74 (1985), pp. 196–223.

Lynd, Alice, and Staughton Lynd, eds., *Rank and File: Personal Histories by Working-Class Organizers* (1973).

Lynd, Staughton, "The Possibilities of Radicalism in the Early 1930s: The Case of Steel," *Radical America*, 6 (1972), pp. 37–64.

McElvaine, Robert S., *The Great Depression: America, 1929–1941* (1984).

———, ed., *Down and Out in the Great Depression: Letters from the Forgotten Man* (1983).

McIntosh, Clarence F., "The Significance of the End-Poverty-in-California Movement," *The Pacific Historian*, 27 (1983), pp. 21–25.

McKenney, Ruth, *Industrial Valley* (1939).

Montgomery, David, and Ronald Schatz, "Facing Layoffs," in David Montgomery, *Workers' Control in America: Studies in the History of Work, Technology, and Labor Struggles* (1979).

Mortimer, Wyndham, *Organize! My Life as a Union Man* (1971).

Naison, Mark, *Communists in Harlem During the Depression* (1983).

Norton, Mary Beth, et al., *A People and a Nation: A History of the United States; Vol. II: Since 1865* (1982).

Painter, Nell Irvin, *The Narrative of Hosea Hudson: His Life as a Negro Communist in the South* (1979).

Reisler, Mark, *By the Sweat of Their Brow: Mexican Immigrant Labor in the United States, 1900–1940* (1976).

Roberts, Harold Selig, *The Rubber Workers: Labor Organization and Collective Bargaining in the Rubber Industry* (1944).

Rosen, Dale, and Theodore Rosengarten, "Shoot-out at Reeltown: The Narrative of Jess Hull, Alabama Tenant Farmer," *Radical America*, 6 (1972), pp. 65–84.

Rosenzweig, Roy, "Organizing the Unemployed: The Early Years of the Great Depression, 1929–1933," *Radical America*, 10 (1976), pp. 37–62.

Rudolph, Frederick, "The American Liberty League, 1934–1940," *American Historical Review*, 56 (1950), pp. 19–33.

Schatz, Ronald W., *The Electrical Workers: A History of Labor at General Electric and Westinghouse, 1923–1960* (1983).

Schlesinger, Arthur, Jr., *The Crisis of the Old Order, 1919–1933* (1956).

———, *The Politics of Upheaval* (1960).

Shannon, David A., ed., *The Great Depression* (1960).

Sitkoff, Harvard, *A New Deal for Blacks: The Emergence of Civil Rights as a National Issue; Vol. I: The Depression Decade* (1978).

Strom, Sharon Harman, "Challenging 'Woman's Place': Feminism, the Left, and Industrial Unionism During the 1930s," *Feminist Studies*, 9 (1983), pp. 359–86.

Susman, Warren I., *Culture as History: The Transformation of American Society in the Twentieth Century* (1984).

Terkel, Studs, *Hard Times: An Oral History of the Great Depression* (1970).

Tindall, George B., *The Emergence of the New South, 1913–1945* (1967).

Trotter, Joe William, Jr., *Black Milwaukee: The Making of an Industrial Proletariat, 1915–1945* (1985).

Trout, Charles H., *Boston: The Great Depression and the New Deal* (1977).

Wandersee, Winifred D., *Women's Work and Family Values, 1920–1940* (1981).

Weber, Devra Anne, "The Organizing of Mexicano Agricultural Workers: Imperial Valley and Los Angeles, 1928–34, An Oral History Approach," *Aztlán—Chicano Journal of the Social Sciences and the Arts*, 3 (1973), pp. 307–47.

Williams, T. Harry, *Huey Long* (1969).

Wilson, Edmund, *The Thirties: From Notebooks and Diaries of the Period* (1980).

Worster, Donald, *Dust Bowl: The Southern Plains in the 1930s* (1979).

Zieger, Robert H., *Rebuilding the Pulp and Paper Workers' Union, 1933–1941* (1984).

Chapter 8: Labor Democratizes America

Auerbach, Jerold S., *Labor and Liberty; The La Follette Committee and the New Deal* (1966).

Bernstein, Irving, *Turbulent Years: A History of the American Worker, 1933–1941* (1969).

Boyer, Richard O., and Herbert M. Morais, *Labor's Untold Story* (1955).

Braeman, John, Robert H. Bremner, and David Brody, eds., *The New Deal; Vol. I: The National Level* (1975).

———, *The New Deal; Vol. II: The State and Local Levels* (1975).

Brinkley, Alan, *Voices of Protest: Huey Long, Father Coughlin, and the Great Depression* (1982).

Brody, David, *Workers in Industrial America: Essays on the Twentieth-Century Struggle* (1980).

Burns, James MacGregor, *Roosevelt: The Lion and the Fox* (1956).

Cayton, Horace, and George Mitchell, *Black Workers and the New Unions* (1939).

Chafe, William, *The American Woman: Her Changing Social, Economic, and Political Roles, 1920–1970* (1972).

Cochran, Bert, *Labor and Communism: The Conflict That Shaped American Unions* (1977).

Conkin, Paul K., *FDR and the Origins of the Welfare State* (1967).

Daniel, Pete, Merry A. Foresta, Maren Stange, and Sally Stein, *Official Images: New Deal Photography* (1987).

DeCaux, Len, *Labor Radical: From the Wobblies to CIO: A Personal History* (1970).

Dobbs, Farrell, *Teamster Rebellion* (1972).

———, *Teamster Bureaucracy* (1977).

Dubofsky, Melvyn, and Warren Van Tine, *John L. Lewis: A Biography* (1977).

Fine, Sidney, *Sit-Down: The General Motors Strike of 1936–37* (1969).

Fleischhauer, Carl, and Beverly W. Brannan, eds., *Documenting America, 1935–1943* (1988).

Friedlander, Peter, *The Emergence of a UAW Local, 1936–1939: A Study in Class and Culture* (1975).

Green, James R., *The World of the Worker: Labor in Twentieth-Century America* (1980).

Harris, William H., *Keeping the Faith: A. Philip Randolph, Milton P. Webster, and the Brotherhood of Sleeping Car Porters, 1925–37* (1977).

Hawley, Ellis W., *The New Deal and the Problem of Monopoly* (1966).

Hofstadter, Richard, *The American Political Tradition and the Men Who Made It* (1948).

Huthmacher, J. Joseph, *Senator Robert F. Wagner and the Rise of Urban Liberalism* (1968).

Ickes, Harold L., *The Secret Diary of Harold L. Ickes* (1953–54).

Jones, Alfred Winslow, *Life, Liberty, and Property: A Story of Conflict and a Measurement of Conflicting Rights* (1941).

Josephson, Matthew, *Sidney Hillman: Statesman of American Labor* (1952).

Kessler-Harris, Alice, *Out to Work: A History of Wage-Earning Women in the United States* (1982).

Lens, Sidney, *The Labor Wars: From the Molly Maguires to the Sitdowns* (1973).

Leuchtenberg, William E., *Franklin D. Roosevelt and the New Deal, 1932–1940* (1963).

Lynd, Alice, and Staughton Lynd, eds., *Rank and File: Personal Histories by Working-Class Organizers* (1973).

Marling, Karal Ann, *Wall-to-Wall America: A Cultural History of Post-Office Murals in the Great Depression* (1982).

McQuaid, Kim, "Corporate Liberalism in the American Business Community, 1920–1940," *Business History Review*, 52 (1978), pp. 342–68.

Meier, August, and Elliott Rudwick, *Black Detroit and the Rise of the UAW* (1979).

Milkman, Ruth, "Women's Work and the Economic Crisis," *Review of Radical Political Economics*, 8 (1976), pp. 73–97.

———, "Female Factory Labor and Industrial Structure: Control and Conflict over 'Women's Place' in Auto and Electrical Manufacturing," *Politics & Society*, 12 (1983), pp. 159–203.

Milton, David, *The Politics of U.S. Labor: From the Great Depression to the New Deal* (1982).

Montgomery, David, "American Workers and the New Deal Formula," in David Montgomery, *Workers' Control in America: Studies in the History of Work, Technology, and Labor Struggles* (1979).

Northrup, Herbert R., *Organized Labor and the Negro* (1944).

O'Connor, John, and Lorraine Brown, eds., *Free, Adult,*

Uncensored: The Living History of the Federal Theatre Project (1978).

Park, Marlene, and Gerald E. Markowitz, *Democratic Vistas: Post Offices and Public Art in the New Deal* (1984).

Perkins, Frances, *The Roosevelt I Knew* (1946).

Piven, Frances Fox, and Richard A. Cloward, *Poor People's Movements: Why They Succeed, How They Fail* (1977).

Preis, Art, *Labor's Giant Step: Twenty Years of the CIO* (1964).

Putte, William J., *The Hilo Massacre: Hawaii's Bloody Monday, August 1, 1938* (1988).

Reuther, Victor, *The Brothers Reuther and the Story of the UAW* (1976).

Rosales, Francisco A., and Daniel T. Simon, "Chicano Steel Workers and Unionism in the Midwest, 1919–1945," *Aztlán—International Journal of Chicano Studies Research*, 6 (1975), pp. 267–75.

Schatz, Ronald W., *The Electrical Workers: A History of Labor at General Electric and Westinghouse, 1923–60* (1983).

Schlesinger, Arthur M., Jr., *The Age of Roosevelt* (1957–60).

Simon, Rita James, ed., *As We Saw the Thirties: Essays on Social and Political Movements of a Decade* (1967).

Sitkoff, Harvard, *A New Deal for Blacks: The Emergence of Civil Rights as a National Issue* (1978).

Sklar, Robert, *Movie-Made America: A Cultural History of American Movies* (1975).

Skocpol, Theda, "Political Response to Capitalist Crisis: Neo-Marxist Theories of the State and the Case of the New Deal," *Politics & Society*, 10 (1980), pp. 155–201.

Sternsher, Bernard, ed., *The Negro in Depression and War: Prelude to Revolution, 1930–1945* (1969).

Streater, John Baxter, *The National Negro Congress, 1936–1947* (1981).

Street, Richard S., "The 'Battle of Salinas': San Francisco Bay Area Press Photographers and the Salinas Valley Lettuce Strike of 1936," *Journal of the West*, 26 (1987), pp. 41–51.

Terkel, Studs, *Hard Times: An Oral History of the Great Depression* (1970).

Tugwell, Rexford G., *The Democratic Roosevelt* (1957).

Wolfskill, George, *The Revolt of the Conservatives: A History of the American Liberty League, 1934–40* (1962).

Wright, Gwendolyn, *Building the Dream: A Social History of Housing in America* (1981).

Chapter 9: A Nation Transformed: The Second World War and Its Aftermath

Alperovitz, Gar, *Atomic Diplomacy: Hiroshima and Potsdam: The Use of the Atomic Bomb and the American Confrontation with Soviet Power* (expanded and updated ed., 1985).

Ambrose, Stephen, *Rise to Globalism: American Foreign Policy, 1938–1980* (1980).

Anderson, Karen, *Wartime Women: Sex Roles, Family Relations, and the Status of Women During World War II* (1981).

———, "Last Hired, First Fired: Black Women Workers During World War II," *Journal of American History*, 69 (1982), pp. 82–97.

Arroyo, Luis Leobardo, "Chicano Participation in Organized Labor: The CIO in Los Angeles, 1938–1950. An Extended Research Note," *Aztlán—International Journal of Chicano Studies Research*, 6 (1975), pp. 277–303.

Babson, Steve, et al., *Working Detroit: The Making of a Union Town* (1984).

Barrera, Mario, *Race and Class in the Southwest: A Theory of Racial Inequality* (1979).

Bayor, Ronald H., *Neighbors in Conflict: The Irish, Germans, Jews, and Italians of New York City, 1929–1941* (1978).

Bernstein, Barton J., "America in War and Peace: The Test of Liberalism," in Barton J. Bernstein, ed., *Towards a New Past: Dissenting Essays in American History* (1968).

Bloom, Jack, *Class, Race, and the Civil Rights Movement* (1987).

Blum, John Morton, *V Was for Victory: Politics and American Culture During World War II* (1976).

Boyer, Paul, *By the Bomb's Early Light: American Thought and Culture at the Dawn of the Atomic Age* (1985).

Brody, David, "The New Deal and World War II," in John Braeman, Robert H. Bremner, and David Brody, eds., *The New Deal; Vol. I: The National Level* (1975).

———, *Workers in Industrial America: Essays on the Twentieth-Century Struggle* (1980).

Browder, Earl, *Victory—And After* (1942).

Burnham, Walter Dean, *Critical Elections and the Mainsprings of American Politics* (1970).

Byrnes, James F., *Speaking Frankly* (1947).

Camarillo, Albert, *Chicanos in California: A History of Mexican Americans in California* (1984).

Chafe, William, *The American Woman, Her Changing Social, Economic, and Political Roles, 1920–1970* (1972).

Clive, Alan, *State of War: Michigan in World War II* (1979).

———, "Women Workers in World War II: Michigan as a Test Case," *Labor History*, 20 (1979), pp. 44–72.

D'Emilio, John, and Estelle Freedman, *Intimate Matters: A History of Sexuality in America* (1988).

Dobbs, Farrell, *Teamster Bureaucracy* (1977).

Dower, John, *War Without Mercy: Race and Power in the Pacific War* (1986).

Dubofsky, Melvyn, and Warren Van Tine, *John L. Lewis: A Biography* (1977).

Feis, Herbert, *Churchill, Roosevelt, Stalin: The War They Waged and the Peace They Sought* (1967).

Foner, Philip S., and Ronald L. Lewis, eds., *The Black Worker from the Founding of the CIO to the AFL-CIO Merger, 1936–1955* (1983).

Frank, Miriam, Marilyn Ziebarth, and Connie Field, *The Life and Times of Rosie the Riveter: The Story of Three Million Working Women During World War II* (1982).

Fraser, Steve, *Labor Will Rule: A Biography of Sidney Hillman* (1991).

Freeman, Joshua B., *In Transit: The Transport Workers Union in New York City, 1933–1966* (1989).

Gabin, Nancy, "Women Workers and the UAW in the Post–World War II Period: 1945–1954," *Labor History*, 21 (1979–1980), pp. 5–30.

Gardner, Lloyd C., *Economic Aspects of New Deal Diplomacy* (1971).

Garfinkel, Herbert, *When Negroes March: The March on Washington Movement in the Organizational Politics for FEPC* (1959).

Gilbert, Felix, *The End of the European Era, 1890 to the Present* (1970).

Gilbert, James, *A Cycle of Outrage: America's Reaction to the Juvenile Delinquent in the 1950s* (1986).

Golden, Clinton S., and Harold J. Ruttenberg, *The Dynamics of Industrial Democracy* (1942).

Glaberman, Martin, *Wartime Strikes: The Struggle Against the No-Strike Pledge in the UAW During World War II* (1980).

Green, James R., *The World of the Worker: Labor in Twentieth-Century America* (1980).

Harris, Howell John, *The Right to Manage: Industrial Relations Policies of American Business in the 1940s* (1982).

Harris, William H., *The Harder We Run: Black Workers Since the Civil War* (1982).

Hawley, Ellis W., *The New Deal and the Problem of Monopoly* (1966).

Hofstadter, Richard, and Michael Wallace, eds., *American Violence: A Documentary History* (1970).

Howe, Irving, and B. J. Widick, *The UAW and Walter Reuther* (1949).

Iriye, Akira, *Power and Culture: The Japanese-American War, 1941–1945* (1981).

Irons, Peter, *Justice at War: The Story of the Japanese American Internment Cases* (1983).

Isserman, Maurice, *Which Side Were You On? The American Communist Party During the Second World War* (1982).

Johnson, Daniel M., and Rex R. Campbell, *Black Migration in America: A Social Demographic History* (1981).

Josephson, Matthew, *Sidney Hillman: Statesman of American Labor* (1952).

Kessler-Harris, Alice, *Out to Work: A History of Wage-Earning Women in the United States* (1982).

Koistinen, Paul A. C., *The Hammer and the Sword* (1979).

———, *The Military-Industrial Complex: A Historical Perspective* (1980).

Kolko, Gabriel, *The Politics of War: The World and United States Foreign Policy, 1943–1945* (1968).

Korstad, Robert, and Nelson Lichtenstein, "Opportunities Found and Lost: Labor Radicals and the Early Civil Rights Movement," *Journal of American History*, 75 (1988), pp. 786–811.

LaFeber, Walter, *America, Russia, and the Cold War* (1980).

Lichtenstein, Nelson, *Labor's War at Home: The CIO in World War II* (1982).

———, "The Making of the Postwar Working Class: Cultural Pluralism and Social Structure in World War II," *The Historian*, 51 (1988), pp. 42–63.

Maltin, Leonard, *Of Mice and Magic: A History of American Animated Cartoons* (1980).

Marshall, Ray, *Labor in the South* (1967).

Meier, August, and Elliot Rudwick, *Black Detroit and the Rise of the UAW* (1979).

Meier, Matt S., and Feliciano Rivera, *The Chicanos: A History of Mexican-Americans* (1972).

Milkman, Ruth, "Redefining 'Women's Work': The Sexual Division of Labor in the Auto Industry During World War II," *Feminist Studies*, 8 (1982), pp. 337–72.

———, "Female Factory Labor and Industrial Structure: Control and Conflict over 'Women's Place' in Auto and Electrical Manufacturing," *Politics and Society*, 12 (1983), pp. 159–203.

———, *Gender at Work: The Dynamics of Job Segregation by Sex During World War II* (1987).

Montgomery, David, "American Workers and the New Deal Formula," in David Montgomery, *Workers' Control in America: Studies in the History of Work, Technology, and Labor Struggles* (1979).

Motley, Mary Penick, ed., *The Invisible Soldier: The Experience of the Black Soldier, World War II* (1975).

Nelson, Steve, James Barrett, and Rob Ruck, *Steve Nelson, American Radical* (1981).

Northrup, Herbert R., et al., *Negro Employment in Basic Industry: A Study of Racial Process in Six Industries* (1970).

Perrett, Geoffrey, *Days of Sadness, Years of Triumph: The American People, 1939–1945* (1973).

Phillipe, Robert, *Political Graphics: Art as a Weapon* (1982).

Polenberg, Richard, *War and Society: The United States, 1941–1945* (1972).

———, *One Nation Divisible: Class, Race, and Ethnicity in the United States Since 1938* (1980).

———, ed., *America at War: The Home Front, 1941–1945* (1968).

Preis, Art, *Labor's Giant Step: 20 Years of the CIO* (1964).

Quick, Paddy, "Rosie the Riveter: Myths and Realities," *Radical America*, 9 (1975), pp. 115–31.

Rhodes, Richard, *The Making of the Atomic Bomb* (1986).

Richmond, Al, *A Long View from the Left: Memoirs of an American Revolutionary* (1973).

Schatz, Ronald W., *The Electrical Workers: A History of Labor at General Electric and Westinghouse, 1923–1960* (1983).

Scott, Robin F., "The Zoot-Suit Riots," in Manuel P. Servin, comp., *The Mexican Americans: An Awakening Minority* (1970).

Seidman, Joel, *American Labor from Defense to Reconversion* (1953).

Sherry, Michael, *The Rise of American Air Power: The Creation of Armageddon* (1987).

Sherwin, Martin J., *A World Destroyed: The Atomic Bomb and the Grand Alliance* (1975).

Sitkoff, Harvard, "Racial Militancy and Interracial Violence in the Second World War," *Journal of American History*, 58 (1971), pp. 661–81.

———, *A New Deal for Blacks* (1978).

Sternsher, Bernard, ed., *The Negro in Depression and War: Prelude to Revolution, 1930–1945* (1969).

Terkel, Studs, *"The Good War": An Oral History of World War Two* (1984).

Tobias, Sheila, and Lisa Anderson, "What Really Happened to Rosie the Riveter? Demobilization and the Female Labor Force, 1944–47," in Linda K. Kerber and Jane DeHart Matthews, eds., *Women's America: Refocusing the Past* (1982).

Widick, B. J., *Detroit: City of Race and Class Violence* (1972).

Williams, William Appleman, *The Tragedy of American Diplomacy* (1972).

Wyman, David S., *The Abandonment of the Jews* (1985).

Chapter 10: The Postwar Era

Alexander, Charles C., *Holding the Line: The Eisenhower Era, 1952–61* (1975).

Barnard, John, *Walter Reuther and the Rise of the Auto Workers* (1983).

Bartley, Numan, *The Rise of Massive Resistance: Race and Politics in the South During the 1950s* (1959).

Bell, Daniel, *The End of Ideology: On the Exhaustion of Political Ideas in the Fifties* (1960).

Biskind, Peter, *Seeing Is Believing: How Hollywood Taught Us to Stop Worrying and Love the Fifties* (1983).

Bowles, Samuel, David M. Gordon, and Thomas E. Weisskopf, *Beyond the Waste Land: A Democratic Alternative to Economic Decline* (1983).

Boyer, Paul, *By the Bomb's Early Light: American Thought and Culture at the Dawn of the Atomic Age* (1985).

Branch, Taylor, *Parting the Waters: America in the King Years, 1954–1963* (1988).

Brody, David, *Workers in Industrial America: Essays on the Twentieth-Century Struggle* (1980).

Caute, David, *The Great Fear: The Anti-Communist Purge Under Truman and Eisenhower* (1978).

Chinoy, Eli, *Automobile Workers and the American Dream* (1955).

Cochran, Bert, *Labor and Communism: The Conflict That Shaped American Unions* (1977).

Davis, Mike, *Prisoners of the American Dream: Politics and Economy in the History of the U.S. Working Class* (1986).

Donaldson, Scott, *The Suburban Myth* (1969).

Fraser, Steve, and Gary Gerstle, eds., *The Rise and Fall of the New Deal Order, 1930–1980* (1989).

Gaddis, John Lewis, *The United States and the Origins of the Cold War, 1941–1947* (1972).

Garrow, David, *Martin Luther King, Jr., and the Southern Christian Leadership Conference* (1986).

Gilbert, James, *A Cycle of Outrage: America's Reaction to the Juvenile Delinquent in the 1950s* (1986).

Gordon, David, Richard Edwards, and Michael Reich, *Segmented Work, Divided Workers: The Historical Transformation of Labor in the United States* (1982).

Goulden, Joseph C., *Meany* (1972).

Greenstone, J. David, *Labor and American Politics* (1970).

Griffith, Barbara, *The Crisis of American Labor: Operation Dixie and the Defeat of the CIO* (1988).

Griffith, Robert, and Athan Theoharis, *The Specter: Original Essays on the Cold War and the Origins of McCarthyism* (1974).

Guilbaut, Serge, *How New York Stole the Idea of Modern Art: Abstract Expressionism, Freedom, and the Cold War* (1983).

Halliday, Jon, and Bruce Cumings, *Korea: The Unknown War* (1988).

Hamby, Alonzo, *Beyond the New Deal: Harry S. Truman and American Liberalism* (1973).

Herberg, Will, *Protestant—Catholic—Jew: An Essay in American Religious Sociology* (1960).

Herken, Gregg, *The Winning Weapon: The Atomic Bomb in the Cold War, 1945 to 1950* (1981).

Jacobson, Julius, ed., *The Negro and the American Labor Movement* (1968).

Jezer, Marty, *The Dark Ages: Life in the United States, 1945–1960* (1982).

Kluger, Richard, *Simple Justice: The History of Brown v. Board of Education and Black America's Struggle for Equality* (1975).

Komarovsky, Mirra, *Blue-Collar Marriage* (1967).

Lacey, Michael, ed., *The Truman Presidency* (1989).

Lawson, Steven, *Black Ballots: Voting Rights in the South, 1944–1969* (1976).

Levenstein, Harvey, *Communism, Anti-Communism, and the CIO* (1981).

Levison, Andrew, *The Working-Class Majority* (1975).

Lipsitz, George, *Class and Culture in Cold War America: "A Rainbow at Midnight."* (1982).

Mathews, Jane De Hart, "Art and Politics in Cold War America," *American Historical Review*, 81 (1976), pp. 762–87.

McAuliffe, Mary Sperling, *Crisis on the Left: Cold War Politics and American Liberals, 1947–1954* (1978).

Mills, C. Wright, *The New Men of Power* (1948).

Morris, Aldon, *The Origins of the Civil Rights Movement: Black Communities Organizing for Change* (1984).

Patterson, Thomas, *On Every Front: The Making of the Cold War* (1979).

Radosh, Ronald, *American Labor and United States Foreign Policy* (1969).

———, and Joyce Milton, *The Rosenberg File: A Search for the Truth* (1983).

Rogin, Michael, *McCarthy and the Intellectuals* (1967).

Ross, Andrew, *No Respect: Intellectuals and Popular Culture* (1989).

Stone, Katherine, "The Post-War Paradigm in American Labor Law," *Yale Law Journal*, 90 (1981), pp. 1509–80.

Theoharis, Athan, *Seeds of Repression: Harry S. Truman and the Origins of McCarthyism* (1978).

Tygiel, Jules, *Baseball's Great Experiment: Jackie Robinson and His Legacy* (1983).

Weinstein, James, *Perjury!: The Hiss-Chambers Conflict* (1978).

Wright, Gwendolyn, *Building the Dream: A Social History of Housing in America* (1981).

Zieger, Robert, *American Workers, American Unions, 1920–1985* (1986).

Chapter 11: The Rights-Conscious 1960s

Adamson, Madeleine, and Seth Borgos, *This Mighty Dream: Social Protest Movements in the United States* (1984).

Aronowitz, Stanley, *False Promises: The Shaping of American Working-Class Consciousness* (1973).

Ashe, Arthur R., Jr., *A Hard Road to Glory: A History of the African-American Athlete Since 1946* (1988).

Baritz, Loren, *Backfire: A History of How American Culture Led Us into Vietnam and Made Us Fight the Way We Did* (1985).

Bernstein, Carl, and Robert Woodward, *All the President's Men* (1974).

Branch, Taylor, *Parting the Waters: America in the King Years, 1954–63* (1988).

Breines, Wini, *Community and Organization in the New Left, 1962–1968: The Great Refusal* (1982).

Caute, David, *The Year of the Barricades: A Journey Through 1968* (1988).

Davis, Mike, *Prisoners of the American Dream: Poli-*

tics and Economy in the History of the U.S. Working Class (1986).

Divoky, Diane, ed., How Old Will You Be in 1968? Expressions of Student Outrage from the High-School Free Press (1969).

Echols, Alice, Daring to Be Bad: Radical Feminism in America, 1967–1975 (1989).

Evans, Sara, Personal Politics: The Roots of Women's Liberation in the Civil Rights Movement and the New Left (1979).

Farber, David, Chicago '68 (1987).

Fink, Leon, and Brian Greenberg, Upheaval in the Quiet Zone: A History of Hospital Workers' Union Local 1199 (1989).

Fraser, Ronald, et al., eds., 1968: A Student Generation in Revolt (1988).

Gettleman, Marvin E., Jane Franklin, Marilyn Young, and H. Bruce Franklin, Vietnam and America: A Documented History (1985).

Gitlin, Todd, The Sixties: Years of Hope, Days of Rage (1987).

Goodman, Mitchell, ed., The Movement Toward a New America (1970).

Halberstam, David, The Best and the Brightest (1972).

Hall, Burton, ed., Autocracy and Insurgency in Organized Labor (1972).

Halle, David, America's Working Man: Work, Home, and Politics Among Blue-Collar Property Owners (1984).

Hersh, Seymour, The Price of Power: Kissinger in the Nixon White House (1983).

Hodgson, Godfrey, American in Our Time (1976).

Howe, Irving, ed., The World of Blue-Collar Workers (1972).

Howe, Louise Kapp, Pink-Collar Workers: Inside the World of Women's Work (1977).

Isserman, Maurice, If I Had a Hammer . . . The Death of the Old Left and the Birth of the New Left (1987).

Joseph, Paul, Cracks in the Empire: State Politics in the Vietnam War (1981).

Komarovsky, Mirra, Blue-Collar Marriage (1967).

Kornblum, William, Blue-Collar Community (1974).

Levitan, Sar, ed., Blue-Collar Workers: A Symposium of Middle America (1971).

Makower, Joel, Woodstock: The Oral History (1989).

Matusow, Allen, The Unraveling of America: A History of Liberalism in the 1960s (1985).

McAdam, Doug, Freedom Summer (1988).

Miller, James, "Democracy Is in the Streets": From Port Huron to the Siege of Chicago (1987).

Miller, Marc, ed., Working Lives: The Southern Exposure History of Labor in the South (1980).

Morris, Charles, A Time of Passion: America 1960–1980 (1984).

Parmet, Herbert S., JFK: The Presidency of John F. Kennedy (1983).

Patterson, James, America's Struggle Against Poverty, 1900–1980 (1983).

Peck, Abe, Uncovering the Sixties: The Life and Times of the Underground Press (1985).

Piven, Frances Fox, and Richard A. Cloward, Poor People's Movements: Why They Succeed, How They Fail (1977).

Raines, Howell, My Soul Is Rested: Movement Days in the Deep South Remembered (1977).

Serrin, William, The Company and the Union: The "Civilized Relationship" of the General Motors Corporation and the United Automobile Workers (1973).

Sexton, Patricia Cayo, and Brandon Sexton, Blue Collars and Hard-Hats: The Working Class and the Future of American Politics (1971).

Singer, Daniel, Prelude to Revolution: France in May 1968 (1970).

Small, Melvin, Johnson, Nixon, and the Doves (1988).

Stevens, Robert, Vain Hopes, Grim Realities: Economic Consequences of the Vietnam War (1976).

Terkel, Studs, Working (1974).

Viorst, Milton, Fire in the Streets: America in the 1960s (1979).

Williams, Juan, Eyes on the Prize: America's Civil Rights Years, 1954–1965 (1987).

Zieger, Robert, American Workers, American Unions, 1920–1985 (1986).

Chapter 12: The United States and the Global Economy

Alcaly, Roger, and David Mermelstein, eds., The Fiscal Crisis of American Cities (1977).

Alperovitz, Gar, and Geoffrey Faux, Rebuilding America (1984).

Auletta, Ken, Greed and Glory on Wall Street (1986).

Balser, Diane, Sisterhood and Solidarity: Feminism and Labor in Modern Times (1987).

Bensman, David, and Roberta Lynch, Rusted Dreams: Hard Times in a Steel Community (1987).

Block, Fred, Richard A. Cloward, Barbara Ehrenreich, and Frances Fox Piven, The Mean Season: The Attack on the Welfare State (1987).

Bluestone, Barry, and Bennett Harrison, *The Deindustrialization of America: Plant Closings, Community Abandonment, and the Dismantling of Basic Industries* (1982).

Blumberg, Paul, *Inequality in an Age of Decline* (1980).

Boris, Eileen, and Cynthia Daniels, eds., *Homework: Historical and Contemporary Perspectives on Paid Labor at Home* (1989).

Bowles, Samuel, David M. Gordon, and Thomas E. Weisskopf, *Beyond the Waste Land: A Democratic Alternative to Economic Decline* (1983).

Carroll, Peter, *It Seemed Like Nothing Happened: The Tragedy and Promise of America in the 1970s* (1982).

Cohen, Stephen S., and John Zysman, *Manufacturing Matters: The Myth of the Post-Industrial Economy* (1987).

Condit, Celeste Michelle, *Decoding Abortion Rhetoric: Communicating Social Change* (1990).

Davis, Mike, *Prisoners of the American Dream: Politics and Economy in the History of the U.S. Working Class* (1986).

———, *City of Quartz: Excavating the Future in Los Angeles* (1990).

Edsall, Thomas, *The New Politics of Inequality* (1984).

Ferguson, Thomas, and Joel Rogers, *Right Turn: The Decline of the Democrats and the Future of American Politics* (1986).

Fink, Leon, and Brian Greenberg, *Upheaval in the Quiet Zone: A History of Hospital Workers' Union Local 1199* (1989).

Freeman, Richard B., and James L. Medoff, *What Do Unions Do?* (1984).

Garson, Barbara, *The Electronic Sweatshop: How Computers Are Transforming the Office of the Future into the Factory of the Past* (1988).

Gilpin, Toni, et al., eds., *On Strike for Respect: The Yale Strike of 1984–85* (1988).

Ginsberg, Benjamin, and Martin Shefter, *Politics by Other Means: The Declining Importance of Elections in America* (1990).

Goldfield, Michael, *The Decline of Organized Labor in the United States* (1987).

Green, Hardy, *On Strike at Hormel: The Struggle for a Democratic Labor Movement* (1990).

Greider, William, *Secrets of the Temple: How the Federal Reserve Runs the Country* (1987).

Halliday, Fred, *From Kabul to Managua: Soviet-American Relations in the 1980s* (1989).

Harrison, Bennett, and Barry Bluestone, *The Great U-Turn: Corporate Restructuring and the Polarizing of America* (1988).

Hoerr, John, *And the Wolf Finally Came: The Decline of the American Steel Industry* (1988).

Holland, Max, *When the Machine Stopped: A Cautionary Tale from Industrial America* (1989).

Howard, Robert, *Brave New Workplace* (1985).

Judis, John, *William F. Buckley, Jr.: Patron Saint of the Conservatives* (1988).

Kennedy, Paul, *The Rise and Fall of the Great Powers: Economic Change and Military Conflict from 1500 to 2000* (1987).

Kingsolver, Barbara, *Holding the Line: Women in the Great Arizona Mine Strike of 1983* (1989).

Kochan, Thomas, Robert McKersie; and Harry Katz, *The Transformation of American Industrial Relations* (1986).

Kolko, Joyce, *Restructuring the World Economy* (1988).

Krieger, Joel, *Reagan, Thatcher, and the Politics of Decline* (1986).

Kuttner, Robert, *Revolt of the Haves: Tax Rebellions and Hard Times* (1980).

———, *The Economic Illusion: False Choices Between Prosperity and Social Justice* (1984).

Lekachman, Robert, *Visions and Nightmares: America After Reagan* (1987).

Lukas, J. Anthony, *Common Ground: A Turbulent Decade in the Lives of Three American Families* (1985).

Magaziner, Ira C., and Robert B. Reich, *Minding America's Business: The Decline and Rise of the American Economy* (1982).

Mann, Eric, *Taking on General Motors* (1988).

Mansbridge, Jane J., *Why We Lost the ERA* (1986).

Martz, Larry, and Ginny Carroll, *Ministry of Greed: The Inside Story of the Televangelists and Their Holy Wars* (1988).

Mead, Walter Russel, *Mortal Splendor: The American Empire in Transition* (1987).

Melman, Seymour, *The Permanent War Economy: American Capitalism in Decline* (1974).

Milkman, Ruth, "Women Workers, Feminism, and the Labor Movement Since the 1960s," in Ruth Milkman, ed., *Women, Work, and Protest: A Century of U.S. Women's Labor History* (1985).

Moody, Kim, *An Injury to All: The Decline of American Unionism* (1988).

Newman, Katherine S., *Falling from Grace: The Experience of Downward Mobility in the American Middle Class* (1988).

Noble, David, *Forces of Production: A Social History of Industrial Automation* (1984).

Parker, Mike, *Inside the Circle: A Union Guide to Quality of Worklife* (1985).

———, and Jane Slaughter, *Choosing Sides: Unions and the Team Concept* (1988).

Petchesky, Rosalind Pollack, *Abortion and Woman's Choice: The State, Sexuality, and Reproductive Freedom* (1984).

———, "Fetal Images: The Power of Visual Culture in the Politics of Reproduction," *Feminist Studies*, 13 (1987), pp. 263–92.

Phillips, Kevin P., *The Emerging Republican Majority* (1969).

Piore, Michael J., and Charles F. Sabel, *The Second Industrial Divide: Possibilities for Prosperity* (1984).

Piven, Frances Fox, and Richard A. Cloward, *The New Class War: Reagan's Attack on the Welfare State and Its Consequences* (1982).

Reich, Robert, and John D. Donahue, *New Deals: The Chrysler Revival and the American System* (1987).

Sacks, Karen Brodkin, *Caring by the Hour: Women, Work, and Organization at Duke Medical Center* (1988).

Siegel, Frederick F., *A Troubled Journey: From Pearl Harbor to Ronald Reagan* (1984).

Smith, Robert Ellis, *Workrights* (1983).

Squiers, Carol, "Picturing Scandal: Iranscam, the Reagan White House, and the Photo Opportunity," in Carol Squiers, ed., *The Critical Image: Essays on Contemporary Photography* (1990).

Stacey, Judith, *Brave New Families: Stories of Domestic Upheaval in Late-Twentieth-Century America* (1990).

Strange, Susan, *Casino Capitalism* (1986).

Terkel, Studs, *The Great Divide* (1988).

Thurow, Lester C., *The Zero-Sum Solution: Building a World-Class American Economy* (1985).

Wachtel, Howard M., *The Money Mandarins: The Making of a New Supranational Economic Order* (1986).

Wilson, William Julius, *The Declining Significance of Race: Blacks and Changing American Institutions* (1980).

———, *The Truly Disadvantaged: The Inner City, the Underclass, and Public Policy* (1987).

Zuboff, Shoshana, *In the Age of the Smart Machine: The Future of Work and Power* (1988).

CREDITS

Introduction

xvi: Currier and Ives, 1876, lithograph—Prints and Photographs Division, Library of Congress. **xviii:** Currier and Ives, 1876, lithograph—Prints and Photographs Division, Library of Congress. **xix:** *Frank Leslie's Illustrated Newspaper*, May 20, 1876—American Social History Project. **xxii:** Fernando Miranda, *Frank Leslie's Illustrated Newspaper*, August 5, 1876—American Social History Project. **xxv:** Fernando Miranda, *Frank Leslie's Illustrated Newspaper*, August 4, 1877—American Social History Project. **xxvi:** S. V. Albee, "The Railroad War"—Paul Dickson Collection.

Part One: Monopoly and Upheaval, 1877–1914

2: Chicago Historical Society.

Chapter 1: Progress and Poverty: The Growth of Industrial Capitalism

Documents: 10: "A path is open'd for all time . . .": *The Hand That Holds the Bread*, Cincinnati's University Singers, New World Records (1978). **17:** ". . . This queer conglomerate mass": Jacob Riis, *How the Other Half Lives* (1890). **23:** ". . . Leaves me in poor circumstances": U.S. Senate Report on Labor and Capital, vol. 3 (1883). **24:** ". . . Pay is too small": Fifteenth Annual Report, Massachusetts Bureau of Statistics of Labor (1884). **26:** "Bell time . . .": Philip G. Hubert, Jr., "The Business of a Factory," *Scribner's Magazine* (January–June 1897). **31:** "A very sad, bitter, and ruinous experience . . .": U.S. Industrial Commission (1899). **32:** "Subordination is a cardinal principle . . .": Sigmund Diamond, ed., *The Nation Transformed* (1963). **45:** "All must work under my direction": Grimes Family Papers, Southern Historical Collection, University of North Carolina, Chapel Hill. **49:** ". . . A very sad sight": Robert D. Marcus and David Burner, eds., *America Firsthand* (1989). **57:** ". . . Indebted to her master/mistress": Alexander McLeod, *Pigtails and Gold Dust* (1948).
Illustrations: 6: Thomas Pollock Anshutz, 1880, oil on canvas, 17 1/8 × 24 inches—The Fine Arts Museums of San Francisco, Gift of Mr. and Mrs. John D. Rockefeller 3rd. **8:** Gray Parker, New York *Daily Graphic*, March 20, 1877—New-York Historical Society. **14:** William A. Rogers, *Harper's Weekly*, April 26, 1890—American Social History Project. **15:** Charles Dana Gibson, *The Ladies' Home Journal*, April 1895—American Social History Project. **18:** Dr. Henry Piffard or Richard Hoe Lawrence (for Jacob Riis), 1888—Jacob A. Riis Collection, Museum of the City of New York. **20:** Lewis Hine, 1909—International Museum of Photography at George Eastman House. **22:** Chicago Historical Society. **25:** Jacob Riis, c. 1889—Jacob A. Riis Collection, Museum of the City of New York. **27:** *National Police Gazette*, May 28, 1892—Prints and Photographs Division, Library of Congress. **29:** National Museum of American History, Smithsonian Institution. **35:** Charles Graham, *Harper's Weekly*, April 10, 1886—American Social History Project. **37:** Joseph Keppler, *Puck*, January 23, 1889—New-York Historical Society. **40:** Valentine Museum, Richmond, Virginia. **41:** Valentine Museum, Richmond, Virginia. **47:** Tenth Annual Report, Bureau of Ethnology, #4700—National Anthropological Archive, Smithsonian Institution. **50:** George Trager, "Burial of the Dead at the Battle of Wounded Knee, (South Dakota)," 1891, albumen silver print, 4 5/8 × 7 7/16 inches—Amon Carter Museum, Fort Worth, Texas. **51:** Frederic Remington, *Harper's Weekly*, January 24, 1891—General Research Division, New York Public Library, Astor, Lenox, and Tilden Foundations. **55:** Solomon D. Butcher, 1888—Butcher Collection, Nebraska State Historical Society.

Chapter 2: The Emergence of Working-Class Collectivity

Documents: 62: ". . . The duty of the man of wealth": Andrew Carnegie, *The Gospel of Wealth and Other Timely Essays* (1889); "A Workingman's Prayer": *The Coming Nation*, February 10, 1894. **73:** "You should take allotments . . .": Edward Goodbird, *Goodbird The Indian: His Story* (1914). **76:** ". . . Let us prove ourselves men": *National Labor Tribune*, July 25, 1891. **80:** ". . . Women should do anything they liked that was good": Frances E. Willard, *Glimpses of Fifty Years: The Autobiography of an American Woman* (1889). **82–83:** ". . . A picture of inferno such as Dante never painted": Kate

Richards O'Hare, "How I Became a Socialist Agitator," *Socialist Woman* (October 1908). **86:** "The workingman's club": "The Saloon in Chicago," *The American Journal of Sociology* (November 1900). **88:** "I had no idea of the inward appearance of a saloon . . .": Frances E. Willard, *Glimpses of Fifty Years* (1889). **94–95:** "The most important and fruitful discovery . . .": Oscar Ameringer, *If You Don't Weaken: The Autobiography of Oscar Ameringer* (1983). **98:** "Labor's Catechism": *The People*, December 17, 1887. **100:** "The meat question": *Locomotive Firemen's Magazine*, November 1890. **105:** ". . . We are Starving to death": Lewelling Papers, Kansas Historical Society; ". . . We are robbed of our means": Ignatius Donnelly Papers, Minnesota Historical Society.

Illustrations: 60: Spiegel, *The People*, April 8, 1894—General Research Division, New York Public Library; Astor, Lenox, and Tilden Foundations. **67:** Chicago Historical Society. **70:** Prints and Photographs Division, Library of Congress. **75:** #1388, Cook Collection, Valentine Museum, Richmond, Virginia. **79:** J. S. Pughe, *Puck*, 1900—Scott Molloy Labor Archives. **81:** *Boston Labor Leader*, October 6, 1894—State Historical Society of Wisconsin. **85:** Otto Becker (after a painting by Cassily Adams), 1896, chromolithograph, 32 × 41 13/16 inches—Amon Carter Museum, Fort Worth, Texas. **87:** *Harper's Weekly*, March 21, 1874—American Social History Project. **89:** (A. B. Davis), Anthony Comstock, *Traps for the Young* (1883)—General Research Division, New York Public Library, Astor, Lenox, and Tilden Foundations. **91:** *National Police Gazette*, January 28, 1882—General Research Division, New York Public Library; Astor, Lenox, and Tilden Foundations. **92:** A. B. Shults, *Frank Leslie's Illustrated Newspaper*, April 22, 1882—General Research Division, New York Public Library, Astor, Lenox, and Tilden Foundations. **93:** Samuel D. Ehrhart, *Puck*, January 2, 1889—New-York Historical Society. **96 (left):** *Irish World*, August 11, 1877—American Social History Project. **96 (right):** Matt Morgan, *Frank Leslie's Illustrated Newspaper*, October 24, 1874—General Research Division, New York Public Library, Astor, Lenox, and Tilden Foundations. **101:** Thomas Nast, *Harper's Weekly*, August 19, 1871—American Social History Project. **102:** Theodore Teeple, 1888—Massillon Museum, Massillon, Ohio. **104:** John Donaghy, New York *Daily Graphic*, September 16, 1873—American Social History Project. **106:** Solomon D. Butcher, 1885—Butcher Collection, Nebraska Historical Society.

Chapter 3: Great Upheavals: The 1880s and 1890s

Documents: 113: "Labor is noble and holy": Peter J. Rachleff, *Black Labor in the South: Richmond, Virginia, 1865–1890* (1984). **117:** "Labor headquarters": Mary C. Grimes, ed., *The Knights in Fiction: Two Labor Novels of the 1880s* (1986). **119:** "Eight hours for what we will": *Boston Daily Voice*, August 7, 1886. **121:** "Labor nowhere has its full and fair reward": L. F. Post and F. C. Leubuscher, eds., *Henry George's 1886 Campaign* (1887). **127:** ". . . I die happy on the gallows": Dave Roediger and Franklin Rosemont, eds., *Haymarket Scrapbook* (1986). **134:** "To protect their homes and families . . .": Linda Schneider, "The Citizen Striker: Workers' Ideology in the Homestead Strike of 1892," *Labor History* (Winter 1982). **140:** ". . . An ulcer on the body politic": U.S. Strike Commission, *Report on the Chicago Strike of June–July 1894* (1895). **147:** ". . . Monopoly is the master": W. E. Connelley, ed., *History of Kansas, State and People* (1928). **155:** ". . . Our condition is precarious in the extreme": Herbert Aptheker, ed., *A Documentary History of the Negro People in the United States* (1970). **156:** "The colored

citizens' desire . . . that some action be taken": Herbert Aptheker, ed., *A Documentary History of the Negro People in the United States* (1970).

Illustrations: 108: Thure de Thulstrup, *Harper's Weekly*, March 13, 1886—American Social History Project. **112:** *Frank Leslie's Illustrated Newspaper*, September 13, 1884—American Social History Project. **115:** Joseph Becker, *Frank Leslie's Illustrated Newspaper*, October 16, 1886—General Research Division, New York Public Library, Astor, Lenox, and Tilden Foundations. **116:** Joseph Keppler, *Puck*, October 13, 1886—Scott Molloy Labor Archives. **118:** *Frank Leslie's Illustrated Newspaper*, March 20, 1886—General Research Division, New York Public Library, Astor, Lenox, and Tilden Foundations. **120:** *Life*, May 27, 1887—Scott Molloy Labor Archives. **122:** Grant Hamilton, *Judge*, 1886—General Research Division, New York Public Library, Astor, Lenox, and Tilden Foundations. **124:** Thomas Nast, *Harper's Weekly*, February 17, 1872—American Social History Project. **126:** Chicago Historical Society. **128:** Charles Upham, *Frank Leslie's Illustrated Newspaper*, July 31, 1886—General Research Division, New York Public Library, Astor, Lenox, and Tilden Foundations. **129:** *The New York Detective Library*, August 7, 1886—General Research Division, New York Public Library, Astor, Lenox, and Tilden Foundations. **130:** Joseph Keppler, *Puck*, August 25, 1886—Scott Molloy Labor Archives. **131:** George M. Bretz, "Philadelphia & Reading R. R. and Coal & Iron Police Quarters, Gordon, Pa., Feb'y 23rd, 1888"—Smithsonian Institution. **132:** *Frank Leslie's Illustrated Newspaper*, February 9, 1889—General Research Division, New York Public Library, Astor, Lenox, and Tilden Foundations. **135:** *National Police Gazette*, July 23, 1892—Prints and Photographs Division, Library of Congress. **136:** T. A. Barnard, 1899—#8-X536, Barnard-Stockbridge Collection, University of Idaho Library, Moscow, Idaho. **139:** *Frank Leslie's Illustrated Newspaper*, April 19, 1894—General Research Division, New York Public Library, Astor, Lenox, and Tilden Foundations. **142:** Frederic Remington, *Harper's Weekly*, July 21, 1894—General Research Division, New York Public Library, Astor, Lenox, and Tilden Foundations. **143:** William A. Rogers, *Harper's Weekly*, July 14, 1894—Scott Molloy Labor Archives. **145:** Joseph B. Beale, *Frank Leslie's Illustrated Newspaper*, August 30, 1873—American Social History Project. **148:** William H. Harvey, *Coin's Financial School* (1894)—General Research Division, New York Public Library, Astor, Lenox, and Tilden Foundations. **151:** Frederick B. Opper, *Puck*, September 9, 1896—New-York Historical Society. **157:** H. Ditzler, *Collier's Weekly*, November 26, 1898—Prints and Photographs Division, Library of Congress.

Chapter 4: Working People and Reform

Documents: 162: "Take up the White Man's Burden": Rudyard Kipling, *Rudyard Kipling's Verse: Definitive Edition* (1940). **164–65:** "The American invasion raised great hopes in our breasts . . ." Henry K. Carroll, *Report on the Island of Puerto Rico*, U.S. Treasury Department (1899). **173:** ". . . Mostly we brought rags and bones": *The Independent* (1902); "The machines go like mad all day . . .": *The Independent* (1902). **180:** "Blabyt Er Lign Toyt im Hol": Mark Slobin, *Tenement Songs: The Popular Music of the Jewish Immigrants* (1982). **190:** "A pint of trouble for the bosses . . .": McAlister Coleman, "All of Which I Saw," *The Progressive* (May 1950). **196–97:** ". . . It was a murder and nothing less": New York *World*, May 5, 1913; *Final Report and Testimony Submitted* to *Congress by the Commission on Industrial Relations*, 64th Congress, 1st Session (1916). **201:** "Give the property owner a fair show . . .": Samuel P. Hays, "The Politics of Reform," in Blaine A. Bronell and Warren E. Stickle, eds., *Bosses and Reformers: Urban Politics in America, 1880–1920* (1973). **202–3:** ". . . Hammering at the truth": Virginia Hamilton, ed., *The Writings of W. E. B. DuBois* (1975). **204:** "Then we'd have some cake and coffee . . .": Marie Hall Ets, *Rosa: The Life of an Italian Immigrant* (1970). **206:** "For why must I tell you all my business?": Anzia Yezeirska, "The Free Vacation House," *Hungry Hearts* (1920).

Illustrations: 158: William A. Rogers, *Harper's Weekly*, June 1, 1901—American Social History Project. **163:** Grant Hamilton, *Judge*, July 9, 1898—General Research Division, New York Public Library, Astor, Lenox, and Tilden Foundations. **166:** Prints and Photographs Division, Library of Congress. **168:** National Museum of American History, Smithsonian Institution. **169:** The Carnegie Library of Pittsburgh. **171:** 4 ½ × 6 ½ inches—The Metropolitan Museum of Art, Gift of Mr. and Mrs. Wolfgang Pulvermann, 1969. **174:** *Life*, May 12, 1910—New-York Historical Society. **176:** International Museum of Photography at George Eastman House. **178:** John Sloan, *The Masses*, July 1913—Tamiment Institute Library, New York University. **181 (top):** Chicago Historical Society. **181 (bottom):** Richard F. Outcault, *New York World*, May 3, 1896—Prints and Photographs Division, Library of Congress. **184:** Harry Grant Dart, *Life*, 1909—Prints and Photographs Division, Library of Congress. **191:** The Bancroft Library, University of California, Berkeley. **193:** Charles H. Kerr Publishing Company. **194:** Hyperion Press, Inc. **195:** Archives of Labor and Urban Affairs, Wayne State University. **198:** John Sloan, *The Masses*, June 1914—Prints and Photographs Division, Library of Congress. **200:** Walter Appleton Clark, *Collier's*, November 10, 1906—Prints and Photographs Division, Library of Congress. **205:** People's Institute papers—General Research Division, New York Public Library, Astor, Lenox, and Tilden Foundations. **209:** William A. Ireland, Columbus (Ohio) *Dispatch*, reprinted in *Cartoons Magazine*, November 1912—Prints and Photographs Division, Library of Congress.

Part Two: War, Depression, and Industrial Unionism: 1914–1945

214: Detroit *News*.

Chapter 5: Wars for Democracy

Documents: 224: "Let the capitalists do their own fighting . . .": Frederick C. Giffin, *Six Who Protested: Radical Opposition to the First World War* (1977). **228:** ". . . Have the women organized in separate locals": Rosalyn Baxandall, Linda Gordon, and Susan Reverby, eds., *America's Working Women* (1976). **229:** ". . . Those who harvest the harvester": E. F. Doree, "Gathering the Grain," *International Socialist Review*, June 1915. **230:** ". . . There were dozens to tell her that she must buy fowl": New York *Times*, February 23, 1917. **239:** ". . . Pass us away from here to a better land": Leslie H. Fishel, Jr., and Benjamin Quarles, eds., *The Black Americans: A Documentary History*, 3rd ed. (1976). **241:** ". . . We lost everything but what we had on": Robert Asher, "Documents of the Race Riot at East St. Louis," *Journal of the Illinois State Historical Society* (1972). **243:** "Iron Road": Manuel Gamio, *Mexican Immigration to the United States* (1930). **246–47:** ". . . We don't want other women ever to have to do this over again": Doris Stevens, *Jailed for Freedom* (1920). **254–55:** ". . . These masses of foreigners must be edu-

cated": Rosalyn Baxandall, Linda Gordon, and Susan Reverby, eds., *America's Working Women* (1976). **257:** "You boys give 'em hell for me": William Matthews and Dixon Wecter, *Our Soldiers Speak, 1775–1918* (1943). **260:** "Over Fair": Alfred Harding, *The Revolt of the Actors* (1929). **264:** ". . . We ought to have the right to belong to the union": U.S. Senate, Committee on Labor and Education, *Investigation of Strike in the Steel Industry*, vol. 1 (1919).

Illustrations: 218: Imperial War Museum. **222:** Photography Collection, Harry Ransom Humanities Research Center, University of Texas at Austin. **227:** Herbert Paus, *Collier's*, May 13, 1916—General Research Division, New York Public Library, Astor, Lenox, and Tilden Foundations. **231:** National Archives. **232:** Robert Minor, *The Masses*, July 1916—Tamiment Institute Library, New York University. **233:** General Research Division, New York Public Library, Astor, Lenox and Tilden Foundations. **234:** National Archives. **244:** Sophia Smith Collection, Smith College. **248:** Joseph Pennell, chromolithograph, c. 1918—Prints and Photographs Division, Library of Congress. **249:** Harris and Ewing, 1917—National Archives. **250:** J. R. Schmidt, 1918—National Archives. **252:** Harold Tucker Webster, *Cartoon Magazine*, September 1917—Prints and Photographs Division, Library of Congress. **253:** Archives of Labor and Urban Affairs, Wayne State University. **256:** Henry Ford Museum and Greenfield Village. **259:** Museum of History and Industry, Seattle, Washington. **262 (left):** Orson Lowell, *Leslie's Illustrated Weekly Newspaper*, June 14, 1919—General Research Division, New York Public Library, Astor, Lenox, and Tilden Foundations. **262 (right):** Alfred Frueh, *Good Morning*, May 15, 1919—Prints and Photographs Division, Library of Congress. **263:** William Z. Foster, *The Great Steel Strike and Its Lessons* (1920)—General Research Division, New York Public Library, Astor, Lenox, and Tilden Foundations. **265:** Morgan, Philadelphia *Inquirer*, March 13, 1919—General Research Division, New York Public Library, Astor, Lenox, and Tilden Foundations. **266:** *Labor Defender*, August 1928—General Research Division, New York Public Library, Astor, Lenox, and Tilden Foundations.

Chapter 6: "The New Era": Mass Society and Business Triumph

Documents: 271: "What is th' open shop?": Leon Litwack, *The American Labor Movement* (1962). **279:** ". . . We rode the public a little ourselves": "Confessions of a Ford Dealer, as Told to Jesse Rainsford Sprague," *Harper's Monthly Magazine*, June 1927. **283:** ". . . A single maiden, never wed": Robert Sklar, ed., *The Plastic Age (1917–1930)* (1970). **286–87:** "The nations most important asset . . .": Molly Ladd-Taylor, *Raising a Baby the Government Way: Mothers' Letters to the Children's Bureau, 1915–1932* (1986). **292:** "Amoskeag did all this to keep harmony . . .": Tamara K. Hareven and Randolph Langenbach, *Amoskeag: Life and Work in an American Factory-City* (1978). **298–99:** "Let's stand together, workers": Jacqueline Dowd Hall, James Leloudis, Robert Korstad, Mary Murphy, Lu Ann Jones, and Christopher B. Daly, *Like A Family: The Making of a Southern Cotton Mill World* (1987); Liston Pope, *Millhands and Preachers* (1942). **301:** "They raised the people's children . . .": Susan Tucker, *Telling Memories Among Southern Women: Domestic Workers and the Employers in the Segregated South* (1988). **306:** ". . . I could not eat the poems I wrote": *Freedomways* (1963). **308:** "Red bandanas I detest . . .": Manuel Gamio, *Mexican Immigration to the United States* (1971). **309:** "We didn't join American organizations . . .": John Bodnar, ed., *Workers' World* (1982). **313:** "There was another unusual feature of the flower shop basement . . .": John Kobler, *Ardent Spirits: The Rise and Fall of Prohibition* (1973).

Illustrations: 268: Maher & Co., Chicago, 1926, 48 × 36 inches—Courtesy of Allan Sekula & Sally Stein (Photo: Steve Callis). **273:** Prints and Photographs Division, Library of Congress. **274:** Hugo Gellert, *New Masses*, February 1928—Prints and Photographs Division, Library of Congress. **276 (top):** Anna Leach, "Science in the Modern Kitchen," *Cosmopolitan*, May 1899—American Social History Project. **276 (bottom):** Prints and Photographs Division, Library of Congress. **280:** From the collections of Henry Ford Museum and Greenfield Village. **282:** *The Ladies' Home Journal*, February 1927—American Social History Project. **284:** Prints and Photographs Division, Library of Congress. **285:** National Archives. **289 (top):** *Life*, February 18, 1926—Prints and Photographs Division, Library of Congress. **289 (bottom):** General Research Division, New York Public Library, Astor, Lenox, and Tilden Foundations. **291:** J. R. Williams, *Labor Age*, March 1929—American Social History Project. **296:** Harold M. Talburt, Cleveland *Press*, 1924 (*Labor Age*, October 1924)—Tamiment Institute Library, New York University. **303:** New York *Times*, November 23, 1922—American Social History Project. **304:** *The Negro World*—Schomburg Center for Research in Black Culture, New York Public Library, Astor, Lenox, and Tilden Foundations. **307:** *The Crisis*, May 1929—Schomburg Center for Research in Black Culture, New York Public Library, Astor, Lenox, and Tilden Foundations. **310:** George Bellows, 1923, lithograph, 9 × 16 ½ inches—Courtesy of the Trustees of the Public Library of the City of Boston. **311:** Prints and Photographs Division, Library of Congress. **312:** New York *Daily News*. **314:** UPI/Bettmann Newsphotos.

Chapter 7: The Great Depression and the First New Deal

Documents: 319: ". . . The hawk had come": Milton Meltzer, *Brother Can You Spare a Dime? The Great Depression, 1929–1933* (1969). **327:** "Where women go . . .": Meridel LeSueur, *Women on the Breadlines* (1984). **333:** "And then we were in California . . .": Studs Terkel, *Hard Times* (1970). **342–43:** "Weren't no use under God's sun to treat colored folks like we been treated . . .": Dale Rosen and Theodore Rosengarten, "Shoot-Out at Reeltown," *Radical America*, November–December 1972. **350:** "The rope was tied in a hangman's knot . . .": H. L. Mitchell, *Mean Things Happening in This Land* (1979). **352–53:** ". . . A real mother to the nation": Robert S. McElvaine, *Down and Out in the Great Depression: Letters from the "Forgotten Man"* (1983). **364:** ". . . Labor was in control": Mike Quin, *The Big Strike* (1949). **368:** "Every man a king . . .": Huey P. Long and Castro Carazo, *Every Man a King* (1935).

Illustrations: 316: Milton (Pete) Brooks, July 1930, Detroit *News*—Detroit *News*. **321:** Courtesy of the Trustees of the Public Library of the City of Boston. **323:** John Tinney McCutcheon, Chicago *Tribune*, 1931—Chicago Tribune Company, used with permission. **325:** J. Lee, March 30, 1933—#20102, Special Collections Division, University of Washington Libraries. **330:** *Daily Worker*, October 20, 1934—Scott Molloy Labor Archives. **331:** Franklin D. Roosevelt Library. **332:** Dorothea Lange, 1936—Prints and Photographs Division, Library of Congress. **334:** Dorothea Lange, 1936—Prints and Photographs Division, Library of Congress. **335:** Richard Decker, *The New Yorker*, March 5, 1932—General Research Division, New York Public Library, Astor, Lenox, and Tilden Foundations; copyright 1932, 1960 The New Yorker Magazine, Inc. **336:**

Literary Digest, November 21, 1931—General Research Division, New York Public Library, Astor, Lenox, and Tilden Foundations. **337:** Art Young, *The Unemployed*, December 1930—General Research Division, New York Public Library, Astor, Lenox, and Tilden Foundations. **344:** August 31, 1932—Scott Molloy Labor Archives. **345:** National Archives. **348:** Pare Lorentz, *The Roosevelt Year: A Photographic Record* (1934)—American Social History Project. **351:** Louise Boyle—Southern Tenant Farmers Union Papers #3472, Southern Historical Collection, Library of the University of North Carolina at Chapel Hill. **356:** United Steel Workers of America Archive, Pennsylvania State University. **358:** The Bancroft Library, University of California, Berkeley. **363:** San Francisco Archives, San Francisco Public Library. **365:** Elzie Crisler Segar, "Thimble Theatre," 1934—Copyright King Features Syndicate, Inc., 1989. **369:** Cleanthe, Huey P. Long, *My First Days in the White House* (1935)—American Social History Project.

Chapter 8: Labor Democratizes America

Documents: 379: "We done it!": Ruth McKinney, *Industrial Valley* (1939). **382:** "President Roosevelt is a friend to the laboring man . . .": George Korson, *Coal Dust on the Fiddle* (1943). **388–89:** "Solidarity forever . . .": *Solidarity*, January 9, 1915. **397:** ". . . Made in the USA": Thomas Bell, *Out of This Furnace* (1941). **400–1:** "The ultimate arbiter is the people . . .": Staff of the Living Newspaper, "Triple A Plowed Under," *Federal Theatre Plays* (1938). **404–5:** "I am hanging on to the principles of the New Deal . . .": Alfred Winslow Jones, *Life, Liberty, and Property* (1941). **408:** ". . . Nothing but good to say about the CIO": Ann Banks, *First-Person America* (1981). **411:** "Almost everybody was there . . .": Ann Banks, *First-Person America* (1981). **414:** ". . . A large group of girls in this office very much interested in having the union": Ellen Cantarow, *et al.*, *Moving the Mountain: Women Working for Social Change* (1980). **418:** ". . . A bloodstained field of battle": Isabel Leighton, ed., *The Aspirin Age, 1919–1941* (1949). **420:** ". . . The charge has been made that this article of yours is entirely Communistic": Eric Bentley, *Thirty Years of Treason: Excerpts from Hearings before the House Committee on Un-American Activities, 1938–1968* (1971).

Illustrations: 372: Harold Ellwood, San Francisco *Examiner*, September 17, 1936—California Section, California State Library. Copyright 1936 San Francisco *Examiner*. Reprinted with permission. **381:** The George Meany Memorial Archives, AFL-CIO. **385:** Archives of Labor and Urban Affairs, Wayne State University. **386:** Scott Molloy Labor Archives. **387:** Archives of Labor and Urban Affairs, Wayne State University. **390–91:** Archives of Labor and Urban Affairs, Wayne State University. **393:** Detroit *News*. **398 (top):** Orr C. Fisher, *The Corn Parade*, 1941, oil on canvas—National Archives. **398 (bottom):** Paul Cadmus, *Pocahontas Rescuing Captain John Smith*, 1939, mural—National Archives. **400:** Library of Congress Federal Theatre Project Collection at George Mason University Library. **402:** Walker Evans, 1936—Prints and Photographs Division, Library of Congress. **403 (top):** Museum of Modern Art/Film Stills Archive. **403 (bottom):** Museum of Modern Art/Film Stills Archive. **406:** *Public Housing: The Work of the Federal Public Housing Authority* (1946)—General Research Division, New York Public Library, Astor, Lenox, and Tilden Foundations. **412:** Denys Wortman, New York *World-Telegram*, March 25, 1937—General Research Division, New York Public Library, Astor, Lenox, and Tilden Foundations. **417:** Chicago Historical Society. **419:**

Grand Jury Exhibit 33, Hawaii State Archives. **422:** Dorothea Lange, 1938—Prints and Photographs Division, Library of Congress.

Chapter 9: A Nation Transformed: The Second World War and Its Aftermath

Documents: 428–29: "Always the waves from Europe breaks like thunder . . .": The Academy of American Poets, *The Official Poem of the New York World's Fair, 1939, and Other Prize Winning Poems* (1939). **439:** "We were fighting and sleeping in one vast cesspool . . .": William Manchester, "The Bloodiest Battle of Them All," New York *Times Magazine*, June 14, 1987. **442:** "You can't fight all of them . . .": Gordon Parks, *A Choice of Weapons* (1966). **450:** "I'm as loyal as anyone in this country . . .": Michi Weglyn, *Years of Infamy: The Untold Story of America's Concentration Camps* (1976). **455:** "We're looking for zoot-suits to burn . . .": Carey McWilliams, *North From Mexico* (1968). **458:** ". . . We were determined to stay": Miriam Frank, Marilyn Ziebarth, and Connie Field, *The Life and Times of Rosie the Riveter* (1982). **462:** "Is that giving labor a square deal?": Richard Polenberg, ed., *America at War: The Home Front, 1941–45* (1968). **464:** ". . . The walking dead": Yaff Eliach and Brana Gurewitsch, eds., *The Liberators: Eyewitness Accounts of the Liberation of Concentration Camps*, vol. 1 (1981). **467:** ". . . They were dealing with a new sickness": John Hersey, *Hiroshima* (1974). **474:** "It is none of your damned business . . .": Irving Howe and B. J. Widick, *The UAW and Walter Reuther* (1949).

Illustrations: 424: The West Point Museum, United States Military Academy, West Point, New York. **427:** Marx Memorial Library, London. **430:** Queens Museum. **431:** Harold Lavine and James Wechsler, *War Propaganda and the U.S.* (1940)—American Social History Project. **433:** Scott Molloy Labor Archives. **434:** *PM*, June 6, 1941—General Research Division, New York Public Library, Astor, Lenox and Tilden Foundations. **437 (top):** Arthur Szyk, *Collier's*, December 12, 1942—American Social History Project. **437 (bottom):** Victor Ancona and Karl Koehler, *This Is the Enemy*, 1942, offset lithograph, 34 ¼ × 23 ¾ inches—Poster fund, The Museum of Modern Art. **438:** Copyright Bill Mauldin. **443:** *McCall's*, August 1942—American Social History Project. **445:** Jean Carlu, *America's Answer! Production*, 1942, offset lithograph, 29 ⅞ × 39 ⅝ inches—The Museum of Modern Art, Gift of the Office for Emergency Management. **448:** American Social History Project. **449:** War Relocation Authority Photo 210-GID-B3, from Edward H. Spicer, Asael T. Hansen, Katharine Luomala, and Marvin R. Opler, *Impounded People* (1969)—Used by permission of Rosamond B. Spicer. **454:** Detroit *News*. **455:** *Mercury Herald and News*, April 25, 1943—Capp Enterprises. **456:** *McCall's*, September 1942—American Social History Project. **457:** Dorothea Lange—Prints and Photographs Division, Library of Congress. **464:** Ben Brown. **465:** AP/Wide World. **466:** National Archives. **468:** Yoshito Matsushige—Hiroshima Peace Culture Foundation. **471:** American Social History Project.

Part Three: The Rise and Fall of the *"American Century": 1945–1991*

478: State Historical Society of Wisconsin.

Chapter 10: The Postwar Era

Documents: 493: "White people wake up . . .": Samuel Lubell, *The Future of American Politics* (1951). **498:** "Never talk . . . about controversial issues": Thurman Arnold, "How Not to Get Investigated, Ten Commandments for Government Employees," *Harper's Magazine*, November 1948. **504:** "If you had a fast car . . . you were a big man": George Lipsitz, "They Knew Who We Were: Drag Racing and Customizing," *Cultural Correspondence*, Summer-Fall 1977. **509:** "UAW Americanism for us": Samuel Lubell, *The Future of American Politics* (1951). **511:** "Sweetheart deal": Allen Friedman and Ted Schwarz, *Power and Greed: Inside the Teamsters Empire of Corruption* (1989). **514–15:** ". . . We consider this part of the city to be ours": Juan Flores, ed., *Divided Arrival: Narratives of the Puerto Rican Migration, 1920–1950* (n.d.). **518:** ". . . Modern music should be fast and complicated": Richard O. Boyer, "Profiles: Bop," *The New Yorker*, July 3, 1948. **519:** ". . . One can never be certain where the observation stops": William O'Neill, ed., *Women at Work* (1972). **533:** ". . . They behave as if drugged": James Gilbert, *A Cycle of Outrage: America's Reaction to the Juvenile Delinquent in the 1950s* (1986). **540–41:** "We were prepared. . . .": Henry Hampton and Steve Fayer, with Sarah Flynn, *Voices of Freedom: An Oral History of the Civil Rights Movement* (1990).

Illustrations: 482: Elliott Erwitt/Magnum. **484:** *School Executive*, August 1951—Special Collections, Milbank Memorial Library, Teachers College, Columbia University. **487:** Jackson Pollack, 1948, oil on canvas, 68 inches × 8 feet 8 inches—The Museum of Modern Art. **489:** *The Reporter*, September 26, 1950—General Research Division, New York Public Library, Astor, Lenox, and Tilden Foundations. **495:** Tamiment Institute Library, New York University. **499:** Photofest. **501:** AP/Wide World Photos. **502:** Michael Barson Collection. **507:** Photofest. **517:** UPI/Bettmann Newsphotos. **520:** Elliot Erwitt/Magnum. **522:** Richard Gerstell, *How to Survive an Atomic Bomb* (1950)—General Research Division, New York Public Library, Astor, Lenox, and Tilden Foundations. **524:** Margaret Bourke-White, *Life* magazine, copyright Time Warner, Inc. **526:** Prints and Photographs Division, Library of Congress. **529:** Virgil Finlay, *Amazing Stories*, October–November 1953. **531:** Photofest. **532:** Prints and Photographs Division, Library of Congress. **534:** "Rock, Baby, Rock" (1957)—Frank Driggs. **536:** Schomburg Center for Research in Black Culture, New York Public Library, Astor, Lenox, and Tilden Foundations. **537:** Schomburg Center for Research in Black Culture, New York Public Library, Astor, Lenox, and Tilden Foundations. **539:** Dan Weiner—Courtesy Sandra Weiner.

Chapter 11: The Rights-Conscious 1960s

Documents: 547: "They shot the tires out . . .": Milton Meltzer, ed., *The American Promise* (1990). **554:** ". . . We are poor, but we know what we want": Lynward Stevenson, Woodlawn Organization *Newsletter*, April 14, 1965. **560–61** ". . . Fight them, and you'll get your freedom": George Breitman, ed., *Malcolm X Speaks* (1966). **566–67:** "The women have to be involved": Ellen Cantarow *et al.*, *Moving the Mountain: Women Working for Social Change* (1980). **570:** "But we are not alone . . .": Jan Berry and W. D. Ehrhart, eds., *Demilitarized Zones: Veterans After Vietnam* (1976). **575:** ". . . Assembly lines in the universities": Immanuel Wallerstein and Paul Starr, eds., *The University Crisis Reader*, vol. 2, *Confrontation and Counterattack* (1971). **585:** ". . . He was just a person": *Ann Arbor*

News, August 28, 1991. **592–93:** "We are inside you . . .": Karla Jay and Allen Young, eds., *Out of the Closets: Voices of Gay Liberation* (1972). **594–95:** ". . . Personal problems are political problems": Anita Shreve, *Women Together, Women Alone: The Legacy of the Consciousness-Raising Movement* (1989).

Illustrations: 542: Charles Moore, copyright Black Star 1963. **545:** State Historical Society of Wisconsin. **548:** Danny Lyon/Magnum. **549:** Federal Bureau of Investigation. **557:** Copyright 1967 The Detroit *News*. **562:** Pirkle Jones—Ruth-Marion Baruch and Pirkle Jones, *The Vanguard: A Photographic Essay on the Black Panthers* (Boston: Beacon Press, 1970). **563:** AP/Wide World Photos. **564:** *1199 News*, Local 1199, Health Care Employees Union, New York City. **565:** American Social History Project. **566:** Madeleine Adamson. **569:** Hiroji Kubota/Magnum. **571:** Ron Haeberle, *Life* magazine, copyright 1969 Time Warner, Inc. **576:** Marc Riboud/Magnum. **577:** Leonard Freed/Magnum. **578 (left):** Harvey Hacker, 1969. **578 (right):** Karen Killinghast, Jay Cantor, 1969—Joshua Freeman. **579:** Gilbert Shelton, *Gothic Blimp Works*, 1969—Copyright Rip Off Press, Inc. **581:** *Rolling Stone*, December 7, 1968—General Research Division, New York Public Library, Astor, Lenox, and Tilden Foundations. **584:** Bruce Darrow, Chicago *American*, August 22, 1968—Chicago Historical Society. **587:** Copyright Charles Harbutt/Actuality, Inc. **589:** AP/Wide World Photos. **591 (top):** Frank Giorandino, New York *Daily News*, March 9, 1970. **591 (bottom):** Bettye Lane, August 20, 1977. **594:** Bettye Lane, 1970. **607:** *Ramparts*, August–September 1973—Edward Sorel.

Chapter 12: The United States and the Global Economy

Documents: 614–15: ". . . Disabled women can learn from the women's movement": Yvonne Duffy, *All Things Are Possible* (1981). **618–19:** "A war against working people . . .": *Radical History Review*, Fall 1978. **629:** ". . . Keepers at home": Robyn Rowland, ed., *Women Who Do and Women Who Don't Join the Women's Movement* (1984). **636–37:** "You know you get desperate . . .": David Bensman and Roberta Lynch, *Rusted Dreams: Hard Times in a Steel Community* (1987). **643:** "There is blood in every dollar I make . . .": Interview conducted by Ying Chan, New York City, 1990. **646–47:** "It's the freon . . .": Diana Hembree, "Dead End in Silicon Valley," *The Progressive*, October 1985. **648:** "You don't have to know how to cook": Barbara Garson, *The Electronic Sweatshop: How Computers Are Transforming the Office of the Future into the Factory of the Past* (1988). **650:** ". . . I fear for my children": *Homeless with Children*, WNYC-TV, June 1991. **656:** "It is against this denial of Yale's own values that we witness": Toni Gilpin *et al.*, *On Strike for Respect: The Yale Strike of 1984–85* (1985). **665:** ". . . I'm a Daughter of Mother Jones 14": Kathy Scott *et al.*, producer, *Drawing the Line at Pittston*, Paper Tiger-TV, 1990. **666:** "Which side was I on? . . .": Martha Southgate, "Sticking with the Union," *Glamour*, March 1991.

Illustrations: 608: Reuters/Bettmann. **613:** Lionel J-M Delevigne. **617:** New York *Daily News*, October 30, 1975. **624:** Stanley Forman. **626:** Jerry Valente/Sipa Press. **627:** Donna Binder/Impact Visuals. **628:** Donna Binder/Impact Visuals. **632:** National Archives. **633:** Photofest. **635:** Evan Johnson/Impact Visuals. **639:** Patricia Morrisroe, "The Yupper West Side: The New Class," *New York*, May 13, 1985—Diego Goldberg/SYGMA. **642:** U.S. Border Patrol. **645:** Andrea Ades Vásquez—American Social History Project. **649:** George Cohen/Impact Visuals. **653:** Los Angeles Professional Air Traffic Controllers' Organization, 1981. **655:** Hardy Green. **658:** AP/Wide World Photos. **661:** Henry Chalfant/City Lore. **663:** Mario Suriani, AP/Wide World Photos. **664:** Donna Binder/Impact Visuals. **668:** Hometowns Against Shutdowns/Commercial Catering and Allied Workers Union of South Africa.

CONTRIBUTORS

DAVID BENSMAN, contributing author, is chair of the labor education department at Rutgers University. He is the author of *The Practice of Solidarity: American Hatters in the Nineteenth Century* (1985) and coauthor of *Rusted Dreams: Hard Times in a Steel Community* (1987).

SUSAN PORTER BENSON, contributing author, is an associate professor of history at the University of Missouri, Columbia. She is the author of *Counter Cultures: Saleswomen, Managers, and Customers in American Department Stores, 1890–1940* (1986), and is currently working on a social history of working-class consumption.

STEPHEN BRIER, supervising editor, cofounded the American Social History Project and has been its director since 1981. He also served as the producer of the ASHP's *Who Built America?* video series. Brier coedits the "Critical Perspectives on the Past" series at Temple University Press and has written a number of articles on race, class, and ethnicity in the coalmining industry.

JOSHUA BROWN, visual editor, has been the art director and scriptwriter of ASHP's video productions since 1981. Among Brown's published artwork and writing, he is coeditor of *History from South Africa: Alternative Visions and Practices* (1991).

DAVID BRUNDAGE, who teaches community studies and history at the University of California, Santa Cruz, was an ASHP staff writer from 1983 through 1985. He is the author of *The Making of Western Labor Radicalism: Denver's Working People, 1878–1905* (1992).

BRET EYNON, contributing author, is ASHP's education director. He coproduced several ASHP videos and edited the series of accompanying viewer guides. He now coordinates ASHP's programs for classroom enrichment and educational change. He is a coauthor of *1968: A Student Generation in Revolt* (1988).

JOSHUA FREEMAN, an associate professor of history at Columbia University, was an ASHP staff writer from 1984 through 1986. He has written extensively on twentieth-century American labor, including *In Transit: The Transport Workers Union in New York City, 1933–1966* (1989).

HERBERT G. GUTMAN was Distinguished Professor of History at the Graduate Center of the City University of New York. He cofounded the ASHP and supervised its work until his death in 1985. His books include *Work, Culture, and Society in Industrializing America* (1976), *The Black Family in Slavery and Freedom* (1976), and *Power and Culture: Essays on the American Working Class* (1987).

BRUCE LEVINE, now at the University of Cincinnati, was the ASHP's director of research and writing from 1981 through 1986. He is the author of *The Spirit of 1848: German Immigrants, Labor Conflict, and the Coming of the Civil War* (1992) and *Half Slave and Half Free: The Origins of the American Civil War* (1992).

NELSON LICHTENSTEIN, contributing author, is a professor of history at the University of Virginia. He has written articles on labor history and industrial relations, is the author of *Labor's War at Home: The CIO and World War II* (1982), and is coeditor of *Essays in the History of Auto Work* (1990), *Major Problems in the History of American Workers* (1991), and *Industrial Democracy: Past and Present* (1992).

BRYAN PALMER, contributing author, is a professor of history at Queen's University, Kingston, Ontario. He is the author of articles and books on working-class history and historical theory, including *Dreaming of What Might Be: The Knights of Labor in Ontario, 1880–1900* (1983), *Descent into Discourse: The Reification of Language and the Writing of Social History* (1990), and *Working-Class Experience: Rethinking the History of Canadian Labor, 1800–1990* (1992).

ROY ROSENZWEIG, consulting editor, is an associate professor of history at George Mason University and is the author of books and articles on nineteenth- and twentieth-century social and cultural history, including *Eight Hours for What We Will: Workers and Leisure in an Industrial City, 1870–1920* (1983) and (as coauthor) *The Park and the People: A History of Central Park* (1992).

INDEX

Page numbers in *italics* refer to illustrations or sidebar documents.